GARLAND OF VISIONS

THE PUBLISHER AND THE UNIVERSITY OF CALIFORNIA PRESS FOUNDATION GRATEFULLY ACKNOWLEDGE THE GENEROUS SUPPORT OF THE RICHARD AND HARRIETT GOLD ENDOWMENT FUND IN ARTS AND HUMANITIES.

GARLAND OF VISIONS

Color, Tantra, and a Material History of Indian Painting

Jinah Kim

UNIVERSITY OF CALIFORNIA PRESS

Parts of chapter 2 appeared in "Painted Palm-Leaf Manuscripts and the Art of the Book in Medieval South Asia," *Archives of Asian Art* 65, no. 1/2 (2015): 57–86.

University of California Press
Oakland, California

Cataloging-in-Publication Data is on file at the Library of Congress.

ISBN 978-0-520-34321-4 (cloth : alk. paper)

Printed in Malaysia

29 28 27 26 25 24 23 22 21 20
10 9 8 7 6 5 4 3 2 1

For Aroon and Myungkoo Kang

The five basic colours (*mūlaraṅga*) are said to be white (*śveta*), yellow (*pīta*), red (*vilohita*), blue (*nīla*) and black (*kṛṣṇa*). [But] O king, other [colours] are in hundreds. By combining the primary colour (*purvarangavikāreṇa*) using one's imagination (*bhāvakalpanayā*) and discretion one could make hundred, even thousand-fold colours.

CITRASŪTRA, *ADHYĀYA* 40, V. 16–17

Everything that is differentiated is all born of the mind.
The distinguishing of white, yellow, red and the like arises from the mind.

***MAHĀVAIROCANĀBHISAṂBODHI SŪTRA*, CHAPTER VII (T 18.848 21C)**

CONTENTS

ACKNOWLEDGMENTS

THIS BOOK IS ABOUT color and Indian manuscript painting. The genesis of this book happened when I came across the announcement for the Getty Research Institute's scholar year theme in fall 2011: the theme for 2012–13 was color. I must start by thanking Joanna Williams for trusting what was obviously a half-baked idea and Patricia Berger for seeing the potential of the project even from a jumble of random and abstract thoughts. Their encouragement and support laid the bridge to the road that I might not have taken otherwise. My fascination with C.G. Jung's *Red Book* as a handwritten manuscript that materialized a person's vision through vivid, chromatic painting drove the very first draft of the fellowship proposal that I shared with Williams and Berger in October 2011. While this enthusiasm had to be curbed and put aside, most ideas expressed in my proposal for the Getty-NEH postdoctoral fellowship have remained pertinent to the project. A year spent at the Getty Research Institute as part of a cohort of scholars working on the theme of color was an absolute boon. I thank Alexa Sekyra, Sabine Schlosser, Rebecca Zamora, Amy Meyers, and all the staff of the Getty Scholar Program for making my time at GRI a successful one. Being part of the residential scholarly community at the Getty Scholar Housing, lovingly called the "Pink Palace," provided an ideal environment for discussions and inspirations across many fields of art history. I learned a great deal from everyone's research, and I thank my cohort for lending ears and providing insights, among them, Jennifer Stager, Noa Turel, Jennifer Josten, David S. Mather, Valérie Kobi, Tiziana D'Angelo, Cindy Kang, Sophia Rochmes, Ann-Sophie Lehmann, Philipp Blom, Ulrike Heinrichs, Dunja Hersak, Gordon Alan Hughes, Jenny King, Vanessa R. Schwartz, and Lothar von Falkenhausen.

The research for this project required many archival searches and field visits to different parts of the world because the manuscripts and paintings studied in this book are found in repositories across the globe. I accrued mountainous karmic debts during each visit: working on manuscripts often requires many levels of interventions, whether it is permission to access a manuscript, or helpful caretakers who fetch manuscripts/objects. Here, I attempt to thank those who helped my research over the years, but I apologize in advance for my memory's failure. For Kolkata, I'd like to start by thanking Subir Sarkar, the ever-so generous and supportive officer of the American Institute of Indian Studies' Kolkata Office. The staff at the AIIS guest house in Kolkata provided a home away from home over the years, and I am grateful for their care. I thank the general secretary and the staff of the Asiatic Society, Kolkata, for providing me access to manuscripts in that collection. I thank Dr. Keka Banerjee in charge of the museum of the Asiatic Society, Kolkata, for her generous help with my research and permissions, and Dr. Bandana Mukherjee, Dr. Sangamitra Chowdhury, and Dr. Mitali Chatterjee for facilitating my research there. Another important repository in Kolkata that I spent many days in looking at objects is the Indian Museum. I am deeply indebted to Dr. Anasua Sengupta who has been my fairy godmother since my doctoral research began fifteen years ago. Dr. Nita Sengupta has also been a generous supporter. Mr. Debesh Chandra Raj helped me examine manuscript folios in the museum's conservation lab. I thank Dr. Jayanta Sengupta for inviting me to share my research at the Indian Museum and Dr. Sayan Bhattacharya for facilitating my visit. Also, in Kolkata, I must thank Dr. Kalyan Chakravarty for his enthusiastic and unflagging support of my research. He went above and beyond to help me get access and permission to study manuscripts and objects not only in Kolkata but also in Delhi. I would like to thank Dr. S.V. Tripathi, Mr. Rehman, and Dr. B.R. Mani, all at the National Museum, New Delhi, for their help. I am grateful that Dr. Tripathi, who is now an expert consultant at the National Manuscript Mission, came back from retirement to show me manuscripts in the National Museum's collection. I also thank the American institute of Indian Studies Delhi Office, especially the director general, Purnima Mehta, and caretakers of the AIIS Delhi guesthouse for their help. In Mumbai, I thank Mr. Sabiyasachi Mukherjee of the Chhatrapati Shivaji Maharaj Vastu Sangrahalaya (CSMVS, formerly Prince of Wales Museum of Western India), and Ms. Vandana Prapanna and Ms. Aparna Bhogal for helping me examine manuscripts in the CSMVS. I was fortunate to study manuscripts in the Asiatic Society, Mumbai. I thank Prof. Vispi Balaporia for her unwavering support of my research and Amalina Dave for helping me examine palm-leaf manuscripts in person. I also thank Dr. Sonya Mehta, Zeenia Framroze, and Dr. Maya Avasia for facilitating my research at the Asiatic Society, Mumbai. I thank Dr. J.B. Shah, director of the L.D. Institute of Indology, and Dr. Preeti N. Pacholi for helping me view some Jain manuscripts in the L.D. Institute. I also thank Dr. Ratan Parimoo and Ms. Balbal Hinglajra at the N.C. Mehta Gallery.

Research for this project took me to Rajshahi, Bangladesh, twice, and I would like to thank everyone who ensured my safe travel and research: Abdul Muyeed Chowdhury, Sumala Chowdhury, Zirwat Chowdhury, Shihab Uddin Ahmed, Shanul Haque Sumon, and Zissan Ahmed. In Dhaka, I thank Professor Abdul Momin Chowdhury, and Professor Perween Hasan. I also thank Dr. Biswas Swapan of the National Museum of Bangladesh for his patience and generous help. In Rajshahi, I would like to thank the staff of the Varendra Research Museum for their help with my research, without which chapter 4 would not exist. Dr. Sultan Ahmed and Professor Kanailal Ray Chittaranjan Misra helped me with access, and I am grateful to M.D. Zakaria, M.D. Muktar Hussain, and M.D. Ziaul Kabir for helping me examine the manuscripts. I also thank M.D. Abdul Kuddus, VRM's conservation officer, for teaching me about the dire state of conservation of palm-leaf manuscripts in the Bangladeshi collections. For Nepal, I would like to thank the staff of the National Archives of Nepal for their help with my research. I thank Rajendra Prasad Neupane for his excellent photography of manuscripts and Manita Neupane for her kindness during my research. I am also grateful to Nirmal and Padma Tuladhar for their hospitality.

In the United Kingdom, I thank the staff of the Asian and African Studies Reading Room at the British Library. I also thank Dr. Pasquale Manzo for helping me examine some of the Mewar Rāmāyaṇa folios and other fragile manuscripts in the British Library collection in person. I thank the kind staff of the manuscript reading room at the Cambridge University Library for their help. I would also like to thank the team behind the Cambridge Digital Library for making many Sanskrit manuscripts available for further examination. This digital tool made a huge difference in my research and analysis and will benefit future scholars for generations to come. I am grateful to Michael Willis who helped me access manuscript folios and book covers in the British Museum. I would also like to thank the Sam Fogg Gallery in London for opening its doors and letting me examine manuscripts in their collection. I have visited numerous collections in the United States for this research, and many curators helped me examine manuscripts and paintings in their collections: John Guy at the Metropolitan Museum of Art, Darielle Mason at the Philadelphia Museum of Art, Katherine Paul at the Newark Museum, Joan Cummins at the Brooklyn Museum, John Henry Rice at the Virginia Museum of Fine Arts, Sonya Rhie Mace at the Cleveland Museum of Art, and Bindu Gude at the Los Angeles County Museum of Art. I am grateful for their generosity and willingness to help despite their busy schedules. Sonya Rhie Mace did not only accommodate my research visits but also hosted my Indian painting seminar group with open arms and grace.

Closer to home, I would like to thank Laura Weinstein at the Museum of Fine Arts, Boston, for her generous support over the years. Also, at the MFA, a special note of thanks is due to Joan Wright who has encouraged my endless queries about material and pigments. She remained an enthusiastic supporter of this project since our very first meeting in 2012. It was Joan who first introduced me to the magic of microscopic viewing of pigment layers on Indian miniature painting and other analytical methods of physical examination. I cannot forget the excitement I felt looking into a high-power microscope in the Asian paper conservation studio for the first time. Joan has always been patient and generous, teaching me how to handle and read these objects materially. It was also through her support and leadership that I was able to work with Michele Derrick, one of the conservation scientists at the MFA who conducted pigment analysis for this project, allowing deep investigation of pigments on Indian painting of pre-1500 CE. My interest in pigments and material history of painting grew over the years, and I am lucky to have worked with colleagues at the Harvard Art Museums and the Straus Center for Conservation and Technical Studies. My research profited from working closely with Katherine Eremin and Penley Knipe at the Straus Center, and I owe them a debt of gratitude. Also at the Straus Center, I thank Narayan Khandekar, Francesca Bewer, and Julie Wertz. My research on pigments and material history of painting also benefited from teaching a course on Painting of India. Mary McWilliams's support was crucial in setting up the course, and Mary Lister's logistical support ensured all appointments and study center sessions ran smoothly.

Such multisited and multiyear research required many grants, starting with the Getty-NEH postdoctoral fellowship in 2012–13. Multiple grants from the Harvard Asia Center, the Lakshmi Mittal and Family South Asia Institute (LMSAI), Ann and Jim Rothenberg Fund for Humanities Research, the Department of History of Art and Architecture, and the Faculty of Arts and Science at Harvard supported research for this book over the years. Publication grants from the Asia Center, the LMSAI, and the Arts and Humanities Dean's office at Harvard enabled color reproduction of images in the book. I thank Robin Kelsey, Dean of Arts and Humanities at Harvard, for his support. The LMSAI's logistical and administrative support was helpful in doing research in South Asia. I thank the LMSAI's executive director Meena Hewett for going above and beyond to connect me with specialists on the ground, and Tarun Khanna, director of the LMSAI, for his continued interest in my project. I must thank our department's amazing administrative staff: Deanna Dalrymple, our DA emerita, and Ann Janik, our current DA, have been extremely patient and supportive. Sean Fisher, Thomas Batchelder, Clayton Scoble, and Ligia Alfonzo helped along the way. I also thank the Harvard Asia Center's former director, Karen Thornber, and associate director, Holly Angell, for inviting me to share my research, giving me a valuable opportunity to get feedback on chapters 1 and 2.

I was able to share parts of my research for this book at various academic institutions: twice at Stanford (thanks to Hanna Marcus for the Humanities Center symposium, and thanks to Paul Harrison for the Center for Buddhist studies); University of Denver (thanks to Ben Norse); at Harvard-Yenching seminar (thanks to Changhong Zhang); at the Buddhist Art workshop at Harvard convened by Leonard van der Kuijp; at the Trace Symposium at Harvard; at the CSMVS; and the Indian Museum, Kolkata. I thank the participants and audience at each event for their feedback and comments. I also have had the good fortune to get feedback from eminent scholars on various issues along the way. I thank Phyllis Granoff, Rob Linrothe, Tansen Sen, and Indrani Chatterjee in particular for sharing their insights on various aspects of this research. My numerous inquiries to Phyllis about textual sources and Jain manuscripts were always promptly answered, and I appreciate her generosity. Janice Leoshko and Rick

Asher provided insightful comments on the entire manuscript. I also thank the anonymous reviewer who helped me sharpen some nebulous points in the earlier version. Padma Kaimal's encouragement and support of the project is also much appreciated. I am grateful to Deborah Klimburg-Salter, Christian Luczanits, Gudrun Melzer, Claudine Bautze-Picron, Eva Allinger, Sonal Khullar, James McHugh, Frank J. Korom, Peter Skilling, Masahide Mori, Kimiaki Tanaka, and Nobuyoshi Yamabe for answering my queries and sharing their expertise.

I have been most fortunate to be part of a collegial department with brilliant colleagues. In the Department of History of Art and Architecture at Harvard, I am deeply grateful to my colleagues for sharing their expertise and wisdom, among them David J. Roxburgh, Yukio Lippit, Eugene Wang, Jeffrey Hamburger, Thomas B.F. Cummins, Carrie Lambert-Beatty, Melissa McCormick, Ioli Kalavrezou, Gülru Necipoğlu, Ewa Lajer-Burcharth, and Irene Winter. Jeffrey Hamburger read three chapters of this book with unparalleled enthusiasm, erudition, and editorial rigor. Tom Cummins read the chapter on color and material history and provided many salient references on pigment analysis. The inimitable David J. Roxburgh has been an important interlocutor throughout the whole process of research and writing. In addition to being a peerless and supportive department chair, David read the entire manuscript with meticulous attention to editorial details amid his demanding schedule. Kio, Eugene, and Melissa ensured an ideal scholarly environment for collegial collaboration and research. Carrie Lambert-Beatty not only read parts of this book but also provided moral support. I also thank Parimal Patil for many lunches during which he always listened attentively and gave me timely advice. Todd Lewis at the College of the Holy Cross has also been a generous supporter. While I acknowledge the help from my eminent colleagues, any errors contained within this book remain entirely mine.

Many hands were involved in making this book come to fruition. My graduate students, Sonali Dhingra, Nandita Punj, and Louis Copplestone, helped in myriad ways, from library errands to researching and organizing primary and secondary sources. Sonali accompanied me to sites in Odisha and navigated access to local museums and temples. Lee Ling Ting compiled primary sources for references collected in Coomaraswamy's 1930 essay, and Francesca Penty assisted me with organizing pigment analysis data. I also thank students in the Indian Painting seminar for their inquisitive questions and enthusiastic participation: Bronwen Gulkis, Sophia Nasti, Gwendolyn Collaco, Rahul Kulka, Sunitha Das, Hannah Hyden, and Chassidy Winestock. A note of thanks is also due to Max Meehan for sharing his expertise from chemistry in art history classes. I thank Cynthia Col for proofreading the entire first draft and preparing the index for the book. At UC Press, I thank Nadine Little for believing in this project. I hope its publication makes her proud as one of her last projects at UC Press. Archna Patel has been a steady force behind the book's production, and I appreciate her gentle but effective steering. I also thank Reed Malcolm for his initial question about the genealogy of Tibetan thankas, and for taking on my first book—absence of color plates in that book in a way further fueled my interest in the materiality of color.

The long journey of writing this book was helped by many friends. I thank my Bengali didi, Sarothi Roy, and Mrs. Subhasree Tagore. Sudha Manghi and her family helped me feel at home in Mumbai, and I thank them for their hospitality. In Cambridge, many friends cheered me on to help me stay on track: Lilian Handlin, Leanna McGrath, Jie Lu, Christine Whitmore, the Bouchard-Koelpin family, the Lim family, and the Tsai-SanClemente family. I thank Chris, Sue Zmijewski, and Jason Lim for their friendship and child care support—Chris and Sue saved the day on many occasions while I was traveling for research. Katarina Tsai's friendship and moral support helped sustain me through injuries and mishaps with many nutritious meals. Many friends from afar provided their friendship and encouragement, among them Jennifer Stager, Bokyung Kim, Deborah Stein, Tracy Miller, and Lisa Julien. Catherine Becker has seen this project grow from its very inception, and her wise council and friendship have helped avert practically every crisis that arose in researching and writing this book—my gratitude to her cannot be expressed in words.

Finally, I thank my family for all their cheers and emotional support over the years. My parents, Drs. Seongsoo Kim and Jungguk Kim, are the most loving and patient parents that one can ever hope for. My mom's faith in my capacity to do things that initially seemed beyond my measure has been a constant source of energy and support, while my disciplinarian father's encouragement and care helped me stay focused. My siblings, Hyoyun and her husband, Seonghyun, and Jaebum and his wife, Jieun, have been understanding and supportive of this big sister, showering me with gifts and cheers for every occasion, and excusing me from my constant delinquency in all family matters. Last but not least, I am eternally grateful to my husband, Myungkoo Kang, for his patience, love, and wisdom, and to our son Aroon, for his love and perseverance. Aroon was only four when I started this project—he tirelessly accompanied his mom on many adventures to different cities and sites. The father-son duo often managed without me while their itinerant mother and wife traveled after manuscripts. This book would have not been possible without their loving support and understanding.

ABBREVIATIONS

AsP	*Aṣṭasāhasrikā Prajñāpāramitā*
BK	*Bṛhatkathā*
KsS	*Kathāsaritsāgara of Somadeva*
MMK	*Mañjuśrīmūlakālpa*
NsP	Benoytosh Bhattacharyya, ed., *Niṣpannayogāvalī of Mahāpaṇḍita Abhayākaragupta*, Gaekwad's Oriental Series, vol. 109. Baroda: Oriental Institute, 1949.
ORP	Ananda K. Coomaraswamy, "One Hundred References to Indian Painting," *Artibus Asiae* 4, no. 1 (1930): 41–57.
SM	Benoytosh Bhattacharyya, ed., *Sādhanamālā*, vols. 1 and 2, Gaekwad's Oriental Series, vols. 26, 41. Baroda: Oriental Institute of Baroda, 1925–28; reprint, 1968.
SSB	*Sarvatatthāgatādhiṣṭhāna-sattvāvalokana-buddhakṣetrasandarśanavyūha sūtra*
VA	*Vajrāvalī-nāma-maṇḍalopāyikā of Abhayākaragupta*

INTRODUCTION

IN THE TWELFTH REGNAL YEAR OF GOPĀLA (IV)—a Pāla king who ruled parts of India in what is now Bihar and West Bengal during the first half of the twelfth century—a lay woman named Aṇaghākā commissioned a sumptuously painted palm-leaf manuscript of an important Mahāyāna scripture, the *Perfection of Wisdom in Eight Thousand Verses* (*Aṣṭasāhasrikā Prajñāpāramitā*, henceforth *Perfection of Wisdom*). The commission was intended to benefit her "priest, teacher, parents, and all sentient beings in attaining supreme knowledge."[1] Only six out of the 206 folios of the manuscript were subject to painting. In these six folios, the unnamed miniaturist executed every given space with dexterity and finesse. On each folio, surrounding the two prebored holes for binding, were placed decorative bands filled with swirling vegetal patterns emerging from a monster's mouth: the dark green tendrils are accentuated with light yellow highlighting and shaded with deep blue against a vibrant red backdrop with yellow borders (figure 0.1). Each band measures about 2 cm in width, and it would have required a brush that was about 2/100 mm in diameter to execute the fine lines.

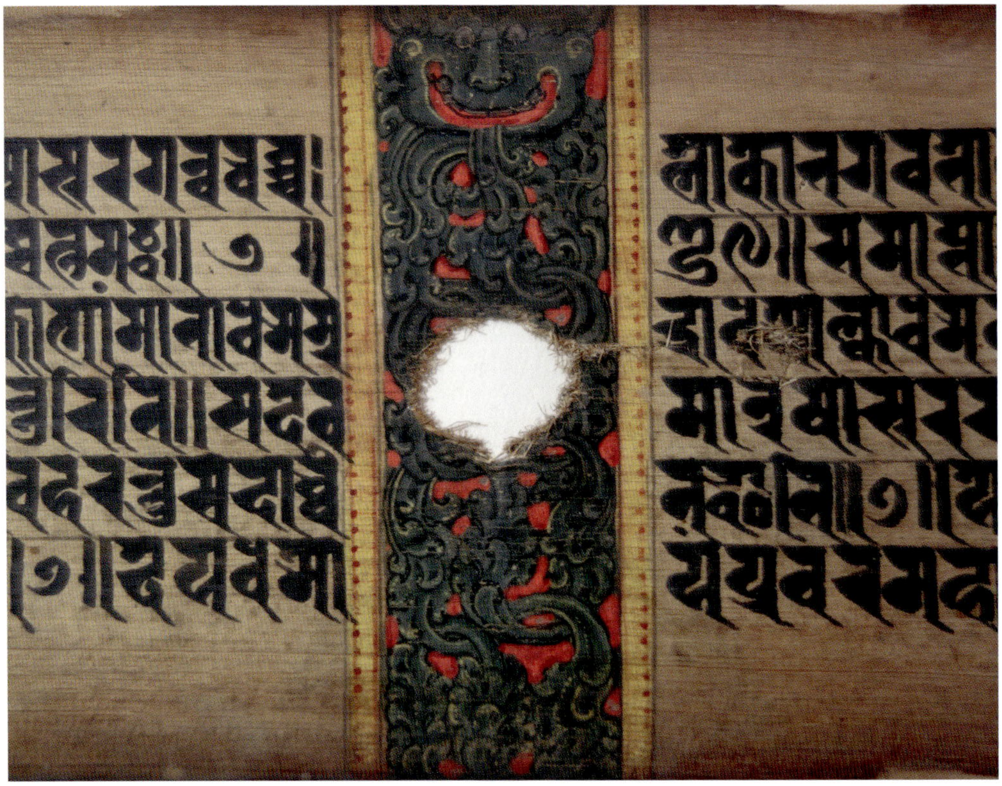

FIGURE 0.1
Decorative pattern on the band around the string hole. Detail of figure 0.2.

The vibrancy of color is absolutely stunning nearly nine hundred years after its production. On the last folio of the manuscript, three painted panels contain a red goddess flanked by blue and yellow bodhisattvas (figure 0.2). Kurukullā, the red goddess in the center panel, is adorned with intricate jewelry and an ornate crown. She is seated within a golden yellow shrine-like frame decorated with a swirly motif and a *haṃsa* (swan) on either end, supported by two *vyāla*s (mythical lions). The large cushion behind her displays an intricate textile pattern in organic blue and red (most likely indigo and lac)—the same colors that would have dyed contemporary textiles. The lotus seat where she sits cross-legged, drawing a flower bow, is rendered with blue, red, and green petals with yellow outlines. This acme of color pops even more brilliantly against the light brown palm leaf whose veins and suppleness still retain their organic character. The Sanskrit text in black ink is written in an ornamental *kuṭila* (hooked) script, a calligraphic variety of the cosmopolitan *siddhamatṛka* script. Its flamboyance supports the brilliance of the painting.

Although this folio (along with a fragment of folio 101) was separated from the original manuscript, and now resides in a museum, it is worth remembering that it once belonged to

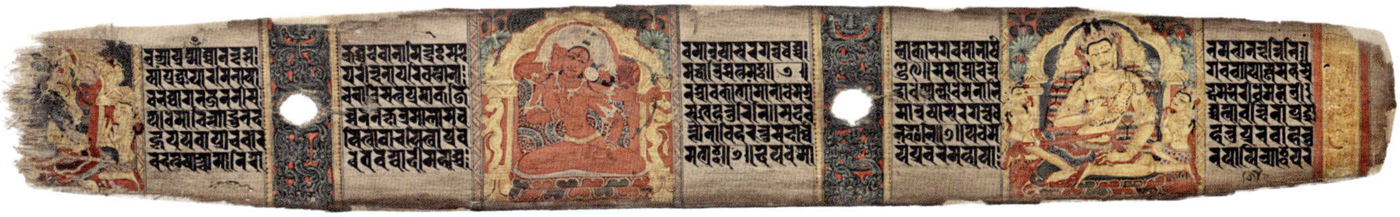

FIGURE 0.2
Folio 206r, *Perfection of Wisdom* manuscript, date: ca. 1143 CE (twelfth regnal year of Gopāla [IV]), patron: laywoman Anaghākā, West Bengal. Organic and mineral pigments and soot ink on palm leaf, size: 6.7 × 48.6 cm. Philadelphia Museum of Art, 1987-52-14. Photo courtesy of Philadelphia Museum of Art.

a manuscript.[2] This was not a codex, but a special type of manuscript called *pothi* in Hindi, unique to Indic manuscript cultures. Among other things, a *pothi* was a portable object, and it often traveled far. Under the original donor's colophon on this same folio, another donor recorded his pious actions with the manuscript. This time, a hereditary Buddhist monk (*śākyabhikṣu*) named Śrī Amṛtadeva, a resident of Tvam vihāra in Bhaktāpur, performed a *pratiṣtha* ritual to renew and install the manuscript as a cultic object.[3] No date is given in this later colophon, but it seems reasonable to suppose the manuscript left the territory of Gopāla in eastern Bihar or West Bengal sometime after its production and came into the possession of Amṛtadeva in Bhaktapur, Nepal, probably no later than the year 1300.

While it is impossible to reconstruct the historical circumstances underlying the manuscript's production and transregional migration, two things might be said about it: first, as a *pothi*-format palm-leaf manuscript, it was portable—even with more than two hundred folios, each measuring about 6.5 × 56 cm—and easily packed for travel to distant destinations; and second, the artisanal intelligence required to make miniature paintings in brilliant primary colors on the surface of palm leaves, depicting a complex iconography known by few outside ritual specialists, existed by the mid-twelfth century in certain parts of India. These two aspects adumbrate two of the central questions motivating this book: Why do primary colors dominate the palette of Indian miniature painting? And how did individual color choices and their collective palette structure knowledge and experience for the viewer?

This book examines the development of Indic manuscript painting during the first half of the second millennium to answer these questions. It takes color—which along with materiality is acutely understudied in South Asian art—as a primary vector of investigation. It contends that the adoption of a *pothi*-format manuscript by visionaries, ritual specialists, and artists as a medium for painting in Indic religious circles enabled the material translation of a private and internal experience of "seeing" into a portable device. In this process, color was neither decorative nor representational; it was the material link between a vision and its artistic output. To understand these manuscript paintings from an emic perspective, this study follows transsectarian and transregional approaches to its subject and uses analytical methods adopted from the study of material culture. Manuscripts are portable objects; as precious religious gifts, powerful cultic objects, or insignia of religious authority, they can move, even within a single location—from a store room to a pedestal, for instance—and at times change hands, sometimes over great distances. The geographic area explored in this study is extensive, connecting Silk Road sites like Khotan and Dunhuang with centers of manuscript production in the South Asian subcontinent. A southern limit to its scope is provided by the Narmada River, since most of the manuscripts I discuss hail from regions north of the traditional boundary between north and south India.[4] Its temporal field is the period between 1000 and 1500 CE—within a "medieval" time frame in global reckoning. A final caveat: although this study proposes alternative ways to approach the history of Indian painting, it is not an exhaustive survey of medieval Indian manuscript painting. Instead, it focuses on the many guises that *pothi*-format manuscripts assumed while functioning as archives, envoys, teachers, and translators of various forms of knowledge across time and space.[5]

To answer the question of why primary colors dominated the palette of Indian miniature painting, we must turn to what Ananda K. Coomaraswamy—the first curator of Indian art in North America and its preeminent savant—called the "blank" period, a time in India when there was "no one great religious inspiration." In the early decades of the twentieth century, when Coomaraswamy was active, the prevailing assessment of Indian tantric traditions was that they were degenerate and corrupt forms of religion; hence, the view that the religious landscape of medieval South Asia provided no great inspiration for artistic activity.[6] As we will see, however, tantric communities made substantial contributions to the art of painting in at least two areas: color theory and material culture. By devising procedures for seeing transcendent objects in a specific set of colors, tantric visionary practice provided a color scheme, based on primary colors, that could be harnessed for artistic purposes, namely, the translation of visionary experience into paintings that would circulate beyond the immediate locus of their productions. In certain tantric communities, there also were seekers (*siddhas*) pursuing transmutation through alchemical tantras who experimented with the ritual use of cinnabar (mercuric sulfide), the mineral source of vermilion.[7] Since the main ores for mineral cinnabar were outside the South Asian subcontinent, vermilion was a precious commodity when it was introduced to artisanal practice in medieval South Asia.

The skills required to produce a miniature were intimately tied to the art of the book. Manuscripts in South Asia were traditionally prepared with birch bark and palm leaves cut to uniform size and strung together through one or two prebored holes. Wooden book covers were provided to protect the folios. A *pothi*-format manuscript was normally oblong, a shape determined by the source material, usually palm leaves measuring 5–6 cm in width (in the case of the so-called talipot palm, *Corypha umbraculifera*, the most common type of palm used in the material examined for this study). With this material, the maximum available space on a given page does not exceed 6 × 55 cm. Given the limited space available to painters, each painted panel on a folio typically measured around 5 × 5.5 cm.

A miniature painting on a page in a Buddhist manuscript, such as the goddess Kurukullā in figure 0.2, rarely finds mention in most narratives of the history of Indian painting, especially after the arrival of the Mughals. The nominally Buddhist subject matter might prompt us to look for more ready comparisons in Buddhist communities nearby. In fact, most early examples of manuscript painting from South Asia come from Buddhist circles, with some exceptional examples hailing from Nepal. We remember that Aṇaghākā's manuscript was taken to Bhaktapur in the Kathmandu valley, where it remained in ritual use, and the iconography of a four-armed red goddess holding a red lotus and drawing a flower bow finds a close parallel in a painting in another manuscript prepared in Nepal (dated 1071), now in the Asiatic Society, Kolkata (A15, folio 152v). The goddess Kurukullā also appears in a number of later Tibetan *thangkas*, suggesting that a Himalayan connection in the development of manuscript painting in South Asia might reward exploration. A sectarian transregional model, however, provides little room to consider the legacy and the contributions of Buddhist manuscript painters in the later history of Indian painting. Here, let us consider an alternative transregional model.

TRANSREGIONAL AND TRANSTEMPORAL CONNECTIONS

As portable objects traveling across different regions, South Asian manuscripts have survived many centuries of use, opening windows to distant connections across time and space. The painting in figure 0.3 was prepared on a vertically oriented sheet of paper. The top register occupying about one-eighth of the page contains a vernacular text (most likely a form of Braj) written in black ink. In comparison to the Sanskrit script in figure 0.2, the scribing seems less controlled, even casual, coinciding with the conversational tone of the text. The text is a cajoling message from Kṛṣṇa that the *sakhi* (the go-between and confidante) delivers to Rādhā, telling her how Kṛṣṇa is love stricken and longing to see her and urging her "come, go and meet Kṛṣṇa struck by Kāma's arrow!"[8] Below this text the scene unfolds in three compartments: the top section shows Rādhā in her apartment being swarmed by bees and addressed by the *sakhi,* whose standing position and lowered left hand connect Rādhā's space to the dense forest where Kṛṣṇa dejectedly longs for his lover; opposite Kṛṣṇa's forest is an inverted *U*-shaped bower, in which a female figure seated on a fully opened lotus draws a flower bow with a lotus stem as an arrow. This figure is commonly taken to be Kāma, or his female consort, Ratī. The accompanying text tells us that Kṛṣṇa is struck by Kāma's arrow. The comparison to Kurukullā's bow and arrow is inevitable.

As the goddess of desire, Kurukullā was regarded in tantric Buddhist communities as a personal deity of some importance.[9] It is unlikely that Kṛṣṇa's painter, identified as Sāhib Dīn (Sahib al-Din), a Muslim painter who served the Hindu Mewar court in seventeenth-century Rajasthan, would have been aware of any recondite Buddhist iconography.[10] Yet images of Kurukullā continued to be made in central Tibet and remained popular from the sixteenth century on. Indrani Chatterjee suggests that through "monastic geographicity" the Himalayan and trans-Himalayan regions remained connected to the rest of the South Asian subcontinent from the thirteenth through nineteenth centuries. Tibetan tantric and Mahāyāna Buddhist lineages "occupied the same terrain" as "the Sufi, Vaiṣṇava, and Śaiva lineages of the fifteenth to nineteenth centuries," yet are forgotten in colonial and postcolonial scholarship.[11] The earliest surviving miniature painting of Kurukullā places her on the Kurukullā peak in present-day Gujarat, and the iconography of the goddess may

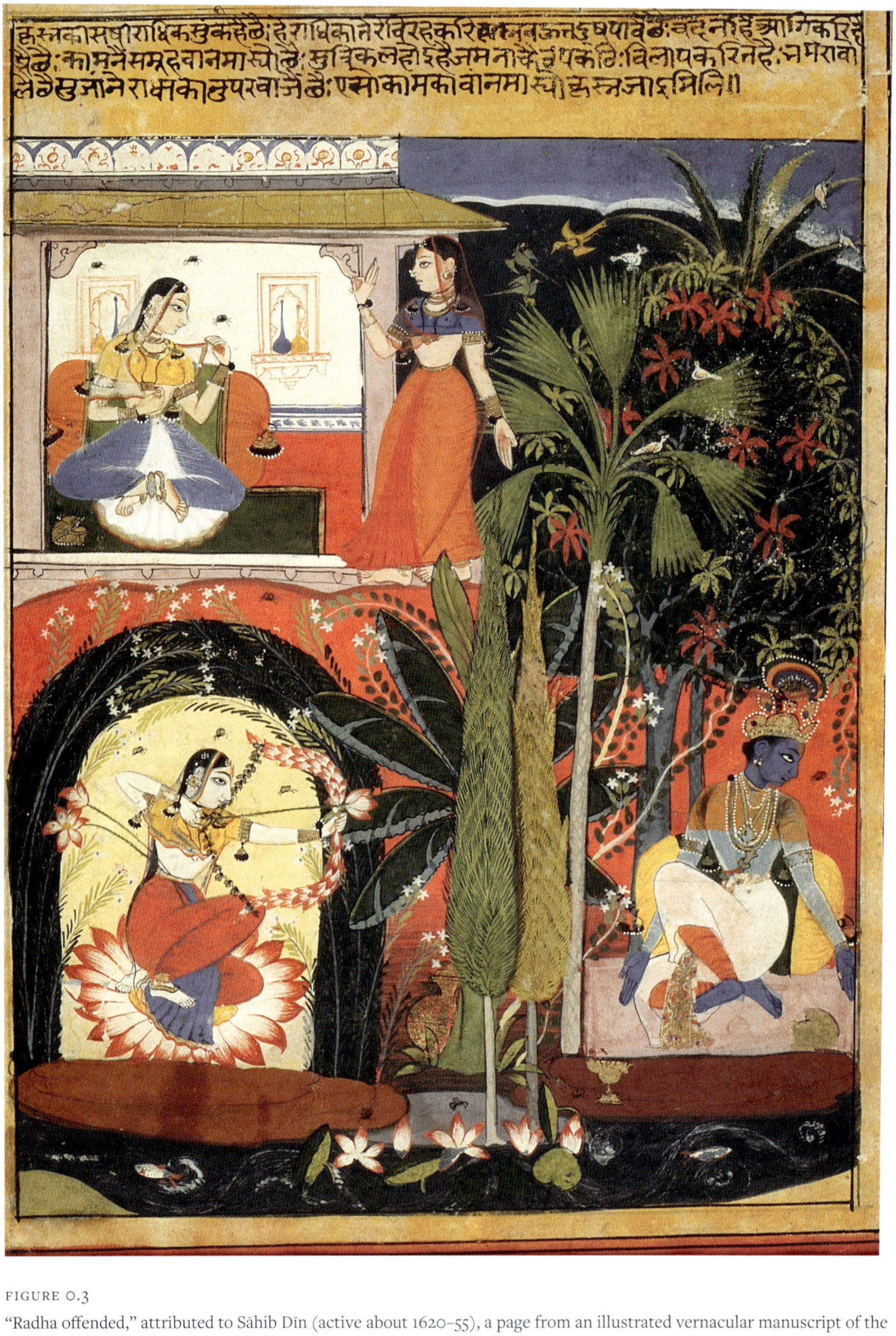

FIGURE 0.3

"Radha offended," attributed to Sāhib Dīn (active about 1620–55), a page from an illustrated vernacular manuscript of the *Gīta Govinda* of Jayadeva, ca. 1635–40 CE, Mewar, Rajasthan. Organic and mineral pigments and soot ink on paper, size: 27 × 21 cm, Kanoria collection, Patna, GKK 187. Image: Regents of the University of Michigan, Department of the History of Art, Visual Resources Collections.

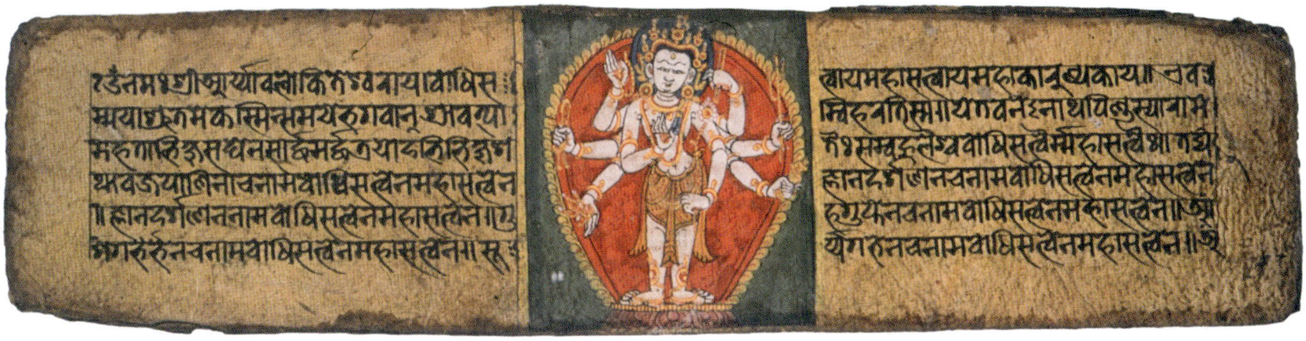

FIGURE 0.4
Folio 1v, *Karaṇḍavyūha* manuscript, dated N.S. 751 (1631 CE), Nepal. Ink and pigments on arsenic treated paper. CUL Add. 1330. Reproduced by kind permission of the Syndics of Cambridge University Library.

in fact have had a non-Buddhist origin. A potential connection between this small detail in a seventeenth-century Rajput painting and earlier Buddhist exemplars may seem inconsequential, but it is worth keeping in mind when we consider the genesis of the Indic manuscript-painting tradition.

The vertical format of the painting is unlike the horizontal *pothi*-format of the manuscript, but the choice of yellow as a backdrop for the band of text at the top of the page invites us to remember the color of a seasoned palm-leaf folio, poeticized as golden. The yellow backdrop is commonly seen in other Rajput court paintings with accompanying texts, and it is close to the color of contemporary Nepalese paper manuscripts. As seen in figure 0.4, the yellow paper folios with text written in black ink in a vernacular, informal hand of a painted manuscript of the *Kāraṇḍavyūha*, dated 1631, resemble the text band in Sāhib Dīn's painting. The materials are different: the Nepalese paper was probably prepared with pulp from the bark of certain bushes or shrubs (for example, *Daphne papyracea*),[12] and its color was produced by an application of arsenic (orpiment) to the surface of the page in the final stage of preparation before scribing. In the Rajput folios, in contrast, the color is the result of a pigment called Indian yellow, said to have been produced from the urine of cows that were only fed mango leaves.[13] The Indian yellow pigment does not seem to have insect-repelling properties, unlike the orpiment used on the Nepalese paper. In any case, formal affinities such as carefully produced color and the proportions of text pages do not necessitate direct contact between artistic traditions, and more historical research is needed before a hypothetical interaction between the seventeenth-century courts of the Rajput rulers and the Malla rulers of the Kathmandu valley can be confirmed.[14]

Recent studies of transregional movements agree that the colonial-era model of Himalayan insularity, which held that Nepal and other kingdoms across the Himalayan foothills were sealed off from the rest of the world, has long been overdue for serious revision.[15] Transregional connections between the Indian plain and a number of Himalayan sites, together with those across the Himalayas, are presently being reconstrued in various fields,

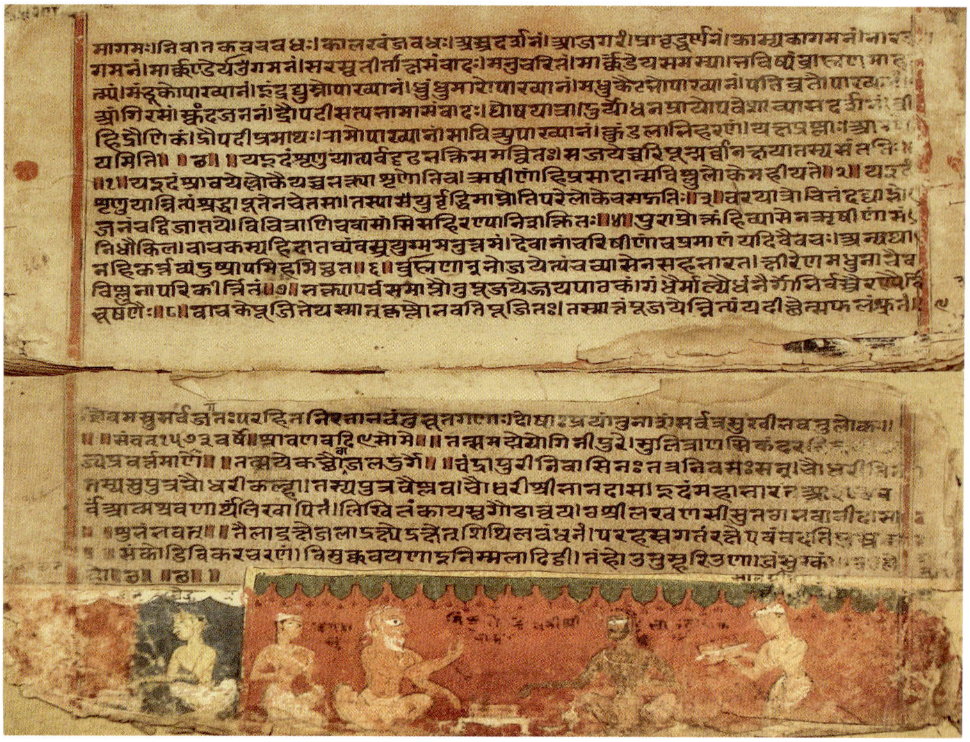

FIGURE 0.5
Folios 361v–362r, the Āraṇyaka Parvan of the *Mahābhārata*, dated V.S. 1573/1516 CE, Delhi. Pigments and ink on paper, Size: 16.5 × 37 cm, Asiatic Society, Mumbai, Acc. No. 966. Image courtesy of the Asiatic Society of Mumbai.

including architecture.[16] As mobile objects, manuscripts may sometimes constitute the only traces of long-ago travels across a network of connectivity now lost to us. Can they be fruitfully engaged to expand our understanding of the premodern era? In one instance, we can see that a sixteenth-century Bengali scribe was employed, in the area of present-day Delhi, in writing out a fully illustrated paper manuscript of the *Āraṇyaka Parvan* (figure 0.5). According to the colophon on folio 362r, the scribe (*kayāstha*) named Bhāvanidasa, son of Lakhaṇasi of the Gauḍa lineage, wrote the manuscript in 1516 (samvat 1573) in Yoginipura (today's Delhi) during the reign of the Sultan Sikandar.[17] Where in Gauḍa his family may have hailed from is difficult to ascertain, but the manuscript bears witness to a scribal family's migration from eastern India to Delhi in the fifteenth century.

THE ART OF THE JAIN SCRIBE

Pursuing transregional Himalayan connections can serve to correct prevailing narratives concerning Buddhism's place in the history of premodern India, but a preoccupation with Buddhist materials risks neglecting an equally strong manuscript tradition that developed among the Jain.[18] Both Buddhist and Jain communities were at the forefront in the

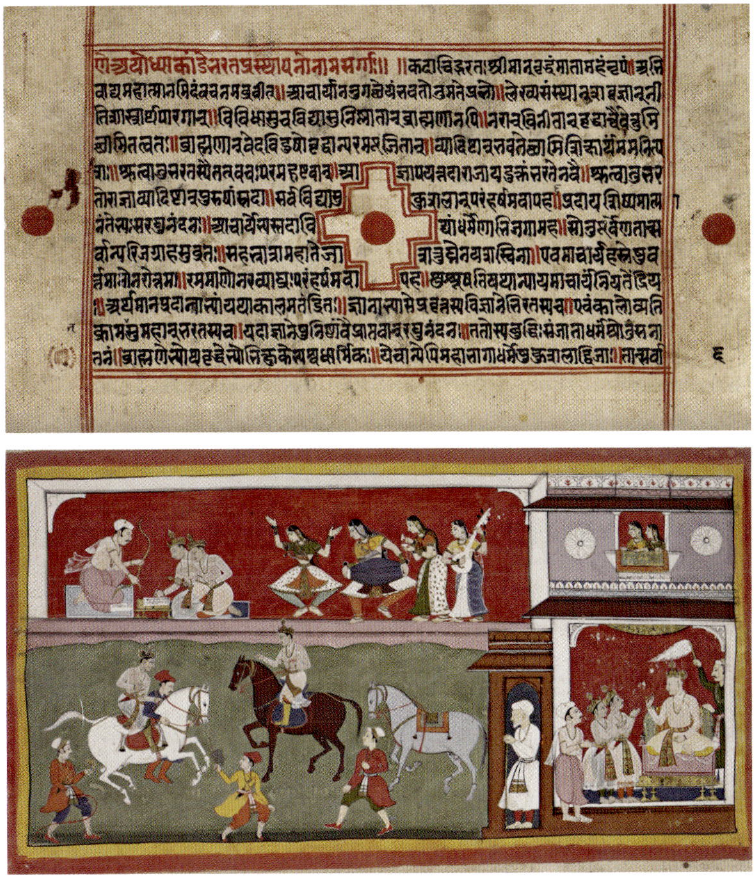

FIGURE 0.6
Folio 6v–7r, Book 2, Ayodhyākāṇḍa of the Mewar Rāmāyaṇa. British Library. Add. MS 15296(1). www.bl.uk/turning-the-pages/?id=68b0d8eb-787f-4609-9028-8cd17ff05c96&type=book.

development of manuscript cultures in South Asia. In an orthodox Brahmanic society where Vedic traditions taught the supremacy of oral instruction, both were considered heterodox. The preservation of their teachers' teachings in written form played an important role early in their respective histories well before the beginning of the Common Era. The manuscript examples we will examine in this study are only selectively drawn from a vast corpus of surviving Jain manuscripts made before the sixteenth century. It is important at the outset to establish that the expertise in manuscript production that the Jain were known for was also held in high esteem by patrons in non-Jain communities. For example, in the Rajput court of Jagat Singh, it was a Jain scribe, Mahātma Hīrānanda, who was commissioned to write the monumental Mewar *Rāmāyaṇa*, an undertaking that would require seven volumes of paper manuscripts in *pothi* format. The first book was completed on December 31, 1649.[19] The Mewar *Rāmāyaṇa*'s importance in art history is largely the result of Sāhib Dīn's work as the painter of the *Yuddhakāṇḍa* and two other books of the *Rāmāyaṇa* that have been attributed to him; the efforts of its scribe and the context in which he worked have gathered little attention so far.

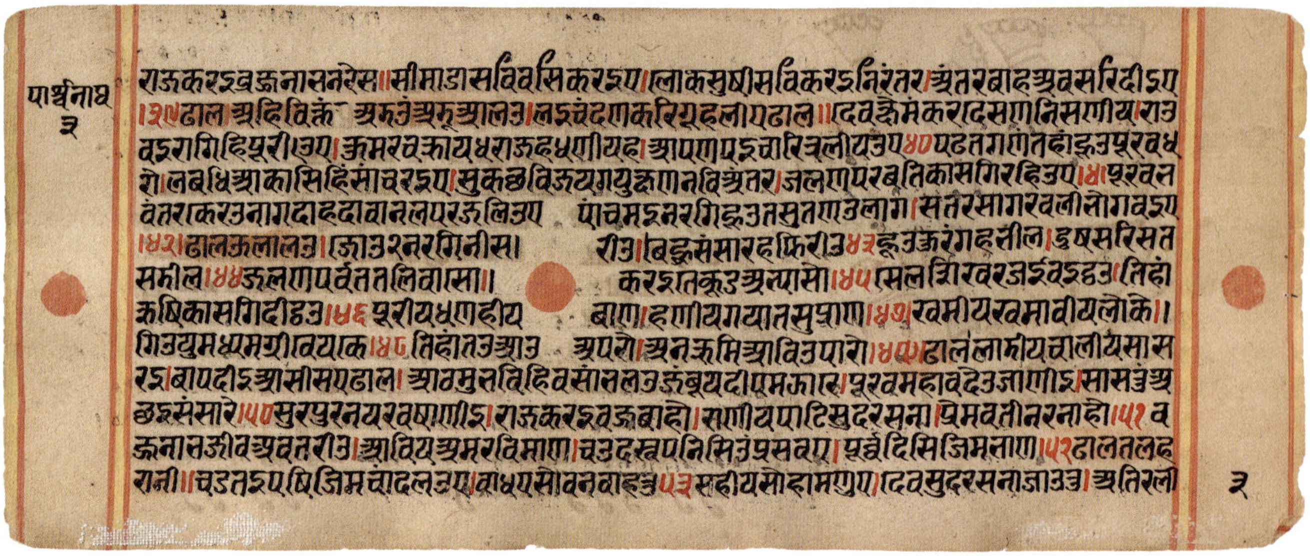

FIGURE 0.7
Folio 3v, Jain manuscript of the *Ratnasāra*, dated Samvat 1633 (1576 CE), Gujarat? Pigment and ink on paper, 10.5 × 26.5 cm. Museum of Fine Arts, Boston, 17.2280, Ross-Coomaraswamy Collection. Photograph © 2021 Museum of Fine Arts, Boston.

As the digitized version available at the British Library website shows, the scribing in the *Bālakāṇḍa*—the first book of the Mewar *Rāmāyaṇa*—is neat and consistent throughout, with all the *daṇḍa*s (punctuation) and chapter (*sargā*) endings finished in red ink, except for a few folios (58r, 97(1)v, and 97(2)v) where the coordination between painting and scribing seems to have gone awry. In the second half of the manuscript, Hīrānanda introduces a distinctive arrangement of the letters in the center of the folio by leaving extra spaces of different length in successive lines, creating a square with four projections, an architecture-based shape with antecedents in earlier Jain manuscript folios.[20] The beginning of the second book brings to bear a singularly expressive signature of a Jain scribe. As figure 0.6 shows, the text side (verso) of the first seven folios of the manuscript features three prominent red dots, placed at the center and both ends of the page in the middle of the folio. This feature appears regularly in early Jain paper manuscripts as if tracing the holes in the folios of an earlier manuscript form. The red dots appear throughout the sixteenth and the seventeenth centuries in other Jain manuscripts (figure 0.7), but in the Mewar *Rāmāyaṇa* it only appears at the beginning of the second book. One could imagine a scenario in which, after successfully completing the first book, the scribe was inspired to bring in a motif from his own tradition but was discouraged or prevented from continuing in that vein.[21] There is much more to learn about the art of the scribe in this princely project to produce an illustrated manuscript of the *Rāmāyaṇa*, especially now that it has become available for digital analysis and reconstruction.

THE GARLAND OF INDIC MANUSCRIPTS

That the painted folios of the Mewar *Rāmāyaṇa* belonged to a manuscript may seem an obvious statement, but it is a fact that most early manuscript pages of "Hindu" subjects have been treated conventionally as belonging to an "illustrated picture series" rather than a manuscript.[22] For example, a painting of Kṛṣṇa seated with adoring *gopis* is commonly identified as belonging to the "dispersed *Bhāgavata purāṇa* series" (figure 0.8). The so-called dispersed *Bhāgavata purāṇa* seems to have been an ambitious project to celebrate Kṛṣṇa, the beloved human incarnation of Viṣṇu, by illustrating the tenth book of the *Bhāgavata purāṇa*; more than two hundred painted folios survive.[23] The text of this manuscript has long been treated merely as an accompaniment to the illustrations despite its presence on the verso of each folio. This concept of an "illustrated picture series" was first deployed by Coomaraswamy in his seminal publication *Rajput Painting* (1917):

> Rajput painting has no connexion with book illustration, and indeed there never was a genuine Indian art of that kind. . . . Whenever Indian painters desired to illustrate a particular story, as often happened, they prepared a series of portfolio pictures consecutively numbered, and either without any text, or with the appropriate text inscribed behind, or sometimes above or below. Such series are not to be described as illuminated manuscripts, but are like the wall-paintings, for example, at Degaldoruwa in Ceylon, if we imagine these transferred to paper and cut up into separate panels.[24]

The analogy between murals and manuscript paintings touches on an important aspect of manuscript design: the internal logic of conceiving it, from an architectural perspective, as a three-dimensional space, a topic to which we will return in chapter 2. Here we might simply note that the use of geometric and vegetal motifs for borders, frames, and other decorative elements, as well as the rhythm of placing painted panels at certain intervals, all point to a perspective on design borrowed from temple architecture.[25] One suspects Coomaraswamy might have had an underlying political agenda in claiming precedence for Rajput paintings by virtue of a link to antiquity, the murals in the Buddhist caves at Ajanta (first to fifth centuries), over the more recent lineage of Mughal paintings, which he placed in the tradition of Persian manuscript illumination.[26] In any case, he was unable to see a painted manuscript as an integral production. Even the "*Rāmāyaṇa* pictures" from Jammu in his study—pages from a *pothi*-format paper manuscript of the eighteenth century—were described as "handsomely endorsed (doubtless by a pandit, not by the painter) with Devanagari texts" rather than as illustrated pages of a manuscript.[27]

Coomaraswamy's rejection of illustrated books as a valid expression of the art of the book in India found expression in subsequent art-historical inquiries that separated manuscript paintings from their physical context for scrutiny, a perspective that echoed the habits of collectors who literally cut manuscripts into pieces so that folios could be displayed as individual paintings.[28] To propose an alternative view, a pioneering exhibition by J.P. Losty, *The Art of the Book in India,* was mounted at the British Library in 1982, initiating serious investigation of the

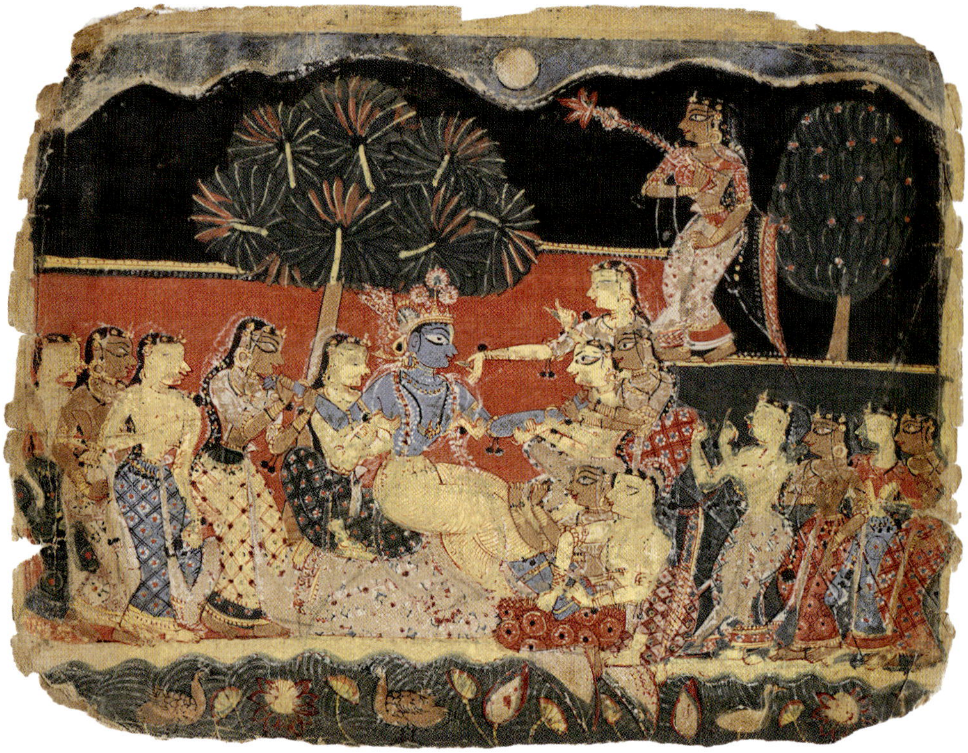

FIGURE 0.8
Krishna with gopis, from the dispersed Bhagavata purāṇa series, ca. 1540, possibly Mathura. Pigments and ink on paper, 17.5 × 23.5 cm. Harvard Art Museums/Arthur M. Sackler Museum, Gift of Mr. and Mrs. Peter Bienstock, 1974.724. Photo © President and Fellows of Harvard College.

manuscript cultures of South Asia. More recently, the National Mission for Manuscripts, established in 2003 under India's Ministry of Tourism and Culture, has worked to build public awareness of Indian manuscript traditions as an important cultural heritage, their initial efforts culminating in a landmark exhibition, *The Word Is Sacred, Sacred Is the Word: The Indian Manuscript Tradition,* held at the National Archives of India in 2007.[29] But despite growing scholarly interest in South Asian manuscript cultures, no serious attempt has yet been made to examine the history of Indian painting with insights gained from manuscript studies.[30]

Shifting focus from painting schools and sectarian styles to an exploration of how the unique manuscript cultures of India participated in the development of manuscript painting brings into view the genesis of specific artistic solutions and their dissemination along various transregional networks. Finding an early painted manuscript of the *Devī-Māhātmya* (now in the Shimla State Museum) or a now dispersed "Tantric Devī series" in the Punjab Hills, both painted in brilliant primary colors, is no longer a surprise. Rather, it might even be expected in an area that lies so close to the innovative Himalayan and trans-Himalayan regions where manuscript culture flourished, as will be discussed in chapter 1.[31]

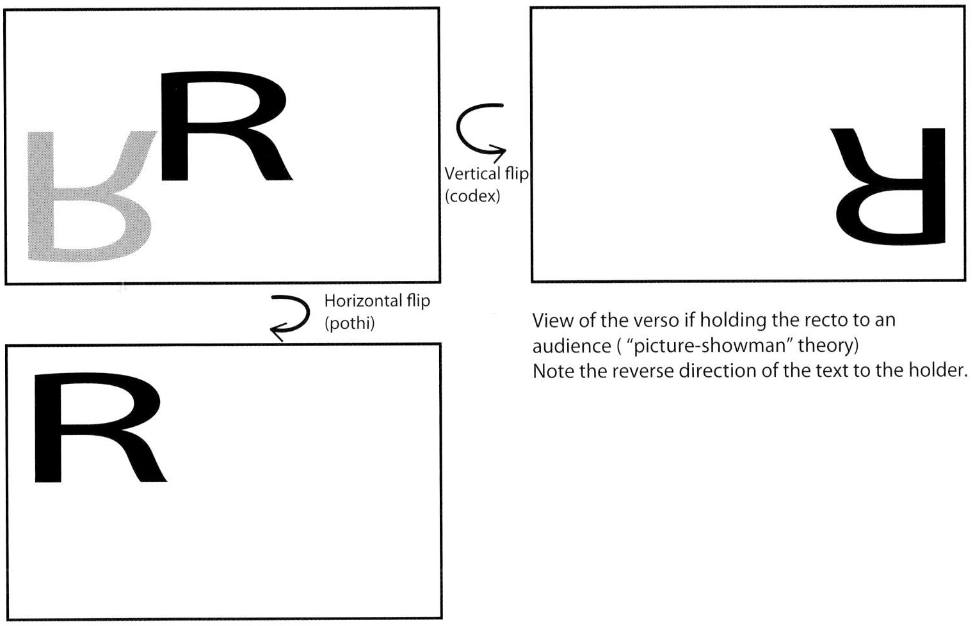

FIGURE 0.9
Orientation and directionality between verso and recto in a *pothi* manuscript. Image © Jinah Kim.

Traditions of manuscript painting developed in the context of religious manuscript production during the first centuries of the second millennium, with prominent contributions from Buddhist and Jain communities. By looking at the materiality of a painting, its *thingness*, and particularly at the *pothi*-format manuscript as a support medium for painting, we examine components in the process of making a manuscript and their social and ritual implications.[32] Recognizing dispersed folios as belonging to a manuscript, for example, introduces experiential aspects of the original context in which each painting was prepared and used. The text on the other side of the painting invokes a directionality in how each folio must be handled, since folios in a *pothi*-format manuscript need to be flipped horizontally to give legibility to the text. In other words, if one holds the painting out to the viewer as in public storytelling, the text on the back of the folio, faced from behind, runs in the opposite direction, making it difficult if not impossible to read (figure 0.9).

In the *Bhāgavata purāṇa* series, the paper folios have nearly three times the height and one-half the width of a folio in a typical *pothi* manuscript in palm leaf. By the seventeenth century, the vertical format typical of a codex began to be seen in "Hindu" courtly painting production, indicating growing awareness of Islamic and European manuscripts and books bound in a codex format. That the shift toward taller vertical formats in manuscript production took several centuries in South Asia suggests the strength of a strong indigenous manuscript tradition committed to a different conception of the format of a book. As was seen in the case of the Mewar *Rāmāyaṇa*, the choice of the *pothi* format signaled in many ways a

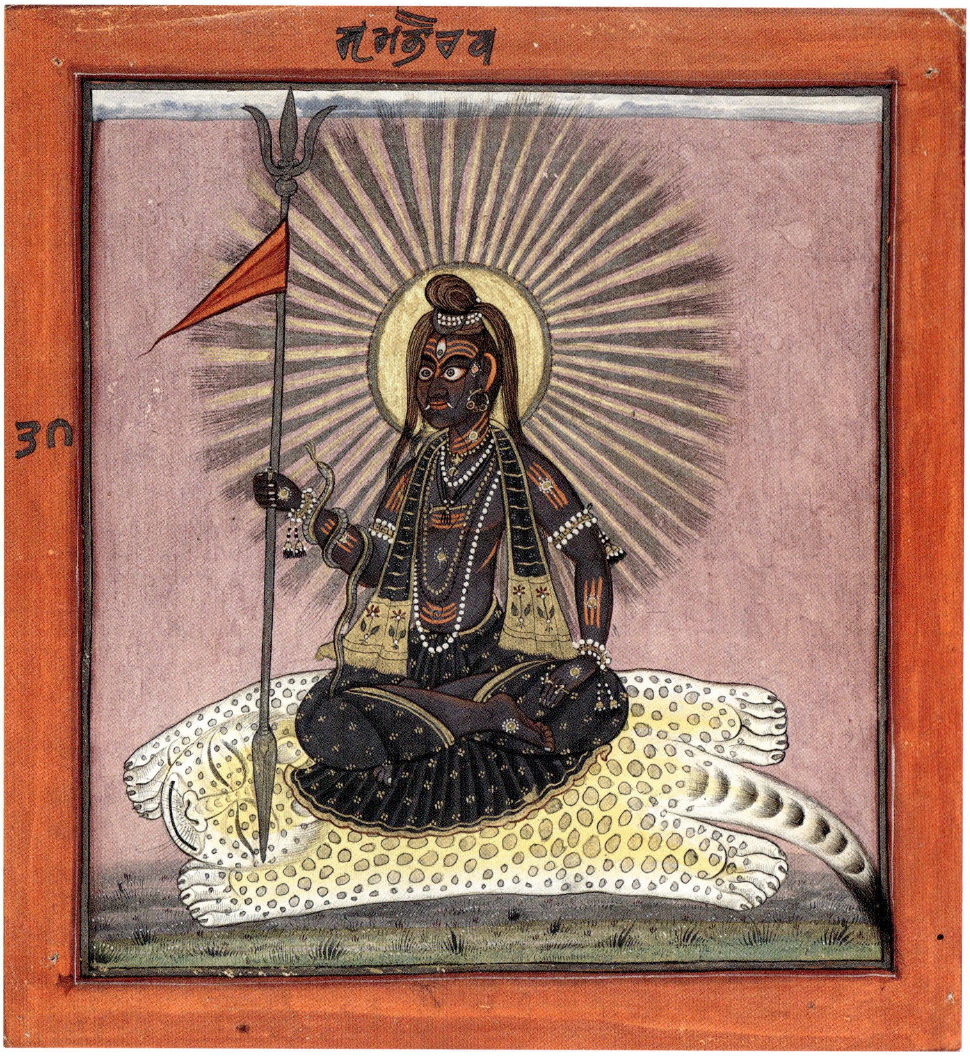

FIGURE 0.10
Bhairava, "Tantric Devī series," ca. 1660–70, Basohli, Punjab Hills. 22 × 21 cm, image: 18.2 × 16.8 cm. Museum of Fine Arts, Boston, 17.2792, Ross-Coomaraswamy Collection. Photograph © 2021 Museum of Fine Arts, Boston.

respectful invocation of the Indic manuscript tradition. It served to articulate their own cultural identity over against that of the Mughals.[33]

Even when a folio is square or slightly longer in height than width, the directionality of text and image on either side of a folio suggests that the folio should be turned horizontally. For example, a seventeenth-century folio depicting a light-emitting image of Bhairava seated on a surprisingly sweet-looking leopard skin against a pink backdrop, now in Boston's Museum of Fine Arts, measures 22 × 21 cm (figure 0.10). The folio once belonged to the so-called Tantric Devī series, believed to hail from Basohli, a small town in the Himalayan foothills (average altitude 460 m) in the present-day Indian state of Jammu-Kashmir.[34] On the back of the painting is a three-line Sanskrit text neatly written in *nagari* script. Each of the paintings in the Tantric Devī series similarly bears a short meditational text on the back. The collection as a whole presents a set of fantastic visions of the goddess expressed both poetically and visually.

Leaving aside the question of whether it was conceived as a manuscript or not, it is significant that the text runs in a direction opposite to that of the image; each folio is to be flipped horizontally rather than vertically. This gives a clue to understanding an embodied knowledge shared by the makers and patrons of the image: they lived in a world whose orientation, at least in this one respect, was determined by *pothi*-format manuscripts, where turning a page horizontally rather than vertically was habitual.

The Tantric Devī series has been recognized as a unique occurrence in Indian art because of its "encyclopedic immensity" and seriality.[35] Yet precedents for both qualities can be found in Buddhist manuscripts from five centuries earlier, when some manuscript makers and knowledge experts in Indic Esoteric Buddhist circles of the twelfth century embraced a *pothi*-format manuscript of the *Prajñāpāramitā*, a famous Mahāyāna scripture, as a fitting medium to contain and circulate colorful painted images of the multifarious visions encountered in tantric visionary practice (*sādhana*). In a late twelfth-century manuscript of the *Prajñāpāramitā sūtra,* now in the Varendra Research Museum, Rajshahi, discussed in chapter 4, for example, painted panels depicting various Buddhist deities and transcendental beings mark the beginning and end of each chapter and the beginning and the end of the book. Placed in the middle of each page of the text, which is written without a break (*scriptura continua*) along "hanging" lines on the top, the painted panels are connected through the lines of the text. Visually, the panels appear like colorful beads on a string of text. Indeed, the structural logic of their placement turns the painted manuscript into a *māla,* a garland or rosary.

Whether it is a *puṣpamāla* (flower garland) or an *akṣamāla* (prayer beads), a *māla* is an essential component of daily devotional life in South Asia. Structurally, a *pothi* manuscript is also a type of *māla* with folios strung through prebored holes. No text dictates that a manuscript be designed as a *māla*. But as a design principle, the *māla* concept can help us attain an "emic" (within the tradition, indigenous) view of the art of the book as it developed in medieval South Asia. Making a *māla* requires that a series of objects follow one another in a sequence without being governed by a rigid hierarchical principle. Accordingly, the most common pattern one sees in Indic painted manuscripts is a series of paintings, each contained in a rectangular frame, placed in a manuscript to create a visual rhythm of its own. In a way, Coomaraswamy's insistence on the idea of a "series" was not completely misplaced, for seriality, though of a different kind, seems to have been a core characteristic of the production of Indic painted manuscripts. Even when narratives were chosen to be illustrated, the design of the manuscript limited the appearance of painted scenes to self-contained, framed panels. The popularity of the painted Rāgamāla(s)—often designated as sets, series, or cycles—at "most Indian courts, from Gujarat to Bengal and from the Himalayan foothills to the Deccan" from the late sixteenth century on bears witness to the widespread dissemination of the *māla* idea as a template for painted manuscript production.[36]

MENTAL IMAGES, COLOR CODING, AND PIGMENTS

The text on the back of the Bhairava painting conjures the image of a dark (*śyāma*) and youthful Bhairava, protector of the three worlds, dressed in dark clothes to be worshipped and holding a victory banner, with which one should meditate while recollecting the goddess who resembles the sun and the moon rising above the peak in one's heart.[37] The unusual depiction of alternating gold and silver light rays behind Bhairava's head suggests a close relation between the text and the image. The painting creatively invokes the image of the goddess as described in the text; she is like the sun and the moon rising above the peak, and Bhairava's head with matted hair is shaped like a mountain peak behind which the sun (a golden disc) and the moon (a silver disc behind the golden one) rise up. The relation between the painted image and the text is deeply intertwined; physically appearing on either side of a sheet of paper, they confirm and substantiate each other—one as an instruction for meditating on a mental image and the other as a pictorial articulation of the mental image in full color. The unnamed artist has translated an internal vision held in one's heart into shimmering rays of light carefully executed in gold (with powdered gold) and silver.

In tantric visionary practice, a *sādhana* (lit. accomplishing or conjuring a deity) requires a practitioner (a *yogin* or *mantrin* in Sanskrit *sādhana* texts) to identify with a chosen deity and achieve transcendence through prescribed ritual techniques. The core techniques involve three basic elements: controlled movement of the body, which assumes certain postures (*āsanas*) and hand gestures (*mudrās*); inward vision of a figural image of the divine, often transforming from a circle to a letter to a figure; and utterance of sound. For example, a short *Kurukullā-sādhana* (SM177) states that after preliminary rituals, one should become Lady Kurukullā (*kurukullā-bhaṭṭārikā*), whose red, four-armed form rises from the letter *tāṁ*, seen also in red on a solar disc that appears on a red night lotus, after which the mantra *oṁ kurukulle hrīḥ svāhā* should be recited. The process of identifying the vibrating sound of auspicious syllables with visual forms in tantric visionary practice produces an internal experience that "appears on the mind-sky in flashes and sparks," according to Benoytosh Bhattacharya.[38] Although Bhattacharya's characterization of the experience may sound alarming, production of a visionary image during *sādhana* is said to be controlled and deliberate, far from the chaotic profusion of colors often used to evoke psychedelic experiences in contemporary media.

The element of color has often been used as a tool to convey information, as the systems of color coding that can be found in every society in human history demonstrate. In a recent project of the Gallant lab at the University of California at Berkeley, RGB colors were assigned to twelve semantic categories in order to map the brain's responses to hearing a story: red for "social," blue for "outdoor," yellow for "body part," green for "visual," purple for "mental," brown for "place," pink for "violence," light green for "number," and so on.[39] Using functional magnetic resonance imaging (fMRI) to measure brain activity, the project reveals a cerebral cortex filled with color.[40] Although the human brain does not light up in different colors to register intellectual or emotional responses, this visualization of a complex data set disambiguates an otherwise monochromatic picture and helps to make its components and their relationships comprehensible. It is also undeniable that the ensuing 3D model of the brain, in vibrant color, has a certain visual appeal as well.

Color is the essence of vision. It captures the most primal aspect of internal visionary experience.[41] In the context of tantric visionary practices, color is neither superficial nor decorative. As the dark (*śyāma*) color of Bhairava or the redness (*rakta*) of Kurukullā suggests, color constitutes an important piece of visual information in the articulation of a figural form of the divine—that is, a chosen deity—in a *sādhana*. Although color is often treated cursorily as one of the attributes in iconographic studies, it is not only symbolically meaningful but is also the material link that can help unpack the constructive relationship between vision and art. Sustained art-historical inquiry on color can shed light on artistic processes that contributed to shaping visionary experiences.

In what for convenience I will call an Indian Esoteric Buddhist (IEB) color system, a set of five colors is used to represent the five Buddha families and the five directions: (1) blue—Akṣobhya—east; (2) red—Amitābha—west; (3) white—Vairocana—center; (4) yellow—Ratnasambhava—south; and (5) green—Amoghasiddhi—north. This system became an important tool for systematizing and encoding a prodigious amount of visual knowledge in Esoteric Buddhism. While the notion of a scheme of five primary colors was present in South Asia from at least the sixth century, as attested by the five root colors mentioned in the *Citrasūtra* section of the *Viṣṇudharmottara Purāṇa*, the directional five-color system documented in Buddhist *sādhana* literature seems to have been adopted in the eleventh century. Was it coincidental that this was also the time when painted manuscripts began to appear in Indic Buddhist communities?

In fact, the systematic adoption and widespread application of the pentad system in image making in the twelfth century occurred in tandem with an increase in color opacity in manuscript painting. As discussed in chapter 5, the application of five colors painted in brilliant opaque pigments seems to have become the norm in Indic Buddhist painting by the end of the twelfth century. At the same time, technical breakthroughs in the preparation of pigments and the artistic methods for applying them also contributed to the dissemination of the IEB color system.

Thus, tantric visionary practice and its artistic expression in manuscript painting can be identified as signaling an important technological advance in the transmission of visual information. Images that externalized visions of deities, translating them into pictorial form, gave to manuscript culture an inestimable resource for conveying how such visions were to be imagined and experienced. Although it is impossible to determine whether the goddess Kurukullā in figure 0.2 or any of the other images in Aṇaghākā's manuscript bore any relationship to actual *sādhana* practice, it seems plausible to suggest that the makers and users of the manuscript may have been aware that the images were externalizations of internal visions rooted in tantric practice. We know that specific images were carefully chosen to empower a manuscript as a cultic object. It is equally plausible that these miniature paintings informed the ways in which such visions were to be experienced. It is worth bearing in mind that the portable medium of a *pothi*-format palm-leaf manuscript functioned as a vessel enabling the visual information generated in visionary practice to circulate in color and in a set.

At the intersection of science and art, this study integrates the results of scientific analysis of pigments with historical analysis of the use of color in Indic manuscript painting. As Teun Goudriaan once remarked, the color terms in Sanskrit religious texts are bewildering.[42] This response is not unique to the study of South Asia, as the experience of color is highly subjective and the semiotic challenges posed by color terms are present in any language.[43] As it happens, the fluid semantic range in Sanskrit makes it especially challenging to identify which color a color term denotes, since its meaning has likely changed over time and differs depending on the context. Given the brilliant blue coloring of the beloved Hindu god Kṛṣṇa seen in figures 0.3 and 0.8, we may imagine that the term *kṛṣṇa* points to "blue." However, as we will see in chapter 6, the history of Kṛṣṇa's "blueness" owes a great deal to historical interventions, especially the artistic intelligence that employed different types of mineral pigments, such as ultramarine (lapis lazuli) and cobalt, to produce a new and brilliant blue.

With data gleaned from scientific analysis of pigments and by attending to the physical aspects of paintings, we can learn more about the material conditions and artistic processes that went into the creation of the formal characteristics of a painting. As one example, a strong pulse of calcite in an XRF analysis indicates that the artist(s) must have applied an extra layer of white pigment to obtain colors of higher opacity.

The ongoing discussions of color in art history have been greatly helped by recent research in conservation science and the technical underpinnings of art history. A multidisciplinary research project on color in European medieval illuminated manuscripts led to a landmark exhibition, *Colour: The Art and Science of Illuminated Manuscripts,* held in 2016. Color has also been an important area of exploration in pre-Columbian and Latin American art with a number of studies actively incorporating pigment analysis data,[44] and a number of recent studies have explored color and its material and political history in early modern Europe and North America.[45] However, there is still a dearth of historical data for medieval South Asia, and we have little or no information on individual artists engaged in the production of manuscript paintings. In this circumstance, letting objects tell a story of their own making and use based on a careful reading of the visual and material evidence pursued in this study is all but necessary and crucial for the study of color.[46]

OVERVIEW OF THE CHAPTERS

In three parts, this book is concerned with the manuscript as an artistic medium, vision, and color. Part 1 examines the development of the *pothi*-format manuscript as a painterly medium that uniquely encompasses textuality, visuality, and materiality. Chapter 1 challenges the common scholarly assumption that treats paintings in all mediums as if they belonged to a single artistic tradition—even despite evidence to the contrary. The adoption of the manuscript as a medium for painting is a relatively late phenomenon; and this chapter explains the circumstances that may have inspired such a move and discusses the subsequent impact of this development. It also highlights the importance of a trans-Himalayan manuscript culture where the practice of making painted manuscripts flourished.

Chapter 2 proposes that religious architecture was an inspiration and a potential model for the development of the art of the book. The regulated placement of painted panels containing images of deities within the three-dimensional space of a manuscript turned them into miniature temples that were not only portable but also potent cultic objects. The chapter concludes with a transsectarian comparison of images and textual sources documenting how the *pothi*-format manuscript became a fitting vehicle for the transmission of knowledge and authority in medieval South Asia.

Part 2 delves into the world of tantric vision, its associated practices, and the role of painted manuscripts in the dissemination of esoteric visual knowledge. Chapter 3 examines the process by which painted palm-leaf manuscripts became vessels for circulating images of visionary practice. Painted manuscripts, in particular, were embraced as an important medium for the transmission of esoteric visual knowledge. Passages relating to the art of the book in the *Vajrāvalī* (lit. "garland of vajras") by Abhayākaragupta conclude the chapter by situating painted manuscripts within the world of Esoteric Buddhist rituals.

Chapter 4 identifies the *māla,* or garland, as a distinctly Indic model for the design of painted manuscripts. As a case study, it focuses on a late twelfth-century manuscript of the *Perfection of Wisdom,* now in the Varendra Research Museum (VRM), Rajshahi, Bangladesh, which demonstrates how the inherent seriality and spatial ordering of images accommodated by the *pothi* format can help record, compile, and circulate tantric visual knowledge tied to initiation linages. It explores the iconographic structure of the VRM manuscript and explains in detail some of the unusual Esoteric Buddhist iconography in it.

Part 3 turns to one of the central questions of the study and explores why primary colors dominate the palette of Indian painting by examining how primary colors became prominent features of the art of painting in India during the second millennium. I seek answers to this question in patterns of historical change: the adoption of color as an encoding tool for systematization of esoteric visual knowledge by medieval tantric groups, especially in Buddhist circles, and increased interest in the potency of certain materials generated by tantric practitioners. This is especially evident among those seeking transmutations of matter, such as siddhas seeking mercury, which is deeply tied to vermilion, the pigment responsible for the brightest, most powerful color in many paintings. Chapter 5 examines the history of the five-color system developed in Indian Esoteric Buddhism as a tool for encoding visual knowledge. This investigation uncovers changing attitudes toward color and provides clues to why primary colors in high opacity became important in painting in medieval South Asia, a development that presaged the spread of painted manuscripts. This chapter also discusses color theory as articulated in medieval Indic religious traditions to explore the symbolic meaning and function of color in medieval South Asia.

Chapter 6 discusses the material evidence of color use in manuscript painting in addition to close readings of texts, including artistic treatises and ritual manuals like the *Nāṭyaśāstra,* the *Citrasūtra,* and the *Vajrāvalī* that can help explain the Indic theory of color. Through laboratory research conducted in Boston and Cambridge, Massachusetts, we have new information on the material composition of pigments used in Indic manuscript paintings, especially in the period before 1500. Identifying these pigments in conjunction with a close study of contemporary treatises explaining Indic theories of color affords us a glimpse into the artists' intimate, embodied knowledge of each color's material properties.

The book ends with an epilogue that discusses the methodological and historiographic implication of the book's analytical focus on color. The question of why primary colors dominate Indian miniature painting is thus addressed by examining the centrality of color in tantric visionary practice that was intimately tied to the development of the art of manuscript painting in India. Through an art-historical reading of material analysis of colorants, we get a glimpse of the artistic intelligence that shaped the color experience in painting.

PART ONE

MEDIUM

1

PAINTING AND ITS MEDIUM

A PAINTING IN HAND

In figure 1.1, we see a congregation of eleven men on a balcony under a canopy delicately decorated with flowering creepers in pink. In the center of the scene is the main protagonist, the figure for whom the painting must have been prepared. Dressed in a pink robe with gold trim, he wears a multicolored, bejeweled turban on his head, holds the stem of a hookah in his left hand and a small picture in his right, and he leans against a large white pillow. In the composition of this figure, the prominent status of Maharaja Sansar Chand (r. 1775–1823) of Kangra is unmistakable. The creator of the painting, possibly Purkhu of Kangra (c. 1780–1820), further ensured that his patron's stature would stand out through a subtle manipulation of pictorial elements. The pipe stem Sansar Chand is holding is connected to the hookah placed at the bottom left via a snaking long tube; at the same time, a standing attendant at the top right waves a giant whisk, or chowry, over his head, adding to his aura. The varying sizes of the figures around him, although seemingly perspectival as if capturing spatial arrangements, achieve a hierarchical scaling that is set off from the figure of Sansar Chand by the large

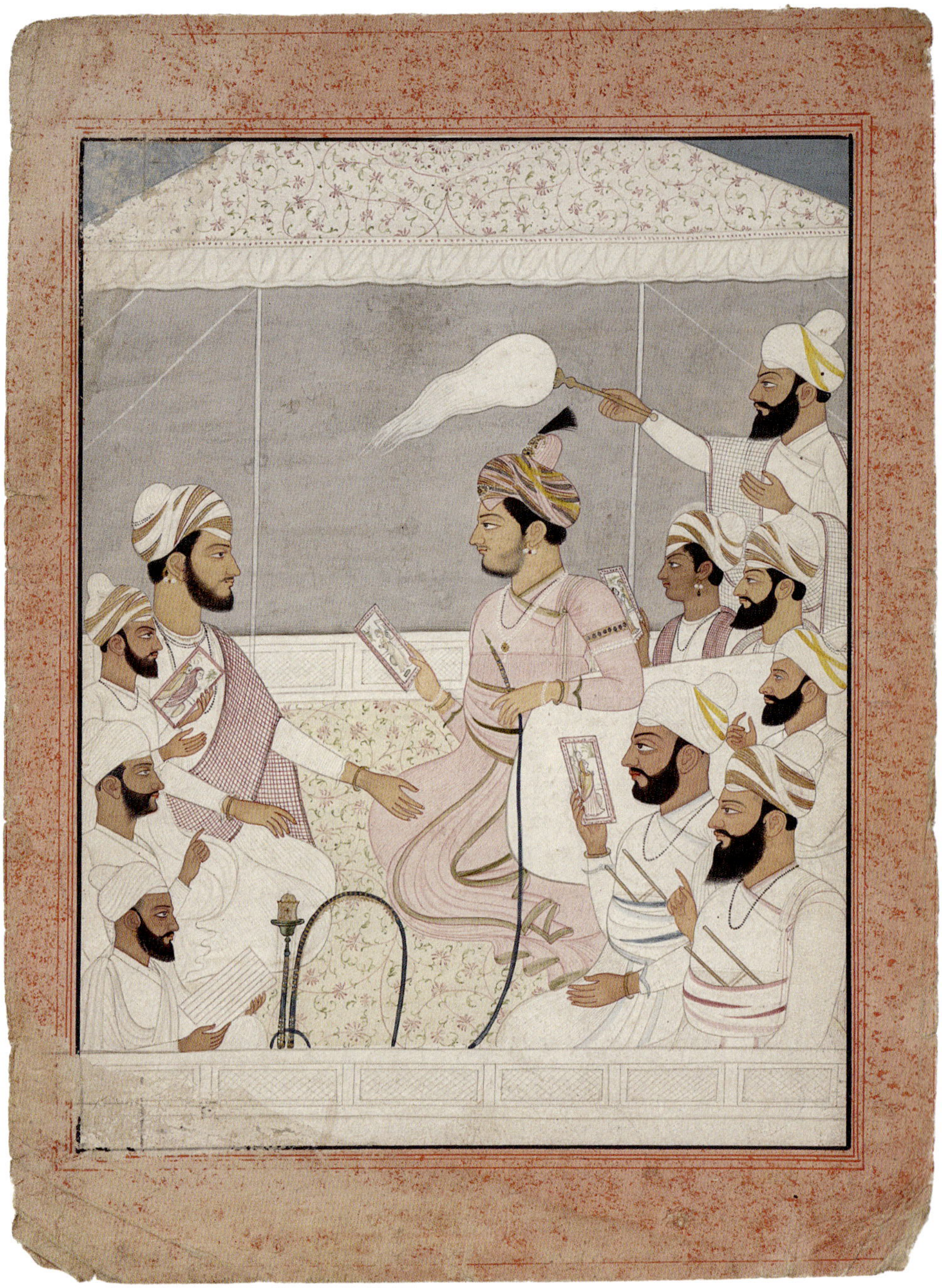

FIGURE 1.1
Raja Sansar Chand (r. 1775–1823) of Kangra inspecting pictures at court, ca. 1810–20, Kangra. 29 × 22 cm page, 23 × 18 cm painting, Acc. No. 2005.9. Museum Rietberg Zurich, Legacy Balthasar Reinhart. © Photo: Rainer Wolfsberger, Museum Rietberg Zurich.

white bolster, which also serves as a plain frame against which a courtier is seen holding a rectangular object, a painting of ladies. While the pictorial convention of depicting faces in strict profile obscures the angle of engagement between the courtier's eyes and the painting, this courtier holds the painting close to his face and appears to be looking at it intensely. What the painting evidently depicts is Maharaja Sansar Chand and his circle of courtiers viewing paintings of women in an informal and intimate setting.

Because Rajput rulers like Maharaja Sansar Chand of Kangra are known to have been avid patrons of the art of painting, finding a painting depicting paintings in use is not entirely unexpected in the work of artists from the Punjab Hills. There is a long history of painting within painting in South Asia; for example, a painting by Abd al-Samad, produced in the 1550s, depicts Akbar presenting a painting to his father Humayun.[1] Another sixteenth-century example is a narrative scene depicting a lady presenting a *paṭa* (painting on cloth) stretched between two sticks, which appears in a Jain manuscript of the *Ādi-purāṇa* dated 1540.[2] Yet this Kangra painting is exceptional because it is so clearly self-referential as an object intended to be held in the hand and viewed intimately. Printed images of the painting do not fully convey this sense, but when examined in close proximity, its intended mode of experience becomes clear. The painting is on thick paper, and at about 29 × 22 cm (23 × 18 cm without borders), its scale is similar to that of the paintings held by four of the noblemen, including Sansar Chand himself. Those who are not holding a painting are gesturing as if commenting on the paintings held by their neighbors. Each of these paintings within the painting is enclosed within a pink border, as is the encompassing painting itself. *This* painting is designed to be held in one hand and viewed close up—just as the men in the painting do. Although more recent than most of the objects discussed in this study, this painting about paintings opens our discussion because it portrays two of this chapter's main themes: painting's materiality and a person's experience of a painting.

There is a tacit scholarly assumption that the practice of painting on manuscripts organically developed from early traditions of mural painting and scroll painting on cloth in ancient India.[3] Another common assumption is that a tradition of manuscript miniatures must have existed, although no material evidence from before the tenth century survives, a circumstance attributed to hostile climates. Apart from these assumptions, is there any evidence to document the origin of manuscript painting? That painting was an important art form widely practiced in ancient India is well established in Indian art history, largely on the basis of the earliest references collected and published by Ananda Coomaraswamy in the 1930s.[4] But the overarching narrative of painting in India that results when all genres and types of painting are merged regardless of their medium and contexts of use has limited our ability to perceive the specific historical circumstances that led to new forms of painting practice and use as well as to our appreciation of certain moments of innovation. This is particularly the case for the period of Indian painting that concerns us in this study, 1000–1500 CE. In this period, various Indic religious communities embraced *pothi*-format manuscripts as a medium for circulating visual knowledge, and the art of the book began to develop in earnest on the South Asian subcontinent.

Painting on the folios of a manuscript prepared from long, narrow palm leaves requires a different approach than painting on walls or cloth—most notably, adjustment to a miniature scale. For viewers, too, the physical manuscript constitutes an entirely different visual and material environment for experiencing painting. From the perspective of manuscript production and use, what may be difficult to grasp at first is that adding colorful pictures to folios did not occur as a natural step in an evolutionary process.

Why this step was taken cannot be explained with a single origin story. Combing through the surviving textual sources that are frequently cited in early histories of Indian painting can provide clues to understanding the genealogy of manuscript paintings, especially when we pay close attention to the media of painting and their contexts of use. Metapaintings, or paintings depicting the use of paintings, such as the Kangran exemplar considered at the beginning of this chapter, can also help us glean the ontological status of painting in premodern South Asia.[5] Weighing the existing clues, is it a surprise to find that the introduction of paintings into handheld manuscripts seems to have been well timed to meet the ritual, theological, and devotional needs of certain religious communities in South Asia? A manuscript with an inherent textual value provides a special medium for painting, and the painted manuscripts of medieval Jaina, Buddhist, and Brahmanical communities were understood to possess a capacity to be much more than a simple repository of pictorial vocabularies for the transmission of style and iconography. As we will see in subsequent chapters, that potential was realized by unnamed, innovative manuscript makers who served Indic religious communities.

ON COOMARASWAMY'S "ONE HUNDRED REFERENCES"

In looking for clues regarding the materials and contexts of use for paintings in India before 1500, Coomaraswamy's compilation of over one hundred references to Indian painting (henceforth ORP) provides a convenient port of embarkation. Coomaraswamy's aim was to establish the antiquity and longevity of painting traditions in India, and so he made room in his list for a number of "references" that merely mention painting, sometimes as an analogy ("beautiful like a painting") or as a backdrop of a scene (painted walls and ceilings of a building).[6] As seen in table 1.1, more substantive references were found in narrative genres, including religious texts; nearly half are taken from Buddhist (thirty-four references, including an inscription from Ajanta) and Jain texts (fourteen).

Although there are obvious limitations to using ORP as a historical data set,[7] perhaps more telling for our purposes is the lack of a clear working definition of "painting." Some of his references point to pictures in a person's mind, while others may better fit under a broader category of "image"; some have to do with drawings, others are about colorful, decorative patterns.[8] In the analysis that follows, the idea of painting will be restricted to three-dimensional material objects laden with colorants.

The premodern textual sources surveyed in ORP identify three types of support medium for painting: walls (Skt. *bhittī*), woven cloth (Skt. *paṭa*), and (wooden) tablets (Skt. *phalaka*). Grouping these references, we find that fifty-three are related to murals, a predominance consistent with the strong evidence of mural painting surviving from the first millennium

TABLE 1.1 **TYPES OF SOURCES COMPILED IN COOMARASWAMY'S 100 REFERENCES TO INDIAN PAINTING (1930)**

Type	Number of references	[ORP nos.]
Vedic	1	
Early Buddhist	7	Nikāya and Vinaya [2–4]; Therā-therigāthā (later text)][5–8]
Early Jaina	3	Āyāraṃga Sutta [9]; Kalpasūtra [10–11]
Epic	1	Mahābhārata [12–13]
Later Pali Buddhist	15	Jātakas [14–21]; Visudhimagga of Buddhaghoṣa [22–24]; Mahāvaṃsa [25–27]; Aṭṭhasālinī [28]
Sanskrit Buddhist	8	Avadānas [29; 33; 35, 36] Sūtrālaṃkaras [30, 31], Saṃyuktavastu [32]; MMK [34]
Early Tamil	2	Paṭṭinapalai [34]; Maṇimekhalai [38]
Technical Sanskrit literature	3	Kāmasūtra [39, 40]; Nāṭyaśāstra [41]
Kāvya (including drama)	27 [42–68]	Mostly Sanskrit dramas: i.e., Bhāsa's [44, 45, 46, 47], Kālidāsa's [48], Mṛcchakaṭikā of Śūdraka [51, 52] Bāṇa's [54–64], Uttararāmacarita of Bhavabhūti [65] also includes Medieval texts like Prabodhacandrodaya [67] and Mudrarākṣasa [68]
Other Sanskrit literature	8 [69–76]	Includes KKS [73, but not the story of Vikramāditya's painter]
Medieval Jaina literature	11	
Inscriptions	3	Ajanta [88]; Ceylon [89]; Ceylon (AD 1593) [90]
"Vernacular"	9	3 Hindi [91, 92, 93], 5 Sinhalese [94, 95, 96, 97, 98], 1 Newari [99]
Chinese	1	Huaqi, 1167 CE

CE in South Asia—most famously, on the walls of the Buddhist cave temples of Ajanta. In addition, there are nineteen references to paintings on woven cloth and three references to painting on a tablet. *Phalaka*s were made from wooden panels and were relatively petite in size, meant to be handheld. The three references to *phalaka* appear under the *kāvya,* or Sanskrit poetry, category in ORP, their use occurring only within a secular context, typically as an object moving between the parties in a romantic affair.

SUPPORT MEDIA FOR PAINTING

PAINTING ON WALLS

The importance of wall painting in ancient India is well attested even though only a tiny fraction of this practice is visible at surviving archaeological sites.[9] Technical treatises on painting in Sanskrit, such as the *Citrasūtra* section of the *Viṣṇudharmottara Purāṇa,* datable to the period between 450 and 650, include detailed discussions on how to prepare a wall for painting, as does the section on royal enjoyments in the *Mānasollāsa* of a Calukya king, Someśvara III (r. 1124–1138).[10] In ORP, nearly half of the references to murals (about twenty-seven) are passing references to painted walls, in the sense of a decorated space. The other references include a few (e.g., Nos. 47 and 96) that suggest a conceptual grasp of the inherent characteristic of a wall as a two-dimensional, immovable surface for painting. References to wall paintings may be divided into four types: decorative, narrative, figurative, and iconographic. (These are not exclusive categories, since narrative, figurative, and iconographic can all fulfill decorative functions.)

The iconographic references point to murals that contain a programmatic wall design, such as a cosmological landscape (No. 20, from the *Mahā-ummaga jātaka*) or a symbolic representation of *samsara* (Nos. 32 and 36, from the *Saṁyuktavastu* and the *Divyāvadāna*). The *bhavacakra* depicted on the northern wall of the entrance veranda area of Ajanta's Cave 17 supports the notion that wall paintings like it were traditionally placed in the most visible area of the architectural space,[11] a discrimination implying an understanding of that space as a public, environmental medium that artists and patrons could use for instructional purposes.

References to narrative murals such as those depicting the *Rāmāyaṇa* or the life stories of the Buddha appear in textual sources dating to the fifth century and later. In the *Visuddhimagga* (lit. "Path of Purification," a Pali text) by Buddhaghoṣa (active ca. fifth century), there is a mention of a cave with painted scenes of the Buddha's great renunciation, which a group of visiting monks admires (No. 22).[12] A more explicit reference to narrative painting on walls appears in the *Uttararāmacarita* of Bhavabhūti (ca. eighth century), where the pregnant Sītā and Rāma are said to admire the painted scenes of their adventures in a picture-corridor in their palace (No. 65).[13] Bhavabhūti uses these vivid descriptions as a literary device to present flashbacks to earlier moments in the story, and while it is possible that visual props may have been prepared for performances of the play, no evidence of it has survived. We only have a glimpse of how the *Rāmāyaṇa* might have been depicted in a wall painting from carvings on temple walls that likely were painted at the time of their creation, such as the eighth-century relief carvings on the Kailasa Temple at Ellora.

A rare pictorial representation of a narrative wall painting appears in a sixteenth-century manuscript of the *Chandayan* now in the Manchester Library (Hindusthani no. 1). Not cited in Coomaraswamy's ORP, the *Chandayan,* a Sufi love poem written in Hindavi by Maulana Daud (completed in 1379), is a great resource for the period that concerns us in this study. Drawing heavily on folktales then circulating in northern India,[14] the poem describes the scene when the hero, Laurik, secretly enters the room where the heroine, Chanda, sleeps (figure 1.2):

> All corners of the walls were colored in red. And on this, painting was done in gold water. Lanka was drawn (where) Vibhiṣaṇa was. Ten-headed Rāvaṇa was also added to it. The abduction of Sītā and Rāma's battle (with Rāvaṇa), the Pāṇḍava group and the battlefield of Kurukṣetra, (were also drawn). Cheating and dice rolling of the gambling scene [from the *Mahābhārata*] were depicted, and the city of Ujjain and Vaitala were drawn. In the middle, the poetry of Pāṇḍava [*Mahābhārata*] was written and placed, and the *Cakravyūha* was (also written/drawn) with which enemies were observed. Lion, tiger, deer, deer forest, and a beast (fierce animal) [in impossible manner] were (depicted). Ślokas of the *kathā kāvya* [narrative poem; probably the *Rāmāyaṇa*] and *Naṭyārāmbha* (*naṭya grantha*) were written and placed in four lines.[15]

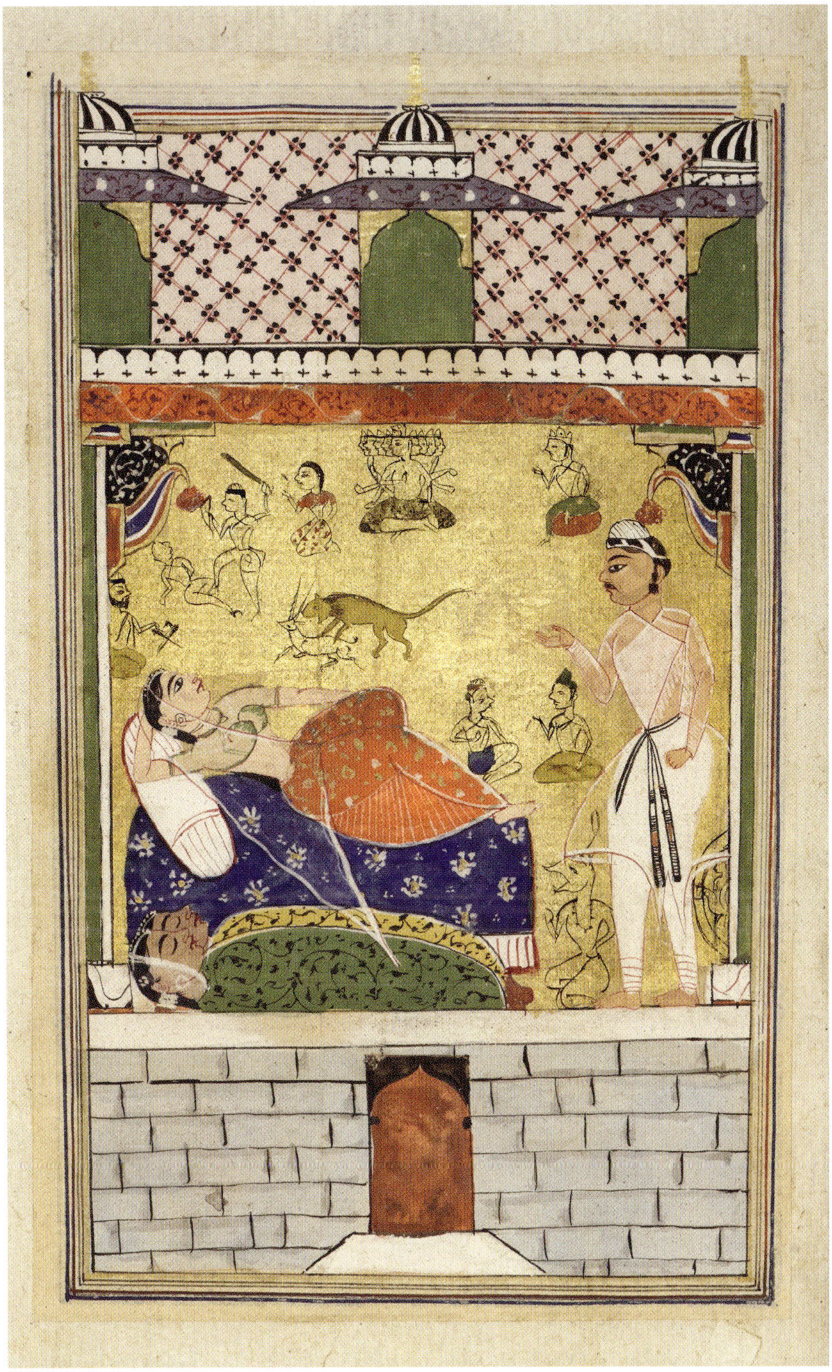

FIGURE 1.2

Folio 160r, Laurik enters Chanda's bedroom, Laur-Chanda manuscript, ca. 1530–40, Mandu(?). The University of Manchester Library, Hindustani MS 1. Image: Copyright of the University of Manchester.

For the most part, the illustrations in the Manchester manuscript follow the narrative content of the *Chandayan* quite closely.[16] While other illustrated *Chandayan* manuscripts fill the interior spaces with decorative patterns to convey the opulence required of royal palaces,[17] the painter(s) of the Manchester manuscript concentrate on depicting the narrative elements mentioned in the text. Although the wall color is gold instead of vermilion, the figures drawn in black line on top of the gold layer follow the description closely. Centered at the top of the painting is the ten-headed demon king Rāvaṇa, his donkey head neatly arranged above his other nine heads. Vibhiṣaṇa, the king of Laṅka, is seated facing Rāvaṇa, just above the head of the standing figure of Laurik.[18] The female figure kneeling in front of Rāvaṇa and facing left is most likely Sītā. The two figures engaged in combat in front of her may be a condensed reference to the text's evocation of the battle in the *Rāmāyaṇa* and the battle in the *Mahābhārata*.[19] At the left edge of the painting, above the head of the sleeping Chanda, is a male figure with a cross-legged book stand. As the only figure without a counterpart in the text, he could represent a storyteller with a manuscript in front of him, in effect a reference to the poems that were supposed to have been written on the wall. The concise representation of each narrative element matches the text's concise style of narration. Yet the succinct nature of pictorial depiction on a page does not attempt to pose as a realistic rendition of a wall mural; both the manuscript and its fourteenth-century text assume not only the audience's intimate knowledge of the Indic epics but also their familiarity with the practice of putting a narrative painting on walls.

PAINTING ON CLOTH

The references in ORP to paintings on cloth fall into two groups: narrative and figurative. Of the four references to narrative painting on cloth, only the *Dūtavākyam* (No. 44), a Sanskrit drama by Bhāsa, clearly describes a scene from the *Mahābhārata* as a painting is being closely examined and admired for its color and execution.[20] The other three references just mention a *paṭa* or piece of woven cloth, and their inclusion as narrative references presumes that the use of paintings on cloth scrolls was an established practice of storytellers in ancient India.[21] For example, in a seventh-century account of the *Harṣacarita* (Deeds of King Harṣa), Baṇa provides a vivid description of a marketplace performance by a *yamapaṭika,* a man using a painted scroll as the primary object of the spectacle. Painted depictions of the various hells captivate his audience as he elaborates on the tortures and torments awaiting wrongdoers in the next life. A similar type of cloth painting, known as *saṃsāra-cakra paṭa,* is described in a late eighth-century Prakrit text, the *Kuvalayamālā-kahā,* by a Jain author, Uddyotana Sūri.[22] Hemacandra's *Triṣaṣṭiśalākāpuruṣacarita,* written sometime between 1057 and 1173, contains a detailed description of a narrative painting on cloth: in a story about one of Ṛṣabhanātha's former lives, the nurse Paṇḍitā prepares a painting on cloth depicting the heroine Śrīmatī's previous life and displays it in an open space for everyone to see.[23] Presumably, cloth is specified as the painting medium in this story because of the need to depict consecutive narrative events in a convenient, portable package.

The format of these scrolls, whether vertical or horizontal, is difficult to ascertain from the textual descriptions. Most of the surviving traditions of narrative scroll painting—the *paṭa* paintings of Bengal, for example—are vertical in orientation, prompting us to surmise that the historical examples probably were also vertically oriented. On the other hand, there are narrative scroll paintings surviving from Nepal (e.g., *Svayambhūpurāṇa bilampau*) and Rajasthan (Pabuji's *phad*) that are horizontal in orientation.[24] The Nepalese Buddhist practice of displaying narrative scroll paintings (especially long horizontal *bilampaus*) during the festival of Gumlā also warrants attention as a possible connection between narrative murals and narrative scroll paintings on a horizontal format.[25] The main difference between the two would seem to lie in the portability of paintings on cloth—they can be rolled up for easy transportation—as well as the controlled access and temporally conditioned viewing experience they provide.

In the figurative category, the references to painting on cloth can be divided into two groups, secular and religious, based on the context of use. While the sources collected in ORP are far from clear on the secular uses of *paṭa* paintings, other texts occasionally specify *paṭa* as the support medium for painted portraits that figure in secular, often romantic affairs.[26] Religious images painted on cloth are mentioned far more often, and there are many surviving examples. The Buddhist use of scroll paintings on cotton or silk is well known from a number of examples found in Dunhuang's Library Cave, some of which date from as early as the eighth century (figure 1.3). The Dunhuang examples range from painted banners and streamers used as devotional offerings to a full articulation of a maṇḍala scheme, often centered on the bodhisattva Avalokiteśvara. They served liturgical, cultic (often funerary), and devotional purposes. Although no *paṭa* painting securely identifiable as originating from a Buddhist site in India survives, the vast number of surviving Tibetan *thangka*s and Nepalese *paubha*s testify to the widespread use of paintings on woven cloth in Buddhist devotional, liturgical, and esoteric ritual practices.

In ORP, a well-known Buddhist ritual text, the *Mañjuśrīmūlakālpa* (henceforth MMK), possibly compiled sometime during the eighth century, provides the most detailed account of the religious production of paintings on cloth and attests to the medium's importance—especially for performing Esoteric Buddhist rituals. As Matthew Kapstein's analysis shows, every step toward the completion of a *paṭa* painting is governed by a ritually strict set of rules—from the production of cotton thread to the weaving of the fabric, to the final stage of painting.[27] The MMK is certainly not a painter's manual, and it does not provide practical guidance for the makers of the painting.[28] The text's main concern is to establish and maintain ritual purity and efficacy by focusing on control of the environment. In this, the MMK underscores the ritual importance of *paṭa* as a support medium for painting; the whole enterprise is dedicated to the transformation of a raw material—in this case, cotton—into a woven fabric through sanctified labor.

Most of the references in ORP to the religious use of *paṭa* paintings date from the eighth century or later. A Buddhist text known from manuscripts found in Gilgit and dated to around the sixth century, the *Sarvatatthāgatādhiṣṭhāna-sattvāvalokana-buddhakṣetrasandarśanavyūha sūtra* (lit. a "splendid vision" of beholding the Buddha field, abode of all tathāgatas, observing sentient beings; henceforth SSB), provides an earlier reference to woven cloth as a support

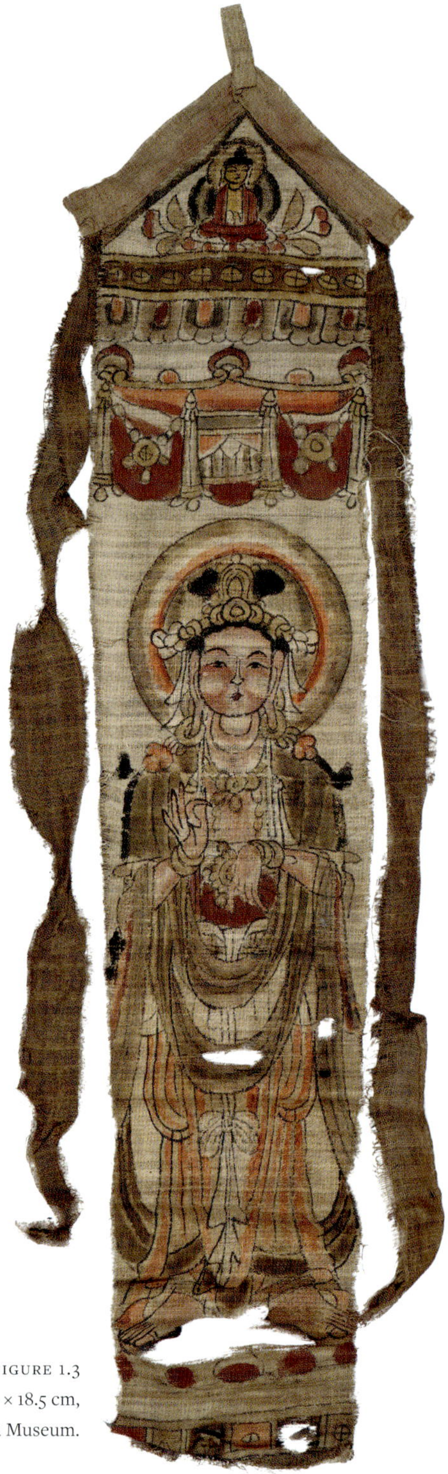

FIGURE 1.3
Painted banner on hemp, ca. 901–50 CE, Dunhuang Cave 17. 100 × 18.5 cm, British Museum 1919,0101,0.147. © Trustees of the British Museum.

medium for painting. As a treasure trove on Buddhist ritual, "especially on the ritual of the *paṭa*,"[29] the SSB includes the following instruction given by the goddess Bhima:

> Suppose someone really wants to see me in my own form (*svarūpa*). On the eighth day of the half month, he should have a painter (*citrakara*) who has taken the eight *upavasa* vows paint the following scene on a piece of cotton. The cotton's fringes should remain uncut, and loose threads (*keśa*) should be removed. With pure colors that are not mixed (*aśleṣairaṅgaiḥ*) and with paints stored in new pots (*navabhājanasthaiḥ*), he should paint an image of the tathāgata teaching the dharma, placing it in the middle. On the right, he should paint noble Avalokiteśvara giving a discourse. On the left, the great goddess Bhima, golden like a stalk of sugarcane (*śarakāṇḍagaurī*), adorned with all ornaments, dressed in white, holding a pitcher of water and vial of medicine, in the gesture of comforting.[30]

The instruction to use a piece of cotton that retains its material quality as a woven fabric with fringed edges recalls the painted banners and scrolls prepared on hemp found in Dunhuang (see figure 1.3). Some banners feature a standing bodhisattva, most often identified as Avalokiteśvara, and the rustic quality of the hemp with loose threads complements the simple color choices and design.

The banners found in Dunhuang, as likely devotional offerings prepared for a funerary ritual, could be hung on a pole for procession; whether painted banners like these were used in Indian Buddhist communities remains a matter of speculation.[31] In the MMK, the completed *paṭa* is "to be affixed to the western side of a reliquary *caitya* and worshipped with offerings of butter lamps."[32] In the SSB, the passage quoted is followed by the injunction to perform a ritual *pūjā* (adoration) with a lamp, flowers, incense, and sandalwood. The difference between the two texts may simply be due to the differing esoteric affiliations of the MMK and SSB authors, the latter, in particular, seeming to be more mindful of the worldly efficacy of the ritual. Nevertheless, in each author's world, the paintings on cloth were never intended to be merely looked at; their value as ritual objects meant to be acted on with sound (mantra recitation) and physical actions (that would inevitably leave material traces) was a temporal construction undertaken by a community, occurring within a controlled environment, and determined at every step by specific rules and directives.

An early visual depiction of a *paṭa* in use, on the Muhammad Nari stele from Gandhara, possibly represents a precursor to the practice of using a painting on cloth as a focus of meditation. This magnificent example from around the third to fourth century presents a dramatic vision of a Buddha-field (figure 1.4).[33] John Huntington has identified two rectangular panels on either side of the central Buddha's head, each bearing an image of a seated bodhisattva in meditation, as *paṭa* representations.[34] With a plain fabric streamer draped and flowing from above, these nearly three-dimensional representations are indeed reminiscent of painted cloth banners hung on celebrative and ritual occasions. However, their iconographic significance seems to be different from that of a painted banner used as a devotional offering. The carved banners contain the only representations of meditation in

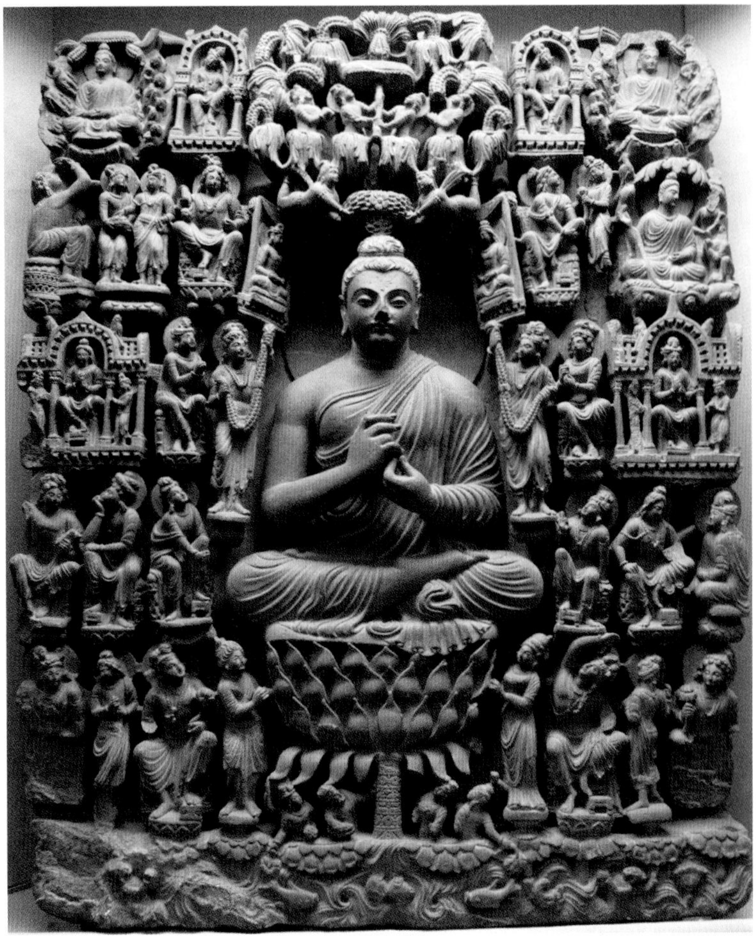

FIGURE 1.4
Preaching Buddha (Muhammad Nari stele), Gandhara, Pakistan, ca. third to fourth century. Lahore Museum. Photo © Juhyung Rhi.

the entire Buddha-field. Hovering in midair and supported by a small lotus, the two seated bodhisattvas flank the Buddha's head with considerable negative space between them. This space seems to have been left purposefully empty, as if to echo the Buddha's mental process. The Buddha is gazing forward with what now looks like a blank stare, but what his inner eye sees may be bodhisattvas in meditation, floating slightly above his head. The two *paṭas* carved in stone may thus represent what is given to the insight of a Buddha. This reading does not relinquish the materiality inherent in the representation: slightly turned to the side as if to reflect the light emanating from the Buddha's head, the two miniature "slabs" representing *paṭas* also function as visual shields framing the central event of the stele.

PAINTING ON WOODEN PANELS

The last category of support media for painting identifiable in ORP is that of the *phalaka,* literally a slab or tablet, most likely made of wood. Only three references in ORP use the term *phalaka* (Nos. 43, 49, and 64); interestingly, the first two use the term in a metaphorical

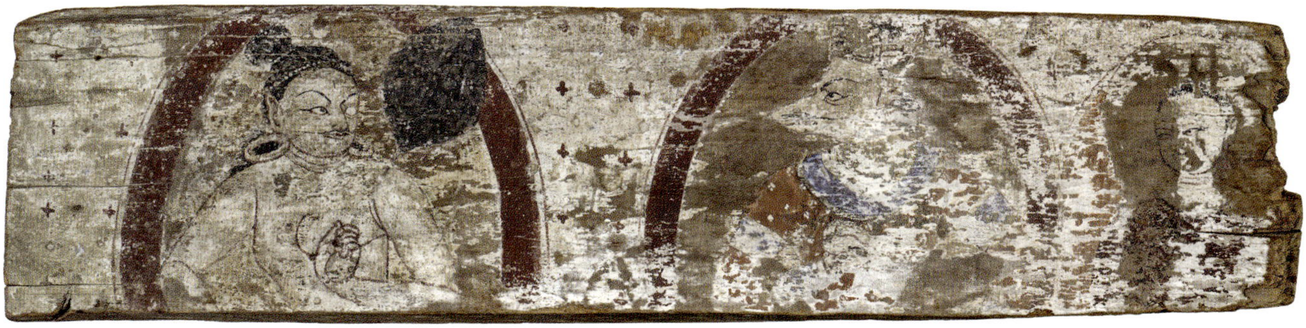

FIGURE 1.5
"Rat King?" double-sided wooden panel, seventh to eighth century(?), Khotan. Dandan-Uiliq, D. IV.5. H: 10.6 cm. British Museum 1907,1111.68. © Trustees of the British Museum.

sense—as in the image of the beloved "on the heart's tablet" (*hṛdaya-phalaka*). This use of the term derives from the appearance of *phalaka*s as part of the plot machinery in Sanskrit dramas. For example, in Kālidāsa's *Śakuntalā,* the lovelorn hero King Duṣyanta orders his maid to bring a *phalaka,* on which he "paints a picture of Śakuntalā with his own hand." In Śūdraka's *Mṛcchakaṭikā,* the heroine Vasantasenā is busy gazing at a painting, on a *phalaka,* of Chārudatta. The term of art in these dramas, *citra-phalaka,* means an object that can be intimately held and viewed and easily moved.

Despite their appearance in literary texts, there is little material evidence that such devices were made for or used in private, romantic affairs in early India. An interesting group of painted wooden panels excavated from a Khotanese site at Dandan-Uiliq (Dandān Oilik, now in China's Xinjiang autonomous region) provides a glimpse of how paintings on wood were used in a Buddhist milieu. Given the close connection between these panels and the earliest surviving painted book covers found in Gilgit (discussed below), they are worth our attention. Wooden panels with at least three different shapes have been found: (1) rectangular panels with an arched top, (2) rectangular panels with a vertical orientation, and (3) rectangular panels with a horizontal orientation. Some panels are double sided, like the panel with Śiva and a Khotanese male deity; others are single sided, like the horizontal wooden panel depicting the "story of the silk princess."[35] The double-sided wooden panel with a conjectural rat king (a Khotanese king who fought the Xiongnu, according to Stein) shows three figures depicted from the waist up (figure 1.5), creating the impression, given the truncation of the male figure's lower right arm and right hand, that there may have been another wooden panel depicting the bottom half.[36] The variety in panel format and sizes suggests that experimenting with wooden boards may have occurred during the sixth through the eighth centuries in the area around Khotan, an important node in a widespread Buddhist network.

The relatively small size of several painted panels also suggests that they were intended to be viewed at arm's length, like the *citra-phalaka*s used to illustrate romantic affairs that are described in the *Śakuntalā* and the *Mṛcchakaṭikā*. Of the three types of support media for painting discussed here, wooden panels were the smallest. As a portable object, each panel's spatial limits constrained the amount of visual information it could carry, making it, from a viewer's perspective, the most intimate medium for painting.

MANUSCRIPTS AS A MEDIUM FOR PAINTING

From a medium-specific perspective, it is striking that the references assembled in ORP do not indicate any awareness of manuscript-painting traditions. There is a single reference to painted book covers, and it comes from a fifteenth-century Sinhalese text, *Girā Sandeśaya* (1457–65 CE), which is one of the seven major "classical Sandeśas" (*sandeśa kāvya:* Sinhalese messenger poem) written under royal patronage in the fifteenth century.[37] A long-held view takes a verse in the *Mānasollāsa,* an encyclopedia of courtly life attributed to a twelfth-century South Indian king, Someśvara III (r. 1124–1138), as a reference to an established tradition of painting on manuscripts. However, if we look at the text carefully, it does not seem to make any reference to "miniature painting on palm leaves," as previous scholarship has suggested.[38] In a short section on the qualities of a painter, we find that a painter should be "skilled in *patra-lekhana*" (*patralekhanakovidaiḥ*). Whether this *patra-lekhana* has anything to do with painting on palm leaves is questionable. The term *patra* denotes "leaf," but the qualities described before and after this particular phrase all relate to the technical skills of a painter: "being proficient in fine lines" (*sūkṣmarekhāviśāradaiḥ*) and "being competent in composition according to proper rules" (*vidhinirmāṇkuśalaiḥ*); then "being skilled in *patra-lekhana,*" immediately followed by "being expert in filling colors" (*varṇapūraṇadakṣaiḥ*). In this context it is unlikely that *patra-lekhana* means the "technique of miniature painting on palm leaves." The technical qualities of a painter under discussion here form a prologue to an extensive discussion of the technique of painting on walls (*citrabhitiḥ*) in the next section. Moreover, in the *Citrasūtra,* a slightly earlier Sanskrit treatise on painting, the term *patra* is used to name a technique for drawing a type of line.[39] Following Parul Dave Mukherji's reading of that text, *patra* seems to indicate a discontinuous treatment of line: "the *patra* [type] of line rendering is drawn by lines which are partly done and partly undone."[40] In this light, it seems more likely, then, that the *Mānasollāsa* passage describes a skill in line handling rather than competence in miniature painting on palm leaves.

In Buddhist manuscripts, the earliest surviving evidence for painted manuscript production suggests that the tradition began in earnest close to the year 1000.[41] Although a lack of textual references to manuscript painting does not mean that it was not practiced, the consistent lack of both material and textual evidence dating before the eleventh century does suggest that painting on the pages of a manuscript was not widely practiced in South Asia until about the end of the tenth century. The production of painted manuscripts in Buddhist and Jain communities during the eleventh century marks the earliest phase in the history of manuscript painting in India. It is worth bearing in mind how innovative and transformative it was to use the pages of a manuscript for painting. Two areas of investigation can help us appreciate this aspect as well as understand the historical circumstances leading to the

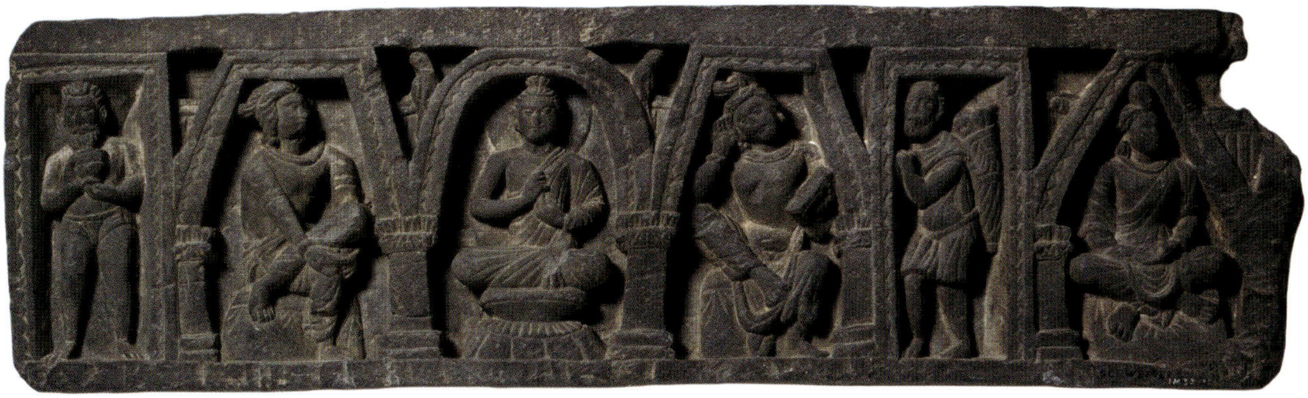

FIGURE 1.6
Bodhisattva Mañjuśrī holding a *pothi* in left hand, Preaching Buddha relief panel, third or fourth century?, probably from the Swat Valley, Pakistan. Schist, 20 × 71.5 cm. V&A IM.53-1936. © Victoria and Albert Museum, London.

introduction of manuscript painting: the changing status of a manuscript as a fitting vessel for knowledge transmission; and the trans-Himalayan connections that provided a catalyst for promoting the material importance of manuscripts in different parts of South Asia.

The earliest surviving painted manuscripts suggest that they were considered important objects on which patrons should dispense extra resources. In India, writing or the written word was traditionally held under suspicion, based on the insistence in the Vedas on the supremacy of oral instruction. As a result, the earliest evidence for the recognition of a manuscript as a physical vehicle fit for the transmission of knowledge and authority is found in Buddhist and Jaina circles.[42] Although textual sources attesting to the elevated status of a manuscript date from as early as the beginning of the Common Era—for example, the "cult of the book" promoted in early Mahāyāna sūtras—in practice, it is likely that the "sound" of teaching remained more important than what was written on a manuscript during the next few centuries.

A Gandharan relief panel now in the Victoria and Albert Museum features a bodhisattva figure that Anna Maria Quagliotti identifies as the earliest representation of Mañjuśrī (figure 1.6).[43] Flanking the Buddha at the center of the panel, this youthful bodhisattva holds a *pothi*-format manuscript (a narrow rectangular object with incised lines on the side indicating folios) in his left hand. The bodhisattva holds his right hand around his ear and tilts his head toward the Buddha in mid-discourse at the center, portraying the act of listening. The manuscript in his left hand, although it is prominently displayed and held out toward the viewer, seems to be secondary. Listening—to the sound of teaching—is the main action, and the iconography here emphasizes the importance of the oral-aural aspect of Buddhist teaching in juxtaposition with a written document. In the next chapter, I will turn to a consideration of visual representations of manuscripts that articulate their status as a material vessel for the transmission of knowledge and authority. Here, I would like to direct our attention to an interesting story about a book that was once used to circulate a painting.

A BOOK AS A VESSEL FOR VISUAL KNOWLEDGE

The story is narrated in Somadeva's *Kathāsaritsāgara* (lit. "Ocean of rivers of story"; henceforth KsS), composed toward the end of the eleventh century (c. 1070).[44] Its author, Somadeva, was based in Kashmir, and it belongs to the tradition of the *Bṛhatkathā* (henceforth BK), or Great Story, a lost text believed to have been composed during the early centuries CE.[45] Various later adaptations and compilations exist, such as Budhasvāmin's *Bṛhatkathā-ślokasaṃgraha* (recently translated in the Clay series as *The Emperor of the Sorcerers*);[46] the *Vasudevahiṇḍi* by Saṅghadāsagaṇi, a Jain author;[47] Kṣemendra's *Bṛhatkathāmañjarī* (lit. "Bouquet of the great story");[48] and Somadeva's KsS. This last version, the KsS, includes a number of stories about characters who are not found in other versions. The story we are interested in does not appear in any of the other BK-related texts.

Book 18 of the KsS narrates the story of King Vikramāditya.[49] In the third "stream" of the story, a painter appears who is named Nagarasvāmin. He has served the king, Vikramāditya, by painting "a picture of a girl . . . taking care to exemplify different types of beauty" every two or three days.[50] But he is in a predicament one day when he forgets to prepare his painterly tribute to the king: "He pondered what he should give to the king, and at this very moment a traveler from a faraway land suddenly arrived and placed a book in his hand and departed. Intrigued, the painter opened the book and saw in it a painting of a girl on cloth [*paṭe*]."[51] The king is immediately attracted to the painted beauty and sees her in a dream in which he cross-dresses as a woman in order to find and marry her. The girl in the painting and in his dream turns out to be a princess named Malayavatī, who is from the great city of Malayapura on a faraway island—the identification of which depends on another painting on cloth, a painting of the city the king saw in his dream. Based on that image, the king draws the city, and it is identified. In this intricate tale, the device of a painting in a book may seem a passing detail, but weighing its significance gives us a chance to consider a hitherto unnoticed role that a book as a material object can play.

At the outset, we can note that it is the painting delivered in a book by a stranger that triggers the entire Malayavatī saga. In other words, a book is used as a container to carry a painting on cloth, and it is given to the painter (and the king) by a traveler. The traveler is unnamed, but the fact that he has come from a distant land is clearly noted in the text. Instead of handing over the painting directly, the traveler puts a book (*pustikām*) in Nagarasvāmin's hand and then leaves. Concealed in the book is the painting; only by opening the book does Nagarasvāmin see a wondrous painting of a girl on cloth.[52] At the same time, the story suggests that the handy size of the book made it suitable for long-distance travel, which again heightens the mystery of the drama. Here the author of the story is exploiting the book's material properties—its portability and potential for concealment and revelation—to maximize the story's dramatic effects.

That Somadeva, an eleventh-century author based in Kashmir, includes this intriguing detail in his story gives us a new context in which we can discern positive recognition of the value of a manuscript as a physical vessel for transmission of knowledge. Among the extant texts, the branching narrative of the KsS unfolds like a piece of oral storytelling that introduces subsidiary stories within a simple, easy to remember frame story, at a length suitable for a narration in a single sitting.[53] It is likely that Somadeva was a writer who had at his command the stories that circulated in the region and were known to him in a Kashmiri *katha* style.[54] As we will see, Kashmir seems to have been a place where the notion of a manuscript as a physical vessel lay embedded in the cultural fabric of the land.

THE TRANS-HIMALAYAN MANUSCRIPT CULTURE

Belief in the primacy of the oral text, a value inherent in the Vedic traditions, had a profound impact on the development of manuscript cultures in South Asia.[55] As Benjamin Fleming demonstrates, many Hindu manuscripts had the aim of being "functional in an oral or ritual context, often with less attention to aesthetics," an orientation that stood in contrast to the "cult of the book" attitude that seems to have characterized Buddhist manuscripts.[56] It may be tempting to extend this insight and see the cultural factors affecting the production and use of manuscripts as exemplifications of a sectarian divide, but such a large generalization is not warranted—nor would it be productive.[57] For example, by limiting the time frame of our analysis to around the end of the twelfth century, we can discern an interesting geographical pattern that is not predicated on sectarian differences.

It happens that a large number of early manuscripts datable to between the ninth and twelfth centuries came from Nepal. These are mostly in Sanskrit and written on palm leaves in the *pothi* format, consisting of loose rectangular folios oriented horizontally and tied together with string run through prebored holes to form a stack; the format is typical of the manuscript cultures of South and Southeast Asia. In fact, some of the texts mentioned in previous sections were recovered from manuscript copies in this format that were prepared or discovered in Nepal. The printed edition of the *Mañjuśrīmūlakalpa* published by T. Gaṇapati Śāstrī as part of the Trivandrum Sanskrit Series (1920–25), for example, was prepared from a single palm-leaf manuscript found near Padmanabhapuram (in the kingdom of Travancore, in today's Kanyakumari district, Tamil Nadu) in 1909; it is now housed in the Oriental Research Institute and Manuscripts Library of the University of Kerala (manuscript no. C. 2388).[58] Judging from its paleographic and codicological features, the manuscript was ostensibly prepared in Nepal.[59] Another example is Buddhsvāmin's *Bṛhatkathā-ślokasaṃgraha* (henceforth BkS), known only from a Nepalese palm-leaf manuscripts so far.[60] The BkS text features a clear reference to a scribe as a respected professional, and it also describes writing instruments and the activities of reading and writing.[61] The earliest manuscript of the *Niśvāsatattvasaṃhitā*, described as the "earliest surviving Śaiva Tantra," also hails from Nepal and is datable to sometime between 850 and 900.[62] The list goes on.

Today, the importance of Sanskrit and other Indic-language palm-leaf manuscripts for the study of medieval religious, and especially tantric, traditions in India is widely acknowledged. However, in textual studies focused on using sound philological methods to produce better critical texts from manuscript sources, the material age and provenance of manuscripts hold little significance. That a manuscript may have been prepared in eleventh-century Nepal is considered a happenstance of the text's survival. Arguably, the subtropical and tropical climates prevailing elsewhere in South Asia proved hostile to perishable materials like palm leaves and tree bark, the two primary materials used in manuscript making. In this view, the milder climate of the Kathmandu valley was indeed more likely to protect manuscripts that would have been destroyed elsewhere. But can there be more to this survival pattern than geographical and environmental factors? Is it possible that social elites in Nepal—scholars, priests, capable donors—were fonder of their Sanskrit books than were their counterparts elsewhere in South Asia? For reasons still to be discovered, the relatively small area of "*nepāla maṇḍala*," as the Kathmandu valley is designated in medieval epigraphic records and literary sources, seems to have had a remarkable concentration of scribes and manuscript makers by the turn of the first millennium CE.[63]

Let us consider a hypothesis: during the first millennium, were manuscripts regarded as physical vessels of the written text and therefore held in higher esteem in the areas around the Himalayan mountain range and its foothills than in the rest of South Asia? If valid, this hypothesis might lead us to designate the region from the Bamiyan valley to the Brahmaputra valley, an area contiguous with the Tibetan plateau, as a cradle for the development of a distinctive trans-Himalayan manuscript culture (map 1.1).[64] Could it be that this is one of the reasons we have so many early manuscripts from Nepal as well as even earlier ones from the northwestern parts of the subcontinent, such as Gilgit, the Kashmir valley, and the Bamiyan valley (in today's Afghanistan)?[65] To this list of early manuscript-production centers, Assam could be added, bringing the Brahmaputra Valley into the picture.[66]

Assam's proximity to China is an interesting clue to consider as we weigh the implications of a trans-Himalayan network facilitating the development of manuscript cultures in South Asia. The relevance of its proximity to China was certainly not lost on a seventh-century Assamese king, supposedly named Kumāra, who repeatedly sent for Xuanzang while the monk was in residence at Nālandā. At length, Xuanzang set out to meet him. When they met, Kumāra is said to have remarked on the greatness of China, especially its love of learning: "All the countries of India today have sung their praises for the Qin king of the Mahacina country (Mahacinadeśa)."[67] The Assamese king described in Xuanzang's record of his travels is none other than the king Bhāskaravarman who dispatched the gift of manuscripts recorded in Baṇa's *Harṣacārita*. Xuanzang's recounting of an Assamese king's praise of Tang China is not to be taken at face value given the political aspiration of Xuanzang to please the Tang emperor implicit in such praise. However, Assam's geographical proximity to China was a real consideration: based on the information he gathered from locals, Xuanzang mentions that one could reach the Shu region (present-day Sichuan) from Assam in two-months' time—a statement that indicates there was a known through route to the east from the area of Assam at the time.[68] However, while a road through Sichuan and Yunnan may have represented a shorter distance to travel to or from the Tang capital of Chang'an (present-day Xian), this was not the route taken by the pilgrim monk, for a variety of reasons.[69]

The Chinese connection is tantalizing, especially since a manuscript culture developed very early in China, during the second half of the first millennium BCE.[70] The search for written texts by Chinese monks, as well as the demand by Indian Buddhist missionaries

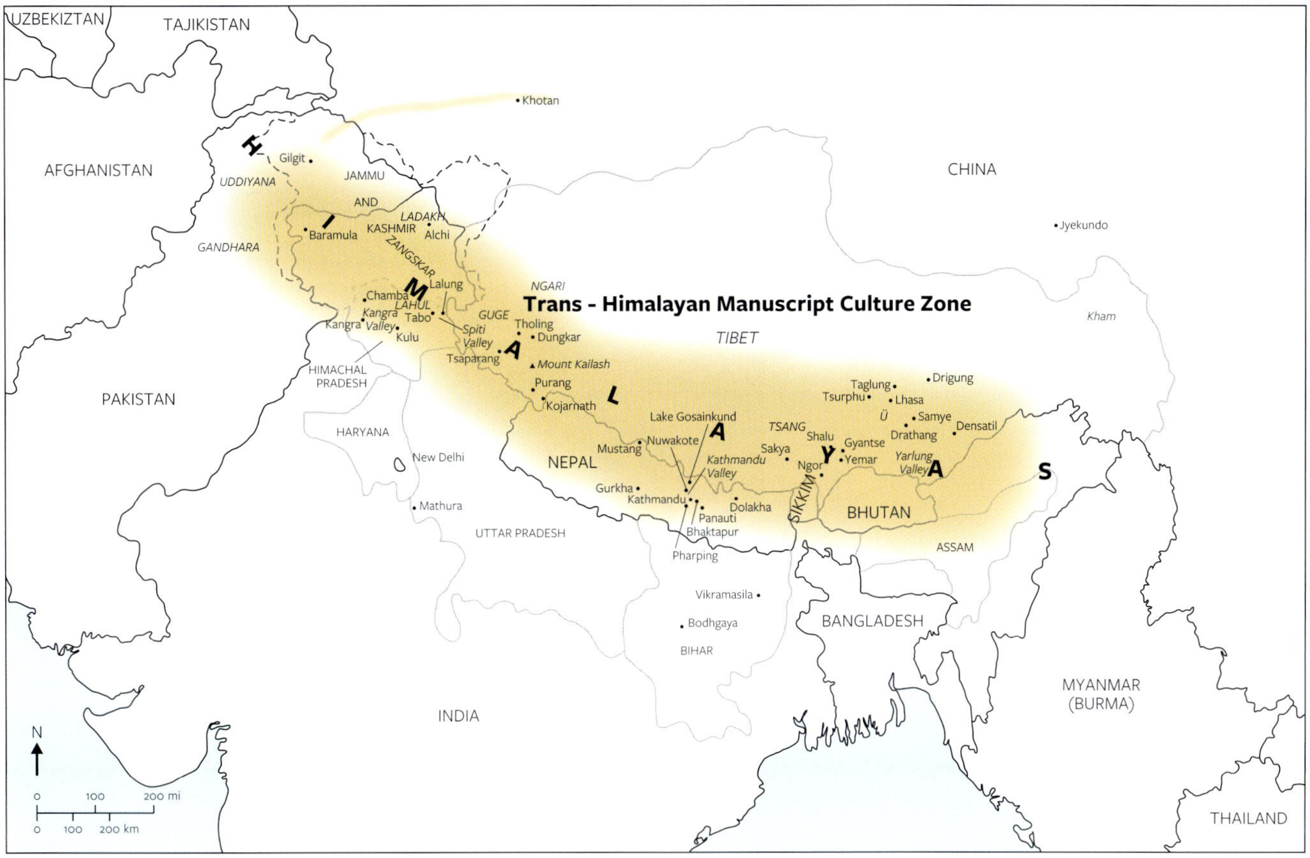

MAP 1.1

Trans-Himalayan manuscript culture zone.

aspiring to travel beyond India, might have triggered increased manuscript production in Buddhist centers in South Asia, since growth in a manuscript culture was inevitably linked to the expansion of commercial and religious networks that sought to transfer goods and knowledge beyond existing boundaries. A mapping of the trans-Himalayan centers of manuscript production and their trade routes could connect to the Silk Road networks through which all sorts of commodities, including manuscripts, were circulated.[71] Such a connection invites us to think about the role increased contact with cultures in which manuscripts were traditionally held in high esteem—be it China or western Asia (Mesopotamia in earlier centuries; the Muslim world after the emergence of Islam)—may have played in stimulating the growth of manuscript cultures in South Asia.

Studies by Deborah Klimburg-Salter among others have established the importance of trans-Himalayan trade routes for comprehending the Buddhist art of the region. By examining the formal similarities in Buddhist manuscript covers from two regions, Klimburg-Salter reconnects the art of the greater Gilgit region in northern Pakistan to that of the Tibetan

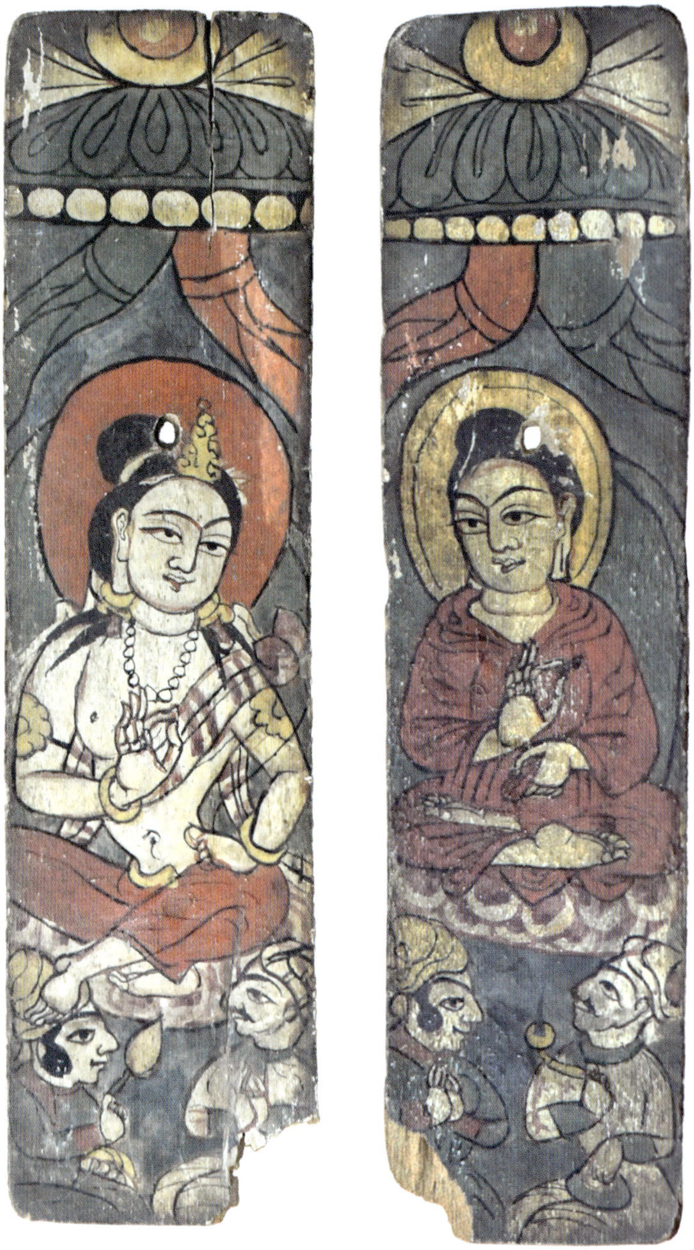

FIGURE 1.7
Manuscript covers (MSC 1), ca. seventh century, Naupur, Gilgit district, Pakistan. Pigments and ink on wood, 25 × 6 cm. Sri Pratap Singh Museum, Srinagar. Photo © Robert N. Linrothe.

plateau.[72] A recent exhibition, *Collecting Paradise: Buddhist Art of Kashmir and Its legacies* (2015), further demonstrates how the artistic legacy of the Kashmir valley was clearly influential in the art of western Tibet during the first centuries of the second millennium.[73] By extending the investigation of interregional cultural connections across the Himalayas, my hypothesis of a trans-Himalayan zone of manuscript culture explores an alternate and

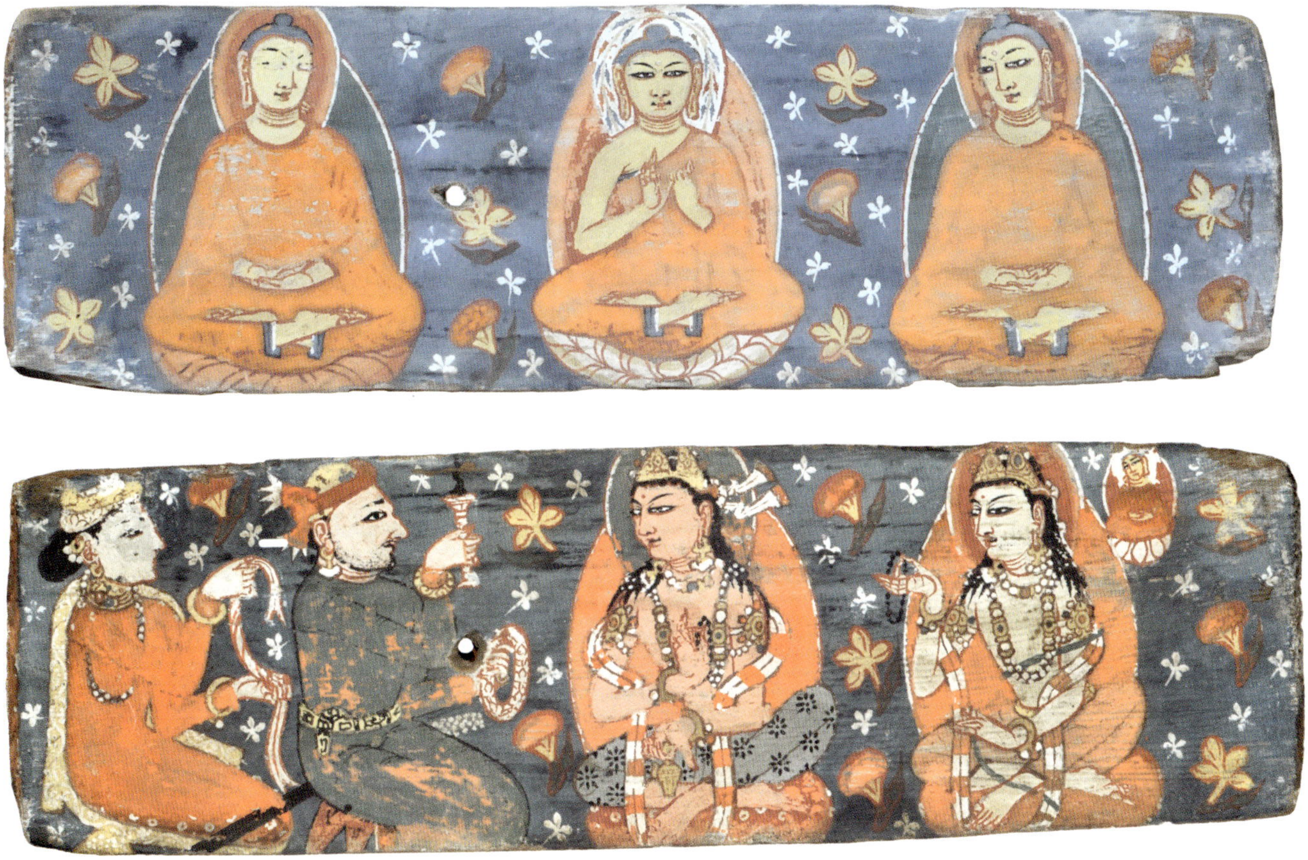

FIGURE 1.8
Manuscript cover (MSC3), late eighth or ninth century, Naupur, Gilgit district, Pakistan. Pigments and ink on wood, 8.3 × 28 cm. Sri Pratap Singh Museum, Srinagar. Photo © Robert N. Linrothe.

complementary approach to the "Silk Road"–centered narrative of the flow of cultural artifacts in Asia during the first millennium.

KHOTAN AND GILGIT: PAINTED BOOK COVERS

At the outset, books were embellished in the same way that the surface of a temple or a palace building was painted. In other words, books (Skt. *pustaka*) were treated as a cultic object that artists were employed to embellish, and the urge to include pictures in a book may have emerged from that practice. The earliest evidence for the addition of painting to a *pothi*-format manuscript is found in a group of Buddhist manuscripts discovered in the Gilgit region in northwestern Pakistan.[74] In the Gilgit manuscript corpus, no surviving folio bears any painting, but three sets of painted wooden covers for protecting manuscripts were found among the considerable cache of Gilgit manuscripts (figures 1.7, 1.8). One of the manuscripts with a painted cover, the *Saṃghātasūtra* (MsC2), has a long colophon that identifies the main patron of the manuscript as Queen Devaśirikā, most likely a member of the Palola Ṣāhi dynasty that ruled in the Gilgit region from the late sixth through the eighth centuries.[75] She was joined (*tathā sārdham*) by fourteen other individuals for the merit that sponsoring the manuscript's production accrued.[76]

It is possible that all three manuscripts with covers were prepared sometime during the seventh and early eighth centuries, when many Palola Ṣāhi royal donations of Buddhist objects were commissioned. It is not clear if the painted wooden covers were prepared at the same time as the manuscript folios.[77] Various dates have been proposed for the covers, on the basis of stylistic variations in the painting.[78] Art historians generally agree that the covers that accompany the manuscript of the *Samghātasūtra* may be the latest: Klimburg-Salter proposes a date of creation sometime in the ninth century, while Rob Linrothe suggests a possible late eighth-century or early ninth-century date.[79] The painted covers for the other two manuscripts (MSC 1 and MSC 2) may date to the seventh century.

The large number of manuscripts discovered in the Gilgit area suggests the existence of a thriving scriptorium, as has been noted in previous studies.[80] Be that as it may, manuscript production was not a completely standardized affair. While most manuscripts were written on sheets of birch bark, at least one was prepared on palm-leaf folios. Most intriguing for this study is the variety of formats in the painted manuscript covers. Two sets (MSC 1 and MSC 2) are vertically oriented (figure 1.7), while MSC 3 is horizontal (figure 1.8). The vertical orientation of MSC 1, moreover, appears incongruent with the text orientation of the folios they protect.[81] As Klimburg-Salter observes, the Gilgit book covers that are vertical in orientation may have resulted "from the functional convergence of the small painted wooden panels used as votive objects—known in archaeological contexts in Kyzil and Khotan—and the wooden boards used to enclose manuscripts in Central Asia."[82] While this is an apt characterization, there is still room to explore how a developing manuscript culture began to embrace painting in its ambit.

The somewhat confusing orientation of manuscript covers that read crosswise to the direction of the text folios they protect can be more fully explained in the context of early Buddhist manuscript production across Central Asia, where different sites produced manuscripts in varying formats, including long rolls made with paper, *pothi*-format manuscripts made with tree bark, palm leaves, or occasionally paper, and folded booklets in paper. The vertical orientation of MSC 1 and MSC 2 would be suitable, for example, in a frontispiece for a text written vertically, such as a Buddhist sūtra written in classical Chinese.[83]

Three illustrated folios found at Dunhuang exemplify the diversity of written cultures that manuscript makers at a nodal point like Dunhuang had to negotiate during the ninth century and after (figures 1.9 and 1.10). Collected by Aurel Stein from the Library Cave (Cave 17), the folios must have been part of a *pothi*-format manuscript in paper. Each folio has an elongated rectangular shape with a single hole on the long side of the folio at about one-third of the width. Both sides of each folio contain writing and illustration. It is thought that the original manuscript may have had five or more folios and was prepared for a specific ritual use—in this case, offering protection to small children.[84] Each page contains a

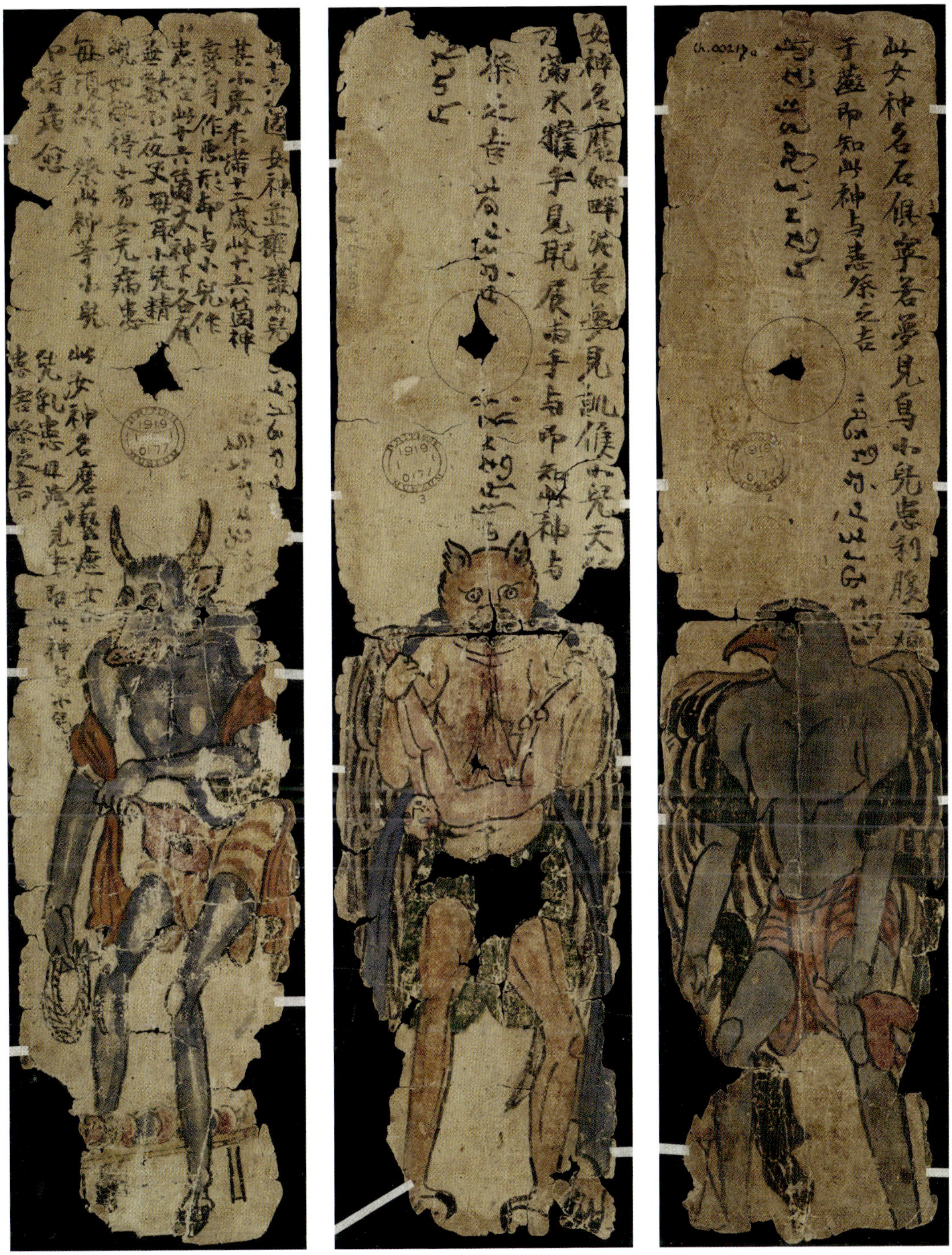

FIGURE 1.9

Folios 2r, 8v, 7v (from *left to right*), animal-headed female spirits (女神), Cave 17, Dunhuang, Tang, ninth century. Ink, color on paper. Each leaf: H: 33 cm. British Museum OA1919.1-1.0177 (1–3) (Ch. 00217 a–c) © Trustees of the British Museum.

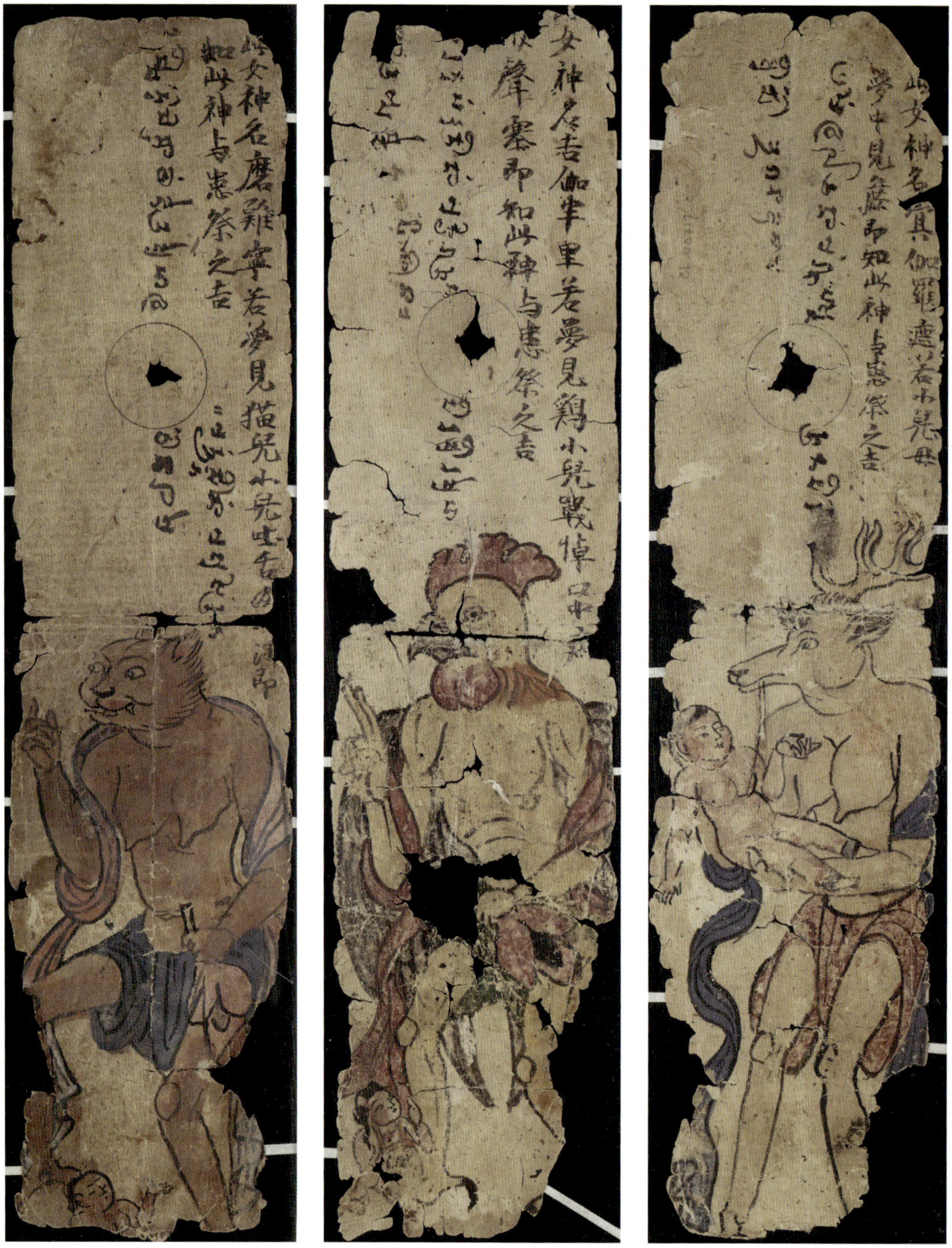

FIGURE 1.10

Folios 7r, 8r, 2v (*left to right*), animal-headed female spirits (女神), Cave 17, Dunhuang, Tang, ninth century. Ink, color on paper. Each leaf: H: 33 cm. British Museum OA1919.1–1.0177 (1–3) (Ch. 00217 a–c) © Trustees of the British Museum.

bilingual text written in two scripts, Chinese and late Khotanese, and a painted image of an animal-headed goddess.

There are six goddesses, one on each page: a cow- or goat-headed goddess (folio 2r, Ch. 00217c) named Miṃjukā or Maṃgicā (written Mo-yi-zhe in Chinese), a stag-headed goddess (folio 2v, Ch. 00217c) named Miṃkhalacā or Mṛgarāja (Ch. Ming-gia-luo-zhe), a cat-headed goddess (folio 7r, 00217a) named Mattrānaṃdī (Ch. Mo-nuo-ning), a crow-headed goddess (folio 7v, 00217b) named Śakuni (Ch. Shi-ju-ning), a rooster-headed goddess (folio 8r, 00217a) named Kirakapaṃdanī (Ch. Ji-jia-ban-li), and a half-bird, cat-headed goddess (folio 8v, 00217a) named Mukhamaṃḍā (Ch. Mo-jia-pan-pa). Henrik Sørensen, following observations made by Matsumoto Eiichi in the 1930s, suggests that this incomplete manuscript may have been an abbreviated version of a bilingual *Huzhu-tongzi-tuolounijing,* a *dhāraṇī* text for protecting children (Taisho 1028A). Accordingly, the animal-headed goddesses have been described in subsequent publications as demons that bring various troubles and illnesses to small children.[85] However, the Chinese text on these folios may be from a different source. The Chinese text cited by Sørensen describes female demons/evil spirits that molest children and explains a ritual and a long dhāraṇī that will control them. Each text in Chinese on these folios states that it deals with a "goddess" or "female spirit" instead of a demon, and each offers a prognosis based on the content of a dream vision and the symptoms of a child.[86] For example, the text on folio 7v (figure 1.9 *far right*) reads, "The name of this goddess (is) Shi-ju-ning. If one sees a bird in a dream and the child has an acute stomach ailment, one should know that this goddess is the cause of the trouble. A ritual (to this goddess) will be auspicious." The accompanying Khotanese texts are much shorter and resemble abbreviated phrase clusters used in a cheat sheet. The Khotanese text on folio 7v reads, "Śakunī by name; in the form of a bird./line1/She makes weak/bad; causes diarrhea./line2/."[87]

The bilingual texts appear to run seamlessly from Chinese to Khotanese at first glance as the letters are similar in size and both are written in black ink. Yet to read the Khotanese text, one needs to rotate the page ninety degrees counterclockwise, placing the folio in a horizontal orientation. This is because the Chinese text runs vertically along the long edge from right to left in defiance of the normal orientation of a *pothi*-format manuscript folio, where the writing would run horizontally along the long side from left to right. Whether the manuscript was written by two different scribes, each following the calligraphic conventions appropriate to his own language,[88] or one scribe who was familiar with both languages, the folios suggest a flexible attitude toward manuscript layout as late as the ninth century.

Given the close connection between the Buddhist community of Gilgit and its counterpart in Khotan,[89] a characterization of Khotanese wooden panels as votive offerings may be due for reconsideration, as indicated in the discussion of *phalaka*s earlier in this chapter. According to Stein's report, some of the panels were found near the images within shrines.[90] The ones he describes were substantial in size, a few measuring close to 50 cm in width. Curiously, some are close in size to the manuscript folios found at the Khotanese sites.[91] It is unlikely that all of the painted wooden panels from Khotan were designed as book covers, but there is a strong possibility that some of them were. Although this is seldom noticed,

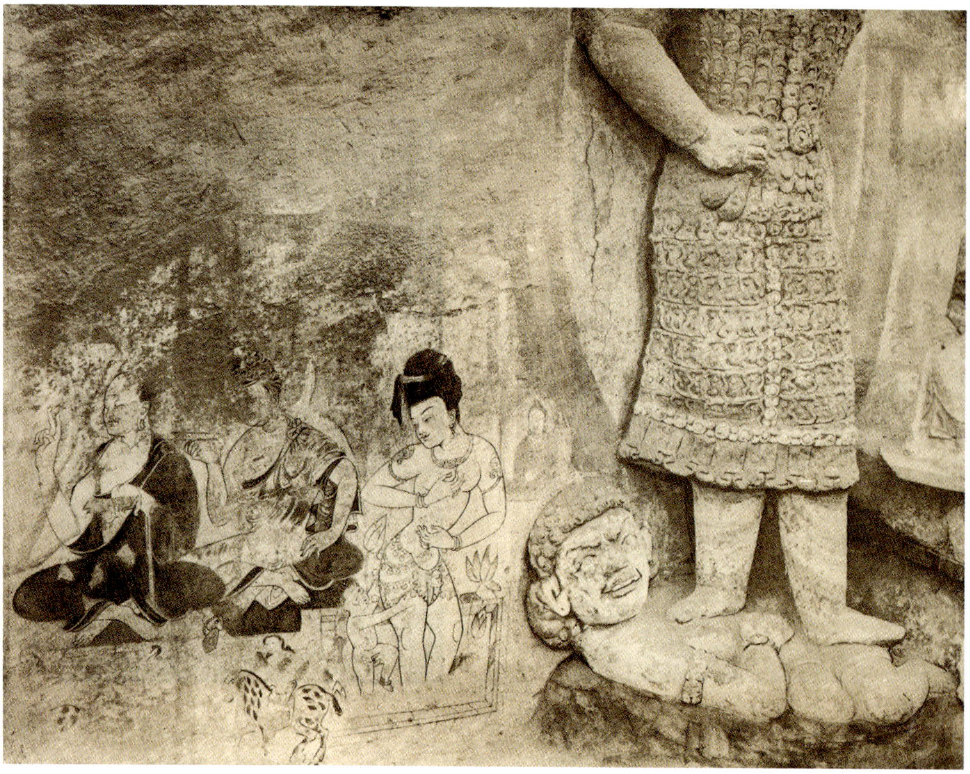

FIGURE 1.11
Wall painting in Small Cella of Shrine D.II. Dandan Uiliq, after Stein, *Ancient Khotan* (1907), vol. 2, plate II.

Stein reports that the manuscript leaves found in Shrine D-X at Dandan Uilique "were placed between various painted panels." He concluded that the manuscripts, many of them in a fragmentary state, "had been deposited as votive offerings by some of the last worshippers at the shrine" because of where they were found, placed on the rim around the foot of the pedestal, and because of red traces on the leaves, akin to *pūjā* marks made with vermilion and sandalwood powder.[92] This remark makes it clear that the painted wooden panels were votive objects only to the extent that they were bound to manuscripts that were venerated and worshipped, as was practiced in the Mahāyāna Buddhist book cult.[93]

The small cella attached to Shrine D-II, where Stein found the first group of painted wooden panels, gives us an intriguing glimpse of the context in which painted book covers may have been used at the site. On the eastern wall of the southeastern corner of the shrine space where the painted panels were found, there was a wall painting that depicted a celebrated standing figure (identified by Joanna Williams as Kinnari in the Sudhana jātaka, and by Stein as a Nāginī that a minister to the Khotanese king volunteered to marry to restore water to the kingdom). In front of this figure sit two monks, and both hold manuscripts in their hands (figure 1.11).[94] The monk in front holds a manuscript in his left hand while the figure seated behind him holds a manuscript in his right hand. The manuscripts they are holding conform to the rectangular *pothi* format of Indic manuscripts—recall, for instance, the *pothi*-format manuscript held by the bodhisattva in the Gandharan relief (see figure 1.6). The main difference is that the monk who is holding a manuscript in his left hand holds up his right hand in a confident gesture signifying that he is giving a discourse. The manuscript in his hand seems to be a clear symbol of the monk's authority to deliver the teaching. The only record we have of this painted wall is the black-and-white photograph that Stein took, as this section remained at the site after his excavation and was subsequently lost.[95]

Unfortunately, twentieth-century collecting practices have separated many book covers from the manuscript folios to which they were once bound. Many of the painted wooden book covers have gone to private collections and museums while the text folios are deposited in libraries and archives to be microfilmed and scanned for further study.[96] In the case of Gilgit book covers, the prevailing understanding that the painted covers were later additions to the manuscripts may have contributed to their consignment to a separate repository from that of the text they once protected. This is also true for many of the wooden panels discovered around Khotan.

PAINTED MANUSCRIPTS AND THE VISUALITY OF TEXT

In Indic religious communities, manuscripts came to be seen as fitting vessels for the transmission of knowledge and authority, and the introduction of painted images on manuscript pages—like the use of painted book covers—began in an effort to embellish religiously meaningful objects. Perhaps it was the inherent textuality of a manuscript, combined with a sensitivity on the part of its readers to the visual properties of its text, that turned it into a natural support medium for painting?[97] That a text's visual properties—its text-visuality—was part of a manuscript's visual appeal for both its makers and (some of) its users can be gleaned from the abundant evidence of a highly cultivated awareness of the visual aspects of writing in medieval South Asia.

Although oral performance remained central to all Indic ritual traditions, written letters—often as the permanent physical record of an action—were actively employed in religious institutions and eagerly cultivated in statecraft from the early centuries of the common era.[98] Royal grants and donative grants that were memorialized on metal sheets and stone surfaces are in fact carefully and beautifully inscribed. The same is true of a multiscript *virudha* on a seventh-century Pallava royal temple in Kanchi as well as of a ninth-century Pāla royal land grant inscribed on a heavy copper plate with a royal emblem soldered on top.[99] In addition to royal emblems soldered in low relief, some copper plates include an incised line drawing. The plate found by D.P. Ghosh in "the wilds of Sunderban bordering the Bay of Bengal" in the 1930s, now in the Asutosh Museum, Kolkata, depicts an image of a seated Viṣṇu with Garuḍa paying homage to him.[100]

Despite a commonly held view that the art of calligraphy was largely absent in pre-Islamic India, the epigraphic evidence reveals that the visual properties of a text were viewed and invested with a growing importance throughout the first millennium. At a Buddhist site in

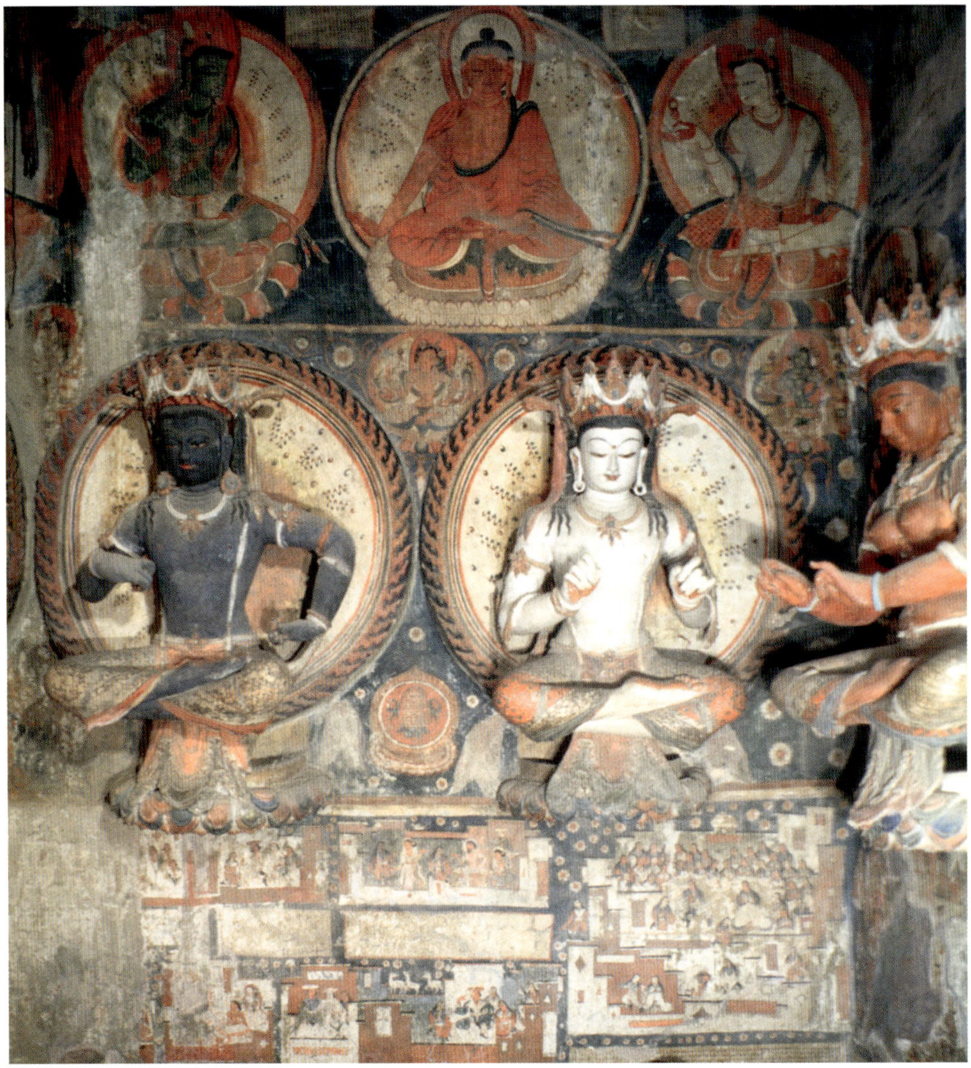

FIGURE 1.12
View of the southern wall at the western end, Main Assembly Hall, Tabo, ca. 996 CE/1040 CE. Photograph by Jaroslav Poncar, 2001. Photo courtesy of the Western Himalaya Archive Vienna.

the western Himalayas, the inclusion of long text panels in the painted program on the walls of the Tabo monastery in the Spiti Valley (present-day Himachal Pradesh), completed in 1042, indicates the veneration with which the visual presence of a written text was treated. On the southern wall of the assembly hall of Tabo's main temple, text panels of the *Gaṇḍavyūhasūtra,* represented in long horizontal rectangles, are interspersed with mural scenes depicting the same text (figure 1.12). The text in the panels, a series of passages forming an abbreviated redaction of the oldest Tibetan translation of the sūtra,[101] is written in

Tibetan in black ink on a white primed background with clearly delineated edges, creating frames resembling manuscript pages. Altogether, the written text occupies nearly half of the space given to the visual program of the *Gaṇḍavyūhasūtra*. Compared to earlier Buddhist sites where narrative depictions show the influence of a strong tradition of oral storytelling, Tabo's murals conjure a world where the written text—and its visual presence as such—was seemingly invested with as much, if not more, importance than the oral text. The text's visibility on a temple wall, combined with the pictorial language of painting, localized the sūtra while simultaneously giving it an immediate presence as an object of devotion.[102]

The ambitious program at Tabo was a product of the period of *phyi-dar,* the second transmission of Buddhism to Tibet, which inspired intense exchanges between Indian Buddhist masters and their Tibetan counterparts and patrons. Written texts, especially in the form of manuscripts, were centrally important vehicles in what amounted to a vast translation project. The presentation and display of writing became important parts of this cultural landscape, and the incorporation of painted images in manuscripts gains in resonance when seen against this backdrop.

ACTIVATING THE TEXT

In Indic religious communities, the visual aspects of written text were cultivated through two modes of active presentation: first, script as image, where a written text is presented as itself, functioning ritually as its own image; and second, substantiation of an image through written letters or text. The earliest surviving example of the former may be found among Jaina *paṭa*s, some of which date from the late fourteenth century.[103] In the *paṭa* dated to 1447 (V.S. 1504), most of the visual field is covered by a text arranged diagrammatically to form a grid with four cardinal points and a center, marked by five enlarged letters (figure 1.13). It has been identified as *a vijaya yantra* (victory banner) used in a rite to ensure victory, although this terminology may be somewhat misleading.[104] Among the surviving *paṭas* containing so-called ritual diagrams, or "mystical syllables," this monumental painting, measuring 137 × 110 cm, is a rare early example in which the written letters dominate the visual field. It is also unusual in that most of the letters are numeric. Except for the two columns crossing in the center that divide the field into quadrants, each square of the grid is filled with numbers. In those two columns, there is seriality in the arrangement of the letters within them (i.e., akā-akhā-agā-agha-ana-aca-acha), and though one might also be able to discern a pattern in the arrangement of the numbers, the actual meaning of the grid remains elusive.

Under a giant umbrella attended by two female figures with two hovering peacocks above, the enlarged red letter written against a blue backdrop at the top is *hrīṃ*—the fundamental mantra syllable of the Jain traditions, it heralds the entire field of numerals and letters. The bottom of the central column is marked by another common mantra syllable, *krom,* and the letter *klīm* marks either end of the central horizontal column. An emboldened letter marking the center of the grid is damaged, but it seems to have encircled numerals within it. This sea of letters is framed by delightfully painted registers that feature auspicious symbols,

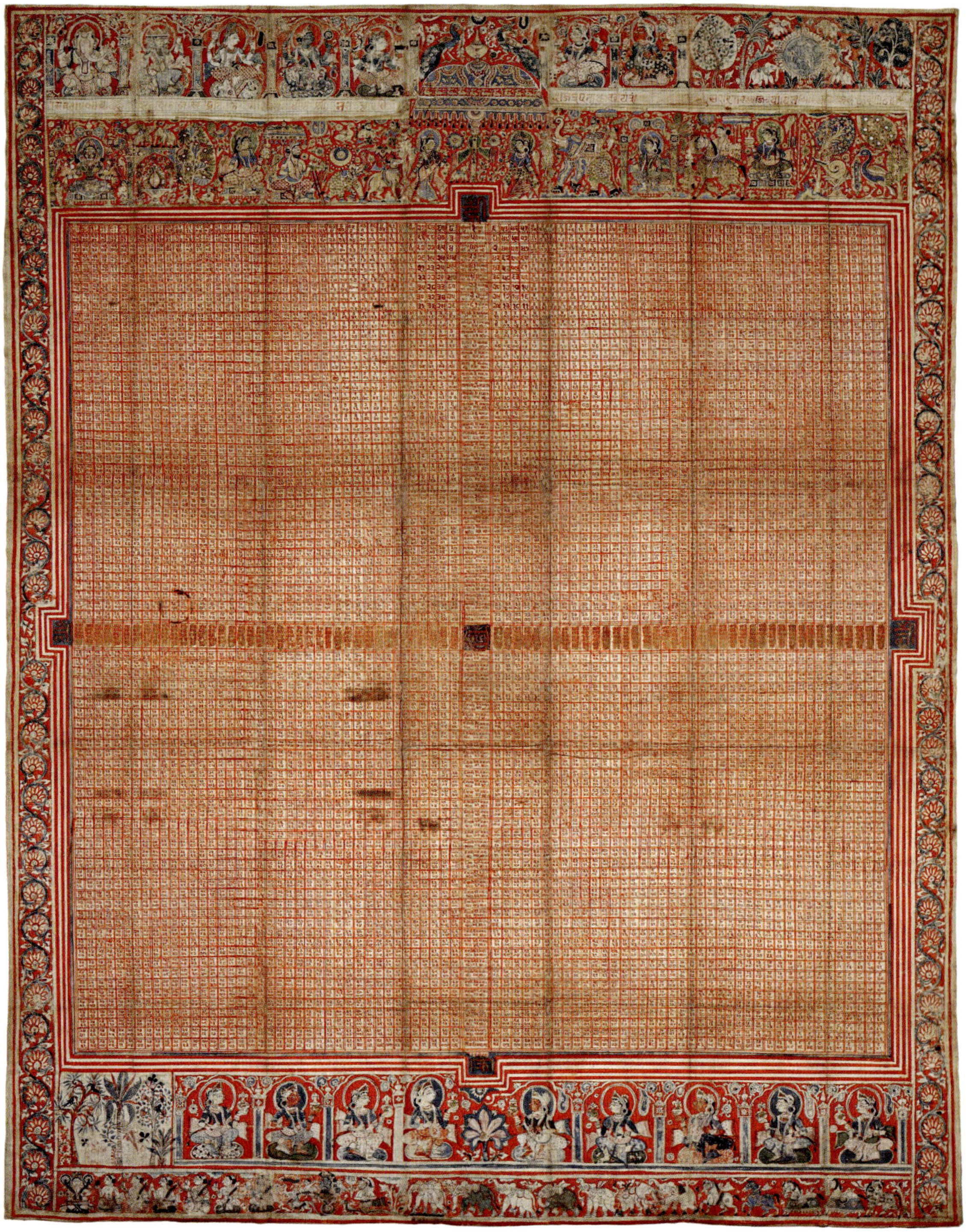

FIGURE 1.13

Victory banner, ca. 1447 (V.S. 1504), Gujarat. Pigments on cloth, 137 × 110 cm. V&A IM 89-1936 © Victoria and Albert Museum, London.

fantastic landscapes, Hindu gods (Gaṇeśa, Brahma, Śiva, and Viṣṇu), the goddess Sarasvatī, the nine planets, seven elephants, and five horses, and other important elements of Jain cosmography.

The Jain *paṭas* containing ritual diagrams, such as the *Suri-mantra paṭa,* the *Ṛṣimaṇḍala paṭa,* and the *Vardhamana vidya paṭa,* have been compared to Buddhist maṇḍalas on cloth. A maṇḍala (lit. circle) is usually a composition outlining the structure of the force field of a central deity, and paintings of this type are known as *thangka* in Tibet and *paubha* in Nepal. The structural and functional similarities that can be observed between maṇḍalas and Jain *paṭas* may arise from common elements in the tantric practices they were created to serve. As Andhare notes, however, the Jain *paṭas* are distinctive in their "liberal use of syllables and even the entire texts of esoteric rites. The mantras therefore become an integral part of the [Jaina] yantra in a way that is rare in Buddhist or Hindu mandalas."[105] The liberal attitude toward the written text that underlies the script-as-image presentation of Jain *paṭas* may also underlie a more open-ended and pragmatic approach to layering and adding texts in Jain manuscripts, a topic to be discussed in chapter 2.[106]

Buddhist examples in which a written text functions as an image are rare in India, but medieval Buddhist communities elsewhere cultivated the practice of using a mantra letter to represent a deity, most notably in the "seed syllable" images used in Shingon rites during the Kamakura period in Japan.[107] Earlier examples are known to have been used in Chinese Buddhist communities. In a sizeable woodblock print sheet containing the *Great Dhāraṇī of Wish Fulfillment* (Skt. *Mahāpratisarā*), dated 980, and found by Stein in Dunhuang's Library Cave, we find twelve seed syllables (Skt. *siddham*) imprinted as enlarged letters in dark ink on lotus seats in the circles marking the four directions, in the inner space, and the eight cardinal and intercardinal points in the outer band (figure 1.14).[108] Tibetan Buddhist examples such as the "tenfold mighty one" (seven interwoven letters with three additional signs), representing the root mantra of the Kālacakra maṇḍala ritual, and the inclusion of the mantra syllables in the outer ring of the Kālacakra maṇḍala (as seen in the creation of a sand maṇḍala), indicate that the script-as-image idea may also have been cultivated in certain Indian Buddhist communities. This conjunction would be consistent with our sense of the underlying history, since the Kālacakra tantra was one of the last of the great tantras to develop in Indic Buddhist circles.

We will come back to the complex text-image relationships articulated in tantric visionary practice in chapter 3. Here we should note that the second mode of active visual presentation of written text, namely, substantiation of an image through written letters or text, is also closely related to the development of tantric visionary practice. While written letters may seem absent on the vibrant visual field of a *thangka* like the fifteenth-century Four Maṇḍalas of the Vajrāvalī from the Ngor monastery in central Tibet, the other side of the cloth is strewn with mantras arranged and written in black ink to correspond to the images on the front (figure 1.15; see figure 3.1).[109] It is as if the written letters are substantiating the color-filled visible forms from behind. In a way, the text-image relationship here, a version of materialization if not transmutation, resembles what is seen in Japanese paintings of the jeweled-pagoda maṇḍala. In a pagoda (or reliquary) composed almost entirely of the letters of a scripture

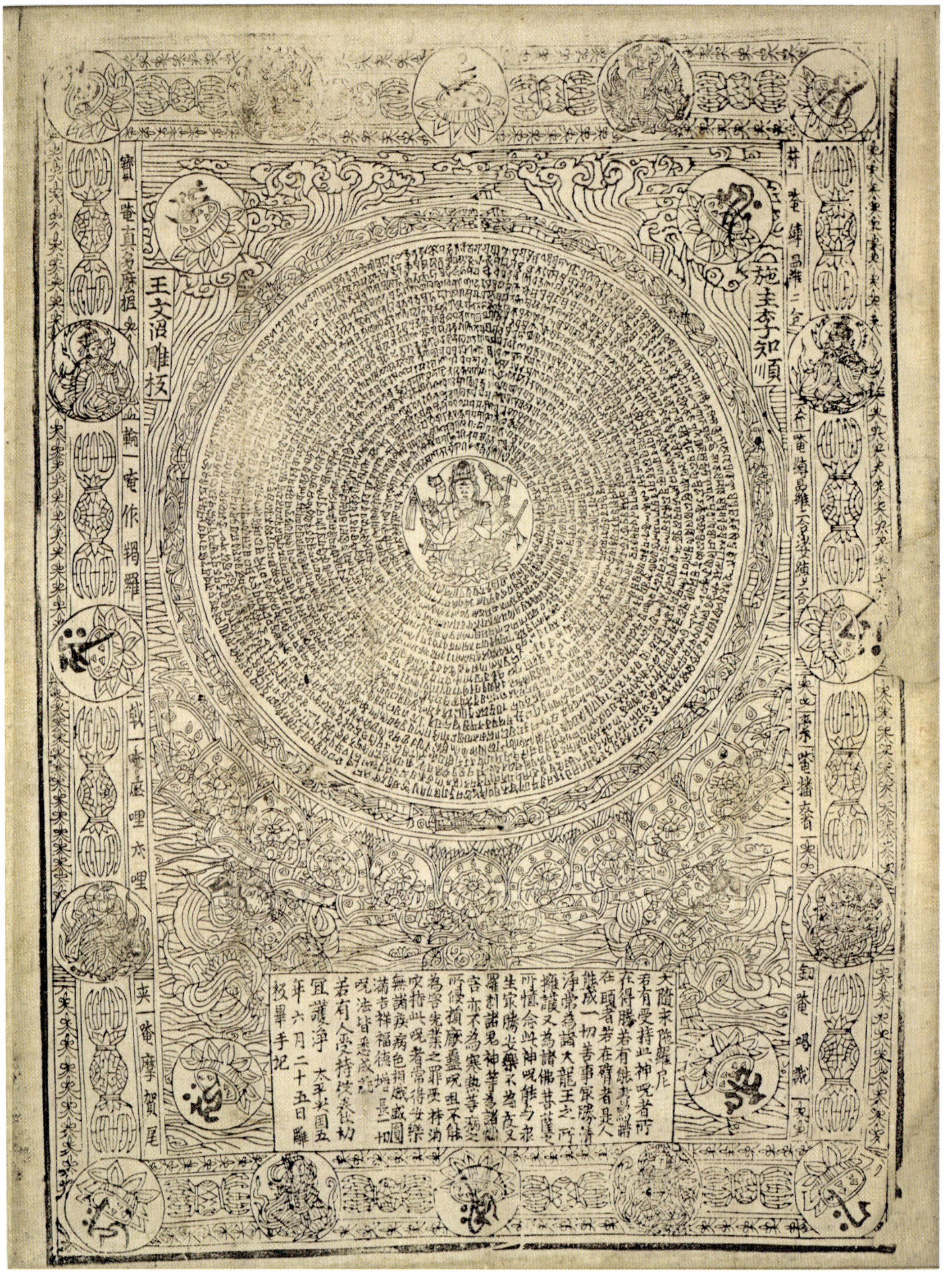

FIGURE 1.14

Mahāpratisarā dhāranī (大隨求陀羅尼) dated 980 CE. Woodblock print, ink on paper, 41.7 × 30.3 cm. British Museum, 1919,0101,0.249 © Trustees of the British Museum.

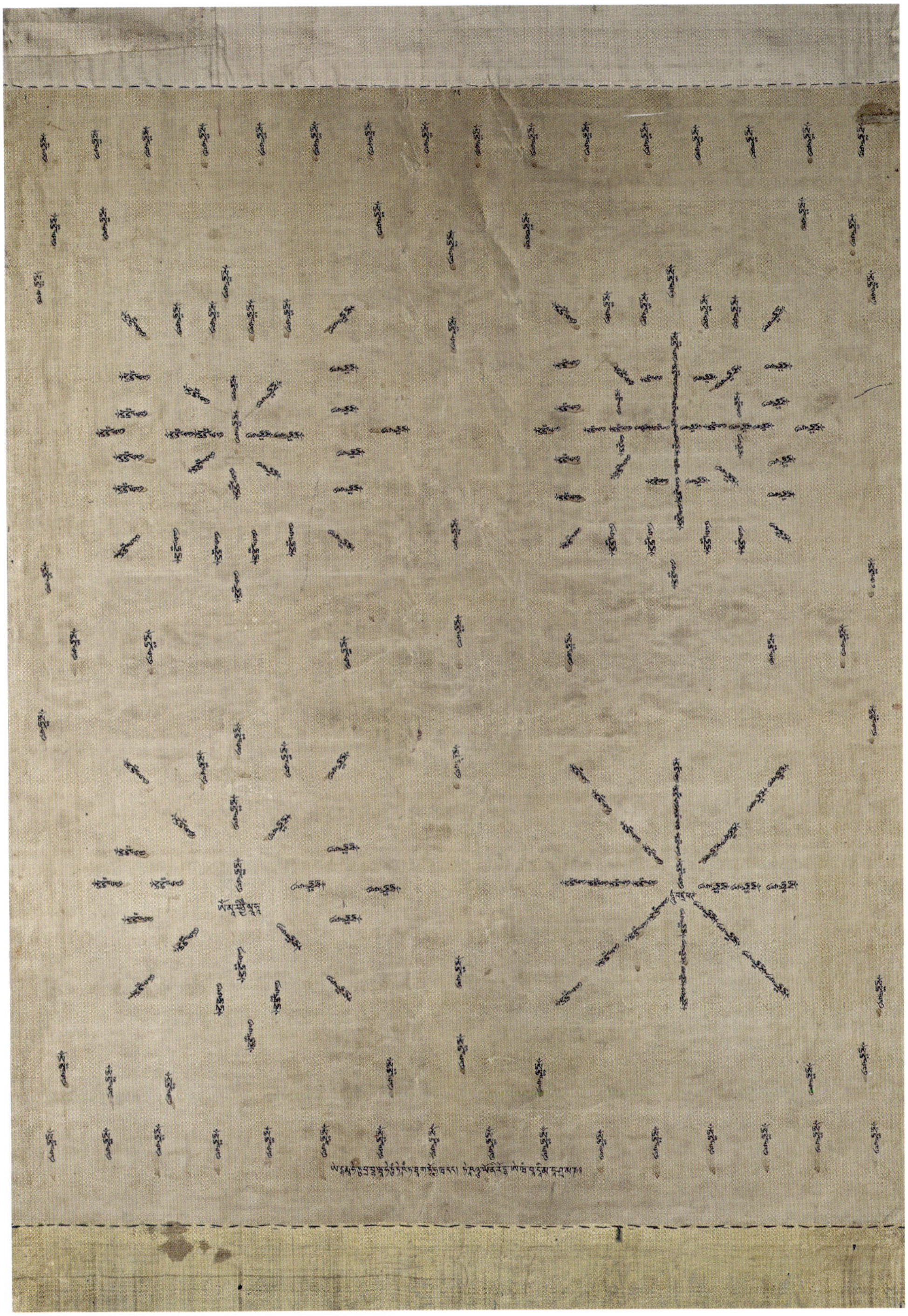

FIGURE 1.15
Reverse side of the Four Maṇḍalas of the Vajrāvalī (see figure 3.1), ca. 1450, Tibet (Sakya-Ngor monastery). Pigments on cloth, 81.9 × 73.6 cm. Rubin Museum of Art C2007.6.1 (HAR 81826). Image courtesy of the Rubin Museum of Art.

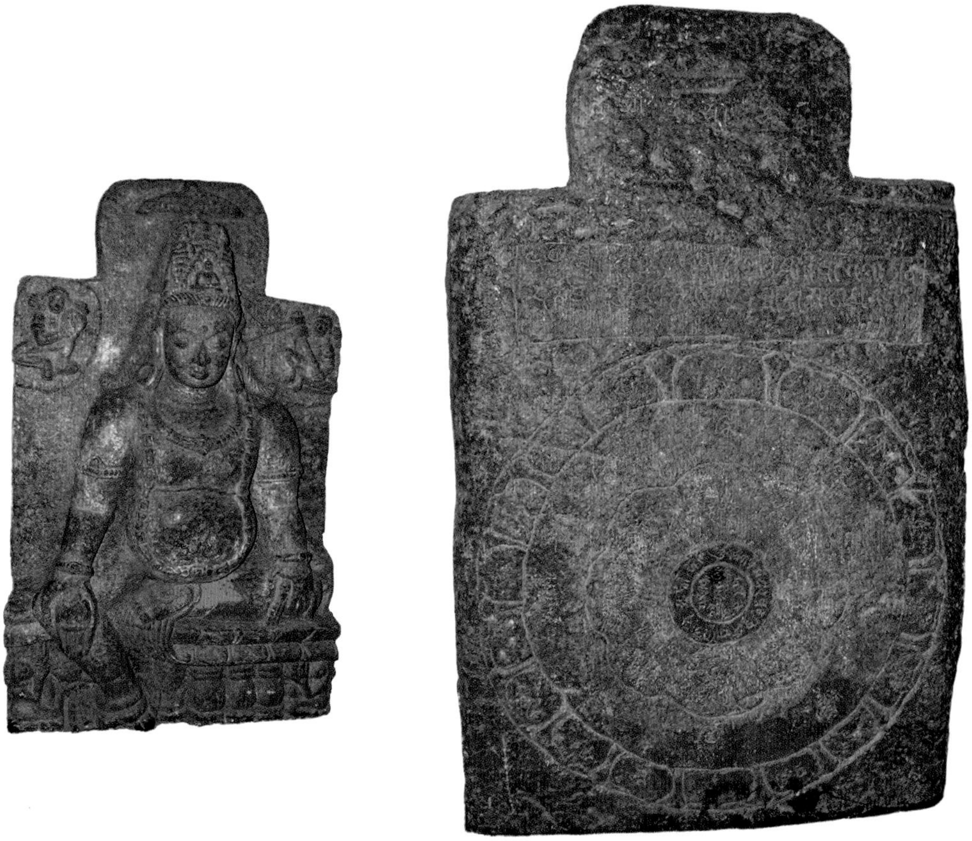

FIGURE 1.16
Jambhala, ca. tenth century, Ratnagiri (Monastery 1), Odisha. Stone, H: 67.3 cm. ASI Site Museum, Ratnagiri. Photo © Jinah Kim.

(here the *Lotus sūtra*), Halle O'Neal finds "a profound visualization of the multiplicity of the Buddha," achieved through the "ultimate indivisibility of word and image."[110]

While no painting on cloth like the Ngor monastery *thangka* survives from India, a much earlier stone image with mantra inscriptions on the back was found at the Buddhist monastic site of Ratnagiri in Odisha. According to Debala Mitra, the inscribed image of Jambhala was found "on the stone basement of the rear porch" of Monastery I, "leaning against the eastern pilaster."[111] Jambhala is a god of wealth often found in the threshold area of a Buddhist establishment in India, and he also takes on (or is given) a wrathful form like many *krodha* or protector deities in the late Indian Buddhist pantheon. Dated to the ninth or tenth century on the basis of style, archaeological evidence, and paleography, the Ratnagiri image follows an early iconographic type in presenting a pot-bellied giver of wealth who holds a jewel-vomiting mongoose in his left hand and a jewel in his right hand (figure 1.16). Despite the conventional iconography, the six-Buddha crown on his head signals that this image is to be understood in the context of Buddhist tantras that assume the five-tathāgata system (such as the *Sarvatathāgatatattvasaṃgraha,* which Linrothe identifies as a "Phase Two" text), which anticipates the introduction of the sixth, the primordial teacher of *ādi*-Buddha. For the present discussion, the significance of the image is found in the maṇḍalaic diagram with mantras on the back of the stele. This side is divided into three text-diagrams, the most prominent being the seventeen-petal lotus that encircles an eight-petal lotus with two inner circles in the bottom two-thirds of the space. Each of these circles and every lotus petal contains mantra letters, starting with *jaṁ* at the very center, which is surrounded by *oṁ jambhala-jālendrayasvāhā,* the beginning mantra of the Jambhala *sādhana* (practice) collected in the *Sādhanamālā,* in the next circle out. The eight petals of the inner lotus contain the eight mantras to be recited in the *sādhana,* while the sixteen petals of the outer lotus contain the mystic syllables *jaḥ, huṁ, vaṁ,* and *hloḥ* at the four cardinal points, together with the names of the eight offering deities and syllables referencing the four musical instruments in the remaining petals.[112]

Unlike the Ngor *thangka,* the letters here do not correspond to the specific image(s) on the front; however, the lettered lotus maṇḍala substantiates the image as a whole. The mantra *oṁ ā hūṃ svāhā,* which is inscribed in the open space across the top of the stele and shaped, unusually, like a protruding bar, seems to imbue the whole stele with the most fundamental mantra of tantric *sādhana.* The long horizontal rectangular bar that runs above the lotus maṇḍala contains the so-called Buddhist creed, beginning with *ye dharmāhetu.*[113] Characterized as a "dharma relic" in older scholarship, this consecration verse commonly appears on Buddhist images from the eighth century on, a phenomenon that reinforces the notion that there was an enhanced awareness of text-visuality at play during this period. The *ye dharmāhetu* verse on the back of the Ratnagiri Jambhala stele is inscribed on a chiseled, slightly recessed surface, within a clearly demarcated rectangular space. It is as if a piece of the essential text were literally embedded in the stele to imbue it with its presence just as a seal of this dharma verse was affixed on bronze statues for consecration.[114]

Although the relationship between the inscribed text on the back and the Jambhala image on the front of the stele may seem more distant than that of the Ngor monastery *thangka,* the mechanism is the same, and the effect is to infuse the images with a special power that is invoked by means of the tantric ritual. Whether in stone or on painted cloth, the images embrace and exploit the written text as a visual trace of a continual performance that empowers it. The *ye dharmāhetu* verse also appears on the back of the Ngor monastery *thangka,* at the bottom of the entire mantra-filled field, consecrating the painting as a whole. Although it is written in Tibetan *uchen* script, it does not seek to translate the meaning of the verse into Tibetan. Rather, it transliterates the Sanskrit text, retaining the *sound* of the letters so that they can operate in the same way as the syllables of the mantras above; in other words, their foremost significance is sonic and visual—in a word, physical. That text can meaningfully operate in a material rather than a discursive domain is worth bearing in mind as we move on to explore the adoption of manuscripts as a medium for painting. It is striking that the tradition of painted manuscripts developed in a cultural and religious milieu in which great discoveries of exceeding philosophical and theological subtlety were also being made in the nature of language. Strategies to manipulate the dynamic interactions between text and image were being made at the same time—especially in tantric circles.

A PAINTING AS A MATERIAL OBJECT

A painting realizes an image. In our day, it may be pixelated into an idea, an abstraction that exists as a mental representation. Thus, when we talk about a painting, we frequently discuss its iconography, style, and other formal aspects while losing sight, in the process, of its weight—its material presence in a space. A painting, whether on cotton canvas, on paper, on a palm-leaf folio, or on a wall, is a substantial object carrying the weight of its colorants—pigments in a binding medium, as well as ink. In an age of boundless opportunity for the digital reproduction of images, a painting can easily circulate—in fact, can more easily circulate—without its physical vehicle. But it is worth concentrating on a painting's materiality when we can, since it gives us access to the history of art on a tactile and experiential level and draws us closer to the culture in which it was created.

On May 22, 1909, the Russian explorer Pyotr Kuzmich Kozlov and his companions made an exciting discovery during their second exploration and excavation in Khara Khoto, located near present-day Edzina (Ejin Qi) in western Inner Mongolia. Excavating what he called "Illustrious suburgan"—in effect, a ruin of a monumental stūpa—his team found numerous treasures of the Tangut Empire (kingdom of XiXia). In great excitement, they forgot to document the process of excavation, but Kozlov later gave a detailed description of his experience:

> I shall equally never forget in particular the powerful impression made on myself and my companions by two Chinese icons on a muslin like material. As we unrolled them, we were enthralled to see magnificent seated figures, bathed in a soft pale blue and pink radiance. From these sacred Buddhist relics there emanated something living, something expressive, something unalloyed; we simply could not take our eyes off them, so inimitably fine were they. . . . Yet, did we but raise one edge of either canvas, a large segment of the paint lifted off, and instantly all the enchantment disappeared, wraith-like, leaving only a vague memory of the beauty that had been.[115]

As Kira Samosyuk notes, it is impossible to identify which of the many *thangka*s and their fragments now housed in the State Hermitage Museum in Saint Petersburg may once have been those two enchanting beauties.[116] But Kozlov's dramatic description expertly conveys the tactile nature of a physical encounter with a painting laden with pigments on cloth. As we will see, methods for painting on cloth and manuscript painting developed during the first centuries of the second millennium, and efforts to harness the most brilliant colors possible from organic and mineral pigments emphasized the layered surfaces and texture of painting. These artisans and artists (an ex post facto distinction) were fully aware of the materiality of painting as they labored to create objects with an abiding physical presence. At this remove, it certainly seems easy to appreciate the presence and material properties of a *thangka* laden with a swath of green from powdered malachite, traces of gold, raised details painted in kaolin (calcium-based) white, and a thick layer of vermilion (cinnabar). Manuscripts are not essentially different from *thangkas*, except in scale—especially those containing paintings. In any case, manuscripts and paintings on cloth were never too far from each other in the ritual spaces for which they were created. This is especially the case in a Buddhist context, as Kozlov reminds us.

> In the center of the stūpa stood a wooden pole, around which were arranged, facing inwards, something in the order of twenty life-size clay statutes "resembling lamas, conducting a religious ceremony in front of hundreds of manuscripts in Tangut script, stacked one upon the other.[117]

Among the illustrated manuscripts now kept in the Institute of Oriental Studies of the Russian Academy of Sciences in Saint Petersburg are a few in *pothi* format, such as Tang 159 (Inventory No. 5654). Certainly, some of these must have been among the manuscripts found with those encircling statues, empowering the site with their material presence.[118]

2

THE ART OF THE BOOK IN MEDIEVAL SOUTH ASIA

THE DESIGN PRINCIPLE

ARCHITECTURAL INSPIRATION

In writing about Jain manuscript paintings in the Museum of Fine Arts Collection, Boston, Ananda Coomaraswamy, the first curator of Indian Art in North America, remarked, "Indian art has never developed book illustrations as such."[1] While his comment reflects the restricted understanding of "book illustrations" of his time, Coomaraswamy, when he asserts, "the square panels [of painting] . . . must be regarded as excerpts from the surfaces of painted walls . . . reduced in size and added to the written page," also provides an insight regarding the art of the book in India.[2] Coomaraswamy emphasizes the connection between manuscript painting and wall painting to write a continuous overall history of Indian painting, the narrative for which begins with the celebrated fifth-century Buddhist mural paintings of Ajanta. Many scholars followed in Coomaraswamy's footsteps, defining Ajanta's murals as the gold standard of India's pictorial art, praising the refined modeling of the body, the subtle yet brilliant use of shading, and the remarkable representation of volume and depth, as seen in the famed images of bodhisattvas flanking the walls to the main chamber in Cave 1 at Ajanta. It is no wonder that India's modern artists sought artistic inspiration in the Ajanta murals during their search for "Indianness" in the early twentieth century.[3] It is an ongoing project of the field of South Asian art to rethink this canonical understanding and to reconsider the contributions of Coomaraswamy and other first-generation scholars of Indian art history in a new light.

Coomaraswamy's remark is insightful, not necessarily on account of his having connected temple murals with the manuscript paintings in terms of their pictorial values, as is often discussed in subsequent scholarship, but for the analogy itself. That the temple walls and painted manuscript pages are compared on equal footing helps us conceptualize Indian book art as exemplifying a distinct mode of visual and material production that promoted the circulation of specific types of knowledge and authority.[4] The manuscript paintings are not just "excerpts from painted walls" but the building blocks of a sacred structure that they create and sustain inside a small portable object in the form of a book (*pustaka* in Sanskrit).[5] This chapter argues that a manuscript was designed like a special ritual space with its unfolding interior space filled with carefully written text in an ornamental/formal script and with strategically placed colorful miniature paintings.[6]

This chapter explores the development of the art of the book in South Asia within the Indic religious landscape by considering the design principles of religious architecture as a potential indigenous model for Indian book art. Three different types of evidence support my conceptualization of architecture as a design model for understanding miniature painting in *pothi*-format manuscripts: first, internal visual evidence seen in iconographic and decorative programs in painted manuscripts; second, images of books in use in the surviving artistic record; and third, textual sources that discuss how books were used and treated in medieval South Asia. Trans-sectarian comparisons of images of books in use combined with a contextual analysis of contemporary textual sources regarding the art of the book help us understand that *pothi*-format manuscripts became an important marker of authority as a fitting material device for knowledge transmission in medieval South Asia.

A multimedia approach helps us to see both the interior and the exterior of a manuscript as a ritual, liturgical object. Regulated placement of painted panels containing images of deities inside a three-dimensional space of a manuscript makes a manuscript a portable miniature temple and, ultimately, a potent cultic object.[7] When architecture is taken as a theoretical principle, a specific design pattern of temple architecture developed in North India can also help locate the art of the book as an indigenous cultural practice in medieval South Asia.

Buddhist examples demonstrate the innovative and creative approaches medieval Indian manuscript makers took to design a painted manuscript, which emphasize the book's three-dimensional quality as a material container of the sacred. This attitude toward the book as a special sacred object was not limited to the Buddhist tradition. Even a cursory examination of early painted palm-leaf manuscripts of the Jain and Hindu traditions reveals a similar attitude toward a book's significance in medieval Indian religious contexts as a sacred object that conveys doctrinal authority and the presence of the divine or as the ultimate teacher. By approaching the production and use of *pothi*-format palm-leaf manuscripts as a distinctive

South (and Southeast) Asian cultural practice and by exploring their material cultural origins as well as their historical development, we can appreciate the historical, artistic, and religious values of the medieval painted palm-leaf manuscripts prepared in *pothi* in the world of painted manuscript production during the first few centuries of the second millennium.[8]

A *pothi,* a Hindi term for a book, is a uniquely Indic format. It is prepared with uniformly sized loose palm-leaf or birch-bark (or paper) folios that are bound through prebored holes (often two holes marking one-third of the length from each side in the case of palm-leaf Buddhist manuscripts) using a cord or two metal sticks.[9] The folios stay loose in this format as one can untie the cord or remove the metal fastener to open a manuscript, and a pagination system was introduced from early on, much earlier than its debut in Islamic manuscripts, probably to ensure a manuscript's integrity as an orderly object with a textual flow. What follows is not an exhaustive or definitive study of the art of the book in medieval South Asia; it is, rather, meant to provide a starting point for further exploration.

A MANUSCRIPT AS A TEMPLE

INNOVATIONS IN BUDDHIST MANUSCRIPT DESIGN

A twelfth-century painted manuscript of the *Pañcarakṣā sūtra,* the text containing hymns and incantation formulas (*dhāraṇī*-s) of the five protective goddesses now in the collection of the National Archives of Nepal in Kathmandu, offers a place to begin our exploration of the conception of a manuscript as a miniature temple.[10] The five goddesses representing the text along with the Buddha Amoghasiddhi are placed at the beginning (folios 1v–2r), in the middle (folios 57r–58v), and at the end of the manuscript (folios 171r–172r). It was prepared for Hīrakā, a lay female donor who was a wife of a certain ṭhakkura Śrībahudhana, probably somewhere in today's West Bengal.[11] Through the addition of a sheet of paper in front of each panel, which functions as a curtain or veil like those placed in front of Tibetan *thangka* paintings, the painted images in this manuscript were treated as if they were deities worshipped in a temple (figure 2.1).[12] These paper curtains are, of course, later additions, but it is important to note that paper curtains were inserted to prevent the paintings from touching each other, not only as a protective measure to prevent rubbing, but also as a physical divider to keep the deities segregated in their own quarters.[13] Traces of vermilion powder visible on top of the painted panels further suggest that the painted images of the goddesses are treated as divinities living in the book. In other words, *tilaka* (a touch of vermilion on a deity's or a person's forehead as an act of veneration and protection) has been put on each panel.[14] At some point in the life of the manuscript, the goddesses, who are already represented as installed within shrine structures, began to be considered as living in this manuscript-house.

Visual strategies of representing deities inside shrine structures were constantly employed in manuscript design during the twelfth century. For example, a manuscript (British Library, Or. 6902) of the *Perfection of Wisdom* prepared in the Vikramaśīla monastery for a monastic elder (śākyabhikṣusthavira), Sumatiśrīmintra, in the mid-twelfth century (Gopāla's fifteenth year, ca. 1147 CE), bears six painted panels placed at the beginning (folios 1v–2r), the middle (folios 163v–164r), and the end (folios 226v–267r). All but one panel have the central image

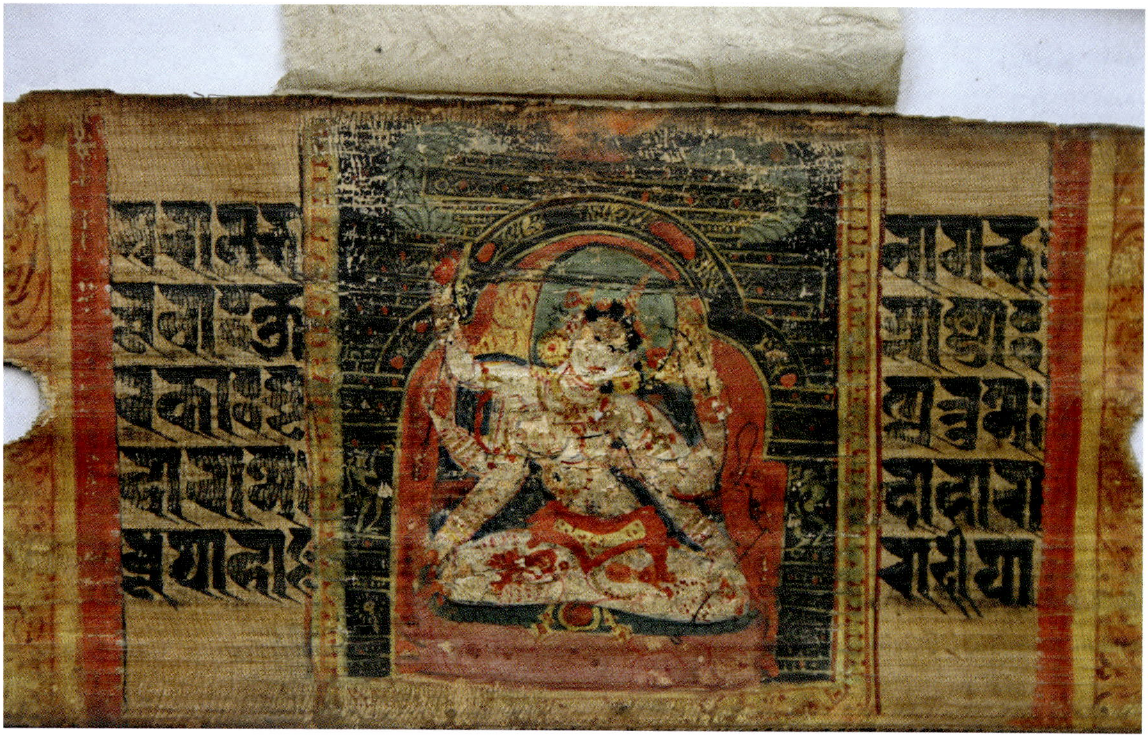

FIGURE 2.1
Mahāśītavatī, folio 57v, *Pañcarakṣā sūtra* manuscript, Govindapāla's sixteenth year (ca. 1181 CE). National Archive, Kathmandu, Acc. No. 5.83.

framed inside a shrine structure. On folio 163v, bodhisattva Maitreya is seated inside a shrine structure that is drawn with yellow outline and colored with brown, orange, and blue, showing various patterns including the lotus petals on the tri-lobed arch and the diamond and triangular shapes on the surface of each tier of the superstructure (figure 2.2). The geometric patterns used to delineate the details of the shrine structure function as miniaturized versions of the patterns seen in the decorative borders framing the painted panel on the same page. These decorative columns mark not only the space inside a page but also the book as a whole with a systematic rhythm, like decorative pillars inside a temple.

Contemporary Nepalese examples make it clear that painted panels often depict the images installed in a temple space through various visual devices such as hanging canopies, tassels, and garlands. A beautifully written manuscript of the *Perfection of Wisdom* provides one such case (figure 2.3). According to the colophon on folio 188r, the manuscript was also written in Vikramaśīla for a Nepali monk (*nepāladeśīyabhikṣu*), Āryaśrīmintra, in 1117 (or 1119) CE (N.S. 237 or 9).[15] The manuscript, which bears witness to the transregional movement of people and objects in twelfth-century South Asia, was written in the Vikramaśīla monastery in India for a Nepali donor and was most likely painted in Nepal where the date colophon and

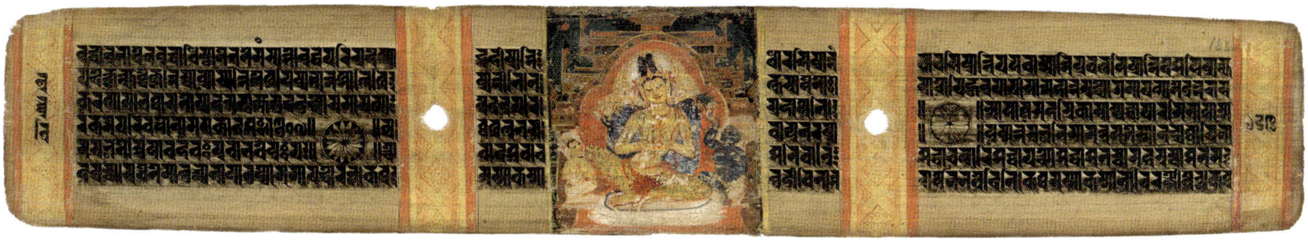

FIGURE 2.2
Folio 163v, *Perfection of Wisdom* manuscript, Gopāla's fifteenth year (ca. 1147 CE), Vikramaśīla monastery. British Library Or. 6902. © The British Library Board.

the mention of the production site seem to have been added.[16] The name of the Nepali monk, Āryaśrīmintra, indicates a connection to the Indian monastery, as suggested by the same ending—"*śrīmintra*" (a scribal variant for *śrīmitra*)—of the name "Sumatiśrīmintra," the donor of the other known painted manuscript from the Vikramaśīla monastery (British Library, Or. 6902).[17] The Cleveland manuscript was originally prepared with six painted folios (folios 1v–2r, 89v–90r, and 186v–187r) and painted wooden book covers, but folio 2 is missing.[18]

The artist(s) purposefully represented the painted panels on folios 1v and 89v as if floating in space by delineating a smaller area for each deity on a larger thinly painted white background. It is as if the first sets of images in this manuscript, that is, the panels on the first folio, probably also on the missing second folio, and the first folio of the middle section (folio 89v), occupy niches leading to the main image on the central panel of folio 90r, which represents the goddess Prajñāpāramitā, the celebrated, rightful center of this book-shrine space, who is represented on a raised platform under an elaborate canopy. If we imagine these panels in a three-dimensional architectural space, we can see that the panels in the first two painted folios and the first of the middle painted folios form a secondary enclosure with the niches perhaps leading to the main shrine. The painted panels on the interior of the two wooden book covers also convey the sense of a shrine space by representing canopies and hanging tassels above each "enshrined" image.

Other visual devices also suggest that the painted images depict deities installed inside the ritual space of a temple. The manner in which the diaphanous orange shawl is represented, as if draped over an image of the offering goddess on folio 89v, is unique to this manuscript. Shawls enveloping deities are often represented draped over their upper arms or shoulders but not over and around the halos. This particular visual device is reminiscent of the offerings of cloth over clay statues in living Buddhist temples from the Himalayan regions.[19]

The conception of a manuscript as a three-dimensional Buddhist temple is also realized in a late twelfth-century palm-leaf manuscript of the *Perfection of Wisdom* from Bengal (formerly Sam Fogg Collection). The manuscript is dated with the Govindapāla's elapsed (*gata*) regnal year 30 (*gata-samvat,* indicating that he is no longer a reigning king), ca. 1195 CE. According to the colophon on folios 217v–218r, it was written by a scribe (*lekhaka*),

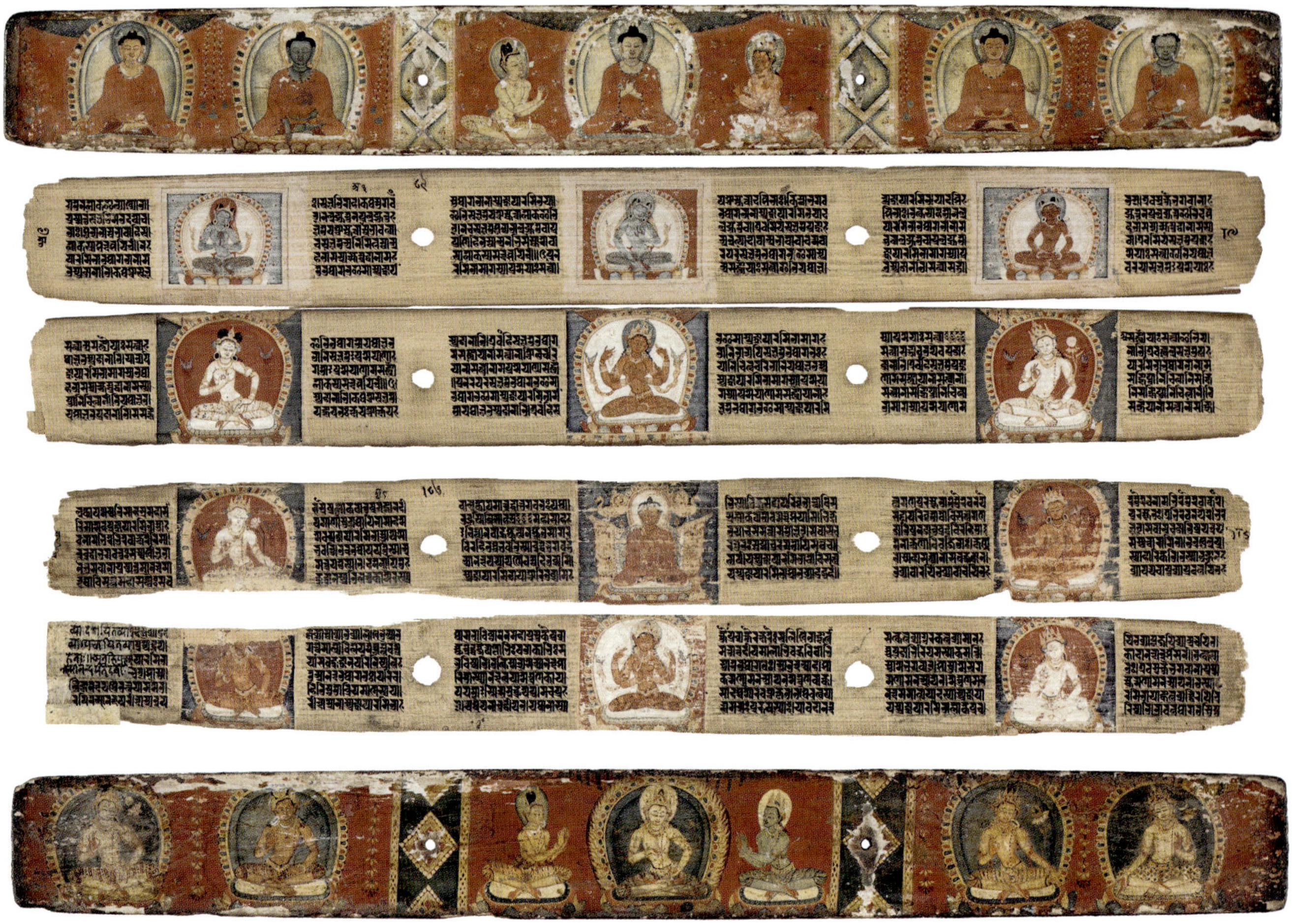

FIGURE 2.3
Painted book covers (*top and bottom*) and painted folios (folios 89v–90r, 186v–187r), *Perfection of Wisdom* manuscript, N.S. 237 or 9? (ca. 1117 or 1119 CE), Vikramaśila monastery. Cleveland Museum of Art, Acc. No. 1938-301.

Devarāja-devarakha, in the town of Kodanda-maṇḍala, the present location of which is difficult to identify.[20] It was prepared for a lay Mahāyāna Buddhist donor whose name tentatively reads "Maitaka, son of Cchinna" (*cchinnasutamaitakasya*).[21] The donor is identified as a resident of Śaucayagrāma or Śaucaya village (*śaucayagramāvasthita*), the location of which is also difficult to establish with currently available epigraphic and topographic evidence. It was originally prepared with six painted folios (folios 1v–2r, 109v–110r, and 216v–217r), but the first two were damaged and later replaced with folios made of yellow Nepalese paper. Each surviving panel in this manuscript depicts a deity (various bodhisattvas and Buddhist goddesses) seated inside a multitiered shrine structure.

Thin yellow lines over a black background are used to inscribe intricate patterns on the architecture, such as the roundels on the tri-lobed arch visible in the central section of

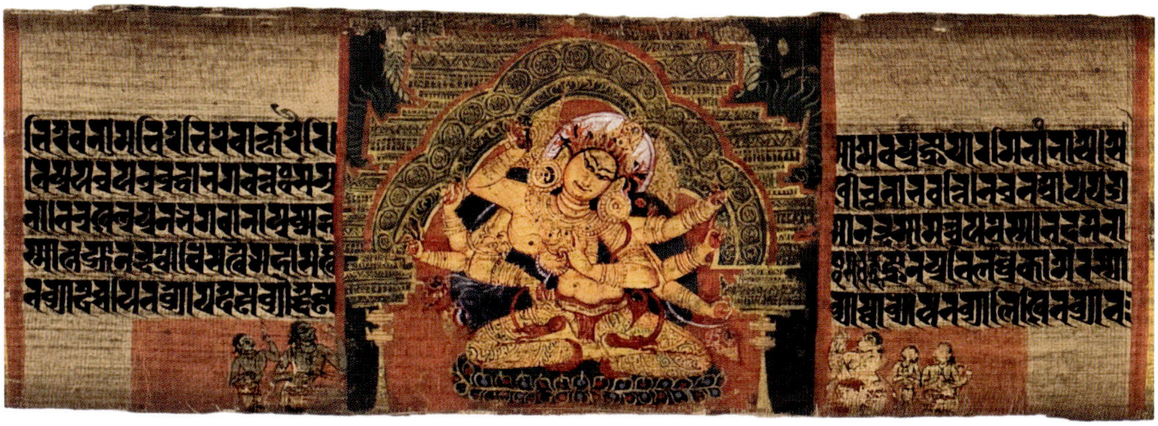

FIGURE 2.4
Vajratārā with devotees, 216v. *Perfection of Wisdom* manuscript, date: Govindapāla's thirtieth year (ca. 1195 CE). Sam Fogg Ltd. Photo courtesy of Sam Fogg, London.

the panel on folio 216v, which depicts the eight-armed goddess Vajra-Tārā (figure 2.4). When the two painted folios are open for viewing, the architectural motifs appear rhythmically to punctuate and structure the pictorial space. When, for example, the last two painted pages are open, an identical multitiered shrine structure serving as a framing visual device of each painted panel appears six times, three per folio. More importantly, the depiction of human figures supplicating to the goddess Vajra-Tārā on folio 216v provides a unique example in which one can see realized the concept of the manuscript's interior as a temple space.

Donor figures are rarely represented in eastern Indian Buddhist manuscripts.[22] When they are included, they are depicted in a separate panel engaged in a ritual action relating to book worship.[23] The donor family in the Sam Fogg manuscript is represented outside the frame of painted panels. The family appears to occupy a temple space while paying homage to the goddess Vajra-Tārā installed inside a main shrine, surrounded by the deities installed in their respective niches. As seen in figure 2.4, on either side of the Vajra-Tārā panel appear small human figures against small vermilion red rectangular blocks that repeat the background color surrounding Vajra-Tārā inside the shrine. Two green male figures on the right side of the goddess most likely represent the main donor holding what may be an incense burner and his eldest son with the offering of a garland in his hands. Three yellow female figures representing the female members of the donor's family are seated to the left of the goddess. Due to the fact that the same vermilion color envelops the goddess and connects the two spaces (the goddess's and the donors') visually, the backdrop for the donor figures gives the impression that they inhabit the shrine space within which the goddess is installed.[24] When seen together in the context of an open book, the bodhisattvas and the other goddess surrounding this scene bless the donors and bear witness to their devotional act of paying homage to the goddess.

The use of the shrine structure as a framing device in manuscripts, such as those discussed here, has been taken as evidence of a regional pictorial style, most probably that of the ancient regions of Aṅga and Varendra in the twelfth century.[25] That this school existed is plausible given paleographic and stylistic characteristics, but one should be mindful that the evidence for identifying a manuscript's provenance on this single formal feature is not as strong as it could be, partly because the argument essentially rests on a single manuscript, the British Library manuscript of the Vikramaśīla monastery (Or. 6902).[26] More than just regionally specific motifs, the architectural framing devices in painted panels represent a concerted effort on the part of twelfth-century Buddhist manuscript makers to enhance visually the conception of a book as a temple.

UTILITARIAN APPROACH

EARLY JAIN PAINTED MANUSCRIPTS

The twelfth-century Buddhist manuscripts discussed above lend the most elaborate articulation to the idea of the manuscript as a temple. From the very beginning of the practice, however, the fundamental structure of an iconographic program in a painted Buddhist manuscript shared the prevailing template for designing a three-dimensional sacred structure such as a shrine, a temple, or a stūpa.[27] A rectangular (occasionally square) space for a painted panel is always demarcated and framed in a systematic manner similar to the niches and framing devices rhythmically present in a temple's iconographic program. A similar structural layout is seen in early painted palm-leaf Jain manuscripts. For example, a thirteenth-century palm-leaf manuscript of the *Savaga Padikkamana Sutta cunni* (henceforth, *SP*), a commentary on the Jain monastic code of conduct now in the Museum of Fine Arts (MFA) in Boston (Acc. No. 30.1), features six painted panels: two sets of two panels at the beginning (folios 1v–2r) and two panels at the end where the text ends and the colophon appears on folio 285v. Each painted panel is framed by red lines on either side clearly demarcating the pictorial space from that of the text (figure 2.5). According to the colophon on folio 285v, the manuscript was prepared in Āghāta (identified as Ahar near present-day Udaipur in southern Rajasthan) by a scribe, Kamalacandra, a disciple of Paṇḍit Rāmacandra in 1260 CE (V.S. 1317).[28]

The first painting in the manuscript depicts Jina Parśvanātha, as indicated by the snake hood surrounding his head and the blue color of his skin. Facing this panel is a scene of a seated monk whose disciple holds a folio of a manuscript, with the rest of the book open on a cross-legged book stand between them. It is important to note that the placement of this scene, facing the *tīrthānkara* (lit. "ford-maker," a term referring to a Jina) on folio 1v, rather than on the same folio, represents a specific visual choice. The two goddesses Ambikā and Saraswatī on the right side panels of folios 1v and 2r respectively are depicted as looking toward this scene of teaching (folio 2r) in front of Jina tīrthāṅkara (folio 1v). Together, they form a visual barrier to direct our view to the scene. On the other hand, the two goddesses on folio 285v face each other in a mirroring fashion, their upper bodies swaying to the op-

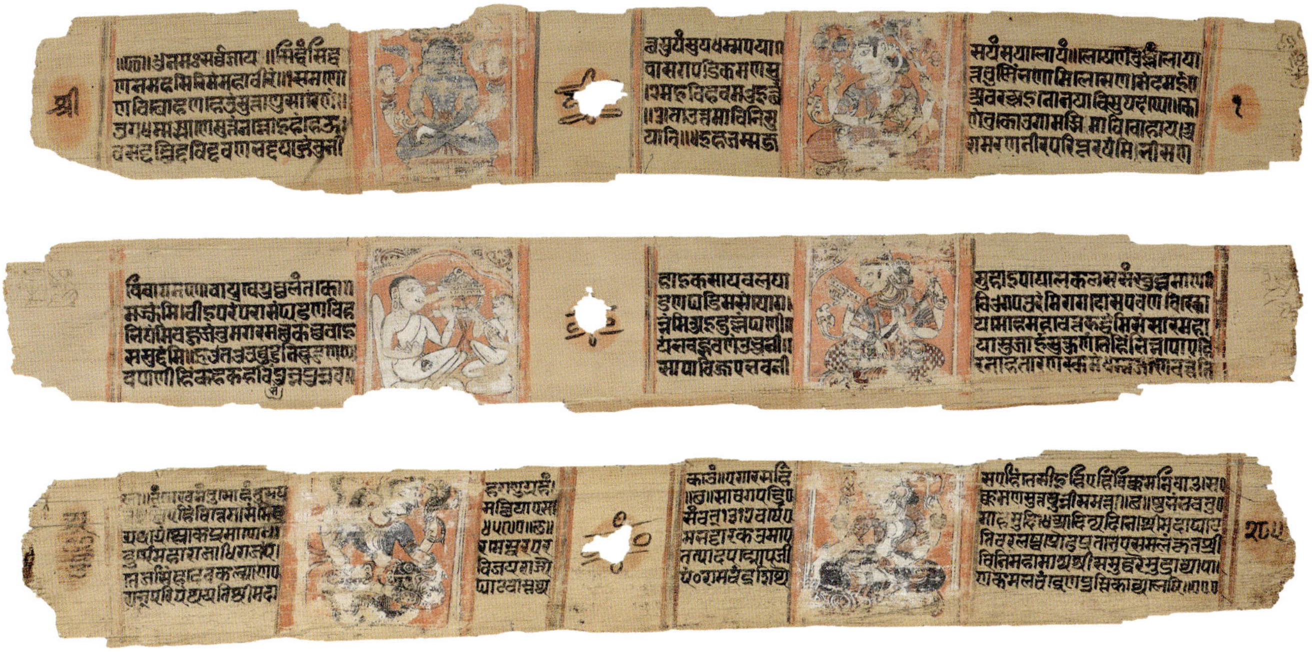

FIGURE 2.5
Painted folios (1v, 2r, 285r) of the *Savaga Padikkamana Sutta cunni*, V.S. 1317 (1260 CE), Ahar near Udaipur, Rajasthan. Museum of Fine Arts, Boston, Acc. No. 30.1, Denman Waldo Ross Collection. Photograph © 2021 Museum of Fine Arts, Boston.

posite side and showing varadā mudrā in their lowered hands facing each other, as if created in the process of a fold-over painting. They create a visual field that ultimately encases the whole text and closes the door of the manuscript.[29] These two snake goddesses, with a clear reference to the *yakṣā-yakṣī* couple Dharanendra and Padmavatī, relating back to Parśvanātha represented on the first folio, form a group with the two goddesses on the first two folios.[30] This is a familiar strategy witnessed in the earliest group of painted Buddhist manuscripts prepared during the eleventh century. There exist, however, some notable differences between the painted Jain manuscripts and the Buddhist examples.

In comparison to those in contemporary Buddhist manuscripts from eastern Indian monastic centers, in the twelfth-century Jain SPS manuscript prepared by Kamalacandra, the folios are much shorter. In Kamalacandra's manuscript the leaves are not of uniform size or in the best possible condition. Careful examination of each folio of Kamalacandra's *SP* manuscript in the MFA demonstrates that the scribe worked with damaged leaves that were already in odd shapes and uneven in size at the time the manuscript was made. The folios were not prepared with the highest quality palm leaves found in painted Buddhist manuscripts from eastern Indian monastic sites. When placed side by side with a nearly contemporary painted Buddhist palm-leaf manuscript from eastern India, such as a twelfth-century manuscript in the MFA's collection (Acc. No. 20.589), the MFA's Jain manuscript appears to have been made with whatever palm-leaf folios were available.[31]

Jain manuscripts were also designed like temples. Nonetheless, a distinct formal scheme was used to stimulate the experience of encountering architecture. As Nachiket Chanchani demonstrated in a recent study, Jain scribes and painters of early *pothi*-format paper manuscripts creatively designed the area around the hole (through which folios were strung) to frame "glimpses of absent lords." According to Chanchani, the design around the perforation reveals a ground plan of an auspicious building (temple: *prasada*) with four projections (i.e., *sarvatobhadra*). During a Jain festival like Jñānapañcamī (celebrated by both Digambaras and Śvetāmbaras) with public recitation and veneration of the texts, Jain manuscript folios designed with a distinct layout and ornamental features would have generated an experience similar to beholding an auspicious temple or a "great tīrtha" in miniature.[32]

Early painted Jain manuscripts include diverse types of texts, unlike the singular dominance of the *Perfection of Wisdom* among the painted manuscripts of the Buddhist tradition. The best known texts found in painted palm-leaf Jain manuscripts, which are celebrated as representing the epitome of the western Indian painting style, are the *Kalpasūtra* and the *Kālakācarya-katha*.[33] These texts are closely linked to the Jain veneration of the book. A surprising number of commentary texts like the *Savaga Padikkamana Sutta cunni* also appear in early painted palm-leaf Jain manuscripts.[34] Contemporary compositions such as the *Yogaśāstra*[35] and the *Siddhahemaśabdānuśāsana* (grammatical rule book), both by the famous Jain polymath Hemacandra (1089–1172),[36] were prepared as painted manuscripts.[37]

In comparison with their Buddhist counterparts, surviving Jain painted palm-leaf manuscripts demonstrate a noticeable interest in the human world and greater didacticism.[38] In contrast to painted Buddhist manuscripts from eastern India, figures of lay donors, monks, and nuns are frequently depicted.[39] The historical figures in Jain manuscripts often are identified by labels above or near them. For example, partly thanks to clearly written labels accompanying the painted scenes, the dynamic scenes painted on a wooden book cover (*patlī*) can be identified as depicting an important historical event in the history of the Śvetāmbara Jain community.[40] The panels depict scenes leading to the doctrinal debate between the Śvetāmbara monk, Devasūri, and the Digambara monk, Kumudacandra, which, according to a fourteenth-century text, the *Prabandha Cintāmaṇi,* convinced the king Siddharāja Jayasiṁha of Patan (Gujarat) to support the Śvetāmbara monks over the Digambara sect.[41] A scene of instruction on the left side of the exterior of the *patli* features two Śvetāmbara monks seated facing each other with a book on a book stand between them. Above the two figures are written the words "*śrīdevasūrayaḥ*||" and "*pa•māṇikyaḥ*||," identifying the figure seated on a raised throne-like seat as Devasūri (figure 2.6). Narrative moments are also identified through written labels such as "*kumudacandraḥ sarppaṁpasyati*" (lit. "Kumudacandra sees a snake"). The practice of labeling seems to have been widespread in Jain circles,[42] and it continued into the fourteenth century and beyond.[43]

From these examples it can be surmised that in Jain painted manuscripts there was little to no reservation about writing on the painted surfaces. In fact, there seems to have been a

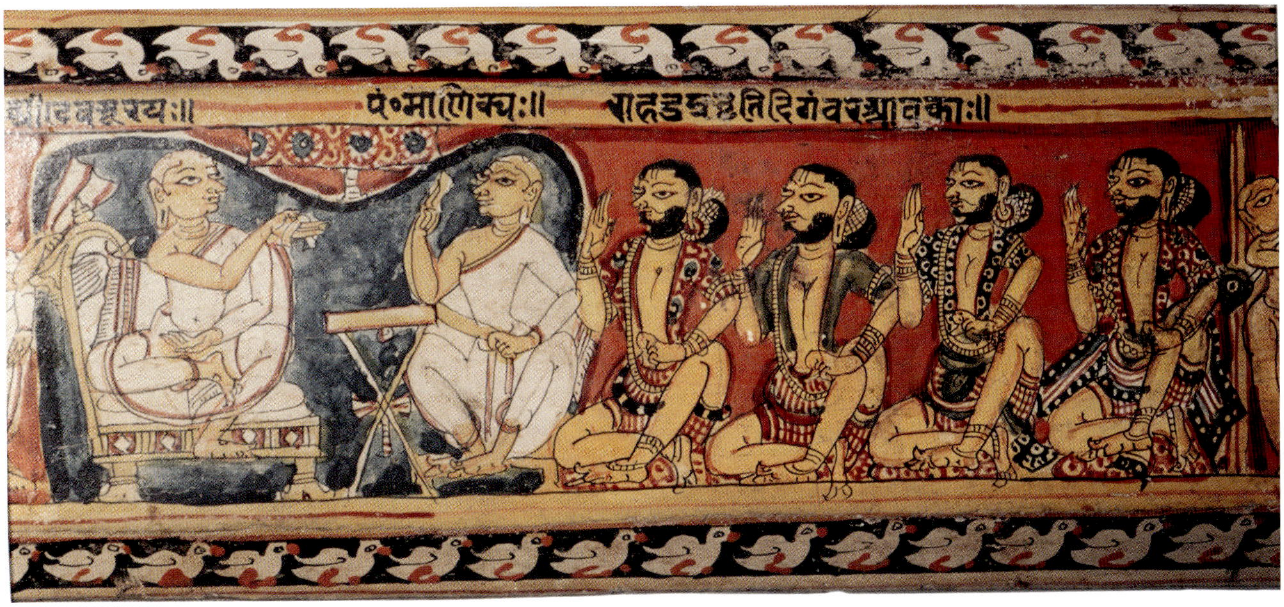

FIGURE 2.6
Discourse between Śrīdevasūri and Paṇḍita Māṇikya with a group of lay devotees, detail from a painted wooden book cover, ca. thirteenth century CE (?), Gujarat. Private collection. Photo courtesy of Catherine Glynn.

more open-ended, pragmatic attitude than is found in the Buddhist examples. Many glosses and editorial notes were added to the pages of painted Jain manuscripts. At times, these are placed in the margins in miniscule, but they are often written in a bold manner highlighting the textual presence. This is quite distinct from the subtle practice seen in Buddhist manuscripts.[44] The correction of Buddhist painted palm-leaf manuscripts is subtle and purposefully hidden or carefully erased, as if attempting to preserve an "aura" of a seemingly perfect object.

The frequently occurring self-referential scenes depicting the books in use by Jain monks and accompanying lay devotees underscores the importance of manuscripts in Jain monastic discourses during the early centuries of the second millennium. If the Buddhist manuscript makers of twelfth-century eastern India were concerned with making their painted manuscripts the most holy, potent cult objects by designing a sacred space within them, their Jain counterparts in western India sought, rather, to convey a manuscript's doctrinal authority and present-oriented historical values. For example, in the panel depicting a scene of teaching on folio 2r in the SPS in the MFA, the artist labored to represent the folio held in the disciple's hand as a written text with scribbles running across the page. The disciple who sits to the right of the viewer holds a long rectangular folio with scribbles, implying a page with written text. His projecting right eye suggests that he looks upward toward the teacher. This common pictorial convention of projecting eyes not only shows how his gaze and the teacher's intersect in the space between them, it also effects a comparable intersection between the gaze of the teacher and that of the viewer. Here an open book with two facing folios is displayed on a simple three-legged book stand with an ornamented support for the seat. That a manuscript on a book stand with an ornamental backdrop serves not simply as a ceremonial object but also provides textual (i.e., doctrinal) authority is suggested by the artist's interest in representing the writing on the manuscript's pages, despite the cursory, scribble-like quality of its execution.

PAINTED VISIONS: EARLY HINDU MANUSCRIPTS

We have very little knowledge of early painted palm-leaf manuscripts of what may be called "Hindu" texts, in part because few examples appear to have survived from the period under study.[45] Perhaps a book was not held in the same regard among the Śaivas, Vaiṣṇavas, and Śaktās of the time as in Buddhist and Jain contexts. If, however, we expand our purview in South Asia to include the art of the book in the trans-Himalayan region, examples of what are arguably "Hindu" texts were prepared as painted manuscripts in the early centuries of palm-leaf manuscript production in South Asia. In Nepal, where painted Buddhist manuscript production took off almost simultaneously with that of eastern India from the beginning of the eleventh century, we find eleventh- and twelfth-century manuscripts of Śaiva, Vaiṣṇava, and Śaktā texts prepared with splendidly painted wooden book covers. They are rarely brought into the discussion of Indian painting, and a sustained study on these painted book covers is lacking partly because many are known in Western collections without any context. As the recent return of the painted book covers that had disappeared from the National Archives of Nepal collection only to appear in the Christie's auction in March 2013 (Lots 354 and 355) shows, the book covers as desirable art objects can easily be divorced from the manuscripts. For example, a precious thirteenth-century *nilapatra* (blue-black paper written in gold ink) manuscript of the *Śivadharma* (Acc. No. 4/2537) may be missing painted panels, as someone deliberately and neatly cut the first two folios to remove the area of painted panels. The prevailing attitude toward the study of manuscript painting that focuses only on the aesthetic and art-historical merits of the painting does not help the situation.[46]

A palm-leaf manuscript of the *Niśvāsatattvasaṃhitā*, an early Śaiva *tantra* text (National Archives of Nepal, Kathmandu, Acc. No. 1/277, Microfilm Reel No. A41/14), which is dated to the late ninth century on paleographic grounds, survives with painted book covers (figure 2.7).[47] On one is the happy family of Śiva: the loving couple of Śiva and Pārvatī surrounded by four goddesses in the center panel and the couple's two sons, Kartikeya and Ganeśa, each with two attendants on left and right panels respectively. On the other cover is Śiva-Maheśa, a four-armed, three-headed form, in the center accompanied by eight four-armed goddesses.[48] In this remarkable example, the motif of bejeweled pillars that define the spatial boundaries are already in use. On each book cover, four such columns appear against a vermilion-colored background; they divide the long rectangular area into three spatial units and help convey a sense of architectural, temple-like space within which the deities are positioned.

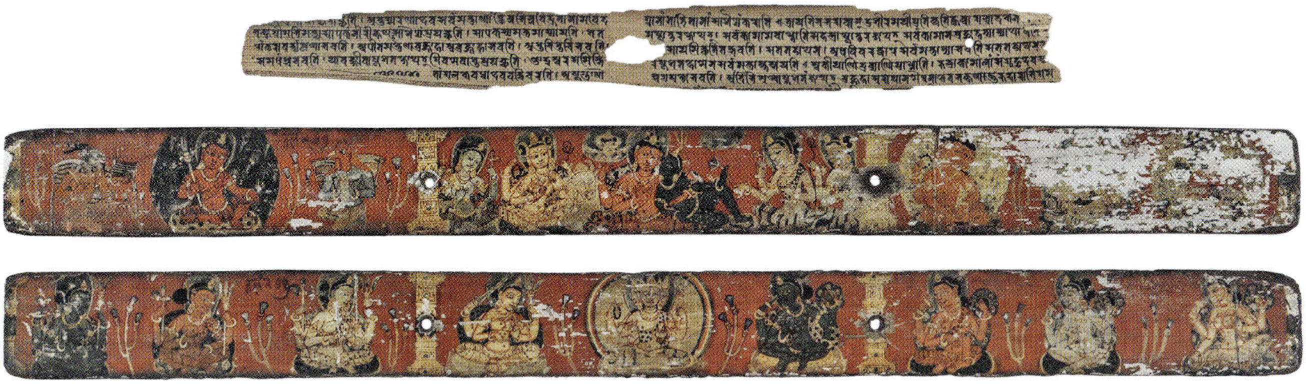

FIGURE 2.7
Painted book covers and a folio of a palm-leaf manuscript of the Niśvāsatattvasaṃhitā, ca. late ninth century CE, Acc. No. 1/277, National Archives of Nepal, Kathmandu. Photograph by Rajendra Prasad Neupane. Photo courtesy of National Archives of Nepal.

Most surviving painted book covers of Nepalese Purāṇic and tantric (what may be roughly termed "Hindu") manuscripts of the twelfth and the thirteenth centuries feature the architectural elements of a temple like those seen in a Buddhist manuscript of the *Perfection of Wisdom* discussed earlier. Along with ornamented columns seen on the book covers of the *Niśvāsatattvasamhitā* manuscript, canopies of richly decorated textiles, hanging tassels, and flower garlands function as spatial dividers and frame the painted space, as on the painted book cover of a *Viṣṇudharma* manuscript dated N.S. 210 (1090 CE), which was recently returned to the National Archives of Nepal (Acc. No. 1/1002, Microfilm no. a. 1080/4).[49] Architectural framing devices, such as the intertwined *kirti-mukha* and *makara* flaming arch found in contemporary Newari *paubhas* (cloth paintings) or Tibetan *thankas* executed by Newari artisans are actively adopted in thirteenth-century Nepalese manuscript cover designs.[50] A book cover depicting various forms of Viṣṇu standing under the repeating decorative arches in an early thirteenth-century blue-black paper manuscript of the Viṣṇudharma prepared in N.S. 340 (1220 CE) (National Archives of Nepal, Kathmandu, Acc. No. 5/344, Microfilm reel no. A 1163/1) offers an excellent example (figure 2.8).[51]

Surviving examples suggest that from the ninth century onward it was a common practice in Nepal to prepare a "Hindu" manuscript with painted book covers in a manner similar to that used to design a temple space. It is, however, rare to find an early palm-leaf Hindu manuscript with painted folios as in the previously discussed Buddhist and Jain examples. An early twelfth-century palm-leaf manuscript of the *Kubjikāmatam*, a tantric text relating to the worship of a goddess, now in the National Archives of Nepal (Acc. No. 1/1363, Microfilm reel no. A 1307/2), offers a precious example.[52] The manuscript has lost its painted covers, and the first and last folios have been damaged considerably.[53] It is unfortunate that the last folio has lost one-third of its surface area, as it carries a date colophon bearing the name of a Pāla king, Rāmapāla (ca.

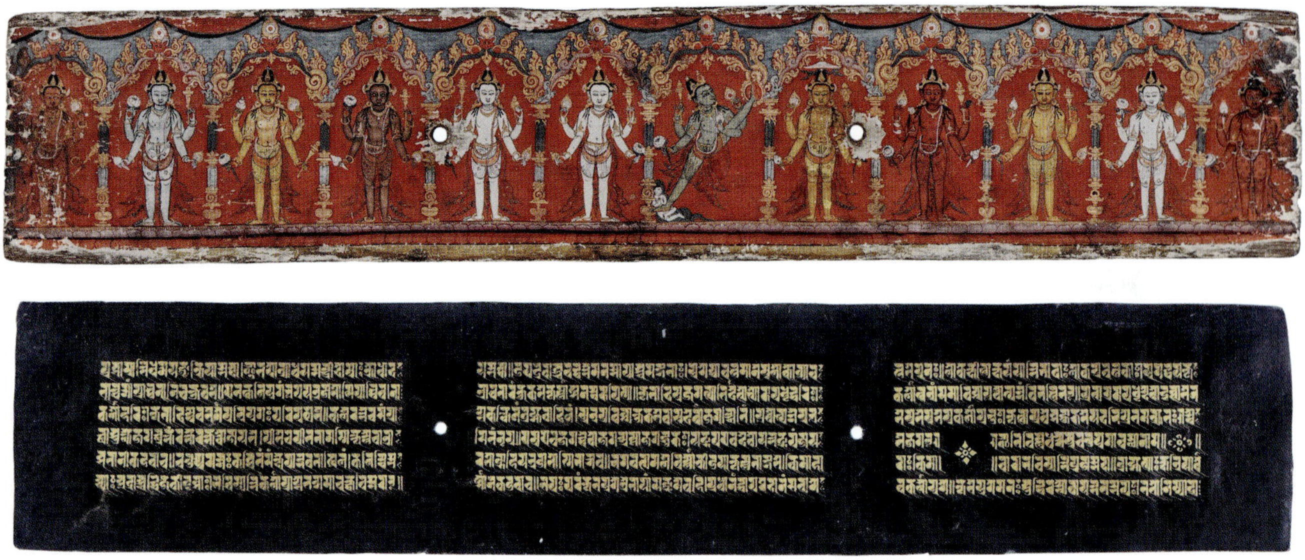

FIGURE 2.8
Painted book cover with a folio, a *nīla-pātra* (blue-black paper) manuscript of the Viṣṇudharma, dated N.S. 340 (1220 CE), National Archives of Nepal, Kathmandu, Acc. No. 5/344. Photograph by Rajendra Prasad Neupane. Photo courtesy of National Archives of Nepal.

1077–1131 CE), and the name of the donor.[54] The donor of the manuscript may have been one Rāmadeva whose intriguing epithet reads "son of a yoginī." The manuscript is much smaller than the other manuscripts discussed thus far, with each folio measuring 31 × 5 cm, considerably smaller than most early twelfth-century painted Buddhist manuscripts from Nepal and eastern India, whose width typically measure about 50 cm.

Two painted panels face each other on folios 1v and 2r. At first glance, the pages do not look so different from those in a contemporary Buddhist manuscript. The decorative framing columns, painted predominantly in yellow patterned with reddish-orange swirly motifs and colored jewel motifs, appear prominently in a painted Buddhist manuscript from eastern India (figure 2.9). The panel on folio 1v features a ten-armed blue Bhairava embracing his female consort against a flaming background, and on the facing panel (folio 2r) there is a red twelve-armed goddess with an unnerving grin, perhaps representing Kubjikā herself.[55] The historical value of this manuscript is immeasurable because it bears rare painted depictions from the early twelfth century of these tantric deities. It was possibly prepared in the Pāla territory in eastern India by an extremely fine hand.[56] If the localization to Magadha is accepted, this may be the sole example of a "Hindu" manuscript that survives from medieval India. The conventional wisdom has it that "there is no sign of any (Hindu manuscript) before the middle of the fifteenth century."[57] The manuscript is also of unmistakable textual importance as it collects an uncommon variation of the *Kubjikā tantra* corpus containing sections from both the *Kulālikāmnāya* and the *Laghvikāmnāya*.[58]

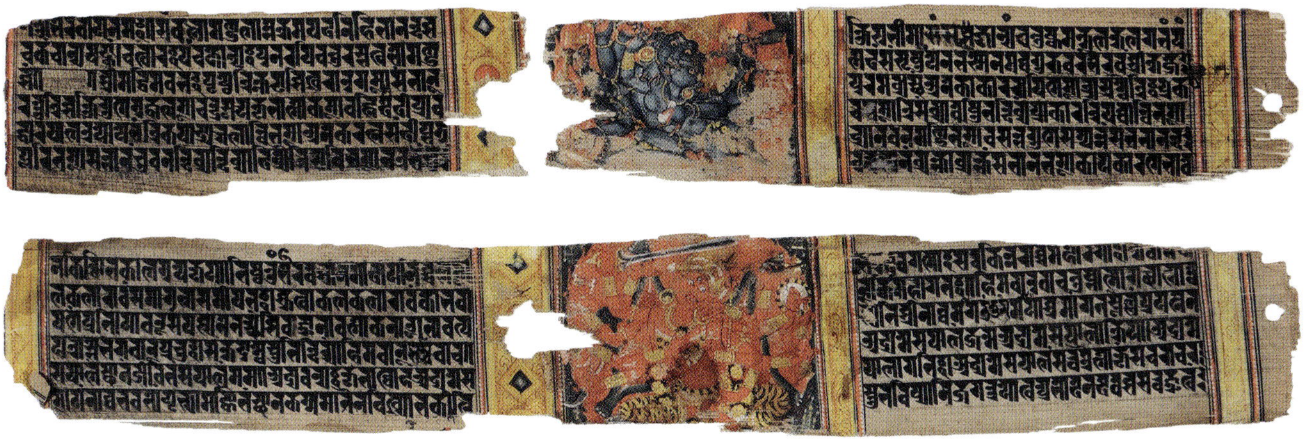

FIGURE 2.9
Folios 1v (Bhairava)–2r (Kubjikā), *Kubjikāmata* manuscript, ca. early twelfth century, dated with the Rāmapāla's regnal year (ca. 1077–1131 CE), National Archives of Nepal, Kathmandu, Acc. No. 1/1363. Photograph by Rajendra Prasad Neupane. Photo courtesy of National Archives of Nepal.

PAINTED MANUSCRIPTS OF THE *DEVĪMĀHĀTMYA*: VISIONS OF THE GODDESS IN A BOOK

In light of the painted manuscript of the *Kubjikāmatam,* it is interesting to note that other early known "Hindu" painted palm-leaf folios also relate to the goddess (devī). Among these is a folio, now in the British Library (BL Or. 13860), depicting the goddess Durgā slaying the buffalo demon with devotees.[59] Most surviving painted palm-leaf manuscripts of the Hindu traditions are of the *Devīmāhātmya* (*DM*) section of the *Markaṇḍeyapurāṇa,* which glorifies the martial triumphs of the great goddess.[60] There exist a good number of painted palm-leaf manuscripts of the *DM* (or alternatively, *Durgāsaptaśatī*). How they relate to later paper manuscripts of the same text, such as the *Simla Devīmahātmya* of the sixteenth century[61] and the *Tessitori Devīmāhātmya* of the seventeenth century,[62] is an important question for both the history of Indian painting and the history of the art of the book. While a full examination of this question awaits another occasion, a manuscript of the *Devīmāhātmya* (CUL Add. 1556) suggests that sumptuous manuscript production was popular among Nepalese communities for whom the *DM* was an important devotional text from as early as the twelfth century.

A complete manuscript of the *DM* was acquired by Daniel Wright in Nepal along with many other Sanskrit manuscripts and presented to the Cambridge University Library (CUL) by William Wright in 1876.[63] Add. 1556 is a black paper manuscript in *pothi*-format; its entire text is written in ornamental and formal *rañjana* script using metallic silver ink.[64] Each folio measures 6.5 × 21 cm and is perforated with a single hole placed off center about 10 percent to the left. The manuscript survives with two stunning wooden covers encased with superbly executed gilt repoussé. The quality of carving, the artistic excellence, and the material of gilded repoussé all suggest that this was a luxury production. The depiction on what may be the top cover features a sage with two male figures on either side. This possibly represents sage Sumedha relating the story of the Goddess to King Suratha (on his right) and merchant/commoner Samadhi (on his left); this scene sets the opening stage for the manuscript (figure 2.10 *top*).[65] The other cover depicts the goddess in her six-armed form; she is shown victorious over the buffalo demon under her left foot, piercing it with a long spear while her lion charges toward the buffalo under her right leg (figure 2.10 *bottom*). The artist who designed these covers cleverly set both scenes amid swirly foliage patterns. In the bottom cover, this dramatic background is creatively used to capture in a single frame the multiple episodes of the vanquishing of demons accomplished by the Great Goddess. In addition to the buffalo subdued under her left foot, two male figures are depicted falling on either side. Both demons have dropped their respective weapons—a sword and a club—and have turned their heads up to look angrily at the goddess. Only their upper bodies are visible, and they seamlessly emerge from behind the goddess and blend into the swirly foliage pattern. These figures likely represent the Buffalo Demon's troupe; at the same time, they effectively recall the pairs of demons, such as Śumbha-Niśumbha and Caṇḍa-Muṇḍa, who in the *DM* are defeated by the Goddess.

The manuscript has, from the time it entered the collection, been dated to the sixteenth century on account of a reading of the colophon (probably by Wright) on a piece of paper pasted inside the front cover reading: "*Hara-nayana* [3]-*sate*' [hundred]-*suryabāhādi* [*sic*] [7] yukte [with] which, being transposed in Nepāl Sam-vat 703 = AD 1583." In his catalog of the Sanskrit manuscripts in the Cambridge University Library, published in 1883, Bendall identified the manuscript as marking the beginning of an "archaic revival in Nepalese writing," with its letter numerals showing "remarkable revivals of XIth-century Bengali forms."[66] Contrary to Bendall, and on the basis of paleographic, art-historical, and historical evidence, I propose reading the date given by the Sanskrit chronogram as 307, which in Nepalese era, that is, *nepāla samvat* (established in October 879, henceforth, N.S.), is equivalent to 1187 CE. The initial proposal to read number three as the lowest unit and to read seven as the highest is based on the assumption that dates written in Sanskrit chronograms should be read from the lowest units to the higher orders. This, however, is not always the case, and the way in which the numbers are written out in Nepal differs from chronograms used in Sanskrit inscriptions from other parts of South Asia. The whole sentence reads, "*prāpte nepālakābde haranayanaśate sūryavāhādhiyukte*"; this should be translated as "completed/attained in the Nepali year three hundred combined with seven." Paleographically speaking, the writing in *DM* manuscript Add. 1556 is consistently much closer to other surviving black or blue-black paper manuscripts from the twelfth century written in metallic ink. Examples of such manuscripts include two in the British Library (Or. 2202 and Or. 13971A-B, the latter dated 1184 CE). The style of the script can also be compared with the hand in the *Kubjikāmata* manuscript discussed above. In addition, it is noticeably different from Add. 1355, another manuscript in CUL that Bendall identifies as an archaic revival. Apparently prizing control over ornateness, the scribe of Add. 1556 varies the thickness of his strokes and treats various consonants and medial vowels in a manner consistent with those found in twelfth- and thirteenth-century Nepalese manuscripts.[67]

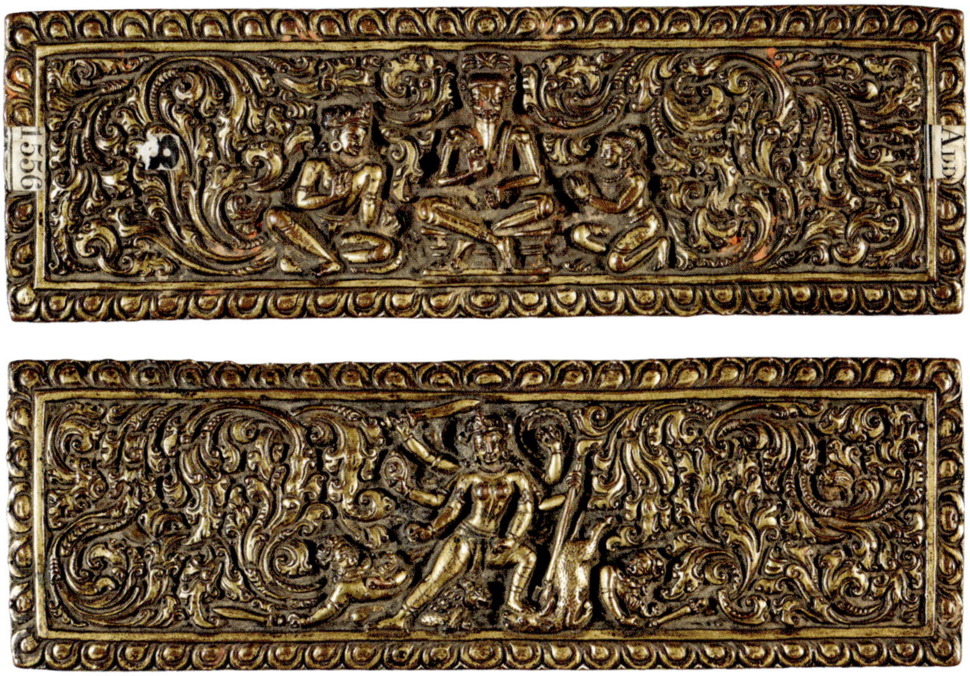

FIGURE 2.10
Repoussé book covers, *Devīmāhātmya* manuscript, 1187 CE (N.S. 307), Kantipur, Nepal. CUL Add 1556. Reproduced by kind permission of the Syndics of Cambridge University Library.

More important for the present discussion, the manuscript features polychrome miniatures that, in terms not only of style but also of color, signal a twelfth-century rather than a late sixteenth-century date. The *DM* consists of thirteen chapters, the end of which are marked by the rubric "thus (*iti;* in the sense of "the preceding was") . . . of the *Devīmāhātmya* in the age of Manu-Sāvarṇi from the Mārkaṇḍeyapurāṇa." In most *pothi*-format manuscripts from eleventh- through thirteenth-century South Asia, each rubric is marked by leaving an empty space that usually occupies the height of two lines. The empty space that brackets the rubric provided an opportunity for manuscript makers to embellish a page within the text; indeed, like a tiny thumbnail icon on a computer screen, the earliest evidence of manuscript illumination appears in this empty space. Early examples of "thumbnail" images appear in the form of a small geometric motif: a wheel or a schematic rendering of a lotus are typical examples. In some twelfth-century Buddhist examples, more fanciful types of thumbnail images appear; among such types of images are flowers, birds, animals, decorative patterns (like foliage-patterned lozenges used in temple architecture), and even *kirtimukha* (lit. victory-face). In manuscripts without any painted folios, these images were most likely executed by the scribes. Those with painted folios sometimes feature polychrome rubric images; their presence signals access to painterly knowledge. In the case of Add. 1556, the manuscript is strewn with bright vermilion thumbnail images that are strategically placed to bracket each rubric of

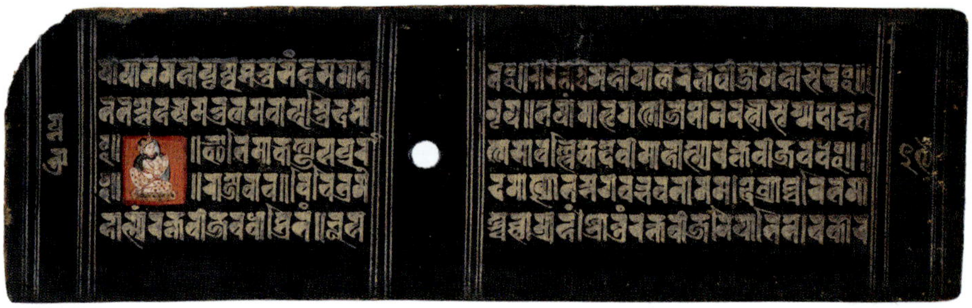

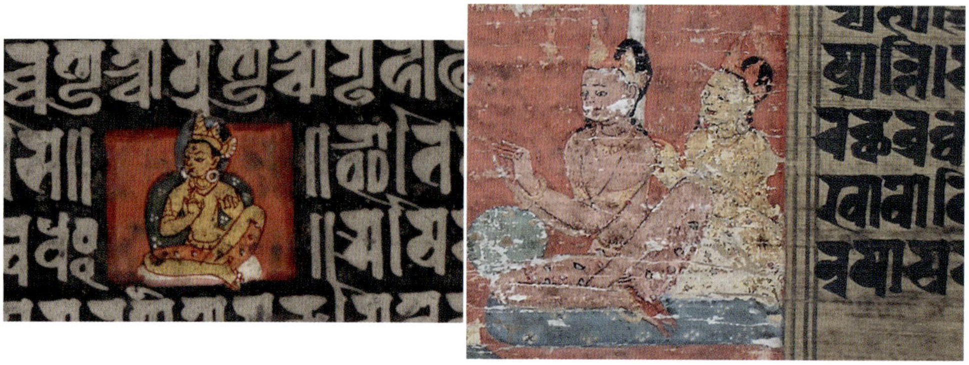

FIGURE 2.11 ▲

Folio 49v, *Devīmāhātmya* manuscript, 1187 CE (N.S. 307). 6.5 × 21 cm, silver and color on black paper, CUL Add 1556. Reproduced by kind permission of the Syndics of Cambridge University Library.

FIGURE 2.12 ▼

Detail of a rubric from folio 42v (*left*), *Demvīmāhātmya* manuscript, CUL Add 1556; folio 298v, *Perfection of Wisdom* manuscript, dated 1148 CE (N.S. 268), Asiatic Society Kolkata G.4203 (*right*).

its thirteen chapters (figure 2.11).[68] Despite their minute size, mostly measuring about 1–1.5 cm in height, their splashes of color stand out against the black and silver backdrop.

In addition to the brilliance of vermilion, each thumbnail features a delightful miniature painting, including eight auspicious symbols: longevity knot, lotus (the end of chapter 1), victory banner (*dhvaja*), vase (*purṇagaṭa*) (chapter 2), flywhisk (chapter 4), double-fish, umbrella (chapter 5), and conch (chapter 6); these are followed by three human figures (one each at the end of chapters 7, 8, and 9), an elephant (chapter 10), a horse (chapter 11), and three flaming weapons of the Goddess (chapters 12 and 13). These images showcase the talent of an unnamed miniature painter. For example, on folio 49 verso in a space barely exceeding 1.5 × 1.5 cm, a carefully rendered painting of a lady seated with her hands held together in devotion marks the end of the story about Devī's victorious killing of the demon Raktabīja (see figure 2.11). Facing the text of the rubric, the woman seems to be paying homage simultaneously to the written text and the glorious power of the goddess extolled in the text. Despite its minute size, this image is clearly comparable to those seen in other twelfth-century Nepalese manuscript paintings. The woman's three-peaked crown, the treatment of physiognomic features, like a slight line under her lip marking the three-quarter profile view of her chin, and the depiction of her diaphanous shawl and the circle-patterned lower garment are similar to what we see on a superbly painted wooden cover of a Śivadharma manuscript dated N.S. 290 (1170 CE), now in the National Archives of Nepal (Acc. No.1/1075; Microfilm No. B 7/3).[69] Although not as refined, perhaps due to scale, a rubric image of a male figure seated tall in the middle of folio 42v is akin to the treatment of figures found in a *Perfection of Wisdom* manuscript now in the Asiatic Society Kolkata (G 4203) dated N.S. 268 (1148 CE) (figure 2.12). The overall color scheme is also analogous to known twelfth-century Nepalese manuscript paintings: dominant use of vermilion along with light blue (most likely indigo), yellow, green (most likely a combination of indigo blue and orpiment yellow), white, and the use of a reddish-brown line for outline and details.[70]

To the best of my knowledge, twelfth-century paper manuscripts of the *Devīmāhātmya* are virtually unknown. To find an example that is so delightfully designed with marvelous miniature paintings marking the end of each chapter (or a text segment/unit) like charms on a string comes as a surprise. The text is beautifully written although not without scribal errors. The manner in which repeating lines of the text in a hymnal sequence are arranged to capture their amplifying effects by aligning the line breaks and the rhymes (for example, see folios 30v–32r) visually testifies to the scribe's interest in presenting the text in a visually pleasing manner. The use of the rubric space for painting suggests that designing this manuscript followed the same logic as contemporary Buddhist manuscripts in which painted panels and rubric images are placed at the end of each chapter and at the beginning and end of the manuscript. While the manuscript lacks an eye-catching opening picture on the first page, an elaborate repoussé book cover portraying a sage with two male figures stands in for the opening scene that appears on the first folios of slightly later painted *DM* manuscripts.

A few palm-leaf manuscripts of the *DM* from Nepal that predate 1500 CE have survived. These bear a close relationship to the earlier mode of painted manuscript production. We can observe this relationship in a late fourteenth- or fifteenth-century painted palm-leaf manuscript of the *DM* now dispersed between the collections of the Bharat Kala Bhavan, BHU (four painted folios, Acc. Nos. 9518, 9519, 9520, 9521) and the Chhatrapati Shivaji Maharaj Vastu Sangrahalaya (henceforth CSMVS, formerly the Prince of Wales Museum of Western India; forty-six folios with eight painted folios and painted book covers, Acc. No. 56.45). Instead of repoussé on the exterior, the interior of the book covers bears a painted iconographic program with twelve deities—six on each cover, featuring various forms of the Goddess described in the text (the goddess Durgā killing the buffalo demon, "eight mothers" that came out of the Great Goddess during a battle against the demon Raktabija (chapter 8) along with her benign form) with Dancing Śiva at the beginning and Gaṇeśa at the end (figure 2.13).[71] The manuscript opens with two painted panels on folios 1v–2r, the first of which depicts the sage Mārkaṇḍeya as an emaciated figure preaching to a white male figure holding two lotuses on either side that most likely represent Sāvarṇi as Sūrya's son (figure 2.14).[72] The subsequent painting facing this page is another sage. Looking younger and smaller in scale, he is preaching to two male figures;

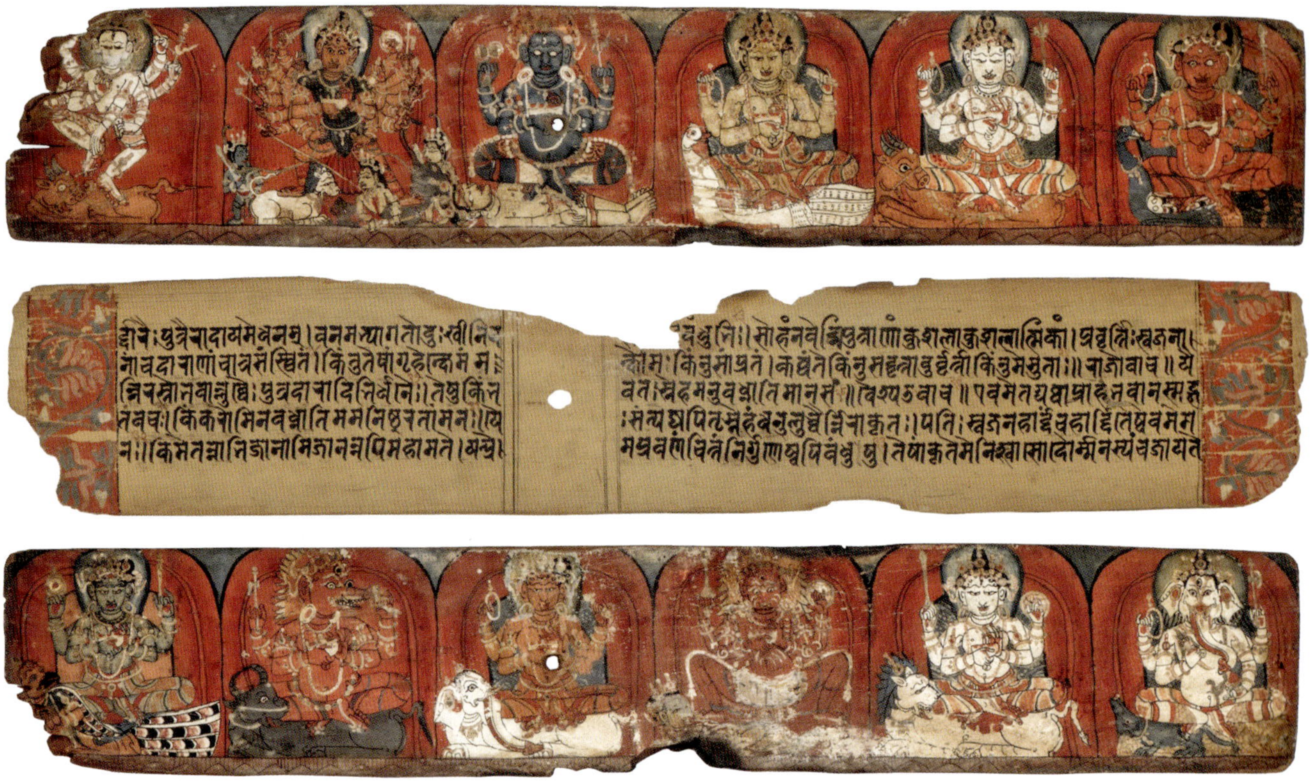

FIGURE 2.13
Painted book covers and a folio, *Devīmāhātmya* manuscript, ca. late fourteenth century, Nepal. Ink and pigments on palm leaf with painted wooden covers. CSMVS Mumbai Acc. No. 56.45. Courtesy of the Trustees of the Chhatrapati Shivaji Maharaj Vastu Sangrahalaya.

most likely these figures represent the sage Sumedha with King Suratha and Vaiśya Samadhi. The artist clarified the hierarchical relationship between the two framing narratives by making Mārkaṇḍeya the largest figure in the two panels. These opening scenes, like all other painted panels in this manuscript, are set against a vibrant red background.

The compositional structure of each painted folio of this dispersed *Devīmāhātmya* manuscript is more or less identical: a painted panel is placed at the end of a narrative segment, and painted borders bearing decorative motifs of floral-vine patterns of about 2.4 cm in width are placed at either end of each painted page. For example, on folio 34r on which a painted panel shows a four-armed goddess piercing a purplish demon figure, the fourth line of the text reads: "Thus completed the destroyer of Niśumbha (section) in the *Devīmāhātmya* in the *Mārkaṇḍeya purāṇa* of Sāvarṇi (eighth Manu)'s time (||*iti mārkaṇḍeyapurāṇe sāvarṇṇike manvatare devīmāhātmye niśumbhavadhaḥ samāpta*||)." Both sides of each painted folio have painted border patterns similar to the ones seen in painted Nepalese Buddhist manuscripts of the twelfth and thirteenth centuries. The folios are systematically color coordinated with a red border for

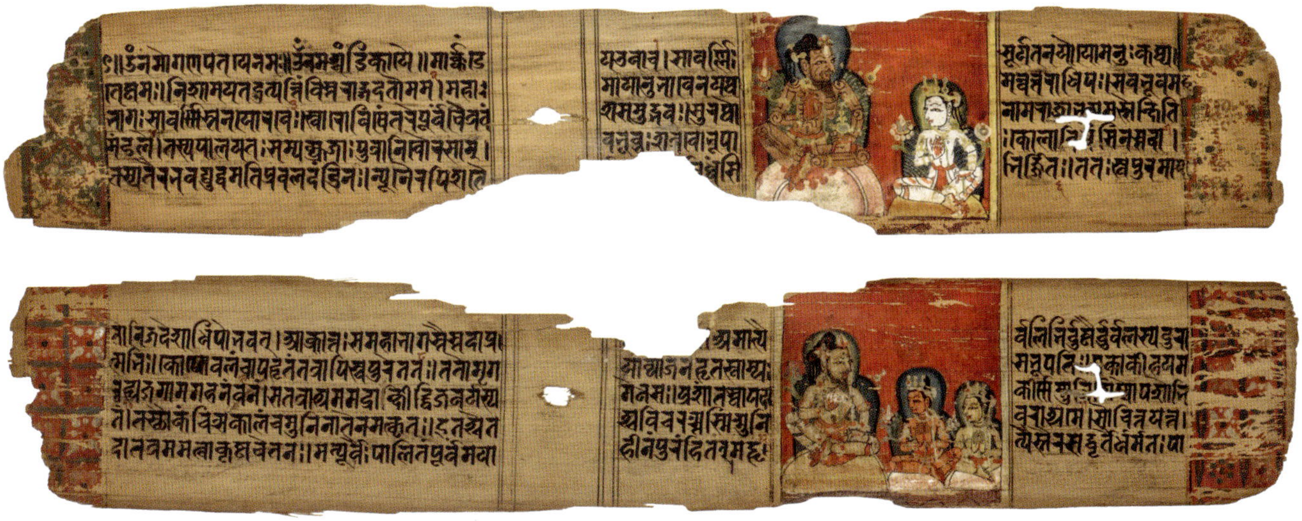

FIGURE 2.14
Folios 1v–2r: Markaṇḍeya with Sāvarni (folio 1v)–Sage Sumedha with King Suratha and Samadhi (folio 2r), *Devīmāhātmya* manuscript, ca. late fourteenth century, Nepal. CSMVS Mumbai Acc. No. 56.45. Courtesy of the Trustees of the Chhatrapati Shivaji Maharaj Vastu Sangrahalaya.

the recto of a page and a green border for the verso of a page. These brightly colored borders frame each manuscript page harmoniously. The visual effect is such that the painted panel seems to subsume the letters of the text under it; in other words, the painted panel depicting the victorious goddess seems to draw up all the essence of the text and pop out like an icon.

While the painted panels in a *Devīmāhātmya* manuscript represent a narrative, the design strategy for the overall structure of its pictorial program is similar to that of the painted Buddhist manuscripts. Such adherence to what may then have been an older model for a book design is remarkable, since by this time other options for designing illustrated manuscripts were known in the Indian subcontinent.[73] The painting need not be contained in niche-like panels as in the famed late fifteenth-century Jain manuscript known as the Devasano Pado *Kalpa-sūtra* and *Kalakācārya-kathā*.[74] Full-page illustrations for narrative contents with various spatial layouts would soon become the norm regardless of sectarian affiliations, as one can see in an illustrated manuscript of the *Āraṇyaka Parvan* of the *Mahābhārata* prepared in 1516 CE at Yoginīpura (Delhi).[75] To elucidate the reasons behind the similarities and differences in design strategies of painted manuscript production in medieval Indic religious traditions, further research is required. In part because of the close interregional connection between manuscript production centers in Bihar, Bengal (West Bengal, India, and Bangladesh), and Nepal during the period concerned, painted Buddhist manuscripts and painted tantric and *śaktā* manuscripts seem to follow similar strategies when it comes to creating sacred structures. The close connection between the Śaiva and Śaktā tantric communities and tantric Buddhist communities, whether in competition or in emulation, is possibly also reflected in their adoption of similar approaches to manuscript design. Perhaps the Hindu manuscripts discussed here were prepared with elaborate painted covers and occasionally with painted folios, as were the painted manuscripts of Buddhist communities, to celebrate their cultic importance as well as their doctrinal authority.

THE GODDESS AND THE BOOK

The existence of early painted manuscripts of the *Kubjikā* and the *DM* signals an interesting theological and cultic relationship among goddess worship, the production of painted manuscripts, and the veneration of a book as a cultic object.[76] As Pal has noted, in Gujarat and Bengal "the goddess is frequently worshipped as a book."[77] This practice may be analogous to the Buddhist cult of Pañcarakṣā goddesses in Nepal, where a book with the goddesses residing within became the most important object of worship. Just as an exquisite manuscript of the *DM* is the earliest known surviving Hindu painted manuscript on paper, the earliest known surviving painted manuscript on paper from South Asia is a Nepalese Pañcarakṣā manuscript dated 1105 (N.S. 225) in the Asutosh Museum.[78] It may, therefore, not be entirely accidental that we find depictions of a manuscript in use on a tenth-century temple dedicated to a goddess: the Ambika Mātā temple in Jagat, near Udaipur in southeastern Rajasthan (established in V.S. 1017 = ca. 960 CE). While depictions of *ācāryas* with books are not rare in the corpus of Hindu temple sculptures, that the scenes representing a book in use in a ritual and instructional setting appear on one of the earliest temples dedicated to a goddess suggests an important connection between the cults of book and goddess in the early medieval religious milieu of South Asia.

Scenes depicting a book in use frequently appear on sculptures of goddesses, like Prajñāpāramitā and Tārā. A rare depiction of a book's ritual use in a Hindu context also appears on a sculpture of a goddess. In a superbly carved and preserved twelfth-century stone stele of the Goddess Pāravatī from Mohammadpur (Comilla, now Bangladesh), in the Indian Museum, Kolkata (IM no. 9481/A25209), the goddess stands tall, making a boon giving gesture (*varada mudrā*) with her right hand and holding an *utpala,* a blue lotus or night lily, conventionally depicted in an upturned triangular shape.[79] Her male entourage, Gaṇeśa, Brahma, Śiva, Viṣṇu, and Kartikeya, hover on the top of the stele, and to either side two female attendants guard her. In its combination of iconographic and decorative motifs, the stele strongly resembles contemporary Buddhist examples.[80]

The bottom register of this stele consists of tripartite projections. On the left side of the bottom register (on Pārvatī's right), sits a group of royally attired donor figures. On the opposite side (on Pārvatī's left), sits a yogi-like male figure with matted hair and a diadem around his head facing the front (figure 2.15).[81] His hands are neatly placed on his lap in meditation. Next to him to the viewer's right is a familiar rectangular object on a pillar-like stand, a manuscript with three flower-like nobs on top. The placement of this meditating male figure under the slightly protruding double lotus pedestal of Pārvatī's attendant creates the illusion that he is seated under a huge umbrella. Other visual devices, such as the relatively small scale of the lion next to him, also contribute to marking the importance of both

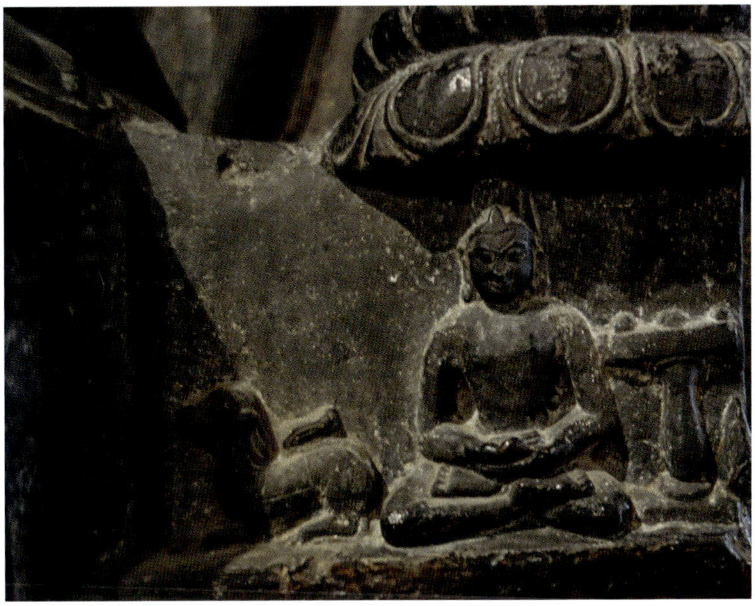

FIGURE 2.15
A *siddha* or *yogi* in meditation with a book, right side bottom register of the Pārvatī stele, ca. twelfth century, Mohammadpur, Bangladesh, black stone. Indian Museum, No. 9481/A25209. Photo © Jinah Kim.

this meditating figure and the book. The book is ceremonially present as if marking his authority. Whether such a manuscript in a Hindu ritual context would have been a painted manuscript is difficult to say with certainty, but it is a plausible hypothesis that a beautifully made book was a fitting offering for the goddess. The connection between the goddess and a book in a Hindu (and perhaps Indic) context is tantalizingly close.

The historical and theological relationship between the goddess cult and the book cult is a complex topic that merits a separate study. One aspect, however, must be discussed here: the better-known linking of book production and book worship in "Hindu" practice, evidence of which comes from the *Devīpurāṇa* (DP) as attested in twelfth-century *nibandha* literature on gifting, such as the *Dānakāṇḍa* section of the *Kṛtyakalpataru* of Lakṣmīdhara (active in Kashmir during the early twelfth century).[82] A passage in the *Devīpurāṇa* discusses how a book should be written beautifully on palm leaves with letters that are "neither too crammed together, nor too spread apart and that are neither sleek nor rough."[83] In addition to providing a detailed description of how a book should be made and how a book as a gift of knowledge (*vidyadāna*) should be ceremoniously prepared and bestowed on the right person (such as the knower of *śāstras*, that is, Brahmins), the passage discusses the religious merits one gains by donating various materials required for the production and ceremonial use of a book. According to a section of the *Devīpurāṇa*, "by giving a very beautiful cloth of appropriate measure to wrap a book in, as well as a thread with which to bind it, a wise man obtains a gift of knowledge [DP verse 79]. In addition, when either a book-holder, girdle, seat or staff and seat are given to someone in the habit of reciting knowledge, they grant kingship [DP verse 80]. And when pigments for the eyes and feet, land, a house, or a field are given to someone utterly devoted to knowledge, they grant the rewards of heaven and kingship [*āñjanam netrapādānām dattaṃ vidyāparāpaṇe| bhumigṛhantu kṣatrantu sarvarājyaphalapradam||* DP v. 81]."[84]

Although nothing is stated about how to create a beautifully painted book, it is clear that the text addresses the art of the book. The fact that the text emphasizes that the letters should be written beautifully in a regionally specific script indicates a concern for the aesthetic quality of a manuscript's appearance (that is, calligraphy). The passage cited from the now-lost *Nandipurāṇa* in the "Dānakāṇḍa" section also explicitly states that the covers need to be painted beautifully and that the text should be written in black or blue-black ink (or in red lotus–like color) and ornamented with crescent-moon patterns of peacock feathers. It is telling, then, that an early twelfth-century stone stele of the goddess Pārvatī has a ritual scene with a book placed on a pedestal, since making a beautiful manuscript and giving and venerating it is known to be one of the most appropriate meritorious activities to honor and worship the goddess.

BOOKS IN USE: TRANS-SECTARIAN COMPARISON

A book's significance as an object is not universal; rather, such meanings are culturally specific. The general lack of detailed information about historical circumstances surrounding the donation and use of manuscripts may be compensated for by a survey of images of books in visual records. These images demonstrate how a *pothi*-format manuscript was understood and used in different ritual and religious settings. The iconographic and symbolic meaning of a book seems to have been relatively stable in religious image-making in South Asia. A book as an iconographic attribute signaling wisdom (*prajñā*) or knowledge (*vidyā*) is the most typical manner in which they appear in ancient and medieval South Asian art. The earliest known example in which we see a book depicted in South Asia is in a third-century stone image of the Goddess Sarasvatī from Kankali Tila, Mathura, now in the Lucknow Museum.[85] The Brāhmī donor inscription is clearly visible on the double pedestal on top of which the now-headless goddess squats holding a book in her left hand. A book in *pothi*-format, a long rectangular object held in her left hand appears as an iconographic attribute. This demonstrates that by the third-century Jain context the conception of a book as a marker of divine authority is articulated visually. Iconographers and image-makers in Buddhist circles also adopted a book as an important attribute for wisdom-related deities and bodhisattvas; thus, a book on a lotus serves as an important marker signaling Mañjuśrī, the bodhisattva of wisdom.

A second category of visual evidence suggests a changing conception of a book as an important material instrument: images that depict people doing things with their books. Examples depicting *pothi*-format manuscripts in use appear in visual records from the fifth century onward. For example, a terra-cotta image probably from Aichcchatra, Uttar Pradesh, depicts two conversing sages (Nara-Nārāyaṇa) next to a manuscript placed on a low stool (figure 2.16). The figure on the right holds a manuscript in his hands. The book is held horizontally, suggesting a *pothi* manuscript. In the visual representations of books in use from

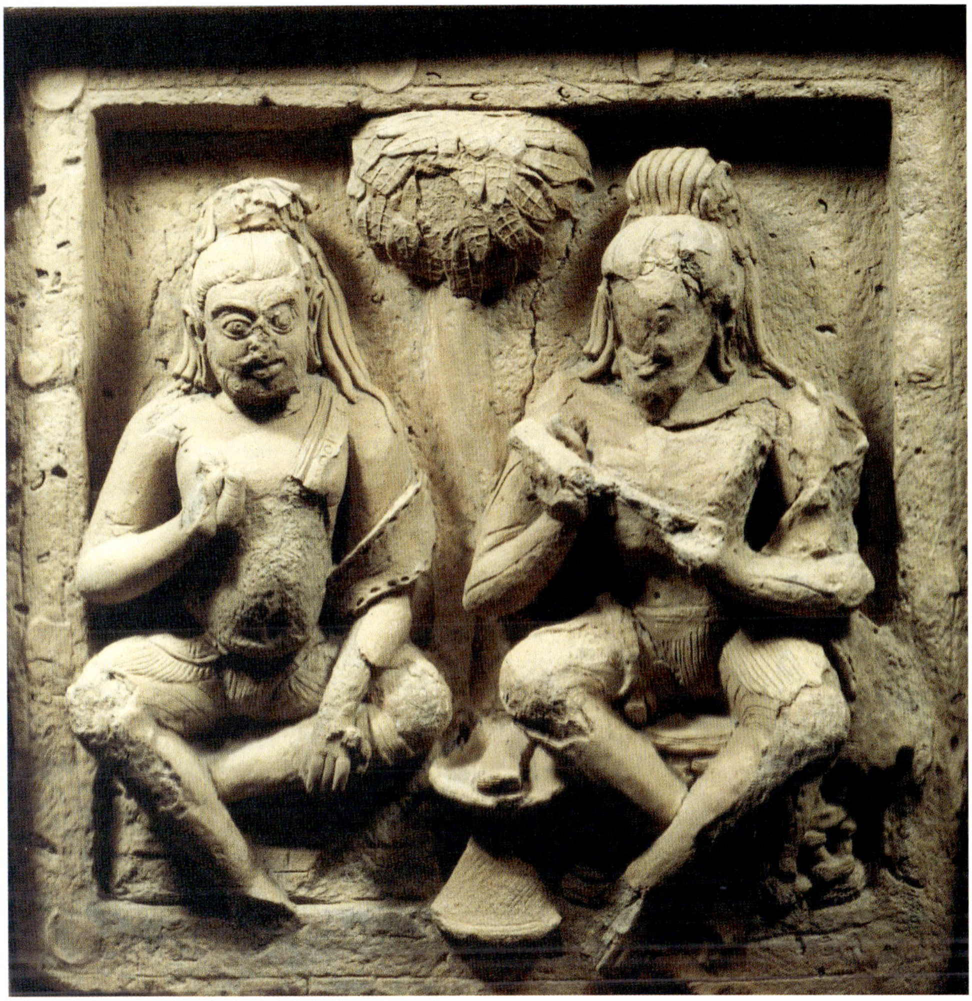

FIGURE 2.16
Nara-Nārāyaṇa, ca. fifth century, Ahichchhatra(?), Uttar Pradesh. Terra-cotta, H: 57.15 cm. LACMA M69.38. Image: Regents of the University of Michigan, Department of the History of Art, Visual Resources Collections.

medieval South Asia, there are two situations in which a book is employed centrally: instruction/knowledge transmission, and a cultic ritual.

As noted in previous studies, a manuscript is a central object of veneration in many surviving stone steles of Buddhist deities made during the Pāla period (ninth through twelfth centuries).[86] One superb example that articulates the power of the book as a cultic object of vision and authority in a Buddhist context is a stone stele of the Buddhist goddess Tārā now in the National Museum of Bangladesh, Dhaka. On this twelfth-century stele, which was found in Somapārā, a hamlet of the village of Vajrayoginī (Dhaka district), a ritual master wearing a cone-shaped hat and holding a *vajra* and a bell, like a Vajrācārya of Newari Buddhism, sits

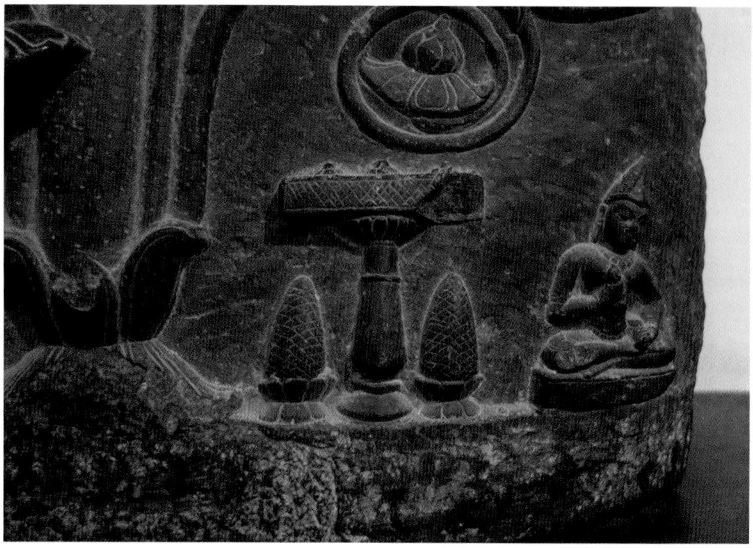

FIGURE 2.17
Vajrācārya with a book, bottom register, stone stele of Tārā (Aṣṭamahābhayā-Tārā), ca. early twelfth century. Black stone. Sompārā, in the village of Vajrayoginī, Dhaka district. National Museum of Bangladesh, Dhaka. Photo © Jinah Kim.

toward the left end of the bottom register (figure 2.17).[87] He is the human equivalent of Vajrasattva, the primordial teacher of all transcendental Buddhas.[88] Next to him toward the middle is a narrow rectangular manuscript on a pillar-shaped book stand. Two food offerings carved in the shape of a pinecone are placed on either side of the book stand.

As a larger-than-life central object that rhythmically mimics the shape of the rising lotus pedestal on which the goddess Tārā sits, this book, with a gracefully carved lotus bud hovering over it, connects the human world with the divine vision of the goddess Tārā and her multiplying forms unfolding above the double lotus seat. It is as if the master artist of this fine sculpture of the goddess Tārā played with the varying scales of depicted images beyond the customary hierarchical scaling so that different levels of visions can simultaneously be accessed and connected in the viewer's mind: the human world of donors and their *ācārya* (ritual master) and the world of the divine, in this case, of the Goddess Tārā.[89] The presence of a book in a ritual scene like this one also serves as a statement of authority, reinforcing the "situatedness" of the power of the vision materialized above this register.

THE CULT OF THE BOOK AND BOOK STANDS

Given the so-called Mahāyāna cult of the book, the employment of a book as a focal point of a ritual may be expected from quite early on: the *Perfection of Wisdom* is the central text that promotes the worship of the book, and its core text dates to the beginning of the Common Era.[90] The offerings described in the early Mahāyāna sūtra, like the *Perfection of Wisdom*—especially flowers, incense, perfumes, unguents, garlands, aromatic powders, clothes, and also rows of lamps—are also present in the ritual worship of the book in contemporary Nepal.[91] Ritual scenes with books that appear frequently on sculpted images from medieval eastern India seem to represent "book worship" (*pustaka pūjā*), which suggests remarkable continuity in the cultic use of books in Indic Buddhist traditions. There is a caveat here. The idea of venerating with all offerings mentioned in the *Perfection of Wisdom* seems to have remained persistent throughout the centuries. Nevertheless, those offerings of flowers, incense, unguents, garlands, aromatic powders, clothes, and rows of lamps are common devotional offerings across the sectarian borders in Indic religions. Importantly, such offerings are not unique to Buddhist traditions, and they have been included in offerings over at least two millennia. In other words, the description of ritual offerings from the *Perfection of Wisdom* fits, but it is too generic to be meaningful. More importantly, as in the Tārā image, the manuscript is depicted as being installed on a tall, cylindrical pedestal with a round disc-shaped bottom and a top plate (which may have lotus petals) that supports the book. It is a book stand, but it is impractical in terms of actually using a book—especially in the most common sense, as a text to be read. Placed so tall on top of a thin column, a book looks more like a crowning jewel or capital of a pillar than a book to be touched and handled, let alone to be read.

This tall, pillar-like object supporting the book merits further discussion. Three types of book stands can be identified in surviving visual records: a cross-legged (most likely foldable) stand (what is called *sthāpanācārya* in the Jain context); a pillar-like pedestal stand; and a rectangular table. A cross-legged stand is the most common type. In both Hindu and Jain contexts, it often appears in the context of knowledge transmission/instruction. A pillar-like pedestal stand appears most commonly although not exclusively in Buddhist examples. Their appearance may connect directly with the conception of a manuscript as a miniature temple. A rectangular table is the least common type; it is only seen in a few Nepalese examples and in an example from South India.[92] The context of this book stand is a scene of instruction or the presentation of a ritual object.[93] The "table" is more like a throne on which an elaborate book is installed; that is, the book stand functions as a vehicle for conveying doctrinal authority and marking an object of veneration. The other two types of stands are more common in visual records.

A CROSS-LEGGED TYPE BOOK STAND

It is worth examining further examples to understand some of the unique elements in a book's use and status in relation to particular stands. Most examples appear in scenes of instruction and knowledge transmission. As discussed earlier in this chapter, in Jain manuscripts a book is frequently depicted on a cross-legged book stand in scenes of instruction. A detail from a fifteenth-century Jain painting discussed in chapter 1 shows a kingly figure seated on a throne under an umbrella with a manuscript in front of him (figure 2.18). He holds a folio in his extended left hand. Here, the scene is not of the instruction but of the study at a place of solitude. The scene honors the Jaina teaching, and it appears in the midst of a series of auspicious images. The cross-legged book stand is made of four sticks with pointed peaks crossed to create a stand. This is similar to book stands still used by Jaina monks. Books in use represented in surviving Jain sculptures are rare. As Julia Hegewald

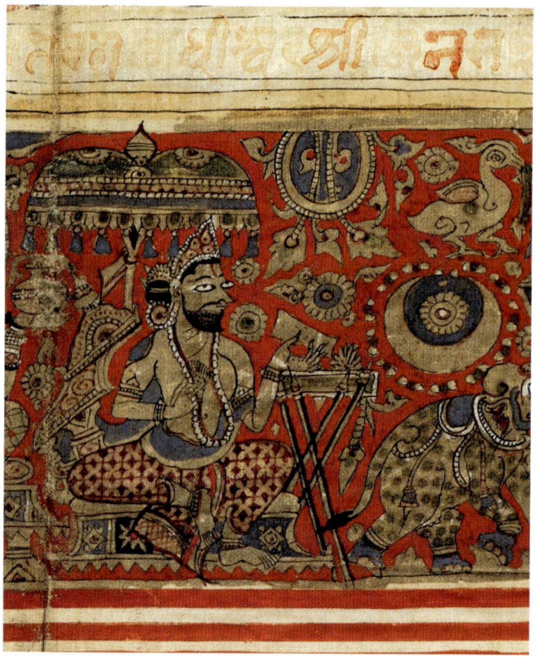

FIGURE 2.18
Detail from Jaina yantra paṭa, dated 1447 CE.
Pigments on cloth, 89 × 59.4 cm. V&A IM89-1936.
© Victoria and Albert Museum, London.

notes, a manuscript depicted in a relief carving on the outer wall of Ellora's Jain Cave suggests "the mediating role of the scriptures in the path from war to enlightenment"; it stands in as a doctrinal authority in the human world.[94] This observation is in agreement with the picture glimpsed during our brief survey of early Jain painted palm-leaf manuscripts, especially in terms of a book's value as a text of doctrinal and exegetical authority—early Jain manuscript makers and users had a more practical and more present-oriented attitude toward the book. Most medieval Jain examples that represent a book in use come from manuscript paintings in which a book seems to hold a more literal textual value. Such value was perhaps greater than its ceremonial and ritual value.

A cross-legged book stand also appears in the context of instruction and knowledge transmission in Brahmanical settings. Intriguing details representing the scenes of instruction in initiate lineages appear on the walls of Mukteshwara temple, an exquisite late tenth-century Hindu temple in Bhubaneshwar, Odisha. In one, a young pupil sits with his master, an emaciated, bearded male figure with matted locks of hair who sits with a *yogapaṭa* (a sign of hierarchic authority in an instruction lineage) wrapped around his legs and back. In between the two figures is a cross-legged stand and a book, on which the pupil has his finger (figure 2.19). The emaciated master holds an interesting object in his raised right hand, which may represent a māla (rosary). In yet another scene, two sages face each other conversing with a book; again, the book is on a cross-legged stand in the middle (figure 2.20). The sage on the right looks slightly younger (no beard) and points toward the manuscript with his right hand while holding what seems to be a manuscript under his arm. The sage on

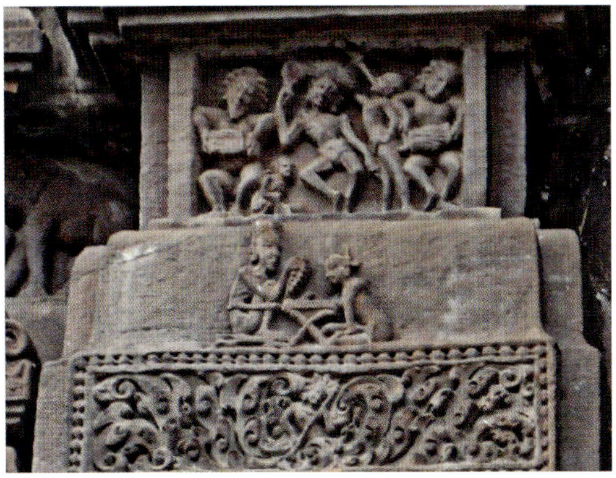

FIGURE 2.19
Detail from Mukteshwar temple, Bhubaneshwar, Odisha, ca. 950–75. Photo © Jinah Kim.

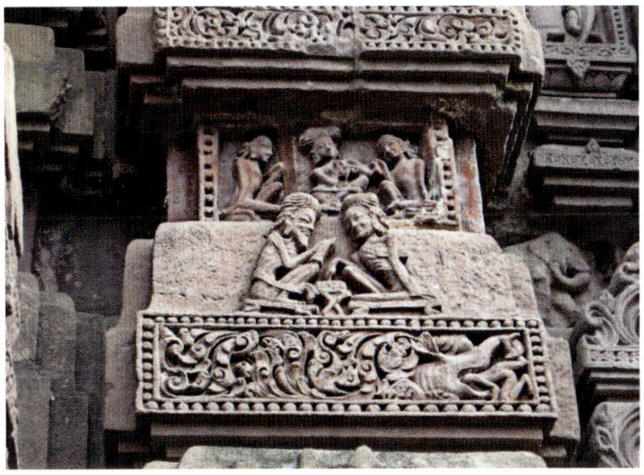

FIGURE 2.20
Detail from Mukteshwar temple, Bhubaneshwar, Odisha, ca. 950–75. Photo © Jinah Kim.

the left is seated with a *yogapaṭa* and holds a folio/manuscript in his hands. The minute but delightful scenes of instruction appear on the upper section of the temple architecture, especially around the place where the shikhara's roof level begins. It seems to occupy the level of transition from the earthly to the next level on temple architecture, fitting the goal of such instructions.

Another late tenth-century example is found on a tenth-century temple dedicated to a goddess, the Ambika Mātā temple in Jagat mentioned previously.[95] On the western side of the temple, on an interlacing, recessed wall (*salilāntara*) next to the projecting center panel (*bhadra*) that depicts the triumphal goddess, a bearded, portly male figure with matted hair is portrayed sitting on a raised seat. Kneeling in front of him, a younger-looking, nearly shaven-headed male devotee carries a gourd-like jar over his shoulder. In front of the elder, priestly figure on the left, a manuscript is placed on a simple cross-legged book stand, and the priest seems to hold the folio with his hands (figure 2.21). This scene is located in the architectural context where we see many pairs of figures engaged in various activities of learning and devotion in the human world. As an iconographic element of a simple transaction between a disciple and a teacher, the book helps articulate the authority of the priestly human teacher.

FIGURE 2.21
An *ācārya* and a disciple with a manuscript on a cross-legged book stand, on the *salilāntara* of the southern *pratiratha* of the western wall, Ambika Mata temple, initial construction, ca. 960 CE, Jagat, Southern Rajasthan. Photo © Jinah Kim.

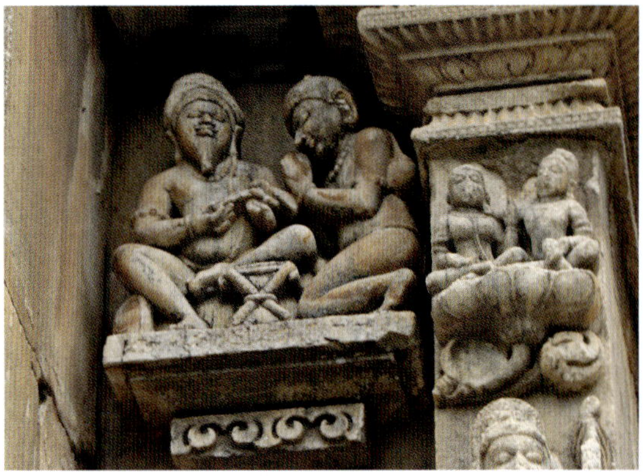

The instructional value of a book as an object that can confirm the authority of a religious lineage is conveyed once again on the northern side of the temple in a similar location on a recessed wall. In this scene, as in the first, another portly bearded figure with matted hair appears, and again in front of him there is a kneeling figure in *añjalī mudrā* with a round, jug-like object behind his shoulder; this time, he has matted hair similar to his teacher's. Between them, again, there is a simple two-legged book stand. Here, the teacher is positioned to face the kneeling pupil more directly, and he now holds a folio in his left hand and holds the right hand in front of his chest as if offering instruction. The novice who came seeking instruction in the previous panel is now fully within the tradition, and the book is the object that confirms this lineage.[96]

Cross-legged book stands also appear in a Himalayan Buddhist site like Alchi's Sumtseg (Three-Story temple), which is famous for its colossal boddhisattva statues and marvelous wall paintings dating to the late eleventh or twelfth century.[97] *Pothi*-format manuscripts placed on cross-legged book stands are depicted among the ritual offerings in various sections of the lower walls. Represented as a horizontally rectangular bar, often two to three stacked together, most manuscripts on cross-legged book stands are portrayed with small flower offerings and streams of fabric or garlands hanging from them. Above all, these are devotional offerings. In some scenes, ritual accouterments that accompany manuscripts—such as conch shells, incense burners, kalaśa pots, along with gestures of meditation taken by the monks—indicate that manuscripts may have been installed as part of a specific ritual like a consecration/empowerment ritual described in the *Vajrāvalī* (VA) discussed in chapter 3 (figure 2.22). Yet another context in which a book appears in the murals at Alchi is educational, as stacks of manuscripts on cross-legged book stands appear in the scene depicting the Buddha-to-be's schooling in his palace on the dhoti of Maitreya: a tall stack of three manuscripts strewn with flowers and garlands marks the apex as if to signal the reverence paid to the presence of knowledge being communicated.[98]

A cross-legged book stand in visual records may represent what is intended when various ritual texts like the *Śivadharmottar*a describe a "foldable seat of iron" (*lohayantrāsana*). According to a passage in the *Pauṣkarasamhitā,* "a white-dressed, pure officiant should place the *śāstrasaṃgrahapustakas* (41.86), enveloped in a cloth, on a foldable seat of iron (*lohayantrāsana* 41.86), and worship them there by means of the twelve-syllable mantra."[99] What is described as *śarayantra* in textual sources like the *Agni purāṇa* discussed by Florinda De Simini may also be something akin to a cross-legged book stand.[100]

A SINGLE-LEGGED PILLAR-TYPE BOOK STAND

A single legged pillar-type book stand appears frequently in Buddhist images from eastern India. As noted, the book in the Dhaka Tārā stele is installed on a tall, bulbous-shaped pillar with a lotus-shaped support on top. This shape is commonly witnessed in Buddhist images depicting a book in ritual settings. On the bottom register of the pedestal of the statue of the goddess Prajñāpāramitā from Mangapur (Puri district), Odisha, for example, a manuscript is centrally depicted as being installed on a tall, cylindrical pedestal with a round disc-shaped bottom and a top plate that supports the book (figure 2.23). Here, as in the Dhaka Tārā stele, a ritual master sits to the right of the bottom register, and under the book there are two food offerings. Three tall objects in front of the ritual master seem to represent ritual implements/offerings, like a butter lamp and an incense burner. A butter lamp, an incense burner, and a vase (*kalaśa*) accompany a book in a ritual scene on a number of stone slabs found around the Mahabodhi temple complex at Bodhgaya, the quintessential pilgrimage site. In one (National Museum New Delhi, Acc. No. 60.547), a book is in the center, placed on a single-legged, pillar-like stand, and the ritual implements along with two tall food offerings surround the book.[101] According to the *Vajrāvalī,* a late eleventh-century Esoteric Buddhist ritual manual, lamps, incense, a supreme vase (*kalaśa*), and a conch shell are among the ritual offerings and implements required for an installation ceremony (*pratiṣṭha*), which is also witnessed in the Alchi mural (see figure 2.22). This ritual refers to the "ceremony of consecration of architectural structures, icons and other such things," which includes books (pustaka) and rosaries (māla).[102] A book's cultic status and use is evident in these images and surviving ritual texts. A ritual text like the VA provides a period eye through which to understand the meaning and the use of manuscripts as cultic objects in Esoteric Buddhist circles.[103] A similar process for an installation ritual is also explained in the *Agnipurāṇa,* but neither text describes the type of "seat" or book stand on which a book is installed. Further exploration in textual and archaeological evidence is needed to answer simple questions like what to call the pillar-like book stand seen in Buddhist images from eastern Indian sites, or how such book stands were made. Surviving art-historical evidence provides interesting clues to understand the formal inspiration for this peculiar pillar-shaped book stand that seems to have enhanced a book's cultic potency.

The pillar-shaped book stand may be regionally specific, as most extant examples occur in images surviving from Bihar, Bengal (West Bengal in India and Bangladesh), and Odisha. This was not the only type of book stand used in these areas. Even within the same locality, we have examples of two different approaches to displaying books. In a relief vignette from

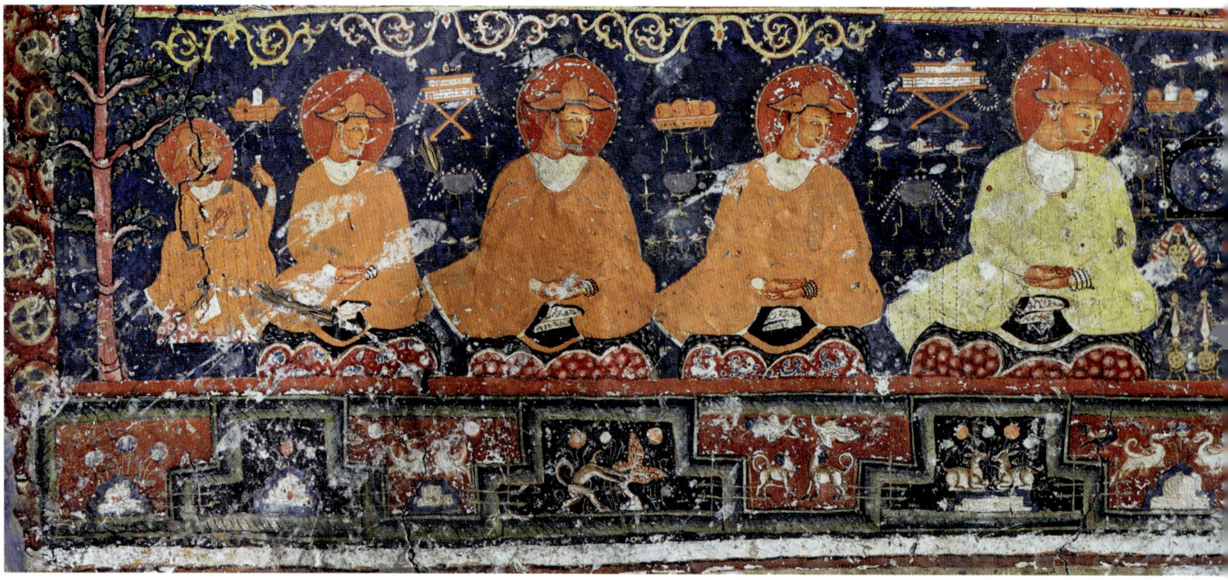

FIGURE 2.22
Monks seated in meditation with ritual implements, Amitābha panel, Avalokiteśvara niche, South Wall, Sumtseg, Alchi, ca. late eleventh or twelfth century. Photo © Peter van Ham.

the Khichakeswari temple, dedicated to the goddess, in Khiching in northern Odisha, a book is placed on a cross-legged book stand, between an ascetic figure and a royal figure in a scene of instruction (figure 2.24). The ascetic figure holds his right hand in a specific gesture pointing on the flat surface in front of him. On a Buddha image now in the Khiching museum, found in the vicinity of the Khichakeswari temple, probably dating to a roughly similar period, a book is shown installed on a bulbous pillar-like book stand (figure 2.25). The scene's exact meaning remains elusive. Donaldson identifies it as *śikṣadāna* (giving the teaching); the activities almost look like those of a scene of initiation given the difference in sizes of figures involved; in particular, the kneeling figure under the book is the smallest of the three figures in the main panel.[104] Here the book is again the center of an exchange. In comparison, however, to the scene of a book in use on a nearby Hindu temple, the book is much enlarged and has a more dominating presence; it looks as if it is a crowning jewel on a pedestal or a capital of a pillar.

This scene is set within an architectural frame, with two bulbous-shaped pillars bookending on either side. These pillars are shaped like a baluster shaft, with a round turned form; its general shape is shared by the pillar-type book stand. In other words, the book stand looks similar to the pillars of the architectural frame of the scene. The formal similarity between an architectural element and a book stand is noticeable in many images depicting books in use from Odishan sites, as also seen in another stone sculpture of Tārā from Ratnagiri (figure 2.26).[105] It hardly seems coincidental that this pillar-like book stand establishes

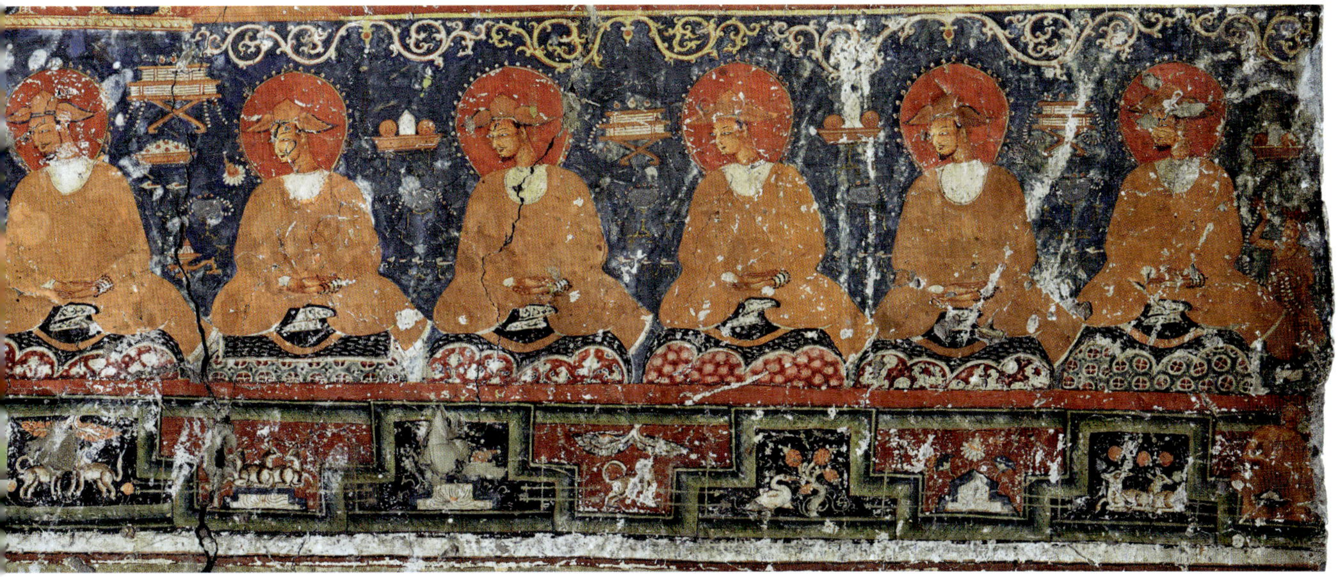

a connection between the architecture and the book—especially given the architectural inspiration behind the design of the interior space of illustrated manuscripts from this period. As we have examined, a number of painted manuscripts were designed like a temple with a three-dimensional space following an architectural logic. The pillar-type book stand turns a book into an architectural part, a pinnacle, loaded with devotional and ritual significance rather than a book to be read.

MINIATURE AND ARCHITECTURE

Painted palm-leaf manuscripts were being produced in various parts of the South Asian subcontinent by the time of the royal compilations of *śāstric* literature like the *Kṛtyakalpataru* of Lakṣmīdhara in Kashmir and the *Dānasāgara* of Ballāla Sena (a Sena king) in Bengal in the early twelfth century.[106] The ideas and techniques relating to a manuscript's production and use discussed in these texts both articulate and highlight the Indian conception of a book, in this case, a "*pustaka*" as a material container of the "*vidya*" or "sacred knowledge." Beautifully painted book covers convey this idea more than sufficiently as they physically encase the text, yet manuscript makers in medieval India did not stop there. Once the practice of painting the text folios was introduced, initially in the Buddhist context of eastern India and Nepal but soon elsewhere for fulfilling various doctrinal and cultic goals, many different iconographic, codicological, and design strategies were experimented with and adopted throughout the twelfth and thirteenth centuries.

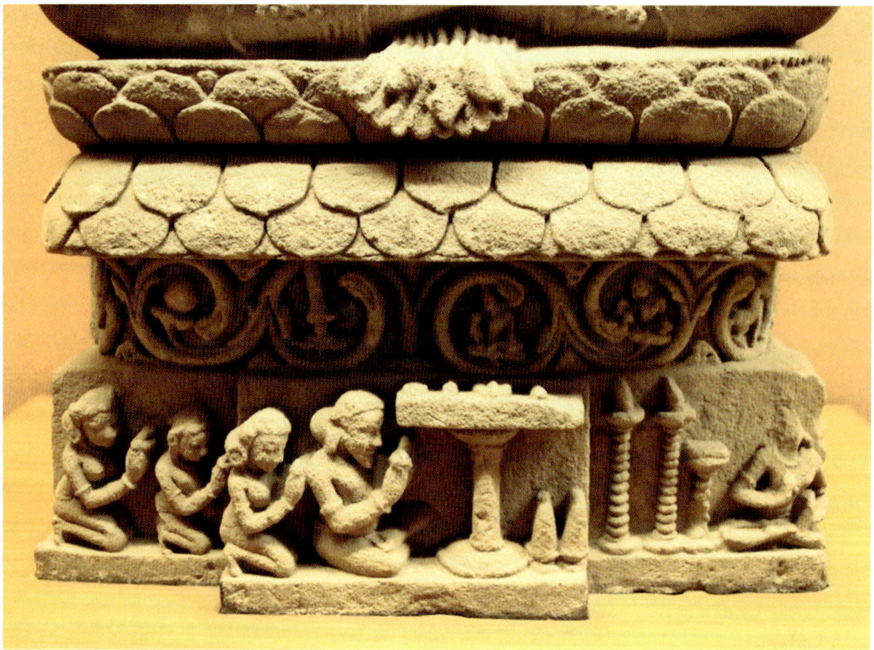

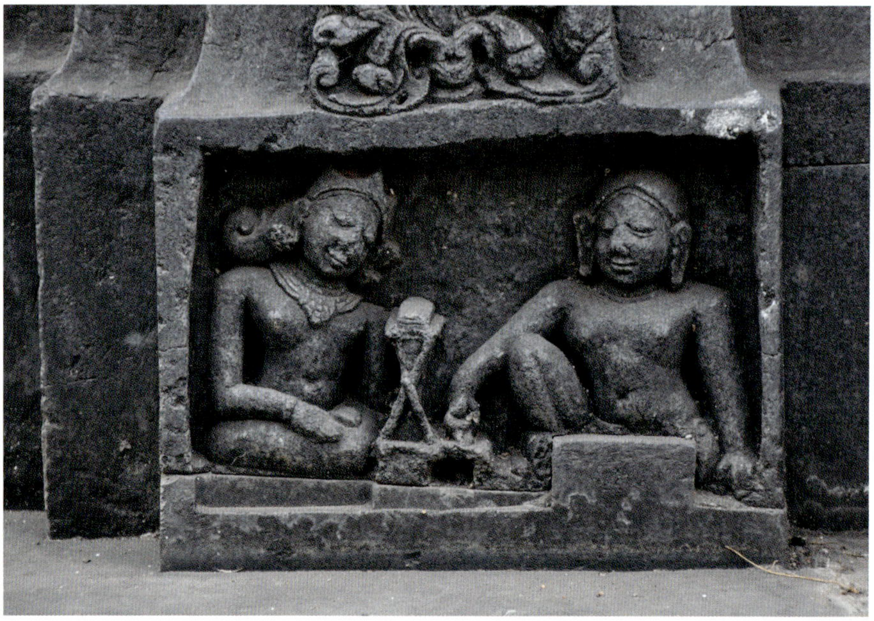

FIGURE 2.23 ▲
Ritual scene on the bottom register, the Goddess Prajñāpāramitā stele, eleventh century, Mangalpur (Puri district), Orissa. Orissa State Museum. Photo © Sonali Dhingra.

FIGURE 2.24 ▼
Scene of instruction-knowledge transmission, Khichakeshwari temple, ca. eleventh century(?), Khiching, Odisha. Photo © Jinah Kim.

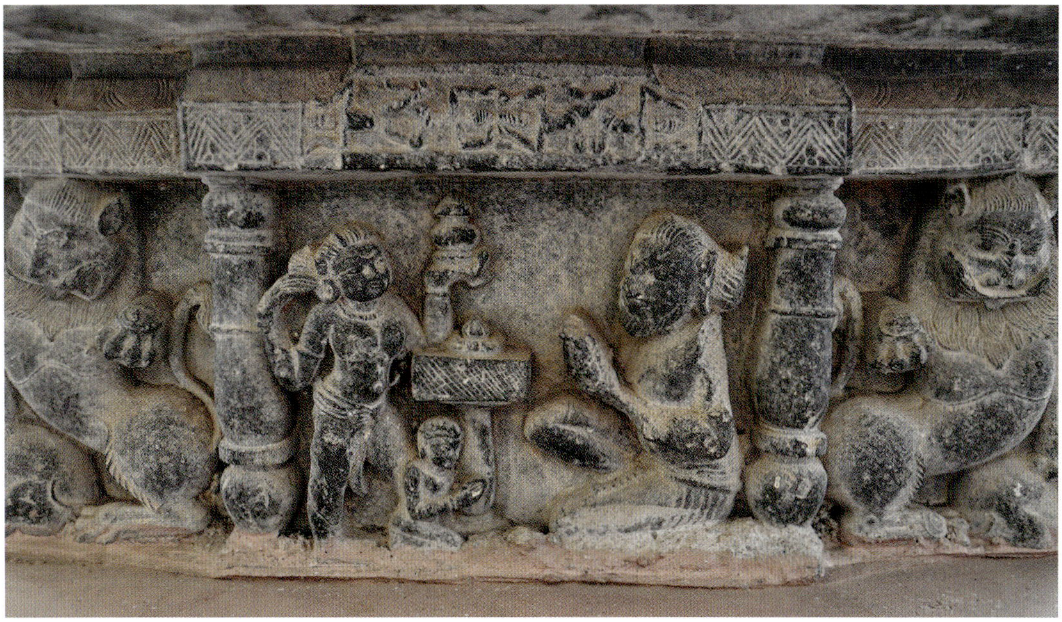

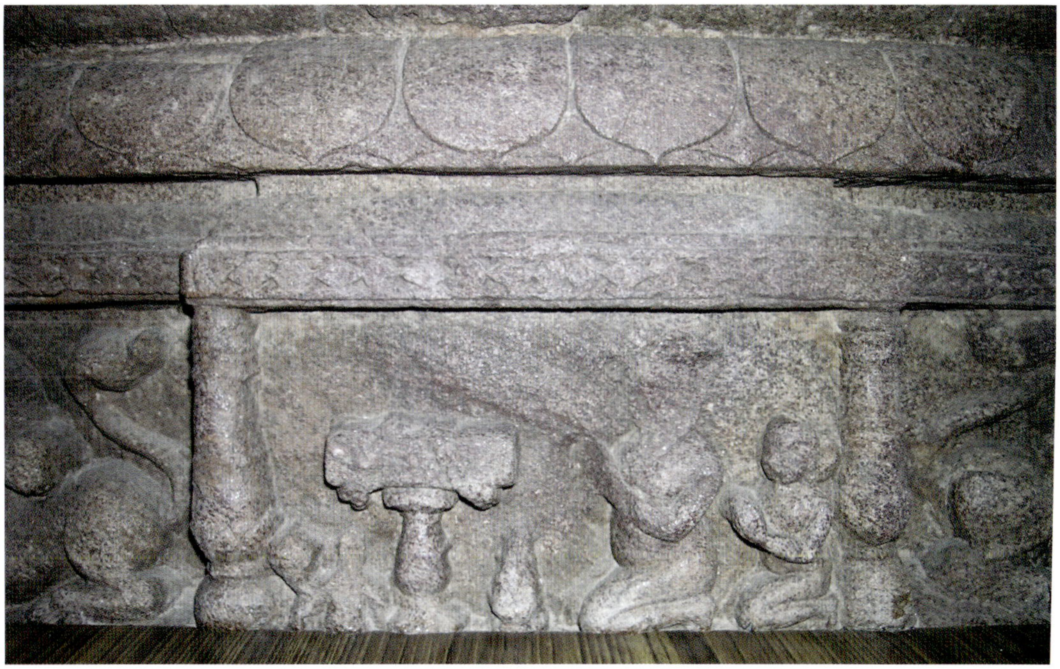

FIGURE 2.25 ▲
Detail of the lower register, Buddha stele, Khiching, ca. eleventh century. Photo © Jinah Kim.

FIGURE 2.26 ▼
Book on a pillar-type stand, bottom register, Tārā stele, ca. late tenth century CE, Ratnagiri, Orissa. Khondalite, H: 137 cm. ASI Site Museum, Ratnagiri.

Further research will reveal a myriad of different local contexts and transregional relationships in which the innovative spirit in the art of the book in medieval India developed and bloomed. Perhaps the ingenious realization of a wondrous temple-like microspace that one could unfold in a palm-leaf manuscript in *pothi* format represented the perfect solution to the theological and cultic demand for more physical space to contain bountifully manifested and immediate expressions of the divine or of doctrinal visions in color and in a miniature, portable package. The art of the book in medieval India developed in a manner not too different from the multiplication of projections and recesses on the walls of the Kandariya Mahadeva temple at Khajuraho, which appears to expand infinitely the physical space for such expressions. In a way, both the temple and the book were designed as sacred space using shared visual strategies.[107] Further research may even reveal that certain design strategies in manuscripts also inspired architectural form or that manuscripts served as a means for transmitting the details of architectural style. For now, having established the importance of a *pothi*-format manuscript as an important medium for painting and transmission of knowledge, we turn to investigate the role of painted manuscripts in the circulation of visual knowledge of tantric vision practices and their bearing on the material history of Indian painting.

PART TWO

VISION

3

VISIONS ON THE MOVE

HOW DID VISIONARY EXPERIENCES OF the transcendence sought by tantric ritual masters get transmitted and circulate in medieval South Asia? In Esoteric Buddhist circles, complex ritual strategies were introduced to stimulate visionary experiences through which a practitioner was to transform the body into that of a chosen deity.[1] Visions and seeing in a designated register played a crucial role in this process. Images, especially portable paintings with their color information, provided a crucial tool to structure visionary experiences and helped to generate shared experiences across generations within specific initiate lineages.[2] Maṇḍala paintings on cloth, like Tibetan *thangka*s and Nepalese *paubha*s, may, in fact, have initially developed to address this need. As we will see in this chapter, *pothi*-format manuscripts also provided a perfect vehicle for transmission and controlled circulation of esoteric visual knowledge because they could capture the uniquely intertwined text-image relationship in tantric visionary practices in a compact, portable package. As discussed in chapter 4, the inherent seriality and spatial ordering of images accommodated by the *pothi* format also promoted specific ways of seeing in stages, as in a mental journey through a carefully orchestrated story-scape, woven from the images that mark stations of halting and transformation. It is equally important to note that awe-inspiring artistic interventions by the unnamed artists frequently helped in shaping a practitioner's visual experience of transformation. The emphasis given to the importance of artistic interventions in shaping the visionary experiences is pursued as a corrective to our heavy reliance on texts in understanding images produced in the service of Esoteric Buddhist communities. Considering how materials and artisanal intelligence shaped certain ways of seeing does not mean that artists were visionaries. Rather, doing so allows us to acknowledge unnamed artists' contribution to shaping the concrete forms in which these visions were experienced beyond what's written in texts and helps us recognize that painting is part of the knowledge or insight being staged.

PORTABLE VISIONS

According to a biography composed in 1688 by Sangs rgyas phun tshogs (1649–1705, Sakya), Ngorchen Kunga Zangpo (Ngor chen kun dga' bzang po, 1382–1456, Sakya master), the founder of the Ngor monastery in central Tibet, commissioned a series of *thangka*s (scroll painting on cloth) from Newar artists sometime between the foundation of the monastery in 1429 and his death in 1456.[3] In particular, "he commissioned from Newar artists the painting of this complete set of maṇḍalas of the Vajrāvalī cycle, together with three additional maṇḍalas from the Kriyāsamuccaya collection."[4] The series of paintings was meant to honor one of his three main teachers, Sazang Pakpa (Sa bzang 'Phags pa gzhon nu blo gros, 1358–1412/24). Due to turmoil in the 1960s, many treasures from Ngor were damaged or lost, and some entered the art market.[5] Eight out of the fourteen *thangka*s of this series are known in Western collections.[6]

The most distinctive aspect of the Ngor Vajrāvalī series is that each *thangka* contains four individual maṇḍalas (figure 3.1). A painting's visual field is divided into four quadrants, and the field also has bottom and top registers. Each quadrant contains a single maṇḍala in figure 1, identified as: (1) Vajradhātu maṇḍala (*top left*, VA19, fifty-three deities); (2) Durgatipariśodhana maṇḍala (*top right*, VA22, thirty-seven deities); (3) Bhūtaḍamaramaṇḍala (*bottom left*, VA23, thirty-three deities); and (4) Mārīcīmaṇḍala (*bottom right*, VA17, twenty-five deities). Placing more than one maṇḍala per painting is a unique organizational scheme that may well have been Ngorchen's innovative contribution to the history of maṇḍala making. By introducing up to four maṇḍalas per painting, this method can accommodate a large number of maṇḍalas on a relatively small number of paintings. The surviving eight *thangka*s contain twenty-six maṇḍalas, twenty-three maṇḍalas from the Vajrāvalī cycle and three maṇḍalas from the Kriyāsamuccaya.[7] These surviving paintings also suggest that Ngorchen organized the maṇḍalas of the VA in a specific sequence. A short inscription above the center of the top register identifies the order in which each painting belongs. The Rubin Museum piece is the "thirteenth painting of the Vajrāvalī (Rdorje phreng ba'i ras bris bcug sum pa'o)." It contains four maṇḍalas in an order different from how they are ordered in the Vajrāvalī.[8]

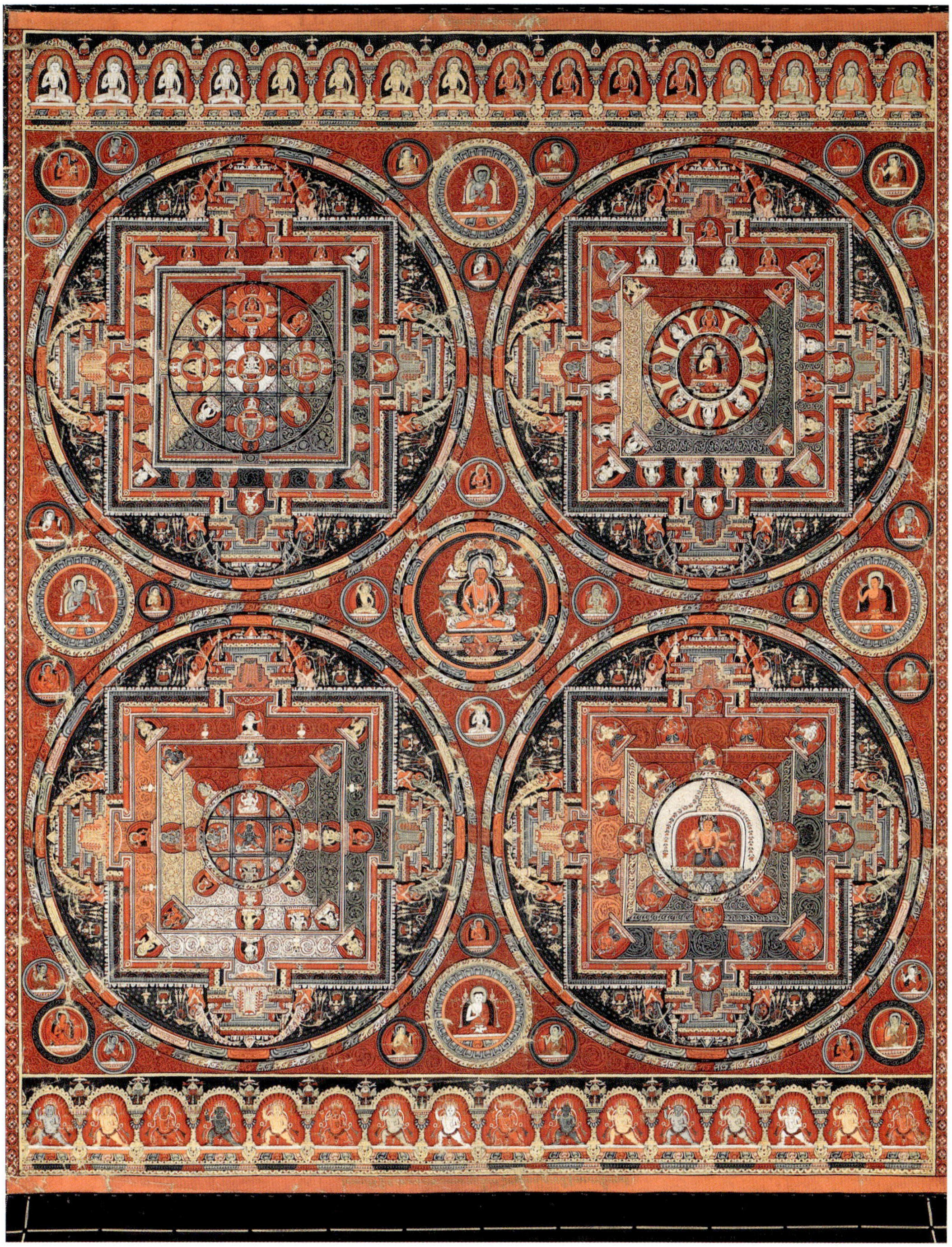

FIGURE 3.1
Four Maṇḍalas of the Vajrāvalī, thirteenth of the Ngor Vajrāvalī series, ca. 1450, central Tibet (Ewam Choden Ngor monastery). Pigments on cloth, 81.9 × 73.6 cm. Rubin Museum of Art C2007.6.1 (HAR 81826). Image courtesy of the Rubin Museum of Art.

At a historical moment when the Sakya order's fortune was waning as the Gelugpa (the so-called yellow hat sect, headed by the Dalai Lamas) was gaining power, Ngorchen was keen on "preserving the integrity of the Sakya tradition."[9] Ngorchen was a renowned tantric master, and he had especially trained in the *Hevajra tantra* and associated rituals of the Lam 'bras ("Path and Fruit") tradition.[10] That Ngorchen commissioned a complete set of the Vajrāvalī series but in a modified sequence sometime after founding of his own monastery, Ngor Ewam Chöden, in 1429 CE, should be understood in this context. The Vajrāvalī is a large group of complex maṇḍalas initially compiled by a twelfth-century Indian Buddhist master, Abhayākaragupta. Ngorchen's project helped him assert authority as a tantric master and to establish the Ngor monastery as a seat of tantric learning with a close Indian connection. The project demonstrated his mastery over the Vajrāvalī and secured his unstated connection to an Indian Buddhist master who recorded exponentially multifarious tantric visionary practices and rituals systematically at the end of the eleventh century. It is important to underscore how the completion of a set of paintings played a foundational role in this authority-building project.

Newar artists who executed these paintings supposedly came to Ngor drawn by some mysterious force, which the biography identifies as "the power of Lama Kunga Zangpo's meditation." Newar artists of the Kathmandu valley were highly sought after by Tibetan patrons, especially from 1200 CE onward. The Sakya order, in particular, had a close connection with Newar artists, as exemplified in an oft-cited story of the Nepali artist Aniko (Anige). Aniko's ascent to fame as a master artist at the Yuan court was facilitated by Chögyal Phagpa (1235–1280), a Sakyapa lama and the imperial preceptor to the Yuan emperor Kublai Khan. There is no doubt concerning the exceptional talents of Newar artists, as seen in the meticulously rendered details in surviving Ngor Vajrāvalī series paintings (figure 3.2). The Kathmandu valley, or "Nepal maṇḍala" in epigraphic records of medieval Nepal, became an important substitute for India when the Buddhist heartland in India became less accessible following the establishment of the Delhi Sultanate and after the conquest of Bengal in 1206. By the turn of 1400, many local Tibetan artists were trained in Newar-inspired visual vocabularies.[11] Employment of Newar artists over local artists must have been a strategic move by Ngorchen as a way to amplify his authority and superiority by expressing his affinity with Sanskritic traditions.[12]

Ngorchen's Vajrāvalī project provides a tangible entry point from which to consider the importance and necessity of a controlled compilation of complex iconographic systems generated in Vajrayana or Esoteric/tantric Buddhism and the role of painting as an artistic medium in presenting visual information, especially regarding color. Tantric rituals were part of an initiation and lineage-based tradition with sworn secrecy in which a hierarchic teacher-disciple relationship was essential for its operation. Their development does not seem to have been centrally controlled by an external or institutional authority. The Vajrāvalī or "Vajrāvalīnāmamaṇḍalopayikā" prepared by the great master Abhayākaragupta ("Mahāpaṇḍitābhayākaraguptaracitā-vajrāvalīnāmamaṇḍalopayikā" on folio 96 of G4835, a twelfth-century Bengali manuscript in the Asiatic Society, Kolkata), was prepared because

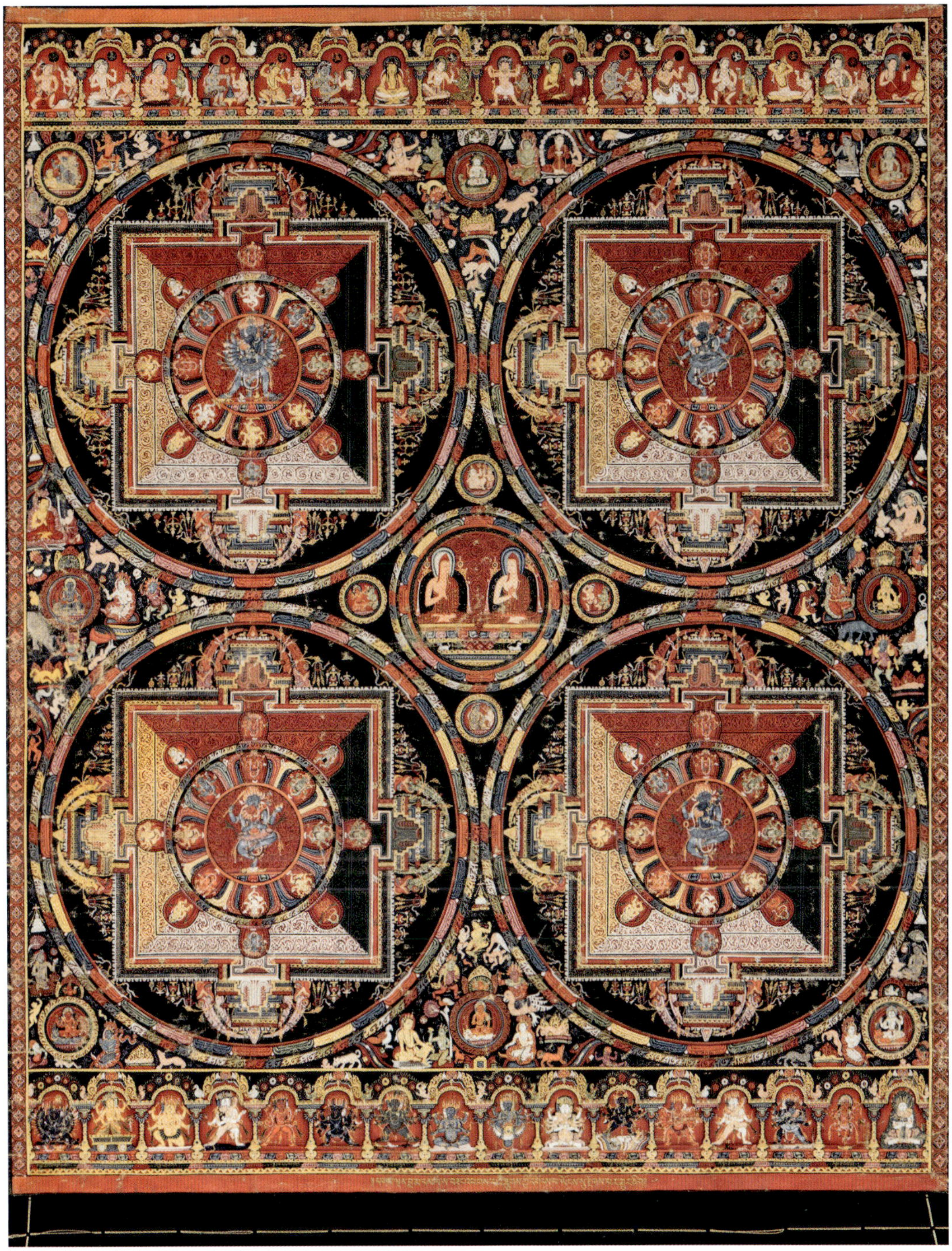

FIGURE 3.2
Four Hevajra Maṇḍalas of the Vajrāvalī, fifth of the Ngor Vajrāvalī series, ca. 1450, central Tibet (Ewam Choden Ngor monastery). 89.5 × 73.7 cm (134.6 × 83.8 cm), Philadelphia Museum of Art 1994-148-635. Photo courtesy of Philadelphia Museum of Art.

Abhayākaragupta, a monastic scholar of tantric Buddhism, felt a great need to systematize tantric rituals that proliferated without much control. According to Masahide Mori, Abhayākaragupta's intent was to "synthesize and systematize the pattern of rituals which were differently performed in various traditions."[13] By the turn of the twelfth century when Abhayākaragupta was active at the Vikramaśīla monastery (near today's Bhagalpur, Bihar, on the southern bank of the Ganges), numerous tantric Buddhist masters had come and gone, and many more were active.[14] We encounter their names in hagiographic literature in Tibet and in tantric ritual manuals (*vidhis*) and vision practice texts (*sādhanas*), many of which survive in Sanskrit and Tibetan translations and also in some Chinese translations. Abhayākaragupta composed two other ritual manuals to complement the VA, the *Niṣpannayogāvalī* (NsP) and the *Jyotirmañjarī-homopāyikā* (JM). The JM is a manual on *homa* fire rituals, and the NsP elaborates on each of the twenty-six maṇḍalas mentioned in the VA. Together with the VA, they are known as the "three garland cycle (*phreng ba 'khor gsum*)" in the Tibetan canon. The NsP is often consulted as an iconographic handbook for Buddhist iconography in modern studies. Abhayākaragupta's intention was to create a handy reference so that a ritual master could envision the specifics of maṇḍalas (*bhāvyamaṇḍala*) in concrete, figurative forms whenever necessary during a consecration/installation ritual as explained in the VA.[15]

Before considering the role of painted manuscripts in tantric visionary practices, two issues need to be understood to contextualize the production of illustrated manuscripts in medieval Indic Buddhist circles: the historical and cultural significance of Abhayākaragupta's compilation efforts, and the characteristics of these texts. The proliferation of tantric practices witnessed in compilations like Abhayākaragupta's suggests that attempts to catalog and systematize were actively pursued in Indian Buddhist monastic circles by the end of the eleventh century. The compilation of Sanskrit *sādhanas*—known as the *Sādhanamālā* (lit. garland of *sādhana,* henceforth SM) in twentieth-century scholarship—also began to be prepared around the turn of the twelfth century, and the genre remained fluid for a few centuries.[16] Written down on small, compact manuscripts like the palm-leaf manuscript from the VA in the Asiatic Society, Kolkata (G4835, size: 5.5 × 29 cm with ninety-six folios), these texts could easily be transported for transregional transmission and circulation; easy transport would have been a crucial characteristic during the period of *phyi-dar* when Indian Buddhist masters and their teachings were actively sought by aspiring Buddhists of the Tibetan plateau and the Nepal maṇḍala. The Kolkata VA manuscript (G4835), which was most likely written somewhere in Bengal, traveled to Nepal soon after its production, as indicated by post colophons in Newari hand (figure 3.3).[17]

Detailed prescriptions of each deity's color, gesture, attributes, and the number of heads and limbs found in these texts underscore the importance of organizing and codifying visual information. These texts demonstrate that visual stimuli were central to *sādhana,* a hallmark of tantric ritual practices. It is also important to remember that the *sādhana* texts share some salient textual characteristics with *śilpaśāstras*, which are technical manuals for artistic and architectural productions. In particular, descriptions of maṇḍalas in Buddhist tantras

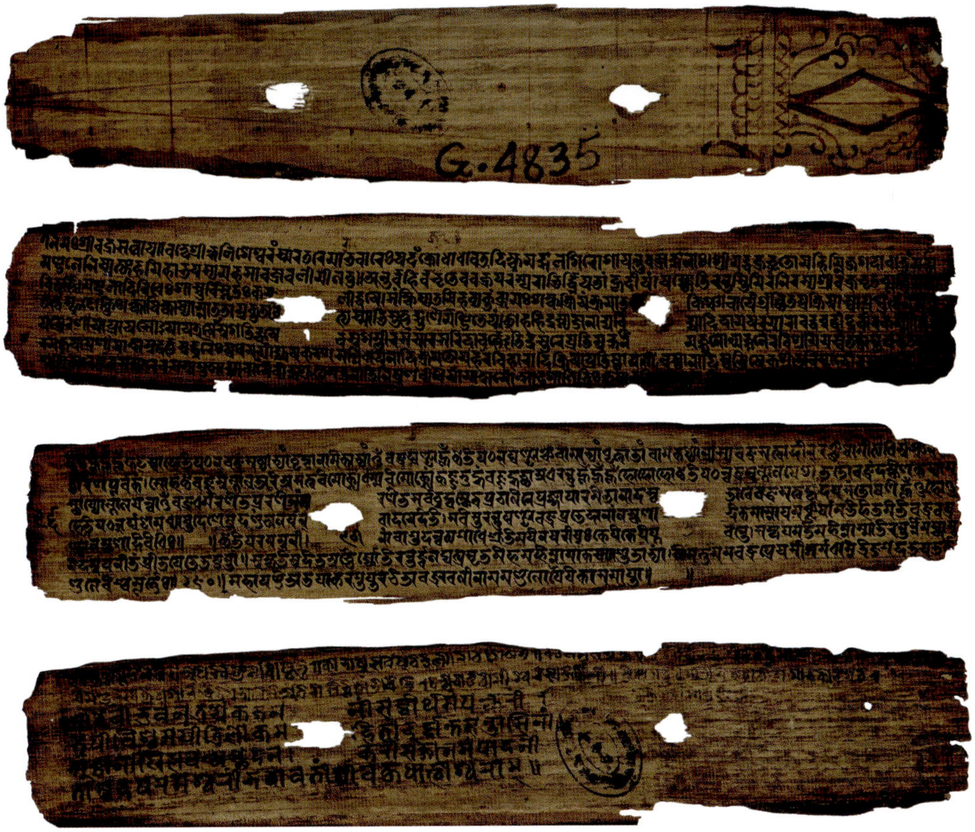

FIGURE 3.3
Palm-leaf manuscript of the Vajrāvalī, ca. twelfth century, Bengal. Size: 5.5 × 29 cm with 96 folios. Asiatic Society, Kolkata G4835. Photo © Asiatic Society, Kolkata.

draw on the technical vocabulary found in the existing literature on architecture (*vāstuśāstra*) by describing a maṇḍala as a palace (*kūṭāgāra*) with four corners, four doors, and four *toraṇa*.[18] For example, in the *Cakrasaṃvara tantra*, a tantric ritual practitioner is instructed to use a thread, "sūtra" for preparing an outline of a maṇḍala, as would an architect preparing a foundation grid for a temple for various Hindu deities. The method remains the same, but the thread in this context is identified as "corpse thread" colored with human blood, updating a traditional method to fit the sanguine and transgressive ritual context of the Cakrasaṃvara tantra.

However detailed, textual descriptions have certain limits in conveying and circulating visual information. A book of drawings does not necessarily convey what and how a practitioner should see or envision these color-filled forms of deities and their maṇḍalas.[19] A handy reference book like *Tibetan Maṇḍalas: Vajrāvalī and Tantra-samuccaya* (1995), published in India by Lokesh Chandra as part of the Śata-piṭaka series founded by his father Raghu Vira, contains numerous diagrams and black-and-white line drawings of maṇḍalas that have been reproduced from early nineteenth-century Mongolian xylographs.[20] While they are informative about structures of maṇḍalas and the number and types of deities, discussion of color is completely absent. As a result, the vivacity with which these visions should be experienced is lost.

A manuscript provided a desirably portable package for assembling a vast amount of visual data in color. A group of surviving twelfth-century palm-leaf manuscripts suggests that a *pothi*-format manuscript of a foundational Buddhist scripture may have been adapted as a fitting medium for transporting visual information generated in tantric Buddhist circles in a controlled manner. Types of images chosen in some twelfth-century Buddhist manuscripts and their iconographic arrangement indicate a potential link between the tantric visionary practices and the production of painted manuscripts in medieval South Asia, at least in Buddhist circles. The interdependent relationship between the rituals described in the VA and the NsP of Abhayākaragupta and painted manuscripts identified in this chapter helps explain this overlooked linkage.

ON TANTRIC VISION PRACTICES

In this study, a "tantric vision practice" refers to a ritual practice described in a type of text called "sādhana" (lit. a means of accomplishing; a means to accomplish "deity yoga"). Its goal is to transform a practitioner into a chosen deity through various ritual techniques. These techniques involve voiced sound (mantra), controlled movements of the body (symbolic hand gestures and postures), and, most importantly for our purpose, visualizing a chosen deity in its fully articulated form to identify with one's self. A simple *sādhana* of bodhisattva Siṁhanāda, a form of bodhisattva Avalokiteśvara, thus instructs a practitioner to do the following:

> Salute to Siṁhanāda! First, the practitioner (the term used in this sādhana is "yogi") who is seated in a comfortable pose after having washed his face, etc., having seen (*dṛṣṭvā*) in his heart the letter *Āḥ* formed in the Sun orb (*sūryamaṇḍala*), having honored the teacher, the Buddha, etc., he should perform the confession of sins, etc. Then, having performed realizing emptiness (*śūnyatā*) etc., he should recall the prayer (*praṇidhi*). Then, meditate on (*dhyāyāt*) the letter *A* transforming into the moon, on which the letter *Oṁ* transforming into a red lotus, on top of which letter *Āḥ* transforming into a white lion, on top of which the letter *Hrīḥ* in a lotus becoming the lord Siṁhanāda, who is white and has matted hair, and who is three eyed and two armed and dressed in ascetic's garb, and who is resting in the posture of royal ease (*mahārājalīlayā*); on top of the lotus held in his left hand [imagine] a rising flaming sword, and on the right, a white trident wrapped by a white serpent, and on the left, a white skull cup filled with a variety of sweet smelling flowers, and [Siṁhanāda] wearing an Amitābha tiara, throbbing five tathāgatas in the great *nirmāṇa* form. [One should] mutter the mantra "*oṃ āḥ hrīḥ siṁhanāda huṃ phaṭ*."—SM 20, p. 51

SM 22 VARIATION

> Salute to Siṁhanāda! First the practitioner (the term here is *mantrī*), having washed his face etc., on a soft *kuśa*-grass seat, having sat down in a comfortable position, in his heart having seen

(*dṛṣṭvā*) a brilliant letter hrīḥ on a moon orb, drawing this light ray evenly together, foremost, meditate on (*dhyāyāt*) the teacher, the Buddha and the bodhisattva. Then having done the pūjā, confession of sins etc., one should realize clearly illumined emptiness (*śunyatā*) through this mantra, "oṃ I in my true self am of the nature of the diamond (*nondual-vajra) knowledge of emptiness (*oṃśūnyatājñānavajrasvabhāvatmako 'ham.*)" Then, at once, the practitioner should imagine/meditate on [*dhyāyāt*] the letter "paṁ" transforming into a red lotus, on top of which the letter "*siṁ*" transforming into a white lion, on top of which, the letter *hrīḥ* in the moon becoming himself in the form of Siṁhanādalokeśvara. Bright/white, with a matted hair diadem adorned by Amitābha, [he is] three-eyed, two-armed, wearing an ascetic's garb, and resting in the posture of royal ease. [Imagine] a flaming sword on top of a lotus held in the left hand, on the right a white trident wrapped by a white serpent, a skull cup filled with a variety of sweet-smelling flowers, trembling five tathāgatas in the great nirmāṇa forms. [One should] mutter the mantra "*oṃ āḥ hrīḥ siṁhanāda huṃ phaṭ*."—SM 22, p. 53

The first section of the text abbreviates a couple of steps as indicated by the use of the term "*adi*" for "etc." It also assumes the knowledge of a full ritual like the one described in the "somewhat detailed sādhana on Tārā (*kiñcidvistaram tārāsādhanam*)" by a monastic author, Anupamarakṣita.[21] Gómez summarizes the "four axes of a visualization session" as follows: "protective magic, philosophical discourse and reflection, devotion, and symbolic transformation of self."[22] This "symbolic transformation of self" is the most important aspect of the sādhana practice. Ritual strategies for pursuing this goal are even more elaborate in sādhanas devoted to deities of "higher" tantras (i.e., mahāyoga and yoginī tantras).[23] While the basic structure of the practice remains more or less similar, ritual strategies become especially complex in terms of the visual information that one needs to control and master to see.[24] In a sādhana practice, "to see" is ultimately "to become" or to generate oneself as the chosen deity. Verbs like √dṛś and √paś, the basic meaning of which is "to see," are common in sādhanas.[25] However, the act here is not to see something external to one's self. As indicated by the phrase "having seen in his heart" in the Siṁhanāda sādhana, an internal vision is the main concern. A practitioner should imagine, and visualize, for example, a letter, *Hrīḥ*, transforming into a figure, here "Siṁhanādalokeśvara." The process elaborated in each sādhana demands the practitioner's deeper background knowledge of the religious system. Likewise, the image that encapsulates the visionary experience also addresses an audience that is already immersed in, or in the process of becoming immersed in, the highly complex religious iconography.

If sādhana texts are for the performance of rituals designed to generate internal visions in a practitioner, how do they relate to "art"—external, material trappings of these visions? What is the meaning and function of the vast array of surviving images of Tantric Buddhism in various media, such as painting, sculpture, and even architecture, when all of the associated practices are supposed to happen in one's mind? And lastly, how do we explain the relationship between the art and the vision when there is a distinct possibility that an artist's intervention provided a seed for a new visionary experience?

On the function of images in Tantric Buddhism, three interpretations prevail: firstly, images, especially painted images of maṇḍalas, as in Tibetan *thangkas*, are aide-mémoire for visualization practices; secondly, they are the material embodiment of the invoked divinity, thus empowering and protecting the space that they habituate; and thirdly, they are tokens of religious merit making, expressing devotion.[26] As Michael Willis points out, there is no explicit instruction in Sanskrit sādhana texts on using the images as meditation aids.[27] The Indian images, especially those myriad stone sculptures of the eleventh and the twelfth centuries hailing from great Buddhist monastic and pilgrimage sites in South Asia, may be understood as "commemorative memorials to those who actually undertook the practice."[28]

Most sādhanas collected in the SM may not state that "painted or carved images are integral" to the vision practice.[29] Many images may be visual and material records of actual religious practices. However, the commemorative memorial theory does not fully explain the proximity between the text and the images and the alternative potential of the images informing the visionary experience. While the historical significance of these images should not be slighted, by relegating images to the realm of historical illustration we miss an opportunity to investigate the intricately intertwined yet parallel text-image relationship that tantric vision practices cultivated to realize the somatic impact of internal transformation.

A painted image of Siṁhānada in a mid-twelfth-century palm-leaf manuscript prepared at the Vikramaśīla monastery now in the British Library (Or. 6902) seems to match the "mental" image described in the sādhana nearly word for word (figure 3.4). This correspondence extends to a red lotus on which the white lion appears, noticeably painted with purplish red (most likely an organic pigment, like lac) instead of vermilion (inorganic pigment based on cinnabar), a blazing sword on a lotus held in his left hand, deliberately represented as held between two bent fingers, and a trident wrapped by a white snake on his right (behind his resting right arm), and a skull cup filled with yellow flowers on his left (next to his bent left knee).[30] With a clearly marked third eye, loftily matted hairdo, and a tiger loincloth representing an ascetic's garb, the synchronicity between the image and the text is unmistakable. The "Throbbing" five tathāgatas emitting from him as in the text are absent in this painting, perhaps due to the space restriction given the miniature size of the panel (about 6.3 × 7 cm). In their stead, we see brilliant vermilion fire with snarly finger-like flames surrounding the bodhisattva, which convey the intensity with which his brilliant white form is to propel the manifestations of the five tathāgatas. The energetic movement of the painted flames—especially when read together with the sādhana—enhances a sense of an animated image actively transformed from letters into a figurative form in sequence, now hovering in midair in the blazing intensity of one's internal vision. Such engulfing flames are not mentioned anywhere in the sādhana. In other words, the unnamed artist has provided an interpretation of what a practitioner is supposed to see. He has brought the practitioner's internal vision to life.

It is difficult to ascertain whether this painted image in the middle of a manuscript of the *Perfection of Wisdom sūtra* may have been a "commemorative memorial" to the practice of the Siṁhanāda *sādhana*. It is possible that that sādhana may have been meaningful for the

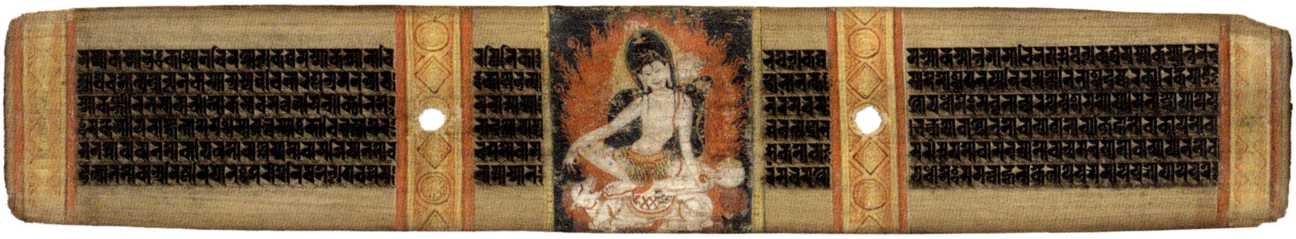

FIGURE 3.4
Bodhisattva Siṁhanāda, folio 164r, the end of chapter 11, *Perfection of Wisdom* manuscript, Gopāla's fifteenth year, ca. 1147 CE, Vikramaśīla monastery. British Library Or. 6902. Photo © The British Library Board.

donor, a monastic elder, Sumatiśrīmintra, who might have requested this image to occupy the heart of the manuscript. The painting's presence most likely enhanced the manuscript's cultic power. Beautifying a manuscript of the *Perfection of Wisdom* with painted panels was certainly a merit-increasing activity. The most questionable hypothesis may be that such an image was used as a memory aid for a sādhana practice. It seems unlikely that this image physically hidden in the middle of a sizable stack of palm-leaf folios was taken out for a specific vision practice.[31] But the image certainly calls to mind the particular practice when the page is open for viewing. One cannot prove or disprove whether such an image was used for a visual practice. The synchronicity between the text and the image in this case may also be due to the preexisting images that informed such a visionary experience. After all, elements of Śaiva iconography embedded in this relatively new form of Avalokiteśvara in the twelfth century were possibly seen and quoted from the preexisting images of Śiva, whose distinct iconographic features such as lofty matted hair, a third eye, a trident, and a snake are without fail incorporated into this new iconography.

A careful reading of sādhana texts and associated ritual texts like those collected in the VA also helps us to understand the phenomenological nature of these tantric ritual practices and the role of images in them. Images as artistic creations were important not only for sādhana practices but also for the education and transmission of tantric ritual knowledge that was so dependent on the vast amount of visual information. It is important to appreciate how an unnamed artist translated a visionary experience into a communicable visual entity.

VISIONS AND IMAGES

A tantric vision practice seeks internal transformation of one's self, but this change is performed through bodily, external means of symbolic actions. To get to the point, when a vision is articulated and experienced, many preliminary steps of actions are required. Each ritual sequence, even a relatively short procedure like the Siṁhanāda-sādhana, requires many preliminary actions: cleansing one's body, preparing the ground, a seat, and offerings. Habitual actions learned in daily life and culturally learned behaviors that do not require instruction, like how one should sit, fold hands, or carry one's body, are not mentioned at all;

nevertheless, these are all necessary actions that take time to perform. So, a procedure for worshipping the "deities with manifold flowers, incense, lamps, perfumed powders, and food" required by the *Vajravārāhī sādhana* would involve a number of hand gestures and movements that are not specified in the text.[32]

A term like "meditation" may call to mind an attitude of silence and stillness, but a sādhana practice was never an absolutely silent affair, especially given the active involvement of vocal chords to sound out mantras and prayers.[33] One of the two quintessential accoutrements of tantric Buddhist rituals is a ghaṇṭa, a bell, which is frequently sounded at opportune moments during a performance of a ritual. Sound also externalizes the process of internal transformation. Through sound (mantra) and actions (including hand gestures), that which should be envisioned internally is acted out and made visible in the practitioner's body. For example, in the last part of the first "meditation stage" in the *Vajravārāhī sādhana* of Umāpatideva, the practitioner is to install and consecrate the "knowledge being (*jñānasattva*)" with water (through water consecration) in the following manner: He should "correctly visualize the tathāgatas in the sky consecrating [you] with the mantra. [Then] see (*paśya*) Vairocana on [your] head [imaging that he has] come forth from the drops of the water remaining from the consecration. The consecration mantra here is "For even as the tathāgatas were bathed as soon as they were born, so I will wash [you], purified, with heavenly water. Thus, *Oṃ sarvatathāgatābhiṣekasamayaśriye huṃ*."[34]

At a first glance, this passage seems to be about internal visions such as seeing in the sky or visualizing tathāgatas and Vairocana on one's head. But the actual performance of this sādhana would require a movement of hands, involving pouring/splashing droplets of water on the practitioner's head. Such a consecration ritual is only briefly mentioned in the sādhana; in part, this is because the necessary ritual knowledge is assumed. Fortunately, Abhayākaragupta's VA provides detailed descriptions of how to perform installation and consecration rituals and allows us to understand the ritual context more fully.[35] The VA compiles fifty "vidhis" (rules for rituals), mainly for consecration (*abhiṣeka*) and maṇḍala construction.[36] Rituals described in the VA create a general sense of projection/identification between the earthly ritual of the practitioner and the ritual imagined/visualized to be performed by a transcendental being, like a tathāgata. As Masahide Mori observes with regard to the water consecration discussed in the VA, the ritual "has two-layers: consecration by the tathāgatas within the visualization of the *ācārya* and the actual consecration by the *ācārya* himself. The consecration by the tathāgatas is ordered by Vajrasattva who is the central deity of the maṇḍala as well as the *ācārya* himself."[37] A ritual sequence performed by the practitioner is synchronized with what is seen/experienced internally and thus manifests this internal experience in flesh. Reading the descriptions of rituals in the VA with the actual performance of rituals in mind (e.g., see the recordings of rituals, like the revival of sādhana ritual at Tabo or the Prajñāpāramitā pūjā in Nepal), one can surmise that realizing the process in life was integral for the successful completion of such a ritual.[38] In other words, the vision is not all in one's head. In order to be efficacious, what is envisioned internally should be enacted bodily.

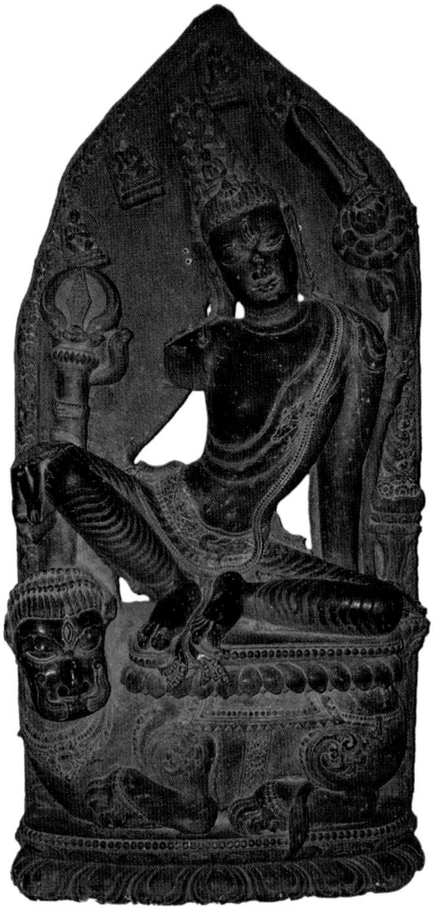

FIGURE 3.5
Siṁhanāda Avalokiteśvara, ca. late eleventh century to early twelfth century, Chitor, Gaya district, Bihar. Patna Museum. Photo © Jinah Kim.

If embodied externalization is essential to a tantric vision practice, one's internal vision would be the only aspect of the ritual that remained completely invisible throughout the process. The inherent mechanism of synchronized externalization in tantric vision practices suggests yet another way to approach the art of Indic Esoteric Buddhism, that is, as external substantiations of vision practices. An image of Siṁhānada does not necessarily serve as an aid for visualization but rather as an outward confirmation and objectification of the internal transformation, which allows communication of what is pursued and experienced internally. Consider a stone image of Siṁhānada now in the Patna Museum (figure 3.5). Whether a practitioner commissioned this image to use during his practice is moot. It would have been clear to an intimate circle of people, whether disciples or lay patrons, if they were present during a ritual in the proximity of such an image, that the magnificent Siṁhānada seen in the sculpture was called on during the ritual. In this regard, images are also essential tools for education and initiation, especially in the training of a disciple in an initiate lineage. Such images of internal visions were advantageous for transmission of tantric ritual knowledge that depended on visual information, in other words, for esoteric visual literacy. Just as a clearly delineated stone image of Siṁhanāda helps us see what a practitioner of the Siṁhanāda sādhana in medieval South Asia may have seen, so too did these images assist those who made and used them. They were meaningful not just as visual memorials of an event; they could also help train a practitioner to see things in specific ways. For example, trembling tathāgatas ("*sphurat-tathāgata*") were to be visualized as if they were popping out of the bodhisattva, engulfed in flame, and in active flying postures. Thus, in the Patna Museum sculpture, the five tathāgatas spring outward from the main deity with their legs bent in active movements instead of seated in meditation posture.

PAINTED VISIONS: ON WALLS, ON CLOTH, AND IN BOOKS

In the stone sculpture of Patna Siṁhānada, it is impossible to see colors that the vision text indicates. As we will see in chapter 5, color is central to Esoteric Buddhist vision practices. Monks and siddhas did not see their visionary world in black and white. It is difficult to say whether carved stone images were painted or not, but certain late eleventh- and twelfth-century sculptures, like the Siṁhānada image, are polished to the point of having an exceptional shine, rendering the surface nearly reflective. Seeing the white color of the bodhisattva's body or the red color of the lotus that the white lion sits on is not impossible on a reflective stone surface lit by numerous burning candles. A stone sculpture would leave the color within the realm of subjective experience. This is where painting as a medium had an advantage. Even a miniature painting like the panel of Siṁhānada conveys detailed information on specific colors in the image. When a sādhana (SM 52 Vādirāṭ sādhanam) describes a vision of bodhisattva Mañjuśrī in the form of Mañjughoṣa as "golden white or bright gold" (*kanaka-gaura*), the value of the color "*kanaka-gaura*" is difficult to determine. A twelfth-century painted panel in a manuscript prepared in Nālandā helps us see how this color was seen and experienced by those who made and used the manuscript (figure 3.6): the manuscript-making crew of scribes/painters (with a possibility of these two categories overlapping), craftsmen, and monastic supervisors, a lay patron, and possibly some monks who had a chance to see the manuscript.

In the SM 52, the image described for a practitioner to see following usual preliminary rituals reads like a description of figure 3.6:[39]

> Again, see (*paśyet*) the letter *A* in the heart. Then, developing (from the letter *A*) a moon orb (*candra maṇḍala*), in the middle of this, the letter *muḥ* is formed. Transforming from this, see oneself in the form of Mañjughoṣa, riding a lion, filled with golden-white color (*kanaka-gaura varṇaṃ*) bedecked with all sorts of ornaments, steadily displaying the *vyākhyā mudrā* (gesture of discourse), on the left side, holding an *utpala* (blue lotus), donned in Akṣobhya crown.* [The text in the SM has *akṣobhyamakuṭinam*, but this must be a misspelling of *akṣobhyamukuṭinam*]. See (*paśyet*) Sudhanakumāra on his right and Yamāntaka on the left. When exhausted from the vision practice [*bhāvanāyāḥ*—holding this image in mind], mutter the mantra, *oṃ vāgīśvara muḥ*.—SM 52, p. 109

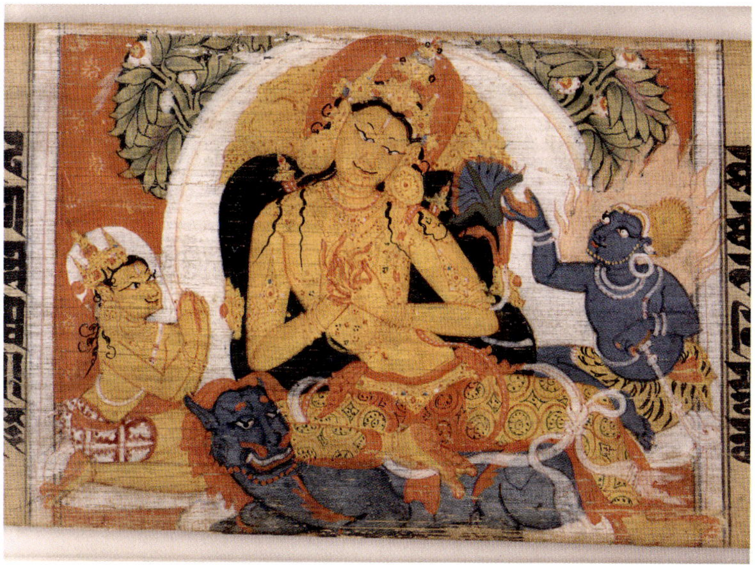

FIGURE 3.6
Mañjuśrī, folio 2r, *Perfection of Wisdom* manuscript, Gopāla IV's eighth year (ca. 1151), Nālandā monastery. Asia Society, New York, 1987.1. Photo credit: Asia Society/Art Resource, New York.

The painting certainly provides more detailed visual information than that offered by a sculpted image, and it goes beyond a single text. This short sādhana does not specify the colors of the attendants Sudhanakumāra and Yamāntaka, but the artist painted them in specific colors, Sudhanakumāra in golden yellow like Mañjuśrī, and Yamāntaka in blue. The flame around Yamāntaka demonstrates the artist's awareness of the iconography of the "Phase Two" Yamāntaka, a fierce, multiheaded, multilimbed, buffalo riding form, surrounded by flames. Instead of deep vermilion like the flame of Siṁhānada in figure 3.4, the flame of Yamāntaka in figure 3.6 is a lighter peachy color, as if signaling his subordinate status (Phase 1) to Mañjuśrī.

Painting presents an important asset for recording and collecting tantric vision practices. Of the four types of painting surveyed according to medium in chapter 1—murals, painting on cloth, painting on wooden panels, and painting on manuscript folios—the first two types, murals and painting on cloth, were extensively used to record and collect the visions of tantric practices in the Buddhist circles across the Himalayas, especially during the period between 1000 and 1500 CE. Colorful maṇḍalas, a beacon of Vajrayana or Esoteric Buddhism, fill the walls of Buddhist temple complexes across the Himalayas, from monasteries at Alchi and Tabo (now in India) to Shalu, Shakya, and Gyantse (in today's Tibet Autonomous Region in China), to name but a few. Among the Buddhist temples with surviving painted layers from the eleventh through the thirteenth centuries, some have multiple maṇḍalas on their walls, although they rarely form a comprehensive group like the Vajrāvalī series. For example, the walls of the main temple (Dukhang, completed toward the end of the twelfth century) at Alchi (near Leh, Ladakh, India), are strewn with a number of maṇḍalas; these include the Vajradhātu maṇḍala, the Dharmadhātu-Vāgiśvara maṇḍala, the Durgati pariśodhana maṇḍala, and a maṇḍala of Prajñāpāramitā.[40] Each maṇḍala seems to be rooted in an important (yoga tantra) text, indicating the doctrinal background of the monastic community that commissioned it. While they do not necessarily form a coherent set, several maṇḍalas strategically placed in a single structure should also be understood as an attempt to compile these maṇḍalas according to a system that a master or the elite group of the monastic community deemed significant.

As the example opening this chapter suggests, by the early fifteenth century in Tibet—building on the herculean efforts to systematize and compile a group of unwieldy and variegated tantric ritual practices begun by Abhayākaragupta in India—a Shakya monastic master like Ngorchen adopted the Vajrāvalī cycle but arranged it into a modified sequence that remained popular in Tibet until the nineteenth century. Ngorchen may not have been the first to commission a full set of paintings of the Vajrāvalī cycle to express his authority over Indic tantric knowledge, and he was not alone in commissioning a set of maṇḍalas for his monastery. For example, earlier examples are known from Shalu where the renowned master, Buston (Bu ston Rin chen grub, 1290–1364, abbot of Shalu from 1320 to 1356) not only commissioned the construction of the "four Maṇḍala temples" but also participated in planning and executing a large number of maṇḍalas.[41] Ngorchen's project is unique because he pursued an efficient and systematic means to record and display the maṇḍalas. In particular, this is reflected not only in his choosing the VA as his system but also in his devising an economical method to present such a large number of maṇḍalas—putting four maṇḍalas into one painting. In Ngorchen's biography, we learn that the painted maṇḍalas of the VA were taken out for display only on specific occasions. If these maṇḍalas had been made individually as forty-four painted thangkas, it would have taken up much more space to store and much longer to install and take them down after their ritual use. The account of the seasonal use of thangkas at Ngor also supports that there was a keen awareness of how the materiality of painting on cloth was quite different from that of immovable murals: they were performative objects to be rolled up and stored, which could also be redisplayed in a new assembly to refresh associated practices.

While there is ample Himalayan evidence to establish the importance of painting for recording and collecting visions of tantric Buddhist deities, there is a dearth of evidence from the Indian plain. It is difficult to determine if monasteries like Nālandā and Vikramaśīla were filled with murals and painted hanging scrolls like their Himalayan counterparts. No "thangka"-like Buddhist painting on cloth survives from India. Moreover, as discussed in chapter 1, the earliest surviving examples of painting on cloth from the Indian subcontinent seem to date later than the thirteenth century, and these are known from Jain examples in today's Gujarat and Rajasthan where the climate is drier than the Gangetic plain. Faint traces of painting on stucco found inside a rectangular temple at Nālandā (Sarai Mound, excavated in 1975–76) certainly suggest that these archaeological sites that now appear monotonous in brick and earth colors may in their heyday have been quite colorful spaces.[42] We will delve into the role of color in tantric vision practices and its relationship to the historical development of Indic painting traditions during 1100–1500 CE in chapter 5. Here, we turn to how and why manuscripts were adapted as an important medium for painting, especially for recording and compiling tantric vision practices during a period when intense transregional transfers of tantric ritual knowledge occurred.

TRANSFORMATION: FROM TEXT TO IMAGE

Synchronized relationships between twelfth-century paintings of Siṁhānada and Mañjuśrī and their descriptions in the sādhanas are not unusual. It is, in fact, common to find such a close relationship between the sādhana text and a manuscript painting in surviving examples from twelfth- and thirteenth-century eastern India. This correspondence hardly seems to be a mere coincidence. The intimate text-image relationships that characterize tantric vision practices constitute one of the clues to consider the use of manuscripts as vessels for containing and compiling images. One of the distinct characteristics of the sādhana practice is a letter-based visualization method in which a letter morphs into a figurative image, relying on a letter's iconicity.[43] Thus, the letter *hrīḥ* transforms into an image of Siṁhanāda in the SM 22 Siṁhanāda sādhana, while the letter *mūh* transforms into an image of Mañjughoṣa in the SM 52 Mañjughoṣa sādhana. These sādhanas, in fact, relay the "nondiscursive character of visual experience" distinct from the theological and philosophical discourse underpinning the practice.[44] At the same time, these visionary experiences require insight into the complex religious system that only those who were initiated and trained in the proper teaching would have had access to.

The process described in the text, which involves a sequence of letters forming into images to build essential components of a picture, provides a sense of animation. For example, in SM 22, the base letter *A* transforms into a moon orb, then into *oṁ* (a red lotus), then into *aḥ* (a white lion), and then into *hrīḥ* (Siṁhanāda). In the process, letters are transformed into figurative elements in sequence to build the vision of Siṁhanāda. Visualizing this animated sequence may be achieved today using computer graphics and digital imaging technology. Metamorphosing from a letter to a figure can be put into an animated "gif" or "png" file and perpetually activated.[45] While completely anachronistic, such visualization techniques of the digital age can help us experience the animated sequence of the visualization of letters transforming into images that tantric vision practices were designed to stimulate in a practitioner's inner vision.

With such practices in mind, let us take a fresh look at the Siṁhanāda image. In figure 3.4, the painted image of Siṁhanāda on folio 164 in the *Perfection of Wisdom* manuscript comes quite close to stimulating such an animated metamorphosis from letters to an image at a purely visual level: a painted panel appears to float in the middle of a sea of letters. It is as if the letters form the material body or the building block sustaining the image. A manuscript folio provides the perfect medium for realizing this visual effect. The context of a manuscript page in which this painting is situated requires a progression from text to image, from reading to seeing, just as the sādhana ritual demands the transformation from a letter to an image. The transformation from text to images demanded by sādhana practices mandates that manuscripts be used as vehicles, first, to stimulate and structure, and second, no less important, to record and codify these visions. Given that the text is neither the Siṁhanāda sādhana nor does it repeat the necessary mantra identified in that sādhana, this interpretation may seem fanciful. After all, the immediate text on this page is the beginning of chapter 12 of the *Perfection of Wisdom* titled "*lokasaṁdarśana*" or "Showing the world" (the page begins with "*m-asmākammātuḥ*" [our mother] and ends with "*gopāyeyur-e*" [protect]), and the content can be summarized as the filial duties of sons for their mothers, including keeping her from harm and all sorts of pain. The content of the text and Siṁhanāda bear no direct discursive relationship. The recognition of the image's significance, and the active transformation from reading to seeing, are only achieved through the preexisting ritual knowledge of sādhana practices.

Without any manual or historical records suggesting the potential use of manuscripts for documenting visions ensuing from sādhana practices, reading this painted image of Siṁhanāda on a folio as somehow activating the potentially animated mental process may seem an ahistorical, twenty-first-century understanding of this sādhana practice based solely on the visual evidence. However, some circumstantial evidence warrants further exploration into the deep connection between tantric vision practices and painted manuscripts of Indic Buddhist circles.

MANUSCRIPTS AND INFORMATION TECHNOLOGY FOR ESOTERIC BUDDHISM ON THE MOVE

As we have seen in chapters 1 and 2, a manuscript's portability lends itself to the transportation and circulation of knowledge. The story of King Vikramāditya's painter in an eleventh-century text suggests the potential use of a book as a vessel for transporting visual knowledge. Paintings on walls were immovable; their content could be conveyed only in reports by those who saw them. Paintings on cloth can be mobile but the weight and the volume can be substantial especially in a compilation project like Ngor production of the Vajrāvalī series that could aid in the circulation of complex visual knowledge of sādhana practices. A manuscript, on the other hand, provides a compact package for carrying images in long-distance travel, especially if artistic competency for miniature paintings exists. The eleventh and the twelfth centuries—the period during which tantric ritual practices were compiled and their manuscripts were prepared in eastern Indian Buddhist circles—witnessed a sizeable increase in communication and movement of people between Indian Buddhist centers and Himalayan Buddhist communities.[46] A large number of surviving Sanskrit manuscripts from India in Tibetan and Nepalese monastic communities testifies that manuscripts were one of these artifacts that moved along with the travelers.

Books were important material agents for confirming authority and power of esoteric knowledge, especially as Esoteric Buddhism moved across Asia in several waves. In an early moment in the history of Esoteric Buddhism's movement across Asia, Amoghavajra, an Indian Esoteric Buddhist master, during his sea journey to Buddhist lands in Southeast Asia in 741, reportedly used a vajra in his right hand and a manuscript of the *Prajñāpāramitā* in his left hand to quell a torrential storm in the sea.[47] Paul Copp examines this story to discuss the use of the Mahāpratisarā dhāraṇī. As he points out, the story is modeled after another tale that emphasizes the power of the dhāraṇī's efficacy for sea-traveling merchants. Whether this account narrates a historically accurate event is not the point. In this account by the Chinese biographer Zhao Qian (fl. 766–75), a vajra and a book are powerful emblems of an Indian Esoteric Buddhist master on the move. A book in particular serves as the emblem of authority and esoteric knowledge that the traveling master embodies. That the particular book in the hand of an Esoteric Buddhist master is of the Prajñāpāramitā is also of great importance, as we will see below.

The choice of the "*kuṭila*" (hooked) script seen in surviving Indic Buddhist painted manuscripts, which most likely served a ceremonial purpose as "deluxe editions," is significant in the context of Esoteric Buddhism on the move (see figure 3.4). The so-called siddhaṃ letters are used for writing mantras in Esoteric Buddhism across Asia. As vehicles for carrying Sanskrit sounds, they are the most visible, external signs of authenticity, linking Esoteric Buddhist traditions elsewhere in Asia back to their Indic roots. The "siddhaṃ" characters used to write seed syllables of mantras in East Asian Esoteric Buddhist contexts share their ancestry with the script used in post-eleventh-century manuscript scribing. They both belong to a lineage of the "Siddhamātṛkā" script that began to develop in the late sixth century in the Gangetic plains. The principal characteristics of the Siddhamātṛkā script lie in the angularity of each letter. Two main formal characteristics of the Siddhamātṛkā are the wedge-like head marks ("nail-headed") and "a strong tendency toward calligraphic elaboration, especially in the treatment of the vowel diacritics and subscript consonants."[48] These features are also found in the scribal practice of fashioning letters flamboyantly in twelfth-century Buddhist manuscripts that are not only of monastic origin and patronage but also of lay patronage and possibly nonmonastic production.

Surviving manuscripts from leading Indian monastic centers, such as Nālandā and Vikramaśīla, suggest that calligraphic perfection was pursued in the production of painted manuscripts, and that Indian scribes developed a formal, ornamental script based on the siddhamātṛkā script used in *praśasti* inscriptions and royal edicts. The ornamental, "hooked (*kuṭila*)" script features a flat head and an angular hook on the bottom of the right-hand vertical line (*daṇḍa*, lit. stick) (see figure 3.4). This feature informs the development of Nepali "Rañjana" (Tibetan *lantsa*), which is an ornamental calligraphic script that was employed for writing the most auspicious texts in Sanskrit. The main formal difference between siddhaṃ letters used in East Asian Buddhist contexts and the script of post-eleventh-century Indian manuscripts is that the latter appears straighter and more standardized in size and shape than the former.[49] Another difference may be that in the manuscripts of the *Perfection of Wisdom*, the text is supposed to have been comprehensible while the mantras written in siddhaṃ letters were used for their phonetic and somatic value.[50]

The calligraphic script of the eastern Indian Buddhist manuscripts was in fact used to write mantras and hymns in Sanskrit on a mid-fifteenth-century Tibetan thangka of dancing

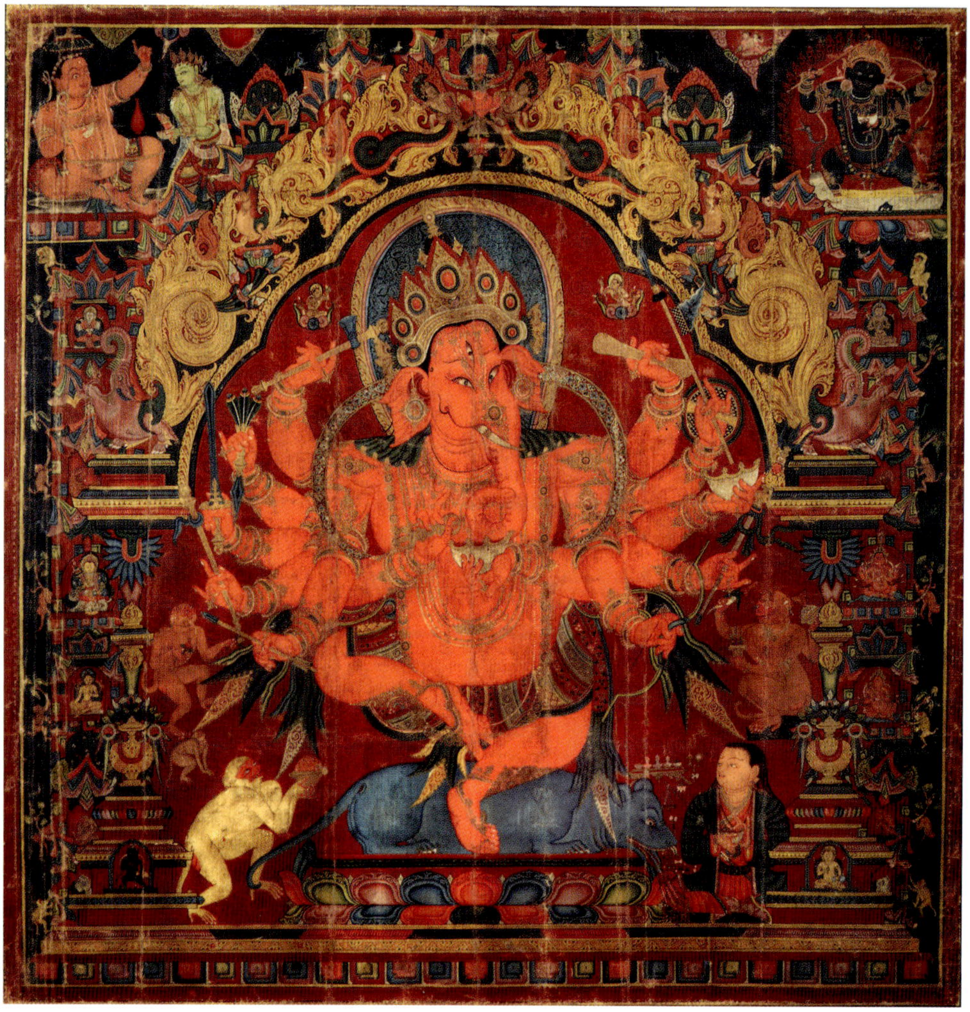

FIGURE 3.7
Dancing Gaṇapati, central Tibet, mid-fifteenth century, H: 68 cm. Private collection.

Gaṇapati (figure 3.7). Attending to the examples like the Gaṇapati thangka that showcase deep Indo-Tibetan connections can help us gain insight into hitherto less known religious and artistic practices of medieval South Asia. Doing so replaces the center-periphery diffusionist model with a globally interconnected network model that also addresses the lasting impact of Sanskrit cosmopolitanism, one of the underlying themes of the current study. The painting is believed to have been prepared for the successful foundation of Tashilhunpo Monastery (founded in 1447 by the first Dalai Lama, in Shigatse, Tibet Autonomous Region).[51] The central image depicts a fantastic twelve-armed form of dancing Gaṇapati, a Hindu god. Gaṇapati, known as the remover of obstacles in Hindu liturgical texts and devotional practices, is framed within a Buddhist context, pronounced by Virupa, one of the

Mahāsiddhas (great perfected beings) important in Tibetan Buddhist lineage systems on the top left corner, and the minor deities represented in the architectural vignettes of the impressive *toraṇa* structure that surrounds the mighty dancing god. A vajra and a skull cup in his primary hands signal Vajrayana Buddhist inflection on the iconography while the four-armed monkey holding a vulva and penis in his raised pair of hands beseeches the viewer to recall the esoteric context from which the iconography emerges.[52] In the historical context of the mid-fifteenth-century central Tibet, the choice of Gaṇapati did not necessarily impart a sectarian meaning, that is, Hindu, but rather a powerful, auspicious sign that directly referenced the Indic culture.

The writing appears on the reverse side of the thangka, carefully arranged to match and support the painted image on the front. The black letters that fill the entire surface are in Sanskrit and written in ornamental Rañjana script, while smaller interlinear writing in red is a Tibetan phonetic transliteration of Sanskrit written in Tibetan *umey* (cursive script). The letters *oṃ, āḥ, huṃ* are placed on the head, the neck, and the throat of each deity painted in the front, and they are written in red as if pictorializing the life force exuding from the three syllables substantiating the deity. The main body of the Sanskrit text appears similar to the sea of letters on a manuscript page. The text is not just a repetition of a Gaṇapati mantra. Rather, it starts with more general and powerful mantras beginning with *oṃ āḥ huṃ vajragurupadmasiddhi huṃ*.[53] Instead of merely listing mantras, the text attempts to simulate a manuscript text by inserting a conjunctive phrase like "*tadyathā*" (lit., namely, in such a manner that follows). In addition to the formal similarities to surviving Indic manuscripts, the Gaṇapati thangka demonstrate the extent to which Sanskritic knowledge—especially the language and its signs—was respected and revered in the Tibetan plateau well into the fifteenth century despite the decline of the Buddhist centers in the homeland.

That an image embodies the text through relational coordination between the letters of the text and the image is not a purely visual argument when considered alongside the notion of the tantric body as a sacred text and vice versa, most clearly articulated in the *Kālacakra tantra* (henceforth KC).[54] According to Vesna Wallace's analysis, the KC and its Vimalaprabha commentary suggest that "right insight into one's own body as a tantric text and its subject matter is a requisite for spiritual transformation." Moreover, this relationship between text and body is explained through the "taxonomic order of syllables." Here, tantras are identified in the body through "their respective classes of consonants, which are the letters of a mantra." The "thirty-six syllables of each consonantal class are declared to be the lords of the cakras in thirty-six tantras in the body, namely, in the ka-vajra-tantra, kha-vajra-tantra, and so on." Such a methodical approach to identifying Sanskrit letters and the transformed body is absent in the text of the *Prajñāpāramitā,* a considerably early Mahāyāna text. Yet, this conception of the letters as the body was known to medieval tantric practitioners of all leanings, as we have seen in the Jain mantra paṭas discussed in chapter 1. Buddhists seem to have embraced this concept in earnest, especially in the KC circles.

In this context, the inclusion of Kālacakra and his consort Viśvamātā in an early thirteenth-century manuscript of the *Perfection of Wisdom* from eastern India hardly seems

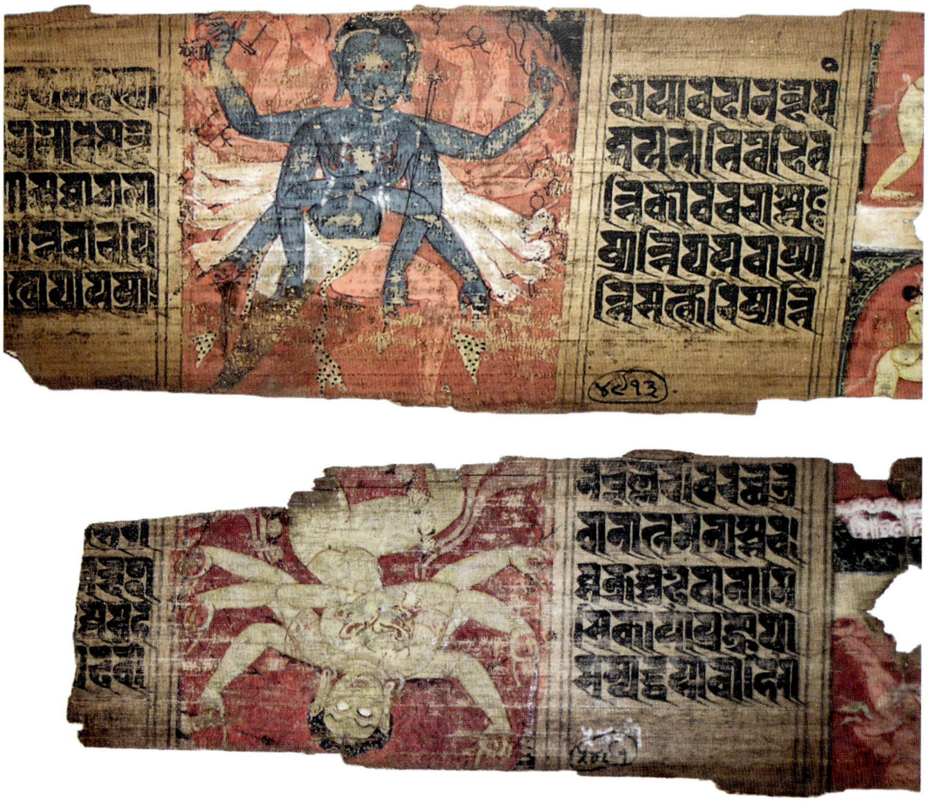

FIGURE 3.8
Kālacakra and Viśvamātā, last two folios, *Perfection of Wisdom* manuscript, Lakṣmaṇasena's forty-seventh year (ca. 1226 CE), Bharat Kala Bhavan, BHU, Varanasi.

coincidental (figure 3.8). The unnamed miniaturist painted each deity's fantastic, rarely seen form, successfully articulating unusual details like the tricolored body of Kālacakra (lit. the wheel of time) by dividing his spraying twenty-four arms into three equal parts, eight per each color, and by allocating blue, red, and white to his upper body, left leg, and right leg, respectively. Despite the damage, the eight-armed image of the yellow-goddess Viśvamātā against a fiery red backdrop with her wide-open eyes, knitted eyebrows, carefully delineated fingers, and fluid rendition of limbs, remains to be the most brilliant and individualistic depiction of the goddess surviving from the Indian subcontinent to date. How to visualize these powerful deities that had been relatively recent additions to the Esoteric visionary practices may in fact have been informed by the visions actualized in painting by the unnamed miniaturist.

Their presence in a *Perfection of Wisdom* manuscript announces the awareness of the teachings of the *Kālacakra tantra* among the group of people who made and used the manuscript—whether the donor Lakṣmīdhara or the maker Mahīdhara or both. Although this is a singular instance, it suggests how the KC and other tantras were understood at the time among the makers and users of painted manuscripts. Inclusion of deities of the mahāyoga tantras like the *Hevajra tantra* and the *Cakrasaṃvara tantra* in manuscripts of ostensibly Mahāyāna texts also suggest how these tantras may have informed the design and the production of painted manuscripts. In addition, it is noteworthy that a Nepalese manuscript of the Vimalaprabhā commentary on the *Kālacakra tantra* now in the Museo Nazionale d'Arte Orientale Giuseppe Tucci (Inv. 20863/30878) is the only ostensibly non-Mahāyāna text among the surviving Sanskrit manuscripts from the twelfth and thirteenth centuries that bears painted panels inside the manuscript. As Karen Weissenborn's analysis of the iconographic program shows, the painted panels are systematically placed to contain the Kālacakra maṇḍala's main framing cakras inside a manuscript along with painted covers (in a private collection).[55] The relationship between the text and the images in this manuscript works in two ways: images form a protective "cage (*pañjara*)" or "frame" of the text, and images collectively emerge as a seeable, outwardly manifestation of the powerful tantra text.

Just as texts of the *Prajñāpāramitā* prevailed as the text of choice for painted manuscript production in Indic Buddhist circles, so too the *Prajñāpāramitā* was important to Buddhist tantric practitioners and exegetists. The story of Amoghavajra suggests that as early as the eighth century, the *Prajñāpāramitā* assumed an important role as a symbol of authority and power within transculturally itinerant Esoteric Buddhism. The *Prajñāpāramitā* expounds the philosophical tenet underlying all groups of tantras.[56] In addition, one of the essential steps in the preliminary rituals for tantric vision practices recorded in the late eleventh and early twelfth century is to realize the insight into "emptiness (*śūnyatā*)": the practitioner should achieve this through a *śūnyatā* mantra, "*Oṃ śūnyatājñānavajrasvabhāvātmako 'ham* (I am identical with the essence of the diamond ["vajra"; nondual] knowledge of emptiness.)"[57] This propaedeutic step is prerequisite to the proper visualization of the deity, and it is included in sādhanas whether the most rudimentary or the most complex. The pervasive appearance of this procedure explains the doctrinal importance of the *Prajñāpāramitā* for Buddhist tantric vision practices of all stripes, as the *Prajñāpāramitā* is the foundational text in which the concept of *śūnyatā* is central. Some twelfth- and thirteenth-century manuscripts of the *Prajñāpāramitā*, like the Rajshahi *Perfection of Wisdom* manuscript examined in the next chapter, feature an array of tantric deities. The text of the *Prajñāpāramitā* was chosen as a vehicle to create a visual compendium of tantric vision practices.

THE VAJRĀVALĪ AND THE ART OF THE BOOK

As a compilation of detailed Buddhist tantric ritual manuals, the VA of Abhayākaragupta supports the hypothesis that the manuscript format was adopted to contain and circulate visions of tantric deities in specific compilations. Scholarship on the VA has been growing steadily; in particular, sustained studies by Masahide Mori during the past two decades have strengthened our understanding of the VA's textual, ritual, and Buddhological significance.[58] Its art-historical implications and merits, however, have remained unexplored. This text holds many important clues to understanding artistic practices in late Indic Buddhist contexts.[59] First of all, as Mori points out, the VA's technical terminology, especially for the construction of maṇḍalas, are adopted from *vastu-śāstra* literature; moreover, as a practical manual, it shares some salient features with the *śāstra* literature.[60] Abhayākara even instructs how artists and scribes need to be compensated to their satisfaction.[61] Second, the VA is sensitive to the materiality of objects used for empowerment rituals, especially of painting. The sections concerning the installation (*pratiṣṭhā*) ceremony include instructions for the offering of liquid substances, such as milk, perfumed water, and oil, or the splashing of water in various occasions.[62] Whereas anointing sculptures and ritual vessels in stone or metal may be performed without any difficulty, painted surfaces are not to be anointed with liquid directly. Instead, this particular step of the ritual involving liquid is to be performed through substitution, through the mediation of a mirrored image. For example, when five kinds of nectar and milk substances are to be applied to objects for consecration, the text makes a provision regarding "paintings on cloth (*paṭa*), manuscripts (*pustakam*), painted statues made from clay, etc. (*paṭapustakamṛnmayādicitritapratimādikaṃ*)": the liquid substances should be offered on their reflections in mirrors.[63] That Abhayākaragupta provided such measures to prevent damage to the surface suggests that he was pragmatic and concerned about potential physical damage to painted objects.

For our purposes, it is important to note that for tantric ritual practitioners served by Abhayākaragupta's VA, manuscripts performed an essential ritual purpose. His instructions for the installation ceremony habitually make a reference to a *pustaka* as an object to be installed along with statues (*pratima*), buildings (*vihara*), and garlands/rosaries (*mālās*). Regardless of the object, the procedure and the method for performing preliminary rituals and the main installation ceremony are nearly identical, whether the object in question is a building, a statue, or a book. Other than the practical consideration for water use, for which mirrored image substitution is suggested, the only difference lies in the type of the pledge-being (*samaya-sattva*, "symbolic-being") invoked for each class of objects.[64] For example, in the preparatory ritual for preparing a book (*pustaka*) according to the VA, "the guru transforms the figure of the scribe (*lekhaka*) into Amitābha. Then he envisages Vākvajra (an epithet of Amitābha) consecrating the material (palm leaves, pen, ink, and such) for the book by reciting the mantras of Amitābha. He further makes them firm by means of the 100 syllable mantra."[65] Further, as Mori summarizes, in the visualization stage for an installation ceremony according to the VA, "the deities visualized as the pledge-being are Amitābha for sacred texts [*pustaka*] and Vairocana for buildings [*vihāra*], and their symbols, a red lotus [for Amitābha] or an eight-spoked wheel [for Vairocana], which is visualized as manifesting its form within either the sacred text or the building."[66]

AMITĀBHA AND THE *PERFECTION OF WISDOM* MANUSCRIPTS

The visualization process in which Amitābha is invoked for making manuscripts becomes particularly meaningful when we consider the surviving evidence. A number of illustrated manuscripts of the *Perfection of Wisdom* that bear Pāla regnal years (mostly from Bihar, India) feature Amitābha on the first page, a peculiar feature that remained an iconographic puzzle (figure 3.9). Of the thirty-five dated manuscripts from eastern India surveyed in my previous study, twenty-four manuscripts are the *Perfection of Wisdom;* among this set of twenty-four manuscripts, six have the Amitābha panel on the first page. To this list, we may also add two dated manuscripts, a fragmented manuscript bearing the date of Gopāla (IV)'s twelfth regnal year, folios of which are now in the Copenhagen Royal Library and in the Philadelphia Museum of Art (see fig. 0.2), and the manuscript formerly in the Sam Fogg collection, dated Govindapāla's elapsed thirty-second year (table 3.1). Most of these manuscripts date to the mid-twelfth to the early thirteenth century. At least three manuscripts bearing Govindapāla's elapsed regnal year (Manuscript Am_5, Manuscript Am_6, and Manuscript Am_7) have Amitābha as a central panel on the first page. One example, Manuscript Am_4, was prepared in Madanapāla's seventeenth year (c. 1160 CE); another, Manuscript Am_3, was prepared in Gopāla (IV)'s twelfth year (c. 1144 CE); Manuscript Am_2 was prepared in Rāmapāla's reign (thirty-sixth year, 1113 CE). Manuscript Am_1, the earliest surviving example, may be from Nālandā and dates to Mahīpāla's sixth year.

When the arrangement is three panels per folio, the red Amitābha occupies the central panel. The Amitābha panel on the first page of a *Perfection of Wisdom* manuscript, which opens with a text of the *Prajñāpāramitā Stuti,* a hymn in praise of Prajñāpāramitā, is paired with a panel of the goddess Prajñāpāramitā on the facing page, unmistakably displaying the gesture of preaching and holding two lotuses often with books on them (see figure 3.9).[67] The appearance of the goddess Prajñāpāramitā fits the textual context perfectly, since the text is of the *Perfection of Wisdom,* that is, the *Prajñāpāramitā* in eight thousand verses, but the appearance of Amitābha has remained a puzzle: Amitābha, as the transcendental *tathāgata* of the Western Paradise and the spiritual sire of Avalokiteśvara, does not have any direct relationship with Prajñāpāramitā, nor is Amitābha prominently mentioned in the text. In a configuration seen on the first folio of Manuscript Am_3, the arrangement of the two life scenes, Śākyamuni's birth and his victory over Māra (*Māravijaya*) on either side of the central panel of Amitābha seems rather out of order (figure 3.10). The unnamed artist carefully distinguished the Amitābha panel from the narrative panels. Amitābha assumes a singular appearance. He is framed by a shrine structure with a tri-lobed opening. He is represented sitting in cross-legged posture and facing forward. Except for his red color, the Amitābha in the central panel is very similar to the Śākyamuni on the right panel. The artist clearly labored to differentiate the two panels unambiguously by enhancing the narrativity of the scene of *Māravijaya* on the right panel. In fact, the scene of *Māravijaya* is the most elaborate narrative representation of the scene on any painted folio among the surviving eastern Indian manuscripts. It includes not only the earth goddess, who appears next to the Buddha's lowered right hand and is raising a water vessel, but also various creatures of Māra's army. These creatures appear amid swirly dark clouds and attack the Buddha from the viewer's left while paying homage to him from the viewer's right.[68]

Alternatively, the central position on this frontispiece place could be adorned very much in tune with the textual context. The surviving corpus of examples presents three possibilities: Preaching Buddha and Prajñāpāramitā (common in twelfth- to thirteenth-century

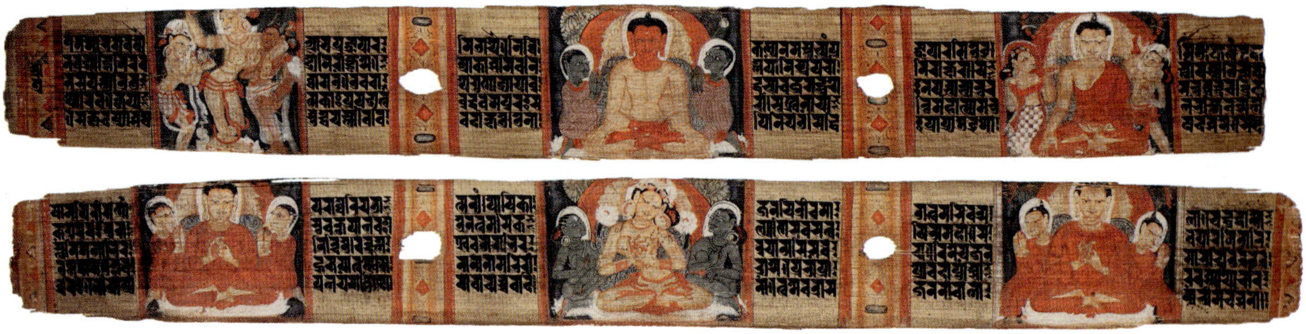

FIGURE 3.9
First two folios with Amitābha and Prajnāpāramitā in the center, folios 1v–2r, *Perfection of Wisdom* manuscript (Am_4), Madanapāla's seventeenth year (ca. 1160 CE), Detroit Institute of Arts 27.586. Photo courtesy of Detroit Institute of Arts.

TABLE 3.1 **DATED EASTERN INDIAN *PERFECTION OF WISDOM* MANUSCRIPTS WITH AMITĀBHA ON THE FIRST FOLIO**

No.	Depository	Text Title	Date	Note
Am_1	Asiatic Society Kolkata G4713	*Perfection of Wisdom*	Mahīpāla 6th year (c. late 10th or late 11th century)	
Am_2	Victoria & Albert Museum, IS4.1958-10.1958	*Perfection of Wisdom*	Rāmapāla 36th year, ca. 1113 CE	Amitābha (fol. 1v c) Avalokiteśvara (fol. 2r c)
Am_3	Philadelphia Museum of Art (1987-52-14) & Danish Royal Library, Copenhagen (Nepal 173)	*Perfection of Wisdom*	Gopāla (IV)'s 12th year (c. 1144 CE)	
Am_4	Detroit Institute of Arts 27.586	*Perfection of Wisdom*	Madanapāla 17th year, ca. 1160 CE	
Am_5	Asiatic Society, Mumbai BI-210	*Perfection of Wisdom*	Govindapāla 32nd year, ca. 1197 CE	
Am_6	Musée Guimet, Fournier Collection	*Perfection of Wisdom*	Govindapāla 32nd year, ca. 1197 CE	
Am_7	Formerly Sam Fogg Collection	*Perfection of Wisdom*	Govindapāla 32nd year, ca. 1197 CE	
Am_8	British Library (Or. 14282)	*Perfection of Wisdom*	Govindapāla's 32nd year? (most likely late 12th century)	
Am_9	Bharat Kala Bhavan (Benares Hindu University)	*Perfection of Wisdom*	Lakśmaṇasena 47th year, ca. 1226 CE	

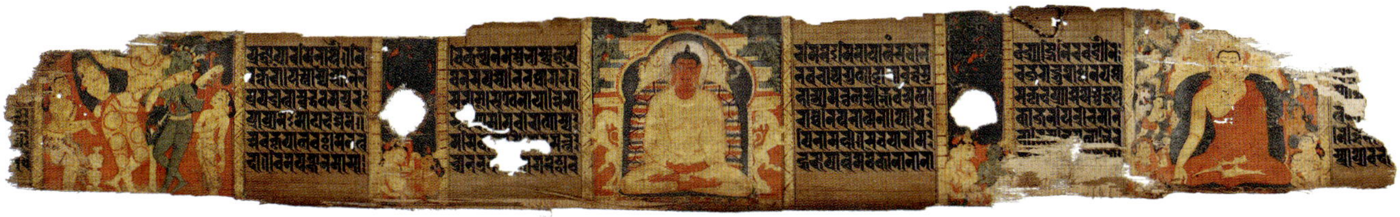

FIGURE 3.10
Folio 1v, *Perfection of Wisdom* manuscript (Am_3), Gopāla's twelfth year (ca. 1143 CE), The Royal Library, Copenhagen, Nepal 173. Photo © The Royal Library, Copenhagen.

Nepalese manuscripts); Prajñāpāramitā and Mañjuśrī (bodhisattva of wisdom); *Māravijaya* (Buddha in earth-touching gesture or Bodhgaya icon) and Prajñāpāramitā. All these options are straightforwardly related to the main text of the *Perfection of Wisdom*: (1) the Preaching Buddha and the goddess Prajñāpāramitā figuratively set the scene of the Buddha preaching the text, personified by the goddess; (2) Prajñāpāramitā and Mañjuśrī together make a fitting icon of the text: Mañjuśrī is the bodhisattva of wisdom and often holds a book of the *Prajñāpāramitā* on a blue lotus as an attribute (especially in a form described in the Vādirāṭmañjuśrī sādhanam, SM No. 51); and (3) The Buddha holding an earth-touching gesture signaling his Enlightenment paired with Prajñāpāramitā encapsulates an important message of the text: the relationship between the *Prajñāpāramitā* and enlightenment.

In the VA, Abhayākaragupta describes the process by which a manuscript is prepared for use in consecration within an installation ritual, during which Amitābha is invoked and visualized within the manuscript. Some painted manuscripts realize this instruction closely. Interestingly, at least as far as can be determined from extant examples, this feature was adopted only in the manuscripts of the *Perfection of Wisdom*, not in the *Karaṇḍavyūha* or the *Pañcarakṣā* corpus or the *Sadharmapuṇḍarīka* (Lotus sūtra), and only in those prepared somewhere in Magadha (today's Bihar) or Aṅga/Varendra (northern Bengal). Although the corpus is small, a trend can nonetheless be discerned. There are two monastic donations. Manuscript Am_1 was prepared in Nālandā.[69] Manuscript Am_4 was prepared for a nun in Ghośalīgrama (probably the area around Gosrawan, northeast of Nālandā.)[70] The two manuscripts prepared for monastics do not feature any tantric deities. In contrast, twelfth- and early thirteenth-century manuscripts prepared for lay patrons include deities of yoga tantra and "higher" tantras. In fact, among the latter group, Manuscript Am_2 (Rāmapāla's thirty-sixth reign) and Manuscript Am_3 (Gopāla's twelfth reign) show a similar attempt at distinguishing Amitābha's panel from the group of panels with which it appears. Just as in Manuscript Am_3, Amitābha's panel on the first folio of Manuscript Am_2 is differentiated from the five other panels of five bodhisattvas that surround it. Amitābha sits inside a shrine structure attended by two bodhisattvas. Because his image is smaller in size than that of the bodhisattvas in other panels, it appears recessed behind the visual plane. These two manuscripts do not have the deities of mahāyoga and yoginī tantras, such as Heruka-Nairātmyā and Cakrasaṃvara-Vajravārāhī. These powerful tantric deities appear prominently in three manuscripts bearing Govindapāla's lapsed regnal years (Am_5, Am_6, and Am_7), all of which were prepared for lay practitioners.

It is difficult to ascertain whether the insertion of the Amitābha panel at the beginning of the manuscript indicates its installation for tantric empowerment/consecration. The manuscripts were certainly powerful cultic objects, and at least one of them, as attested by the post colophon of the Detroit manuscript, was taken out for ritual use in later centuries.[71] In light of the VA, the prominent placement of Amitābha in *Perfection of Wisdom* manuscripts allows us to draw two important conclusions: first, the circle of tantric practitioners that Abhayākaragupta had as his audience must have overlapped with those who made and used painted *Perfection of Wisdom* manuscripts. We do not know if the instruction to invoke Amitābha in the installation ritual for a manuscript inspired manuscript-makers to include Amitābha in the design. It is also possible that Abhayākaragupta recorded what he saw as a common practice locally.[72] The second conclusion is that painted manuscripts of the *Perfection of Wisdom* served as important ritual objects for Abhayākaragupta's audience. Although the VA does not identify this "*pustaka*" as a specific text—Mori translates this term as "sacred text"—the surviving manuscripts suggest that in fact the particular *pustaka* used in Buddhist tantric ritual practices may well have been that of the *Perfection of Wisdom*. The VA's instruction and art-historical evidence support the *Perfection of Wisdom* manuscript's status as an important ritual object for sādhana practitioners.

4

A GARLAND OF VISIONS

MĀLĀ AS AN INDIC MODEL FOR PAINTED MANUSCRIPTS

In discussing a late twelfth-century manuscript of the *Perfection of Wisdom,* whose forty-eight surviving folios are dispersed among five collections, Eva Allinger identifies the painted folios of the second half of the manuscript (from chapter 17 onward) as forming the Akṣobhya maṇḍala from the Piṇḍīkrama, the second maṇḍala of the NsP (*Niṣpannayogāvalī*).[1] The manuscript is arranged in a manner similar to that found in a few other twelfth-century Prajñāpāramitā manuscripts prepared in eastern India: a single painted panel is placed in the center of each painted folio, and the end of each chapter and the beginning and the end of the manuscript are marked by two painted folios. By the twelfth century, Buddhist manuscripts were designed like a sacred religious architecture, as discussed in chapter 2, and some manuscript makers used the three-dimensional space of particular manuscripts to realize an innovative maṇḍalaic configuration inside them.[2]

A book-maṇḍala provides an appropriate model for thinking about the design principle behind a unique manuscript of the *Perfection of*

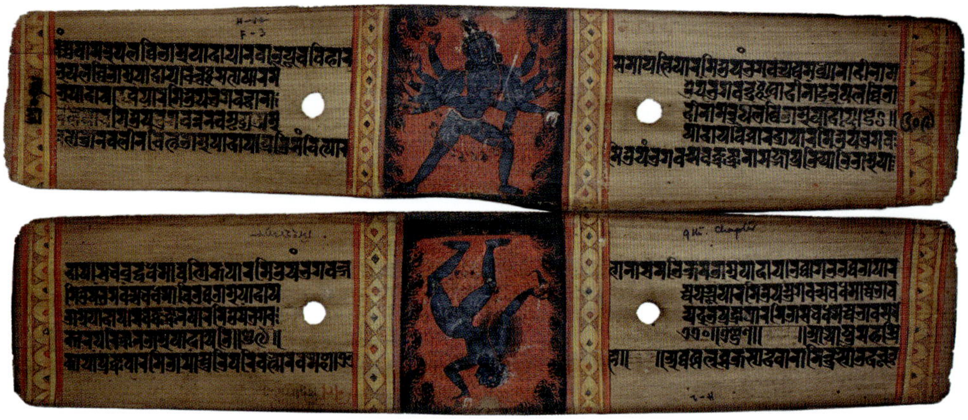

FIGURE 4.1
Folios 209v–210r, VRM manuscript, late twelfth–early thirteenth century. Bengal. Pigments and ink on palm leaf. Average folio size: 6.5 × 31.5 cm. Varendra Research Museum, University of Rajshahi, Bangladesh, Acc. No. 851. Photo © Jinah Kim.

Wisdom now in the Varendra Research Museum, Rajshahi (Acc. No. 851) (henceforth the VRM manuscript). The Rajshahi VRM manuscript, however, offers a different approach to designing from a maṇḍalaic model. It articulates the distinct sexual relationship between male and female deities through inverted images, an approach not found in the five-collection *Perfection of Wisdom* manuscript. From one set to the next, powerful deities of what may be classified in the Tibetan canon as the *anuttarayoga* tantras, punctuate the manuscript (figure 4.1). In this sense, the Rajshahi manuscript does not seem to form a maṇḍala. Various forms of Heruka and Saṃvara embracing their respective consorts appear in a certain sequence, and each couple can reign as lord over a maṇḍala (*maṇḍaleśvara*). The design principle behind the Rajshahi manuscript's structure seems to resemble that informing such compilations as the VA and the SM: that of a garland, a *mālā*.

The *Sādhana-mālā* (lit. sādhana-garland) collects one sādhana after another. Texts like the VA and the SM, in fact, compile tantric visions and are conceptualized as a garland or as an object that is strung together in a series. Such sets have seriality and a sense of completeness, but, unlike a maṇḍala, they lack a hierarchical structure with a center.[3] A garland may be easily expanded or shrunken to fit the wearer's physical size and its purpose. In the case of Vajrāvali of Abhayākara, the title may simply be translated as a "series/row [*āvali*] of Vajra." But a row of vajras, which may encircle the perimeter of a maṇḍala as seen in an eleventh-century Nepalese Cakrasaṃvara painting (Metropolitan Museum of Art 1995.233), is also like a garland in its appearance and structural logic. The Tibetan title of the VA, *rDor rje phreng ba,* indeed translates the title as the "Vajra-Garland," which is often the English title given to the VA.

No text explains that a manuscript may be designed like a *mālā.* Yet, as we will see in the Rajshahi manuscript, the logic behind arranging central deities of various maṇḍalas in a serialized order following chapter endings certainly accords with the principle that informs the compilation of maṇḍalas. The order of the maṇḍalas in the VA establishes a sense not of hierarchy but rather of seriality according to a sequence that varies in later Tibetan use of the series. As an object, a *pothi*-format manuscript resembles a mālā in material terms in that the manuscript folios were literally hung together on a cord through the holes. Moreover, in the VRM manuscript each painted panel appears as if suspended on the page, hanging from lines of text written without breaks. In light of the importance of manuscripts (*pustaka*), especially *Prajñāpāramitā* manuscripts, for tantric practitioners—a topic on which the VA's accounts of rituals offers explicit commentary—to characterize the VRM manuscript as a garland of tantric visions based on its physical and pictorial traits hardly seems conjectural. As a series of visions connected through line after line of the *Prajñāpāramitā,* the ultimate teaching of which is *śūnyatā,* evoked in almost every sādhana, the VRM manuscript resembles the Vajrāvalī series commissioned by Ngorchen from Newar artists in the early fifteenth century discussed in chapter 3. Compared to the set of fourteen thangkas, it is more compact and singular as an object, and the experience more intimate and personal. Each of the Ngor thangkas measures about 89 × 74 cm without their mounts, and they are meant to be displayed on walls.

The design logic of the Rajshahi manuscript, in which central deities of maṇḍalas appear in a serialized fashion, finds an interesting parallel in a much later Tibeto-Mongolian project that compiles the paintings of the three sādhana compilations (*Rin-byun, sNar-thaṅ-brgya-rtsa,* and *rDor-'phreṅ*) into a set of manuscripts. Of such a set the example now in the Völkerkundemuseum of the Universität Zürich, known and published as *Icons Worthwhile to See* (*Bris sku mthoṅ ba don ldan,* henceforth IWS), offers a representative example.[4] The last of the "three sādhana collections" included in this project is in fact, *rDor-'phreṅ,* the Tibetan title for the VA, and here, too, as in the VRM manuscript, only principal deities of maṇḍalas are compiled.

The context of the IWS clearly differs from that of the VRM manuscript; its aim is to compile images of the Tibetan pantheon. In the IWS, the male-female deities in sexual embrace are portrayed in a single panel. Moreover, each folio is divided into three panels with identifying inscriptions but no other visible texts (mantras of each deity are written behind each painting, and thus remain invisible). Although the genealogy of the development of iconographic compendia like the ISW is much more complex and varied than can be elaborated here, the distant connection with the VRM manuscript nonetheless is noteworthy. The VRM *Perfection of Wisdom* manuscript is perhaps one of the earliest extant examples to bear witness to an interest in compiling the tantric visions in color and stringing them together in a *pothi*-format manuscript that lends literal form to the metaphor of a garland of visions.

Recognizing a garland or *mālā* as a design principle behind a painted manuscript helps underscore the deep historical connection between Indic Buddhist circles and Himalayan Buddhist communities. It also assists in identifying a more historically meaningful context for the Indic Buddhist manuscript paintings (and the manuscript culture in general) in the history of Indian painting. The later paintings from the Punjab Hills, such as the famed Tantric Devī series from Basohli (dated ca. 1660–70 CE), are rarely discussed in relation to the Buddhist manuscript paintings of the twelfth century.[5]

No direct line of descent links the two manuscripts. The parallels, however, are instructive. Each folio of the Tantric Devī series bears a meditational text that describes the

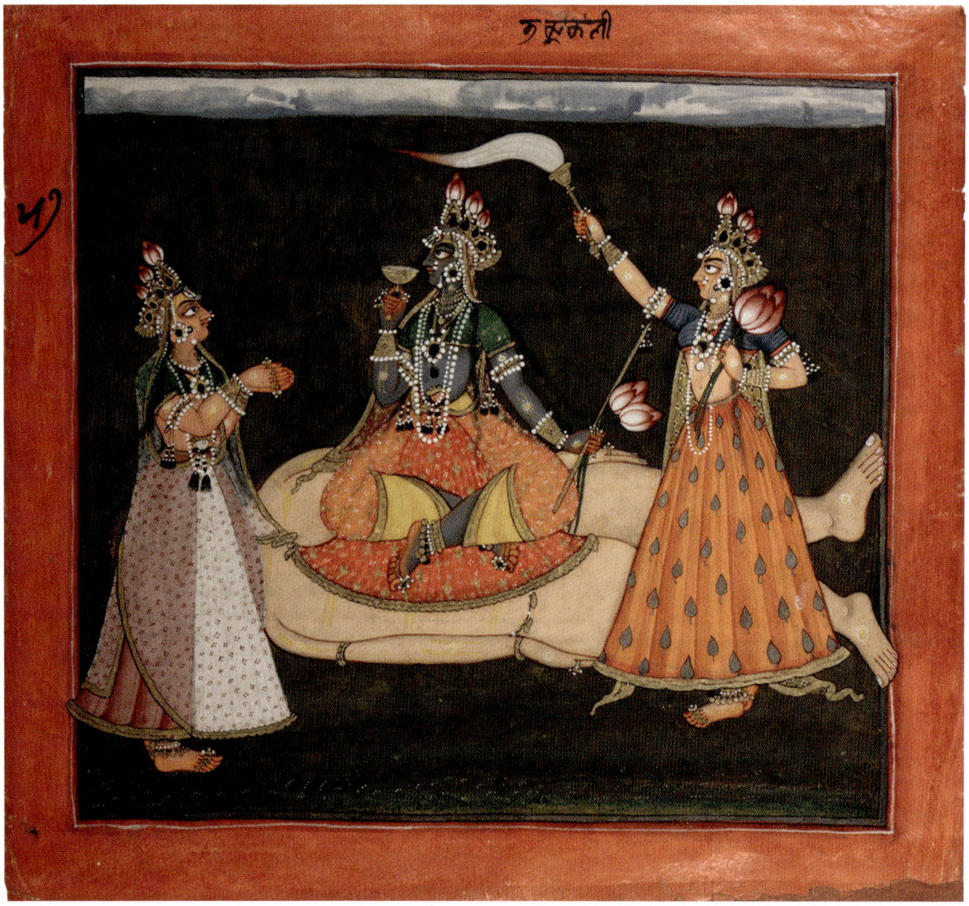

FIGURE 4.2
Bhadrakalī, "Tantric Devī series," folio 57, ca. 1660–70, Basohli, Punjab Hills. 22.5 × 20.6 cm. Philadelphia Museum of Art 2004-149-23. Photo courtesy of Philadelphia Museum of Art.

goddess depicted on the front page. The text on the back of the twenty-fourth figure reads: "In her hand a flute and two full-blown lotuses. She drinks wine seated upon a corpse with the crescent moon adorning her crown, accompanied by companions. In my heart, I meditate upon Bhadrakali with the seed mantra *bhaim*."[6] The vision of the goddess invoked in this text matches what the painting portrays in such details as the two lotuses and a crescent moon on the crown (figure 4.2). The tight relationship among the text, the image, and the ritual language used in the text—in particular, the practice of meditation and the use of a seed mantra—resonates with imagery that informs the twelfth-century painted manuscripts of the *Perfection of Wisdom*. The metatext on which the Tantric Devī series is based has yet to be identified, if—and this is perhaps the crucial point—such a text ever existed.

The insight provided by conceptualizing the VRM *Perfection of Wisdom* manuscript as a garland of visions can be further applied to the Tantric Devī series. It can also be viewed as a painted garland of visions of the great goddess that perhaps served as a structured set of prompts to a personal visionary experience.[7] This tradition did not just spring up in the Punjab Hills in the sixteenth century.[8] As discussed in chapter 2, it is important to remember the Himalayan network in considering the development of manuscript culture in the subcontinent and the close connection between the art of the book and that of "miniature" painting. In catalogs and surveys on Indian painting, it is uncanny to find so many later paintings presented as belonging to a "series"—for example, a "Bhagavata purana series," a "Rasamanjari series," or a "Ragamala series." As a concept, a "series" is used to indicate multiplicity and to suggest a group of pages in sequence. The idea of series may be redefined as a nod to the great Indic manuscript tradition that provided the structure of a mālā as a model for making painted manuscripts. This tradition was kept alive for centuries, well after the popularization of the codex format and album manuscripts through Mughal imperial interventions. Whether it is a *puṣpamālā,* a flower garland, which constitutes an important component of devotional offerings in Indic religious contexts, or an *akṣamālā,* a set of prayer beads, an important ritual implement used by all Indic religious communities, a *mālā* serves as an essential ritual tool and conceptual model for a variety of religious pursuits. Identifying the *mālā* as a distinctly Indic model for designing painted manuscripts provides an indigenous, emic perspective from which to view Indic manuscript traditions and the history of Indian painting.

Here let us turn to take a close look at the VRM manuscript, which demonstrates how a *pothi*-format manuscript could be adapted to record and compile tantric vision practices for the instruction and circulation of tantric visual knowledge tied to initiation. The following analysis attempts to highlight its innovative use of pictures within the medium of the painted palm-leaf manuscript as a means of circulating visual knowledge. The VRM manuscript demonstrates how the inherent seriality and spatial ordering of images accommodated by the *pothi* format promoted specific ways of seeing, prompting a challenging yet rewarding journey through an orchestrated story-scape marked by awe-inspiring images that must have shaped a practitioner's visual experience of transformation. The VRM manuscript's overall iconographic program is complex and packed with numerous unique examples of tantric iconography. This chapter focuses on several exemplary instances. The aim of the following analysis is twofold: to explain the overall iconographic structure to establish the manuscript as a medium for storage and transmission of tantric visual knowledge and to underscore the creativity and diversity of pictorial expressions seen in these paintings of tantric deities that would have powerfully conditioned the visionary experience of the initiated and the novice alike.

THE VRM MANUSCRIPT

The VRM manuscript was first discussed by Sachindra Nath Siddhanta in his descriptive catalog published in 1979.[9] Based on the postcolophon on the last folio, Siddhanta Babu suggested that the manuscript dates to the late thirteenth century, 1273 CE (N.S. 393).[10] Yet, as Gudrun Melzer and Tanaka Kimiaki have each pointed out, the colophon, which is a later addition not marking the completion of the project, clearly reads N.S. 696 (1576 CE).[11] Paleographically, the two last folios bearing the colophon are written in a hand different from that which wrote the

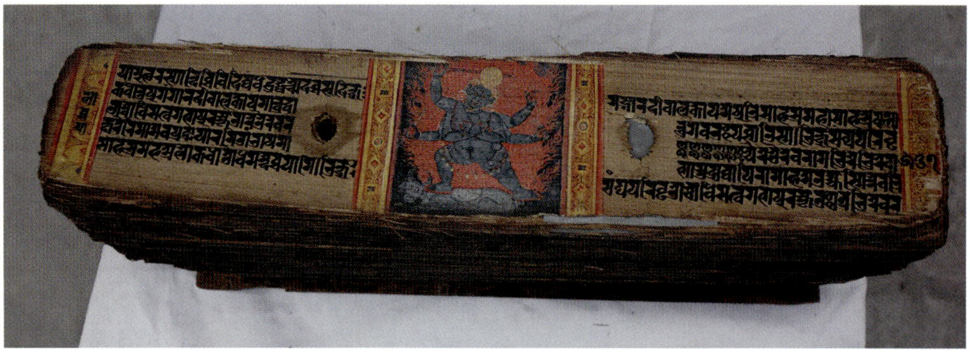

FIGURE 4.3
Perfection of Wisdom manuscript (VRM manuscript) (folio 527v, *on top*), late twelfth to early thirteenth century. Bengal. Pigments and ink on palm leaf. Average folio size: 6.5 × 31.5 cm, height of the stack (without the covers): 11.4 cm. Varendra Research Museum, University of Rajshahi, Bangladesh, Acc. No. 851. Photo © Jinah Kim.

main body of the text, which concludes on folio 530v. At the bottom of the same page the beginning of the *ye dharmahetu* verse (|| *yedharmahetuprabhavāhetunteṣānta*) also occurs. The beginning of the next surviving folio, however, opens with the indicative "*śreyo 'stu*" (Let it be auspicious!), which marks the opening of the postcolophon. In other words, what originally would have been folio 531 is missing; on its recto, it presumably bore an illustrated panel of the goddess of wealth, Vasudhārā, who often was paired with Jambhala, who appears on folio 530v. This missing folio most likely bore the original colophon of the manuscript. In his catalog, Siddhanta notes that when the manuscript entered the Varendra Research Museum, twelve painted folios were missing. Given the lacuna both in the colophon text and in the iconographic program—which lacks Vasudhārā—the manuscript must have lacked thirteen folios. Among these thirteen missing folios, ten are in the Indian Museum (AT.72/101/A-J); one additional folio is in the Jñāna-Pravāha Museum in Varanasi (folio 483).[12] Paleographic, stylistic, and iconographic characteristics suggest that the parent manuscript most likely was made in eastern India during the late twelfth or early thirteenth century. In terms of size and stylistic features, it comes close to the *Perfection of Wisdom* manuscript, dated to Govindapāla's thirty-second year (c. 1193 CE) in the Fournier Collection/Musée Guimet (MA5161).[13]

Measuring 31.6 × 6.3 cm, the manuscript is a *pothi*. The manuscript is shorter in width—by at least 20 cm—than many surviving eastern Indian manuscripts of the *Perfection of Wisdom*. This format is consistent with a few dated late twelfth-century manuscripts.[14] A shorter folio size required more folios to write the same text than those prepared on folios measuring 55 × 5 cm. It is clear that the VRM manuscript was a lavish production in terms of materials. The quality of palm leaves is high, being very supple, light, and sturdy.[15] Folios are evenly cut and neatly shaped. Each folio was spatially laid out: five lines per page with 1.5 cm margins on the left and the right sides as well as a nearly 2 cm margin on the top and the bottom, and two empty square boxes measuring 2 × 2 cm around the two string holes. The project used over 530 leaves to write the text, which is more than double the number usually needed for

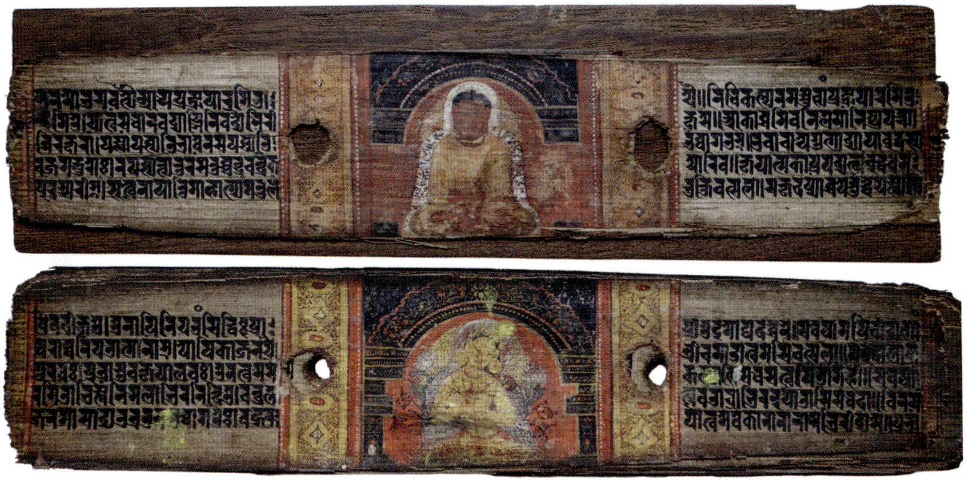

FIGURE 4.4
Folios 1v–2r, Amitābha-Prajnāpāramitā, VRM manuscript. Photo © Jinah Kim.

a painted *Perfection of Wisdom* manuscript from eastern India, which runs around 200–220 folios. Even without the missing folios, the manuscript in the VRM makes an extraordinarily tall and hefty stack of 11.4 cm (figure 4.3).[16] It is certainly not an object to be carried around and taken out when opportune moments arise like Amoghavajra's *Prajñāpāramitā* manuscript mentioned in chapter 3, nor would it be a book secretly carried around by a follower of the *Hevajra tantra*.[17] The shape, the size, and the weight of the manuscript make it look like a chest or a vessel that contains a precious substance.[18] In addition to the neatly written text of the *Perfection of Wisdom*, the manuscript indeed contains unseen treasures.

AMITĀBHA AND PRAJÑĀPĀRAMITĀ

Opening the manuscript to the first two folios reveals two painted panels. On the first, Amitābha sits at the center. Facing him is the goddess Prajñāpāramitā (figure 4.4). The first opening already signals that this manuscript represents an exceptionally deluxe edition. The painted panels occupy nearly half of each page; such a scale is rarely seen in the surviving painted Buddhist manuscripts from the period.[19] By way of comparison, in the previously mentioned Fournier manuscript, a central painted panel and four columns with two columns around the string holes and two much narrower columns on either end of each folio occupy only one-sixth of each page. Even when the painted columns are taken into account, the entire painted surface constitutes less than one-third of each page.

In the VRM manuscript, the text starts with the invocation to the goddess, "*Oṁ* salute to the Lady Excellence Prajñāpāramitā! (*oṁ namo bhagavatyai āryaprajñāpāramitāyai||*)," followed by the hymn to the goddess known as the *Prajñāpāramitā Stuti*, which appears in nearly all east Indian manuscripts of the *Perfection of Wisdom*. Amitābha sits inside a shrine structure, a placement found in some twelfth-century *Perfection of Wisdom* manuscripts.[20]

The goddess Prajñāpāramitā sits inside a shrine structure even more elaborate than that occupied by Amitābha, and her flowing scarves and the two full-blown lotuses to either side of her emphasize the grand presence of the goddess. Marking her centrality was clearly of prime importance to the makers of the manuscript. Demonstrating this emphasis is the larger size of her panel, of which the inner framed area measures 7.6 cm; in comparison, Amitābha's panel measures only 6.8 cm. Drops of yellow smudged on the Prajñāpāramitā panel provide further evidence that the goddess was central to the devotees who employed it. At least in this respect, the iconography presented by the first two folios follows an established model. As one flips through the folios, however, it becomes apparent that this manuscript truly represents a treasure trove of unusual imagery that sheds light on the relationship between tantric sādhanas and painterly practices.

ICONOGRAPHIC STRUCTURE

A detailed analysis of the overall iconographic structure of the manuscript can help recognize a distinct design principle at play in the VRM manuscript. The manuscript was originally designed to include sixty-two painted folios. Of these, sixty are known, the majority of which (forty-nine) are preserved in the collection of the Varendra Research Museum. As laid out in figure 4.5, with the exception of two chapters, two painted panels are placed at the end of each chapter; in addition, there are two painted panels at the beginning and the end of the manuscript. Other than the anomaly of the absence of painted panels at the end of chapters 19 and 22, which will be discussed further below, the overall structure has two painted panels marking the beginning and the end of each chapter. As a whole, such a structure occurs in only a few late twelfth-century manuscripts of the *Perfection of Wisdom,* most notably the undated manuscript in the British Library Or. 12460 and the dispersed *Perfection of Wisdom* manuscript of one "Dharmadatta" (the so-called five-collection *Perfection of Wisdom*). The iconographic program, however, differs, from the five-collection *Perfection of Wisdom*, in which Eva Allinger finds a realization of the Piṇḍīkrama Akṣobhya maṇḍala in the manuscript's latter portion.[21]

The next set of painted panels appears on folios 28v–29r, the point at which chapter 1 on the practice of the knowledge of every mode (*Sarvākārajñatācaryā*) ends. The panel on folio 28v represents a six-armed, white, seated male deity with three faces (*right* blue, *left* red); facing him on folio 29r is a female deity, also white, with six arms and three faces (figure 4.6). Their right hands hold, from the top, a red lotus (*padma*), a wheel (*cakra*), and a vajra; their left hands hold, a sword (*khaḍga*), a jewel (*cintāmaṇi*), and a bell (*ghaṇṭa*). The two principal hands are crossed in front of the deity's chest to indicate the embrace of the female deity who is identical in form. The iconographic attributes fit the description of Akṣobhya embracing a self-born female (*svābhasparśavajra*) in the second maṇḍala of the NsP, the Akṣobhya maṇḍala based on Nāgārjuna's *Piṇḍīkrama* (*Piṇḍīkramoktākṣobhyamaṇḍalam*). In terms of the organization of the arms and attributes, the image is strikingly similar to the seventeenth-century painting of Guhyasamāja Akṣobhyavajra now in the Rubin Museum (acc. no. C2001.1.3).[22] The only difference from both the textual description and the seventeenth-century painting is that the deities are white instead of blue. For example, in the NsP text

Folio		Painted Panel	Note
1v		Amitābha	
2r		Prajñāpāramitā	
28v		Guhyasamāja – Akṣobhyavajra (6 armed, 3 heads, white)	IM AT.72/101/J
29r		Prajñā of the male (6 armed, 3 heads, white)	[R] Chapter 1 ends
44v		Kalpadhāra-Hevajra (16 armed, 4 legged, 1 head, dark blue)	Chapter 2 ends
45r		Nairātmyā (2 armed, 1 head, dark blue)	[R] IM AT/72/101/B
90v		Kālacakra (?, 24 armed, 3 heads, blue-black, yellow, white)	(Chapter 3 ends on 90r) IM AT/72/101/C
91r		Viśvamātā (? ,10 armed, 1 head, dark blue)	
98v	*TN: Hevajra (Śastradhara-Hevajra)	A form of Samvara (?, 24 armed, 3 heads, blue-black, 8 legged)	
99r		Prajñā (? 24 armed, 3 heads, blue-black, 8 legged)	[R] chapter 4 ends
134v		A form of Samvara (?, 16 armed, 3 heads, 2 legs, blue black)	Chapter 5 ends
135r		Prajñā (?, 16 armed, 3 heads, 2 legs, blue-black)	[R]
173v		Prajñā (?, **11-armed,** 3 heads, 2 legs, dark blue	**[R]**
174r		A form of Samvara (12-armed, 3 heads, 2 legs)	Chapter 6 ends
188v		A form of Samvara (12-armed, 3 heads, 2 leg, feet together, knees bent feet together, dark blue)	
189r	TN: Naropa Ḍākinī	Ḍākinī or A form of Vajravārāhī, 2 armed, 1 head, leg position same as male, blue black)	Chapter 7 ends [R]
201v		A form of Samvara (12 armed, 3 heads, 2 leg- feet together legs bent, dark blue)	
202r	TN: Naropa Ḍākinī	Ḍākinī or A form of Vajravārāhī ?, 2 armed, 1 head, similar leg as male, light grey blue (aded)	[R] (Chapter 8 ends on folio 202v)
209v		A form of Samvara (12 armed, 3 faces, *ālīḍha* [right leg stretched, left leg bent] , dark blue)	
210r		Ḍākinī or a form of Vajravārāhī, 2 armed, 1 head, *pratyālīḍha*, dark blue)	[R] Chapter 9 ends
233v		A form of Samvara (12 armed, 3 faces, *ardhaparyaṅkāsana* or dancing, dark blue)	
234r		Prajñā of male (12 armed, 3 faces, the same leg position as male, darker blue)	[R] Chapter 10 ends
255v		8-armed Avalokiteśvara (white, lotus, *kuṇḍi*, rosary)	Chapter 11 ends
256r		Maitreya (yellow, stūpa on the headdress, *nāgapuṣpa* with *kuṇḍi*)	
280v		Māyājala-samvara (12 armed, 1 face, 1 leg, blue black)	
281r		Prajñā (Rūminī bhagavatī, 12 armed- 1 face, 1 leg, blue black)	[R] Chapter 12 ends.
288v		A form of Samvara (12 armed, 3 faces, *ālīḍha*, dark blue)	Chapter 13 ends
289r		Prajñā (12 armed, 3 faces, *pratyālīḍha*)	[R]
296v		Guhyasamāja-Amitābha (8-armed, 3 faced, seated, Red)	IM AT/72/101/F
297r		Prajñā of male (8 armed, 3 faced, seated, Red)	[R] Chapter 14 ends on folio 297v
310v		Missing	
311r		Prajñā of male (? 10 armed, 4 legged, multi-colored, white, blue, red, but faded)	[R]Chapter 15 ends
326v		Vajrabhairava? (36 Armed, 16 L, single buffalo head), dark blue	Chapter 16 ends
327r		Vajravetālī? (16 armed, 4 legged, yellow)	IM AT/72/101/A [R]
345v		Samvara (?, 8 armed, 2 or 3 head, *pratyālīḍha*, blue black)	
346r		Prajñā of male (8-armed, *ālīḍha*, blue black, cross eyed)	[R] Chapter 17 ends
356v		Heruka (?, 4 armed, dancing, blue black, yellow rising hair)	IM AT/72/101/H
357r		Nairātmyā (or Kurukullā?, 4 armed, red, *ālīḍha*)	[R] Chapter 18 ends
371v		Text only	
372r		Text only	Chapter 19 ends
388v		Heruka (4 armed, *kapāla, khaṭvaṅga, vajra, ghaṇṭa pratyālīḍha*, blue black, yellow rising hair)	Chapter 20 ends
389r		Nairātmya (? 4 armed, Prajñā of male, blue black, *ālīḍha*)	[R]
400v		Heruka (4 armed, Vajra, *ghaṇṭa khaṭvaṅga, ḍamaru*, dark blue, dancing,	(chapter 21 ends 400r)
401r		Vajrayoginī (2 armed, naked, long hair, drinking blood, feet together, knees bent, red)	[R]
412v		Text only	
413r		Text only	Chapter 22 ends
418v		Hevajra (10 armed, 3 heads, blue, *ālīḍha*)	Chapter 23 ends
419r		Nairātmyā (?, 8 armed, *pratyālīḍha*, blue)	[R]
425v		Hevajra (? 8 armed- Raised hands above, dancing male, light blue grey- discolored)	Chapter 24 ends
426r		Nairātmyā (? Prajna of the male, 8 armed, dancing, blue)	[R]
435v		Red Male, Samvara? (10 armed, 2 legged, *ālīḍha*)	
436r		Red female, (6 armed, *pratyālīḍha*, red - discolored)	Chapter 25 ends. [R]
445v		Blue Male , a form of Samvara? (10 armed, lighter blue, *ālīḍha*)	Chapter 26 ends
446r		Red Female (4 armed, prajñā of the male?, red, *pratyālīḍha*)	[R]
458v		White Samabra? (12 armed, *ālīḍha*)	IM AT/72/101/E *Chapter 27 ends on the recto?
459r		White yogini (2-armed, white)	[R]
477v		Samvara (? 6 armed, bright blue, completely cross eye, holds a severed head on the raised right hand, noticeably more elaborate white ornaments, blue)	Chapter 28 ends
478r		Prajna of the male (6 armed, *pratyālīḍha*)	[R] IM AT/72/101/G
482v		Guhyasamaja Vajrasattva? (8 armed, white male, seated in *paryaṅka*)	IM AT 72/101/I
483r		Prajna of the male (8 armed, seated in *paryaṅka*)	[R] Jñānapravaha, Varanasi Chapter 29 ends
512v		Yellow Samvara (?, 10 armed, male, feet together, knees bent)	IM AT 72/101/D
513r		Prajñā of Samvara (10 armed female, same leg position, the color here is much lighter than the one in the IM)	[R] chapter 30 ends
527v		Yamāri (6 armed, blue, riding a buffalo)	Chapter 31 ends on fol.527r
528r		Prajñā of Yamāri, (6 armed, blue, riding on buffalo)	[R]
530v		Jambhala	Ch. 32 ends text ends
531r		(Vasudhārā)	Missing

*TN: variant readings by Kimiaki Tanaka (2017). [R] indicates the painted panel's placement in reverse direction to the text.

FIGURE 4.5
Iconographic structure of the *Perfection of Wisdom* manuscript (VRM manuscript). Image © Jinah Kim.

Akṣobhya is supposed to be "*kṛṣṇa*," which may be blue-black.[23] It may be that Guhyasamāja Vairocana in the same text (NsP 2) is described as the white body color as in this painting, but the painting depicts the deity with Akṣobhya's attributes not those of Vairocana.[24] The red lotus held in the upper right hand fits the "*padma*" held by Akṣobhya rather than "*puṇḍarīka*," a white lotus, one of Vairocana's attributes.[25] In addition, Vairocana of the

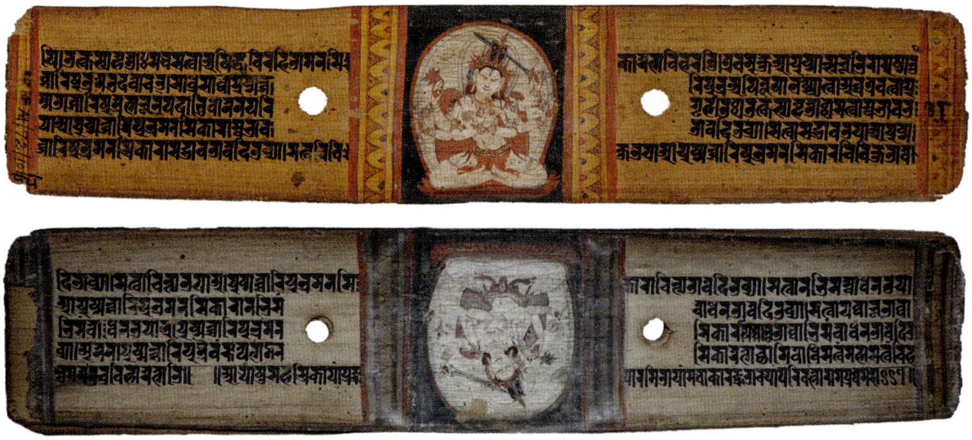

FIGURE 4.6
Folios 28v–29r, VRM manuscript. Top: Indian Museum AT. 7. 2/101J. Photo courtesy of Indian Museum. Kolkata. Bottom: Varendra Research Museum, University of Rajshahi (VRM) Acc. No. 851. Photo © Jinah Kim.

NsP 2 does not embrace his consort of his own form, whereas Akṣobhya of the same maṇḍala does. The female deity, the consort of Guhyasamāja Akṣobhya in folio 29r, is placed upside down vis-à-vis the text.[26] This unconventional arrangement of the text and the images demands an experiential and performative approach that considers how a reader, which, more adequately speaking, should be a Buddhist practitioner, either a ritual master (monastic or nonmonastic) or a lay initiate, would have used and interacted with the manuscript. When open for use, each folio in a *pothi* manuscript is flipped horizontally and the flipped folio joins the stack of already viewed folios. The format would performatively bring the two deities into a physical embrace, head to head and knees to knees, when the folio is flipped, a position in which they would remain when the manuscript is closed.

The presence of these two deities marking the first chapter signals that the reader enters a space dictated by the deities of mahāyoga and yoginī tantras, or what the thirteenth-century Tibetan scholar Buston categorized as texts of the Anuttarayoga tantra class. An image of the male deity and the female partner (characterized as "*prajñā*") in sexual embrace epitomizes the radically transgressive outlook of these texts and their associated ritual practices. All deities appearing after this Guhyasamāja Akṣobhya couple at the end of the first chapter are tantric deity couples depicted in sexual embraces, with the female deities consistently placed upside down vis-à-vis the text, except for the pairings at the center (the end of chapter 11: folios 255v–256r) and at the end of the manuscript (the end of chapter 32: folios 530v–531r).

THE ADVANTAGE OF A MANUSCRIPT FOR CONTAINING COUPLED DEITIES

Realizing the physical embrace between the male and the female deities within the space of a manuscript represents a particularly innovative use of a book in the *pothi*-format. Its exploitation permits the detailed articulation of each deity to be presented in a way that painted images on other surfaces cannot achieve.[27] In short, the format is media specific in the manner in which it takes advantage of its specific form of materiality. The image of the sixteen-armed Heruka (NsP8) on folio 44v (see figure 4.8), which marks the end of chapter 2, faces his female partner, Nairātmā, on folio 45r (see figure 4.9), placed upside down versus the text, ensuring that they remain interlocked in intercourse when the folio is flipped or when the book is closed, that is, most of the time. When open to these two folios, the manuscript presents each deity clearly. In comparison, most painted or even sculpted images of tantric deities in sexual embrace do not allow one to see each deity's body in detail. In a sixteenth-century Tibetan painting of the Hevajra maṇḍala in the Rubin Museum, the interlocked forms of the sixteen-armed and four-legged Hevajra combined with the two-armed Nairātmā do not offer a distinct view of each deity.[28] In such a painting, Nairātmā can only be seen from behind. It is nearly impossible to see the female deity apart from the main male deity, as her body is fused with his. Even when, as in an early twelfth-century Nepalese scroll painting of Cakrasaṃvara maṇḍala, an attempt is made to distinguish the two deities, each deity's bodily form remains indistinct (figure 4.7). Only abstract attributes, such as the number of limbs, heads, and eyes, body color, and the objects held in their hands permit one to see them as Cakrasaṃvara and Vajravārāhī in sexual embrace as described in the seven-syllable Cakrasaṃvara sādhana (*saptākṣara-sādhana*).[29]

The principal advantage of a manuscript format that permits a single painted panel to be devoted to each deity is that each one's form can be appreciated as in the same manner laid out according to the process of visualization described in sādhana texts, moving from one deity to the next in sequence. The image of the sixteen-armed, four-legged Heruka (figure 4.8) closely matches the description in the nine-deity Heruka fourfold maṇḍala (*navātmakaherukacatuṣṭayamaṇḍalam*) in the NsP, and this description appears at the beginning of the text immediately after the description of the maṇḍala's architectural structure.[30] The text first describes the form of Heruka fully, describing his eyebrows as stretched and knitted; next, it moves on to his "prajñā" by the name of Nairātmā (figure 4.9), whose two-armed form is then described in detail. Seeing these two deities in the VRM manuscript in sequence mirrors the process outlined in the NsP text, which describes these two deities to be seen with the mind's eye. The NsP is also authored by Abhayākaragupta as a companion treaty to the VA, and its aim is to help practitioners visualize maṇḍalas in concrete forms during the rituals.

According to the text, Nairātmā's form is "dark blue (*kṛṣṇa*), which is no less naked than that of her lord. Holding a dagger (*kartri*) and a skull cup, in her left arm she embraces the lord (Heruka*, who also appears with a Katvaṅga), and dances in the *pratyālīḍha* posture (right leg bent, and left leg lifted). She is one-faced with three bloodshot, bulging eyes, a gaping mouth with fangs (large teeth), tawny hair rising upward in a blaze, and a sunken forehead. She is ornamented with a five-head garland hanging from her neck and a dried-up human-head garland reaching her ankle, and so on."[31] This frightening form is what is presented to the reader on folio 45r. In other words, the manuscript's pages allow the paired

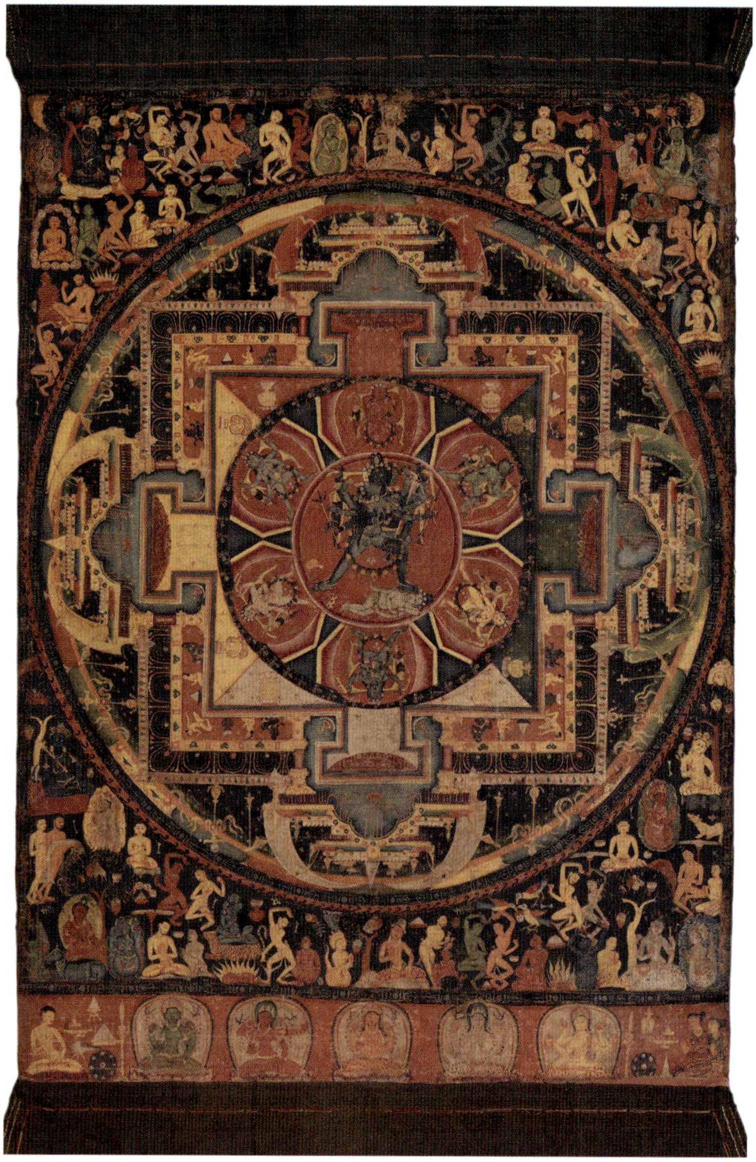

FIGURE 4.7
Cakrasamvara with Vajrayoginī and six yoginīs. Detail of Cakrasamvara maṇḍala, Nepal, ca. 1100. Metropolitan Museum of Art. Acc. No. 1995.233.

images to be presented as they ought to be conjured up in a practitioner's mind before they are imagined coupling in a sexual embrace.

The bewildering inverted placement of the female deities vis-à-vis the text puzzled earlier scholars to the extent that it was characterized as an illiterate artist's mistake.[32] This conclusion, however, underestimates both the sophistication and independence of the manuscript's pictorial program. Not content with effectively signifying the concept of sexual union, the unconventional layout realizes such union in a performative action in which the

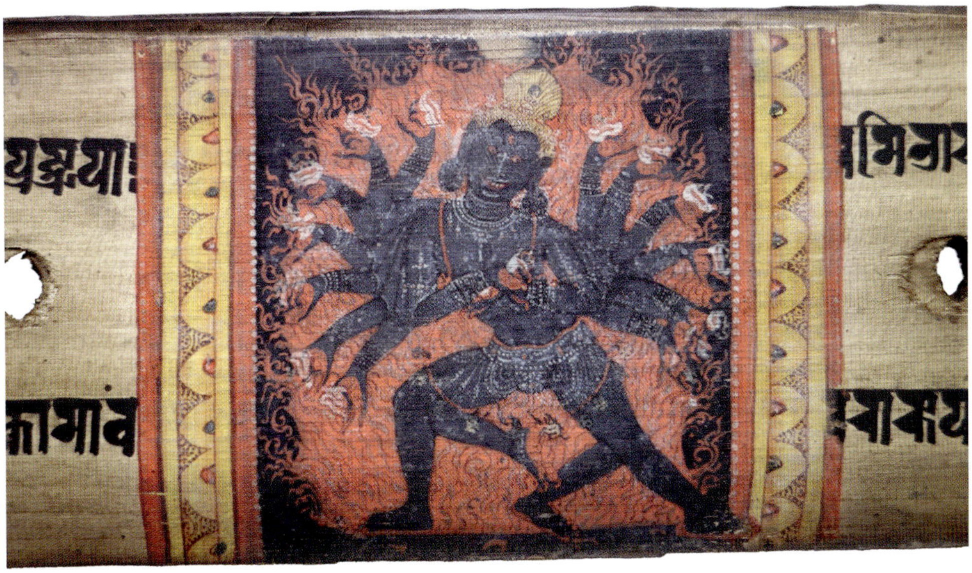

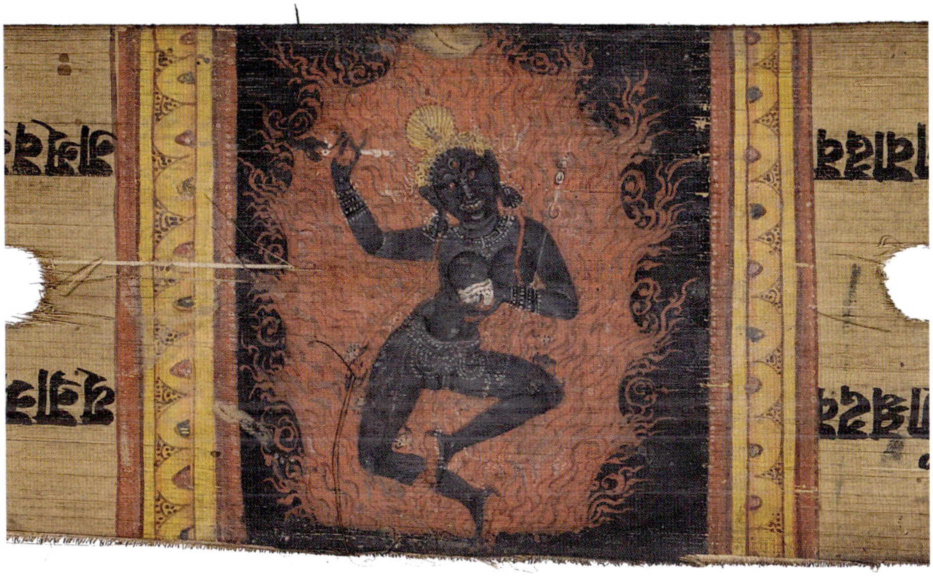

FIGURE 4.8 ▲
Heruka (NsP 8), folio 44v, VRM manuscript. Photo © Jinah Kim.

FIGURE 4.9 ▼
Nairātmā, folio 45r, VRM manuscript. Indian Museum, AT.72.101B. Photo courtesy of Indian Museum, Kolkata.

reader actively participates. Upturned images would not have been out of place in tantric ritual communities in which transgression was integral to a symbolic system of empowerment.[33] The sense of bewilderment aroused by encountering such an image on pages of a manuscript would have captured the bafflement experienced in the first encounter with a group of new antinomian tantras.

The story of a tantric master, named Kukuripā or Kukura (one of the eighty-seven Mahāsiddhas, known as the dog guru, *kukurācārya,* due to his "sacraments with 1,000 dogs") provides an interesting backdrop against which to contextualize upside-down images placed upside-down. In a story recounted in the commentary literature regarding the revelation myth of the Buddhist tantras, Kukura was approached by an official messenger from the King of Zahor, Indrabhūti, to come to his court to explain this newly revealed set of esoteric scriptures.[34] Kukura responded with a request that the king "send these scriptures in advance" so that he could prepare to explain them before coming. "When the scriptures arrived, Kukura took one look at them and he became turned upside down, uncertain on where to look. Throwing himself down in front of the books, he cried out, I have no Lord! I have no Refuge!"[35]

Here we have a tantric siddha throwing himself in front of a stack of books, not knowing where to look, and turning himself upside down. The upturned images in the VRM manuscript similarly disorient our sight, as if to capture the shock value inherent in the experience of seeing something unexpected. Kukura expects to be able to master the text, but the presentation of the manuscripts undoes him; the story itself underscores their status as an independent medium. It is also important to remember that the manuscripts were delivered as physical objects, books, in the face of which Kukura finds himself completely perplexed. The story emphasizes the importance of manuscripts as vessels for the transmission of secret knowledge among Buddhist tantric communities (Jñānamitra's commentary, from which this story is taken, is known from an early ninth-century record). Yet it also demonstrates the importance of vision: the act of perception required to comprehend these texts and the images that accompany them through intuitive insight or by merely looking. Kukura's request to Vajrasattva, who physically appeared before him in response to Kukura's desperate cry, exemplifies the ability "to understand these deep scriptures merely by looking at them."[36]

If the mahāyoga and yoginī tantras (the antinomian tantras) "transcend the [dualist] tantric systems from within," the painted visions of the tantric deities in sexual embrace transcend the text of the *Perfection of Wisdom* from within.[37] Wedemeyer's observation that the Prajñāpāramitā literature is full of "discursive inversion resulting in reinforcement of pre-established values" on which the "nondualism of the antinomian Tantras is predicated," proves useful in understanding why these late Indian *Perfection of Wisdom* manuscripts were adopted for the particular purpose of transmitting and circulating the images of the mahāyoga and yoginī tantras. In using an image of Vajrayoginī from folio 210r of the VRM manuscript for the cover of his groundbreaking book, *Making Sense of Tantric Buddhism* (2013), Wedemeyer probably did not know that the image is oriented in a direction opposite to that of the text and that it faces a twelve-armed form of Saṃvara. Moreover, it is doubtful that he knew that it originates from a manuscript of the *Prajñāpāramitā* that is distinguished by the fact that it holds the most extensive and powerful images accompanying these "antinomian" tantras known from medieval South Asia.[38] The VRM manuscript brilliantly captures the method through which the nondualistic Buddhist tantras relate to and transcend the *Prajñāpāramitā* from within.

ON ARTISTIC VIRTUOSITY AND TANTRIC VISIONS

As observed in chapter 3, the correspondence between textual descriptions of tantric visions and images commonly occurs in painted Indic Buddhist manuscripts of the twelfth and thirteenth centuries. What is remarkable about the VRM manuscript, however, is the extent to which the artists went out of their way to individualize each deity, an effort that showcases remarkable pictorial talent and ambitions on their part. The execution of facial expressions is particularly stunning in their diversity. Nairātmā's face is especially expressive: bloodshot, round, bulging eyes roll in slightly different directions, and multiple black lines and lightly applied white shading mark her sunken forehead (figure 4.9). Her consort is also remarkably individualized. Perhaps to amplify his "contracting brows," Hevajra's face (figure 4.8) is covered with what seems to be either a white net or white-stripe markings drawn on his face. Flipping through the manuscript gives an impression of the diversity of individualized facial expressions, especially in the rendition of eyes, which roll in different directions (cross-eyed, rolling to one side, rolling upward, rolling in opposite directions). This is clearly noticeable in those instances in which the same deity appears in sequence in different forms. For example, a twelve-armed form of Saṃvara appears in a sequence starting from the end of chapter 6, marking the end of chapters 7, 8, 9, and 10, and, as seen in figure 4.10 (a composite reproduction of faces only), these five faces are amazingly animated. In particular, the dancing Saṃvara at the end of chapter 10 (folio 233v) bears an intense expression, with his pupils rolling slightly toward the center and the left eye slightly more blurred than the right, and with his gaping mouth looking as if he is about to explode like the roaring flames around him (figure 4.11).

The expressiveness seen in the eyes of powerful tantric deities like Saṃvara, Hevajra, and Kālachakra are not necessarily just a product of an artist's whim, all the more so given the description of the four gazes known in the *Hevajra tantra* (henceforth HT) corpus. In the eleventh chapter, the HT explains four types of gazes that can cause worldly and magical effects and how to achieve them through controlled breathing. First, the upward-gaze, two eyes directed upward to the forehead, achieves hatred/downfall, which is realized through exhaling; second, the leftward gaze, two eyes thrown to the left, causes subjugation, which is achieved through inhaling; third, the rightward gaze, two eyes thrown to the right and upward, causes conjuring forth (*ākṛṣṭi,* in the sense of attracting an absent person to make him- or herself present or creating something out of nothing; 鉤召眼), achieved through holding the breath; and fourth, the centrally directed gaze, two eyes looking toward the nose, causes petrification, which is achieved through tranquil breathing.[39] Some examples in this manuscript match these four types of gazes, which are rarely articulated or noticed in other visual renditions of such deities in art (see figure 4.10). The NsP and other sādhana texts rarely explain the manner in which the eyes of each deity should be depicted. The

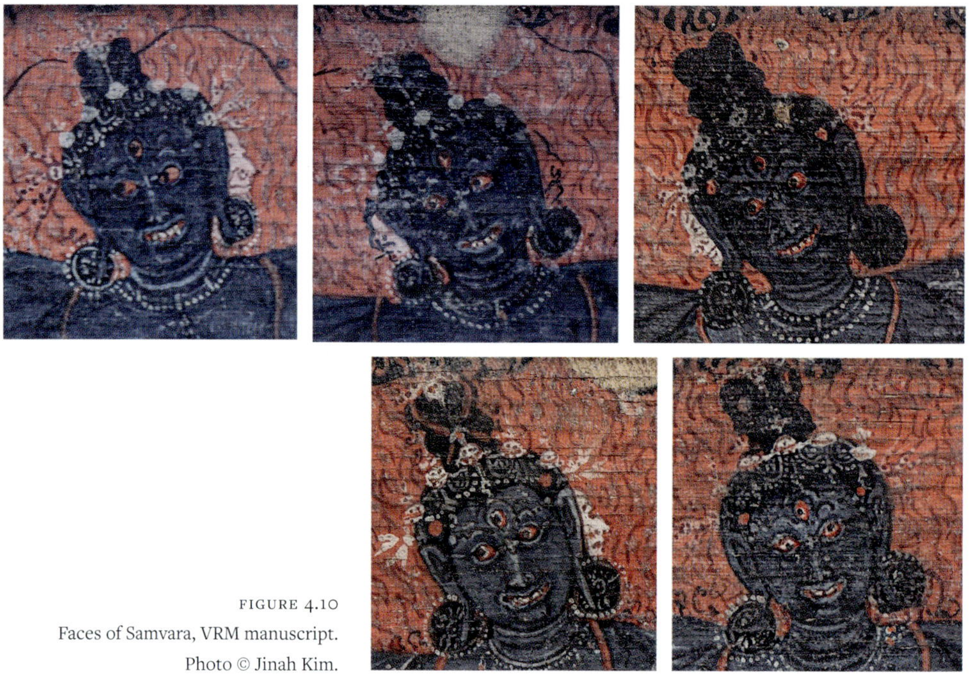

FIGURE 4.10
Faces of Samvara, VRM manuscript.
Photo © Jinah Kim.

examples collected from the VRM manuscript include diverse deities other than those directly related to the HT. The HT's explanation of gazes and their physical effects helps to understand the ritual language through which specific types of gazes were understood and articulated in the tantric Buddhist milieu.

The VRM manuscript most likely represents the product of a collaboration between a trained tantric master well versed in rituals and techniques of the mahāyoga and yoginī tantras as they were being experimented in late Indian Buddhist contexts and an artist (or artists) of great virtuosity who could translate these fantastic visions of tantric deities into pictorial forms with such intensity and vivacity. The six-armed Saṃvara (folio 477v), together with his consort of the same form (folio 478r), shows such liveliness and intensity, especially in his expressive face with eyes drawn to the center, that by comparison the exquisite and controlled depiction of Saṃvara in the Nepalese paubha appears schematic and almost lethargic (compare figures 4.7 and 4.12). Attributes, such as a human skin or a skull diadem, are abbreviated and less articulate on the manuscript page than in the paubha, yet the image in the manuscript captures the essence of this ecstatic form. The energetic flames surrounding him animate the image to such an extent that one can imagine oneself hearing the sound of mantras and seeing the "quivers of high bliss" from which his form has risen. The fact that the sight can cause hearing and bodily sensations does not seem to be out of place given the somatic effects of the gazes explained in the HT. Although somewhat abbreviated in terms of their iconographic detail, the paintings in the VRM manuscript impart a

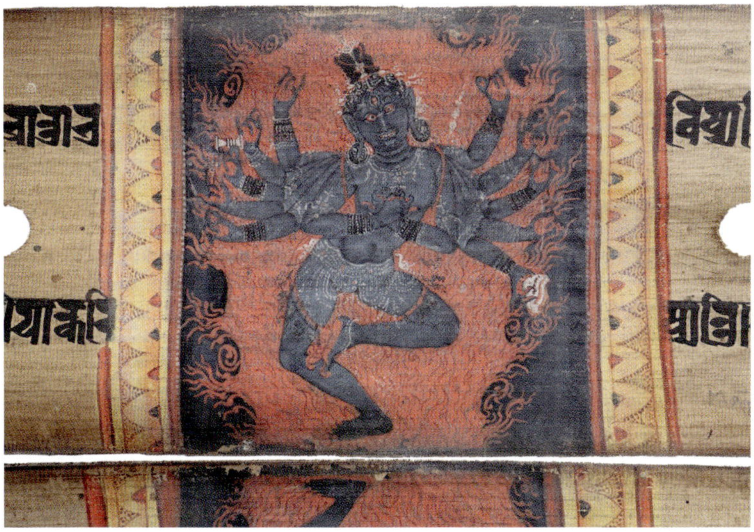

FIGURE 4.11
Folio 233v, dancing Samvara, VRM manuscript. Photo © Jinah Kim.

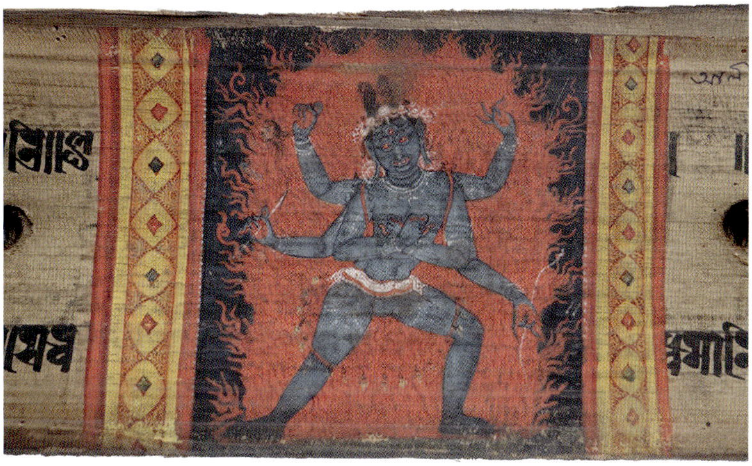

FIGURE 4.12
Folio 477v, six-armed Samvara, VRM manuscript. Photo © Jinah Kim.

powerful sense of presence of these otherwise transcendent beings in such a compelling and powerful visual language that one easily forgets that these painted panels measure only 6.5 cm in height.

TANTRIC ICONOGRAPHY PAR EXCELLENCE

That this project involved a tantric master who had deep knowledge and experience of specific tantric vision practices rooted in variously named tantras and diverse images generated in them and an artist (or artists) of great talent is clear on account of two specific features of the manuscript. First, the program incorporates idiosyncratic iconographies for some of the deities. Second, they made clever use of these unique iconographic elements to

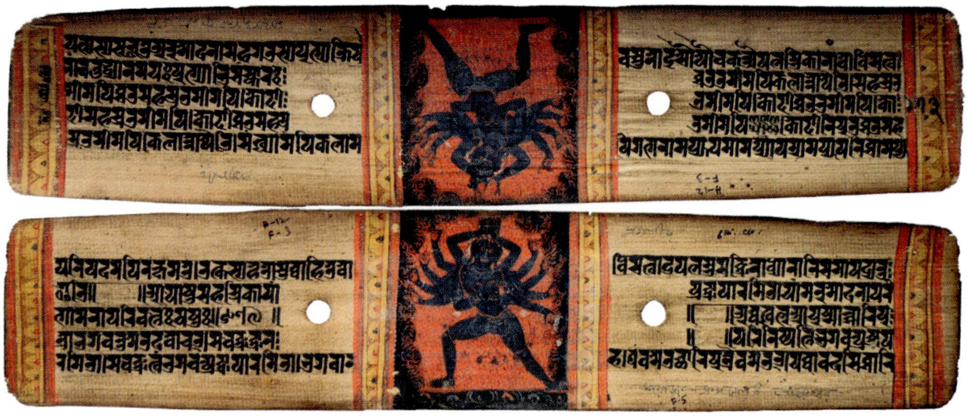

FIGURE 4.13
Folio 173v (eleven-armed female)–174r (twelve-armed male), VRM manuscript. Photo © Jinah Kim.

structure the overall program. If one follows the order of the text in reading these images, the first time one is brought up short by an iconographic oddity occurs at the end of chapter 6, titled "Anumodanāpariṇāmanā, Dedication and Jubilation" (folio 173v). An inverted female deity faces the male deity on folio 174r (figure 4.13). In other words, the female appears first, followed by the male form, an ordering opposite to that employed in every other case. In addition, once one examines the image more carefully, it emerges that the female deity has an odd number of arms, eleven in total, which is completely anomalous in Buddhist iconography. One could dismiss this anomaly as an artist's mistake. It does not, however, seem to be a mere coincidence that the change in direction, which disorients the reader, occurs here; it makes her pause to look again, at which point another oddity commands attention. After this odd moment, the set of images in this manuscript is punctuated by a sequence of three twelve-armed forms of Saṃvara, followed by the most expressive dancing Saṃvara on fol. 233v (figure 4.11). Similarly, the absence of images in the last half of the manuscript, at the end of chapter 19 (folios 371v–372r) and chapter 21 (folios 412v–413r) appears to introduce a sequence of Heruka-Nairātmā images into 1HN ○ 2HN ○2HN or 1HN ○2HN ○ 1HN sets (the two circles stand for the chapters without images).

Two bodhisattvas, Avalokiteśvara and Maitreya, mark the end of the eleventh chapter as if marking the midpoint in the manuscript's overall structure, thereby introducing a complete break from the series of tantric deities. Marking the midpoint of the manuscript with painted panels representing bodhisattvas characterizes many twelfth-century monastic manuscripts like the *Perfection of Wisdom* manuscript prepared in the Vikramaśīla monastery. Their placement in the center along with the placement of Amitābha-Prajñāpāramitā at the beginning and Jambhala-Vasudhāra at the end, suggests that their makers were cognizant of the existing tradition of illustrated *Perfection of Wisdom* manuscripts and consciously responded to it.

This short break from the tantric deities quickly turns in another direction at the end of chapter 12. Here, iconography expresses the fact that the reader has reached the true center

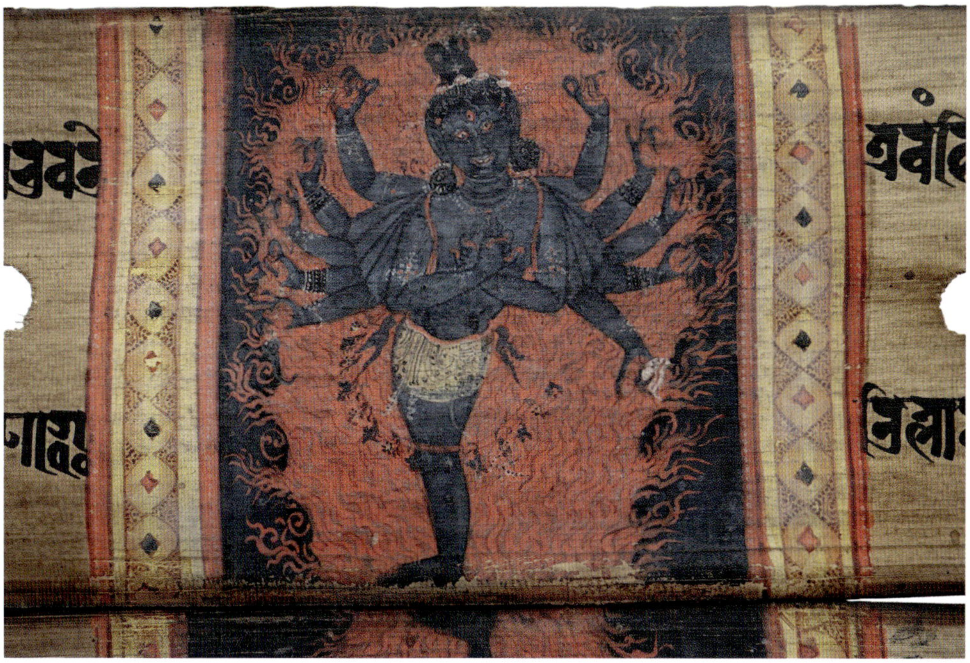

FIGURE 4.14
Folio 280v, one-legged Samvara, VRM manuscript. Photo © Jinah Kim.

of the manuscript, which, in Indian Buddhist manuscripts of the late twelfth and early thirteenth centuries, is often reserved for the most powerful deities. On folio 280v, a single-legged, twelve-armed deity, most likely a form of Saṃvara (identified as Māyājala Saṃvara in another manuscript), embraces a single-legged, twelve-armed female deity on folio 281r who is identical to himself (figure 4.14).[40] Just as the odd number of arms on folio 173v represents a unique occurrence that elicits prolonged looking, so too, a single-legged deity proves disorienting because it is so unexpected.

This one-legged feature immediately recalls the images of "Ekapāda-Śiva," which from the ninth century onward are found in abundance on the exterior walls of Hindu temples in Odisha.[41] Ekapāda-Śiva images from Odisha provide an instructive point of comparison, especially given that, based on their facial expressions and coiffure, the surviving examples are understood to represent Bhairava or the ferocious aspect of Śiva. Tantric Buddhist iconographists (if there ever was such specialization in institutional Buddhism), or, perhaps more reasonably put, the tantric Buddhist *imaginaire*, understood Bhairava to have been crushed under Saṃvara's foot. This unique Ekapāda form of Saṃvara can be understood in the tradition of appropriating powerful Śaiva iconography in tantric Buddhist circles.[42] The one-footed form makes a clear visual citation of Ekapāda Śiva, but in every other aspect, this is a tantric Buddhist image of Saṃvara and his consort. In preceding chapters of the VRM manuscript, we have encountered different forms of the twelve-armed Saṃvara. This instance of the deity repeats the same arrangement of arms, with the main differences being the single leg and the tiger loincloth. The loincloth seems to have been adopted consciously to differentiate this image from Ekapāda Śiva, whose form is always ithyphallic.

It hardly seems coincidental that this idiosyncratic form was chosen to mark the center of the manuscript following the exoteric deities at the end of chapter 11. Given the overall sequence of the related forms of Saṃvara that occur prior to chapter 11, the two panels bearing the single-legged, twelve-armed Saṃvara and his consort, who, like her partner, also is single-legged and twelve-armed, mark a point of transition like double *daṇḍa*s in the sea of letters, which function as "periods" in Sanskrit texts.

The sequence that begins with the unusual Ekapāda images is bookended by another set of iconographies unique in Indic Buddhist art that appears at the end of chapter 16. On folio 326v there appears a thirty-six-armed, sixteen-legged male deity with a buffalo head figure 4.15). Dark blue in color, his dynamic, multilimbed form moves energetically against a red flame. His three eyes, all bloodshot, stare out at the viewer in a most unusual fashion. This buffalo-headed, ithyphallic form resembles images of Vajrabhairava, in Himalayan-based Vajrayana Buddhism understood to be a powerful, terrifying emanation of the bodhisattva Mañjuśrī. Vajrabhairava was important in Tibetan Buddhist communities, especially in the Sakya and Gelug traditions, whose elites introduced Mahāvajrabhairava as the protector deity of the Mongol rulers and the Manchu rulers in China. Although the origin of the Vajrabhairava tantra is often traced to ninth-century Oḍḍiyana (possibly the Swat valley in Pakistan), the tantra and its related corpus are mainly known from Tibetan and Mongolian versions.[43] Vajrabhairava images are unknown in surviving examples from eastern India, which makes the occurrence of this image in a manuscript particularly striking.

Vajrabhairava is most commonly depicted in the nine-headed, thirty-six-armed, sixteen-legged form surrounded by his retinue, as seen in the famous *kesi* tapestry version of the Vajrabhairava maṇḍala in the Metropolitan Museum of Art, commissioned for the Mongol ruler, Tugh Temür (c. 1304–32, Wenzong emperor of the Yuan dynasty, r: 1328–April 3, 1329, and September 8, 1329–32) and his older brother Kusala.[44] In this form, he is nine-headed, thirty-six armed, and sixteen-legged, and his principal hands hold a dagger (*kartri*) and skull cup (*kapala*). In comparison, the version in the VRM manuscript displays a single buffalo head and places his principal hands crossed before his chest, holding a *vajra* and a *ghaṇṭa*. This arrangement of principal hands repeats that which characterizes the images of Saṃvara in preceding chapters of the VRM manuscript. This gesture also indicates a sexual embrace, in this case, of the fantastic sixteen-armed, four-legged yellow female figure on folio 327r (figure 4.16).

The female partner of Vajrabhairava is rarely encountered as an independent image. In later examples, his consort, often identified as Vajravetālī, is depicted in the one-faced, two-armed, two-legged, dark-blue (in painted images) form. The deity on folio 327r is considerably more complex and dynamic than the simple two-armed consort figure of the later Tibetan sādhanas (Figure 4.16). Her principal hands are also crossed in front of her chest and hold a *vajra* and *ghaṇṭa*, as does the buffalo-headed male deity. How these deities were iden-

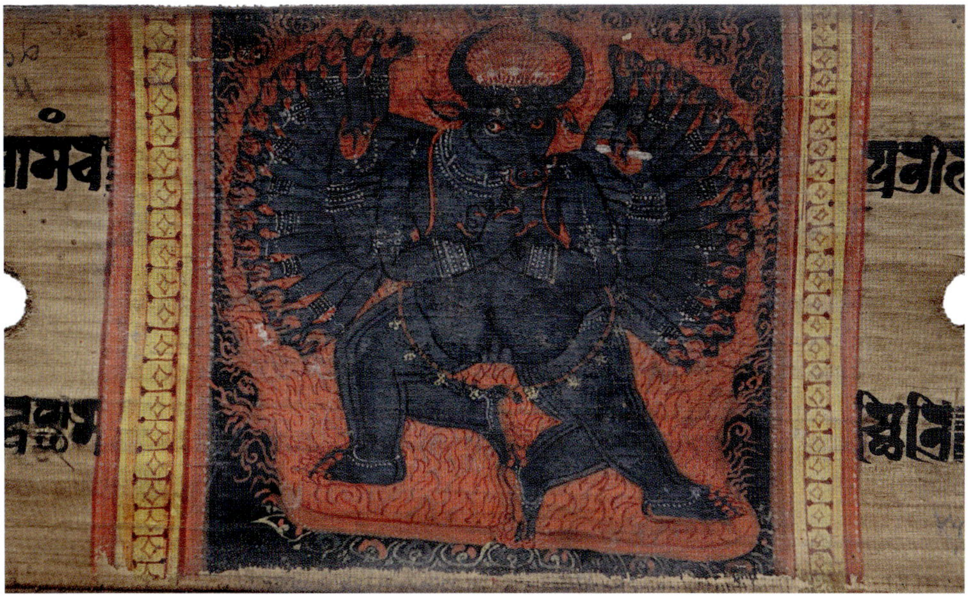

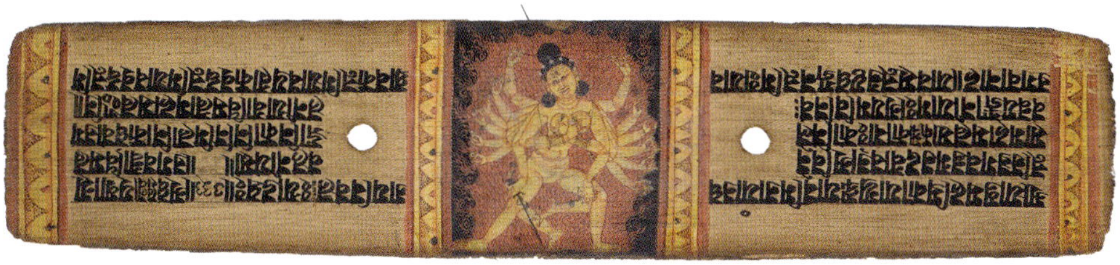

FIGURE 4.15 ▲
Folio 326v, Mahiṣa-Samvara/Vajrabhairava, VRM manuscript. Photo © Jinah Kim.

FIGURE 4.16 ▼
Folio 327r, Vajravetālī?, VRM manuscript. Indian Museum, AT.72.101A. Photo courtesy of Indian Museum, Kolkata.

tified in the immediate circle of the makers and audience for this manuscript is difficult to determine. In the Kathmandu valley, Vajrabhairava is known as Mahiṣa-Saṃvara (lit. buffalo-Saṃvara), an important tutelary deity in the tantric shrines (*āgam*) in the *bahal* (Newar Buddhist) complex of Kathmandu and Patan. Given the buffalo head and the iconographic ties with previous Saṃvara images within the manuscript, especially in terms of the color and the arrangement of the principal hands with a *vajra* and a *ghaṇṭa*, the image may tentatively be identified as "Mahiṣa-Saṃvara."

In Nepal, the iconography of Mahiṣa-Saṃvara and the associated rituals are supposed to remain hidden and unknown to anyone outside the initiated ritual specialists (*vajrācāryas*). To apply this name without any historical study of the associated ritual texts is anachronistic. The manuscript's connection to Nepal, however, is more than a speculation; as recorded in the postcolophon, the manuscript was in use in the Kathmandu valley in 1576 CE. The deity may in fact have been understood as Mahiṣa-Saṃvara among the family of Newar patrons in the sixteenth century: Śākyabhikṣu Jayalakhaju with his two wives and two daughters, and Śākyabhikṣu Śrī Hakuju and his family who were part of the Tarumūla monastery community, today's Shikamu bahal, Kathmandu). This group of individuals used the manuscript for recitation and pūjā in 1576 CE, wishing for long life, happiness, wealth, health, and family prosperity.[45] It is possible that the deity was understood as Mahiṣa-Saṃvara at the time of its production at the turn of the thirteenth century. Mahiṣa as a quintessential buffalo demon destroyed by the goddess Durgā of the Devī-Māhātmyā was widely known in medieval South Asia. The fantastic buffalo-headed deity and his sixteen-armed female companion, although anticipating the later iconography of Vajrabhairava, are distinct from what one finds articulated in Tibetan images of Vajrabhairava and his consort. Their precise meaning awaits further study.

Due to the many idiosyncrasies that are unknown in the familiar corpus of tantric sādhanas (for example, those collected in the SM and those gleaned from the *Hevajra tantra, Cakrasaṃvara tantra,* and *Kālacakra tantra* literature), the identification of each deity in the VRM manuscript remains a challenge. The unparalleled iconography realized in this book may fit the vision of a fantastic tantric body described in an obscure text, as yet unknown, in the vast corpus of such texts. Diverse expressive forms of tantric deities are captured in an extraordinarily vivid fashion. In particular, the yellow, sixteen-armed, four-legged goddess Vetali, the consort of Vajrabhairava (see figure 4.16) appears highly individualized: she sports a deeply frowning forehead, wide-open, sunken eyes, and a clenched mouth. In fact, the artistic virtuosity that permitted the capturing of such diverse and eccentric tantric visions may also have contributed to the multiplication and diversification of tantric visions. As witnessed by the sequence of Saṃvara faces in the VRM manuscript (figure 4.10), an artist's ability to translate a vision into such a vivid pictorial form in itself and independently of any prompts in the accompanying text can inspire further diversification and multiplication with subtle modifications.[46] In the thangkas and paubhas, in which expectations of iconographic correctness and orthodoxy result in the development of rigid iconometric rules (the use of a grid system with a predetermined ratio) and iconographic conformity, such individualization and whimsical expressions are rarely seen. Such individualized instances of pictorial expression, which possibly can be related more closely to personal experience than to the transcendental aspects assumed in later understandings of tantric vision practices, flourish in the realm of painted manuscript production.

Identifying the deities represented by the remarkably individuated images in the VRM manuscript holds out the possibility of advancing our knowledge of tantric iconography as circulated in late Indic Buddhism. Many of these deities are the lords of their maṇḍalas, which may be associated with specific texts. In this regard, being able to link deities with specific names, for example, "Heruka of the Mahāmāyā-tantra" or "Seven-syllable Saṃvara," can advance our understanding of which of the numerous tantric texts recorded and cataloged in the Tibetan Buddhist canon may have circulated in conjunction with practical ritual knowledge in late Indic tantric Buddhist communities.[47] While acknowledging the significance of such a project, it is equally important to remember that the lack of identification in textually attestable verbal forms should not hinder our appreciation of the remarkable achievement represented by this manuscript, which showcases the virtuosity of artistic invention and the diversity of tantric visions in late twelfth- and early thirteenth-century South Asia.

PART THREE

COLOR

5

COLOR AS AN ENCODING TOOL

COLOR IS INDISPENSABLE IN ABSTRACT ANIMATIONS and digital visualization projects. Experimental abstract animations of the 1920s and 1930s, such as Oskar Fischinger's *Circles* (1933) represent early examples of the use of color in capturing mind pictures.[1] His subsequent technicolor *Optical Poem* (1938, MGM) is a seven-minute abstract animation of orchestrated movement; its colorful geometric shapes (mainly circles) visualize *Hungarian Rhapsody No. 2* by Franz Liszt, and the film begins with the following message on screen: "To most of us music suggests definite mental images of form and color. The picture you are about to see is a novel scientific experiment—its object is to convey these mental images in visual form." Such a "novel scientific experiment" that attempts to translate internal, mental image into externalized, visual form continues to be pursued up to the present by specialists in neuroscience, brain imaging, bioengineering, and psychology who collaborate to develop computational models that reconstruct people's visual experiences with the help of functional magnetic resonance imaging (fMRI).[2] The method and the available tools used in modern scientific research projects may be groundbreaking, but translating mind images into visual forms is not a novel or even modern project in human history; it finds an uncanny parallel in *sādhana* practices described in texts over a thousand years old. The process of identification between the vibrating sound of auspicious syllables and a visual form in tantric visionary practices, explored in chapter 3, is similar to what Fischinger's visualization of music achieves. Dizzying effects of fast-moving geometric shapes in various hues and colors in an abstract animation can easily be a twentieth-century rendition of an internal visionary experience during sādhana that, according to Benoytosh Bhattacharya, "appears on the mind-sky in flashes and sparks." Bhattacharya's characterization reads strikingly like a description of a psychedelic experience. Yet, the visionary experience during sādhana is said to be controlled and deliberate, far from the profusion of colors often used to evoke psychedelic experiences in contemporary media.[3]

The contemporary use of color coding in digital visualization projects provides a productive and comparative approach to understanding the role of color use in manuscript painting and tantric visionary practice.[4] A system of color coding is often employed to codify and organize complex information visually. For example, in the Gallant Lab's recent project, brain activities in response to semantic concepts are arranged and recorded by assigning an RGB color to each of twelve semantic categories.[5] The project's online digital tool (a 3D brain viewer) demonstrates how color coding of twelve semantic categories helps map brain activities in an accessible, visual manner.[6] The resulting 3D model of the brain, in vibrant color, appears attractive. The color coding also makes it easier to analyze the data and communicate the result.

In this chapter, I suggest that the need to control and codify the esoteric visual knowledge that tantric visionary practices generated led to the development and the employment of a distinct color codification system (designated as the "IEB system" for convenience) in Indic Buddhist circles. What prompted a pragmatic application of color as a codification tool was not only the overwhelming number of variants but also the complexity and the multiplicity of the vision, especially of powerful tantric deities. The prevalent adoption of the IEB system curiously coincides with the artistic development seen in the production of painted manuscripts in Indic Buddhist circles. This chapter explores how and why the color codification system developed in the way it did and investigates the contribution of manuscript painters in shaping it. The five-color codification system seen in manuscript paintings of the eleventh through the thirteenth centuries also helps us understand how and why primary colors became prominent features in the art of painting in India during the second millennium.

THE FIVE COLORS

In Act Two of the *Nāgānanda,* a five-act drama based on a Buddhist *jātaka* story by Harṣa, who ruled much of northern India during the seventh century (r. ca. 606–47 CE), we find a scene in which the lovelorn hero, Vidyādhara prince Jimūtavāhana, declares to draw the image of his beloved on a moonstone bench (*candrakāntaśilātalam*) under a sandalwood bower: "Friend, I'll draw her on this stone and while away the time with her in the picture. So fetch bits of red pigment from the mountain slope."[7] The term translated as "red pigment" here is "*śilā-śakala*" bits of "red-arsenic" or realgar, a type of mineral similar to orpiment, commonly occurring in hydrothermal sulfide-bearing mineral deposits.[8] His trusted companion, Vidūṣaka, obliges: "You've asked for one color, my friend, yet I brought five colors (*pañcavarṇā*) from the mountain. You now can get drawing."[9] The story unfolds without identifying what these five colors are, and five colors in this context may simply be a figure of speech that marks the intensity of longing (of the prince) requiring a pictorial expression. This passing remark suggests that the concept of five colors was known and circulating at the time of the story's composition in the seventh century. The concept also appears in the *Citrasūtra* section of the *Viṣṇudharmottara* (henceforth VdhM), a Vaiṣṇava text probably written down in Kashmir sometime between 450–650 CE.[10] Chapter 40 of the *Citrasūtra* states in verse 16 that there are five "root colors" (*mūlaraṅgā*), and that they are "white (*śvetaḥ*), yellow (*pītaḥ*), red (*vilohitaḥ*), blue (*nīlaḥ*), and black (*kṛṣṇaḥ*)."[11] While the idea of five colors as primary colors may have been established, specifics of these five colors seem to have remained in flux throughout the first millennium, with some artistic manuals like the *Mānasollāsa* by the twelfth-century king Someśvara III (r. 1124–38) identifying only four pure colors of white (*śveta*), red (*rakta*), yellow (*pīta*), and black (*kṛṣṇa*) in the section on the ingredients of pure colors (*śuddhavarṇadravyāṇi*).[12] We will discuss the significance of the primary colors as identified in these texts for the artistic practice in chapter 6. For now, let us turn to the five-color system as developed in Indic contexts.

DEVELOPMENT OF A FIVE-COLOR CODIFICATION SYSTEM

The most systematic and consistent application of five colors in the Indic context is found in the world of Indian Esoteric Buddhism. Their systematic nature is in stark contrast to what Teun Goudriaan once characterized as "bewildering" in his discussion of the role of colors in meditative vision practices of Indic religions.[13] The history of this five-color system is worth investigating further, as it reveals changing attitudes toward color and provides a few historical clues to explore how and why primary colors in high opacity may have become important in the production of paintings in medieval South Asia. The system of the five Buddha families, or *pañcakula*, which is the most distinctive characteristic of Esoteric Buddhism, assigns five body colors along with five directions to the five transcendental Buddhas, constituting a Buddhist cosmology. In the simplest schema, they are: Akṣobhya-East—Blue, Amitābha-West—Red, Ratnasambhava-South—Yellow, Amoghasiddhi-North—Green, and Vairocana-White—Center (see diagram *a* in figure 5.1). This cardinal-direction five-color system (IEB color system) is clearly in play in the sādhana texts compiled during the late eleventh century like those recorded in the *Sādhanamālā* (henceforth SM) and the *Niṣpannayogāvalī* (henceforth NsP). Most sādhanas collected in the SM provide color values in the description of a deity's form, and the five primary colors of the five tathāgatas—white, blue, red, yellow, and green—are the main colors.[14] However, such color specificity did not exist in the earliest layer of Esoteric Buddhist ritual texts. Sādhanas that lack color specification may indicate an earlier date of composition, as images of bodhisattvas and deities that appeared in the Buddhist pantheon before the codification of this scheme also seem to

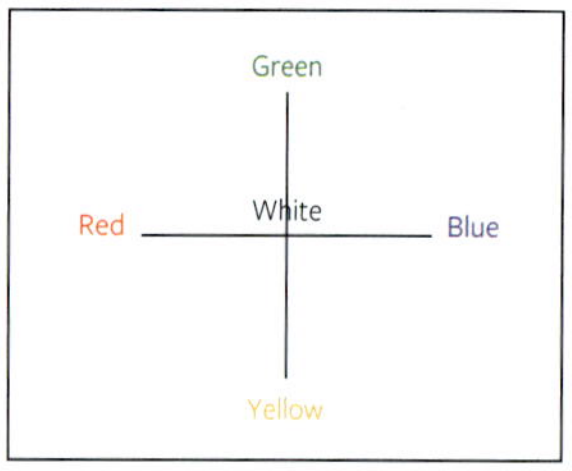

a. Indian Esoteric Buddhist system
NsP 19, Vajradhātu maṇḍala
NsP 21, dharmadhātuvāgīśvaramaṇḍala
Nepalese Pañcarakṣā system

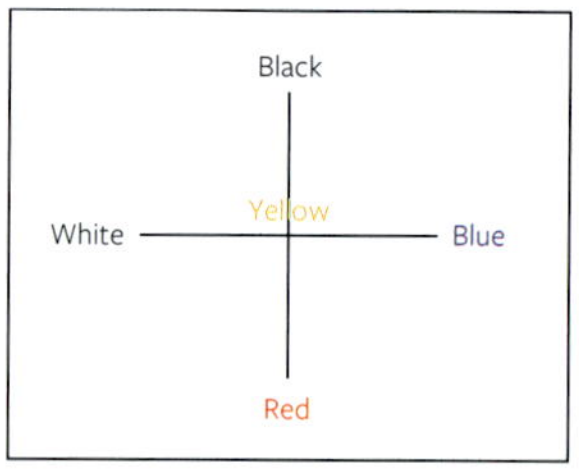

b. Chinese system

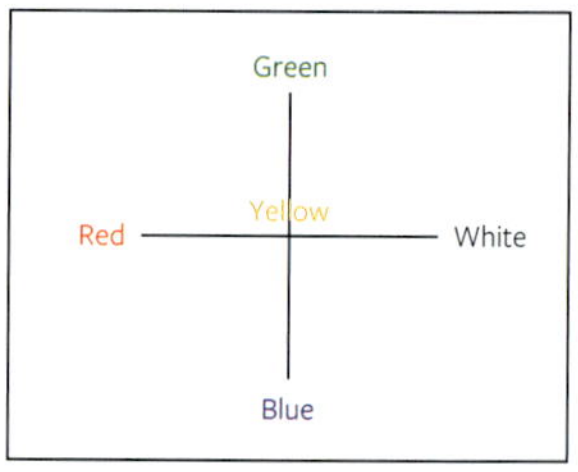

c. Pelliot 2012 diagram scheme, c. 10th century
MG17780 Five Buddha maṇḍala, c. 10th century
MG3579 maṇḍala of Avalokiteśvara,
c. 10th century
T No. 939, translated at the end of 10th century

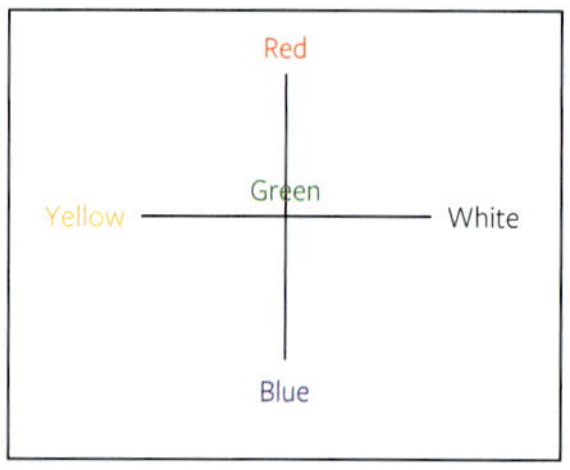

d. Alchemical tantras system
(RC 15.4-12, RRS 1.23-29 AK 1.8-15)

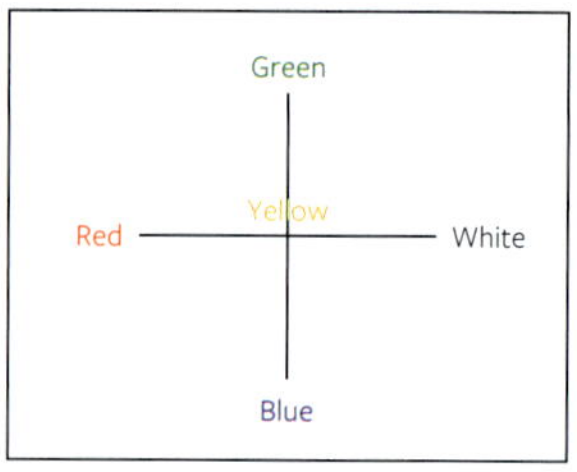

e. Indian Pañcarakṣa system
NsP 18 Pañcarakṣā maṇḍala
NsP 22 Durgatipariśodhanamaṇḍala

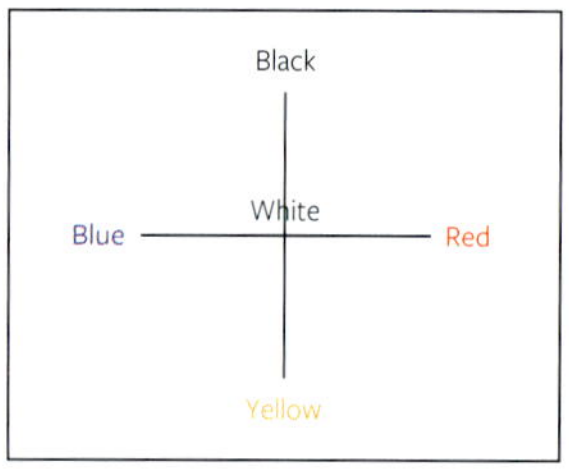

f. Garbhadhātu maṇḍala Snodgrass
(1988) report

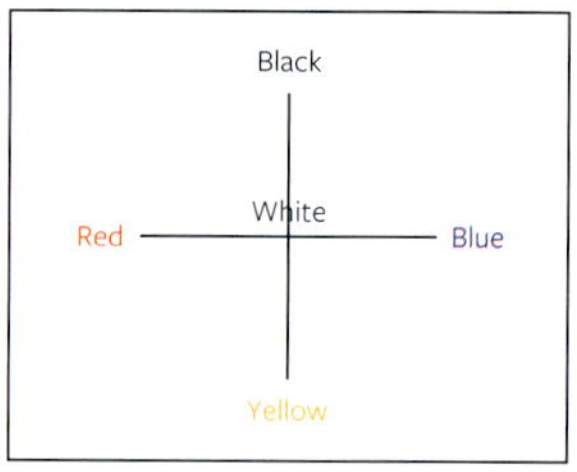

g. Genzu maṇḍala [realized maṇḍala]
Garbhadhātu maṇḍala, Toji, Kyoto
Vajradhātu maṇḍala a la T18, No. 866
by Vajrabodhi trans. in 723
according to Lokesh Chandra (1986),
but not found in T 866

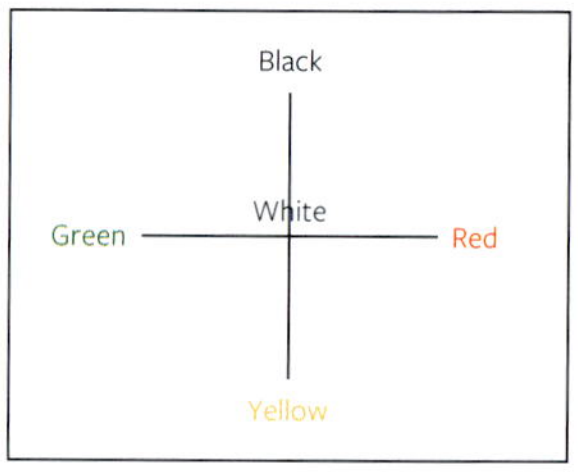

h. T 18, No. 866, trans in 723, the colors
indicated, but the direction is unmarked
in the text.
Suggested based on the order of appearance.

FIGURE 5.1

Diagrams of Color Systems. Image © Jinah Kim.

retain pre-IEB color schemes. Such images are mainly described in terms of their brilliance, as golden and yellow—regardless of which of the five Buddha families each deity was assigned in later practices.[15]

The *Sarvatathāgatatattvasaṃgraha* (henceforth STTS) is one of the most fundamental texts to introduce and articulate the five tathāgata system. This text's circulation in Himalayan and eastern Indian Buddhist circles at the turn of the first millennium—be it in the Spiti valley in the first half of the eleventh century (Tabo); in the Kathmandu valley, Nepal; or in Eastern India—seems to be closely linked to the codification of the cardinal-direction color system of Indic Esoteric Buddhism (see figure 5.1a). The text was already known in the eighth century and circulated widely in the transregional Esoteric Buddhist network, but no evidence of the five-color system in use from an earlier phase is known. Based on a few accounts available in hagiographic literature on Amoghavajra and his teacher Vajrabodhi (or Vajrabuddhi), an early eighth-century South Indian origin of the STTS has been suggested.[16] As Hudaya Kandahjaya and other scholars working on Javanese Buddhism have suggested, the STTS and the *Mahāvairocanābhisaṃbodhi* (henceforth MVS), another crucial yoga tantra text, were important in the Esoteric Buddhist world of maritime Southeast Asia. In the span of the eighth through the mid-ninth centuries, the two texts were used for the realization of Borobudur, Plaosan, and Sewu.[17] None of the Javanese Buddhist sites bear out the color information of the IEB color system.

No surviving example that testifies to the use of the five colors as articulated in the later sādhanas is securely datable before the tenth century. For example, due to the impact of Japanese Esoteric Buddhist master Kūkai (空海), also known posthumously as Kōbō-Daishi (c. 774–835), we have the earliest surviving set of monumental painted maṇḍalas on cloth (*ryokai mandara*) in Tōji; these are the Vajradhātu maṇḍala (Jp. *kongokai* mandara) and the Garbhadhātu maṇḍala (Jp. *Taizokai mandara*), which were painted on silk and completed toward the end of the ninth century. The body colors of five tathāgatas that appear in the center of the Garbhadhātu maṇḍala are not differentiated (figure 5.2). Although deities of different body colors appear in this set of dual-world maṇḍalas, color is not systematically applied, and the color values in these two maṇḍalas are rarely discussed in scholarship.[18] Until the beginning of the tenth century, the unsystematic application of color remains consistent in other surviving examples of the five-tathāgata scheme seen in Buddhist paintings; a typical example is found in a late Tang cave at Dunhuang (Mogao Cave 14), where the four directional Buddhas appear on the ceiling without color differentiation.[19]

There are three possible reasons behind this clearly indeterminate use of color in pre-tenth-century Esoteric Buddhist material: first, existence of multiple systems of five colors in circulation (see figure 5.1)—this accounts for the late date of the codification of the IEB color system; second, predominance of a light-based color theory, one conceptualizing transcendental and divine beings as luminous and light-emitting rather than conveyed by opaque colors; and third, underutilization of portable painting as a medium for conveying visual knowledge in Esoteric Buddhism. Two factors likely contributed to the last point about underutilization: first, images were most commonly circulated in monochromatic drawings; and second, color demarcation was not crucial in the early phase.[20] Thus, color conventions became important when efforts to systematically record and codify Esoteric Buddhist visual knowledge were made from the turn of the eleventh century onward.

A cursory examination of color terms in early Chinese translations of yoga tantra texts suggests that, until the tenth century, the IEB five-color system known in later Sanskrit sādhanas was yet to be codified.[21] Amoghavajra's translation of the STTS datable sometime in 753–55 (Taisho 18, No. 865 金剛頂一切如來真實攝大乘現證大教王) does not include any color terms, partly because it only translates the first part of the STTS.[22] His master

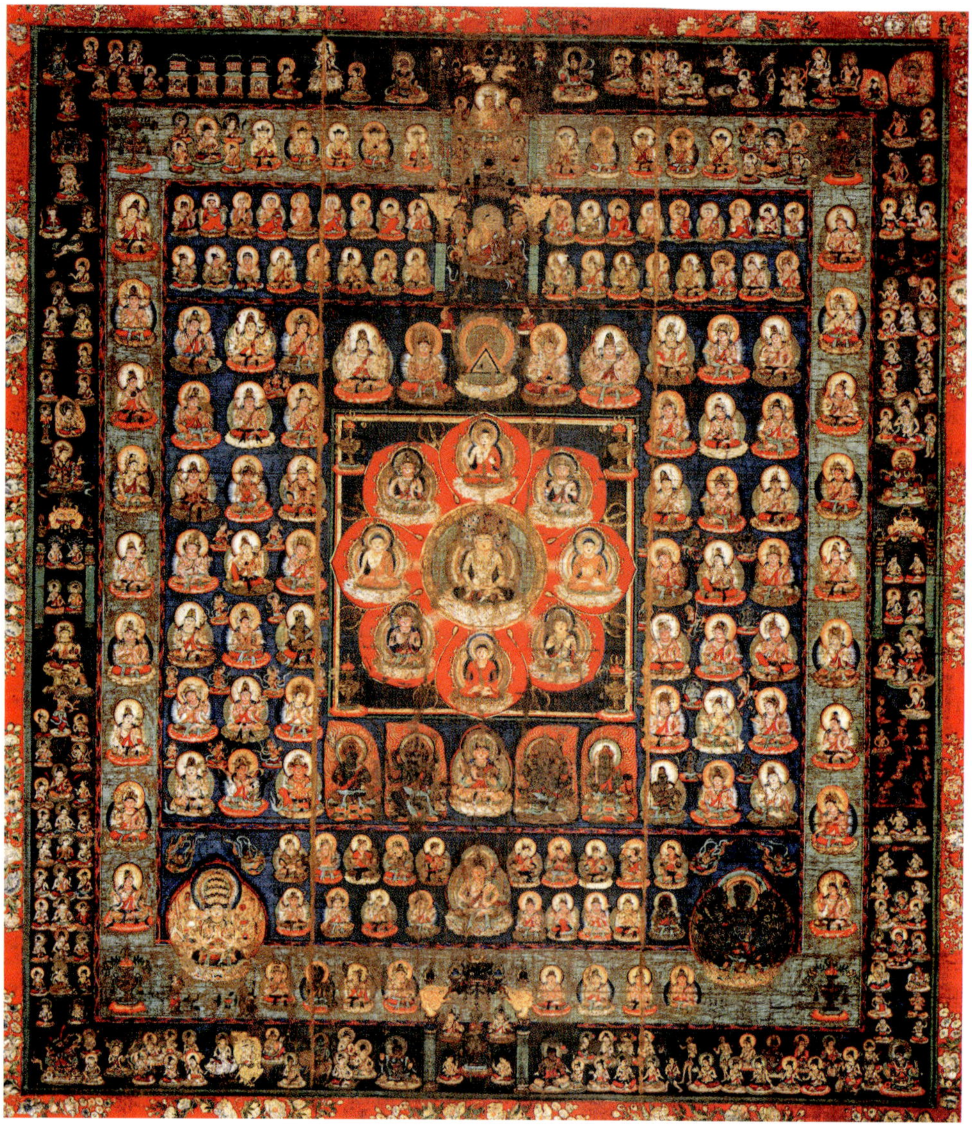

FIGURE 5.2
Taizokai mandara (Garbhadhatu maṇḍala), Kyō-ō-gokokuji (Tōji), Kyoto, Japan, Heian period, ca. second half of the ninth century. Hanging scroll, color on silk. Photo: HIP/Art Resource, New York.

Vajrabodhi's STTS related work translated in 723 (Taisho 18, no. 866, 金剛頂瑜伽中略出念誦經, i.e., Vajraśekhara) does include the term "five colors," with black, gold, and red appearing as specific color terms. Colors identified in the maṇḍala configuration are white, red, yellow, green, and black (T18, no. 866, 0240a17)—different from the five colors of the IEB color system (see figure 5.1h). Whether these colors (W-R-Y-G-Bk) constitute the concept of the "five colors" in the text also remains uncertain. An earlier mention of the five colors in the Chinese canon appears in the *Uṣṇīṣadhāraṇī* (Taisho 19, No. 0970) translated by Divākara; in this text, the light emanating from Buddha's *uṣṇīṣa* (cranial protuberance) that illuminates the whole of the Buddhist universe is described as having the five colors of blue, red, yellow, white, and black.

These five colors are also the primary colors identified in the *Citrasūtra* section of the VdhM as mentioned above, and they, too, are different from the IEB color system. These five colors—blue, red, yellow, white, and black—are identified as the colors of the cardinal-direction five-color system that was long established in China (henceforth, the Chinese system, see fig. 5.1b). According to a recent study by Feng Shi, a Chinese archaeologist, this configuration may have been established as early as the Neolithic age in the third millennium BCE, serving as an essential tool for conceptualizing time and space in traditional China.[23] This indigenous system is different from the IEB system in two ways: inclusion of black instead of green; and the directional values assigned to the colors of white, yellow, and red, which places yellow in the center instead of the white of the IEB system.[24]

Early examples of the artistic use of a five-color system survive from Dunhuang. A painted Five-tathāgata maṇḍala on silk now in the Musée Guimet (Pelliot collection, MG17780) depicts the five tathāgatas and eight offering deities around an offering altar (figure 5.3). A mid-tenth-century date and Uygur patronage have been proposed based on stylistic analysis and indications from donor portraits and their names recorded on the bottom register.[25] The five tathāgatas are arranged in cardinal directions with the South (*top left*)–North (*bottom right*) axis and West (*top-right*)–East (*bottom left*) axis crossing in X with Vairocana in the middle. They appear in bejeweled forms with crowns, earrings, and necklaces: vajra-topped golden five-Jina crowns are on four tathāgatas, while a lofty white crown with five peaks frames the serene face of Vairocana in the center. Each tathāgata holds his hands together in meditation on his lap, on which sits an attribute signaling his lineage/quality: Vairocana (*center*)—wheel (cakra); Ratnasambhava (*top left*)—flaming jewel (*ratna*); Amitābha (*top right*)—lotus (*padma*); Amoghasiddhi (*bottom right*)—*viśvavajra* (or double vajra); and Akṣobhya (*bottom left*)—vajra. Here, five tathāgatas' colors are clearly differentiated. Vairocana in the center is golden yellow. Ratnasambhava on the top left is blue, while Akṣobhya on the bottom left is white. Amoghasiddhi on the bottom right is green. Amitābha on the top right appears almost white, but in comparison to Akṣobhya, Amitābha's color is differentiated and takes on a red hue that renders his color light pink. The five colors used here—yellow, white, blue, red (pink), and green—are the five colors in the Esoteric Buddhist five-color system of the yoga tantra class and beyond. However, their application varies from the IEB color system. Vairocana's color is yellow instead of white, Akṣobhya is white instead of blue, and Ratnasambhava is blue instead of yellow.

There may have been a five-direction color system known in Dunhuang (Dunhuang system) during the tenth century (figure 5.1c).[26] A same color configuration of the five tathāgatas appears in another mid-tenth-century painted maṇḍala from Dunhuang, also in the Musée Guimet (MG 3579) (figure 5.4). The five tathāgatas appear on the top register above the central maṇḍala configuration with a four-armed Avalokiteśvara (holding a noose, a stalk of

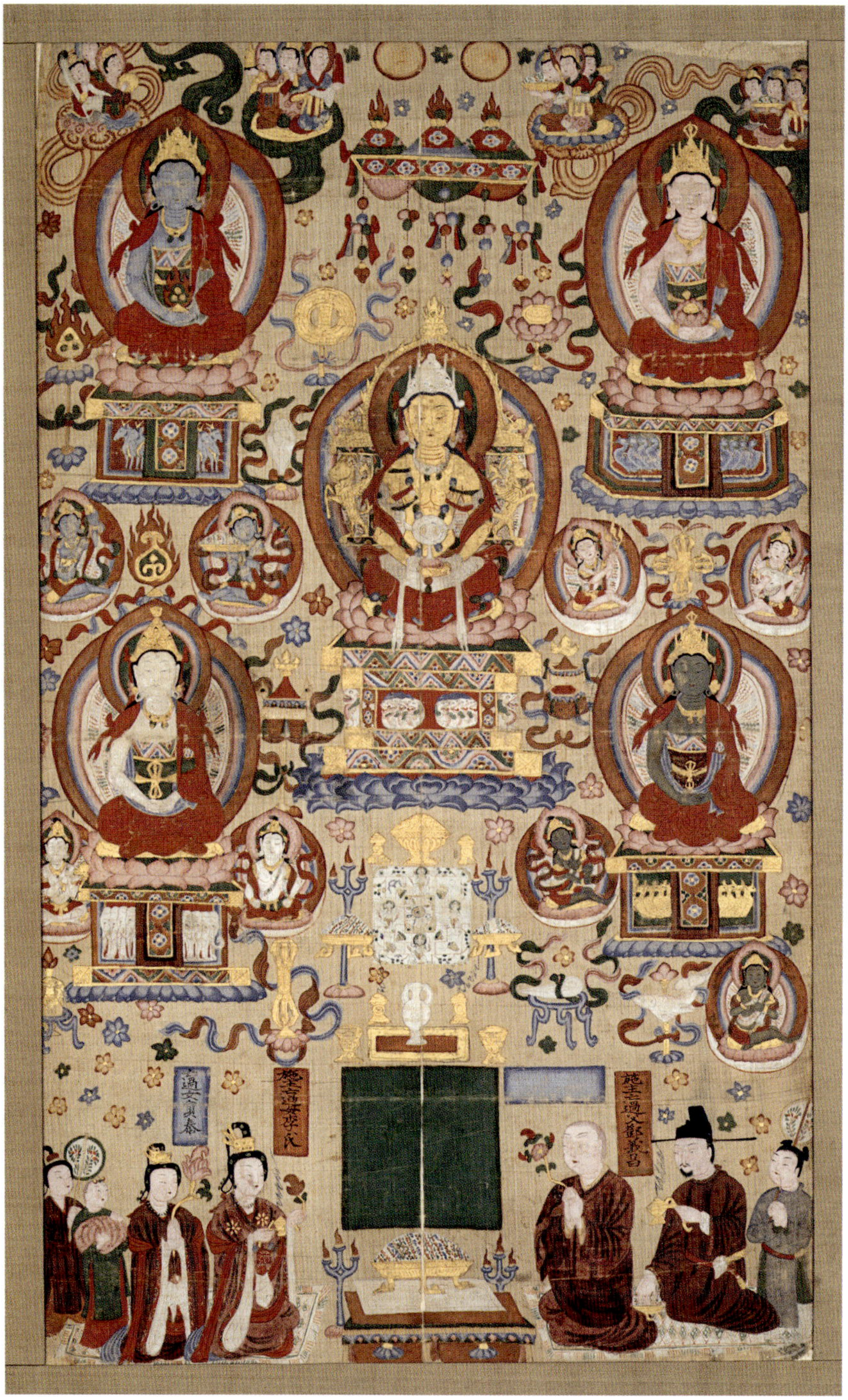

FIGURE 5.3
Five Tathāgata Maṇḍala, ca. 950–1000 CE, pigments and gold on silk, 101.5 × 61 cm, from Dunhuang, Musée Guimet, Pelliot Collection, MG 17780. Photo © RMN-Grand Palais/Art Resource, New York.

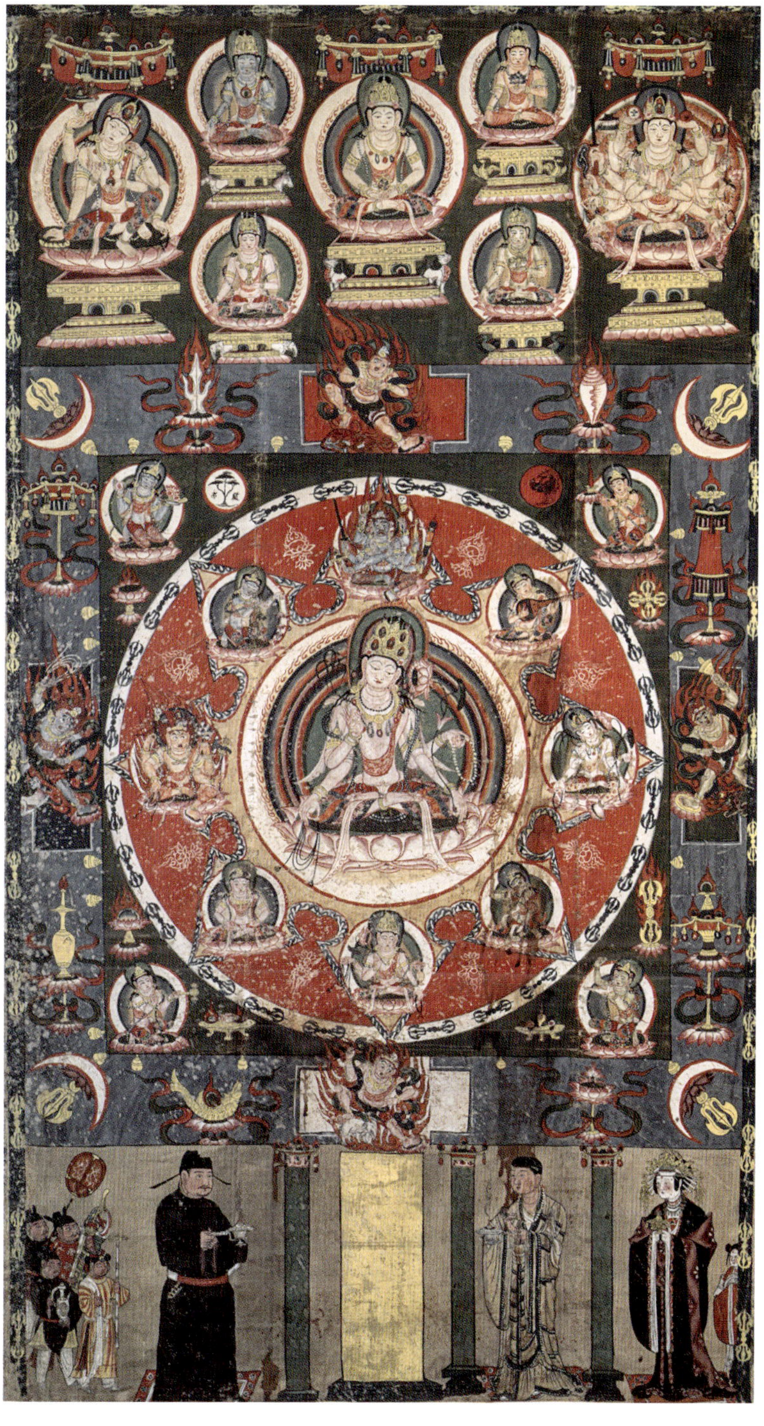

FIGURE 5.4
Maṇḍala of Avalokiteśvara, ca. tenth century, pigments on silk, H: 90 × 63 cm, from Dunhuang. Musée Guimet, Paris (3579). Photo © RMN-Grand Palais/Art Resource, New York.

flowers, a lotus, and a māla) wearing a five-Buddha crown surrounded by four attendants and four of the eight offering deities arranged on the eight spokes of the central wheel (or lotus). The colors of the five tathāgatas are differentiated like the previous one, and it follows the same arrangement as before, with Vairocana holding a wheel in the center. The Dunhuang system is closely related to the IEB system, with the same set of five colors, white-blue-red-yellow-green. But the difference lies in the directional assignment of the five colors. Here, the Dunhuang system seems to retain the Chinese system's idea of yellow as a central color, assigning it to Vairocana seated in the middle. This Dunhuang system with the arrangement of White-East—Akṣobhya and Blue-South—Ratnasambhava is also found in a few Indic-Buddhist examples, as seen in the arrangement of the five goddesses in the Pañcarakṣā maṇḍala of the NsP18 and also in the Durgatipariśodhana maṇḍala of the NsP22 (figure 5.1e). These examples suggest that the Dunhuang system may have been in a broader circulation.

Early examples of maṇḍala diagrams and drawings, like a tenth-century diagram from Dunhuang, Pelliot Chinois 4518 (33), recently discussed by Michelle Wang, point to how colors may have been understood in early Esoteric Buddhist communities and how they were transported in the context of transmitting teachings relating to Esoteric Buddhist rituals.[27] Pelliot Chinois 4518 (33) is a schematic drawing on paper of the Vajradhātu maṇḍala (figure 5.5). The details of the deities are only summarily sketched. A practitioner is supposed to see in the Vajradhātu maṇḍala a basic visual guide to the placement of deities by their types. The drawing also features dabs of color on the ground, assigning colors to each quarter. Next to the central Buddha Vairocana is a dab of brilliant yellow. The eastern quadrant with Akṣobhya is placed on the bottom of the page, where the dabs of color appear consistently dark brown. The dab of blue appears on the left side of the page, marking the southern quadrant with Buddha Ratnasambhava as the head. Above Vairocana is Amitābha, marking the western quadrant. The dab of color appears nearly black. On the opposite side of Ratnasambhava is Amoghasiddhi marking the northern quadrant, and the color here appears light brown, which most likely would have been green. Given the discoloration of green on the page, it is possible that the color scheme here also followed the Dunhuang system (C-Y; E-Wh; S-B; W-R; N-G). The dab of brown on Akṣobhya's eastern quadrant may have been white, while the black dots on Amitābha's western quadrant may have been red. This identification remains a hypothesis until scientific analysis of pigments on this diagram is possible.[28] This diagram and others like it help us understand how visual information concerning Esoteric Buddhist visionary practices may have circulated. As Wang observes following Cynthea Bogel's concept of eidetic contemplation, "there was an inverse relationship between the complexity of the visualization and the amount of visual detail offered in the diagram."[29] Perhaps, it was unnecessary to circulate color information when it was challenging to do so in mostly monochromatic drawings and diagrams that seem to have been prevalently used to transfer visual knowledge during the first phase of Esoteric Buddhism's transmission to East Asia. Even when color notations are introduced, it is difficult to determine in a monochromatic drawing which color was intended at the time of its production,

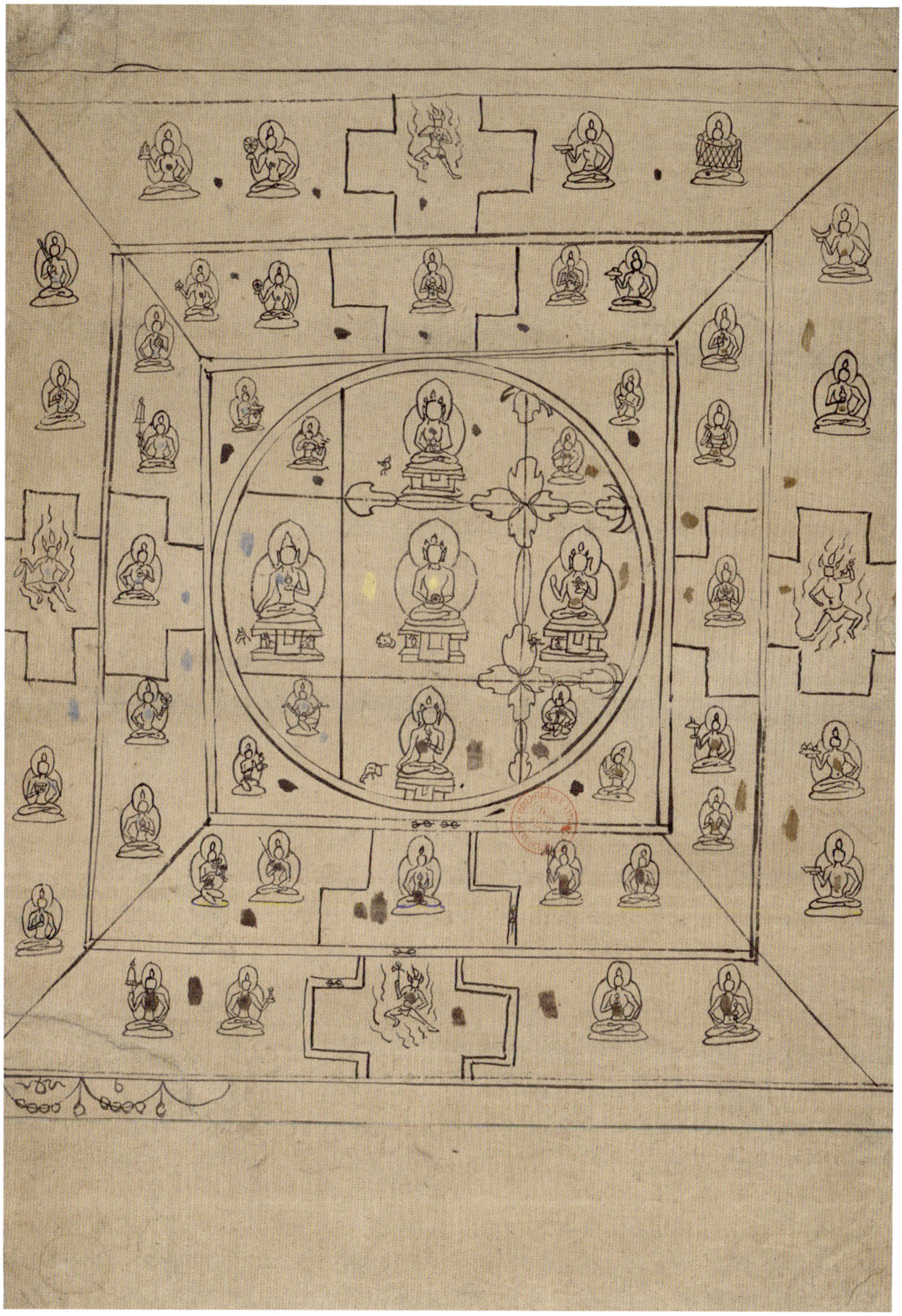

FIGURE 5.5

Diagram of the Vajradhātu maṇḍala, P.4518 (33) ca. tenth century, Dunhuang, China. Ink and light colors on paper, H: 43.6 cm. Image © Bibliothèque Nationale de France.

and which color was expected from each color term if it circulated beyond its original production site and period.[30]

COLOR AS AN ENCODING TOOL FOR SYSTEMATIZING ESOTERIC VISUAL KNOWLEDGE

Once a systematic approach to organizing visual knowledge developed in Buddhist circles, the IEB color system was embraced and established as a tool to organize the vast Buddhist pantheon systematically from the eleventh century onward. That color was adopted as an encoding tool suggests that the circulation of visual information in polychrome was not only possible but also important in the changing Esoteric Buddhist circles in South Asia and the Himalayas. Systematic use of color seen in the application of the IEB color system in artistic production from 1100 CE onward suggests that polychromatic painting became an important medium for circulating the knowledge of Esoteric vision practices.

TRANSREGIONAL INSPIRATIONS: THE ELEVENTH-CENTURY MOMENT

Surviving art-historical evidence for the application of the IEB color system is scarce until the eleventh century. The main assembly hall of the Buddhist monastery of Tabo (located in the Spiti valley, Himachal Pradesh) in the Indian Himalayas, provides the earliest securely datable in-situ example of the IEB color system in art. The five Buddha families and the cardinal direction–five color codification system was instrumental for arranging the spatial and color distribution of deities in a carefully orchestrated iconographic program inside this building. Here, the assembly of clay sculptures and painted upper walls realizes the Vajradhātu maṇḍala in a three-dimensional space (see figure 1.12). Given the state of conservation and the practice of repairing/restoring painting and clay sculptures throughout centuries, it is difficult to discuss what the original colors used in the hall may have looked like. Nonetheless, the surviving wall painting and the sculptures of the Vajradhātu maṇḍala bear out the IEB color system. As scholars like Christian Luczanits and Deborah Klimburg-Salter have observed, the iconographic system is based on the STTS, but it does not exactly follow any of the known versions of the STTS. Its system differs from the earliest known Tibetan translation of the STTS and also from the Chinese translation by Vajrabodhi. The closest may be the new translation of the STTS in the early eleventh century by the famed Tibetan translator Rinchen Zangpo (c. 958–1055 CE). While Rinchen Zangpo's direct association with Tabo cannot be established, the changes that inspired the renovation of Tabo's main assembly hall within only a generation of its foundation (the monastery was initially founded in 996 CE), which according to the renovation inscription was "old," should be taken into consideration along with Rinchen Zangpo's translation activities. Rinchen Zangpo's rise to fame and the foundation and renovation of Tabo are almost certainly connected to transregional movements of Indian Esoteric Buddhist masters and their Himalayan disciples during the period of *phy-dar,* the later transmission of Buddhism to the Tibetan plateau. The sophisticated system of organization realized in the main assembly hall at Tabo suggests that the STTS-based five-Buddha system was well established and widely circulating in the Esoteric Buddhist world by this time. At the same time, most surviving art-historical records that signal the importance of the five tathāgatas (including the IEB color system) as a crucial concept for organizing the Esoteric Buddhist pantheon date from around 1000 CE onward. Prominent art-historical examples that exemplify this system date after the time of Tabo's renovation, which is also linked with an important Indian Esoteric Buddhist master, Atīśa Dīpaṅkara Śrījñāna, whose career embodies the transregional movement of Esoteric Buddhism during this time. Atīśa had spent twelve years in Sumatra with another Esoteric Buddhist master before returning to India and rising to great fame, according to later Tibetan historical traditions.

While the STTS-based five-tathāgata system was not a new phenomenon, surviving evidence suggests that there may have been renewed interest in it as a principle to organize the knowledge generated in Esoteric Buddhist vision practices. A new type of stone stele that incorporated five tathāgatas on the top portion appeared in numerous Indian Buddhist monastic centers and pilgrimage sites around the turn of the eleventh century, with a securely datable image dating to the second half of the eleventh century. Most surviving stone steles from Bihar and Bengal that bear the five tathāgatas in their programs were made in the late eleventh and the twelfth centuries.[31] They often bear the tathāgata of the chosen deity's family—for example, Amitābha for Avalokiteśvara, and Amoghasiddhi for Tārā—as the center or apex of the five-Buddha composition on the top of each stele. A dated example is unfortunately rare among this corpus, but one of the earliest datable stone steles of this kind is a standing Tārā from Tetrawan, a site near Nālandā in today's Bihar (figure 5.6). The five Jina Buddhas appear in the order of Vairocana, Ratnasambhava, Amoghasiddhi, Akṣobhya, and Amitābha, with Amoghasiddhi in the apex. A number of sādhanas identify Amoghasiddhi as a lineage tathāgata of many forms of Tārā including Khadiravaṇī-Tārā (SM 89), which this sculpture represents closely. The stele bears a donor inscription dated with Rāmapāla's second regnal year, identifying its time of production and installation during the second half of the eleventh century.

A five-tathāgata arrangement also appears on top of a painting of a seated Tārā that once belonged to the Reting monastery in central Tibet (figure 5.7).[32] On the top register, the five tathāgatas appear inside seven clear rocky mountain peaks, with the central Buddha, Amoghasiddhi, attended by two bodhisattvas on either side, along with the other four tathāgatas. Despite the discoloration and restoration on the surface, the mudras and surviving colors clearly identify each tathāgata, starting with Ratnasambhava, yellow, *varada mudrā;* Amitābha, red, *dhyāna mudrā;* Amoghasiddhi in the center, dark brown (green), *abhaya mudrā;* Vairocana, white, *bodhyagrī mudrā;* and Akṣobhya, blue, *bhumisparśa mudrā.* The five tathāgatas in five colors are systematically used here and signify the lineage color of Tārā. If the proposed date of the painting, sometime during the second half of the eleventh century, can be confirmed, this painting would suggest that the IEB color system might have traveled across the Himalayas simultaneously as it was being embraced in the eastern Indian monastic centers.[33]

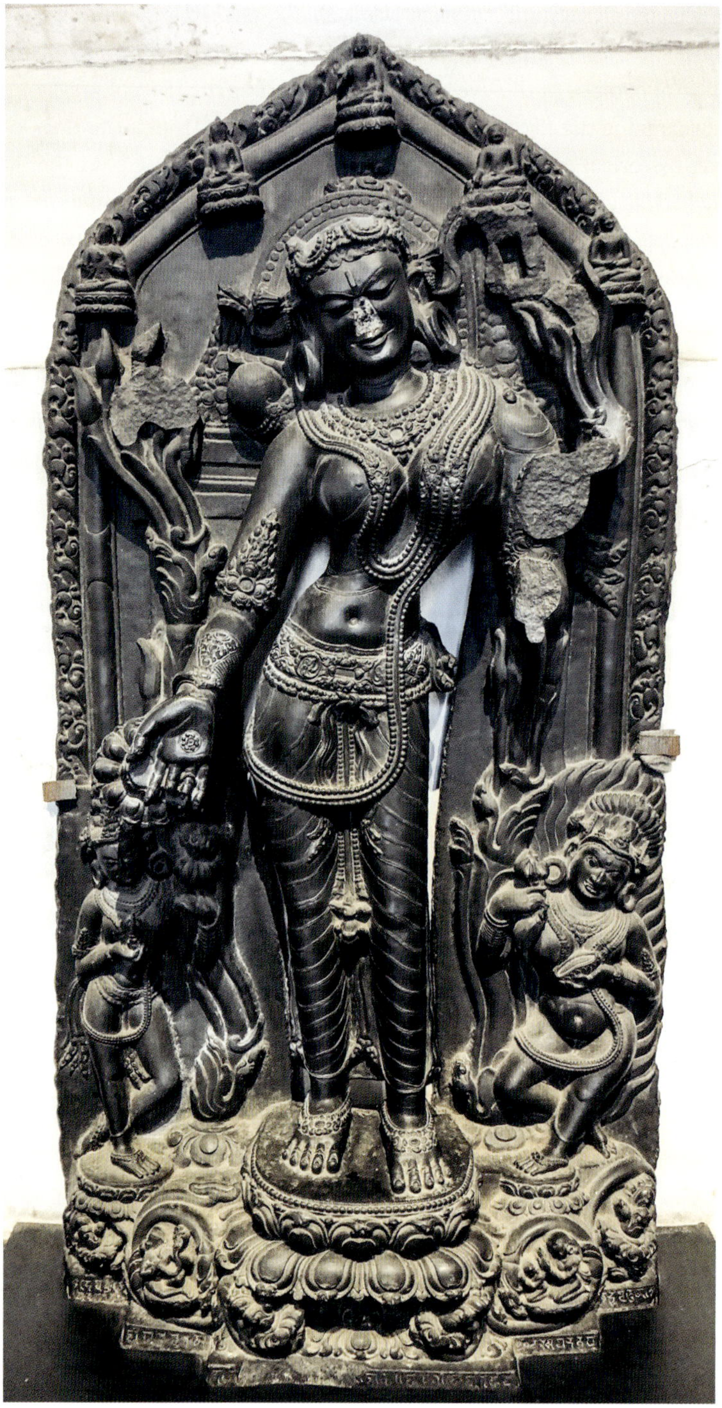

FIGURE 5.6
Tārā, Tetrawan, Bihar, India, second year of Rāmapāla's reign (ca. 1079 CE). Indian Museum. Photo © Jinah Kim.

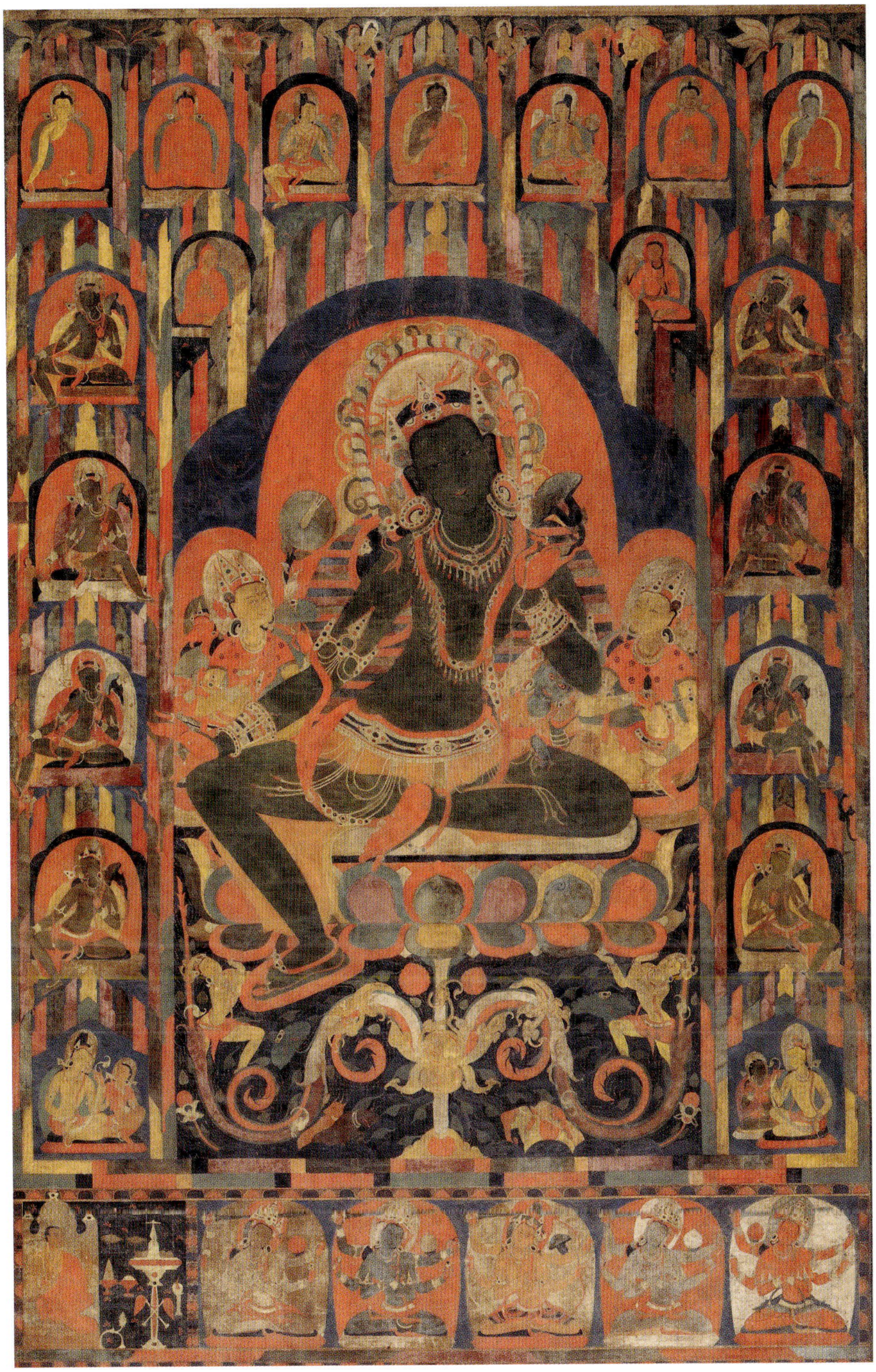

FIGURE 5.7
Green Tārā (Khadiravaṇī Tārā/Aṣṭamahābhaya Tārā), central Tibet, Reting monastery, ca. second half of the eleventh century. Distemper on cloth, H: 122 cm. The John and Berthe Ford Collection. Photo courtesy of the Walters Art Museum.

IEB COLOR SYSTEM

Introduction of this new compositional program (pentad system) in Buddhist sculptures during the second half of the eleventh century may in fact be related to the rising need to catalog Esoteric Buddhist ritual practices systematically, which culminated in ambitious compendium projects like the VA and the NsP by Abhayākaragupta, as discussed in chapter 3. In particular, color seems to have become an important tool for coding this esoteric visual knowledge: every tathāgata lineage is assigned a color. Most every sādhana collected in the SM, which in Bhattacharyya's edition totals 312 sādhanas, gives specific color information (often through the suffix *-varṇa*), down to each face when multiple faces are invoked. When a lineage color is not specified or seems undetermined in a sādhana—for example, as in the case of the form of Mañjughoṣa described in the SM 52, Vādirāṭ sādhanam—the color term is often light-based. (For example, it is "golden" [*kanakagaura*] for Mañjughoṣa of the SM 52.) This "default" may suggest a pre-pentad layer in iconographic conception.[34] The IEB color system as articulated in the later sādhana literature seems to have emerged as a tool used to organize the complex field of Esoteric Buddhist visual knowledge sometime during the eleventh century. Subsequently, it was embraced in earnest within the span of a few generations.

Since it is difficult to speak of color codification through surviving stone sculptures, the most important surviving evidence that demonstrates the adoption of the IEB color system in Buddhist South Asia is found in painted manuscripts.[35] Perhaps due to their portable size and intimate nature, painted manuscripts seem to have been the central medium in which to experiment and incorporate new ideas arising in Indic Esoteric Buddhist circles. Two important observations may be made with regard to the appearance of five tathāgatas in five colors in surviving painted Buddhist manuscripts: (1) the IEB color system appears in the iconographic program of painted manuscripts prepared from the mid-eleventh century onward in two contexts: one as a systematic schema that frames the *Perfection of Wisdom*, and the other as an organizing schema for ordering the five protective goddesses (Pañcarakṣā) in five colors; and (2) the opacity in color increases dramatically from the turn of the twelfth century, which likely relates to color's function as a tool for codifying visual knowledge. Pigments applied in high opacity convey color values much more straightforwardly than thinly applied pigments.

THE IEB COLOR SYSTEM IN THE *PERFECTION OF WISDOM* MANUSCRIPT

Early examples representing the five tathāgatas in the IEB system appear in the painted manuscripts of the *Perfection of Wisdom*. The earliest known surviving manuscript that introduces the five tathāgata system in its iconographic program is in the Wellcome Library. The manuscript was most likely prepared during Vigrahapāla II's reign (c. 1043–69 CE).[36] The five tathāgatas appear on the first two folios (folios 1v–2r) and surround the goddess Prajñāpāramitā in the central panel of folio 2r. Here, Ratnasambhava (yellow, *varada mudrā*), Akṣobhya (blue, *bhūmisparśa mudrā*), and Amitābha (red, *dhyāna mudrā*) appear on folio 1v from left to right, and Vairocana (white, *bodhyagrī mudrā*)–Prajñāpāramitā (yellow, dharmacakra mudrā)–Amoghasiddhi ("green," *abhaya mudrā*) appear on folio 2r from left to right

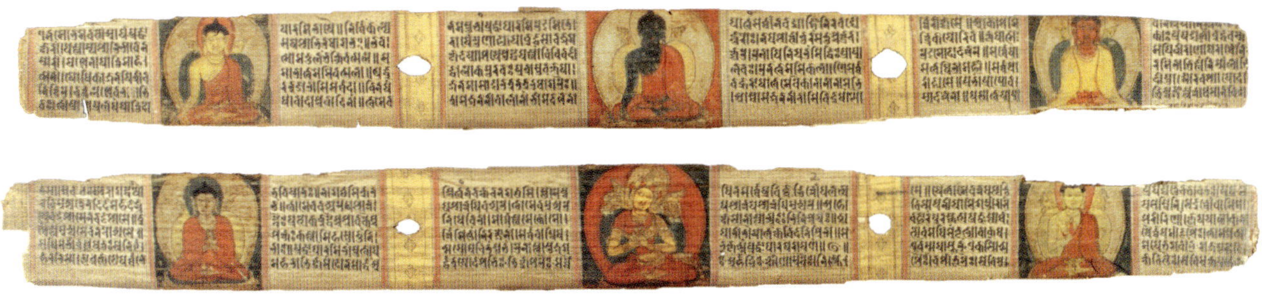

FIGURE 5.8
Folios 1v–2r, *Perfection of Wisdom* manuscript, Vigrahapāla's reign (ca. 1043–69 CE), Wellcome Library, London, Sansk. Epsilon 1. Photo credit: Wellcome Collections, London.

(figure 5.8). The five tathāgatas are not mentioned in the accompanying text of this manuscript, which is a hymn to the goddess, nor do they appear anywhere else in the *Perfection of Wisdom*. Their incorporation on the first two pages establishes a paratextual context in Indian Esoteric Buddhist tradition, one in which the *Perfection of Wisdom* text was being repackaged to support Esoteric Buddhist perspectives through the production of painted manuscripts with sophisticated iconographic programs.[37]

The centrality of Akṣobhya, in particular, signals a new stage in Esoteric Buddhist thinking, as it is in the Phase Three texts (*mahāyoga* and *yoginī tantra*s and their ritual manuals in Indian Buddhist circles) in which Akṣobhya's lineage triumphs and occasionally pushes Vairocana to the side. The Wellcome manuscript remains a sole known example where the five tathāgatas are incorporated into the painted pages. Colors appear rather transparent and not as opaque as what we see in typical post-twelfth-century Buddhist paintings. This is perhaps due to the quality of available pigment (in the case of inorganic mineral pigments, for example, density and particle sizes determine both opacity and shade) and also to the available pigment application technique on a palm-leaf surface.[38] In the IEB system, Amoghasiddhi would be green; however, on folio 2r, he appears nearly indistinguishable from the body color of Ratnasambhava (yellow, on folio 1v), possibly due to the fugitive nature of colorants used. It is also possible that the recipe used to create green here was not as long lasting as the artist had expected it to be. On the other hand, the use of transparent colors may have been an artistic response to the need to pictorialize the tathāgatas as brilliant, light-emitting beings.

Other surviving examples of the *Perfection of Wisdom* manuscripts that include the five tathāgatas in the iconographic program have them on the interior of the book covers. Most of them were prepared in Nepal. Many of these painted manuscript covers, especially when they encase a manuscript without any painted page(s), unfortunately were collected separately as art objects throughout the twentieth century. Most examples of this small but important corpus of surviving portable paintings from medieval South Asia are now divorced from their original manuscript contexts. Fortunately, there are a handful of prominent

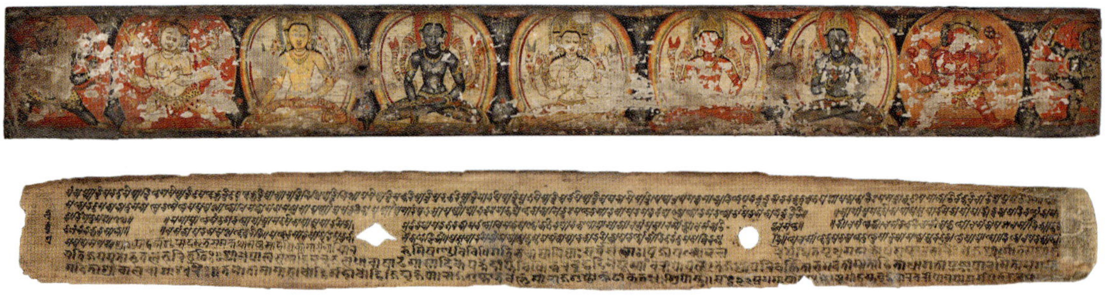

FIGURE 5.9
Front cover (interior view) and folio 261v, *Perfection of Wisdom* manuscript, Nepal, ca. twelfth century. Cambridge University Library Add. 1544. Reproduced by kind permission of the Syndics of Cambridge University Library.

repositories where we find manuscripts and their painted covers together: for example, during the second half of the nineteenth century, Sanskrit manuscripts from Nepal entered Cambridge University Library; the manuscripts that were kept in Nepal were collected in Nepalese archives as part of a modernization project initiated during the early twentieth century. There are a few occasional examples found in Western museums (including two American public museums, the Museum of Fine Arts, Boston, and the Detroit Institute of Arts) that have Sanskrit palm-leaf manuscripts; these examples were collected in the early twentieth century. Here, I introduce a few exceptional examples that help us understand the use of the IEB color system with a hope that some of the following observations may locate stray manuscript covers in a more informed historical context.

A manuscript of the *Perfection of Wisdom* now in the Cambridge University Library (Add. 1544) survives with two painted covers that showcase the IEB color system in use. The manuscript is written in neat, tiny letters that are slanted at about a ten-degree angle from a vertical line (figure 5.9). Unfortunately, the manuscript's original scribe and patron are not credited—the original text ends at "*mahāśramaṇaḥ*||," marking the end of the "*ye dharmāhetu*" verse.[39] An extensive postcolophon dated N.S. 422 (1302 CE) immediately follows the end of the original text; this colophon continues on the recto of the first folio, where another later fourteenth-century colophon is added following the first colophon. The presence of multiple colophons attests to the manuscript's importance for the community that owned it. Stylistic features seen on the painted wooden covers suggest a late eleventh-century date. The stippled treatment of dark-blue background seen on both covers is a technique found in other late eleventh-century and early twelfth-century manuscript paintings.[40] The bottom end cover features seven identical Buddhas displaying the preaching gesture. All seven are yellow—indicating the Buddha's golden body—and all wear red monastic robes covering both shoulders; they are flanked by yellow Maitreya and red Avalokiteśvara.[41] The front cover, which bears extensive physical marks from the ritual worship of the book, reveals a set of the five tathāgatas flanked by four six-armed, three-headed protector deities, two on either side.[42] The five tathāgatas are arranged with Vairocana in the center, flanked by Akṣobhya and

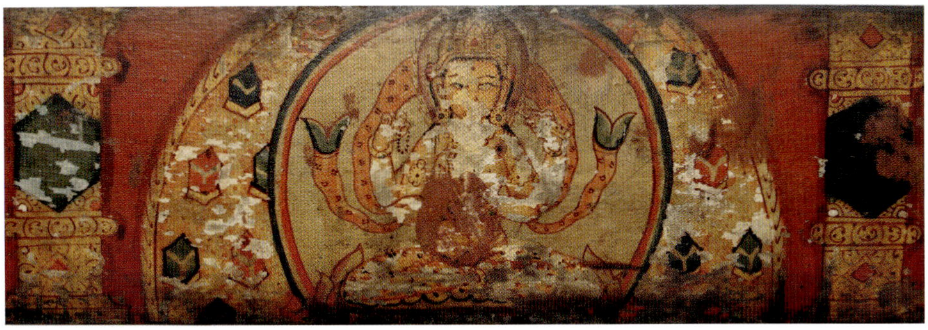

FIGURE 5.10
Goddess Prajnāpāramitā with pūjā marks, detail of figure 5.12.

Amitābha on the right and the left of Vairocana, followed by Ratnasambhava and Amoghasiddhi to the farther right and left. The iconography of Vairocana is unique among the surviving examples of five tathāgatas in manuscript paintings: he is three-faced and four-armed with two principal hands held in *bodhyaṅgī mudrā* (the so-called wisdom fist, also known as *bodhyagrī mudrā*). This four-headed form of Vairocana in the center of the Vajradhātu maṇḍala conforms to that in the STTS. The two additional hands holding a rosary and a book, right and left respectively, emulate the iconography of the goddess Prajñāpāramitā, suggesting an effort to make this form relevant to herald the manuscript of the *Perfection of Wisdom*.

A rosary and a book are the two prominent attributes of the goddess Prajñāpāramitā, often held in the exact manner as we see in a twelfth-century Nepalese painted cover for another *Perfection of Wisdom* manuscript where the central deity is Prajñāpāramitā (figure 5.10). Other than this effort to customize the iconography to fit the manuscript context, the iconographic details of the five tathāgatas are clearly executed with appropriate mudrās and colors assigned to the five tathāgatas as known in the Vajradhātu maṇḍala: Ratnasambhava-varada mudrā with yellow (S), Akṣobhya-bhūmisparśa mudrā with blue (E), Vairocana-bodhyagrī mudrā with white, Amitābha-dhyana mudrā with red (W), and Amoghasiddhi-abhaya mudrā with green (N). The cardinal directions are difficult to indicate in a horizontal arrangement, but by arranging Akṣobhya (E) and Amitābha (W) on the right and the left of Vairocana respectively, the program also imparts a sense of a directional scheme.

The intention of assigning five colors according to the sādhana system is clear, but the color of Amoghasiddhi as we see today is not "green." It appears dull blue, slightly lighter and grayer than the color of Akṣobhya. What color was exactly intended here is difficult to judge from the surviving evidence. Future analysis of pigment layers will help to reconstruct what the original color may have looked like. Akṣobhya and Amoghasiddhi also seem to have been painted translucently. On the body of Akṣobhya, for example, a deeper shade of blue accentuates crevices and defines body parts. Such light application of colorants may have contributed to the loss of the "greenness" on Amoghasiddhi. It is most likely that two colorants—indigo and orpiment—were used to create green.[43] Such translucent and light

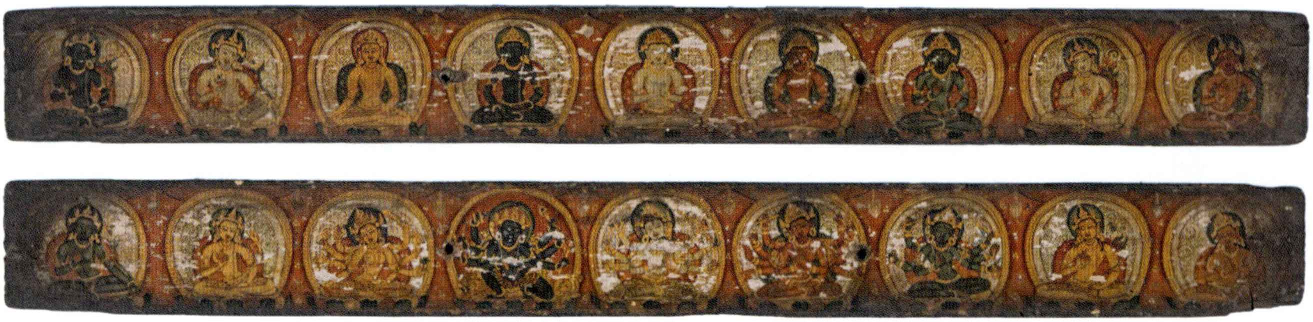

FIGURE 5.11
Painted wooden book covers of a Pañcarakṣā manuscript, dated N.S. 325 (1205 CE), Nepal. 5.5 × 55 cm, Cambridge University Library Add. 1644. Reproduced by kind permission of the Syndics of Cambridge University Library.

application of pigment layers for the body colors of transcendent beings is commonly seen in the surviving eleventh-century Buddhist manuscript paintings from South Asia. This tendency may have developed to capture the idea of the transcendent, enlightened body being bright and light-emitting.

Within a century, the colors became increasingly opaque and vivid; thus, by 1200 CE, bright, solid colors become the norm in Himalayan paintings. Compare the blue of Akṣobhya and the green of Amoghasiddhi in an early thirteenth-century manuscript of the *Pañcarakṣā* (CUL Add. 1644, dated N.S. 325, 1205 CE, see figure 5.11), which are also the colors of two of the five rakṣā goddesses, Mahāsāhasrapramardanī and Mahāśītavatī, respectively. They appear completely opaque and in much deeper shades in comparison to the colors seen on the Add. 1544 manuscript covers.

A *Perfection of Wisdom* manuscript now in the National Archives of Nepal in Kathmandu (Acc. No. 5.195; Microfilm #136/4) suggests a direct relationship between artistic confidence in the IEB color system and the increased opacity in color application in manuscript paintings (figure 5.12). The palm-leaf folios of this manuscript are not illustrated except for the geometric shapes such as floral diamonds, wheels, and lotus roundels in black ink, marking chapter endings. It survives with two wooden painted book covers that were most likely prepared contemporaneously at the time the text was copied. The manuscript bears a dated colophon on the last folio (folio 282v). Unfortunately, the date was revised by a later hand, as were the names of the donor and the reigning king. The current date of completion reads as the fourth fortnight of the bright half in the month of *pauṣa*, N.S. 271 (1151 CE); this makes it a mid-twelfth-century manuscript, but both the single digit and the hundredth digit have been retouched along with the name of the month. Given the paleographic indication of archaic features—for example, the exaggeration of angular curves—and the two-letter name of the king that had been erased, it seems likely that the manuscript was prepared slightly earlier, possibly at the turn of the twelfth century.[44]

Both covers are divided into five compartments with bejeweled pillars as spatial dividers, a reminder of how temple architecture inspired the logic of painted manuscript designs, as discussed in chapter 2. The center of the opening cover is the four-armed goddess

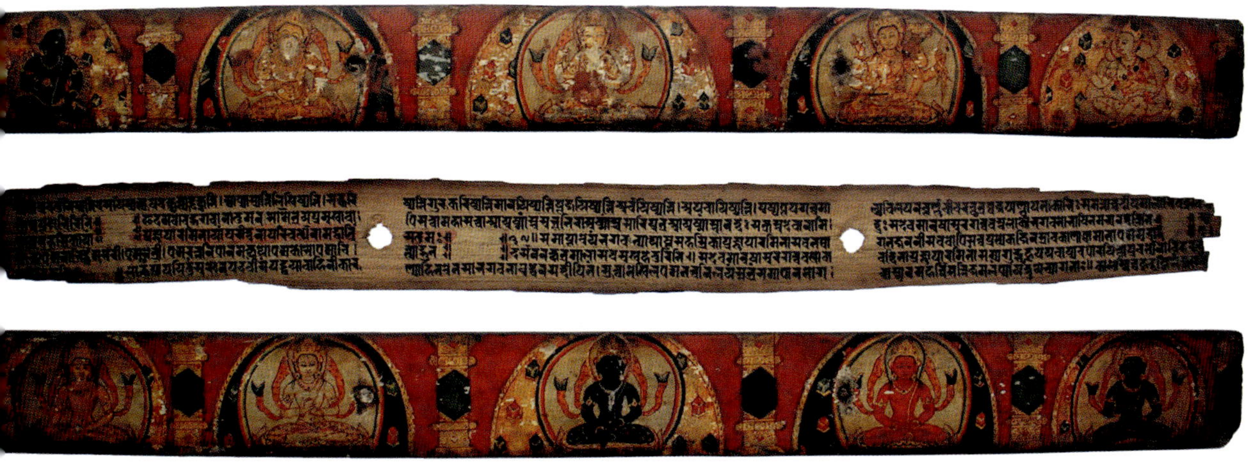

FIGURE 5.12
Perfection of Wisdom manuscript, ca. early twelfth century, Nepal. Pigments and ink on palm leaf and wood. National Archive, Acc. No. 5.195. Photo © Jinah Kim.

Prajñāpāramitā who holds a rosary and a book in her raised hands. That she was the central focus of ritual offerings over the centuries is clear from the prominent reddish-brown stains on and around her that also reveal traces of fingerprints (figure 5.10). These are like *tilak* (Skt. *tilaka*) marks often seen on images that receive devotional offerings. On either side of Prajñāpāramitā there are two-armed Jambhala and six-armed Vasudhārā, deities of prosperity and wealth. Jambhala seems to have received additional devotional actions as he has an additional layer of white sandalwood marks. These three deities are all painted yellow, including their attributes, such as a sheaf of grain and a pot (*bhadraghaṭa*) in Vasudhārā's hands and a jewel-vomiting mongoose and a citron in Jambhala's hands. Yellow seems to have been chosen to signal golden radiance. The deities depicted on either end of this cover are positioned to look toward this central trio. Next to Jambhala to the left end is another Jambhala in dark blue. Although this particular form does not match any of the known sādhanas, it seems to indicate an awareness of a form of a Jambhala that belongs to Akṣobhya's lineage.[45] The other end is an image of Nāgarāja depicted in white with a coiled five-headed snake as his backdrop, holding a jewel-filled bowl in his left hand and offering a jewel in his right hand.

An image of Nāgarāja on a *Perfection of Wisdom* manuscript is rather unusual among surviving examples, but it does not seem out of place on the opening cover to the manuscript of the Prajñāpāramitā, given the popular legend that nāgas protected the teaching of the Prajñāpāramitā until Nāgārjuna retrieved it for mankind.[46] While drawing from the age-old serpentine iconography, the iconographic composition and details found in this particular miniature painting of Nāgarāja are creative outputs of an unnamed artist. In particular, the artist represented the snake king as offering a cubic-shaped, shining green jewel. It seamlessly repeats the shape and the size of the jewels strewn on the yellow mandorla (body-halo) that surrounds him. Such a bejeweled, fantastic backdrop frames each deity in alternate colors of yellow and deep blue, creating a rhythmic pattern that harmonizes both covers. The jewels in these orbs are in three primary colors of the IEB system, green, blue, and red (here most likely in vermilion), and the reflective cubic surface is indicated through its white (uncolored) lines.

The end cover showcases the confidence of the unnamed artist in manipulating the IEB color system to generate a harmonious and brilliant picture. The five tathāgatas appear in the order of Ratnasambhava-Vairocana-Akṣobhya-Amitābha-Amoghasiddhi, with Akṣobhya in the center. Only Vairocana and Akṣobhya switched their place from the arrangement seen in the Cambridge manuscript (Add. 1544), as discussed above. Here, the five colors of the five tathāgatas are represented fully manifested through high opacity in pigment. The IEB color system seems to organize and control the entire visual plane thanks to various artistic interventions. The jewel-speckled orb that surrounds each tathāgata alternates between the yellow and the deep blue of Ratnasambhava and Akṣobhya, enhancing the sense of visual harmony. The blue of Akṣobhya is an opaque, dark blue, possibly achieved through several layers of application. The red of Amitābha is also dense, opaque, and Amitābha's color stands out in contrast to the deep blue bejeweled orb. The green of Amoghasiddhi is no longer indistinguishable, and the artist seems to have mastered how to deliver the color, probably by balancing the ratio between orpiment and indigo. The vision of the five tathāgatas, each surrounded by a brilliant, colorful jewel-strewn orb, appearing in between bejeweled pillars, does not seem to have been a part of a common iconographic repertoire circulating in the twelfth century. The same is true for the arrangement of the goddess Prajñāpāramitā and her retinue in the opening panel. Is this an exceptional surviving example on which the five colors of the IEB system are brilliantly embraced to coordinate the pictorial program? Whatever the answer, its extraordinariness should remind us of possibilities that, during this early period of its history, a manuscript was a portable, intimate object offering artists and patrons a medium for the expression of new ideas and visions in color. This unnamed artist successfully showed how to convey Buddhist divinities in five colors.

IEB COLOR SYSTEM IN THE PAÑCARAKṢĀ MANUSCRIPTS

The IEB color system is clearly in play in illustrated manuscripts of the *Pañacarakṣā*. The text is a collection of five "sūtras," each explicating the power of one of the five goddesses. It provides dhāraṇīs (mystical syllable clusters) of each goddess to use for protection against specific calamities and diseases. The idea of the five goddesses as a set already imparts a Pentad system. Their formulation in this style hosted in a manuscript context is a later phenomenon than the appearance of individual goddesses and their respective dhāraṇīs.[47] Goddesses like Mahāmāyurī and Mahāpratisarā are known independently from early on.[48] Mahāpratisarā, in particular, was well known across early Esoteric Buddhist communities; numerous *Mahāpratisarā-dhāraṇī* amulets (woodblock printed paper sheets) are known from the eighth century onward from Dunhuang and elsewhere in China (see figure 1.14).[49] Independent images of Mahāpratisarā that may be datable between the eighth and the tenth centuries are known in eastern India (especially Bengal) as well as in Java.[50] A *pothi*-format

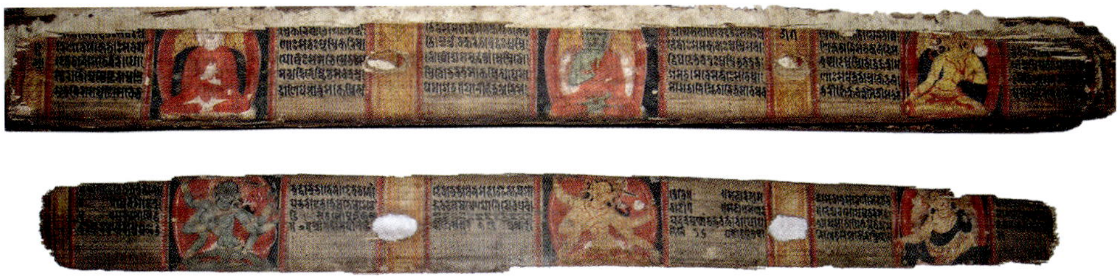

FIGURE 5.13
Folio 57v–58r, Pañcarakṣā manuscript, Rāmapāla's fifty-third regnal year (ca. 1131 CE), Bihar, India. Ink and pigments on palm leaf. National Museum, New Delhi, Acc. No. 67.560. Photo courtesy of National Museum, New Delhi.

manuscript seems to have provided a vehicle to compile the five rakṣās as a set while the Phase Two Esoteric Buddhist emphasis on the five-Buddha system may have encouraged the formulation of their group identity and presentation as a Pentad.[51] In later Nepalese manuscripts dating to the fifteenth century or later, five goddesses are almost always paired with five tathāgatas, but this pairing seems to have been introduced well after the adoption of the IEB color system as an organizing schema for designing illustrated manuscripts of the five goddesses. Once painted manuscripts were introduced to make these powerful protective deities and their spells available for ritual consumption, Nepalese manuscript makers seem to have quickly adopted the IEB color scheme more systematically than their eastern Indian counterparts.[52] The iconography of the goddesses and their color scheme remain consistent in Nepalese PC manuscripts, more or less corresponding to the visions of the goddesses recorded in the *Pañcarakṣāvidhānam* (SM 206).[53]

The earliest known dated manuscript of the *Pañcarakṣā* hails from eastern India, and this important manuscript now in the Cambridge University Library (Add. 1686) was prepared for a queen Uddākā during the fourteenth regnal year of Pāla king Nayapāla.[54] In this mid-eleventh-century manuscript, body colors of deities are undifferentiated; all have an earthly appearance that is similar to the color of the palm-leaf page. Close physical inspection of each painted panel reveals that each may in fact have been uniformly painted in shimmering shell gold. The use of gold effectively represents the idea of divine beings emitting light. Here, color specificity does not seem to have been a concern. The IEB color scheme is used in a PC manuscript dated to the late tenth century (Rāmapāla's fourth year, ca. 1081 CE) now in the Bharat Kala Bhavan, BHU; in this PC manuscript, the five colors of the IEB system (blue-yellow-white-green-red) are assigned to five goddesses.[55] It is not necessarily an organizing principle for the iconographic program, and the colors' tonality remains rather transparent as seen in the washed-green color of the goddess Mahāmāyūrī on folio 2r.[56]

It is only after the turn of 1100 CE that five colors are consistently applied to the goddesses. The IEB color system does not seem to have been fully embraced until the late twelfth century. In a *Pañcarakṣā* manuscript dated with Rāmapāla's fifty-third regnal year (c. 1131 CE) now in the National Museum, New Delhi, the five goddesses and the five

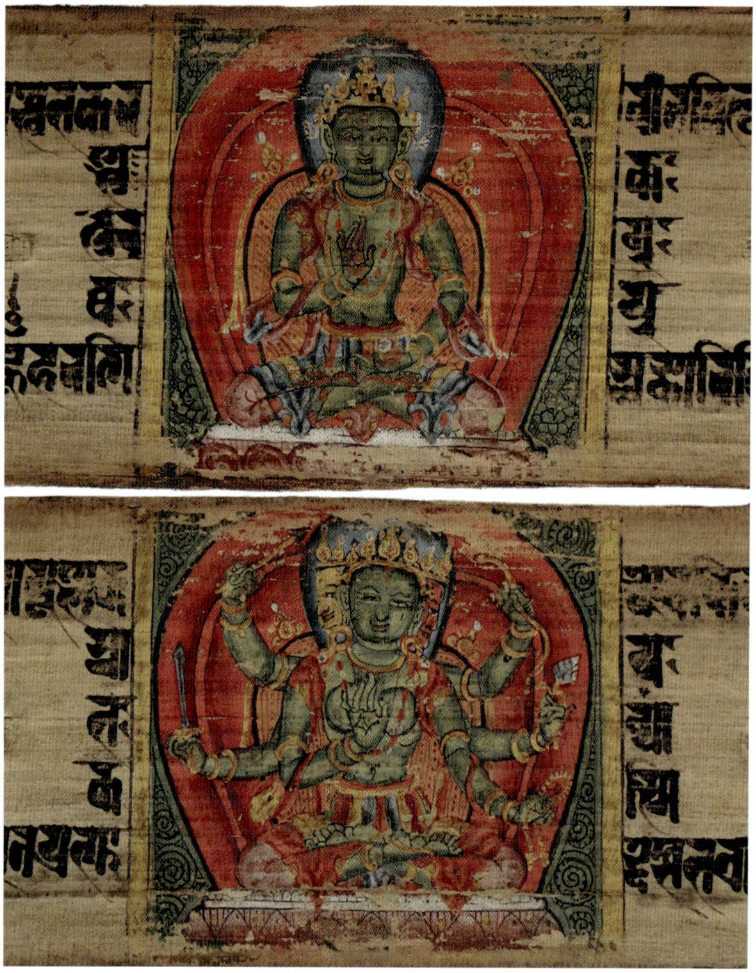

FIGURE 5.14
Amoghasidhi-Mahāśītavatī, folios 155v–156r, *Pañcarakṣā* manuscript, ca. late fifteenth century, Nepal. Kaiser Library Acc. No. 9.105. Photo © Jinah Kim.

tathāgatas appear together, but their body colors are not coordinated (figure 5.13): Yellow Ratnasambhava is facing white Mahāsāhasrapramardanī (folios 1v–2r) while white Vairocana faces green Mahāmāyūrī, and Green Amoghasiddhi faces yellow Mahāpratisarā (folios 57v–58r). By the turn of the thirteenth century, the IEB color system applied in opaque, brilliant colorants seems to have become the norm in manuscript painting in both eastern India and Nepal. For example, in an early thirteenth-century Nepalese manuscript of the Pañcarakṣā (CUL Add. 1644), the five goddesses and the five tathāgatas appear in their opaque colors of yellow, blue, white, red, and green (see figure 5.11). The pairing of the goddesses with the five tathāgatas seems complete, but their consort relationship exists only on a conceptual level. They are relegated to the beginning and the end of the book, respectively, instead of physically and proximately paired with each other. It would be another century before they would appear together physically coupled and facing each other inside a manuscript, as seen, for example, in a late fifteenth-century manuscript prepared during the reign of Ratnamalla (c. 1484–1520 CE) for a resident of Kathmandu (kaṣṭamaṇḍapa), Śantirājasiṁha (figure 5.14).

EMIC UNDERSTANDING OF COLOR

The development of a color codification of esoteric visual knowledge seems to be integrally linked to artisanal knowledge in preparing material and applying colorants in a conclusive manner, for example, with painting in opaque colors. We will return to this material aspect in chapter 6. Here we explore further how color was conceptualized and how certain colors were understood in medieval Indic ritual contexts. The ambiguous use of color terms in textual sources underscores how the use of the IEB color system in the sādhanas and artistic programs ordered and cataloged visual knowledge systematically, aiding the codification of esoteric vision practices and their visual knowledge.

VISIONS IN COLOR

The ways in which colors are identified and described in Buddhists texts demonstrate clearly that early medieval Buddhist authors were aware of the phenomenological qualities of color as well as the semiotic limitations of a color-based systematization scheme. The MVS translated by Yixing and Subhakarasiṁha in 724 CE (T18, No. 848), for example, describes forms of maṇḍala deities in detail, including color specification. But the color information given in this text is approximate and descriptive. For example, Hayagrīva is in "the color of rising sun" [大力持明王晨朝日暉色] T18n8487a; Vairocana is "blazing golden color" [大日勝尊現金色具暉曜] T18n848_7a; Śrī Tārā is a "mixed color of blue and white" [聖者多羅尊青白色相雜] T18n848_6b; one of the *vidyārājas* [月黶尊] is "in the color of summer time rain clouds" (a descriptive translation of monsoon clouds) [夏時雨雲色] T18n848_7a. Such descriptive terms and mixed color terms for the body colors of deities appear in a number of other Esoteric Buddhist texts known in eighth-century Chinese translations.

Descriptive and metaphoric terms continued to denote the body colors of deities in later tantras as well. For example, consider this passage in the *Hevajra tantra*, an important text of the *yoginī tantra* class:

> One should first imagine a corpse which represents the whole of existence, and the yogin, seated thereupon, should conceive himself of the nature of Heruka. In his own heart, he imagines the syllable RAM and a solar disk arising from it, and then upon that the syllable Hūṃ, the nature of which is Wisdom and Means. It is dark in colour and exceedingly fearful is this syllable Hūṃ which has emerged from a Vajra, and one should conceive of the essence of this Hūṃ as abiding in the heart of the Vajra. Then he should envisage the syllable Hūṃ as transformed into (Heruka) whose nature is wrath. This Vajra-born is exceedingly dark like a blue lotus in colour, or one may conceive of him as dark and red (*nīlārunābham*)—as one pleases. (HT I, iii)[57]

This "*nīlārunābham*," which Snellgrove translates as "dark and red," is explained as "the colour of the dawn mixed with dark blue" in a Tibetan commentary, which conjures up an image in a light-based hue rather than of a definitive color. In contrast, descriptions of Heruka's form collected in sādhana literature, for example in the NsP and the SM, consistently identify Heruka with a single, color term, "*kṛṣṇavarṇa*," meaning blue or blue-black colored.[58] The wide semantic range that a color term can denote presents a huge challenge to interpretation.[59] Colors that are seen in internal visions are equally difficult to capture in external expressions, whether in words or in images.

LIGHT-BASED COLOR THEORY

The five colors realized in early Buddhist paintings are rarely opaque, and the resulting images seem to capture the idea of the body of transcendental beings (like a Buddha) being light-emitting. In the Dunhuang Avalokiteśvara maṇḍala, for example, Amitābha's color takes on more orange hue, colors of Vairocana and Akṣobhya are barely differentiated (see figure 5.4). Even the green of Amoghasiddhi (*bottom right*) and the blue of Ratnasambhava (*top left*) are translucent so that traces of shading brushstrokes are visible. A subtle yellow/golden layer envelops the contour of the upper body of each of the four directional tathāgatas, as if to suggest their luminosity. In the Dunhuang Five-Tathāgata maṇḍala, the blue of Ratnasambhava and the green of Amoghasiddhi are rather pale, while the red of Amitābha is indicated only through a pinkish hue (see figure 5.3). In the "glow" behind their bodies, a transparent application of colors is used to portray the transcendent Buddhas. The multicolored wavy lines inside the body mandorlas of the five tathāgatas also convey the idea of transcendental beings with radiant, glowing bodies.

The idea that the body of the tathāgatas (and other transcendental beings) is light-emitting and brilliant is an ancient one. In Buddhist texts, the body color of Śākyamuni is described as "golden-hued" and "bright" in the Pali Canon (both among the thirty-two signs of a *mahāpuruṣa*).[60] In the *Splendid Vision Sūtra* (SSB) known from a sixth-century Gilgit manuscript (discussed in chapter 1), the body color of the goddess Bhima is described as "golden like a stalk of sugarcane" (*śarakāṇḍagaurī*) while she is dressed in white. In this instruction on how to paint an image of the goddess, Bhima is in an assembly with the tathāgata in the center, and the colors of the tathāgata and Avalokiteśvara are not identified. The text instructs the artist to use various unmixed colors, but it does not specify any particular color.

A brief survey of color terms found in Chinese translations of the early Esoteric Buddhist texts from the eighth century reveals that the most common terms used for body colors are related to the idea of light. In these texts, "gold" ("yellow gold," "bright golden color," or "truly golden") is the most predominant color, and the runner up is white.[61] In the *Uṣṇīṣadhāraṇī* (T19n0970), the five-colored light emitting from Buddha's *uṣṇīṣa* illuminates the entire Buddhist universe. In another version of an Uṣiṇīṣavijaya text translated by Amoghavajra in 755 CE (T19n0940), the brilliant light emitting from the Buddha's *uṣṇīṣa* is also multicolored (blue, yellow, red, white, and purple).[62] In the *Guhyasamāja Tantra,* a text understood to be the earliest instance of Phase Three Esoteric Buddhism (classified as *mahāyoga* tantra), the image of light is important and frequently evoked to describe the transcendent beings and their maṇḍalas: "at the centre of space visualize the maṇḍala of

Buddhas, a great hall of clouds of light-rays, the blazing light-rays of the Buddhas, pervaded by the five kinds of light-rays."[63] In addition, the supreme entity is conceptualized as clear light in the GT.[64] As David Gordon White observes in his discussion of alchemical tantras, the conception of a rainbow body or a body of light is fundamental in the tantric alchemy cultivated in Vajrayāna parlance.[65]

COLOR THEORY IN MEDIEVAL INDIC RELIGIOUS TRADITIONS

A light-based theory of color was not limited to the Buddhist tradition. It is common in other Indic religious traditions, as exemplified in the following select cases.[66] The *Niśvāsatattvasaṃhitā* (henceforth NvS), the earliest surviving Śaiva tantra, for example, helps us examine how color was understood in Śaiva tantric visionary practices. According to Goodall and colleagues, the four core sūtras of the *Niśvāsa* "had probably attained their present form by the seventh century."[67] In the *Nayasūtra* of the NvS, a detailed instruction on how to visualize Sadāśiva appears in the third chapter (*paṭala*). The preparatory practice described in one of this text's chapters includes a long list of color terms. A set of four colors—yellow (*pīta*), white (*śukla*), red (*rakta*), and black (*kṛṣṇa*)—are used to describe different aspects of the goddess.[68] However, the colors are not systematically used as in the IEB system. A detailed instruction on multiple stages of visualization, including the use of seed syllables and the identification of different elements located on different body parts, is similar to the ritual practices described in Buddhist sādhanas. After this, the *Nayasūtra* chapter concludes with the following instruction on how a practitioner should see Sadāśiva:

> He should form the posture [called] "six-face" [which involves closing ears, eyes, and nostrils with the fingers] and meditate upon Sadāśiva. Sadāśiva is seen as tenfold by colour. White (*sita*), red (*rakta*), yellow (*pīta*), black (*kṛṣṇa*), green (*harita*), tawny (*piṅgala*), blue (*nīla*), mottled (*citrakavarṇa*), crystalline (*sphaṭikābha*), beautiful (*manorama*). (*Nayasūtra*, 3: 68–69)[69]

Here Sadāśiva is to be seen in the mind's eye in ten different colors, through a physical process that seems akin to suffocation (eyes closed and other upper orifices closed), which would trigger physiognomic responses. It is clear that this conjured image is to be seen internally, and the color seen in this internal visionary experience of Sadāśiva is tenfold. The list includes the five colors of the IEB system, White, Red, Yellow, Green, and Blue, along with "tawny" (*piṅgala*), which is often used to describe the colors of the raised hair of wrathful deities in Esoteric Buddhist sādhanas, and "black" (*kṛṣṇa*). The color term "*citraka varṇa*," which the editors translate as "mottled," is probably closer to "variegated" or even "colorful." With terms like "crystalline (*sphaṭikābha*)" and "beautiful (*manorama*)," the list suggests that one should see colors changing, and not as static hues. It conveys a sense of a spectrum of colors that ultimately cannot be pinpointed by verbal description. The experience of seeing Sadāśiva in ten colors is set up for the yogin ultimately to succumb to the idea of light. Thus: "On seeing all these forms, the wise one should reject them. [Finally] only one should be grasped; the others are subordinate. It is like the orb of the moon, like a mass of

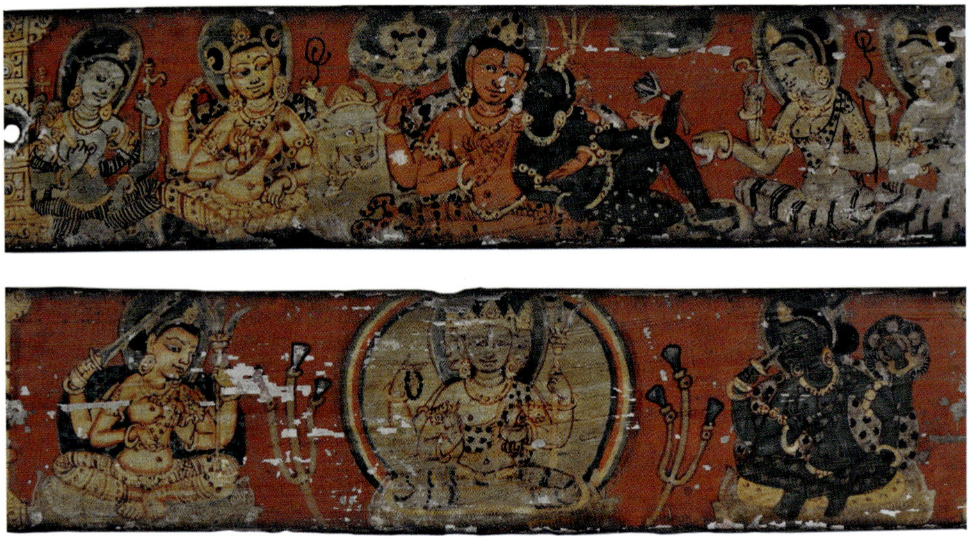

FIGURE 5.15
Painted book covers and a folio of a palm-leaf manuscript of the *Niśvāsatattvasaṃhitā*, ca. late ninth century CE, Nepal. National Archives of Nepal, Kathmandu. Photograph by Rajendra Prasad Neupane. Photo courtesy of National Archives of Nepal.

lightning, its form twinkling like a star; [this] *bindu* is the mark of the Lord" (*Nayasūtra* 3: 70). All the colors are ultimately to be merged in a flash of light, subtle like the moon's glow.

Seeing the divine as light or light-emitting is a common visionary practice in the world religions. This emphasis on light in a visionary experience perpetuates in the *Śāradā-Tilaka Tantra* (henceforth StT), another slightly later Hindu tantric text, believed to have been compiled in the twelfth or the thirteenth century.[70] The venerable mother, *śakti* (*kuṇḍalinī*), resembles "a streak of lightning . . . and shines like ten million moons and suns."[71] A specific color may be identified, but the application of color terms remains unsystematic in the StT. A single color may be described in wide-ranging terms. For example, the supreme deity in the practice of *kuṇḍalinī* yoga is seen as "red like the fresh javā/japā [flower], red lead, and the dawn."[72] A vivid color is conveyed through multiple references, from a reference to a flora that only those in a similar climate environment would understand, to a colorant ("*sindura*"), and to something to be inferred from a natural phenomenon.

Just as the text remains uncommitted to a color system, colors are specified unsystematically in artistic expressions that realize these visions of deities. The circa ninth-century palm-leaf manuscript of the NvS, which is the primary text of the critical edition prepared by Goodall and his team, survives with two painted wooden book covers. These may in fact be one of the earliest surviving portable paintings on wood in "Hindu" themes. It is challenging to date the painted boards for two reasons: painting can be added later than the time of scribing, and the manuscript itself is not dated. The ninth-century date for the manuscript seems likely, based on paleographic indications and the condition of the palm-leaf folios. The painting may date from the time of the manuscript's production, circa ninth century, and most likely no later than the tenth century, given the iconographic and stylistic characteristics.[73] Each cover is divided into three compartments with four jeweled pillars framing each section, and the background is painted in opaque vermilion. In the center of one panel (most likely the front cover) is a four-armed Śiva holding Ūma on his lap, with one of his left arms tightly wrapped around her breast (figure 5.15 *top*). A goddess diving from above Śiva's raised right hand seems to evoke the Gaṅgādhara moment—the descent of the Ganges—which along with the front-facing image of Śiva's bull seems to have been popular in Nepal. This is attested in many Nepalese sculptures of the "Śiva's family on Mountain Kailaśa" dating back to the ninth and the tenth centuries.[74] Accompanying the couple are four goddesses, all of whom are four-armed and single faced.[75] This scene of Śiva and Ūma (Devī) on Kailaśa is the frame setting for the teaching of the *mūlasūtra* of the NvS, which is fitting for the manuscript.

The central focus of the other panel is an image of four-armed, three-faced Śiva, who is white in color and holds a rosary, a trident, and a bowl (figure 5.15 *bottom*).[76] The orb that surrounds him is also white with four colored rims, and this image evokes the light-exuding form of Sadāśiva that ultimately triumphs over the visions of Sadāśiva in other colors explained in the text. This Śiva is surrounded by eight four-armed goddesses, four on each side. Those on the right side of the panel (Śiva's left) hold swords and shields made of peacock feathers, while those on the left side (Śiva's right) hold tridents and elephant goads (*aṅkuśa*), except for the goddess next to Śiva who holds a trident and a sword. The four goddesses on each side are assigned four colors: dark green, vermilion, white, and yellow, from left to right. It is difficult to name the colors without confirmation of pigment analysis, especially the "dark green" that seems to have a greenish and bluish hue. The NvS text names four colors of Vidyā as "white (*śukla*), red (*rakta*), yellow (*pīta*), and black (*kṛṣṇa*)" (*Nayasūtra,* 3: 39), conquering of which makes one a siddha, an accomplished yogin. The four colors of "yellow (*pīta*), red (*rakta*), black (*kṛṣṇa*), and crystalline (*sphaṭika*)" are assigned to the fourfold vision of Śiva's *śakti* whose vision also leads one to connect with Śiva (Nayasūtra 4: 34). This fourfold color scheme in the NvS seems to have been made known to the artist who painted them in four different colors of yellow (pīta), white (*śukla*—also *sphaṭika*), red (*rakta*), and "black" (*kṛṣṇa*). The colorist meaning of the term *kṛṣṇa,* which the editors translate as "black," merits further investigation: the term makes a transition to refer to brilliant deep blue in later paintings and poetic literature.[77] The painter of the NvS manuscript covers took this "kṛṣṇa" as a dark greenish color in a deep shade. He seems to have applied the deepest shade of this color to the goddess Ūma in Śiva's lap to signal her utmost beauty. While colors are used to differentiate the goddesses in the painting, their application is in no way as systematic as in the IEB color system. It is a challenge to identify each goddess based on their attributes and colors.

Jains also adopted a color system to organize their pantheon, especially to differentiate the twenty-four tīrthaṅkaras. Employing a color system for this is similar to the system behind the color codification of the IEB system, but perhaps the code is more complex, and the impulse for systematization may be weaker. As Ellen Gough demonstrates, there are many variations in the system depending on which Jain tradition (Śvetambara or Digambara) is

TABLE 5.1 **COLOR OF TĪRTHAṄKARAS AFTER ELLEN GOUGH (2012)**

Tīrthaṅkara	Color
1. Ṛṣabha	Golden yellow
2. Ajita	Golden yellow
3. Sambhava	Golden yellow
4. Abhinandana	Golden yellow
5. Sumati	Golden yellow
6. Padmaprabha	Red, like lotus
7. Supārśva	Green
8. Candraprabha	White
9. Puṣpadanta	White
10. Śītala	Golden yellow
11. Śreyāṃsa	Golden yellow
12. Vāsupūjya	Red
13. Vimala	Golden yellow
14. Ananta	Golden yellow
15. Dharma	Golden yellow
16. Śānti	Golden yellow
17. Kunthu	Golden yellow
18. Ara	Golden yellow
19. Malli	Golden yellow [Blue]
20. Munisuvrata	Black
21. Nami	Golden yellow
22. Nemi	Black with inner tinge of lotus-red
23. Pārśva	Blue
24. Mahāvīra	Golden yellow

referenced and the period under consideration (table 5.1).[78] Regardless of variations, five color terms are used, with an optional sixth color in the texts that list the colors of the twenty-four *tīrthaṅkaras.* The most common colors identified in sources seem to be golden yellow, red, white, black, and green, with the occasional inclusion of blue in texts dating to the twelfth century or after. A twelfth-century treatise on artistic practices, the *Aparājitapṛcchā,* includes a list of tīrthaṅkaras with their color assignments, which includes blue "*nīla*" in addition to golden (*kāñcana*), red (*rakta*), white (*śveta*), and *śyāma* (black?).[79]

The idea of light was equally important in visualizing these transcendent Jina *tīrthaṅkaras.* As seen in table 5.1, golden yellow is the most prominent color used for fifteen (in the case of Digambaras, sixteen) of the *tīrthaṅkaras,* including the first tīrthaṅkara and the last *tīrthaṅkara,* Mahāvīra, a historical teacher senior to the historical Buddha Śākyamuni. The "golden yellow" color denotes brilliance and luminosity. According to Gough, the *Triṣaṣṭiśalākapuruṣacar-*

TABLE 5.2 **FORMS OF VIṢṆU AND THEIR COLORS AS REPORTED IN GOPINATH RAO'S *ELEMENTS OF HINDU ICONOGRAPHY* (1914)**

No.	Type of Viṣṇu Mūrti	Color as translated by Rao Vol. 1. Part. 1	Sanskrit term for color in Vaiṣṇavadhruvaberāṇi Vol. 1. Part II, Appendix B
1.	Yogasthānakamūrti	Dark page 80	Śyāma page 17
2.	Bhōgasthānakamūrti	Dark page 82	Śyāma page18
3.	Virasthānakamūrti	page 83	Śyāma page 19
4.	Ābhicarikasthānakamūrti	Dark (clothed in black) page 84	dhūmvarṇa śyāmavastradharaṅa
5.	Yogāsanamūrti	White page 85	Śvetā page 20
6.	Bhōgāsamūrti	Dark page 87	Śyāmalāṃgna page 21
7.	Virāsanamūrti	Coral red (draped in black) page 89	Samāsīnam śyāmāmbardharaṃ page 22
8.	Ābhicarikāsanamūrti	Blue (draped in black) page 90	Nīlāṃbha śyāmavastradharana pages 22–23
9.	Bhōgāśayanamūrti	Dark page 92	Śyāmalājña page 24
10.	Viraśayanamūrti	Dark page 94	Śyāma page 25
11.	Ābhicarikāśayanamūrti	Blue page 95	Nīlāṃbha page 25
12.	Yogaśayanamūrti	Mixture of black and yellow page 96	Pītaśyāma page 23

ita, an early twelfth-century Śvetambara Jain text by Jain polymath Hemacandra (c. 1089–1172 CE), reports that statues of the twenty-four *tīrthaṅkaras* at a temple built on Mount Aṣṭapāda were made of precious materials, sixteen were made of gold (*suvarṇa*), two of lapis lazuli, two of crystal, two of *vaiḍūrya,* and two of ruby.[80] All of these statues would have been luminous and light reflective. The colors assigned to the *tīrthaṅkaras* appear standardized within each sectarian group in the post-twelfth-century texts. While the colors of the *tīrthaṅkaras* remained unevenly distributed mathematically speaking (with gold being dominant), the idea of a five-color system seems to have been picked up by later Jain communities, as suggested by the practice of meditation on "Jain Oṃ" in five colors that Gough discusses. However, the set of five colors does not seem to have been adopted as a codifying system for organizing the Jain pantheon, in contrast to the Esoteric Buddhist tradition.

A cursory survey of the use of color terms in iconographic descriptions of deities and divine beings in Indic religious traditions makes it clear that color articulation and codification was taken up most seriously in Buddhist circles. For example, forms of Viṣnu taken from the *Vaikhānasāgama* (a Vaiṣṇava *agama* or doctrinal work), as reported by Gopinatha Rao in his compendium of Hindu iconography, include various and indeterminate color terms assigned to Viṣṇu's body color: "dark" (for *yoga-sthānakamūrti, bhoga-sthānakamūrti, bhogāsamūrti, bhoga-śayanamūrti, vīra-śayanamūrti*); "dark complexion with faded countenance" (for *ābhicārika-sthānakamurti*); "white" (for *yogāsanamūrti*); "coral red" (for *virāsanamūrti*); "blue" (for *ābhicārikāsanamūrti, ābhicārika-śayanamūrti*)"; and "a mixture of black and yellow (for *yoga-śayanamūrti*)" (table 5.2).[81] Thus, Viṣṇu can be seen in at least five different colors according to this compendium. Most surviving images of Viṣṇu before 1000 CE are in plastic

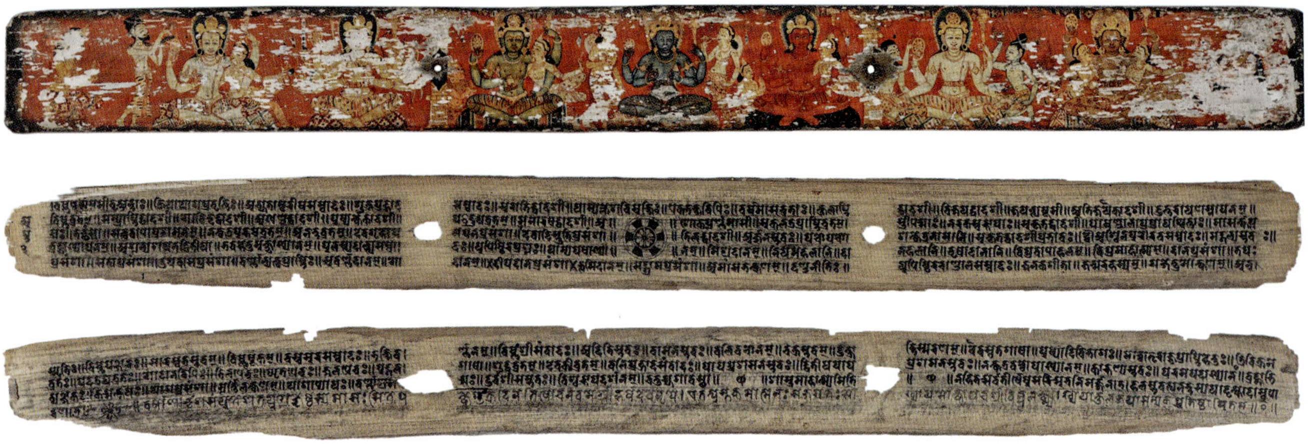

FIGURE 5.16
Painted book cover with folios 143v–144r, a palm-leaf manuscript of the *Viṣṇudharma*, dated N.S. 210 (1090 CE), Nepal. National Archives of Nepal, Kathmandu Acc. No. 1/1002. Photograph by Rajendra Prasad Neupane. Photo courtesy of National Archives of Nepal.

forms, often in stone or metal, from which color information is difficult to glean. One of the earliest surviving painted images of Viṣṇu appears on a wooden book cover of a Nepalese palm-leaf manuscript of the *Viṣṇudharma* now in the National Archives of Nepal, Kathmandu (Acc. No. 1/1002). The manuscript is dated to Jyeṣṭha (second month in the lunar calendar) of Harṣadeva's era, circa 1090 CE (N.S. 210), and the surviving cover seems to have been prepared at the time of manuscript's initial production in the late eleventh century (figure 5.16).[82]

Seven images of Viṣṇu are portrayed, all seated on elaborate textile cushions. Two bejeweled and narrow columns depicted around the two holes for binding cord/sticks divide the long panel into three sections. Three images are in the middle and two on either side, comprising a set of seven images of Viṣṇu. Two devotees, possibly patrons of the manuscript, flank the panel on either side, with a kneeling female in *añjali mudrā* on the left end. The iconography of each of the seven Viṣṇu(s) is differentiated with varying hand gestures and entourage/companions. All except for one are four-armed, and all hold a cakra and a club in their raised hands. Most importantly for our purpose, these images of Viṣṇu are painted in diverse colors. The three in the central panel are colored green, blue, and red, with the blue image in the very center.[83] The two on the left are white and yellow (very light, perhaps golden), and the remaining two on the right are white and light brown (akin to skin color). In comparison to the examples following the IEB color system in Buddhist art, very little attempt seems to have been made to apply color systematically. Color does play an important role in conveying fantastic visions of Viṣṇu. The assignment of colors of deeper tonality—green, blue, and red—in the center conveys a prism of colors in which the divine vision of Viṣṇu can be generated quite vividly. In fact, the combination of green, blue, and red for the body colors of Viṣṇu reminds us of the assignment of the five colors to the five tathāgatas seen on the book covers of Nepalese Buddhist manuscripts of the twelfth century. It is not unlikely that manuscript artists who worked for Buddhist patrons also worked on non-Buddhist commissions. Shared contemporary understanding in artisanal intelligence and artistic practices may have inspired the choice of the specific colors for Viṣṇu in artistic translation—especially since green is not a common color one encounters in the textual descriptions of Viṣṇu, but a standard choice in the IEB system.

THE LEGACY OF THE IEB COLOR SYSTEM

Why do primary colors dominate in Indian painting? This question may have more to do with modern Western perceptions of India that freely associate tropical climates with hot colors.[84] On the other hand, if rich textiles represented in the wall paintings of the Sumtseg (three-storied temple) at Alchi in today's Ladakh have any connection with the historical reality of social elites in small pockets of northern India around 1200 CE, their world was certainly filled with primary colors. According to a computational analysis of the color schemes visible in painted textiles, the six primary colors of red, yellow, white, green, blue, and black, are in use (figure 5.17). Moreover, in all categories, the frequency of red is higher than any other color.[85] It may not be a coincidence that the five primary colors of the IEB color system and black—the main color of the ink for writing—dominate the painted world at an early Western Himalayan Buddhist site.[86]

As suggested in this chapter, once Indian Esoteric Buddhist communities adopted color as a systematic tool to codify and circulate tantric visual knowledge during the eleventh century, a catalyst for the predilection for primary colors in Indic painting traditions may have been provided. Buddhism is the most outwardly oriented religion among the Indic religious traditions, and it seems fitting that Buddhists in medieval South Asia may have been on the frontier of adopting manuscripts as a medium for painting. Some ritual specialists and artists in Esoteric Buddhist circles recognized the extraordinary communicative potential of a *pothi*-format manuscript; in particular, its capacity as a mobile device to codify and convey visions generated in tantric ritual practices, using color for the transregional circulation of Esoteric Buddhist visual knowledge. Esoteric visualization practices in their earliest stages may not have necessarily lacked color, but references to luminosity dominate the descriptions of the transcendental beings. How colorful can a practitioner's internal visionary experience be? Bhattacharyya's characterization of a sādhana practice is worth repeating here:

> When the Bodhicitta combines with *śūnya* in the highest meditation and concentration, an artificial condition akin to deep sleep (*suṣupti*) is brought about, and the deity appears on the mind-sky in flashes and sparks. . . . And the object for which the Yogin undertakes the psychic exercise being different in different cases the deity visualized also becomes different. It is the *bhāvanā* "desire" of the worshipper which is of the nature of a psychic force, which re-acts on *śūnya*s, giving rise to manifold appearances in the concrete shape of deities.[87]

In this sense, color is one component of the form that a practitioner trains the mind's eye to see. It is also a mnemonic tool to guide a visualizing meditator in mapping and navigating

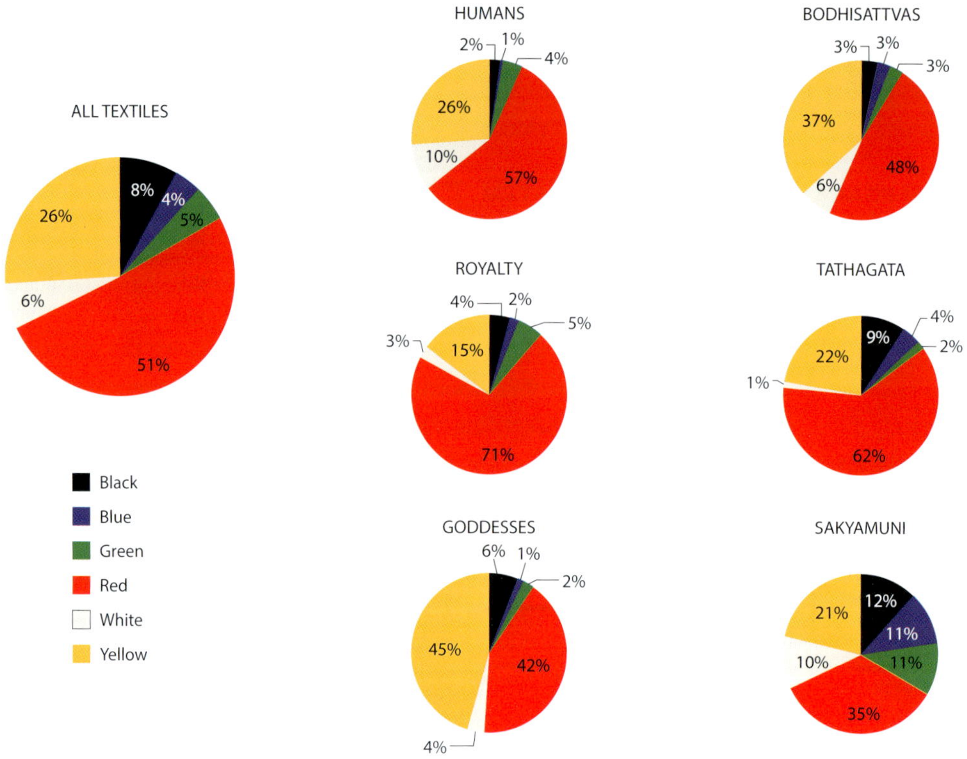

FIGURE 5.17

Computational analysis of color distribution in Alchi Sumtseg's wall paintings based on published documentation of the site in *Alchi: Ladakh's Hidden Buddhist Sanctuary* (1996), data coding and analysis by Max Meehan and Artur Meller. Reproduced by kind permission of Max Meehan.

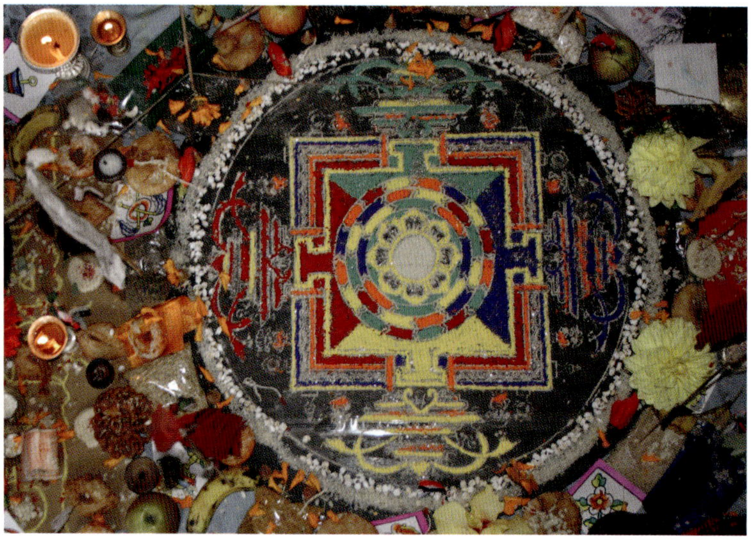

FIGURE 5.18

Pañcarakṣā maṇḍala prepared by Ratna Raj Bajracharya and Hem Ratna Bajracharya for a pūjā, July 13, 2004, Patan, Nepal. Photo © Jinah Kim.

the manifold layers of a complex maṇḍala. The predominance of primary colors in Indic painting traditions in the latter half of the second millennium is a legacy of the IEB color system and a reflection of the use of painted manuscripts in the Indic Esoteric Buddhist tradition. This model of the "Esoteric Buddhist origin of primary color use in Indian painting" requires many more dots to connect before the detailed contours of this connection can be fully specified, taking into account the detailed temporal, spatial, and sectarian instances for the period between circa 1000 and 1500 CE.

The legacy of the IEB color system certainly continues in contemporary Nepal in the most distilled and essential form. In a ritual of Pañcarakṣā-pūjā ("worship of the five protectresses") performed by Newar Vajrācāryas in the Kathmandu valley, Vajrācāryas carefully prepare a Pañcarakṣā maṇḍala with five-colored powder, just as Abhayākaragupta instructs in his *Vajrāvalī* for the "ritual of installing the deity."[88] In a private ritual observed in Patan on July 13, 2004, a Vajrācārya used six packets of colored powder to install a Pañcarakṣā maṇḍala: five colors of IEB system (white, blue, yellow, red, and green) plus orange (figure 5.18).[89] Orange was used to accentuate the architectural elements of the maṇḍala while the five colors embodied the five goddesses in their respective directions. Instead of figural representations, vibrant colors alone encapsulated the five goddesses. As is the case in the Tibetan sand maṇḍalas, the use of powder ensures the understanding of a color's ultimate emptiness, a perception pursued in sādhanas seeking an experience transcending attachment to names and material forms. At a more mundane level, being accustomed to these brilliantly colored temporary maṇḍalas condition one's mind to internalize their powerful symbolic and apotropaic meanings. The repetitive use of color that informs somatic and ritual experiences should be seen as central to the transformative potency of tantric Buddhist practice.

6

COLOR TO MATTER

A Material History of Indian Painting

IN 1941 IN A LETTER TO AN INDIAN ART CRITIC, Khandalavala, Amrita Sher-Gil wrote, "Lovely those Basohli things—especially the Radha-Krishna one—exquisitely painted. The yellow background, the white cloud bank merging into the deep blue sky. As well painted as Matisse and that is saying a great deal. Reminiscent of Gauguin, too."[1] Sher-Gil was a Paris-trained artist of Indian and Hungarian lineage; her father was a Sikh nobleman from Punjab and her mother was a Hungarian. Sher-Gil sought to cultivate "Indian-ness" in her artistic practice against some contemporary critics' skepticism of her "European" background. The intense, primary colors of Basohli paintings from the Punjab Hills certainly seem to have been one of her inspirations: her late paintings are saturated with "hot colors" that the art critic Geeti Sen explains as signifying a "mood," a "taste of the heightened eroticism" of the color symbolism rooted in Indic aesthetic theories.[2] Like a folio from an illustrated manuscript of the *Rasamañjarī* (the bouquet of *rasa*-s) in figure 6.1, the color scheme of a Basohli painting is unmistakably dominated by the hot colors of yellow, orange, and red in maximum opacity. Adding to the feast of colors, the blue skin of the standing male figure (*nāyaka*) wearing a

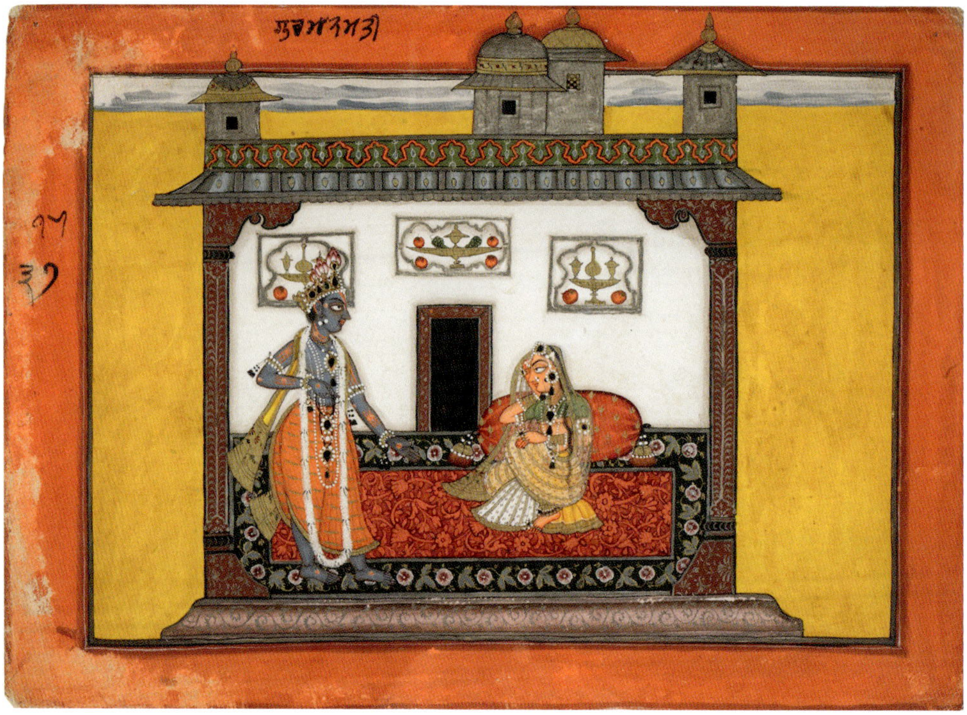

FIGURE 6.1
A nāyikā and her lover, a page from a manuscript of the *Rasamañjarī*, ca. 1660–70, Basohli, Punjab Hills. Harvard Art Museums/Arthur M. Sackler Museum, Gift of John Kenneth Galbraith. 1972.74. Photo © President and Fellows of Harvard College.

brilliant orange dhoti (lower garment) with golden trim, and the green blouse of the heroine (*nāyikā*) seated dejectedly wearing a bright yellow skirt, pop against the white of the interior wall and the red of the bolster respectively. The use of primary colors in high opacity achieving a flat pictorial surface with a hot palette is typical in Indic painting traditions. Sher-Gil's embrace of primary colors—especially red and vermilion—seems justifiably "Indian" in her nationalist bent to express "Indian-ness" in her painting. Why do these primary colors dominate the palette of Indian painting? And how old is this tradition of the "hot colors?" As surveyed in chapter 5, a god or goddess is assigned a specific primary color in Indic religious systems, which speaks to the importance of color in Indic religious communities as iconographic signifiers. The centrality of color in articulating tantric visionary experiences partly explains why color was considered an essential element in conceptualizing "Indian-ness" in art in the nationalist discourse. In this chapter, we turn to the central question of this study by attending to the color's material properties, especially employing the data gleaned from the scientific material study of pigments and locating them in the historical context of a painting's production and use. As we will see, for example, the blue of Krishna (*Kṛṣṇa*) may in fact have been shaped by artistic interventions. A brief survey of color terms in Sanskrit artistic treatises and religious manuals precedes the material discussion to help situate the ensuing analysis of color and pigments in the Indic cultural context. Before exploring color terms in literature, let us first consider the genesis and validity of the hot color = Indian painting thesis to gain a historiographic insight about the historical context and the methodological significance of the following color investigation.

INDIAN PAINTING: THE BRIGHT AND COLORFUL

The brilliantly colorful Basohli painting may be productively juxtaposed to much earlier murals of rock-cut Buddhist cave temples of Ajanta dating back to the fifth–sixth centuries of the Common Era. Both served the artists in Indian nationalist circles in their search for "Indianness." As Sonal Khullar observes, the paintings on the walls of Ajanta's many caves also inspired "Indian artists and intellectuals with anti-colonial nationalist sympathies to embark on a rediscovery of India's ancient past."[3] These included not only those in the circles of Abanindranath Tagore in the Bengal school like Nandalal Bose who visited Ajanta in 1909 and copied paintings there, but also Amrita Sher-Gil, whose earliest "Indian" phase was also inspired by a visit to Ajanta in 1936. Consider Sher-Gil's 1937 painting, *Brahmacharis*. According to Khullar, this painting translates "the aesthetics of Ajanta" into "the idiom of modernist art"; in its color palette, various hues of brown with big patches of austere white dominate. It is also in a nascent anticolonial nationalist spirit that Coomaraswamy labors to establish a direct link between Ajanta's murals and Rajput paintings of the post-sixteenth century. Thus, in his seminal book *Rajput Painting* published in 1916, he suggests "later Hindū schools are directly descended from old Buddhist art such as we see at Ajaṇṭā."[4] As observed in the introduction, Coomaraswamy's insistence on this connection was driven by his nationalist desire to establish the antiquity of Rajput paintings against Mughal painting practices.[5] Here, let us consider the color schemes in these two types of Indian painting that were embraced as signaling "Indian-ness" during the first half of the twentieth century side by side.

Putting aside the limits of reproducibility of murals in perpetually shaded cave temples, Ajanta's murals are famously earthy in tonality. One good example is the area around the western interior wall of Cave 17, which depicts the Chaddanta Jātaka and the Mahakapi Jātaka. White and brown dominate the color palette (figure 6.2). Artists in anticolonialist nationalist circles in 1930s and 1940s also took the murals' earthy and brownish palette as one of the fundamental formal aspects of paintings at Ajanta, as exemplified in a painting like *Jadugriha Daha* by Nandalal Bose (NGMA New Delhi 4798), done ostensibly in "Ajantaesque" style.[6] The murals have undergone many rounds of chemical treatments for conservation and restoration, and given the limitation of lighting inside the caves and the age of the murals, the earthy tonality and the predominantly brownish color palette may be due to the age and the material condition in which we see and photograph them.[7] We are looking at them nearly 1,500 years after their creation. It is difficult to reconstruct what the paintings may have looked like when they were freshly painted—before all the layers of soot from burning lamps, physical damages ravaged by weathering elements, insects and other organisms, and the physical impact of the conservation and the restoration efforts throughout the

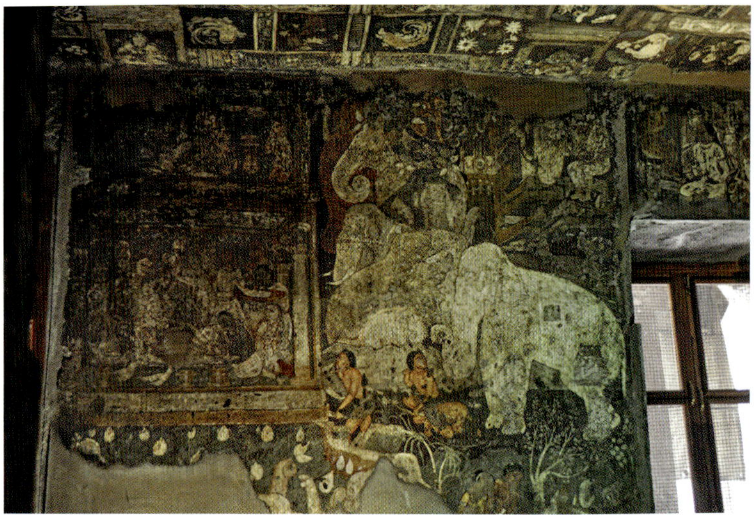

FIGURE 6.2
View of Chaddanta jātaka, Cave 17, Ajanta, ca. fifth century. Photo © Jinah Kim.

twentieth century.[8] In recent decades, advancement in conservation science and constant efforts to better preserve Ajanta's world-renowned paintings have led to more scientific analysis of pigments and supporting matters like mortar and plaster.[9] The colors visible to the eyes today are brown, white, red, orange, yellow, green, blue, and black.

The findings summarized in the table from a recent publication by M. Singh suggest that most colorants were locally sourced and earth-based, such as lime (kaolin = white clay, and calcite) for white, red ocher for red, yellow ocher for yellow, and green earth for green (table 6.1). The use of green earth in particular suggests a creative use of local resources. The geological composition of the site is basalt, and this green earth is supposed to be the product of basaltic rock disintegration.[10] Blue, which is absent from the earliest painting layer, has been identified as lapis lazuli, which may have been imported from present-day Afghanistan.[11] Although the table identifies heavier metal-based pigments—such as red lead (*minium*), vermilion (cinnabar), and organic yellow—according to the lead scientist of the study, Manager Singh, their presence is partly due to the interventions of twentieth-century conservation efforts.[12]

The results of scientific analysis suggest that it is most likely that the painted walls did not appear so brightly colored and dominated by primary colors like what we see in a Basohli painting like in figure 6.1. In purely colorist terms, the most obvious difference between the walls' color schemes is the presence of dominantly "hot" primary colors of yellow, orange, and red in the Basohli painting. The colors of red, orange, and yellow do appear at Ajanta, but they are not as vibrant as what we see in the Basohli painting; this is not just because of their age. The earth-based red ocher and yellow ocher used at Ajanta have different color values of red and yellow than those created from pigments used in the Basohli painting, which include red lead, vermilion, and Indian yellow.[13] Vermilion is one of the primary in-

TABLE 6.1 **PIGMENTS IDENTIFIED AT AJANTA AFTER M. SINGH (2011)**

Color	Pigments	Location
White	Kaolin	All around
	Pure calcium carbonate	Dresses and architecture figures
	Shell white	Lips, necklace, and women decorations
	Lead white	Dress and highlights
Red	Red ocher	All around
	Red lake	Brighter red pigments all around
	Minium	Tools, architectures, inscriptions, and dresses
	Cinnabar (very rare)	Identified at one place only
Yellow	Yellow ocher	Background, animals, dresses, and figures
	Organic yellow	Bright yellow spots
	Orpiment and/or realgar	Decorations, tools, dresses, animals, and composition
Green	Green earth	Leaves, dresses, background of composition
	Orpiment with blue	
Blue	Lapis lazuli	All around (not present in early layer)
Black	Lamp black	All around

gredients that make the later Basohli painting appear "hot"; given its importance in Indic ritual practices and in later Indian art, the absence of vermilion (cinnabar) at Ajanta is particularly striking. Red powder of *sindur* or *kumkum* is very much present in India's many rituals.

This curious absence of vermilion at Ajanta urges us to reconsider what Coomaraswamy called the "blank" period. Coomaraswamy posited that there was "no one great religious inspiration" at this time. Coomaraswamy's view that the religious landscape of medieval South Asia during his "blank" period provided no great inspiration for artistic activities seems to reflect the prevailing negative assessment of tantric traditions as degenerate and corrupt forms of Indian religions during his time. As we will see later in this chapter, the world of medieval tantric practitioners provides some interesting clues to understand how vermilion became so important in Indic religious practices and how it was introduced to the Indian artists' palette.[14] The introduction of this "hot" color and its prominence in artistic practices may have been an early medieval phenomenon.

A COLORIST PERSPECTIVE

Color is an essential element in the art of painting, and a comprehensive understanding of color is important in the history of painting. Yet, color is also a murky analytical tool. When the goddess Mahāmāyūrī (figure 6.3) and the blouse of the nāyikā (see figure 6.1) are described as green, it is difficult to discuss or objectively measure their exact color values. It is challenging to convey in writing how colors in a painting appear to one's naked eyes due to

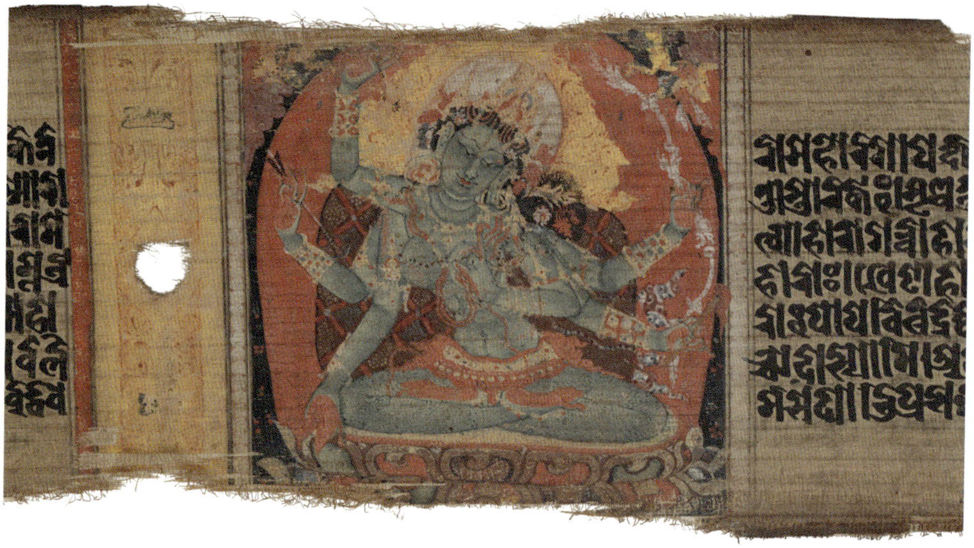

FIGURE 6.3
Mahāmāyurī, folio 29r, Pañcarakṣā manuscript (Ms_B), ca. late eleventh to early twelfth century, Bihar, India. Museum of Fine Arts, Boston, 37.376, Helen and Alice Colburn Fund. Photograph © 2021 Museum of Fine Arts, Boston.

linguistic limitations and the problematic reproducibility of colors.[15] As John Gage puts it, "The visual analysis of color can, in principle, never be at second hand, for different eyes will, as like as not, see quite different things."[16] We may say and read "yellow" but the color "yellow" can have a broad spectrum. You may be thinking of "mustard yellow" while I may mean "butter cream yellow," whatever these color terms may actually mean subjectively. Shades and tonalities are equally difficult to convey without the presence of the object that bears the color under discussion. Even with highly developed digital tools and digitization capacity, it is also extremely challenging to get the color right, as any art historian and artist who has dealt with reproduction will report. The RGB color value system uses numeric codes to make colors consistent across the digital medium. However, colors do not achieve stable and universal values in perception also because the calibration of displays and reproduction settings on machines are not identical. Color values are even more difficult to share when externalizing and circulating what one sees internally, which is precisely what was needed at the time of heightened demand for the circulation of esoteric visual knowledge during the period of *phyi-dar*. It is at times difficult to see what was intended in painting from pre-1500 CE India due to chemical reactions and physical altercations brought on by environmental and human factors.[17]

At the outset, it should be noted that this study follows the color-realist position; that is, it assumes that colors do exist independent of the viewer.[18] By taking this position, it also takes the value of the color's material properties more seriously and incorporates findings of scientific material analysis into the writing of the history of art. Advances in conservation science offer identification of pigments used in manuscript paintings through noninvasive material analysis. For example, noninvasive XRF (X-Ray fluorescence) analysis can help identify most mineral and inorganic colorants on a painted manuscript without taking physical samples from the surface.[19] This process helps to identify hematite on what appears to be dark purple on a cushion behind the goddess Mahāmāyūrī (see figure 6.3). Based on pigment analysis, we may also surmise that the artist working on this manuscript had access to at least three different types of colorants for "red"; starting with vermilion, there is also occasionally reliance on organic red and hematite. Use of three different types of red supports the argument for the agency of artists in making artistic choices in religious image making. The knowledge of colors' symbolic meanings and optical values seems to have informed artists' choice and use of certain colors, often in response to the demands of patrons and knowledge experts. Purely aesthetic consideration of harmony and balance in color composition at times played an equally important role in artistic decisions, and the availability of certain grades of pigments was also a factor. Paying attention to materiality of pigments is particularly relevant in the study of Indian painting because the painterly techniques and practices developed in medieval South Asia suggest that appreciation of the physical, tactile presence of painting was particularly cultivated among artistic communities and their patrons. Identifying pigments in use in close comparison with the colors discussed in theoretical texts and treatises affords us a glimpse into artists' intimate, embodied knowledge of each color's material properties—knowledge probably learned through years of preparing pigments in individual containers, whether in coconut shells as do contemporary *paṭa* painters of Bengal, or in gourds as described in seventh-century Bāṇa's *Harṣacarita*.[20]

ON "BEWILDERING" COLOR TERMS

Color terms are as difficult to pin down as conveying a color objectively. Sanskrit's fluid semantic range compounds the difficulty when dealing with color in historical and textual sources.[21] Color terms in the Vedas are most often expressed in epithets or metonymical terms.[22] Color terms begin to appear more systematically in artistic treatises. One of the earliest attempts in the codification of a color system may be found in the *Nāṭyaśāstra* (NtS) by the nearly mythical sage author Bharata. Considered a foundational text of Indian aesthetic theory (c. 300 CE?), the NtS offers a "vast and comprehensive account . . . of the entire domain of dramaturgy," and *rasas* (tastes) are categorized in color terms: "the erotic is blue-black (*syāma*), the comic is white (*sita*), the tragic is gray (*kapota*), and the violent red (*rakta*); the heroic is golden (*gaura*), the fearful black (*kṛṣṇa*), the macabre blue (*nīla*), and the fantastic yellow (*pīta*)."[23] This list is by no means systematic, and there may be psychosomatic reasons for assigning specific colors to specific emotion-driven *rasas* (tastes) in this treatise on drama. That color terms are used in this manner illuminates the importance of color in Indic communities, and that in a way explains why color became an important signifier of Indian-ness among nationalist artistic circles. Pollock's English translation renders the color terms straightforwardly; for example, *śyāma* for *śṛṅgāra* (the erotic) is translated as "blue-black" or *kṛṣṇa* for *bhaya* (the fearful) is translated as "black." Exactly what color terms may mean with respect to their visual properties remains in the realm of subjective interpretation. The color connotation of these terms may have been far from universal over time.

Chapter 40 of the *Citrasūtra* section in the *Viṣṇudharmottara* (VdhM) deals with color and pigments used for painterly practice. As mentioned in chapter 5, it identifies five primary colors as "white" (*śveta*), "yellow" (*pīta*), "red" (*vilohita*), "blue" (*nīla*), and "black" (*kṛṣṇa*).[24] As observed in copious notes accompanying Parul Dave Mukherji's translation, there remain many unresolved issues especially in verses describing more technical aspects of painterly practices, and this is also the case in the chapter on color. An important technical aspect explained in chapter 40 relates to the "mixing" of colors. In verses 18 through 22, the text discusses how a secondary color like green may be achieved in varying shades and tonalities. Mixing yellow (*pīta*) and blue (*nīla*) results in the green color, here interestingly referred to with a nature-based term, "*palāsa* (leaf)," instead of a color term like "*harita*." This secondary color can be made in various tones depending on the amount and the ratio of the primary colors used.

In the verses relating to the techniques of "shading," Mukherjee changes the translation of the term *nīla* to "black" instead of "blue." This suggestion makes sense since pragmatically speaking, in general, colors can be darkened by adding black and lightened by adding white. The text does mention the use of "white" (*śveta*) to achieve different tonalities, and as an opposite concept to this, Mukherjee takes *nīla* as "black." However, this hermeneutic move seems unnecessary in the context of the text. First of all, the text uses different terms for blue and black, *nīla* and *kṛṣṇa,* respectively in verse 16 where primary colors are identified. Second, it seems unlikely that *nīla* should be the term of choice when "black" is intended in the following verse; at this point, the text clearly differentiates the two colors. That the author(s) of the VdhM continuously use(s) *nīla* in the sense of "blue" is also confirmed in the usage in verse 22b, where blue night lotus (*nīlotpala*) is mentioned. In addition, the term *nīla* that Mukherjee takes as "black" appears in explaining how to make "green." Increasing the amount of "blue" can also help create a darker shade of green. In fact, *nīla* in this case most likely refers to color prepared from indigo-dye-based pigment. This pigment would have been applied with orpiment to create green as observed in surviving paintings.

If any opposition between tinting (lightening of colors) and shading (darkening of colors) is intended in the text, translating the term *nīla* inconsistently as "black" seems to complicate the matter unnecessarily when the term *śyāma* that appears in verses 21 and 24 relates directly to the technique of shading. As Mukherjee notes, discussion on color in chapter 40 makes a clear reference to an earlier chapter in the VdhM, chapter 27 on dramatic art, which discusses color terms and two aspects of tonalities—five tints of brightness (*gaura*) and twelve shades of darkness (*śyāma*).[25] In the context of the VdhM, the term *śyāma* seems to mean "darkness," as in darker shades. As we will see shortly, its colorist meaning remains unstable along with other color terms for dark hues, such as "*kṛṣṇa*" and "*nīla*."

Another challenge in the translation of the color chapter in the VdhM concerns the term *sindūra,* which is often translated as "red lead." Verses 25–26 identify colorants (*raṅgadravyāṇi*): gold, silver, copper, mica, lapis lazuli (lazurite), *sindūra,* yellow orpiment, lime, lac, vermilion (mercury sulfide), and indigo. Taking *sindūra* as "red lead" needs to be qualified with further historical evidence based on material analysis of surviving paintings. At least among the makers of Indic manuscript paintings of pre-1500 CE, red lead does not seem to have been a common colorant in artists' tool cases. Another possibility may be that the term may refer to a plant-based pigment, as the term *sindūra* appears again as a name of a tree whose milk is mentioned in a recipe for a color protective formula in verse 30.[26]

A cursory survey of color terms that appear in post-*Nāṭyaśāstra* Sanskrit texts suggests certain consistencies and variants in color names depending on the color. Most common terms used for "white" in Sanskrit artistic treatises and ritual texts are *śveta* and *sīta,* with the occasional use of *śukla*. *Pīta* for yellow seems to have been the least problematic term. This term remains most consistent among the color terms for primary colors across textual sources of varying dates. *Rakta* is the most common Sanskrit term used to denote the color "red" in lists of colors. VdhM uses *vilohita* to indicate "red." The term *vilohita* is a matter-driven epithet for signifying this color, as the term is derived from *lohita,* with one of its primary meanings as copper. Green is one of the five colors of the IEB system, but it is in fact a secondary color in terms of its color properties. The VdhM authors seem to have been aware of this color's secondary nature. Metonymical terms like grass, green apple, or bean are used to denote green color precisely to overcome this limitation. The term *harita* that is used to denote "green" in a number of post-VdhM texts can refer to a range of colors, from yellow to green.[27] When the term appears with *pīta* in a list of colors, it can be more straightforwardly taken as meaning "green." In the rasa-color system of the NtS, green is missing, but this system includes another secondary/mixed color, "gray" (*kapota*), for the tragic. The meaning of *kapota* as gray derives from the nature, as the color signification comes from the word's meaning being pigeon or dove. This is similar to the case of metonymical terms used to denote "green" in the VdhM. Both of these texts suggest that their authors were aware of semiotic challenges in color names, especially when it comes to mixed or secondary and tertiary colors.

ON *ŚYĀMA*

As seen in table 6.2, color terms for dark hues seem to have been less stable. In the VdhM, *kṛṣṇa* and *nīla* are clearly differentiated; thus, translating *kṛṣṇa* as black in this context seems reasonable. In the case of the *Nāṭyaśāstra* (NtS) rasa color system, the terms, *nīla* and *kṛṣṇa,* are also differentiated; this distinction justifies their translation into English as blue and black respectively. As noted, the NtS also includes another term for dark hue, *śyāma,* which is translated as "blue-black"; however, identifying which hue this term refers to is unclear. In fact, as the "color" of *śṛṅgara* rasa, *śyāma* seems to mean much more than what "blue-black" can convey in English. *Śyāma* can mean the color of the pregnant monsoon cloud, the night sky, the Indian cuckoo bird (whose color may be best described as dark olive green), and an attribute of a beautiful maiden as in "swarthy complexion" among others. The term can help amplify the charged meaning of *śṛṅgāra rasa* (the erotic) in a vivid, visual sense. The VdhM takes *śyāma* as indicating darker shades opposite *gaura* (white or bright). It is difficult to determine how *śyāma* as a color was translated into painting during the time of these texts.

TABLE 6.2 **COLOR TERMS IN SANSKRIT TEXTS**

Text	Color System							
	Blue-black (?)	*White*	*Yellow*	*Red*	*Blue*	*Black*	*Golden*	*Gray*
Nāṭyaśāstra ca. 300 CE	śyāma	sita	pīta	rakta	nīla	kṛṣṇa	gaura	kapotaḥ
	śṛṅgāra (erotic)	hasya (comic)	adbhuta (fantastic)	raudra (violent)	bībhatsa (macabre)	bhaya (fearful)	vīra (heroic)	karuṇa (tragic)
Viṣṇudharmottara purāṇa, chapter 40 (raṅga) ca. 450–750 CE		White	Yellow	Red	Blue	Black		
		śveta	pīta	vilohita	nīla	kṛṣṇa		
Viṣṇudharmottara purāṇa, chapter 27 (varṇa) ca. 450–750 CE		White	Yellow	Red	Green	Black		
		śveta	pīta	rakta	harita	kṛṣṇa		
Aparājitapṛcchā ca. 12th century (Bhuvanadeva)		White	Yellow	Red	Green		Green	All colors
		nāgara	vyantara	drāviḍa	Kalinga		vesara	Yāmuna
		East	West	karnātam	Kalinga		north	All regions
		Brahman	vaiśya	kṣatrya	Mixed caste		vaiśya	All castes
Mānasollāsa, vol. 2, book 2, c. 12th century		White	Yellow	Red (three kinds)		Black		
		śveta	pīta	(a) śoṇa (crimson-darada-cinnabar) (b) rakta (alakṣa-lac) (c) lohita (red ocher)		kṛṣṇa		
Śilparatna, c. 16th century (Śrī Kumāra, Kerala)	Blue-green (?)	White	Yellow	Red		Black		
	śyāma	sita	pīta	rakta		kajjala		
Citrakarmaśāstra	Blue-green (?)	White	Yellow	Red		Dark blue	Lamp black	
	śyāma	śveta	pīta	rakta		kṛṣṇa	añjana	

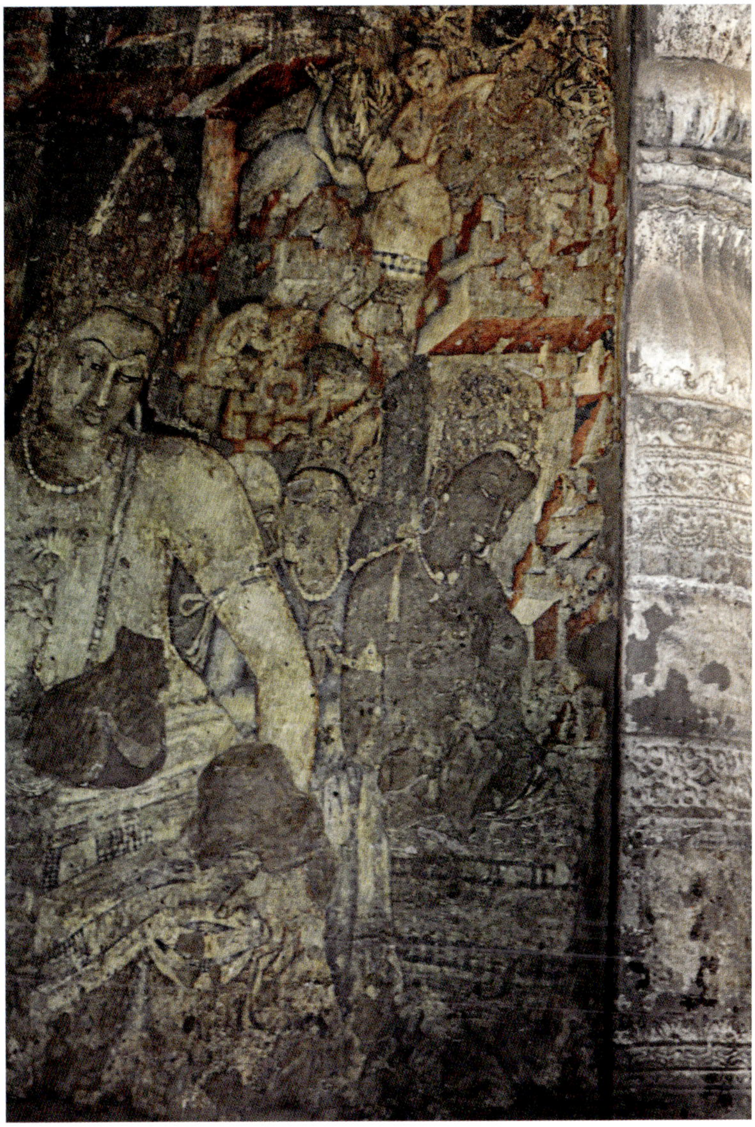

FIGURE 6.4
Tārā, next to Padmapāṇi, Cave 1 left side wall flanking the antechamber to the main shrine, Ajanta, ca. fifth century. Photo © Jinah Kim.

Using these texts to explain aspects of artistic practices and artisanal mastery of every period is a logocentric superimposition and something that should be negotiated with care. It is tempting to see some realization of these ideas on the surviving murals of caves at Ajanta, especially given the temporal proximity to these two texts. The female figure standing behind the famous image of bodhisattva "Padmapāṇi" in the Cave 1 at Ajanta may come close to how this *śyāma* was interpreted in painting (figure 6.4). Sumptuously ornamented with a tall, bejeweled crown and delicately rendered jewelry draped across her bare upper body, this female figure's slanting gaze and her slightly turned body direct our attention to the antechamber of the central shrine. She may not garner as much attention as her male counterpart, the famed bodhisattva image, towering next to her, but her dark complexion seems almost purposefully painted in contrast to the bright, "golden" complexion of the male bodhisattva. Here we may have a case where *śyāma* as a color pictorializes the dark complexion of a female beauty.

It is difficult to see today the exact color that was originally intended by artists and knowledge experts working in Ajanta Cave 1. Nevertheless, this darker greenish tonality certainly seems to come close to capturing the term's visual essence: along with her shape and form, the color helps to evoke how *śṛṅgara rāsa* may have been imagined pictorially. In light of the present discussion about *śyāma* as a color that pictorializes the dark complexion of a female beauty, we may reconsider this female figure's connection with the Buddhist goddess Tārā, especially since she is paired with bodhisattva Padmapāṇi and is represented in this particular dark shade.

In terms of the historical development of the iconography, Tārā initially appeared as an attendant to the bodhisattva of compassion, Avalokiteśvara. Ajanta Cave 1's Padmapāṇi is a form of this bodhisattva. In later Esoteric Buddhist sādhanas, in which the five-color system is consistently used, *śyāma* is frequently used as the color term to describe many forms of Tārā, whether as an attendant to Khasarpana Avalokiteśvara (SM14, Padmakaramati's Khasarpaṇa sādhana) or as a popular form known as Śrī Tārā. By the time when sādhanas were compiled toward the end of the eleventh century, it seems likely that *śyāma* meant green in dark shades. Two-armed forms of Tārā in surviving Indic manuscript paintings are almost always in green whether as an attendant to Avalokiteśvara or as an individual deity. This is also the case in surviving Himalayan paintings from the eleventh through the thirteenth centuries, be it the famous image of Standing Tārā as savioress depicted on the wall of Alchi's Sumsteg (1200 CE), or the seated Tārā in the "Ford Tārā" thangka (see figure 5.7). Śyāma-Tārā is one of the most common epithets of Tārā, and this form is painted in dark green in later Tibetan thangkas. The term *śyāma* and its spectrum of meanings and early visual connection to Tārā may also hold a key to explain why the IEB color system adopted "green" instead of "black" as one of the five primary colors—an adoption that makes this system distinct from the five colors known in the VdhM. Painterly interventions in translating the color of *śyāma* seem to have played an important role.

ON *KṚṢṆA*

Kṛṣṇa is another challenging color term. In the VdhM and the NtS, it may be justifiable to translate this term as "black" in contrast to "blue" of *nīla,* but what this *kṛṣṇa* would have meant at the time of the texts' composition remains elusive. *Kṛṣṇa* is the namesake color of an important form of Viṣṇu, Kṛṣṇa.[28] In today's popular visual culture in South Asia, Viṣṇu is dominantly portrayed in blue, along with his two most revered human incarnations, Rāma and Kṛṣṇa. The fixation of the blue color for Viṣṇu and his human incarnations may in fact be related to the understanding of Kṛṣṇa as blue, which was most likely shaped by artistic interventions.

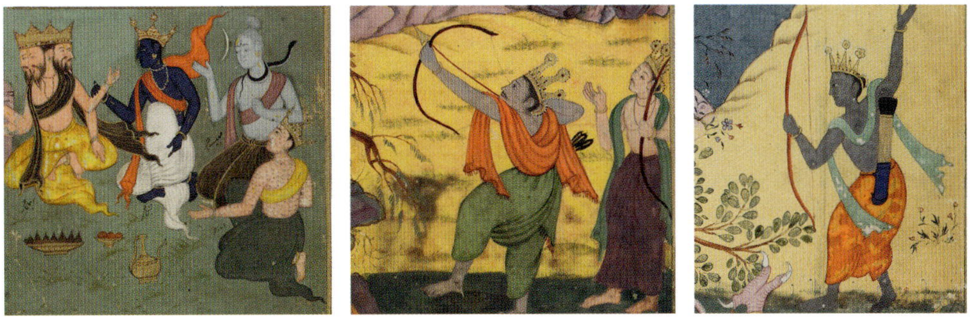

FIGURE 6.5
Details of Viṣṇu and Rāma by different artists: folio 60r by Nadim, folio 117r by Syam Sundar, folio 123r by Qasim, the Freer Rāmāyaṇa, Mughal dynasty, reign of Akbar, ca. 1597–1604. Ink, pigments, and gold on paper, 27.5 × 15.2 cm (H × W). F1907.271.1-172.

The challenges artists faced in translating and painting a color term are exemplified in one of the earliest known illustrated manuscripts of the Hindu epic *Rāmāyaṇa* prepared during the reign of the Mughal emperor Akbar (r. 1556–1605). In the Freer *Rāmāyaṇa* manuscript (c. 1597–1604), the artists rendered Rāma in various dark shades, from light, bluish gray to gray while rendering Viṣṇu in brilliant blue without any hesitation (figure 6.5). This may be an attempt to render Rāma as recorded in the text, whose body color is described as *śyāma;* different artists working on the same manuscript interpreted this dark monsoon cloud-like color differently.[29] The artists seem to have been hesitant to employ bright blue in painting a human form of Viṣṇu. On the other hand, in the famed Jagat Singh *Rāmāyaṇa* manuscripts, there is no hesitation in depicting Rāma as brilliant blue (most likely mineral blue, like lapis lazuli or azurite instead of organic blue like indigo), although there are variations in the tonality of blue in each book coinciding with the stylistic differences of individual workshops (figure 6.6).[30] In the indigenous circles of manuscript production, the blue color of Rāma seems to have been already widely accepted as seen in the illustrated paper manuscript of the Āranyaka Parvan of the *Mahābhārata* dated V.S. 1573 (1516 CE); here, Rāma is consistently depicted in a dark blue color (figure 6.7).

Kṛṣṇa is painted bright blue in early illustrated paper manuscripts of the *Bhāgavata Purāṇa,* like the so-called Dispersed *Bhāgavata Purāṇa* of about 1520–40 CE and an undated illustrated manuscript of the *Gīta Govinda* of the early sixteenth century now in the N.C. Mehta Collection in Baroda.[31] An illustrated manuscript of the *Bālagopāla stuti* has Kṛṣṇa the cowherd consistently painted in blue, and his color stands out against plain red background (figure 6.8). The manuscript is undated, but the painting bears a stylistic similarity to the rare painted scroll on cloth of the *Vasanta-vilāsa* now in the Freer Gallery, dated V.S. 1508 (1451/52), suggesting an early to mid-fifteenth-century date. In all three cases, the bright blue color of Kṛṣṇa is unmistakable, and the confidence and consistency suggest an established understanding that *kṛṣṇa* meant brilliant blue to artists and patrons. Here we may hypothesize that

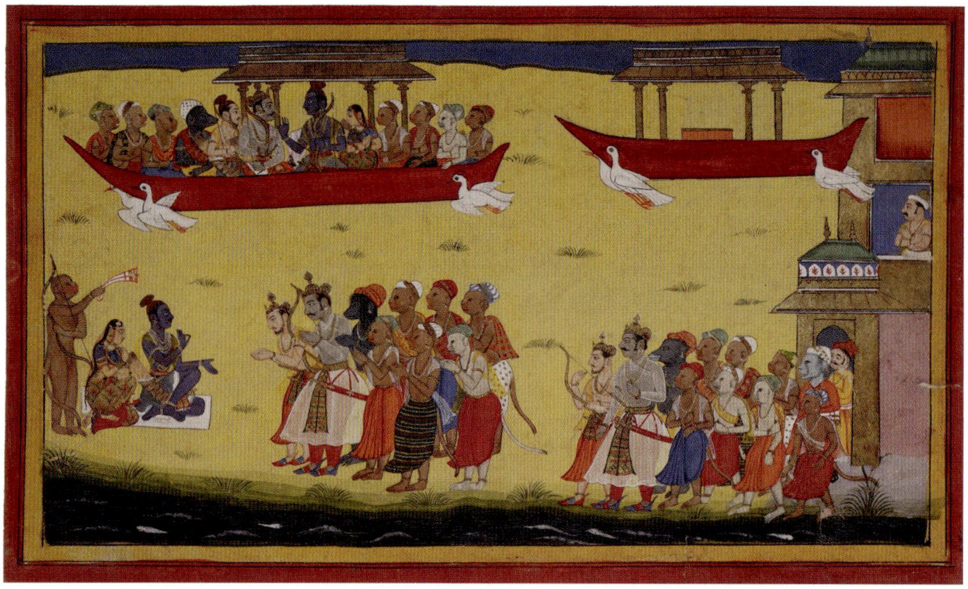

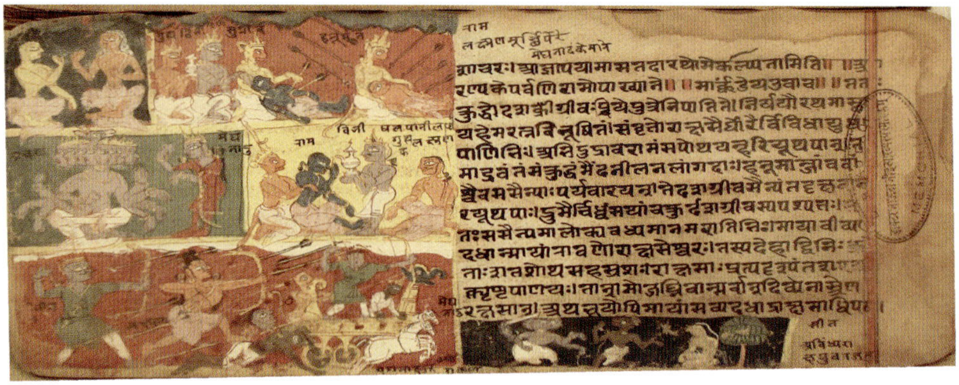

FIGURE 6.6▲
Folio 189v, Vibhīṣaṇa and his troupe bid farewell to Rāma and Sītā as Puṣpaka arrives to take them back to Ayodhyā. Mewar Rāmāyaṇa Book 6, folio 189v. British Library. Add. Ms. 15297(1). © The British Library Board.

FIGURE 6.7▼
Folio 212r, Scenes from the *Rāmāyaṇa*, Āraṇyaka Parvan of the *Mahābhārata,* dated V.S. 1573/1516 CE, Delhi. Pigments and ink on paper, size: 16.5 × 37 cm, Asiatic Society, Mumbai, Acc. No. 966. Image courtesy of Asiatic Society, Mumbai.

availability and the introduction of ultramarine, in particular, may have had an impact on the adoption of the brilliant-blue hue of Kṛṣṇa. Only further research on the material properties of color in these manuscripts would confirm the types of pigments used in early examples. It seems likely that Indian painters had access to both mineral-based pigments (lapis lazuli or azurite) and organic ones (indigo) by the beginning of the fifteenth century, if not before, and that they used them discerningly. The use of lapis lazuli for painting Kṛṣṇa is confirmed on a

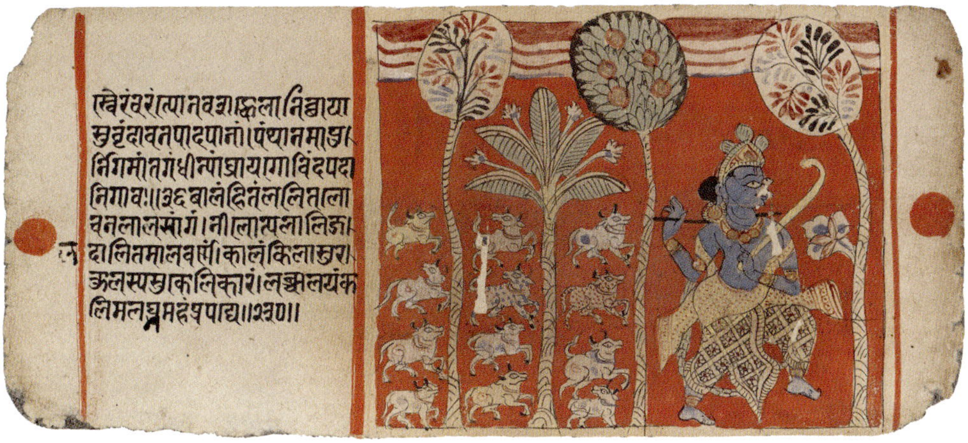

FIGURE 6.8
Kṛṣṇa herding cows, from a *Bālagopāla stuti* manuscript, ca. 1425 CE, Gujarat. Museum of Fine Arts, Boston, 30.106, Denman Waldo Ross Collection. Photograph © 2021 Museum of Fine Arts Boston.

page from the dispersed *Bhāgavata Purāṇa*.[32] Rutherford J. Gettens's scientific analysis suggests that artists working on the Freer *Vasanta Vilāsa* scroll used both lapis lazuli and indigo, saving indigo for nonessential motifs.[33] Lapis lazuli and indigo are also confirmed on an illustrated Jain paper manuscript of the *Uttarādhayana sūtra* now in the Victoria and Albert Museum (IS.2–1972), which dates to the mid-fifteenth century.[34]

THE COLOR TERM *KṚṢṆA* BEFORE "BLUE" *KṚṢṆA*

It is unclear when this formula of Viṣṇu = *kṛṣṇa* = blue may have been introduced. Few paintings depicting Vaiṣṇava iconography that may date to pre-1400 CE survive in northern India. Here transregional and trans-sectarian approaches to Indian painting can be helpful. As noted in chapter 2, painted "Hindu" manuscripts that date as early as the eleventh century survive from Nepal, and painted images of "Hindu" deities are included in some Buddhist manuscripts. The painted wooden cover for a *Viṣṇudharma* manuscript discussed in chapter 5 may be one of the earliest surviving examples of painted images of Viṣṇu, that too, with a blue one in the center (figure 6.9). The idea of Viṣṇu as a blue deity was certainly known to twelfth-century manuscript makers in Buddhist monastic circles in eastern India. Viṣṇu and Śiva are included in the retinue welcoming the Buddha back to earth from his visit with his late mother in the *trāyastriṃśa* heaven, and the four-armed Viṣṇu portrayed in Buddhist manuscript painting is always blue (figure 6.10).

A manuscript of the *Harivaṁśa* prepared in N.S. 292 (1172 CE) survives with painted covers and provides some interesting color information in Viṣṇu's pictorial iconography. The painted covers feature rare narrative renditions of the ten incarnations of Viṣṇu (figure 6.11). These renditions include what may be the earliest surviving miniature painting of the churning of the ocean episode with Kurma (turtle) avatar. Each panel is divided into

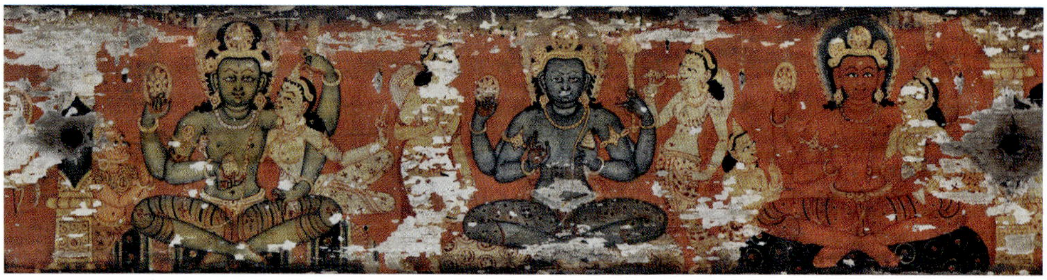

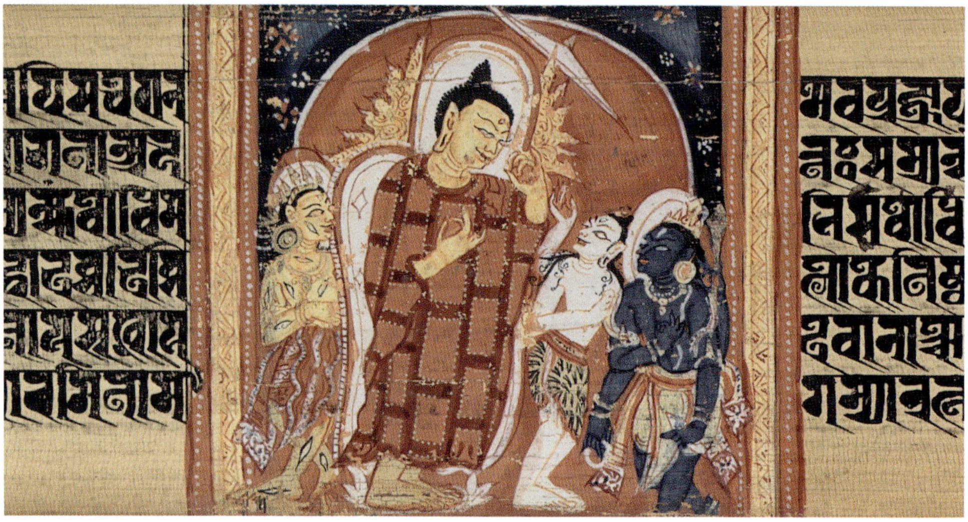

FIGURE 6.9▲
Various forms of Viṣṇu, detail from painted book cover, a palm-leaf manuscript of the *Viṣṇudharma,* dated N.S. 210 (1090 CE), detail of figure 5.16.

FIGURE 6.10▼
Buddha's descent from the Trāyatriṃśa heaven with Indra, Śiva, and Viṣṇu as attendants, a folio from a *Perfection of Wisdom* manuscript, ca. twelfth century, Bengal. LACMA M72.1.23.

five sections. Each section contains one of the ten avatars, starting with Matsya, Kurma, Varāha, Narasimha, and Vāmana-Trivikrama on one, and Paraśurāma, Rāma, Kṛṣṇa, Buddha, and Kalki on the other. The iconography is clear, and an easily recognizable moment is chosen from each story. For example, the panel on Rāma depicts him dressed in armor, engaged in battle against ten-headed Rāvana, who is also dressed in meshed armor, and Rāma is about to release his arrow. Both Rāma and Rāvana ride handsomely decorated horse-drawn war-chariots showcasing the artist's talent in miniature painting and dramatic interpretation of the epic. Rāma and Rāvana are also differentiated in terms of their skin colors, and Rāma here is clearly in a deep orange hue, not blue. The iconography of the Kṛṣṇa panel is the least clear among the ten panels (figure 6.11, *top center*). This is not only because of the damage on the bottom of the panel but also because the iconography of Kṛṣṇa as one of the ten avatars was not necessarily fixed.[35] If Kṛṣṇa is intended in this panel, the dark "blue

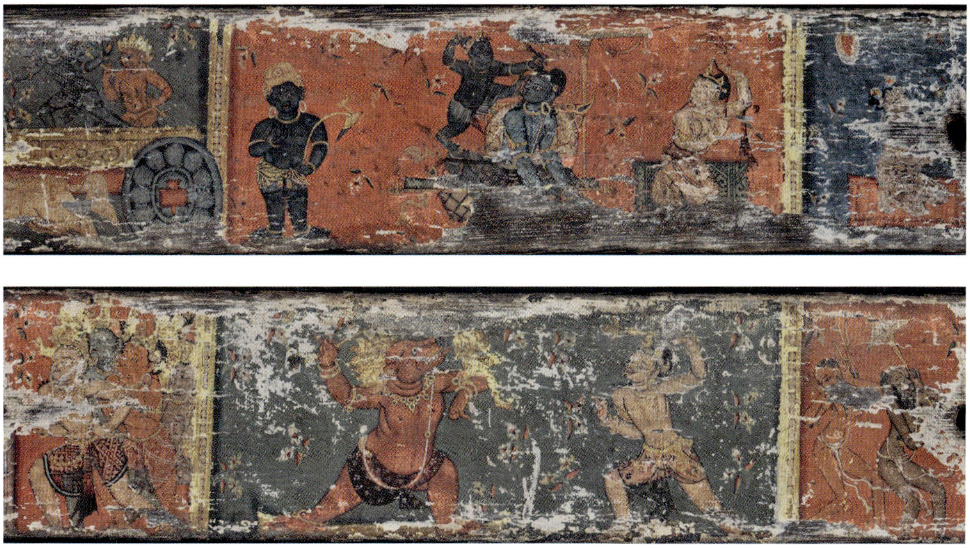

FIGURE 6.11
Kriṣṇa panel (*top center*), detail from a painted cover of a Harivaṃśa manuscript, date of copying—N.S. 292 (1172 CE). Pigments on wood. National Archive of Nepal, Acc. No. 1/455. Photograph by Rajendra Prasad Neupane. Photo courtesy of National Archives of Nepal.

black" skin color of a childlike figure striking a blue male figure in the center may be what the unnamed artist in twelfth-century Nepal envisioned as the color of *kṛṣṇa*.

In the Esoteric Buddhist sādhanas, *nīla* and *kṛṣṇa* are often used interchangeably to denote Akṣobhya's lineage. When sādhanas identify colors of three or more heads of a deity, *nīla* and *kṛṣṇa* are never used in the same configuration for one deity, suggesting that *nīla* and *kṛṣṇa* may have been of the same color value for the authors of Buddhist sādhanas. Color descriptor for the deities of the so-called higher class tantras (the mahāyoga and yogini tantras), especially forms of Saṃvara and Hevajra in Abhayākaragupta's *Niṣpannayogāvalī* (NsP) is always *kṛṣṇa*. That *kṛṣṇa* is the color of frightening deities with chilling smiles or hysterical laughs in these vision texts reminds us of the NtS color scheme, which assigns *kṛṣṇa* to the fearful (*bhaya*).[36] Artists in charge of translating these visions into painting seem to have taken this color to mean "blue." Images of Saṃvara and Hevajra we encounter in surviving Indian Buddhist manuscripts of the twelfth and the thirteenth centuries are always in blue. In some extraordinary cases like the VRM manuscript discussed in chapter 4, the artist(s) pursued exceptional darkness in *kṛṣṇa* to create the fear-striking forms of Saṃvara, Hevajra, and Kālacakra (see figures 4.8, 4.10, 4.11). The artist(s) manipulated the tonality of the dark-blue color to create different visual effects of each deity: deeper and darker blue, which we may aptly call "blue-back," seems to have been applied to more powerful and secretive forms. Application of extremely dark blue or blue-black was most likely a measured effort and not due to the unavailability of blue pigment. Learning about what types of colorants were used to create such varied shades of blue to blue-black or any other unique colors and discoloration in the VRM manuscript would illuminate how the unnamed artist(s) should be understood as active agents and generators of color information who may have fashioned the colors of these visions. A scientific analysis on the paintings' material properties of the VRM manuscript remains a future task. Here we turn to explore some of the lessons that we can glean from material analysis of paintings. Doing so can improve our understanding of the color's function and meaning in the history of painting.

FROM COLOR TO MATTER: TOWARD A MATERIAL HISTORY OF PAINTING OF INDIA

PAINTING AND ITS MATERIALITY

Painting's thingness was highly cultivated in medieval South Asia, as we have seen throughout this book. Primary colors presented in maximum opacity intensify this sense of material presence. The Basohli folio mentioned at the beginning of this chapter provides a good example to appreciate the lavish artistic attention paid to the materiality of painting and the artisanal intelligence that enabled such intense realization of color in painting (see figure 6.1). The Harvard page belongs to a manuscript of the *Rasamañjarī* (Bouquet of Rasa) by a fifteenth-century Brahman poet, Bhānudatta. It is identified as folio 37 by pagination written on the left side border. The text of the Rasamañjarī is inscribed on the back. This Sanskrit text is neatly written in *nagari* script rather than in a local *takri* script, which is used to label the painting.[37] The orientation of the text is horizontal. The text is written in a reversed direction in relation to the painting that appears on the other side. The page retains the codicological feature of a *pothi*-format manuscript page in terms of the relationship between the text and the image (see figure 0.9).[38]

Verse 67 appears on the bottom of the page.[39] It reads:

> When the woman saw her husband's forehead stained by tawny lac from a rival's foot, the pearls at her ear were turned redder than rubies from the flash of anger from the corner of her eyes.[40]

The painting depicts this moment of tension and angst cleverly, and the emotional state and mood of the two protagonists are conveyed through composition and gestures. The standing male figure, who seems to have just walked into the space with his scarf flowing slightly backward, appears apologetic, with his extended left hand lowered and gently gesturing toward the woman as if addressing her in a low tone. In his retracted right hand, he is holding behind him a bejeweled necklace, presumably a gift to appease the woman. The seated woman sits tightly with her right leg close to her upper body as if holding in her anger; her right hand placed behind her ear provides a reddish shade around the outline of her head. Colors play an important role both in the poem and in the painting: "tawny lac" (*laktaka piñjaram*) on the husband's head is the direct cause of "redder than rubies" color denoting her anger in the text. In the painting, the male figure has a blue color that invokes Kṛṣṇa, and extra orange lines added on his forehead and limbs double as markers of extramarital love play indicated in the text; the female figure has vermilion on her right palm against which she rests her angry face—the color cleverly signals her emotional state.

Sustained attention to color allows us to draw a deeper connection between this seventeenth-century painting and earlier paintings on palm-leaf manuscripts. Brilliancy of hot colors in a seventeenth-century Rasamañjarī manuscript page finds a close parallel on paintings on twelfth-century palm-leaf manuscripts. For example, let us compare the Rasamañjarī page to a painted panel depicting the goddess Mahāmāyūrī in a twelfth-century palm-leaf manuscript of the Pañcarakṣā from eastern India (see figure 6.3). The goddess Mahāmāyūrī in her six-armed, green form is seated on a multicolored double-lotus pedestal against a dark-purple cushion and a yellow ornamental throne-back. A bright vermilion orb encircles her, while two yellow celestial beings emerging from purple clouds in the dark sky—indicating inner vision—offer garlands from either side. The painted area of the page, including the ornamented yellow column with a vermilion border around the binding hole, is dominated by bright yellow and vermilion, against which pops the green body of the goddess. The bejeweled goddess anticipates the heavily bedecked heroine of the Basohli painting.

Although executed on two different types of support medium—one on palm-leaflet and the other on paper—the level of opacity appears similar in both paintings. The pigment loss on the left side red border of the Basohli painting is comparable to the pigment loss in the thin line of vermilion to the left of the yellow column next to the Mahāmāyūrī panel. Each goddess panel in the Pañcarakṣā manuscript faces a painted panel that depicts her male counterpart; in this case, it is preaching Buddha. Substantial pigment loss in orpiment on the Buddha's face and upper body reveals the existence of several pigment layers that are visible even to the naked eye (see figure 6.17). A two-dimensional, flat, opaque pictorial surface is composed of physical layers of pigments. Intense vibrancy of colors delays the immediate recognition of such tactility of a painted surface, but its materiality is unmistakable—especially on a palm-leaf surface. Against such a surface, the painting appears jewel-like.

This jewel-like material quality of painting is pushed even further in the later Basohli example (see figure 6.1). The painting's materiality is prominent: the glistening beetle wings exactly cut to the shape of the jewels on the ornaments adorn the bodies, and raised white dots depict strands of pearls; all of these elements enhance the texture of the painting's surface. The light of a candle or a burning oil lamp—which is how its original viewers must have enjoyed the painting—would have made this textured surface even more alluring. Eschewing illusionistic techniques to the minimum, the artist(s) (who may have been Kirpal and his family members according to B.N. Goswamy) achieved the painting's presence through tactility and materiality of the pictorial surface, heavily laden with layers of colorants, many of which are mineral-based, inorganic pigments, and beetle wings.

That painterly practices in Indic artist circles developed to pay exceptional attention to a pictorial surface's texture and materiality is discernable in many earlier examples surviving from the Indian Himalayas.[41] In addition to those Klimburg-Salter mentioned, we can also look at the incredibly textured surfaces of early thirteenth-century murals in Alchi's Sumtseg, located in Ladakh. Good examples are raised white dots for pearls and the use of thick

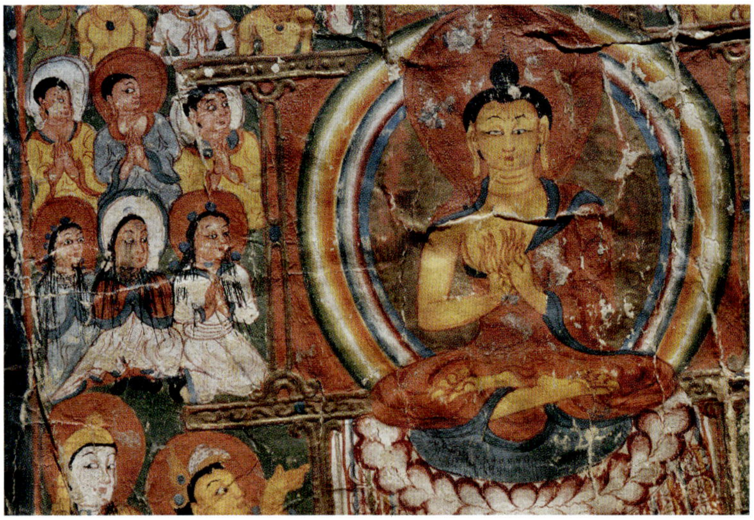

FIGURE 6.12
Detail from a *Perfection of Wisdom* manuscript, ca. twelfth century, Poo monastery, Himachal Pradesh. Pigments and gold on paper. Photo © Peter van Ham.

layers of gold. A manuscript page from Poo, also from the Indian Himalayas (Himachal Pradesh) demonstrates the confident use of raised gold technique to embellish the architectural throne of preaching Buddha on a paper folio (figure 6.12).[42] We may also add the multimedia approach in the art of Jaina caves at Ellora. Here, the sculpting on the rock surface and painting on the plastered surface of this carved rock are integrated to execute the overall design and the iconographic program from as early as the ninth century (figure 6.13).[43] In other words, painterly techniques and practices seem to have developed to engender appreciation of material and tactile properties of painting regardless of their support medium throughout the first half of the second millennium. Such deep attention to the materiality of painting in artistic practice calls for a more materially oriented historical inquiry of Indian painting. Turning to scientific analytical research is not a universalist superimposition on the material. Rather, the material demands such an approach to unearth an emic, that is to say, within the tradition, perspective.

CONSERVATION SCIENCE AND PAINTING OF INDIA

Analytical study of pigments has been the main area of research in conservation science for nearly a century. Continued refinement of scientific methods and utilization of advanced technological tools for art conservation have improved our understanding of the material properties and characteristics of pigments used in painting.[44] As colorful as they are, it seems predictable that pigments used in Indian painting have attracted much attention for technical analysis. An exceptional pigment called "Indian yellow" is believed to have been derived from the urine of cows fed only with mango leaves.[45] This color appears as the first pigment explored in volume 1 of *Artists' Pigments: A Handbook of Their History and Characteristics* published in 1985. This helpful publication follows in the footsteps of Rutherford J. Gettens (1900–1974), a pioneer in conservation science, whose "proposal for the handbook

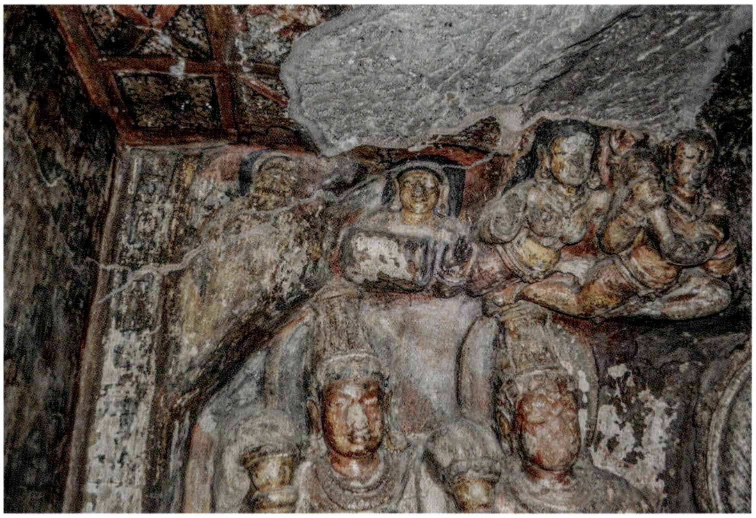

FIGURE 6.13
Celestial beings and attendants, painted sculpture and wall painting, main shrine, Cave 33a (J20), Ellora, ca. ninth century. Photo © Jinah Kim.

on analysis of materials of paintings" published in 1961 generated concerted efforts to systematically analyze and report on pigments. Indian and Buddhist painting loomed large in the life of Gettens, who started his career as a chemist on the staff at the Fogg Museum in Cambridge, Massachusetts, in 1928. Interactions with Langdon Warner, who was the curator of Oriental Art and the lecturer on the Art of Asia certainly propelled him to work on conserving Buddhist wall paintings from China, such as the fragments Warner took from Dunhuang. Having moved to the Freer Gallery to set up the Technical Laboratory in 1951, Gettens analyzed and identified pigments used in a mid-fifteenth-century cloth painting from India of the *Vasanta Vilāsa* (dated 1450–51) using microscopic, microchemical, and x-ray diffraction methods for W. Norman Brown's monograph on the scroll published in 1962.[46] Indian painting, like the Freer *Vasanta Vilāsa,* should have been in his mind when Gettens presented his proposal for the systematic material analysis of paintings in IIC 1961, which laid out a blueprint for a more sustained and systematic study of pigments.[47]

Another technical analysis of pigments used in Indian painting was conducted at the Los Angeles County Museum of Art in 1969, based on the paintings from the Nasli and Alice Heeramaneck Collection.[48] Samples for this analysis included a number of Nepalese manuscripts along with Mughal and Rajput paintings. Here the juxtaposition of Nepalese paintings with Mughal and Rajput examples may have been an accidental one predicated on the nature of the available material in the collection. But this study's result helps us put these often disparately treated materials on the same playing field. This is particularly relevant for the present study because it aims to narrow the categorical gap in scholarly literature between Indian painting and its Himalayan counterparts. Communities and locales in the Himalayan foothills and the Tibetan plateau were very much part of a larger Indic network, whether religious, political, or commercial, as a recent study by Indrani Chatterjee demonstrates.[49] This rather obvious connection is often forgotten and deserves our conscious effort to bring them together.

Since the late 1960s, Himalayan paintings—especially Tibetan thangkas—have also garnered much interest from conservation scientists.[50] As noted in a recent review of the state of the field in conservation of thangkas, Indian conservation scientists like O.P. Agrawal made an important contribution to the field of thangka conservation by bringing culturally sensitive and local tradition-based approaches to the attention of Western conservators.[51] A number of notable studies identifying pigments and materials used in thangkas of various dates have been published. Recent publications on the results of scientific analysis on wall painting in Western Himalayan Buddhist sites like Nako in India also expand our knowledge base for pigments and support materials used for painting in the Indian Himalayas from the twelfth century onward.[52] Our understanding of pigments used in the murals of Ajanta has improved steadily thanks to the efforts by conservation scientists in India.[53] More such studies on medieval wall painting should be carried out to help better preserve the cultural heritage and its artistic treasures.

MANUSCRIPT PAINTING AND PIGMENT ANALYSIS

Murals and manuscript paintings are completely different categories when it comes to material analysis. Unlike murals from which a physical sample for further analysis may be taken, manuscript paintings—often miniature in size and on relatively thin support mediums, whether palm-leaf or paper—present an additional challenge to material analysis as taking a sample of any size poses a greater threat to preserving the integrity of the work in question. When Gettens employed "microscopic, microchemical, and x-ray diffraction methods" to analyze pigments on the Freer *Vasanta Vilāsa*, identification of certain pigments benefited from chemical analysis, which surely required sampling from the surface, however microscopic. This challenge is mitigated by development in noninvasive methods for technical analysis in conservation science, such as XRF, UV imaging, infrared spectroscopy, Raman spectroscopy, and reflectance spectroscopy.[54]

The advancement in the area of noninvasive analysis of pigments in recent decades is fruitfully engaged in an interdisciplinary project, MINIARE (Manuscript Illumination: Non-Invasive Analysis, Research, and Experience) based in Cambridge, in the United Kingdom. This project already resulted in an exhibition held in 2016 and an exemplary publication on color, focusing mainly on European medieval illuminated manuscripts.[55] Initiated at the Fitzwilliam Museum with a focus on European manuscript illumination and Renaissance painting, the project has broadened its scope, taking synergy and inspiration from the University of Cambridge's exceptional collections and multidisciplinary experts. Its current aim is to undertake "non-invasive analysis of Western, Egyptian, Byzantine, Slavonic, Armenian, Persian, Mughal, Ottoman, Sanskrit, and Tibetan illuminated manuscripts (1350 BCE–19th century CE) and a selection of early printed material."[56] An impressively ambitious scope, if realized in its fullest potential, will surely benefit scholars in multiple disciplines, for generations to come.[57] The project's expansive scope already saw a technical study using a noninvasive method for identifying pigments in a late seventeenth-century Tibetan manuscript and a sixteenth-century Tibetan xylograph book with hand-colored panels in the Cambridge

University Library, adding to the growing body of knowledge on material aspects of the culture of Tibetan books.[58]

Identification of a pigment on a work of art often helps to establish when and where certain types of pigments may have been in use. In existing studies on pigments, findings from different analytical processes on different materials are often lumped together to make a general statement about a painter's practice or palette in a broad sweep.[59] This approach does not necessarily help answer the question of how and why certain colors were used, nor does it explain why certain pigments were used in certain ways. Paying deeper attention to specific elements in examples and trying to contextualize the analytical data with art-historical questions can advance our understanding of color and pigments in the history of painting beyond a matter of confirmation of a pigment's use. This is pursued in my digital humanities project, "Mapping Color in History [MCH]" currently under development at Harvard.[60] MCH is a web-based digital tool with a searchable database that contains historical and scientific information on color, based on material analyses of pigments in South Asian and Himalayan painting. Unlike other pigment databases, it takes a deeply historical approach and aims to integrate historical and locally specific information to a pigment profile by taking an object-based data entry method whenever possible. In what follows, I discuss directions and interpretative potentials of a focused, object-based historical approach in the study of pigment and color by sharing my analysis of findings from two ongoing collaborative projects: a pilot study on pigments on a small group of Indic manuscripts done at the Museum of Fine Arts, Boston, and an ongoing research project on pigment analysis of Indian painting at the Straus Center for Conservation and Technical Studies of the Harvard Art Museums.

THE MFA COLOR PROJECT

The Museum of Fine Arts, Boston (MFA), holds three rare examples of complete painted palm-leaf manuscripts from South Asia, two of which are dated. While there exist other institutional collections with more painted palm-leaf manuscripts, the MFA is an ideal site for collaboration on material analysis and pigment research for early Indic manuscript paintings. This is thanks to an in-house conservation studio and a scientific research lab, and to a world-renowned collection of South Asian art, a legacy of Ananda K. Coomaraswamy's tenure as the first curator of Indian art in North America. While Indian painting has been subject to scientific material analysis for nearly a century, early Indic manuscript painting like those on palm-leaf manuscripts dating prior to 1300 CE has rarely been examined for its material properties. Inaccurate information about pigments used in these early palm-leaf manuscripts remains in circulation and repeats itself partly due to the lack of existing research on pigments in early Indic manuscript painting. Thus, the idea that these early Indic manuscript painters used the pigments and a "similar process to that used in the wall paintings of Ajanta," which is completely unfounded, generates an inaccurate list of pigments in the palm-leaf manuscript painting that identifies "white (burnt conch shell), yellow (orpiment), blue (lapis lazuli), vermilion (cinnabar), crimson (lac-dye), Indian red (red ochre), green (terra-verde) and black (lamp black)" mostly based on cursory identification of pigments used at Ajanta.[61] Needless to say, extensive material analysis of palm-leaf manuscript paintings—especially those dated prior to 1400 CE—should be carried out at a much broader scope. With the material turn in art history and the developments in conservation science that allow for more accurate identification of pigments in manuscript painting, it is perhaps only a matter of time before we will start seeing more research in this direction.[62] For now, the analytical results from a small-scale study conducted at the MFA commissioned for the current book in 2017 can help improve our understanding of pigments in early Indic manuscript painting. The following five Indic manuscripts were selected for material analysis in the scientific research laboratory at the MFA. Michele Derrick, Schorr Family Associate Research Scientist, was the lead scientist working with Joan Wright, Bertina Burr Conservator, and her team.[63] My historical analysis is based on the XRF data readings provided by Michele Derrick.

1. Ms_A: Acc. No. 20.589, *Aṣṭasāhasrika Prajñāpāramitā sūtra,* palm-leaf manuscript, Gopāla's fourth year (c. 1136 CE), eastern India (northern Bengal)
2. Ms_B: Acc. No. 37.376 *Pañcarakṣā sūtra,* palm-leaf manuscript, ca. twelfth century, eastern India (Bihar)
3. Ms_C: Acc. No. 30.1, *Savaga Padikkamana Sutta Cunni,* Rajasthan, Udaipur, palm-leaf manuscript, dated 1260 CE
4. Ms_D: Acc. No. 17.2277 Kālpasūtra manuscript, paper manuscript, western India (Gujarat), dated 1497 CE
5. Ms_E: Acc. No. 62.929, Musa (Mosses) and the Great Man, a page from the Khamsa of Amir Khusrau Dihlavi, ca. first half of the fifteenth century, Sultanate

The first three are palm-leaf manuscripts, two of which are dated (two Buddhist; 20.589, dated ca. 1136 CE, and 37.376, and one Jain: 30.1, dated 1260 CE). The fifteenth-century examples are both on paper (Jain: 17.2277, dated 1497 CE).

SOME GENERAL OBSERVATIONS

Contrary to the assumption about the common use of ultramarine in Indic painting traditions, blue pigments used in palm-leaf manuscripts are identified as organic, most likely indigo, which is a well-known plant-based dye.[64] Green in palm-leaf manuscripts is identifiable as a combination of orpiment and organic blue rather than a single mineral or earth-based pigment. Yellow is consistently orpiment. The most common red pigment is vermilion, and vermilion is used in all of our samples. Artists also used hematite (earth-based red ocher) and organic red; this variety suggests the agency of the unnamed artists in making artistic choices that could affect the final outcome. Red lead is nearly absent from all examples. Despite the small sample size, this absence seems to bear out a general pattern in the use of red lead in manuscript painting production in South Asia, since all analyzed manuscripts date to the pre-1500 CE period, and the use of red lead in Indian painting seems to increase in the sixteenth century. The absence of lead-based pigments is noteworthy in palm-leaf manuscripts. Rather than lead-based pigments, material analysis suggests that artists working on palm-leaf manuscripts used calcium-based white (identified as calcite in Derrek's original report, which can be chalk or lime) and clay white (like kaolin, the appearance of Ti [titanium] in the elemental pulse seems to be related to the type of clay used in India for pigments).[65]

It is curious that yellow is visibly absent from the color field of two Jain manuscripts, Ms_C and Ms_D, examined in this study, one on palm-leaf, the other on paper. The thirteenth-century Jain manuscript on palm leaf contains arsenic-based material, of which orpiment as arsenic sulfide is a prime example in a painter's tool box, but this element's presence is not discriminating in terms of optical properties of visible colors in Ms_C. The color spectrum in Ms_C is rather limited, mainly employing four primary colors of red, white, black, and blue. As noted in chapter 2, Ms_C was prepared with leaves that were of uneven quality, and the modest character of painting with a limited palette goes in tandem with its humble appearance. This may well have been a conscious, possibly aesthetic choice rather than one entirely dictated by material conditions of shortage of available resources. The artist(s) used a limited palette cleverly, like creating different shades of red by employing organic red in addition to vermilion and combining various organic colors to create a secondary color like purple.

The absence of orpiment in Ms_D is partly compensated by the extensive use of gold, perhaps closely translating the light-based color theory and the prevalence of "golden yellow" body color of the *tīrthaṅkaras* (figure 6.14). On the surface, Ms_D appears to be a common example of fifteenth-century Jain manuscripts on paper with its liberal use of gold, accentuated by blue, red, black, white, and occasionally green. But material analysis reveals some unusual elements. It is helpful to compare the results with those of two existing studies on pigments in fifteenth-century Indic painting of similar provenance: one by Isacco and Darrah on a painting in a mid-fifteenth-century Jain paper manuscript of the *Uttarādhyayana sūtra*, now in the Victoria and Albert Museum, and the other by Gettens on the Freer *Vasanta Vilāsa* scroll of 1451 CE prepared in Ahmedabad, Gujarat.[66] Although nearly absent in our two Jain examples, yellow appears frequently in surviving paintings of Jain and western Indian origin of pre-1500 CE periods. When yellow is visible, it is most likely arsenic-sulfide (orpiment) as identified in two existing studies. For example, the yellow of the figure's face on folio 23r of the Victoria and Albert manuscript is identified as orpiment (figure 6.15).

The most unusual aspect of Ms_D is that the brilliant blue on its surface turns out to contain cobalt, possibly suggesting the use of smalt (ground form of blue enamel glass).[67] In the other two fifteenth-century examples analyzed in previous studies, indigo and ultramarine (identified as lazurite mixed with silicate in the case of the Freer *Vasanta Vilāsa*) were used. If this is indeed smalt from the fifteenth century, Ms_D may be one of the earliest examples where smalt is in use in manuscript painting.[68] Ms_D also uses copper-based green (possibly malachite) instead of a mixture of indigo and orpiment. Two different types of green, the copper-based "verdigris," and the combination of orpiment and indigo, were used in the Victoria and Alberts manuscript while in the Freer *Vasanta Vilāsa*, only the latter form was found. If green in Ms_D is indeed malachite, this may suggest diversification of

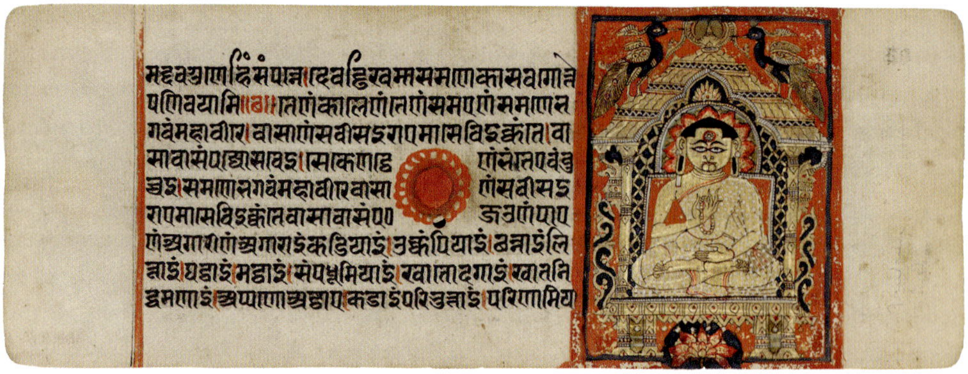

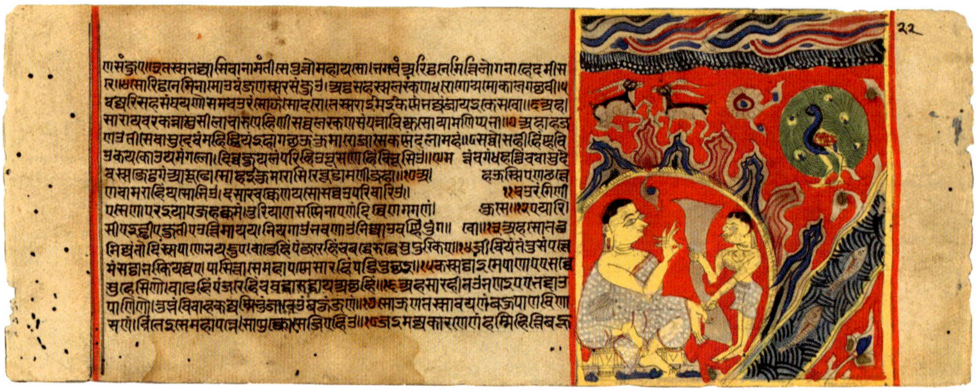

FIGURE 6.14 ▲
Folio 61r, Tīrthaṅkara, a manuscript of the Kalpasūtra and Kālakācārya Kathā (Ms_D), dated 1497 CE, Gujarat(?), 30 × 11 cm. Ink, opaque watercolor, gold, on paper. Museum of Fine Arts, Boston, 17.2277, Ross-Coomaraswamy Collection. Photograph © 2021 Museum of Fine Arts, Boston.

FIGURE 6.15 ▼
Folio 23r, *Uttarādhyayana sūtra* manuscript, ca. 1450, Gujarat. Pigments on paper, V&A IS.2–1972 23r. © Victoria and Albert Museum, London.

pigments available at manuscript artists' disposal. We may hypothesize that new pigments were introduced and experimented with as paper was adopted as a new support medium for painting and manuscript production. Further research is necessary to understand how diverse and experimental pigments used in fifteenth-century Indic manuscript paintings may have been. Paper as a medium seems to have enabled different methods of pigment application from the method used on palm-leaf painting. In Ms_D, almost all colors are applied as additional layers on an expansive swath of gold in each panel: brilliant deep blue, shimmering white, shining red, iridescent green, and matte vermilion appear to have been inlaid into a golden surface like enamel. The pigment application technique in Ms_D that renders the manuscript's surface like enamel jewelry may indicate a potential artisanal inspiration taken from jewelry makers, which may have served well the taste of the Jain patrons that might have been jewelry merchants.[69]

The lone folio from a Sultanate manuscript (62.929) was selected for a comparative benchmark (figure 6.16). The period during which the Indic palm-leaf manuscript painting tradition developed in earnest is also when a very different tradition of the book from the Islamic world was introduced in the subcontinent. The provenance of this folio is unclear, and the material analysis indicates that the folio was repaired and restored heavily in the modern period as suggested by the appearance of lead chromate-based pigments in several points in restored areas.[70] It most likely belongs to a dispersed manuscript of the *Khamsa* (quintet) of Amir Khusraw Dihlavi (d. 1325). The manuscript's date and the production site are unidentified in the surviving folios, but there is a scholarly consensus that it dates to the mid-fifteenth century and was probably prepared somewhere in northern India.[71] In comparison to the examples belonging to the "Indic" manuscript painting tradition, the range of pigments identified on this folio is markedly different. Most notable is the use of lead white and gypsum for white along with the use of azurite, a copper-based mineral blue pigment, a cheaper alternative to lapis lazuli (ultramarine), and the possible use of malachite for green—none of these pigments are found in three palm-leaf manuscripts analyzed for this study. This variety suggests changes in the material world of colors for artists that arrived in South Asia along with the introduction of a different kind of a manuscript culture that had paper and the codex format as its material base, instead of palm-leaf and *pothi*-format. Lead white, for example, is widely used in the Persian painting tradition.[72] The matte, opaque color field is also an established characteristic of Persianate painting in which "areas of color steadfastly maintain their 'thingness,'" as David J. Roxburgh characterizes it.[73]

The packed color field on paper is partly achieved through the process of burnishing. While it is difficult to prove the use of a multistage burnishing technique on the folio Ms_E partly due to damage and later restoration, it seems likely, given the compacted nature of pigment layers. In the Persianate painting traditions, at least two stages of burnishing are recommended, as explained in a sixteenth-century technical treatise by Sadiqi Beg, a royal painter in sixteenth-century Safavid Iran: burnishing the support prior to application of color, and burnishing from the back after the painting is finished. In the case of gold and silver use, burnishing is also recommended in between the stages of color application.[74] Burnishing the ground, or support layer, in preparation for painting is a common step taken in painting in other media in India as well, like wall painting and cloth painting. An early Sanskrit treatise on painting in the VdhM describes this burnishing process in preparation of wall for painting.[75] Burnishing the (gesso) ground on cloth is an important final step of initial preparation stage for painting on cloth as reported from twentieth-century Tibetan thangka painters.[76] Smoothing the painted surface by burnishing from the back of the support medium is desirable and effective on paper, and this particular technique may have been introduced to India with paper as a medium for manuscript production from the Persianate world.[77] After color application, burnishing the painting from the back smoothens the painted surface and enhances its brilliance. The burnishing technique still practiced today by miniature painters in Rajasthan in India includes burnishing during intermediary stages of paint application.[78] A similar technique is also followed in Pahari schools, and it

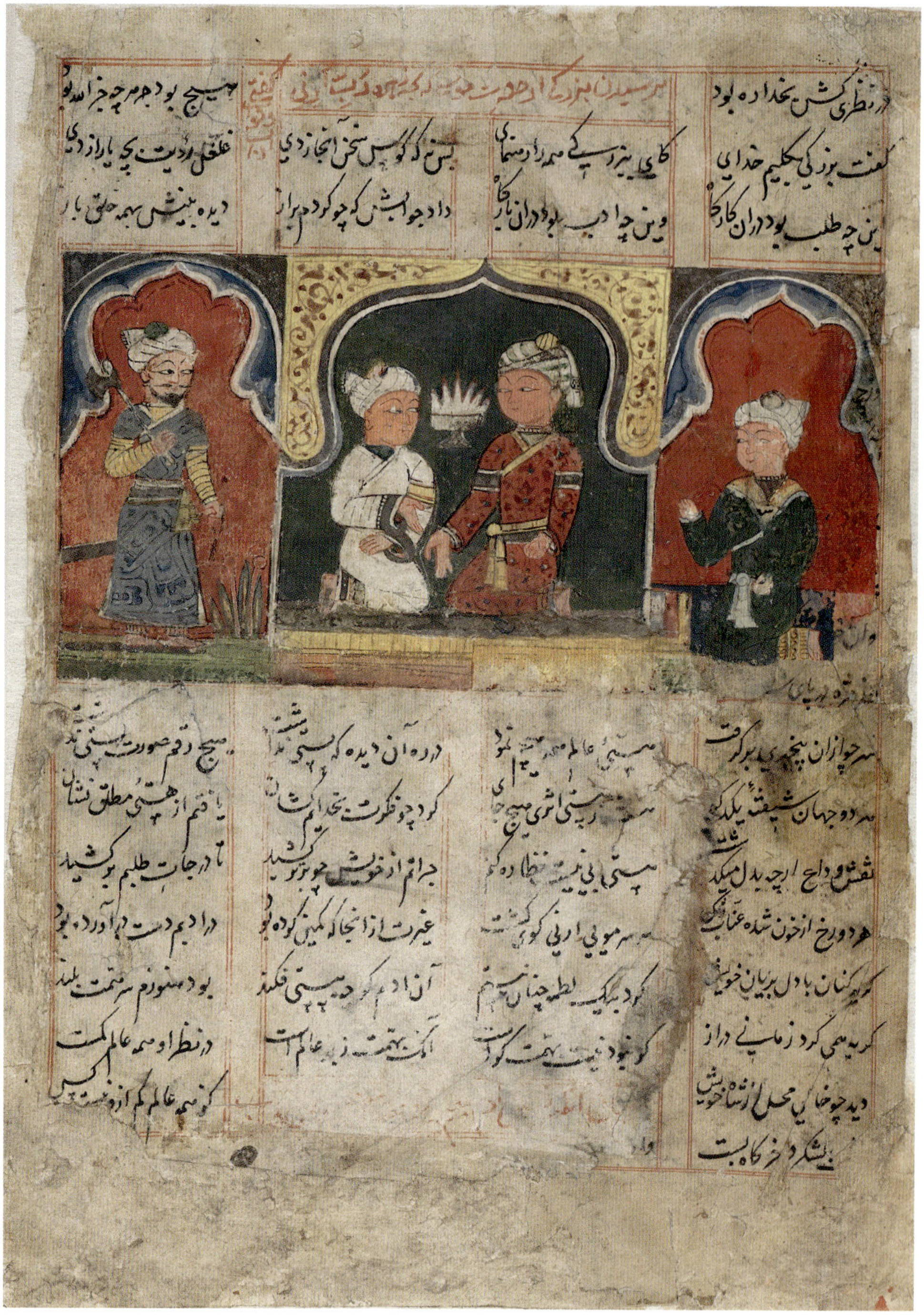

FIGURE 6.16
Musa (Moses) and the great man, a folio from a dispersed Khamsa of Amir Khusrau Dihlavi (Ms_E), ca. first half of the fifteenth century (Sultanate), pigments on paper. Museum of Fine Arts, Boston, 62.929, John Ware Willard Fund. Photograph © 2021 Museum of Fine Arts, Boston.

continues to be taught in the training of traditional miniature painters in Pakistan, notably at the National College of Arts, Lahore.[79] It seems unlikely that this technique of burnishing in multiple stages to enhance the finish was applicable in preparation of miniature painting in palm-leaf manuscripts. A palm-leaf folio may have been burnished to prepare the surface for writing, but a finished painting is unlikely to have been burnished from the back—especially since the text was mostly inscribed on the surface before painting.[80] As noted above, even in the case of a late fifteenth-century Jain paper manuscript (Ms_D), it seems improbable that the final painting was burnished from the back, as additional pigment layers on the golden surface remain tactile and textured.

Another noticeable aspect in Ms_E may be the use of more varied hues, tints, and shades. While mixing colors seems to have remained an artist's prerogative that was not necessarily theorized, methods for color mixing are discussed by Teflisi where mixing lead white with various pigments leads to diversification of colors according to Yves Porter's study: lead white plus indigo for light blue (*bleu clair*), lead white plus *minium* for pink (*rose-clair*), lead white plus lac for rose, lead white plus cinnabar for rose (*ogar-gun?*), lead white plus *vert de gris*, as light green (pale green).[81] As mentioned, in the MFA study, Ms_E is the only manuscript that used lead white. Given the predominance of lead white in Persian sources, we may hypothesize that lead white use may be another marker that signals the Persianate painting tradition as a source of material and artistic knowledge in a pre-1500 CE painting. The control and use of white seem to have been important to diversify colors; moreover, the method for making colors brighter by adding "white" is also discussed in early Indic treaties. The following is a close reading of the results of material analysis of Ms_B, a manuscript hitherto unpublished, which aims to demonstrate how pigments, especially white, may have been used in painterly practice.

OPACITY AND BRILLIANCE OF COLORS: THE ROLE OF WHITE PIGMENTS IN THE MFA PAÑCARAKṢĀ MANUSCRIPT (MS_B)

In Ms_B, a mid-twelfth-century eastern Indian manuscript of the Pañcarakṣā now in the MFA, the body color of each goddess is well articulated in brilliant densely packed colorants (see figure 6.3). Each painted panel successfully masks the biological character of the support material, palm-leaflets with veins, so that it transforms the surface to a material manifestation of a colorful vision of each goddess. This undated manuscript bears witness to the complete translation of the IEB color system in painting in Indian monastic circles.

Ms_B suffered considerable damage prior to coming into the museum's collection in 1937; the damage is extensive on the first folio but it is seen throughout the manuscript (figure 6.17).[82] Originally prepared with ninety-eight folios, the manuscript is missing ten folios and it most likely had two wooden end boards. The original plan for the manuscript's design seems to have been twelve painted panels, two at the beginning of each *rakṣā* text and two at the end of the manuscript. However, folio 94r, which should have contained a painted panel of the goddess Mahāmantrānusāranī, is missing. The last folio has a blank panel delineated for painting—including the area for the border design—but this was never executed.[83]

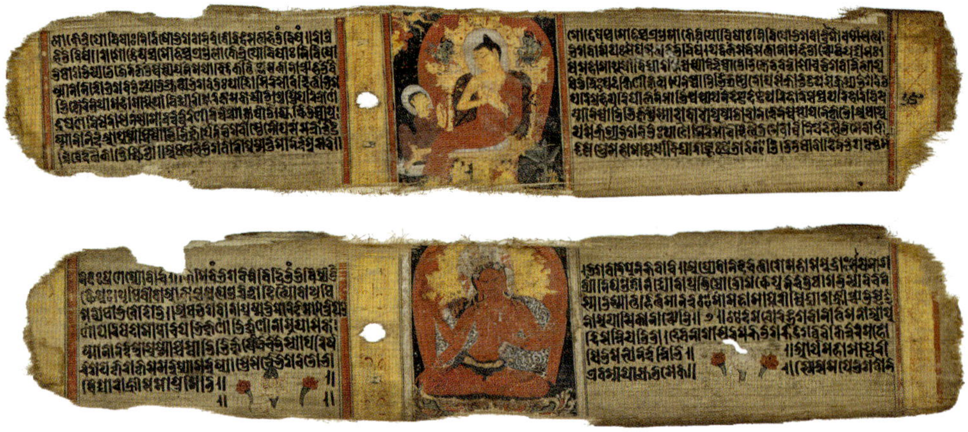

FIGURE 6.17
Preaching Buddha-Goddess Mahāśītavatī, folio 65v–66r, Pañcarakṣā manuscript (Ms_B), ca. late eleventh to early twelfth century, Bihar, India. Museum of Fine Arts, Boston, 37.376, Helen and Alice Colburn Fund. Photograph © 2021 Museum of Fine Arts, Boston.

The manuscript is written in what may be called *bhujimol* or "round top" script often found in Nepalese manuscripts of the twelfth and thirteenth centuries. However, this rounded character of the script does not necessarily indicate Nepal as its production site. A group of manuscripts that are written in the round top script clearly bears Pāla regnal years, and their paintings are executed in what is arguably a visual language of Magadhan monastic sites like Nālandā. Stylistic features such as the oval-shaped head of the goddesses, curved seagull eyes, a swaying upper torso with pronounced breasts of the goddesses, a pointed triangular shaped *uṣṇīṣa* of the preaching Buddha in three-quarter profile, along with many ornamental details—be it jewelry worn by goddesses, textile patterns, the design of throne backs, the shape of halos, or clouds in which celestial beings appear above—find close parallels in the mid-twelfth-century manuscript paintings from Nālandā such as the first two folios of the Rockefeller AsP manuscript now in the Asia Society, New York (see figure 3.6).[84] The script is also distinct from Newari *bhujimol*.[85] Based on paleographic indication and stylistic analysis, it seems reasonable to suggest that the manuscript was most likely prepared in a Magadhan monastic site in the first half of the twelfth century. The goddess iconography clearly follows what Mevissen calls the "Eastern Indian tradition." The iconographic program is unique to this manuscript. Each text is framed as if being preached by the Buddha: the painted panel depicting the Buddha preaching to an audience is always paired with a goddess. Except for the opening panel, every preaching Buddha is shown in three-quarter profile with a listener, either a monk or a lay man, and a flying deva appears amid dynamic clouds from above with an offering of a garland (see figure 6.17, *top*). This is a metonymical representation of the opening scene of each text in which the Buddha preaches the very text personified as the goddess on the facing page in front of a crowd of monks, bodhisattvas, and celestial beings.[86] Such a unique configuration also suggests an eastern Indian provenance rather than Nepalese, because Nepalese examples follow a conventional schema for an iconographic program in Pañcarakṣā manuscripts.

Despite the damage, the painted panels survive with remarkable freshness. Body colors of the goddesses are well differentiated with brilliant opaque colors: Mahāsāhasrapramardanī (folio 2r) in white; Mahāmāyūrī (folio 29r) in green; Mahāśītavatī (folio 66r) in red; and Mahāpratisarā (folio 69r) in yellow. Unfortunately, folio 94 that would have had the goddess Mahāmantrānusāriṇī in blue is missing. Based on the results of the material analysis, pigments for the goddesses can be reasonably suggested as follows: white is most likely from a form of calcite (calcium carbonate white); yellow is from orpiment (an arsenic sulfide mineral); while red is from cinnabar (a form of mercury sulfide). The green of Mahāmāyūrī is most likely created from organic blue (most likely plant-based indigo) with orpiment and calcite. The blue of Mahāmantrānusāriṇī would have been of organic blue given its consistent use elsewhere in the manuscript. The use of brilliant mineral colorants like vermilion and orpiment delivers the color values of the IEB system with exceptional clarity. As noted at the beginning of this chapter, these colorants are less commonly used in earlier centuries of the first millennium, notably in the murals of Ajanta.

Painting in this manuscript appears even more brilliant and opaque in color than that in the other twelfth-century eastern Indian manuscript analyzed for this study: Ms_A, a complete manuscript of the *Perfection of Wisdom* (20.589, Ms_A) with two original painted wooden covers (figure 6.18). According to the colophon on folio 206, the manuscript was completed during the fourth regnal year of a Pāla king, Gopāla (IV) (c. 1136 CE) for a lay patron named Kamalapāṇisiṁha. Painting in Ms_A shows a similar range of visible colors with Ms_B—white, red, blue, yellow, green, and black. Pigments used in both manuscripts seem similar: the use of orpiment can be confirmed in both manuscripts. The predominant use of orpiment in these two manuscripts supports existing scholarly wisdom on orpiment use in the history of Indian painting.[87] Orpiment seems to have been one of the main arsenals of Indian manuscript painters from at least 1100 CE onward. The use of vermilion, a mercurial red, is clear in Ms_B and it is also likely in Ms_A.[88] Paintings in both manuscripts showcase exceptional talents in draftsmanship and artistic creativity in twelfth-century eastern India.

In terms of the quality of color execution, the artist(s) working on Ms_B seems to have been more adept at handling colors: he created varied hues and shades like light blue to dark blue and purple deftly using organic colorants and calcite (white). The exact types of organic colorants are difficult to determine without further material analysis, but it is clear that he had at least three different types of red pigments: vermilion, hematite (Fe in XRF pulse), and organic red. He also had more precious material like gold, the use of which is confirmed on the Mahāmāyūrī panel (for example, one of her attributes, the elephant goad in her extended lower left hand, is in gold). A close reading of the results of XRF analysis also allows us to consider why the painting in Ms_B appears more brilliant and bright to our naked eyes than that in Ms_A when the range of colorants used in both cases remains similar. In addition to access to more precious material like gold and possibly higher-grade pigments, the artist working on the Pañcarakṣā manuscript seems to have used a good quality white pigment,

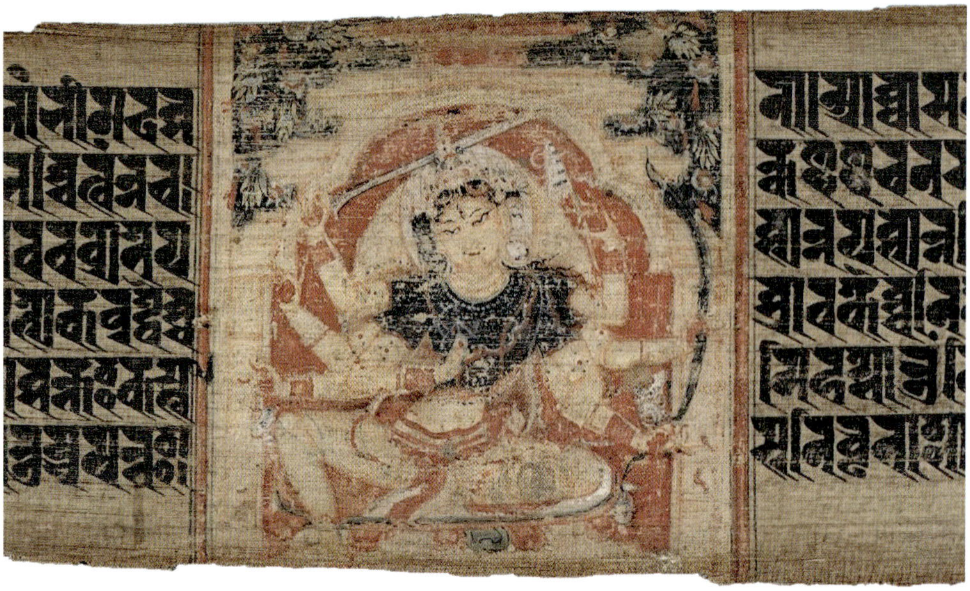

FIGURE 6.18
Vajratārā, right panel, folio 2r (Ms_A), Gopāla's fourth year (ca. 1136 CE), northern Bengal. Pigments and ink on palm leaf. Museum of Fine Arts, Boston, Acc. 20.589, Harriet Otis Cruft Fund. Photograph © 2021 Museum of Fine Arts, Boston.

suggested in the report by the lead scientist Michele Derrick as calcite, and used it well to bring out the intended color. It seems likely that he applied an additional white pigment layer underneath the painted panel and used white whenever a new color was introduced over another color, like light blue over vermilion, vermilion or blue over white, purple over vermilion.[89] The XRF data also suggests that the artist may have been adept at using white pigment to create more pastel colors like purple and light blue, as the "Ca" pulse peaks in the areas where we optically notice these pastel colors.

Surviving examples that have unfinished painted panels like the *Kubjikā* manuscript of Rāmapāla's reign in the National Archive, Kathmandu, discussed in chapter 2, suggest that artists devised a way to prepare the surface of palm leaf better for painting; it is possible that they prepared the ground with white in the same way that artists would have prepared a wall or a piece of woven fabric/canvas (for *paṭa* or *thangka*) (figure 6.19).[90] Further research on material properties in the Indic manuscript painting of the initial phase will be necessary to identify whether white pigment was skillfully used to increase opacity across sectarian and regional boundaries and to confirm whether this method was adopted as a common technique by manuscript painters in twelfth-century India.

Among the surviving examples, it is interesting to note that a group of twelfth-century manuscripts, especially those of Nālandā that are closely associated with Tibetan monasteries, stands out for the extensive use of white pigment and opacity. For example, a twelfth-

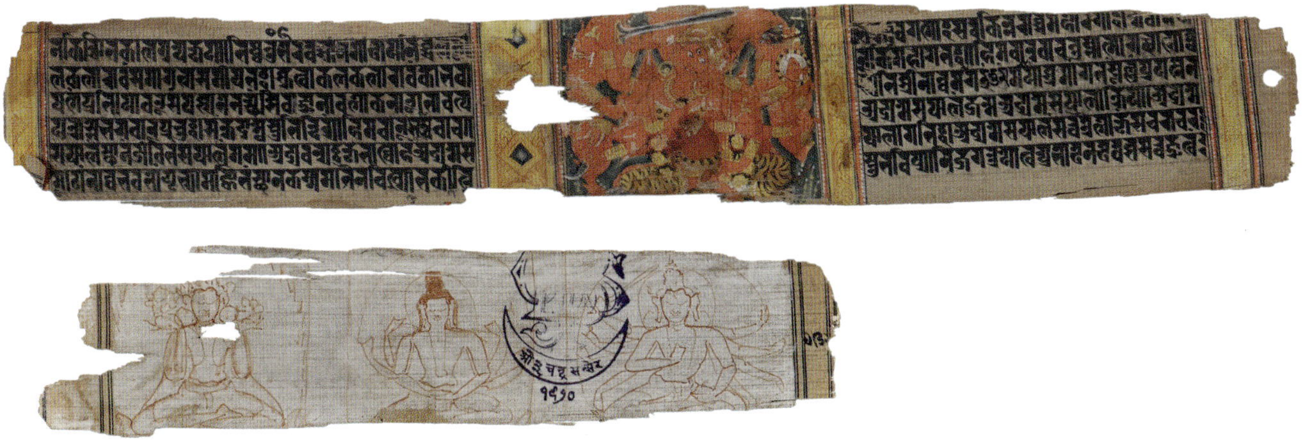

FIGURE 6.19
Folio 2r–last folio v, a painted palm-leaf manuscript of the *Kubjikāmata*, ca. early twelfth century, dated with Rāmapāla's regnal year (ca. 1077–1131 CE), National Archives of Nepal, Kathmandu, Acc. No. 1/1363. Photo courtesy of National Archives of Nepal.

century *Perfection of Wisdom* manuscript prepared in Nālandā for a Tibetan monk is remarkable for its brilliant color and the generous use of white pigment that survives in nearly pristine condition. Introduction of a more diffused pastel color, like "pink" of the monk's robe and light blue on the dhoti (lower garment) of Śakra (Indra, identifiable by eyes all over his body) (figure 6.20), is most likely a result of artistic interventions, which pursued a more varied spectrum of colors that are pleasing to the eye. Another Nālandā manuscript with a known connection to Tibet, the *Perfection of Wisdom* manuscript in the Asia Society New York mentioned above, also survives with two painted folios that were most likely prepared in the mid-twelfth century that stands out for the brilliance of color and the controlled use of white, including the noticeable appearance of more pastel colors like pink, purple, and light blue (see figure 3.6).

The increased opacity and brilliance in color are common in paintings surviving from across the Himalayan region—be it in murals or paintings on cloth (thangkas/paubhas) or manuscript paintings from the twelfth and thirteenth centuries. The Indian examples that showcase exceptional caliber in color handling derive from monastic productions with close ties to Tibet.[91] This pattern indicates a deeper connection in the circulation of artisanal knowledge across this vast Indic Buddhist world that these manuscripts and manuscript makers traversed, along with other knowledge experts like monks, tantric masters, their disciples, and translators.

COLOR AND TANTRA: MERCURIAL RED

Of all the colorants identified in the five manuscripts of the MFA study, vermilion is the only pigment present in all five examples. The consistent use of vermilion across sectarian and

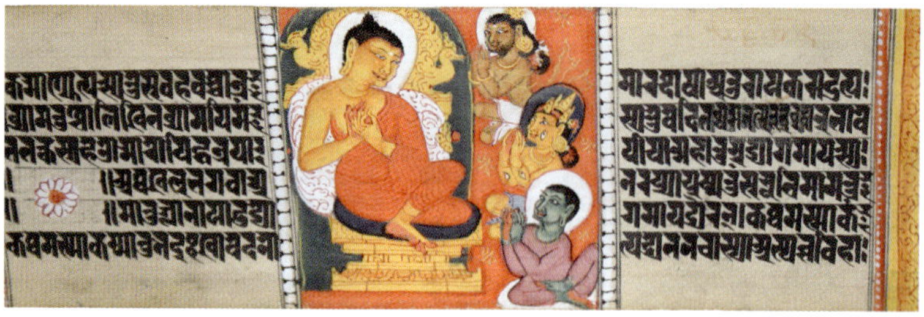

FIGURE 6.20
Preaching Buddha, the end of chapter 11 (Mara's deeds), *Perfection of Wisdom* manuscript, Rāmapāla's thirty-seventh year, ca. 1114 CE, Nālandā. Donor: Vijayakīrti from Tibet. Tibet Museum, Lhasa. Photo © Jinah Kim.

cultural boundaries speaks to the importance of this pigment in Indian manuscript painting. Identification of vermilion is suggested through the presence of mercury, because vermilion's elemental composition is mercuric sulfide. One can obtain this pigment either by finding it naturally or producing it artificially. Vermilion naturally occurs in mineral form as cinnabar, which can be ground. Artificial vermilion can be obtained by combining mercury and sulfur. Two methods are known for synthetic mercury production—dry-process and wet-process. Dry-process is believed to have been invented by the Chinese in the early centuries of the Common Era. This method requires a complex process of sublimation to transform the black-colored initial compound of the two elements into red crystalline pigment. Wet-process is an easier method for vermilion production that requires additional agents (a solution of ammonium or potassium sulfide). Such a process was invented in Germany in the seventeenth century.[92] Many recipes for artificial vermilion production are also reported in Persian literature.[93] Various recipes recommend different ratios between mercury and sulfide; in general, the mercury ratio is higher than sulfide. In Europe, vermilion appears more commonly after the fourteenth century when the synthetic manufacture of vermilion was more widely practiced.[94] Recipes for vermilion are scarce in Indic sources. A reference to vermilion in Indic artistic treatises is rather indiscriminate in terms of its material properties. But its material properties as confirmed in material analyses of surviving paintings provide some important clues to consider in this pigment's connection with tantric communities of medieval South Asia.

Indic artistic treatises may be silent about recipes for vermilion, but methods for transmutation of substances are found in what David Gordon White terms the "alchemical tantras" of the tenth century and onward.[95] The central focus of this alchemical art is "rasa," especially in its sense as "mercury." In the alchemical tantras that White analyzed, mercury and sulfur, the two ingredients of vermilion and the material components of natural cinnabar, are identified as Śiva's semen and "the uterine or menstrual blood" of the Goddess (Śiva's consort) respectively. According to White, cinnabar, as the combination of the two most potent elements, is "a mineral hierophany of the sexual union of Śiva and the Goddess, a union that, according to Hindu tradition, creates and sustains the universe." A potent symbolic meaning is transposed onto the matter. White's discussion underscores the ensuing red color's association with the "life force or vital energy in both India and China."[96] Mercurial red's importance emerged in the alchemical tantras of the post-tenth century. This emergence nearly coincides with appearances of vermilion in Indic manuscript painting. Recognizing this helps to contextualize the persistent use of vermilion observed in the material analyses of Indic manuscript paintings of the first centuries of the second millennium.

However powerful as an alchemical substance, a natural source of mercury, cinnabar ore is not commonly found in the Indian subcontinent.[97] This fact is relevant for the discussion of vermilion as a pigment. Whether artificial or natural, vermilion requires access to cinnabar ore, which provides the source material for mercury. When was vermilion introduced to India? If cinnabar ore is absent in the subcontinent, where did the material come from? Further research is necessary to determine when vermilion became an essential part of the Indic painting traditions' tool kit, but this pigment's prevalence seems to have risen along with the thoughts and practices that informed the development of the alchemical tantras of the post-tenth century that shifted the earlier material focus on gold (as in the *Śatapatha Brāhmaṇa*) to mercury. As for the Indic knowledge of the locus of mercury's natural source such as actual cinnabar ore, the origin myth of mercury told in the alchemical tantras surveyed by White introduces an interesting conception of mercurial wells on earth that are colored according to their cardinal directions: "The mercury of the eastern well is white, that of the western well yellow, and that of the southern well is blue." The mercury of the northern well is red. "The well at the center of this five-sided mercurial maṇḍala contains 'mixed' mercury, called *miśraka*, which is said to be *mayūra* (peacock)." In colorist terms, the central well may be designated as green. As seen in figure 5.1d, the five-color directional scheme according to the alchemical tantras does not match any of the directional color schemes surveyed in chapter 5. But if we take the "*miśraka*" as a peacock-like "green" color, the alchemical tantra system also uses the five primary colors of the IEB system.

Most important for the present discussion, the northern well's mercury is singled out as "red and pure, superior to the other four." White suggests that this idea of the northern well is linked to the understanding of Darada deśa (Dardistan, north of Kashmir) as "a likely overland source of mercury for India in the age of tantric alchemy."[98] Whether the term *darada* could have also meant "cinnabar" as White suggests is debatable. Nevertheless, knowledge of cinnabar ores located beyond the northwestern frontier region of the South Asian subcontinent—such as in present-day Afghanistan—seems to be historically accurate as cinnabar mines are well documented in that area.[99]

In part, vermilion's conspicuous absence at Ajanta and dominance in manuscript paintings may be related to the fragmentary nature of surviving evidence. Further material analysis on murals dating between the fifth and the tenth centuries will help locate when and where this pigment was introduced initially and how widespread its use was before 1000 CE. By the time the walls of the Sumtsek (three-storied building) at Alchi were painted in the late eleventh or late twelfth century, vermilion was certainly in use in this Himalayan location in today's Ladakh (see figure 2.22).[100] An interesting historical parallel can be drawn between sustained interest in mercury in alchemical tantras and vermilion's prominent role in Indic paintings as the most consistently used pigment. Mercury-sulfur's importance in the alchemical tantras does not mean that vermilion is a pigment that was concocted by the tantric activities. This pigment's use in artistic production is documented in other cultures from ancient times. The fact that references to the importance of mercury occur in alchemical tantras that date after the tenth century is relevant for thinking about the historical picture of cinnabar use in artistic production. It suggests a tantalizing possibility that vermilion's bold appearance in early Indic manuscript paintings may be potentially tied to knowledge being generated in the tantric communities. This connection is tangential. The information gleaned from the alchemical tantras may only be relevant to suggest the medieval Indic knowledge of the geographical location of a cinnabar ore.

The generative association of mercury that some tantric communities of medieval South Asia introduced may have had a wider appeal. Tantric communities of various sectarian leanings—be they Śaiva, Bauddha, or Jaina—shared much in terms of iconographic languages and ritual technologies. While no painted manuscript directly related to the alchemical tantras survives, a recent study on a small group of palm-leaf manuscripts associated with the famous Vikramaśīla monastery suggests another connection between tantric communities and mercury that concerns manuscript production. A team of researchers from the University of Hamburg performed a material analysis on a small set of Sanskrit palm-leaf manuscripts that are known to have a connection with Vikramaśīla now kept in Kathmandu, Nepal, in 2013.[101] Using a mobile XRF spectrometer and infrared spectroscopy (FTIR) equipment, the analysis was focused on identifying material properties of ink and possible chemical treatments on palm leaf. Ink recipes known in historical literature and identified in archaeological and art-historical samples all point to a consistent use of carbon-based (like soot) ink. The material analysis conducted by the Hamburg team suggests that there may have been some variations in ink recipes, depending on the region and the period.[102] The most interesting finding for the present discussion is the identification of mercury content in ink used in Vikramaśīla manuscripts. The sample size (three manuscripts) is rather small for generalizing the findings. The level of mercury is not consistent: in one example (KL 128) only a trace amount is detected. Nonetheless, mercury's presence in ink is an interesting phenomenon to consider. The authors of the study opt not to pursue a mercurial connection with Indian medicine and alchemical tantras. Instead, they prudently suggest that the enrichment of ink with mercury may have served "a very practical purpose." Along with arsenic—which is consistently present on palm-leaf folios—mercury provides "additional protection against insect infestation." This is a possibility, but this remains a conjecture as the discussion lacks any reference to the understanding of mercury's pesticidal capacity in known literature.

All of the Vikramaśīla manuscripts examined in the study happen to contain texts that can be classified as Buddhist tantras. Along with Vikramaśīla's reputation as a seat of tantric learning in later Tibetan hagiographic literature, it does not seem improbable to suggest that the addition of mercury to ink—if this was indeed intentional—may have been symbolically meaningful; that is, it would have empowered the text through what is increasingly understood as a generative substance in other tantric circles; erstwhile, it would have acquired a more protective quality physically. Another practical explanation would be the possibility of mercury enrichment affecting ink's thickness and fluidity for easier or smoother scribing.[103] More important for the present study is the question of how mercury ended up in ink.

Mercury is not a naturally available substance commonly found in the Indian subcontinent. The Gangetic plain is an unlikely place to find mercury in nature. Prior to the turn of the first millennium, mercury was an uncommon substance in India. While a possible recipe referencing the procurement of mercury may be identified in a ninth-century (?) Jain text, it is only in a thirteenth-century text that mercury recipes appear more substantially developed for use. It takes another three centuries before mercury is transformed into a perfect medicine in *ayurvedic* literature.[104] The most likely source of mercury for a monastic scriptorium like Vikramaśīla in the twelfth century would have been vermilion, a pigment favorably used in manuscript paintings of the period. None of the manuscripts examined by the authors were painted, but there are surviving Vikramaśīla manuscripts with miniature paintings. The mid-twelfth-century *Perfection of Wisdom* manuscript in the British Library (Or. 6902) is such an example (see figure 3.4). An accidental use of an inkpot that may have contained vermilion previously could certainly explain a mercury pulse as a minor element in an XRF reading. The data shared in the published report is unclear on the level of mercury content in each case, as identifying information on the vertical axis is missing.[105] If the amount is substantial, it is also possible that vermilion was intentionally added to soot ink to make it more potent, if the meaning generated in the alchemical tantras had any significance among Buddhist tantric circles. The addition of vermilion in a black-ink recipe would have not changed the optical appearance of the ink substantially. All of these suggestions remain hypothetical until further research in the scientific material analysis of palm-leaf manuscripts provides further data. Nevertheless, it seems reasonable to suggest that the presence of mercury in ink of manuscripts associated with the Vikramaśīla monastery indicates the use of a mercury-based pigment—vermilion (possibly as a piece of cinnabar, a geological form in which it can travel easily across vast distances)—in the scriptorium.

EXPANDING COLOR KNOWLEDGE

In the *Nāgānanda,* the Vidyadhāra prince Jimūtavāhana requests "bits of red pigment" to be fetched from the mountains to paint his beloved on the surface of a moonstone bench. It seems reasonable to assume that his companion most likely brings him earth-based pigments—like red ocher, yellow ocher, and clay white; these are the most common pigments found in Ajanta's murals. Pigments that produce more brilliant hues like orpiment and vermilion are extremely toxic: orpiment is essentially an arsenic sulfide mineral and vermilion is a combination of mercury and sulfur. Lead-based pigments, like lead white and lead red, are also toxic. In artistic practices according to today's toxicology and health standards, none of these pigments would be available or deemed safe to use.[106] Long-term exposure to arsenic can cause malevolent changes in one's skin and circulatory and peripheral nervous disorders as well as adverse effects on liver and kidney function.[107] Mercury's harmful effects on the nervous system are well known. If vermilion was processed from cinnabar, it may have been less toxic than dealing with other forms of mercury. Cinnabar is less poisonous to humans than other forms of mercury, like quicksilver. For example, a recent study on the mercury toxicity in pre-Hispanic use of cinnabar for face/body painting finds medical dangers posed by cinnabar use less likely than expected.[108] These pigments were also matters or by-products of some of the powerful substances used in traditional medicine and magico-religious rituals. It is unlikely that their toxicity and hazardous impact on artists' health were a major concern.[109] However, for artists who may have had to prepare the pigment, its ill effects due to long-term exposure would have been more likely than for those involved in its occasional ceremonial use such as pre-Hispanic Peruvian elites. These pigments were most often traded in a concentrated cake or mineral form. Artists would have ground the chunks to a desirable fineness before application, a process that would have increased the chance of accidental inhalation and further exposure to chemical toxicity. In addition to toxicity, the production of pigments like indigo is extremely labor intensive and even "bloody" in the context of the British colonial rule in India, as Natasha Eaton poetically terms it. Prized for its vibrant yellow hue, the production of Indian yellow supposedly required feeding live animals an exclusive diet of mango leaves. This cruel practice was under criticism and pressure to cease production from 1866 onward until its prohibition in 1908.[110] The development of synthetic pigments bolstered by the "chemical revolution of the nineteenth century that emerged from the search for easily reproducible, cheap, standardized colors and drugs" made more diverse and brilliant colors readily available for artists' use. However, as Taussig points out, this availability came at the cost of environmental alternations that chemical pollutions produced in industrialized cities.[111] Although the discussion of the politics of color and pigments may seem far from the work of conservation science labs, both touch on concerns with distancing from immediate optical qualities, the allure of color, and interest in the physical properties of color.

A recent material analysis performed on the Harvard Rasamañjarī folio at the Straus Center for Conservation and Technical Studies confirms that the jewel-like appearance of the Basohli paintings that enthralled Amrita Sher-Gil in the early twentieth century are thanks to their physical properties (see figure 6.1). The page is literally laden with metallic substances, including gold and silver in the architecture and in the details of jewelry. The silver has tarnished over the centuries and the architecture does not shine as brightly, but its metallic quality is still unmistakable on close viewing. Silver and gold were rather liberally used, indicating a sumptuous production value. Even the thin decorative lines on the pillars are delineated in silver. The artist (possibly Kirpal or someone in his circle) used four different pigments to achieve various hues in red; both red lead and vermilion are used for the opaque red color, while organic red is used to accentuate decorative patterns and subtle shading. The brownish-red color on pillars and doorways contains a combination of hematite and red lead. The artist seems to have been enthusiastic about reaping the benefits from the diversity of available pigments and to have experimented with different hues that can be achieved with available pigment resources. He used two different types of green; the bright green on the blouse of the heroine, *nāyikā,* is a copper chloride, and the green on the roof is a mixture of indigo and Indian yellow. The bright yellow backdrop that fills the earth up to the high horizon in the painting is Indian yellow, so is the yellow skirt and scarf of the *nāyikā*. The orange dhoti of Kṛṣṇa/*nāyaka* is in fact a combination of Indian yellow and red lead. The extensive use of Indian yellow adds the luminous quality to the painting along with gold, silver, and iridescent beetle wings. Indian yellow fluoresces under UV light, and the painting would have nearly fluoresced even under sunlight. These artistic choices make the painting appear exquisite. Here we also find the seventeenth-century use of smalt, a cobalt-based pigment that is chosen to convey the double-identity of the male figure (*nāyaka*) as Kṛṣṇa.

The use of smalt identified on a late fifteenth-century Jain manuscript in the MFA study raises a question of whether it may be a later adulteration because smalt's use as pigments is understood to happen later in time.[112] On the other hand, much of the knowledge we have at hand regarding pigments and their characteristics and history of use is not based on an extensive study of pigments in Indian painting, and our current knowledge is greatly lacking. The appearance of zinc white in sixteenth-century miniature paintings prepared in India like the Cleveland *Tūtīnāma* ("Tales of a Parrot") manuscript may be deemed problematic as a later alteration, as the documented production and use of zinc white as a pigment is believed to begin only at the end of the eighteenth century.[113] But zinc smelting and zinc's general usage were well known in India from ancient times. An intact ancient zinc distillation furnace has been found that is believed to have been in operation in the fourteenth century or earlier. It was found in a zinc mine in Zawar, located on the Aravalli hills in southern Rajasthan, whose operation goes back to a few centuries before the beginning of the Common Era.[114] Just as an observant artist's chance encounter with the dried up urine of a cow or a kettle showing brilliant yellow particles may have inspired the eventual production of Indian yellow, the adoption of zinc white by some resourceful Indian artists much before its production in European factories may be a distinct possibility—especially given zinc's abundant production and medical use in ancient and medieval India.[115] According to Sonya Rhie Mace, experimental spirits that come through in the variety of styles in the Cleveland *Tūtīnāma* are equally evident in the diversity and the idiosyncrasy of pigments used, some of which have been recently identified in the Cleveland Museum's conservation studio.[116] Further material and scientific investigations into the world of Indian painting of the second millennium may reveal hitherto unknown early instances of certain pigments. As conservation science opens more doors for art-historical studies, it is important to acknowledge the inherent bias in existing knowledge on pigments and to be open-minded about the resourcefulness of these artists of premodern South Asia that contributed to expanding an ordinary person's ability to see things more colorful.

EPILOGUE

HOW BLUE IS KRISHNA (KṚṢṆA)? In contemporary popular imagination, including devotional prints, children's cartoons, and blockbuster movies, blue skin color is an obvious iconographic trait of the beloved Hindu god. It is unclear exactly when Kṛṣṇa's blue color became a definitive attribute. However, among surviving miniature paintings, the earliest known pictorial rendition of Viṣṇu's blue color may be found in twelfth-century Nepalese manuscripts (see figure 6.9). The medieval Indic manuscript artists' painterly intervention of translating "*kṛṣṇa*" as blue—first in indigo, soon followed by the use of mineral pigments like ultramarine and azurite—certainly inspired enduring poetic imagination around the blue color of Kṛṣṇa.

The oft-cited opening couplet (*doha*) of the *Satsai* by Bihāri Lāl (ca. 1595–1663) uses colorist terms to poeticize the impact of Kṛṣṇa's beloved Rādhā. Even coming in contact with her shadow turns his dark color (*śyāma*) into a greenish brightness.[1] In an early twentieth-century Hindi commentary, Ramvriksh Benipuri (1899–1968) explains the poet's clever usage of color terms as suggesting the mixture of two colors:

blue (*nīla*) of Kṛṣṇa and golden yellow (*kāñcana*) of Rādhā.[2] It is perhaps no surprise that the poet capitalized on color chemistry to capture the image of the devotee's union with the divine, which is central to the Kṛṣṇa bhakti movements. As a court poet, Bihāri may have been familiar with painterly practices. In fact, this poet's use of the term *śyāma* instead of *nīla*, or even *kṛṣṇa*, takes on an interesting art-historical significance when considered together with the painted images of Kṛṣṇa that appear in the now dispersed illustrated manuscript of the *Rasikapriyā* (the so-called Boston Rasikapriya).

In each scene in this manuscript, Kṛṣṇa is consistently portrayed with a darker skin color than everyone else: although at times appearing grayish, he never is in blue (figure 7.1). This convention is similar to the painterly strategy of rendering Rāma's skin tone in the Freer Rāmāyaṇa and other imperial Mughal illustrated manuscripts of the Hindu epic in Persian (see figure 6.5). Although the Boston Rasikapriya unfortunately does not survive with a colophon page,[3] the Rajput court of Amber near Jaipur about 1610 CE has been suggested as a possible provenance based on style and historical circumstances.[4] Coincidentally, it was also under Raja Jai Singh I (1611–1667) of Amber that Bihāri is said to have composed the *Satsai*. We cannot prove that Bihari had access to the Boston Rasikapriya at the court of Raja Jai Singh I; however, Mughal imperial painterly interventions initially pictorialized "*śyāma*" in the dark monsoon cloud color of Rāma. Bihāri's poetic talent was first appreciated at the Mughal imperial court before his career as a court poet under Jai Singh, who was one of the closest Hindu allies of the Mughal empire.[5] The Mughal-inspired painterly translation of Kṛṣṇa in *śyāma* may have shaped Bihāri's understanding of Kṛṣṇa's color. But unlike the idea of blue, a primary color, this dark skin color as articulated in the Boston Rasikapriya pages is difficult to describe and convey. This is perhaps why its occurrence seems to be limited to courtly circles that were in intimate contact with the Mughal imperial court and its painting workshop.[6]

By the time Bihāri Lāl composed his couplets, miniature painters familiar with the Indic manuscript tradition had introduced various brilliant hues for Kṛṣṇa, painting him in deep blue with pigments like ultramarine and azurite. Some began to experiment with other pigments like smalt (see figure 6.1). Several painting workshops went back to creating a much darker blue-black seen in the earlier phase of Indic manuscript tradition.[7] The darker blue-black is reportedly achieved by combining indigo with other pigments, like smalt and red lac.[8] How and why did these artistic changes happen? What factors affected color choices in each instance? A new visionary experience and its poetic revelation? Or discovery and introduction of a new colorant? The artistic effort to capture, share, and universalize what is essentially a fleeting and subjective individual spiritual experience may be akin to capturing one's sight in a thousand-mirrored room, with every mirror positioned at a slightly skewed angle under a light source timed to turn on at different intervals.[9] Each translation is subtly different but deeply connected as each facing mirror informs each other and the adjacent ones.

By identifying pigments used in early Indic manuscript paintings and by locating the scientific findings in historical contexts, we can trace the history of artistic interventions that cleverly combined old concepts with newly available materials to formulate colorants.

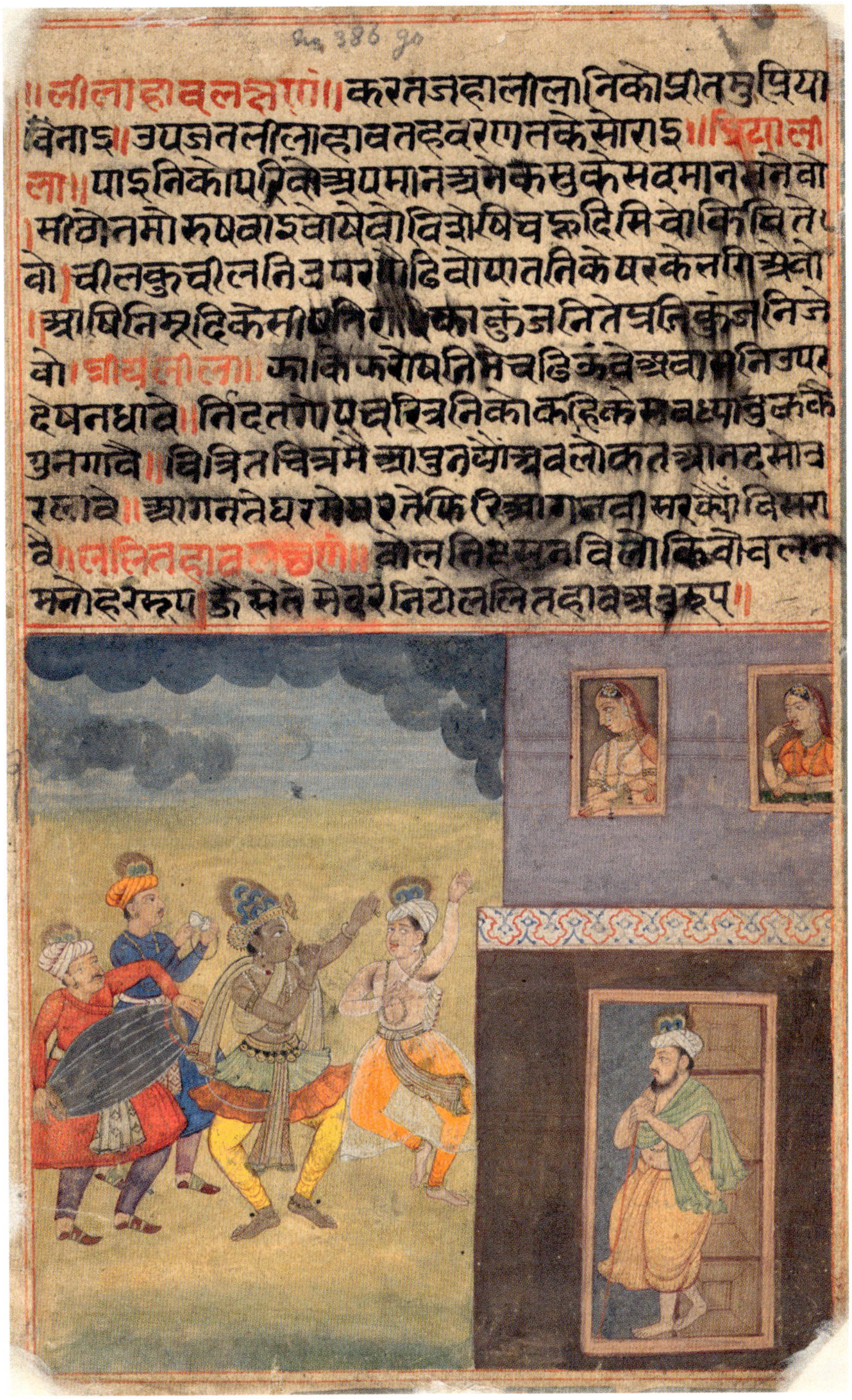

FIGURE 7.1

Kṛṣṇa Dancing, page from the dispersed "Boston" Rasikapriya, ca. 1610, Amber, Rajasthan. Ink, opaque watercolor, and gold, on paper. Sheet size: 22.9 × 14.3 cm. Metropolitan Museum of Art. 18.85.5a.

Painting conditioned the way color was imagined and experienced in each community. An analytical focus on color also illuminates the lasting legacy of the Indic manuscript painting tradition and the formative influence of Indic religions—especially those belonging to the tantric traditions—in shaping the history of Indian painting through the second millennium.

The period before 1500 remains obscure in our understanding of the history of Indian painting partly because of the paucity of surviving evidence but also due to the received notion of what constitutes painting worthy of study. In a general historical narrative of Indian painting, this period is overshadowed by the study of Mughal and Rajput paintings of subsequent centuries. The religious nature of early painted manuscripts and the schematic rigidity of their pictorial conventions have further contributed to the lack of scholarship. Belonging to the "blank period" in Coomaraswamy's reckoning, the medieval Buddhist and Jain paintings were considered mere stepping stones and ugly cousins that had no prominent place in connoisseurship-driven approaches to Indian miniature painting.

Yet religion is central to understanding manuscript art. *Pothi* manuscripts were sacred objects. As written and material manifestations of doctrinal teaching and mythological narratives, manuscripts became fitting vessels for signaling religious authority and sacred presence. The centrality of color in articulating tantric visionary practices for initiation and instruction was a perfect catalyst for shaping the development of the art of manuscript painting. Painted manuscripts were portable, intimate objects. Such a format allowed them to circulate color-coded visual knowledge to distant lands with adequate secrecy and authority. Furthermore, pigments helped convey sensorial experiences, not just visually but also in tactile and perhaps even aromatic terms. If color was a key component of a sacred visual knowledge, some pigments like vermilion were also sanctifying materials. Pigments can carry meaning through their raw materials.

Whether Jaina, Buddhist, or Hindu, the divine iconography serving Indic religious communities is colorful. Why is Kṛṣṇa blue? Or why is Amitābha red? Color assignment often encodes further theological and religious meanings. For instance, Buddhist narratives are embedded in the five-color directional system of Indian Esoteric Buddhism, and these convey layers of spiritual and liturgical meaning. Five colors help map the Buddhist universe onto the life of the Buddha and vice versa. Blue of Akṣobhya represents the color of dawn, with the rising sun in the east. Akṣobhya's iconography also assumes the form representing the Enlightenment of the Buddha under the bodhi tree at dawn. The color of sunset is assigned to Amitābha, who is said to reside in the Western Paradise. His gesture of meditation is also the gesture that signals the penultimate moment of the Buddha's biography, his acceptance of the bowl of honey from a monkey in Vaishali.[10] Centered between these two Buddhas that set the sun's course, Vairocana is white, representing the bright midday sky.[11] Just as Akṣobhya's gesture of Enlightenment and the color of dawn mark the beginning of the Buddha's career at Bodhgaya, Vairocana's preaching gesture and the color of midday sun, brightness, combine to signal the teaching of the Buddha, frequently represented by the images of his first sermon at Sarnath. Ratnasambhava in the south is yellow, bright, and warm like the afternoon sun. His gesture of giving is also the gesture representing the Buddha's descent from the Trāyatriṃśa heaven when he was greeted by the nun Utpalivarṇā. Amoghasiddhi in the north is green, pictorializing *śyāma* or the darkness, where the sun's reach is short. The fear-not gesture of Amoghasiddhi signals the episode of the Buddha's taming of an intoxicated elephant at Rajagriha. The five colors are instrumental to making the narrative weave of the Buddha's teachings transcendentally meaningful.

Color is a deceptively simple tool that can capture the essence of individual experience while simultaneously conveying universal and transcendental significance. Color enables the abstraction of individual experience. In Indian art, abstraction is achieved through figuration as Dehejia's "body as leitmotif" theory demonstrates.[12] Bodily forms can represent concepts and even embody the universe. Color brings theological and philosophical concepts to the level of figuration. This is perhaps why color became an essential tool in capturing the tantric visionary experiences: color is an essential element in authentic meditative states.

Clearly, color was the stuff of inner vision. To project it across various geographic and temporal boundaries required artistic interventions. Painters translated these conceptual color notions to the stuff of matter, by using organic and mineral colorants, like indigo, orpiment, calcite, and vermilion; their crafting methods also made each resulting color as loud and clear as possible. Sometimes, these artistic interventions completely set the way a color was to be experienced. The dark gray skin tone in the Boston Rasikapriya may be how Bihāri imagined Kṛṣṇa's color as *śyāma*. This dark color of the north, *śyāma,* was pictorialized as green, one of the five primary colors of the Indian Esoteric Buddhism, as seen in medieval Indic Buddhist paintings. For example, the popular Buddhist goddess Tārā is described as *śyāma* in several Buddhist vision texts, and is consistently painted green. As numerous surviving paintings of the Green Tārā attest, this artistic intervention left a strong resonance in Himalayan Buddhist art. Artists' choice can have far-reaching effects on our conceptualization of the divine.

In Sanskrit literature, the association between *śyāma* and green hue may be found in poetic references to emerald. In Kālidāsa's *Raghuvaṁśa* (c. fourth century), the appearance of a "*śyāma*" Banyan tree covered with fruits is likened to a "heap of emeralds mixed with rubies."[13] This emerald connection is perhaps the inspiration behind the artistic translation of *śyāma* as green. Emerald suggests a range of fecund imagery and precious beings. But emerald is not a material that could constitute the green color in painting. In addition, this emerald connotation coexisted with other connotations of the term, such as monsoon clouds and the erotic *rasa* (established in the *Nāṭyaśāstra,* see chapter 6). In other words, the emerald connotation was an old idea, and artists came up with ways to capture this color with various recipes. What the unnamed artist(s) used to paint the green image of "Lady Tārā in Samataṭa (*samataṭe buddhardhi bhagavatī tārā*)" in eleventh-century Nepal is yet to be explored (figure 7.2). Perhaps it was a combination of indigo, orpiment, and calcite as in the twelfth-century painting of Mahāmāyūrī (see figure 6.3)?

Early Indic manuscripts that demonstrate an extreme mastery over chromatic brilliance demand a deeper investigation of the developing artistic knowledge of pigments and color

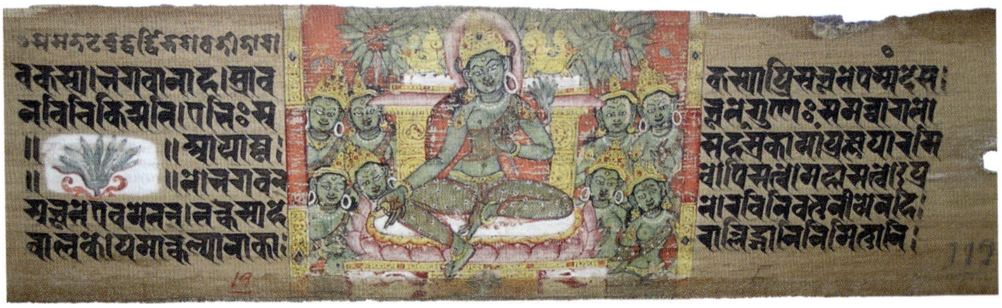

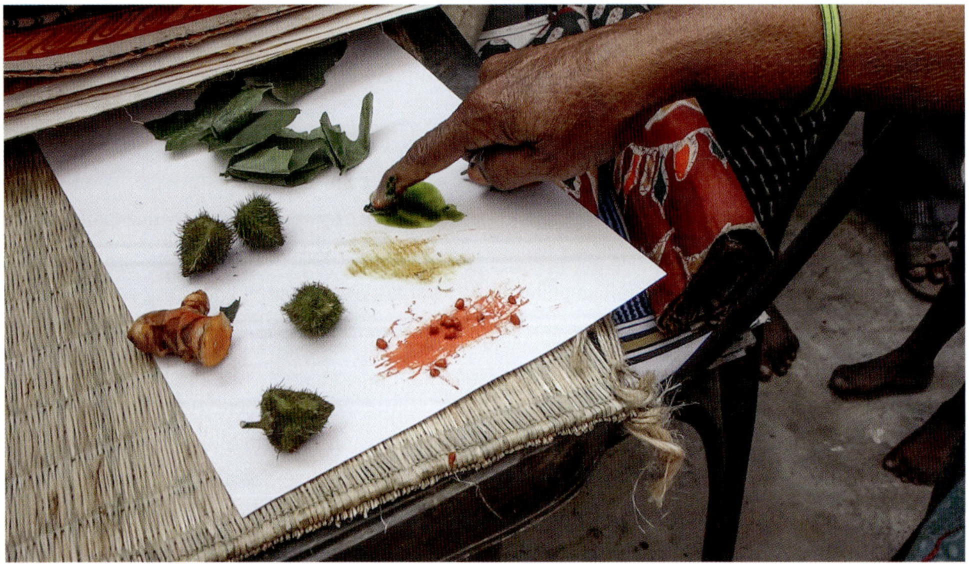

FIGURE 7.2 ▲
"Tārā (Candragomi's Aṣṭamahābhaya Tārā?) in Samataṭa (Southern Bengal)," folio 119v, the end of chapter 17, *Perfection of Wisdom* manuscript, dated N.S. 191 (1071 CE), Nepal. Pigments and ink on palm leaf. Asiatic Society, Kolkata, A.15. Photo © Jinah Kim.

FIGURE 7.3 ▼
Turmeric root, achiote seeds, and three types of leaves used as colorants by Patua artists in Bengal (Naya village, Mednipur, West Bengal), India. Photo © Jinah Kim.

in medieval South Asia. Such an investigation will explicate how the material knowledge and artistic intelligence may have shaped the ways certain visions were experienced and circulated. Conventional wisdom assumes the use of mineral pigments like malachite in many Tibetan thangkas and Himalayan paintings. But the surmise of the actual usage of malachite in Indic and Himalayan painting still requires further scientific analysis on a number of surviving examples. Many questions on the materials and the processes of making also remain to be explored: When did painters in South Asia begin to use copper-based greens? When images with copper-based green appear, was the color produced by following the same recipe? Are there variations in the material composition and application methods? How and why did these changes occur? If we start mapping the appearance of pigments geographically and chronologically, the ensuing color map can provide insight into a locality-specific understanding of painterly practices. It will also reveal hitherto little recognized patterns of change and currents not only in artistic practices but also in aesthetics, patronage, trade, and in light of other sociopolitical and religious factors.

The jewel-like appearance of painted panels on palm leaf may invite a ready comparison with colors of precious gems. After all, precious gems support the light-based Indic theory of color discussed in chapter 5. In the case of the Mahāmāyurī panel (figure 6.3), the scientific analysis of pigments helps us understand that this dazzling jewel-like appearance was actually due to the clever combination of organic and mineral pigments that increased its opacity and luminosity. No precious stone other than gold seems to have been used on this painting. While we need much more concrete data to chart the appearance of certain precious pigments in Indian painting, I end this study by musing over an imaginary scenario: the possibility of an old metonymical reference to the color of a gemstone in the *Arthaśāstra*, the ancient Sanskrit text on statecraft, inspiring artists more than a thousand years later to use cow's urine, an auspicious substance in Hinduism, to make a pigment. The text reads, "the beryl [*vaiḍūrya*] (is), of the color of the night lotus [*utpala*] . . . . *puṣya* (flower) color, of cow's urine [*gomūtraka*]."[14] The foremost meaning of *gomūtraka* is "similar to the course of cow's urine," which relates to how it flows in a zigzag rather than to its color. The text is certainly not a recipe for the famous pigment, "Indian yellow." How well such a passage from the *Arthaśāstra* would have been known in the second millennium requires further investigation. This passage may ultimately not relate to the invention of Indian yellow at all. But just as names of colorful things in nature often signify color in Sanskrit texts, contemporary village artists use color in nature as pigments, for example, achiote seeds for red, turmeric roots for yellow, and a mixture of three types of leaves for green (figure 7.3).[15] With a deep admiration for the Indian artists' resourcefulness—that I witnessed in painters' villages and workshops over the years—I cannot but wonder about the tantalizing possibility that it was the artists who turned their poetic imagination into a powerful colorant in the search for ever more luminous means to capture the color of light.

NOTES

INTRODUCTION

1. The colophon reads, "*deyadharmoyaṁ pravaramahāyānayāyinyāḥ-para*/ [*mopaśikā*xx]*cira-vadhūśrīaṇaghākāyāyadatrapuṇyaṃtadbhavatācāryopadhyāya mātāpitṛpūrvaṅgamaṁ kṛtvā sakalasatvarāścaranuttarajñānaphalāvāptayaiti*|| @|| *śrīmadgopālarājyesaṁvat* 12 *kārttikadine* 29" folio 206v. This is a common donative formula used in medieval South Asia. Throughout this study, transcription and translation from manuscript sources are by the author unless noted otherwise.
2. Some thirty-eight folios in varying states of conservation, including two painted folios, nos. 1 and 100, are in the Danish Royal Library, Copenhagen (Nepal 173); see Hartmut Buescher, *Catalogue of Sanskrit Manuscripts: Early Acquisitions and the Nepal Collection* (Copenhagen: NIAS, 2010), 7 14.
3. Tvam vihāra in Bhaktapur may be the Tom baha that is one of the three *ādibāha*s (original monasteries) of Bhaktapur, but this is a conjecture. On Tom baha, see John K. Locke, *Buddhist Monasteries of Nepal* (Kathmandu: Sahayogi Press, 1985), 439–40.
4. Some early Jain painted palm-leaf manuscripts survive from what is today's Karnataka; see, for example, Saryu Doshi, *Masterpieces of Jain Painting* (Bombay: Marg Publications, 1985), 43. The relationship between the southern manuscript tradition and its northern counterpart is an important puzzle that awaits further study. On the manuscript culture of South India, see Saraju Rathe, *Aspects of Manuscript Culture* (Leiden: Brill, 2012); and for an overview

of manuscript culture in general, see Dominik Wujastyk, "Indian Manuscripts," in *Manuscript Cultures: Mapping the Field* (Berlin: De Gruyter, 2014), 159–81. A huge corpus of palm-leaf manuscripts survives from Sri Lanka, but they all date from the eighteenth century or later. The curious absence of surviving material from earlier times remains to be explored more fully; see Stephen Berkwitz, "Materiality and Merit," in *Buddhist Manuscript Cultures: Knowledge, Ritual, and Art* (London: Routledge, 2009), 35–49.

5. Transhistorical and geographically diverse comparisons are made alongside careful examination of emic uses and the materiality of artistic processes. Some of the examples discussed here, while falling outside the focal period of this study, serve to demonstrate both the historical continuity of the format and the wide extent of its use.
6. Through the work of art historians in postindependence India, what Coomaraswamy identified as the "blank period" in the history of Indian painting is no longer devoid of interest. A generation of scholars like Moti Chandra, Karl Khandalavala, and C. Sivaramamurti have brought to light many treasures of Indian painting that date to the period between 650 and 1427 (the beginning and end dates of Coomaraswamy's void). Jain manuscript paintings—many of them dating to the "blank" period—received scholarly attention as early as 1933 with Norman Brown's *The Story of Kalaka* (Washington, DC: Smithsonian Institution, 1933), and the field has witnessed steady growth ever since. Recently, *Jaina Painting and Manuscript Culture* (Berlin: EB-Verlag, 2015), edited by Julia Hegewald, has added significantly to our understanding of the manuscript culture in Jain traditions; and "The Art of the Book in India under the Sultanate" (2014) and other studies by Éloïse Brac de la Perrière (*L'art du livre dans l'Inde des Sultanats,* 2008) have shed new light on paper manuscripts from the Indo-Islamic sphere in northern India.
7. David Gordon White, *The Alchemical Body: Siddha Traditions in Medieval India* (Chicago: University of Chicago Press), 186–96.
8. This folio has been identified as an illustration of the *Gīta Govinda*'s tenth canto. The text is based on the *Gīta Govinda*, but it is not the *Gīta Govinda* by Jayadeva, which is in Sanskrit. The text here is clearly a local dialect: the line translated reads "eso kāmakāvānamasyo kṛ sna jāi mili||"
9. Miranda Shaw, *Buddhist Goddesses of India* (Princeton, NJ: Princeton University Press, 2006), 432–47.
10. The clever use of bees in the composition (e.g., Ratī's bow strung by a row of bees; swarming bees around Ratī and Rādhā) indicates Sahib Din's intimate understanding of the *Gīta Govinda* in which the poetic motif of buzzing bees is repeatedly used to deliberate the erotic mood (*śṛṅgara rasa*). Despite being composed in twelfth-century Bengal when Brahmans were reportedly hostile to institutional Buddhism, Jayadeva's *Gīta Govinda* harbors a sympathetic attitude toward Buddhism. Kunal Chakrabarti, "A History of Intolerance: The Representation of Buddhists in the Bengal Purāṇas," *Social Scientist* 44, no. 5/6 (2016): 11–27.
11. Indrani Chatterjee, *Forgotten Friends: Monks, Marriages, and Memories of Northeast India* (New Delhi: Oxford University Press), 2.
12. Jesper Trier, *Ancient Paper of Nepal: Results of Ethno-Technological Field Work on Its Manufacture, Uses, and History—With Technical Analyses of Bast, Paper, and Manuscripts* (Copenhagen: Jutland Archaeological Society, 1972), 197–201; also see Agnieszka Helman-Ważny, *Archaeology of Tibetan Books* (Leiden: Brill, 2014), 23–25 and 43.
13. Reported in Moti Chandra, *Technique of Mughal Painting* (1949), based on a firsthand report by T. N. Mukharji (1883), this explanation has recently been scientifically tested using a variety of analytical methods. See, for example, R. Ploeger et al., "Late 19th Century Accounts of Indian Yellow: The

Analysis of Samples from the Royal Botanic Gardens, Kew," *Dyes and Pigments* 160 (2019): 418–31. Scholarly communities' interest in this exceptional pigment are also attested in the fact that this is the first pigment in the compilation of pigments published under the aegis of the National Gallery of Art in the United States. See Robert L. Feller, *Artists' Pigments: A Handbook of Their History and Characteristics* (Washington, DC: National Gallery of Art, 1986), 1: 17–36.

14. Pratapaditya Pal, *Arts of Nepal,* vol. 2, *Paintings* (Leiden: Brill, 1978), 141–44. Pal recognizes in seventeenth-century paintings from Nepal and the Punjab Hills traits he ascribes to stylistic inspiration from the art of the Rajput courts, but he is hesitant to explore the connection further because "the Punjab Hills and Nepal are similarly isolated from the plains" (143).

15. For example, vol. 45 of *Ars Orientalis* (2015), edited by N. Chanchani and T. Sears, is dedicated to transregional movements.

16. For example, see Nachiket Chanchani, "From Asoda to Almora, the Roads Less Taken: Māru-Gurjara Architecture in the Central Himalayas," *Arts Asiatiques* 69 (2014): 3–16; Robert N. Linrothe, *Collecting Paradise: Buddhist Art of Kashmir and Its Legacies* (New York: Rubin Museum of Art, 2014); Deborah Klimburg-Salter, "Along the Pilgrimage Routes between Uḍḍiyāṇa and Tibet: The Gilgit MSS Covers and the Tibetan Decorated Book Cover," in *Tibet in Dialogue with Its Neighbours: History, Culture, and Art of Central and Western Tibet, 8th to 15th Century* (Arbeitskreis für Tibetische und Buddhistische Studien and China Tibetology Research Center, 2015), 392–406; and Andrea Acri, ed., *Esoteric Buddhism in Mediaeval Maritime Asia: Networks of Masters, Texts, Icons* (Singapore: ISEAS, 2016).

17. Karl J. Khandalavala and Moti Chandra, *An Illustrated Āraṇyaka Parvan in the Asiatic Society of Bombay* (Bombay: Asiatic Society, 1974). An earlier instance of a Bengali scribe working elsewhere is seen in the Khajuraho inscription of the Chandella king Yaśovarman, dated samvat 1011 (953–954 CE), which identifies the scribe as a *kāyastha* from Gauḍa named Jadda; see Jinah Kim, "Seeing in between the Space: Aura of Writing and the Shape of Artistic Productions in Early Medieval South Asia," in *History and Material Culture in Asian Religions,* ed. Benjamin Fleming and Richard Mann (London: Routledge, 2014), 51.

18. Studies by scholars such as Moti Chandra, Karl Khandalavala, Saryu Doshi, and more recently Nachicket Chanchani underscore the importance of early Jain painting in the history of Indian painting.

19. See J. Losty, *The Ramayana: Love and Valour in India's Great Epic* (London: British Library, 2008). For a physical description of the books in the Mewar *Rāmāyaṇa,* see "Art Historical Overviews of the Mewar Rāmāyaṇa Books," available as a pdf from the British Library website, www.bl.uk/ramayana. We have little historical information about Hīrānanda, who presents an interesting historical puzzle. In the colophon to the *Yuddhakāṇḍa,* folio 206r, BL, Add. Ms 15297(1), he identifies the place where he wrote it as Dharmaghoṣa gaccha, whereas in the colophon to the *Uttarakaṇḍa* a different name, Sūrāṇā-gaccha, is given. Dharmaghoṣa gaccha is thought to have been a monastic group, or possibly the residence of such a group, and it is possible that Hīrānanda belonged to this *gaccha.* Sūrāṇa gaccha is yet to be identified in historical records, but it would be unusual for a person to switch from one monastic lineage to another. According to John Cort, it is possible that it was a name of his family lineage (*gotra*). John Cort, personal communication, May 2018. In any case, the use of the locative with *gaccha* in these colophons is intriguing, because a Jain mendicant order would not have been tied to a specific site or place.

20. Chanchani suggests a connection between this shape and the architecture of the Jain worship hall (*samavasaranas*); see Nachiket Chanchani, "Paper Prasada," *Artibus Asiae* (2016): 132–33.

21. The most likely reason for such an intervention would have been economic, as painting red dots on every page would have consumed a significant quantity of red pigment, either red lead or vermilion, a precious commodity at the time.

22. Andrew Topsfield defends this convention by emphasizing the autonomy of the painting's illustrative capacity. In this formulation, "illustrated picture series" were prepared for noble patrons who were ignorant of Sanskrit and their illiterate ladies; see Topsfield, *Court Painting at Udaipur: Art under the Patronage of the Maharanas of Mewar* (Zurich: Museum Rietberg, 2007), 29.
23. The first, and so far only, complete survey of the dispersed BP is Daniel Ehnbom's dissertation, "An Analysis and Reconstruction of the Dispersed '*Bhagavata Purana*' from the Caurapancasika Group" (PhD diss., University of Chicago, 1984).
24. Ananda K. Coomaraswamy, *Rajput Painting* (London: Oxford University Press, 1916), 3–4.
25. See the discussion in Kim, "Painted Palm-Leaf Manuscripts and the Art of the Book in Medieval South Asia," *Archives of Asian Art* 65, no. 1/2 (2015): 57–86; and Chanchani, "Paper Prasada."
26. For a recent discussion of other dichotomies set up by Coomaraswamy, see Molly Emma Aitken, *A Magic World: New Visions of Indian Painting* (Mumbai: Marg, 2016), 10–19.
27. Coomaraswamy, *Rajput Painting,* 17.
28. Chapter 2 herein has some examples.
29. B.N. Goswamy, *The Word Is Sacred, Sacred Is the Word: The Indian Manuscript Tradition* (New Delhi: Niyogi Books, 2007).
30. In a rare instance, Pramod Chandra mentions Indian traditions of book painting in his "Notes on the Study of Indian Miniatures," in *Indian Miniatures: The Ehrenfeld Collection* (New York: Hudson Hills Press, 1985), 15.
31. See B.N. Goswamy and Eberhard Fischer, *Pahari Masters: Court Painters of Northern India* (Zurich: Artibus Asiae Publishers, 1992), 16–27; Tryna Lyons, "The Simla 'Devi Mahatmya' Illustrations," *Archives of Asian Art* 45 (1992): 29–41; and Catherine Glynn, "A Sixteenth Century 'Devīmāhātmya' Manuscript" (PhD diss., University of Southern California, 1979). For the Tantric Devī series, see Terrence McInerney, "Mysterious Origins: The Tantric Devi Series from Basohli," in *Devi: The Great Goddess,* ed. Vidya Dehejia (Washington, DC: Smithsonian Institution, 1999), 119–35.
32. In recent decades, materiality and artistic process have been an important analytical anchor in numerous art historical inquiries, marking what may be termed the "material turn." In this study, I take excavating historically contextual information as an important component of the material- and process-oriented approach. For a succinct theoretical outlook, see, for example, Michael Ann Holly, "Notes from the Field: Materiality," *Art Bulletin* 95, no. 1 (2013): 15–17.
33. See Molly Emma Aitken, *The Intelligence of Tradition in Rajput Court Painting* (New Haven, CT: Yale University Press, 2010), 60–70.
34. The painter of this series is proposed to be Kripal of Nurpur (active during ca. 1660 to 1690). See B.N. Goswamy and Eberhard Fischer, *Pahari Masters: Court Painters of Northern India* (Zurich: Artibus Asiae Publishers, 1992), 31.
35. McInerney, "Mysterious Origins," 120.
36. Tusara Bindu Gude, "Between Music and History: Ragamala Paintings and European Collectors in Late Eighteenth-Century Northern India" (PhD diss., University of California at Los Angeles, 2009), 2.
37. *"śyāmam ṣoḍaśahāyanam dhvajakaraṃ trailokyarakṣāparam smerāspaṁ smara-darpa-yukta hṛdayam / śyāmāmbarodbhāsitam̄|| udyatkoṭiśaśāṅkasūryasadṛśīṁ devīṁ smaraṁ taṃ hṛdādhyāyec ce/tasi śyāmabhairavam upastambhena saṁpūjitaṃ||21||"*
38. B. Bhattacharyya, Introduction to *Niṣpannayogāvalī of Mahāpaṇḍita Abhayākaragupta* (Baroda: Oriental Institute, 1949), 16.

39. Alexander Huth et al., "Natural Speech Reveals the Semantic Maps That Tile Human Cerebral Cortex," *Nature* 532 (2016): 453–58.
40. http://gallantlab.org/huth2016/.
41. Intense color-filled pages in C.G. Jung's *Red Book* provide great examples that underscore the central role color plays in externalizing internal visionary experience. As a handwritten manuscript that materializes Jung's visionary experience in colorful painting and calligraphic text, the *Red Book* can, in fact, be considered analogous to painted manuscripts from medieval South Asia that record the tantric visionary experience.
42. Teun Goudriaan, *Māyā Divine and Human: A Study of Magic and Its Religious Foundations in Sanskrit Texts, with Particular Attention to a Fragment on Viṣṇu's Māyā Preserved in Bali* (Delhi: Motilal Banarsidass, 1978), 163–210.
43. For a helpful overview of color discussions in art history, see John Gage, "Color in Western Art, an Issue?" *Art Bulletin* 72, no. 4 (1990): 518–41.
44. Notable recent studies include Gabriela Siracusano, *Pigment and Power in the Andes: From the Material to the Symbolic in Andean Cultural Practices, 1500–1800* (London: Archetype Publications, 2011); and Diana Kerpel, *The Colors of the New World: Artists, Materials, and the Creation of the Florentine Codex* (Los Angeles: Getty Research Institute, 2014). I thank Thomas B.F. Cummins for these references.
45. For example, Ewa Lajer-Burcharth's *The Painter's Touch: Boucher, Chardin, Fragonard* (Princeton, NJ: Princeton University Press, 2018), demonstrates how deep attention to a painting's materiality can lead to a new understanding of a relatively well understood period like eighteenth-century France. Also see Michael T. Taussig, *What Color Is the Sacred* (Chicago: University of Chicago Press, 2009); Laura Kalba, *Color in the Age of Impressionism: Commerce, Technology, and Art* (University Park: Pennsylvania State University Press, 2017); Regina Lee Blaszczyk, *The Color Revolution* (Cambridge, MA: MIT Press, 2012); and Natasha Eaton, *Colour, Art, and Empire: Visual Culture and the Nomadism of Representation* (London: I.B. Tauris, 2013).
46. In this sense, this approach is more in line with art historians who "study how objects are made." Joseph Leo Koerner, "Factura," *RES: Anthropology and Aesthetics* 36 (1999): 5. On the thing-oriented methodology and its application across fields, see, for example, Lorraine Daston, *Things That Talk : Object Lessons from Art and Science* (New York: Zone Books, 2004). Uncovering the artistic process is only one part of the exploration of the painting's objecthood. Investigating how something is made helps excavate and weave the deeper historical meaning of art especially when surviving historical data is scarce.

CHAPTER 1. PAINTING AND ITS MEDIUM

1. See Sheila Canby, "Abd al-Samad," in *Masters of Indian Painting: 1100–1650* (Zurich: Artibus Asiae Publishers, 2011), 102–5.
2. See Saryu Doshi, *Masterpieces of Jain Painting* (Bombay: Marg Publications), 32.
3. See Ananda K. Coomaraswamy, *Rajput Painting* (New York: H. Milford; Oxford University Press, 1916); John Guy, "Indian Painting from 1100 to 1500," in *Masters of Indian Painting: 1100–1650* (Zurich: Artibus Asiae Publishers, 2011), 15–28; John Guy and Jorrit Britschgi, *Wonder of the Age: Master Painters of India, 1100–1900* (New York: Metropolitan Museum of Art, 2011).
4. Ananda K. Coomaraswamy, "One Hundred References to Indian Painting," *Artibus Asiae* 4, no. 1 (1930): 41–57.

5. On metapainting in Europe, see Victor Stoichita, *The Self-Aware Image: An Insight into Early Modern Meta-painting* (New York: Cambridge University Press, 1997).
6. In some cases, "painted" can just mean "decorated," as Coomaraswamy acknowledges; on the other hand, it is worth remembering that the term *citra* can mean "image," which holds broader semantic values than "painting."
7. As he noted himself, it was by no means an exhaustive list. Although the scope of sources he was able to amass is impressive, and his decision to include a section covering "vernacular references" was pioneering, they only represent the literary and textual sources known to Coomaraswamy at the beginning of the twentieth century. Many more sources have been made available for critical analysis during the last few decades, including better critical editions of classical texts. Yet, for the period under consideration in this study, 1000 to 1500, the sources surveyed in ORP still form a reasonable nucleus for analysis.
8. For example, "*citrapaṭa*" can be a colorful fabric, a type of chintz, either woven with multicolor thread or dyed to be multicolored; see Phyllis Granoff, "Luxury Goods and Intellectual History," *Ars Orientalis* 34 (2004): 151–81.
9. For example, the famed Kailasa temple at Ellora bears traces of painting on its surface, and the excavation of the Sarai Mound Shrine at Nālandā revealed traces of murals. See Mira Seth, *Indian Painting: The Great Mural Tradition* (New York: Abrams, 2006); and Birendra Nath, *Nalanda Murals* (New Delhi: Cosmo Publications, 1983).
10. See Parul Dave Mukherji, ed., *Citrasūtra of the Viṣṇudharmottara Purāṇa* (New Delhi: Indira Gandhi National Centre for the Arts and Motilal Banarsidass Publishers, 2001); and G.K. Shrigondekar, ed., *Mânasollâsa of King Someśvara* (Baroda: Baroda Oriental Institute, 1939).
11. Buddha's instruction on placing a *bhavacakra* at the entrance of a monastery is found in the *Mūlasarvāstivāda vinaya;* see Stephen Teiser, *Reinventing the Wheel: Paintings of Rebirth in Medieval Buddhist Temples* (Seattle: University of Washington Press, 2006), 50–75.
12. Caroline A.F. Rhys Davids, ed., *The Visuddhi-Magga of Buddhaghosa* (London: Pali Text Society, 1920), 38.
13. Sheldon Pollock, ed., *Rāma's Last Act by Bhavabūti* (New York: New York University Press, 2007), 80.
14. See Aditya Behl, "Creating a New Genre: The Cāndāyan," in *Love's Subtle Magic: An Indian Islamic Literary Tradition, 1379–1545* (New York Oxford University Press), 59–108; and Naseem Akhtar Hines, *Maulana Daud's Cāndāyan* (New Delhi: Manohar Publishers, 2009).
15. Translation after P. Lal Gupta, ed., *Cāndāyana* (Mumbai: Hindi Grantha Ratnakara, 1964), 188–89.
16. Qamar Adamjee, "Strategies for Visual Narration in the Illustrated *Chandayan* Manuscripts" (PhD diss., New York University, 2011), 141.
17. Adamjee, "Strategies for Visual Narration in the Illustrated *Chandayan* Manuscripts," 125–36.
18. Interestingly, the king's posture is nearly identical to that of Vibhiṣaṇa in the Freer *Rāmāyaṇa* manuscript, vol. 2, folio 273r (see https://asia.si.edu/object/F1907.271.173-346/#txtMetaData).
19. The two male figures facing each other on the wall between Chanda's bent right leg and Laurik's right hand may represent the gambling scene. The image also includes what must be Vaitala or the fierce beast in between Chanda's bed and Laurik's legs.
20. C.R. Devadhar, *Dūtavākyam: A Sanskrit One Act Play by Bhāsa* (Poona: Oriental Book Agency, 1957), verse 7.
21. In his oft-cited essay published in 1929, Coomaraswamy suggests that a passage in Patañjali's *Mahābhāṣya* (c. second century BCE) should be taken as indicating that "the practice of picture showmen explaining their own pictures has been so general and wide spread in India." "Picture Showmen,"

Indian Historical Quarterly 5, no. 2 (1929): 182. The number of narrative scrolls in ORP is meager partly because Coomaraswamy excluded references that he had already discussed in "Picture Showmen."

22. U.P. Shah, *More Documents of Jaina Paintings and Gujarati Paintings of Sixteenth and Later Centuries* (Ahmedabad: L.D. Institute of Indology, 1976), 5.
23. The painting was "spread out on the highway"; see Helen M. Johnson, trans., *Triṣaṣṭiśalākāpuruṣacarita; or, The Lives of Sixty-Three Illustrious Persons* (Baroda: Oriental Institute, 1937–62), 61. This scene is mentioned in Coomaraswamy's "Picture Showmen."
24. Kavita Singh draws attention to the resemblance between the *phad* and the Iranian *parda* while cautioning us against tracing a direct causal connection between the two; see Kavita Singh, "Transfixed by the Arrow of Time," in *Indian Painting: The Lesser-Known Traditions,* ed. Anna L. Dallapiccola (New Delhi: Niyogi Books, 2011), 112–13; and John D. Smith, *The Epic of Pābūjī: A Study, Transcription, and Translation* (Cambridge: Cambridge University Press, 1991). The existence of Nepalese examples supports Smith's speculation about *phad*'s indebtedness to the mural traditions. For an analysis of the text-image relationship in a Nepalese *paubha,* see Siegfried Lienhard, ed., *Svayambhūpurāṇa: Mythe du Népa; Suivi du Maṇicūḍāvadāna: Légende du Prince Maṇicūḍā* (Suilly-la-Tour: Éditions Findakly, 2009); also Alexander von Rospatt, "On the Monumental Scroll of the *Svayambhūpurāṇa* Now Kept in the VMFA Collection," in *Dharma and Puṇya: Buddhist Ritual Art of Nepal,* ed. Jinah Kim and Todd Lewis (Leiden: Hotei Publishing, 2019), 166–86.
25. A good example is discussed in Gautam Vajracarya, *Nepalese Seasons: Rain and Ritual* (New York: Rubin Museum of Art, 2016), 89–96. On the religious function of these scrolls, see Todd Lewis, *Popular Buddhist Texts from Nepal: Narratives and Rituals of Newar Buddhism* (Albany: State University of New York Press, 2000); Lewis, "The Tradition of Vajrācārya Storytellers," in Kim and Lewis, *Dharma and Puṇya: Buddhist Ritual Art of Nepal,* 156–60.
26. Robert DeCaroli, *Image Problems: The Origin and Development of the Buddha's Image in Early South Asia* (Seattle: University of Washington Press, 2015), 109.
27. Matthew Kapstein, "Weaving the World: The Ritual Art of the Paṭa in Pāla Buddhism and Its Legacy in Tibet," *History of Religions* 34, no. 3 (1995): 256.
28. The text assumes that specialists hired for the job will have the necessary practical knowledge. For example, it omits a crucial step in preparing the fabric for the application of pigments: without a priming layer, the pigments will not adhere to the surface.
29. Gregory Schopen, "Sukhāvatī as a Generalized Religious Goal in Sanskrit Mahāyāna Sūtra Literature," *Indo-Iranian Journal* 19, no. 3 (1977): 185n13. Here, we should also add the recent study by Ronald Davidson, who found another important Gilgit manuscript-based text that discusses the procedure for making of painting, *Mūlamantra,* which he dates to the early sixth century. The basic procedure is extremely similar. See Ronald Davidson, "Revisiting the Mañjuśriyamūlakalpa's Painting Chapters," in *Reasons and Lives in Buddhist Traditions: Studies in Honor of Matthew Kapstein,* ed. Dan Arnold, Cécile Ducher, and Pierre-Julien Harter (Somerville, MA: Wisdom Publications, 2019), 78–83.
30. Richard Cohen, *The Splendid Vision: Reading a Buddhist Sutra* (New York: Columbia University Press, 2012), 38–39. Cohen's translation of this passage has been adapted with slight modifications based on Dutt's edition; see N. Dutt, *Gilgit Manuscripts* (New Delhi: Sri Satguru, 1984), 76. A very similar instruction is given by another goddess, Anopamā Mahāyakṣiṇī, for a person who wants to see her. The goddess is again bright like a stalk of sugarcane (*śarakāṇḍagaurī*) and clothed in white garments.
31. See Money L. Hickman, "Notes on Buddhist Banners," *Boston Museum Bulletin* 71, no. 363 (1973); and Robert Jera-Bezard and Monique Maillard, "Origine et montage des bannières peintes," *Arts Asiatiques*

40 (1985): 83–91. That banners were used is confirmed by a *vinaya* instruction documented in Gregory Schopen, "Taking the Bodhisattva into Town" *East and West* 55, no. 1 (2005): 299–311; whether they were painted is another matter.

32. Kapstein, "Weaving the World," 251.
33. The meaning of the stele is the subject of an ongoing debate. See Paul Harrison and Christian Luczanits, "New Light on the Muhammad Nari Stele," *Special International Symposium on Pure Land Buddhism* (Kyoto: Research Center for Buddhist Cultures in Asia, 2011), 69–126; John Huntington, "A Gandharan Image of Amitāyus' Sukhāvati," *Annali Istituto Orientale di Napoli* 40 (1980): 651–72; and Juhyung Rhi, "Early Mahāyāna and Gandhāran Buddhism," *Eastern Buddhist* 35 (2003): 152–202.
34. Huntington's captions for figures 21 and 22 identify these panels as "banners" held by the standing bodhisattvas below. Upon close inspection, it is quite clear that the standing bodhisattvas carrying the flower garlands stand in front of the negative space around the Buddha's head while the seated bodhisattva in each *paṭa* hovers within that space on a lotus pedestal.
35. See British Museum 1907, 1111.73.
36. Two Uṣṇīṣavijayā maṇḍalas found at the Tangut capital of Khara Khoto were painted on multiple wooden panels; see M.B. Piotrovsky, *Lost Empire of the Silk Road: Buddhist Art from Khara Khoto (X–XIIIth Century)* (Milan: Thyssen Bornemisza Foundation and Electa, 1993), 144–45. In one of these (X-2406), six wooden panels each measuring about 18 × 130 cm were conjoined to create a 108 × 130 cm surface for painting. The Khotanese painted wooden panels are much older than these Tangut examples, suggesting that the technique of using wooden panels as a medium for painting circulated for a long time along the Silk Road before the idea was creatively adapted to suit the requirements of putting a maṇḍala with text and images on a single surface.
37. The earliest "*sadeśa kāvya*" is in Sanskrit (Kalidasa's Meghadūta, ca. fourth–fifth century), and the poetry tradition saw a unique development much later in fourteenth-century Sri Lanka. Being "messenger poems," the genre allowed poets to demonstrate their prowess in describing the world they lived in, and it includes many descriptive passages, in one of which a reference to a painted wooden book cover appears. See Dhanesh Wisumperuma, "Elephants in 'Sandēśa Kāvyas,'" *Journal of the Royal Asiatic Society of Sri Lanka,* n.s., 57 (2011): 71–94; Anuththaradevi Widyalankara, "Mapping Urban and Social Space of Mediaeval Cities as Depicted in Sandeśa Kāvyas," *Journal of the Royal Asiatic Society of Sri Lanka,* n.s., 57 (2011): 95–12.
38. Guy, "Indian Painting from 1100 to 1500," 18n14. Guy's characterization is based on Moti Chandra's *Studies in Early Indian Painting,* which cites a statement in the *Mānasollāsa* to the effect that an accomplished painter was "not only a fresco painter but also well versed in the technique of miniature painting on palm-leaves (*patra-lekhaka*)."
39. In Adhyāya 41, verse 5 identifies three types of line rendering: "*patrajā* (leaf born), *acchaidikā* (unbroken), and *bindujā* (dot-born)." Mukherji, *Citrasūtra,* 159.
40. Mukherji, *Citrasūtra,* 161.
41. See Jinah Kim, *Receptacle of the Sacred: Illustrated Manuscripts and the Buddhist Book-Cult in South Asia* (Berkeley: University of California Press, 2013), 43–52.
42. See Benjamin Fleming, "The Materiality of South Asian Manuscripts," *Manuscript Studies* 1, no. 1 (2016): 28–51; Jinah Kim, "Seeing in between the Space: Aura of Writing and the Shape of Artistic Productions in Early Medieval South Asia," in *History and Material Culture in Asian Religions,* ed. Benjamin Fleming and Richard Mann (London: Routledge, 2014); and C. Mackenzie Brown, "Purāṇa as Scripture: From Sound to Image of the Holy Word in the Hindu Tradition," *History of Religions* 26, no. 1 (1986): 68–86.

43. Anna Maria Quagliotti, "Mañjuśrī in Gandharan Art: A New Interpretation of a Relief in the Victoria and Albert Museum," *East and West* 40, no. 1/4 (1990): 99–113.
44. A recent publication providing a general index to this text facilitates access and use of it for historical research; see Willem Bollée, *Cultural Encyclopaedia of the Kathāsaritsāgara* (Halle an der Saale: Universitätsverlag Halle-Wittenberg, 2015).
45. See Donald Nelson, "Bṛhatkathā Studies: The Problem of an Ur-Text," *Journal of Asian Studies* 37, no. 4 (1978): 663–76.
46. See Félix Lacôte, ed., *Budhasvāmin-Bṛhat-Kathā Çlokasaṃgraha* (Paris: Imprimerie Nationale, 1908); and James Mallinson, ed., *Emperor of the Sorcerers by Budhasvāmin* (New York: New York University Press, 2005).
47. This is claimed to be the oldest version and the closest to the lost original. J.C. Jain pushes the date back to the first and second centuries; see J.C. Jain, "Stories of Trading Merchants and Vasudevahiṇḍī," *Annals of the Bhandarkar Oriental Research Institute* 55, no. 1/4 (1974): 73–81. According to the introduction in a Gujarati edition by H.C. Bhayani and R.M. Shah, Dharmasenagaṇi's date is placed "in the vicinity of, say, 700 AD," and Saṅghadāsagaṇi's date to around the fifth century. I thank Phyllis Granoff for the reference.
48. M.M. Shivdatta and K.P. Paraba, *Bṛhatkathāmañjarī of Kṣemendra* (New Delhi: Panini, 1982; originally published 1931).
49. A legendary king, he is famous in epigraphy and history through Candragupta II's use of the epithet Vikramāditya.
50. C.H. Tawney and N.M. Penzer, eds., *The Ocean of Story: Being C.H. Tawney's Translation of Somadeva's Kathā Sarit Sāgara*, vol. 9 (London: Chas J. Sawyer, 1928), 35.
51. Nalini Balbir et al., *Océan des rivières de contes* (Paris: Gallimard, 1997), 1281. Also see Bollée, *Cultural Encyclopaedia*, 64, entry on "Book."
52. Since no unrolling of cloth is mentioned, we may conjecture that the painting is miniature in scale.
53. As Nelson puts it, a reading of the KsS gives one "the experience of an audience hearing *puraṇa* recitation, rather than that of readers of novels." Nelson, "Bṛhatkathā Studies," 672.
54. On Kashmiri *śloka-kathā* style, see Whitney Cox, "Literary Register and Historical Consciousness: A Hypothesis," *Indian Economic and Social History Review* 50, no. 2 (2013): 133.
55. See Dagmar Wujastyk, "Indian Manuscripts," in *Manuscript Cultures: Mapping the Field*, ed. Jörg B. Quenzer, Dmitry Bondarev, and Sobisch Jan-Ulrich (Berlin: De Gruyter, 2014); and Richard Salomon, "Origin of the Early Indian Scripts," *Journal of the American Oriental Society* 115, no. 2 (1995): 271–79.
56. See the discussion in Fleming, "Materiality of South Asian Manuscripts."
57. While Fleming is able to elaborate the differences between Buddhist and Hindu scribal practices, he also draws our attention to their "interconnection." Fleming, "Materiality of South Asian Manuscripts."
58. Sudha Gopalkrishnan, ed., *Vijñānanidhi: Manuscript Treasures of India* (New Delhi: National Mission for Manuscripts, 2007), 113–15.
59. The writing is similar to the hand seen in a Nepalese *Prajñāpāramitā* manuscript in the Cambridge University Library, Add. 866, dated 1008 (N.S. 128), and it is a long, narrow folio divided into three blocks, as was typical of Nepalese Sanskrit MSS. Two holes with blank columns serve as dividers, and letter numerals appear on the verso on the left-hand side. How this manuscript got from Nepal to the southern tip of the subcontinent remains to be investigated.
60. According to the text's editor, Félix Lacôte, MSS A and B are palm-leaf manuscripts from Nepal, both dating (probably) to the twelfth century.

61. In Canto 10, the hero goes on a carriage ride where he meets a "long-eared, educated scribe in a long gown . . . carrying an inkpot . . . and a pen behind his ear" and is taken through a courtesans' district, where he reports seeing girls studying (reading) on written tablets (*paṭṭikā*). Mallinson, *Emperor of the Sorcerers,* 229–33.
62. Dominic Goodall, Alexis Sanderson, and Harunaga Isaacson, eds., *The Niśvāsatattvasaṃhitā* (Paris: École Française d'Extrême-Orient, 2015), 103–8. The manuscript is discussed in subsequent chapters herein.
63. Very little is known about these early practitioners in Nepal. A project to collect and analyze the available manuscript colophons will help shed light on this vital piece of history.
64. Indrani Chaterjee's *Forgotten Friends* underscores the importance of the Brahmaputra valley in premodern South Asian history. Hearing her call to recognize this connection, I propose to look back further in history with it.
65. A number of ongoing research projects have shed new light on early manuscript cultures, including the Early Buddhist Manuscripts Project led by Richard Salomon and based at the University of Washington. See the project website: https://asian.washington.edu/early-buddhist-manuscripts-project.
66. Although most of Assam's surviving manuscripts are datable to the period after 1500, the aloe-bark manuscript tradition goes back to at least the seventh century, if Bāṇa's accounts in the *Harṣacārita* have any credibility: the precious gifts that the king of Kāmarūpa (Assam), Bhāskaravarman, sent to Harṣa include poetry manuscripts and *subhāśita*s, all made from the bark of the agaru tree (*agaru-valkala-kalpita-śañchayāni* ca *subhāśita-bhāñji pustakāni*); see V.S. Agrawala, *The Deeds of Harsha: Being a Cultural Study of Bāṇa's Harshacharita* (Varanasi: Prithivi Prakashan, 1969), 203; 217. The aloe-bark manuscript tradition remained strong in Assam, as numerous illustrated aloe-bark manuscripts produced for Vaiṣṇava patrons during the seventeenth and the eighteenth centuries attest; see Biman Hazarika, "World of the Sattriya School of Painting in Assam," in *Pelagic Passageways: The Northern Bay of Bengal before Colonialism,* ed. Rila Mukherjee (Delhi: Primus Books, 2011), 425–42.
67. See Samuel Beal, ed., *Si-Yu-Ki: Buddhist Records of the Western World by Hsüan-Tsang* (London: Trübner, 1884), 197. We should, of course, read Xuanzang's account while keeping his ultimate motive in mind, which was to impress and earn the favor of Tang Taizong; see Tansen Sen, "In Search of Longevity," *Journal of World History* 12, no. 1 (2001): 5–6.
68. A late nineteenth-century report by Huang Maocai on routes between western China and eastern India is instructive. Huang was sent by the governor of Sichuan province to document the possible expansion routes open to the British from the eastern states of India. He traveled from Sichuan through Yunnan to Burma (Rangoon) and arrived in India (Kolkata) by ship. See the discussion in Tansen Sen, "Changes and Exchanges and Good Karma: Chinese Diplomatic Missions to Middle India in the Seventh Century," *India International Centre Quarterly* 36, no. 3/4 (2009): 41–42.
69. Deadly challenges such as the "fatal snakes, destructive vegetation, and pestilent air" cited by Xuanzang may have contributed to the long-standing communication gap between eastern India and western China. Divergent worldviews also seem to have posed challenges to bridging that gap. For example, Xuanzang mentions how the people at the frontiers of the Kāmarūpa territory were like the Man (蠻), the "southern barbarians" in the Han Chinese conception of the world. Politically, southwestern China (Sichuan and Yunnan) was not under Tang control, and it is expected that Xuanzang chose to follow an established commercial route rather than try to cross a dangerous territory to a Tang citizen.

70. See Dirk Meyer, "Bamboo and the Production of Philosophy: A Hypothesis about a Shift in Writing and Thought in Early China," in *Material Culture and Asian Religions: Text, Image, Object,* ed. Benjamin J. Fleming and Richard D. Mann (New York: Routledge, 2014), 21–38.
71. See Deborah Klimburg-Salter, *The Silk Route and the Diamond Path: Esoteric Buddhist Art on the Trans-Himalayan Trade Routes* (Los Angeles: UCLA Art Council, 1982).
72. Deborah Klimburg-Salter, "Indo-Tibetan Miniature Painting," in *Tibetan Studies: Proceedings of the 6th Seminar of the International Association for Tibetan Studies, Fagernes, 1992* (Oslo: Institute for Comparative Research in Human Culture, 1994), 441–53; and Klimburg-Salter, "Along the Pilgrimage Routes between Uḍḍiyāṇa and Tibet."
73. Robert N. Linrothe, *Collecting Paradise: Buddhist Art of Kashmir and Its Legacies* (New York: Rubin Museum of Art, 2014).
74. The spot is near Nurpur; see M.S. Shastri, "Report on the Gilgit Excavations," *Quarterly Journal of the Mythic Society* 30, no. 1 (1939): 1.
75. For Palola Ṣāhi inscriptions and their history, see Oskar von Hinüber, *Die Palola Ṣāhis: Ihre Steininschriften, Inschriften auf Bronzen, Handschriftenkolophone und Schutzzauber: Materialien zur Geschichte von Gilgit und Chilas* (Mainz: P. von Zabern, 2004). Von Hinüber assumes the contemporaneity of the painting and the text.
76. The total number of proper names given in the colophon is seventeen, including the name of the scribe, Śa[śi-] varddhana (Śrīvarddhana?), whose father's name, Maṇiyakabhagi, is also given. It seems that some of the names were added at a later date, on an additional blank folio, now folio 121. See Von Hinüber, *Palola Ṣāhis,* 25–27.
77. Following Von Hinüber, Rebecca Twist accepts the date of the manuscript, "*samvatsare* 3," datable to 627/28, as the date of the painting; see Twist, "Patronage, Devotion, and Politics: A Buddhological Study of the Patola Sahi Dynasty's Visual Record" (PhD diss., Ohio State University, 2008), 397.
78. Klimburg-Salter has discussed these book covers extensively; see, for example, "The Gilgit Manuscript Covers," in *South Asian Archaeology, 1987* (Rome: Istituto italiano per il Medio ed Estremo Oriente, 1990) and "A Note on the Origin of Tibetan Book Cover Decoration," *Tibet Journal* 16, no. 1 (1991): 115–27.
79. Klimburg-Salter, "Along the Pilgrimage Routes," and "Painted Covers of the Saṃghāṭasūtra," in *South Asian Archaeology 1989* (Madison, WI: Prehistory Press, 1992); and Linrothe, *Collecting Paradise,* 41–54.
80. See Gregory Schopen, "On the Absence of the Urtexts and Otiose Ācāryas: Buildings, Books, and Lay Buddhist Ritual at Gilgit," *Écrire et transmettre en Inde classique* 30 (2009): 189–219.
81. Klimburg-Salter, "Along the Pilgrimage Routes," figure 4.
82. Klimburg-Salter, "Along the Pilgrimage Routes," 400. See also Pratapaditya Pal and Julia Meech-Pekarik, *Buddhist Book Illuminations* (New York: Ravi Kumar 1988).
83. It is unclear when an illustrated frontispiece and a decorated exterior cover began to be added to manuscripts of Buddhist texts written in classical Chinese. The earliest known examples from East Asia date from the eighth century, and the oldest printed book in the world, a woodblock print copy of the *Diamond sūtra* (*Vajracchedika Prajñāpāramitā*), dated 868, also features an illustrated frontispiece. See W. Zwalf, *Buddhism: Art and Faith* (London: British Museum, 1985), 40–90.
84. The page with the most writing, which may be the beginning of the series, states that these sixteen goddesses are propitiated to protect a child—especially from illness caused by evil spirits. Maggi suggests that the folios were used as an amulet based on the text's tenuous connection with the Mahāpratisarā dhāraṇī. However, given the prescriptive nature of the text and the surviving codicological features—for example, string holes for binding the folios as a *pothi*-format manuscript—Joanna

Williams's observation that they were not used as amulets seems more reasonable. Mauro Maggi, "A Chinese-Khotanese Excerpt from the Mahāsāhasrapramardanī," in *Convegno internzionale sul tema la Persia e l'Asia Centrale da Alessandro al X Secolo* (Rome: Academia nazionale del Lincei, 1996), 123–37; Joanna Williams, "The Iconography of Khotanese Painting," *East and West* 23, no. 1 (1973): 109–54.

85. Henrik Sørensen, "Typology and Iconography in the Esoteric Art of Dunhuang," *Silk Road Art and Archaeology* 2 (1991/92), 294–95. Sørensen calls them "child-devouring demons of anthropomorphic cast with the heads of various animals." See also Prods Skjærvø, *Khotanese Manuscripts from Chinese Turkestan in the British Library: A Complete Catalogue with Texts and Translations* (London: British Library, 2002).

86. Negative connotations of the term *demon* can undermine our understanding of the healing strategies developed in Indic religious traditions. That a malevolent force causing bodily harm could be tamed and turned into a protective and healing entity is attested in the story of the goddess Hāritī, a protectress of children, who used to be a child-devouring *rakṣasī*. In a similar vein, the smallpox goddess Śītalā not only causes the disease but also can cure it by taking it away. See, for example, Tony K. Stewart, "Encountering the Smallpox Goddess," in *Religions of India in Practice,* ed. Donald Lopez Jr. (Princeton, NJ: Princeton University Press, 1995), 389–97.

87. Skjærvø, *Khotanese Manuscripts,* 583; Maggi, *Chinese-Khotanese Excerpt,* 130. Maggi suggests a connection with the *Mahāsāhasrapramardanī dhāraṇī*. Similar names appearing in that text suggest a connection, but the relationship between this manuscript's text and the dhāraṇī is far from clear.

88. Direction of writing is a custom developed over time. There is at least one example from Dunhuang where Khotanese script is written vertically, which again suggests the complexity and diversity of the manuscript culture in a place like Dunhuang; see Mauro Maggi and Anna Filigenzi, "Pelliot Tibétain 2222: A Dunhuang Painting with a Khotanese Inscription," *Journal of Inner Asian Art and Archaeology* 3 (2008): 83–89.

89. See Lore Sander, "Remarks on the Formal Brāhmī Script from the Southern Silk Route," *Bulletin of the Asia Institute* 19 (2005): 133–44.

90. Aurel Stein, *Ancient Khotan: Detailed Report of Archaeological Explorations in Chinese Turkestan,* vol. 1 (Oxford: Clarendon Press, 1907), 250. The silk princess panel, for example, was found standing against the base of a stucco image in a shrine. Stein also reports seeing "fragments of leaves . . . pasted across the two painted panels previously described" (255), suggesting a possibility that they may have been book covers.

91. The seventh-century *Sadharmapuṇḍarīka* MS found in the neighborhood of Khotan, possibly at the Khadalik stūpa, OMPB Or. 9613, measures 18 × 56.5 cm.

92. Stein, *Ancient Khotan,* 261.

93. See Gregory Schopen, "The Book as a Sacred Object in Private Homes in Early or Medieval India," in *Medieval and Early Modern Devotional Objects in Global Perspective,* ed. Elizabeth Robertson and Jennifer Jahner (Hampshire, UK: Palgrave Macmillan, 2010); and Kim, *Receptacle of the Sacred,* 23–41.

94. They may belong to a later layer of painting than the narrative scene below.

95. No further attempt to retrieve or photograph it has been made. There have been a few explorations of the Khotanese sites since Stein, most recently in 2002 when a joint expedition team from the Xinjiang Cultural Relics Bureau, the Xinjiang Archaeological Research Institute, and the Niya Research Institute of Bukkyo University in Japan discovered a new Buddhist temple with wall paintings. See *Dandanwulike yi zhi* (Dandan oilik site: Report of the Sino Japanese Joint expedition) (Beijing: Wenwuchubanshe, 2009).

96. Even when a manuscript was acquired in its entirety, text folios without any trace of illustration or painting are sometimes given a secondary status or no status at all and are kept separately from painted folios and book covers.

97. Jeffrey F. Hamburger and Brigitte Miriam Bedos-Rezak, *Sign and Design: Script as Image in Cross-Cultural Perspective* (Washington, DC: Dumbarton Oaks, 2016). See also Jeffrey F. Hamburger, "The Iconicity of Script," *Word and Image* 27, no. 3 (2011): 249–61.

98. On epigraphic evidence, see Richard Salomon, *Indian Epigraphy: A Guide to the Study of Inscriptions in Sanskrit, Prakrit, and the Other Indo-Aryan Languages* (Oxford: Oxford University Press, 1998), 7–42. On inscriptions as a physical record of ritual performance, see Benjamin J. Fleming, "Making Land Sacred: Inscriptional Evidence for Buddhist Kings and Brahman Priests in Medieval Bengal," *Numen* 60, no. 5–6 (2013): 559–85.

99. Salomon, *Indian Epigraphy,* 146–68; Kim, "Seeing in between the Space."

100. D.P. Ghosh, *Mediaeval Indian Painting* (Delhi: Sundeep Prakashan, 1982), 6. Numerous examples are known from the tenth century on.

101. See Ernst Steinkellner, *A Short Guide to the Sudhana Frieze in the Temple of Ta Pho* (Vienna: Institute for Tibetan and Buddhist Studies, University of Vienna, 1996).

102. The use of the local language together with images, both of which were set against the Sanskrit text they supposedly translated, effectively gave a transregional asset a local or regional presence, making it their own. In a similar way, Nachiket Chanchani finds in the Freer Vasanta Vilāsa "an emergent regional language (old Gujarati), an older trans-regional language (Sanskrit) and visual vocabularies in fifteenth century Gujarat" combining to create a "climate in which these self-conscious practices to make the medieval modern" could unite. Chanchani, "Telling Tales: The Freer Vasanta Vilāsa," *Artibus Asiae* 72, no. 1 (2012): 123.

103. Moti Chandra proposes the third quarter of the fourteenth century. Moti Chandra, *Jain Miniature Paintings from Western India* (Ahmedabad: Sharabhai M. Nawab, 1949), 46–49.

104. Shridhar Andhare, "Jain Monumental Painting," in *The Peaceful Liberators: Jain Art from India,* ed. Pratapaditya Pal (Los Angeles: Los Angeles County Museum of Art, 1995), 78. According to the colophon written in red in the top section of the painting, the banner is a *yantraṃ* called "*jatra-patāka*" (*jatrapatākākhy*[*a*]*-yantram*), written and installed by Śrī Jinabhadrasūri, a master of a Śvetambara Jain order, on the day of Divali. If any success or victory was to be attained with it, it is likely to have occurred in the realm of *siddhi* (ritual powers), not on a literal battleground. This is also discussed in Nick Barnard, "Jaina Paintings and Manuscripts," in *Jaina Painting and Manuscript Culture,* ed. Julia Hegewald (Berlin: EB-Verlag, 2015), 96.

105. Andhare, "Jain Monumental Painting," 81.

106. Most of the Jain communities where the visual dimensions of a written text were exploited most forcefully were located in present-day Gujarat, southern Rajasthan, and northern coastal Maharashtra, a region that maintained strong trade connections to the Arab world from at least the eighth century on, especially thriving from the eleventh through the fifteenth centuries. It would be surprising if exposure to the Arab and Persian manuscript cultures had not played a role in fostering the sensitivity to written letters that characterized these communities.

107. The "Maṇḍala of the Two Worlds" of Entsuji, Koyasan, painted on silk and prepared in the fourteenth century, is a good example. An earlier example dating from the ninth century was used at Toji in Kyoto. See Susan Dine, "Sanskrit beyond Text" (master's thesis, University of Washington, 2012), figure 12.

108. They are what Paul Copp calls "a proto-typical image of eidetic contemplation." Paul Copp, *The Body Incantatory* (New York: Columbia University Press, 2014), 124. Copp discusses this image in the context of *dhāraṇī* amulets, and the text of this sheet certainly underscores its protective function.

109. There are inscriptions on the front as well, one line at the top and a second line at the bottom, the former identifying the series to which the painting belongs and the latter the patron's wish or intention. Written in gold ink on a red ground, their presence seems to be more important than their visibility.
110. Halle O'Neal, "Performing the Jeweled Pagoda Mandalas: Relics, Reliquaries, and a Realm of Text," *Art Bulletin* 97, no. 3 (2015): 279–300.
111. Debala Mitra, *Ratnagiri,* vol. 1 (New Delhi: Archaeological Survey of India, 1981), 229–31.
112. This is based on Debala Mitra's reading.
113. A number of khodalite slabs inscribed with the text of the *Pratītyasamutpāda gātha,* from which the "*ye dharmāhetu* . . ." verse was taken as its essence, were excavated as deposits within stūpas at Ratnagiri. See Daniel Boucher, "The Pratītyasamutpādagāthā and Its Role in the Medieval Cult of the Relics," *Journal of the International Association of Buddhist Studies* 14, no. 1 (1991): 1–27.
114. A number of bronze statues from Achutrajpur hoard bear an affixed seal either on the back or inside of the pedestal. See Jinah Kim, "Unorthodox Practice: Rethinking the Cult of Illustrated Buddhist Books in South Asia" (PhD diss., University of California, Berkeley, 2006), 322–25.
115. Piotrovsky, *Lost Empire of the Silk Road,* 44.
116. If we trust Kozlov's judgment about the "Chinese" style of the painting, and given the rarity of pastel colors resembling "soft pale blue and pink" on (Indo-Tibetan inspired) painted Tangut *thangka*s, I wonder if the two silk scrolls of Mañjuśrī and Samantabhadra (X-2447 and X-2444) might be considered candidates. Another possibility might be paintings of Guanyin, such as X-2437.
117. Piotrovsky, *Lost Empire of the Silk Road,* 44.
118. The variety of formats of Tangut manuscripts, together with the diversity of languages, Tangut, Tibetan, and Chinese, they contain, speaks volumes about the multicultural nature of the kingdom's affairs. Some are scrolls, yet others are xylograph woodblock prints in concertina format; still others are what is called a "butterfly book"—in effect, a codex. But unlike a codex, the text in them can run across the full width of the two leaves. In some examples, illustrated pages were created from engraved block prints, while the rest of the manuscript was handwritten, such as Tang 164 (Inventory No. 206; Cat. 79) or Tang 334 (Inventory No. 1446; Cat. 80), both of which are from the *Prajñāpāramitā.* See Piotrovsky, *Lost Empire of the Silk Road,* 257–78; catalog entries are on 72–87.

CHAPTER 2. THE ART OF THE BOOK IN MEDIEVAL SOUTH ASIA

1. Ananda Coomaraswamy, *Catalogue of the Indian Collections in the Museum of Fine Arts, Boston,* Part IV (Boston: Museum of Fine Arts, 1924), 32. Jeremiah Losty makes a similar suggestion for understanding the Indian manuscript paintings as "scaled-down versions of icons as wall painting," making a clear reference to the connection with the wall paintings of Ajanta, in his discussion of the unique narrative painting of the *Vessantara jātaka* on the manuscript cover now in the National Museum, New Delhi. J.P. Losty, *Art of the Book in India* (London: British Library Board, 1982), 35.
2. Coomaraswamy, *Catalogue of the Indian Collections,* 32.
3. For example, the visit of Amrita Sher-Gil (1913–1941) to Ajanta in 1936 and her appreciation of the vibrant and subtle tonality of the murals and bodily forms making up a pictorial space contributed to the painterly achievements seen in the *Bride's Toilet* (1937) and *Brahmacharis* (1937), among others. See the discussion in Sonal Khullar, "National Tradition and Modernist Art," in *The Cambridge Companion to Modern Indian Culture,* ed. Vasudha Dalmia and Rashmi Sadana (Cambridge: Cambridge University Press, 2012), 163–82. Nandalal Bose (1882–1966) and his students created copies of Ajanta

murals on the walls of Visva-Bharati University in Santiniketan, and Ajanta's painting style is credited as being one of the main sources of inspiration for Bose's prolific stylistic output, as the artist himself acknowledges in his 1944 letter. Nandalal Bose, *Vision and Creation*, trans. K.G. Subramanyam (Calcutta: Visva-Bharati Publication, 1999), 271. Also see Pramod Chandra and Sonya Rhie Quintanilla, "Nandalal Bose and the History of Indian Art," in *Rhythms of India: The Art of Nandalal Bose* (San Diego: San Diego Museum of Art, 2008), 26–41.

4. I use the terms *book* and *manuscript* interchangeably in this study. The word *book* is used to emphasize its material and physical quality as an object, whereas *manuscript* is used to discuss folios and its fluid, open structure, but their usage is not exclusive. Approaching a "book" as a cultural artifact and a physical object has already yielded fruitful results in other art historical fields. See, most notably, David J. Roxburgh, *The Persian Album, 1400–1600: From Dispersal to Collection* (New Haven, CT: Yale University Press, 2005). More than a decade ago, Roxburgh raised important methodological issues relating to the study of the art of the book and proposed a new direction for the study of paintings and painted manuscripts from a phenomenological and material culture perspective, and his discussion provides valuable insights for researchers studying the art of the book in other areas of the world. Roxburgh, "The Study of Painting and the Arts of the Book," *Muqarnas* 17 (2000): 1–16.
5. Pratapaditya Pal notes the Sanskrit term "*pustaka*" is "a loan word from Old Persian and could not have been introduced before the sixth century." Pratapaditya Pal, "Early Paintings of the Goddess in Nepal," *Ars Orientalis* 12 (1981): 47. This observation needs to be explored further.
6. For the idea of a manuscript as a three-dimensional sacred object in a medieval Indian Buddhist context, see Jinah Kim, *Receptacle of the Sacred: Illustrated Manuscripts and the Buddhist Book Cult in South Asia* (Berkeley: University of California Press, 2013).
7. In Western medieval manuscripts, architectural frames also play a crucial role as exemplified in the use of architectural Canon Tables in Gospel books. I thank Jeffrey Hamburger for this reference.
8. It is important to remember that the introduction of painted manuscripts around 1000 CE is not a belated phenomenon in comparison to other manuscript cultures of the world. Most surviving "illustrated" manuscripts from the Islamic traditions, whether in Arabic or Persian languages, date later than the eleventh century, although the inclusion of didactic and functional images like schematic drawings are reported in the tenth-century sources. See, for example, Houari Touati, *L'armoire à sagesse: Bibliothèques et collections en Islam* (Paris: Aubier, 2003), 113–16; Eva R. Hoffman, "The Beginnings of the Illustrated Arabic Book: An Intersection between Art and Scholarship," *Muqarnas* 17 (2000): 37–52; Anna Contadini, ed., *Arab Painting: Text and Image in Illustrated Arabic Manuscripts* (Leiden: Brill, 2007). I thank David J. Roxburgh for these references. During the period concerned here, Islamic books began to be introduced to the Indian subcontinent. Whether these books were recognized among their contemporaries as the same kind of objects should be explored further. The codex format of Islamic books does not have a profound impact until the fifteenth century in South Asia, when, coinciding with the wider circulation of paper as the medium for manuscript production, a decisive change in the manner of production of painted manuscripts seems to have taken place. On the impact of paper on manuscript production, see Jonathan M. Bloom, *Paper before Print: The History and Impact of Paper in the Islamic World* (New Haven, CT: Yale University Press, 2001).
9. "*choti pustaka*" is the definition given in H. Bahri's *Rajpal Hindi Shabdakosha* (Delhi: Rajpal and Sons, 1999). The term "pothi" is a Middle Indo Aryan (MIA) term derived from the Sanskrit (Old Indo Aryan or OIA) term "pustaka." See the discussion in Camillo Alessio Formigatti, "Sanskrit Annotated Manuscripts from Northern India and Nepal," PhD diss. (University of Hamburg, 2015), 17–20

10. For a detailed discussion of this manuscript's iconographic program and the cultic value, see Jinah Kim, "A Book of Buddhist Goddesses," *Artibus Asiae* 71, no. 2 (2010): 259–329.

11. In the donor colophon on folio 172v, the scribe initially forgot to record the name of Bahudhana's town and made an effort to identify the place with an insertion mark (·) in front of his name as the "resident of Vakalāṅgala (*vakalāṅgalāvasthita*)." With the present state of knowledge of ancient and medieval topography, we do not know the location of Vakalāṅgala. Folio 172v, *Pañcarakṣā sūtra*, National Archive, Kathmandu, Acc. No. 5.83.

12. The use of curtains over images in a manuscript is also known in Christian medieval illuminated manuscripts where textile curtains, often in silk, were stitched to protect painted areas. For their use and potential liturgical significance, see Christine Sciacca, "Raising the Curtain on the Use of Textiles in Manuscripts," in *Weaving, Veiling, and Dressing: Textiles and Their Metaphors in the Late Middle Ages*, ed. K.M. Rudy and B. Baert (Turnhout: Brepols: 2007), 161–90. I thank Jeffrey Hamburger for this reference.

13. If it were only for the purpose of preventing them from rubbing each other, a single sheet on one side of the folio would have sufficed. Each panel has a paper curtain attached to it, which means there are two sheets of paper in between two facing painted folios when the manuscript is closed.

14. Touching the divine images with offerings of vermilion powder is a common devotional practice still seen in Nepal and India.

15. The donor colophon reads, "*deyadharmoyaṁ pravaramahāyānayāyinaḥ śrīmannepāladeśīyabhikṣu āryaśrīmintrasya yadatrapuṇyantadbhavatvācāryopādhyāyamātāpitṛpūrvaṅgamakṛtvāsakalasatvarāśer-anuttarajñānaphalāvāptaiti*||" Here, "—mintra" is a variant of "—mitra." The identification of the donor's regional identity as "a monk of Nepal (*nepāladeśiyabhikṣu*)" (instead of a location in the Kathmandu valley, which is usually the case in a Nepalese manuscript from this period), suggests that the manuscript was most likely written in the Vikramaśīla monastery in India rather than in Nepal. The incongruity seen in the calligraphy of the two manuscripts prepared in the Vikramaśīla monastery may be explained by the fact that the British Library Or. 6902 was prepared a generation later than the Cleveland Museum manuscript, which shows a hand closer to that responsible for a Nālandā manuscript of a similar date (Rāmapāla's thirty-fifth regnal year) now in the Tibet Museum, Lhasa. This colophon was discussed by Pal as one of the problematic cases. P. Pal, *Arts of Nepal*, Vol. II Painting (Leiden: Brill, 1974), 32.

16. The provenance colophon reads, "~*samvat ālañca* (237 or 9) *aṣvaniśuklāṣṭamyāṃ*|*śrīvikramaśīlamahāvihare*||." The last letter numeral "ñca" of the samvat era is unusual, and may be taken as 7 or 9. I thank Shin'ichiro Hori and Hanunaga Isaacson for sharing their thoughts on this number. A different hand with distinctive features seen in contemporary Nepalese manuscripts wrote this colophon. This hand is similar to the one in the heavily painted *Perfection of Wisdom* manuscript in the Asiatic Society, Kolkata, dated 1071 CE (N.S. 191), A15. The form of the letter "*śrī*," for example, is different from the one used in the main text and the donor colophon, which, I believe, were written in the Vikramaśīla monastery in India.

17. There is a tantalizing possibility that these two monks related to the Vikramaśīla monastery belonged to the "*śrīmitra*" (*śrīmintra* being a scribal variant of *śrīmitra*) lineage charted by a well-known *praśāsti* inscription of a monk named Vipulaśrīmitra from Nālandā. Tuladhar-Douglas speculates that a "*śrīmitra*" lineage of scholar monks from Nālandā and Vikramaśīla had a significant Nepalese connection. Will Tuladhar-Douglas, *Remaking Buddhism for Medieval Nepal: The Fifteenth Century Reformation of Newar Buddhism* (London: Routledge, 2006), 127–28. His historical evidence linking Nālandā and Vikramaśīla with Nepal through a lineage of monks is rather weak, but the Cleveland Museum manuscript may hold a key to understanding this tantalizing connection through art historical evidence.

18. Given the damaged state of folio 1, which shows the conservation effort of the previous generation of Nepalese owners of the manuscript in the yellow paper used to support the folio from the back, it is possible that the second folio was also damaged and possibly lost in the course of the manuscript's life as a cultic object in Nepal. On Nepalese methods of manuscript conservation, see the discussion in Jinah Kim, "Unorthodox Practice: Rethinking the Cult of Illustrated Buddhist Books in South Asia" (PhD diss., University of California, Berkeley, 2006), 341–50.
19. See, for example, the images collected under the auspices of the Western Himalayan Archives, Vienna (WHAV) on Christian Luczanits's website, http://luczanits.net/pictures/TaboAHGeneral/index.html. Also see Christian Luczanits, *Buddhist Sculpture in Clay: Early Western Himalayan Art, Late 10th to early 13th Centuries* (Chicago: Serindia, 2004).
20. It is interesting to note the use of different orthography for the letter "kha" in the same sentence. The letter "kha" in the second part of the name "*devarakha*" is written in a manner similar to the Bengali "kha," showing what can be categorized as a proto-Bengali hand, but the same letter is written in a typical *siddhamātṛka* manner in the term "*lekhaka*" and the verb "*likhita*" in the same sentence. This seems to reveal what Losty characterizes as certain "Bengalism." I do not think there is any reason to consider his name as being repeated twice, once as "Devarāja" and the next instance as "Devarakha" as Losty posits. J.P. Losty, "The Perfection of Wisdom (Prajnaparamita sutra)," entry 1 in *The Art of Enlightenment: Buddhist Manuscripts from the Himalayas, India, China, Japan, and South-East Asia*, October 30—November 21, 2008 (an online exhibition catalog, Sam Fogg London).
21. My reading is based on the photographs of the colophon pages kindly provided by Katie Boycott Trevor of Sam Fogg Ltd. I concur with Losty that this manuscript must have been prepared somewhere in West or North Bengal, probably in the ancient region of Varendra or Aṅga.
22. In Nepal (the Kathmandu valley in this study), this situation changes over time, and donor portraits become an essential part of a painted manuscript by the sixteenth century.
23. For example, the scene depicting a lay donor and a monk venerating a book on a pedestal is depicted on the last folio of a painted *Prajñāpāramitā* (c. 1100 CE) from Bengal. See Kim, *Receptacle of the Sacred*, figure 6-5.
24. This is despite the fact that the shrine structure is depicted against a dark backdrop with trees growing behind it, as if suggesting a shrine standing in a night landscape. The trees hovering around such shrine structures were part of a common pictorial strategy in this type of painted manuscript from the period as seen behind other shrine structures in the same section.
25. J.P. Losty, "Bihar, Bengal, or Nepal? Problems of Provenance in 12th Century Illuminated Buddhist Manuscripts," part 1, *Oriental Art* 35, no. 2(1989): 86–96.
26. Losty also cautions that the use of the shrine structure does not always indicate a single provenance.
27. Kim, *Receptacle of the Sacred*, esp. 47–52.
28. The entire colophon as read by L.D. Barnett is quoted in full in Ananda K. Coomaraswamy, "Illustrated Śvetambāra Jaina Manuscript of A.D. 1260," *Eastern Art* 2 (1930): 237–39. The entire manuscript is digitized and available on the museum's website: http://www.mfa.org/collections/object/sravakapratikramasutra-curni-of-vijayasimha-605509.
29. Here, I am helped in understanding the mechanism of *dhāraṇī* practices by Janet Gyatso's conceptualization of the "*dhāraṇī* door." Janet Gyatso, "Letter Magic: A Peircean Perspective on the Semiotics of Rdo Grub-chen's Dharani Memory," in *In the Mirror of Memory: Reflections on Mindfulness and Remembrance in Indian and Tibetan Buddhism* (Albany: State University of New York Press, 1992), esp. 180–90.
30. In this case, we may call the goddess with snakes in her hands Dharanendrī, as Coomaraswamy identified her. Coomaraswamy, "Illustrated Śvetambāra Jaina manuscript."

31. What prompted such economic usage of palm leaflets needs further exploration. It may have been prompted by the diminishing supply of talipot palm, which requires a wetter climate to grow and is not native to Gujarat and Rajasthan. Two hypotheses may be entertained to explain a decrease in palm-leaf supply: potential impact of climate change during the "little Ice Age," and the impact of a more widespread introduction of paper that may have rendered palm-leaf supply business less profitable than in previous centuries. According to a story in the Kumārapālacarita of Jinamaṇḍanagaṇi written in 1492, King Kumārapāla was horrified at the thought of sacred texts being written on paper, which suggests that paper was becoming a common source material to make manuscripts. I thank Phyllis Granoff for this reference and insight.
32. Nachiket Chanchani, "Paper Prasada," *Artibus Asiae* 76, no. 2 (2016).
33. This characterization is partly due to the pioneering works by early twentieth century scholars such as W. Norman Brown. As the parenthetical subtitle of his 1934 volume, "as executed in the early Western Indian style," suggests, Brown's study played a definitive role in the history of Indian painting in the subsequent canonization of the Jain manuscript paintings as the epitome of the "early Western Indian style." In the author's own words, "taken as a whole this work should form a guide to the *Kalpasūtra* miniatures, by means of which almost any scene in any series of manuscript illustrations of that work executed in that style can be identified at a glance without the necessity for special research." W. Norman Brown, *A Descriptive and Illustrated Catalogue of Miniature Paintings of the Jaina Kalpasūtra* (Washington, DC: Smithsonian Institution, 1934), iv.
34. For example, the earliest known dated painted palm-leaf Jain manuscript now in Jaisalmer (Jain Trust) is identified as a text on monastic rules, the *Oghaniryukti.* It bears the date of V.S. 1117 (1060 CE) as seen in the reproduced sections of the two painted folios. See Saryu Doshi, *Masterpieces of Jain Painting* (Bombay: Marg Publications, 1985), 33–44, and figure 3.
35. For example, two painted folios in the Cleveland Museum of Art, Acc. No. 1971.128 and 1971.129, mark the beginning of Hemacandra's *Yogaśāstra.*
36. The two painted palm-leaf folios in the Los Angeles County Museum of Art, M. 88.62.1–2, are now identified as bearing the text of the *Siddhahemaśabdānuśāsana,* according to Phyllis Granoff's recent reading. They were identified as "two folios from a *Kalpasutra* manuscript" in P. Pal's catalog of the museum's Indian painting collection. Pratapaditya Pal, *Indian Painting* (Los Angeles: Los Angeles County Museum of Art, 1993), 86–87.
37. It is possible to generalize on this point as we find various titles such as "*Nripadeshamala,*" "*Pravachana-Saroddhar-Vriti-Saha,*" "*Prakarana Pothi,*" and "*Visheshavashyaka-vriti*" in the "illustrations" list in Saryu Doshi's chapter on early painted Jain manuscripts. Doshi, *Masterpieces of Jain Painting,* 44.
38. This is also reflected in the way in which a painted manuscript was prepared and handled in Jain traditions after the introduction of paper as the main medium in the fifteenth century. Even in the manuscripts of the *Kalpasūtra,* the most ceremonial text-object created for Paryuṣan, a Śvetāmbara Jain festival, we see numerous corrections and additions written directly on the page without hesitation whereas in the painted Buddhist manuscripts the near-contemporary copyediting hands are very discreet and often hidden.
39. The situation is somewhat different in Nepal. Depictions of the donors begin to appear in a painted program from the twelfth century.
40. The date of this book cover has been suggested as sometime immediately after the historical event, around 1125–1150 CE, but a recent identification of the two painted folios in the Cleveland Museum of Art by Granoff as that of Abhayatilaka Gaṇi's commentary to Hemacandra's *Dvyāśrayamahākāvya,*

which was composed in 1312 V.S. (1255 CE), questions this dating because the paintings on these folios bear remarkable stylistic similarities to the painting on the book covers. I thank Sonya Rhie Mace of the Cleveland Museum of Art for providing this information.

41. Also see Doshi, *Masterpieces of Jain Painting,* 34 and figures 15 and 16.
42. For example, in an early twelfth-century manuscript of the Jñātasūtra reported to have been in the Śāntinātha temple (Nagin Dās) Bhaṇḍār, Cambay in Gujarat (dated V.S. 1184; 1127 CE), we find written labels identifying the names of the male donors seated on either side of the standing goddess Saraswatī. Brown, *Descriptive and Illustrated Catalogue of Miniature Paintings*, 18 and 116, plate 1, figures 1–2.
43. An interesting comparison may be drawn between the Jain practice and label inscriptions used in post–Iconoclast Byzantine portraits of saints. According to Henry Maguire, their use helped define and control sacred portraiture. Label inscriptions in Jain examples seem to have functioned similarly. Henry Maguire, *The Icons of Their Bodies: Saints and Their Images in Byzantium* (Princeton, NJ: Princeton University Press, 1996).
44. It is worth noting that these interlinear writings and marginal notations are found even in a *Kalpasūtra* manuscript, which is prepared as a ceremonial object, as we see in a manuscript in the Brooklyn Museum collection, dated 1472 CE. See Paul Dundas, "Victorious across Eternity: The Lives of the Jain Tīrthaṅkaras," in *Victorious Ones: Jain Images of Perfection,* ed. Phyllis Granoff (New York: Rubin Museum of Art; Ahmedabad: Mapin Publishing, 2009), 17–33, esp. 27–31.
45. The editors of the Sanskrit text of the *Dānakāṇḍa,* where giving of a book is characterized as an act of knowledge-giving (*vidyādāna*), express their belief in the "prejudice against the substitution of books for oral instruction in ancient India" citing a term such as "seller of the *veda.*" Rangaswami Aiyangar, ed., "Introduction to the *Dānakāṇḍa,*" in *Kṛtyakalpataru of Bhaṭṭa Lakṣmīdhara,* vol. 5, *Dānakāṇḍa* (Baroda: Baroda Oriental Institute, 1941), 110. This assumption has been effectively called into question. For example, see C. Mackenzie Brown, "Purāṇa as Scripture: From Sound to Image of the Holy Word in the Hindu Tradition," *History of Religions* 26, no. 1 (1986). James McHugh, "The Hindu Love of Writing, and the Manuscript as Event," paper presented at the workshop *Writing and the Inscription of Power in South Asia,* Duke University, April 5–6, 2013.
46. The plight of the lost painted book covers came to light in part thanks to the work done by the Nepal-German Manuscript Preservation Project that documented these manuscripts in the 1970s, which were used in the pioneering study by Savitri Mainali, *Hindu Miniature Paintings of the Kathmandu Valley* (Kathmandu: Bishwa Kanta Mainali, 2009). This book provides valuable data regarding the tradition of Hindu manuscript paintings. Unfortunately, it repeats the same exclusive attitude toward painting found in previous scholarship on Indian painting, in which only painted panels are discussed, in a highly focused manner, for their pictorial qualities.
47. The calligraphy in this manuscript is similar to that in the painted folios belonging to a *Perfection of Wisdom* manuscript that was once in the Shalu monastery (Sāṅkrityāyana's list: Shalu monastery—XXVIII, no. 288) photographed by Rāhula Sāṅkṛityāyana during his second visit to Tibet in 1936. Sāṅkrityāyana found the writing in this manuscript less than appealing, as he notes, "Calligraphy of this Ms is not so good, but it is beautifully illustrated. Ms. is worn out, and at the end few leaves are missing." Sāṅkrityāyana, "Second Search of Sanskrit Palm-Leaf Mss. in Tibet," *Journal of the Bihar and Orissa Research Society* 23, part 1 (1937): 42. The black-and-white photographs of the painted folios of this manuscript appear in S.K. Pathak, ed., *The Album of the Tibetan Art Collections* (Patna: K.P. Jayaswal Research Institute, 1986), plates 25–29. At least two folios from this manuscript are now in the Los Angeles County Museum of Art, M. 71.1 43 and M. 72.1.21, and are most likely to have been taken from Shalu by Giuseppe Tucci.

48. For further discussion of the painted panels, see chapter 6 herein.

49. According to the colophon on folio 144r, this manuscript was prepared during the reign of Harṣadeva. The painted book covers are discussed in chapters 5 and 6 herein.

50. On the characteristics of this design element used in Tibetan painting, see David P. Jackson, *The Nepalese Legacy in Tibetan Painting* (New York: Rubin Museum of Art, 2010), 88–92. Jackson identifies this motif as one of the uniquely Newari elements in Tibetan painting, or of what he calls the "Beri" style.

51. The other book cover of this manuscript is in the Bhaktapur Art Gallery. See Savitri Mainali, *Hindu Miniature Paintings of the Kathmandu Valley* (Kathmandu: Bishwa Kanta Mainali, 2009), plate 22.

52. Mainali, *Hindu Miniature Paintings,* 64–84.

53. I would like to note that the painted book covers belonging to this manuscript are currently housed in the Musée Guimet, Paris, as they were on display at that museum in 2009 (MA5996). I thank Nathalie Bazin, curator of the Nepal/Tibet section of the Musée Guimet, for kindly providing accession and provenance information for the covers. According to the museum's records, the pair was given to the museum as a gift in 1993.

54. The available area of the colophon reads, "*yoginīputraśrīrāmadevasya parameśvara-paramabhaṭṭāraka-paramasaugata-mahārājādhirāja-śrīmadrāmapāladevasya pravarddhama.*" This colophon is intriguing because it gives the full royal title of a Pāla king, Rāmapāla, including a great Buddhist epithet, "*paramasaugata,*" customarily used to identify him in other known Rāmapāla-era Buddhist manuscripts prepared in the famous Nālandā monastery (Bodleian Library Sansk a.7, dated Rāmapāla's fifteenth year, and a *Perfection of Wisdom* manuscript in the Tibet Museum, Lhasa, dated Rāmapāla's thirty-seventh year). The writing in "flat-bottomed *kuṭila*" script in fact looks extremely similar to the Tibet Museum's manuscript, raising the tantalizing possibility that this manuscript was indeed prepared somewhere in Magadha (present-day Bihar in India).

55. Mainali identifies this as an image of Bhairava, but it clearly represents a goddess, as the tiger skin garment around her chest and the round shapes indicating full breasts suggest. Mainali, *Hindu Miniature Paintings,* 126.

56. Dehejia notes that numerous *Kubjikāmata* manuscripts survive in Nepal but that there is remarkably little evidence of thriving cultic practices for yoginīs there. Vidya Dehejia, *Yoginī: Cult and Temples—A Tantric Tradition* (New Delhi: National Museum, 1986), 81–82. This painted manuscript provides a glimpse into the visions of the yoginī cult as realized in eastern India and Nepal of the twelfth century.

57. Losty, *Art of the Book in India,* 48.

58. J.A. Schoterman, "*Kubjikāmata Tantra:* The *Laghvikāmnāya* Version," in *The Sanskrit Tradition and Tantrism,* ed. Teun Goudriaan (Leiden: Brill, 1990), 76–95. According to Sanderson, this manuscript is also the earliest surviving manuscript of the middle-length redaction of the *Kubjikāmata Tantra.* Alexis Sanderson, "Remarks on the Text of the Kubjikāmatatantra," *Indo-Iranian Journal* 45 (2002): 1–24.

59. Losty, *Art of the Book in India,* 36, see plate II.

60. Pal, "Early Paintings of the Goddess in Nepal," 41.

61. Catherine Glynn, "A Sixteenth Century 'Devīmāhātmya' Manuscript from Kangra" (PhD diss., University of Southern California, 1979); Tryna Lyons, "The Simla 'Devi Mahatmya' Illustrations: A Reappraisal of Content." *Archives of Asian Art* 45 (1992); B.N. Goswamy and Eberhard Fischer, *Pahari Masters: Court Painters of Northern India* (Zurich: Artibus Asiae Publishers, 1992), 16–27.

62. Alessandro Passi et al., eds., *Devī-māhātmya: MS. 4510 of the "Vincenzo Joppi" Municipal Library in Udine* (Udine: Società Indologica "Luigi Pio Tessitori," 2008).

63. The entire manuscript is digitized and available on the University of Cambridge Digital Library website. https://cudl.lib.cam.ac.uk/view/MS-ADD-01556.

64. It is most likely a combination of silver and gold (or some other pigment). Silver has tarnished in general, but the mild degree of tarnish and the slight yellowish tint suggest that it may have been a special recipe. In Nepal, metallic ink prepared with silver and gold was often used on black or blue-black paper manuscripts. The earliest surviving examples date from the twelfth century. See W. Zwalf, *Buddhism: Art and Faith* (London: British Museum, 1985), 127–30.

65. The figure on the left (who sits on the sage's right side) is larger and wears a crown and also shows *abhaya mudrā,* while the figure on the right (on the sage's left) does not wear a crown and kneels in veneration, representing Suratha and Samadhi, respectively.

66. Cecil Bendall, *Catalogue of the Buddhist Sanskrit Manuscripts in the University Library, Cambridge* (Cambridge: Cambridge University Press, 1883), xxxi–xxxii.

67. That the colophon is missing any reference to a reigning king also goes well with its late twelfth-century date of 1187 CE; this is believed to have been a time of political chaos with at least three rulers acknowledged within a decade. Luciano Petech, *Medeiaeval History of Nepal* (*c.* 750–1482) (Rome: Instituto Italiano per il Medio ed Estremo Oriente, 1958), 71–77.

68. There is a total of fifteen rubric images. When the rubric line runs across two pages (from recto to verso), the beginning and the ending are given separate rubric images (folios 10r–10v and 37r–37v). The scribe aligned the text in a way that a single rubric image can mark both the end and the beginning of the rubric. Folio 67v is an exception where two rubric images appear on the same page, marking the end of chapter twelve and the beginning of the last chapter. The end of chapter 3 is missing an image. Instead, there is a smudged outline of some sort.

69. See Mainali, *Hindu Miniature Paintings,* plates 3, 4. They went missing from the National Archives sometime after their documentation in the 1970s by the Nepal-German Manuscript Preservation Project and appeared in the Christie's New York auction in 2013. They were safely returned to the National Archives later that year.

70. Identifying pigments used in these manuscript paintings requires scientific material analysis as discussed in chapter 6. A systematic survey of pigments used in early Indic manuscript painting awaits further collaborative research.

71. Such an iconographic program with eight mothers is seen in many painted manuscripts related to DM with some variations in additional deities. In fact, the painted book covers prepared for the Kubjikāmata manuscript previously discussed (now in the Guimet Museum, MA5996) also feature eight mothers and two other forms of the Goddess described in the DM.

72. This is most likely an artist's interpretation of a character in the epic.

73. For a discussion of the complex formats of manuscripts available between the thirteenth and the sixteenth centuries, see the discussion in Losty, *Art of the Book in India,* 37–54; Losty, "Indian Painting from 1500 to 1575," in *Masters of Indian Painting: 1100–1650*, ed. Milo Beach, Eberhard Fischer, and B.N. Goswamy (Zurich: Artibus Asiae, 2011), 67–76.

74. For the most recent assessment of the Devasano Pado manuscript, see Saryu Doshi, "The Master of the Devasano Pado Kalpasutra and Kalakacharya Katha," in Beach, Fischer, and Goswamy, *Masters of Indian Painting: 1100–1650*, 53–66.

75. Karl Khandalavala and Moti Chandra, *An Illustrated Āraṇyaka Parvan in the Asiatic Society of Bombay* (Bombay: Asiatic Society of Bombay, 1974). Also see figure 6.7 herein.

76. It is important to note that the rituals prescribed in the worship of the goddess Kubjikā put emphasis on the materialization of the letters, as in a ritual involving written mantras and another involving a *mālā* (rosary) of fifty letters (i.e., the Sanskrit alphabet), the former conquering time and the latter conquering death. See Teun Goudriaan, "Some Beliefs and Rituals Concerning Time and Death in the Kubjikāmata," in *Selected Studies on Ritual in the Indian Religions: Essays to D.J. Hoens*, ed. Ria Kloppenborg (Leiden: Brill, 1983), 92–117.
77. See the discussion in Kim, "Book of Buddhist Goddesses."
78. The Asutosh Museum Pañcarakṣā manuscript is prepared on Thmelaeaceae paper made from fibers of high-altitude species (from plants found over 1,800 m, like *Daphne bholua*), which is consistent with its age. See Jesper Trier, *Ancient Paper of Nepal: Results of Ethno-Technological Field Work on Its Manufacture, Uses, and History—With Technical Analyses of Bast, Paper, and Manuscripts* (Copenhagen: Jutland Archaeological Society, 1972), 199 and 207. The material property of the CUL DM manuscript remains to be examined.
79. Jinah Kim, "Painted Palm-Leaf Manuscripts and the Art of the Book in Medieval South Asia," *Archives of Asian Art* 65, no. 1/2 (2015): figure 25.
80. The five deities hovering on top recall the five *tathāgata*s who often appear on top of contemporary Buddhist steles of Avalokiteśvara and Tārā. The flying celestial beings, the animal motifs decorating the throne-back, such as an elephant surmounted by a *vyāla* with a rider, and a *kinnarī-kinnara* couple standing on top of a *makara*-head marked crossbar, are all common visual motifs seen in contemporary sculptures transcending sectarian divisions.
81. The exact identity of this figure remains unclear. He seems nearly naked—whether there is a loincloth is not indicated as he is seated firmly cross-legged. His meditating hands certainly drew devotees' (and visitors') attention as the exceptional shine on them suggests many touching the surface on that spot.
82. I thank Parimal Patil for informing me about the existence of this rich body of literature.
83. Translation after David Brick, "The *Dānakāṇḍa* ('Book of Giving') of the *Kṛtyakalpataru:* A Critical Edition and Annotated Translation" (PhD diss., Harvard University, 2009). I thank James McHugh for this valuable reference.
84. Translation after David Brick, "The *Dānakāṇḍa* ('Book of Giving') of the *Kṛtyakalpataru.*"
85. The sculpture bears a dated inscription, "year 54." It is believed to be in the Kaniṣka era, and some argue for a second-century date while others suggest a third-century date. I concur with Catherine Ludvik in following van Lohuizen-de Leeuw's proposal of an early third-century date (232 CE). Catherine Ludvik, *Sarasvatī Riverine Goddess of Knowledge: From the Manuscript-Carrying Vīṇā-Player to the Weapon-Wielding Defender of Dharma* (Leiden: Brill, 2007), 231–35.
86. Claudine Bautze-Picron, "Between Men and Gods: Small Motifs in the Buddhist Art of Eastern India, an Interpretation," in *Function and Meaning in Buddhist Art,* ed. K.R. van Kooij and H. van der Veere (Groningen: Egbert Forsten, 1995), 59–80; Jinah Kim, "Performing Texts, Engendering Merits: Manuscripts and Paubhas as Ritual Objects," in *Dharma and Puṇya: Buddhist Ritual Art of Nepal,* ed. Jinah Kim and Todd Lewis (Leiden: Hotei Publishing, 2019), 88–99.
87. For discussion of images of Newar Vajrācāryas using manuscripts, see Kim, "Performing Texts."
88. On Vajrasattva's status as a teacher and his relationship to human practitioners, such as Vajrācāryas, see Robert Linrothe, "Mirror Image: Deity and Donor as Vajrasattva," *History of Religions* 54, no. 1 (2014): 5–33.
89. See Kim, "Painted Palm-Leaf Manuscripts," figure 23.
90. Kim, *Receptacle of the Sacred,* 23–41.

91. Kim, "Performing Texts," 88–89.
92. A set of painted wooden covers for a Jain manuscript now in the Oriental Institute, Mysore, shows a number of activities involving a *pothi*-format book, including scribing and venerating. Some manuscripts are shown hanging from above while others are placed on a rectangular table, which seems to have elaborate legs. See B.N. Goswamy, *The Word Is Sacred, Sacred Is the Word* (New Delhi: Niyogi Books, 2007), 99.
93. For example, such a book stand appears in the scene of instruction by Dharmodgata in a twelfth-century Nepalese manuscript of the *Perfection of Wisdom*. See Jinah Kim, "Iconography and Text: The Visual Narrative of the Buddhist Book-Cult in the Manuscript of the *Aṣṭasāhasrikā Prajñāpāramitā* Sūtra," in *Kalādarpaṇa: The Mirror of Indian Art*, ed. Arundhati Banerji and Devangana Desai (New Delhi: Aryan International, 2008), plate 30.2.
94. Julia A.B. Hegewald, "The Multiple Meanings of Manuscripts in Jaina Art and Sacred Space," in *Jaina Painting and Manuscript Culture*, ed. Julia A.B. Hegewald (Berlin: EB-Verlag, 2015), 75–77.
95. On the Ambika Mātā temple, see R.C. Agrawal, "Khajuraho of Rajasthan: The Temple of Ambika Mātā at Jagat," *Arts Asiatiques* 10, no. 1 (1964): 43–65; more recently, Deborah L. Stein, *The Hegemony of Heritage* (Oakland: University of California Press, 2018), esp. 30–41.
96. I suggest a temporal sequence between the two scenes based on the notion of clockwise circumambulation around a temple.
97. Alchi's three-storied temple (*sum-tsek*) is famous for its murals, which have been a subject of a number of book-length documentations and studies. See, for example, Roger Goepper, *Alchi: Ladakh's Hidden Buddhist Sanctuary: The Sumtsek* (Boston: Shambhala, 1996); and Peter van Ham, *Alchi Treasure of the Himalayas: Ladakh's Buddhist Masterpiece* (Munich: Hirmer Verlag, 2018). Sumtsek's date is under debate.
98. Christian Luczanits, "The Life of the Buddha in the Sumtsek," *Orientations* 30, no. 1 (1999): 30–39. For an image, see http://luczanits.net/pictures/AlchiMaitreya/source/alchists_jp84_0109.html.
99. Chapter 41 of the *Pauṣkarasamhitā*, from Florinda De Simini, *Of Gods and Books: Ritual and Knowledge Transmission in the Manuscript Cultures of Premodern India* (Berlin: De Gruyter, 2016).
100. "Having revered in a propitious maṇḍala the manuscript lying on a *śarayantra* seat (*śarayantrāsane sthitam*), [both] the exemplar and the apograph, [he] will worship the teacher, the knowledge, Hari."—*Agnipurāṇa* 1.63.10, from De Simini, *Of Gods and Books*, 350.
101. These slabs at Bodhgaya may relate to funerary rites performed at the site for the deceased.
102. Masahide Mori, *Vajrāvalī of Abhayākaragupta* (Tring, UK: Institute of Buddhist Studies, 2009), 23.
103. For the relationship between the VA and the painted manuscripts, see chapter 3 herein.
104. Thomas E. Donaldson, *Iconography of the Buddhist Sculpture of Orissa* (New Delhi: Indira Gandhi National Centre for the Arts, 2001), figure 422. In Donaldson's photograph, there is an additional scene with devotees on the very bottom register that depicts food offerings and an incense burner. This scene is now covered by the pedestal.
105. A balustrade pillar is not a common functional element on surviving Odishan temple architecture, but it does appear frequently in depictions of architecture in sculptural programs, especially of secular architecture or those relating to the human realms.
106. The text was completed in 1169–70 CE. Bhabatosh Bhattacharya, ed., *Dānasāgara of Ballāla Sena* (Calcutta: Asiatic Society, 1956), introduction, xxiii; McHugh, "Hindu Love of Writing, and the Manuscript as Event."
107. In her study of artistic treatises, Isabella Nardi argues, "at this theoretical level of the creative process there is no textual boundary between sculpture and painting." While we should caution against an

ahistorical reading of Sanskrit treatises that Nardi's study adopts, her observation may be expanded further to include architecture. Most of these Sanskrit treatises, in fact, concern buildings. Isabella Nardi, "Re-evaluating the Role of Text in Indian Art," *South Asia Research* 29, no. 2 (2009): 104.

CHAPTER 3. VISIONS ON THE MOVE

1. The ultimate goal of these Esoteric Buddhist practices is to attain a state of being akin to the Buddha, realizing *śūnyatā*, in one's body. The ritual technique of identifying with one's chosen deity as articulated in *sādhana* practices was developed to help a practitioner on this goal.
2. We do not have much historical information about these lineages in late Indian Buddhist circles. Later Tibetan hagiographies report a number of tantric and/or teaching lineages of great Indian Buddhist masters in Tibetan Buddhism. Some *sādhana*s identify the originator of the vision, which may have been of a lineage master. The selective employment of specific types of images suggest that images may have been used to signal the patrons' initiation into a specific lineage. A guru-disciple relationship made a central tenet of any tantric community's operation in premodern South Asia.
3. The biography was written in 1688 by Ngaripa Sanggye Phuntsho (mNga' ris pa Sangs rgyas phun tshogs, 1649–1705), twenty-fifth abbot of the Ngor monastery.
4. Sangs rgyas phun tshogs, 254.5 (60b–61a), as cited in David Jackson, *The Nepalese Legacy in Tibetan Painting* (New York: Rubin Museum of Art, 2010), 184.
5. The monastic complex was completely destroyed in 1966. Rebuilding and reconstruction took place in 1985.
6. Although the paintings have been known since the 1960s, their identity as a group was only recognized in the 1990s. David Jackson first identified this group as belonging to Ngor monastery in his 1996 study. Despite Ngorchen's efforts to order them, confusion persists over the individual identification of the paintings. For example, a painting in the Philadelphia Museum of Art (1994-148-636) is published as catalog number 21, "Four Cakrasaṃvara Mandalas from a Vajrāvalī Set," in *Wisdom and Compassion* (1991), but the painting illustrated in the published catalog presents a different painting from the same set of the same museum's collection (1994-148-635); the illustrated painting contains four Hevajra maṇḍalas. Also, in Rae Dachille's recent dissertation on the polemics between Ngorchen and Mkhas grub rje, figure 5 is identified and discussed as the Four Hevajra Mandalas painting in the Philadelphia Museum of Art (1994-148-635); however, the image depicts a painting in the Zimmerman collection bearing three maṇḍalas of Vajrayogini and one Hevajra maṇḍala.
7. The painting now in the Kimbell Museum of Art (AP 2000.01) is the fourteenth painting in the series, and it contains one maṇḍala from the VA cycle: the Pañcarakṣā maṇḍala (VA18). The other three are drawn from the *Kriyāsamuccaya* (= KS). The KS is an extended compilation by Darpaṇācārya, a Buddhist master who was active in the mid-twelfth century. The KS combines the entire text of the *Niṣpannayogāvalī* (NsP) with the VA. Gudrun Bühnemann, "Some Remarks on the Text of the Niṣpannayogāvalī as Found in Jagaddarpaṇa's Kriyāsamuccaya," *Zentralasiatische Studien des Seminars für Sprach-und Kulturwissenschaft Zentralsiens der Universität Bonn* 22–24 (1992): 20. Three maṇḍalas in the Kimbell painting follow those described in the KS, the *Grahamātṛkā-svatsyayana-vidhi* (KS 428–433), the *Vasudhārā dhāraṇī pāṭha-vidhi* (KS 433–436), and the *Uṣṇīṣavijayā pāṭhavidhi* (KS 436–441). In the exhibition catalog *Wisdom and Compassion*, the first of these is inaccurately identified as "the mandala of the Bhagavati Mahavidya." Marylin M. Rhie and Robert A.F. Thurman, *Wisdom and Compassion: The Sacred Art of Tibet* (New York: Asian Art Museum and Tibet House with Abrams, 1991), 227.

8. The Kālacakra maṇḍala is the eleventh painting in the series, and the Ṣaṭcakravarti-maṇḍala is the eighth. The former appears as the twenty-sixth maṇḍala in the VA and the latter is the twenty-fifth. The order of maṇḍalas in the Ngor VA series is similar to the arrangement of maṇḍalas by an eighteenth-century Mongolian Gelugpa scholar, Changkya Qutuytu Ngawang Lozang Chöden (lCang skya ngag dbang blo bzang chos ldan) in his "The stages of practice of the rituals of the NsP and VA, set out so as to be easy to practice," rDzog 'phreng dang rdor 'phreng gnyis kyi cho ga phyag len gyi rim pa lag tu blangs bde bar dgod pa, TTP, No. 6236, Vol. 162, 184.5.7ff. The complete set would have had forty-four maṇḍalas with slight variation in their order.
9. Rae Erin Dachille, "The Body Mandala Debate: Knowing the Body through a Network of Fifteenth-Century Tibetan Buddhist Texts" (PhD diss., University of California at Berkeley, 2015), xxii. Dachille calls him the "hero of the Sakyapa legacy" (x).
10. Dachille, "Body Mandala Debate," xxi–xxv; Jackson, *Nepalese Legacy in Tibetan Painting;* Michael Henss, *The Cultural Monuments of Tibet,* 2 vols. (Munich: Prestel, 2014), 689–94.
11. David Jackson refers to the Newar-inspired art in Tibet as the "Beri style."
12. Nepal was a center of Sanskrit manuscript production—Sanskrit seems to have been preferred over Newar literary outputs. See Kim, "Performing Texts, Engendering Merits: Manuscripts and Paubhas as Ritual Objects," in *Dharma and Puṇya: Buddhist Ritual Art of Nepal,* edited by Jinah Kim and Todd Lewis (Leiden: Hotei Publishing, 2019), 90, 95.
13. Masahide Mori, "The *Vajrāvalī* of Abhayākaragupta: A Critical Study, Sanskrit Edition of Selected Chapters and Complete Tibetan Version" (PhD diss., SOAS, University of London, 1999), 102.
14. See Ronald M. Davidson, *Indian Esoteric Buddhism: A Social History of the Tantric Movement* (New York: Columbia University Press, 2002).
15. Mori, "Vajrāvalī," 49.
16. Benoytosh Bhattacharyya's effort makes it seem as if there were a single tradition; however, as English (*Vajrayoginī: A Study of Her Visualizations, Rituals, and Forms*) demonstrates partly based on Bünemann's earlier study, there were at least two or three different compilations.
17. This is the Manuscript B in Mori, "Vajrāvalī," 105. He corrects Sastri's reading and suggests a date of 1530 CE (N.S. 650), but this is erroneous. First of all, the number appearing right before the end of the text colophon is unlikely to be a date. And it does read 250. Paleographic features with clear proto-Bengali elements, such as the placement of medial vowels over a letter and the size of the manuscript, consistently suggest a twelfth-century date. Writings on the blank recto side of the first folio are in two different Newari hands.
18. Drawing a deeper connection between *śilpaśāstra*s and the tantric vision text can lead to further historical understanding of both genres of texts. As Felix Otter notes in his study of the *Samarāṅgaṇa-sūtradhāra,* an eleventh-century architectural treaty attributed to Pramara king Bhoja (c. 1010–1055 CE), "the meaning of technical architectural terms in Sanskrit is not as fixed as it is in most modern languages." Felix Otter, *Residential Architecture in Bhoja's Samarāṅgaṇa-sūtradhāra* (Delhi: Motilal Banarsidass, 2010), 38. Bearing in mind such an awareness of temporally and spatially specific architectural practices when closely reading technical manuals will help us to understand the artistic practices that informed the general shape and form of maṇḍalas used in tantric vision practices.
19. A tenth-century Dunhuang diagram of the Vajradhātu maṇḍala, Pelliot 4518 (33), survives with interesting color marks; another example, Pelliot Chinois 2102, actually has color notations. See Michelle M. Wang, "Changing Conceptions of 'Mandala' in Tang China: Ritual and the Role of Images," *Material Religion* 9, no. 2 (2013): 186–217.

20. The images of maṇḍalas are taken from the *Rin-'byung sNar-thaṅ-brgya-rtsa rDor-'phreṅ bcas-nas gsuṅs-pa'i bris-sku: Mthoṅ-ba don ldan bzhugs-so,* composed by the fourth Panchen Lama, Tenpei Nyima (Bstan pa'i ni ma phyogs las rnam rgyal, 1781–1854). In 1810, he traveled to Mongolia from Tibet. On this occasion or "to mark this occasion, a set of block prints was commissioned depicting the deities of three great cycles of empowerments. They comprised 507 small images, printed three to a page in the usual loose-leaf format of Tibetan books." Raghu Vira and Lokesh Chandra, eds., *Tibetan Maṇḍalas: Vajrāvalī and Tantra-Samuccaya* (New Delhi: International Academy of Indian Culture, 1995). These xylographs have been hand painted in color. A copy is now in the University of Zurich collection. Lokesh Chandra's reproductions are from a set that he originally claimed was purchased by his father, Raghu Vira, from a monk in Ulan Bator in 1956. This set is also known as the "Five Hundred Gods of Narthang," but they were not from Narthang. The Tibetan title actually translates to "Icons worthwhile to see." Also see the bibliographic reference on https://www.tbrc.org/#!rid = W1PD159377.
21. Luis Gómez provides a full translation of the text and divides the actions into fourteen headings. Luis O. Gómez, "Two Tantric Meditations: Visualizing the Deity," in *Buddhism in Practice,* ed. Donald Lopez Jr. (Princeton, NJ: Princeton University Press, 1995).
22. Gómez, "Two Tantric Meditations," 319.
23. For example, in the Vajravārāhī-sādhana composed by Umāpatideva, the Four Meditation stages (Bhāvanākramas) present increasingly complex visual programs. Elizabeth English, *Vajrayoginī: A Study of Her Visualizations, Rituals, and Forms* (Boston: Wisdom Publications, 2002), 109–204.
24. For example, the fourfold meditation stages of the Vajravārāhī sādhana and the exceptionally large number of deities in the Kālacakra.
25. Other verbs include "√dhyai" (to imagine, meditate) and "√bhū" (to be, become), both of which are used in the imperative.
26. The first type of interpretation prevailed in early scholarship on Tibetan *thangka*s. See the discussion in Donald S. Lopez Jr., *Prisoners of Shangri-La: Tibetan Buddhism and the West* (Chicago: University of Chicago Press, 1999), 135–55. The second interpretation has gained popularity in recent decades. See the discussion in Robert H. Sharf and Elizabeth H. Sharf, *Living Images: Japanese Buddhist Icons in Context* (Stanford, CA: Stanford Univeristy Press, 2001).
27. Michael Willis, "Avalokiteśvara of the Six Syllables: Locating the Practice of the 'Great Vehicle' in the Landscape of Central India," *Bulletin of the Asia Institute,* n.s., 23 (2009): 226.
28. Willis, "Avalokiteśvara of the Six Syllables."
29. Willis.
30. The sādhana clearly distinguishes the position of these attributes vis-à-vis the body, for example, being held in the left hand versus being placed on the left side.
31. Placed in a manuscript of the *Perfection of Wisdom sūtra,* along with five other painted panels of "Wisdom deities" strategically placed in the beginning, the middle, and the end, it is unlikely that the folio would have been singled out for such a practice. The six painted panels do not form a known sequence or a maṇḍala.
32. English, *Vajrayoginī,* 227.
33. The audibility of these sounds was not important, however, as these mantras and prayers were often supposed to be muttered. As observed in today's rituals by Newar Buddhist masters (*Vajrācāryas*), these sounds were probably neither audible nor were they comprehensible. The point was to create unordinary sounds, outside of a common speech pattern.
34. English, *Vajrayoginī,* 242–43.

35. Mori ("Vajrāvalī of Abhayākaragupta") provides a useful introduction to the text and the Sanskrit and Tibetan editions. Also see Masahide Mori, "The Installation Ceremony in Tantric Buddhism," in *From Materials to Deity: Indian Rituals of Consecration,* ed. Shingo Einoo and Jun Takashima (New Delhi: Manohar Publishers, 2005), 199–237.
36. Abhayākaragupta begins his text by identifying the fifty rituals for maṇḍala construction; this topic comprises more than one-third of the VA. Mori, "Vajrāvalī," 49–50.
37. Mori, "Installation Ceremony," 214.
38. Donald Lopez Jr. characterizes this enactment aspect as: "The tantric sādhana is . . . the making of the world of the Mahāyāna sūtras." Lopez, *Elaborations on Emptiness: Uses of the Heart Sūtra* (Princeton, NJ: Princeton University Press, 1998), 116. For example, see the video footages of Newar Buddhist rituals compiled on the exhibition website for "Dharma and Puṇya: Buddhist Ritual Art of Nepal," https://dharmapunya2019.org/rituals/.
39. As should be clear from the imperative mood expressed in verbs, sādhanas are prescriptive not descriptive.
40. Christian Luczanits, *Buddhist Sculpture in Clay: Early Western Himalayan Art, Late 10th to Early 13th Centuries* (Chicago: Serindia Publications, 2004), 128–37.
41. According to Buston's own writing, he "traced the outlines together with the explicative inscriptions, of the paintings of four sides of the temple Zhva lu," and "laid more than 70 maṇḍalas of the Kalachakra and of the yoga tantras, chiefly the Vajradhātu," and drew plans of 500 maṇḍalas of various tantric cycles." Henss, *Cultural Monuments,* 616–17; Sarah Aiofe Richardson, "Painted Books for Plaster Walls: Visual Words in the Fourteenth-Century Murals at the Tibetan Buddhist Temple of Shalu" (PhD diss., University of Toronto, 2016).
42. Nālandā murals are published in black-and-white plates, and the issue of color is rarely addressed. For example, Gouriswar Bhattacharya in his analysis of the murals discusses the iconography without ever mentioning the colors used. G. Bhattacharya, "The Newly Discovered Buddhist Temple at Nalanda," *South Asian Archaeology* 2 (1995). One wonders if he has even seen the murals in person. Existing scholarship on eastern Indian Buddhist art tends to be color blind. Perhaps due to the nature of surviving material, there is little to no attention paid to the issue of color, as if color information is superfluous to the whole discourse that focuses solely on the discussion of iconography. As we will see in the next chapter, color is essential in tantric vision practices. By recognizing the importance and significance of color in esoteric Buddhism as it was practiced in India, we do get to a deeper understanding of the history of Indian painting during 1100–1500 CE and the legacy of Indic Buddhist traditions on that history's later development.
43. A similar trend is found in Christian medieval manuscripts. See the discussion in Jeffrey Hamburger, "The Iconicity of Script: Writing as Image in the Middle Ages," *Word and Image* 23, no. 3 (2011): 259–61.
44. As Hamburger eloquently explains in his discussion of female spirituality in medieval Christian art, the "nondiscursive" does not mean that the practice assumes an illiterate, ignorant audience. See Jeffrey Hamburger, *The Visual and the Visionary: Art and Female Spirituality in Late Medieval Germany* (New York: Zone Books, 1998), 29; 110–48.
45. This is an imagined scenario inspired by the sequence of flashing images in animated features, like Nina Paley's *Sita Sings the Blues* (2008). www.sitasingstheblues.com/watch.html. See also a series of recent works by Chitra Ganesh, "Face of the Future" and "The Scorpion Gesture," at the Rubin Museum http://rubinmuseum.org/events/exhibitions/chitra-ganesh. Ganesh embraces digital animation to make historical examples of religious art more widely meaningful.

46. See Ronald Davidson, *Tibetan Renaissance: Tantric Buddhism in the Rebirth of Tibetan Culture* (New York: Columbia University Press, 2005).
47. Taisho no. 2056, vol. 50: 292c. For an English translation of the passage, see Paul Copp, *The Body Incantatory: Spells and the Ritual Imagination in Medieval Chinese Buddhism* (New York: Columbia University Press, 2014), 137 and n. 77.
48. Salomon identifies these features as indicating the "influence of pen-and-ink writing on the epigraphic script." Richard Salomon, *Indian Epigraphy: A Guide to the Study of Inscriptions in Sanskrit, Prakrit, and the Other Indo-Aryan Language* (Oxford: Oxford University Press, 1998), 39–40.
49. It is important to separate and trace the historical development of scripts of the Siddhamātṛkā type. The term *siddhaṃ* and *siddhamātṛkā* are often used rather indiscriminately when there are many local and temporal varieties. This work remains to be done. Also see the discussion in Salomon, *Siddham across Asia: How the Buddha Learned His ABC* (Amsterdam: J. Gonda Fund Foundation of the KNAW, 2015).
50. The literal meaning of the *Prajñāpāramitā* text, however, is difficult to comprehend, as the long-standing commentarial literature on the *Prajñāpāramitā* demonstrates. Whether a scribe copying the text, or the donor, would have understood the doctrinal aspect of the text, line by line, is doubtful. However limited and superficial, it is likely that the chapter headings and the general gist of the text were understood. On the other hand, the *Pañcarakṣā* manuscripts exemplify the writing down of meaningless syllables in an ornamental script for the apotropaic efficacy of the text. The *Pañcarakṣā* contains mantras and dhāraṇīs with many letters that are meaningful only for their phonetic values.
51. Steven M. Kossak and Jane Casey Singer, *Sacred Visions: Early Paintings from Central Tibet* (New York: Metropolitan Museum of Art, 1998), 173–77.
52. Gudrun Bühnemann, "Erotic Forms of Gaṇeśa in Hindu and Buddhist Iconography," in *Script and Image: Papers on Art and Epigraphy,* ed. A. Gail, G. Mevissen, and R. Salomon (Delhi: Motilal Banarsidass, 2006), 15–28.
53. This mantra is understood to be the mantra of Padmasambhava (Guru Rinpoche) in the Nyingma tradition. This is followed by "*oṃ āḥ namovajradharaya huṃ svāhā| oṃ munimunimahāmunaho svāhā|*" Most of the text is indeed dedicated to Gaṇapati. The mantras seem to be extended variations on the version of mantras in the Gaṇapati sādhanam (SM 307, 592–93).
54. The parallel drawn between the book and the body is hardly unique in the medieval Indian materials. For the discussion of the relationship between body and book in Christian materials, see Jeffrey Hamburger, "Body vs. Book: The Trope of Visibility in Images of Christian-Jewish Polemic," in *Ästhetik des Unsichtbaren: Bildtheorie und Bildgebrauch in der Vormoderne,* ed. David Ganz and Thomas Lentes (Berlin: Reimer 2004), 112–45.
55. For the iconographic scheme, see table C.6 in Karen Weissenborn, *Buchkunst aus Nālandā: Die Asaṭasāhasrikā Prajñāpāramitā-Handschrift in der Royal Asiatic Society, London (Ms. Hodgson 1) und Ihre Stellung in der Pāla-Buchmalerei des 11./12. Jahrhunderts* (Vienna: Universität Wien, 2012), 114. A painted panel from the manuscript is published as figure 50. For the book covers in the private collection, see figure 49. Weissenborn dates the manuscript as late twelfth century. Weissenborn, *Buchkunst aus Nālandā,* 73–74. Also see Francesco Sferra, ed., *Sanskrit Texts from Giuseppe Tucci's Collection* (Rome: Istituto Italiano per l'Africa e l'Orient, 2008), 66, figures 18–21.
56. A number of recent studies supports this general characterization. In late tenth-century Tibetan manuscripts of the Mahāyoga from Dunhuang, Sam Van Schaik finds clear indication of the prevalent use of "prajñāpāramitā-based discourse." Sam Van Schaik, "A Definition of Mahāyoga: Sources from

the Dunhuang Manuscripts," *Tantric Studies* 1 (2008): 54–55. Also see Gregory Max Seton, "Integrating Non-Tantric and Tantric Doctrines through Prajñāpāramitā at Vikramaśīla during the Mid-Eleventh Century," paper presented at the XVIIth Congress of International Association of Buddhist Studies, Toronto, University of Toronto, August 2017.

57. English, *Vajrayoginī,* 231. Luis Gómez's translation of the Tārā-sādhana has it: "*Oṃ,* I in my true self am of the nature of [this] diamond of the knowledge of emptiness."

58. Mori, "Vajrāvalī"; Yong-Hyun Lee, "『금강의 화환』(Vajrāvalī)에서 관정(灌頂)에 대한 아바야카라굽타의 해석 (Abhayākaragupta's Interpretations on the Consecration Ceremony of the Vajrāvalī)," 인도연구 (*Journal of the Korean Association for Indian Studies*) 17, no. 1 (2012): 51–84.

59. I was first drawn to the VA's connection with painted manuscripts due to a passing remark by D.C. Bhattacharyya. D.C. Bhattacharyya, "The *Vajrāvalī-nāma-maṇḍalopāyikā* of Abhayākaragupta," in *Tantric and Taoist Studies in Honour of R.A. Stein,* ed. Michel Strickmann (Brussels: Institut Belge des Hautes Etudes Chinoises, 1981), 73. Unfortunately, his translation is inaccurate; the text does not state that manuscripts were painted.

60. This relationship requires much more space to explore than possible here. Anna Ślączka's book is a step closer to using *śāstra* texts for understanding artistic practices. Anna A. Ślączka, *Temple Consecration Rituals in Ancient India: Text and Archaeology* (Leiden: Brill, 2007). Also see Sheldon Pollock, "The Idea of Śāstra in Traditional India," in *Shastric Traditions in Indian Arts,* ed. Anna L. Dallapiccola et al. (Stuttgart: Steiner Verlag Wiesbaden, 1989).

61. "At the end of the procedure of both rituals, the guru must satisfy the craftsman (śilpinoṣaṇa) and the scribe with food, just as he does in the case of the construction of a building." This is explained in the "preliminary ritual for the construction of buildings." According to Mori, "This is done because the Tantric Buddhists followed the traditional architectural rituals whenever devising the ritual procedure for the maṇḍala construction." Mori, "Vajrāvalī," 82.

62. As Masahide Mori explains, the installation ceremony in the VA is "a particular type of consecration or empowerment of statues, buildings, books, or other religious artifacts after they have been produced." Mori, "Vajrāvalī," 82.

63. Mori, " Installation Ceremony," 207.

64. The concept of pledge-being is difficult to grasp. Alex Wayman follows Tsongkhapa's explanation in the *sNgags rim chen mo* and explains it as "the yogin who has identified himself with a deity he has evoked or imagined." F.D. Lessing and A. Wayman, eds., *Introduction to the Buddhist Tantric Systems* (Delhi: Motilal Banarsidass, 1978), 162–63. According to VA usage, the term seems to indicate the transcendent being to be invoked for visualization.

65. Mori, "Vajrāvalī," 84; this is a loose translation of the passage cited by D.C. Bhattacharya, also a VA manuscript in CUL, folio 5v–6r, CUL Add. 1703, N.S. 549 (1429 CE).

66. The term Mori translates as "sacred text" is *pustaka.* To indicate the material quality of particular items, I take this term more straightforwardly as "manuscript" or "book."

67. The only exception among the dated examples mentioned here is Am_2.

68. For the discussion of the significance of narrative panels depicting the Buddha's biography in the *Prajñāpāramitā* manuscripts, see Kim, *Receptacle of the Sacred,* 73–87.

69. In my earlier study, I've identified this manuscript as the late tenth-century manuscript, one of the earliest surviving eastern Indian example. Jinah Kim, *Receptacle of the Sacred: Illustrated Manuscripts and the Buddhist Book-Cult in South Asia* (Berkeley: University of California Press, 2013), 223–24. In light of the historical trend identified here, which places Amitābha's inclusion in an AsP (Aṣṭasāhasrikā

Prajñāpāramitā) manuscript mostly in the twelfth century, it seems possible to reconsider the date of the colophon as Mahīpāla II's reign year, thus of the late eleventh century rather than the late tenth century. If it belongs to Mahīpāla I's reign, the makers of this manuscript truly set the "archetypal pattern" for the production of painted Prajñāpāramitā manuscripts in eastern India.

70. Jinah Kim, "Unheard Voices: Women's Roles in Medieval Buddhist Artistic Production and Religious Practices in South Asia." *Journal of the American Academy of Religion* 80, no. 1 (2012): 200–232.
71. Jinah Kim, "Emptiness on Palm Leaf: A Twelfth-Century Illustrated Manuscript of the 'Aṣṭasāhasrikā Prajñāpāramitā,'" *Bulletin of the Detroit Institute of Arts* 82, no. 1/2 (2008): 76–91.
72. Unfortunately, he does not explain why a specific *tathāgata* should be invoked for a specific category of objects, for example, Amitābha for a book or Vairocana for a monastery. There may be a commentarial literature on this aspect that awaits further exploration.

CHAPTER 4. A GARLAND OF VISIONS

1. Eva Allinger, "A Pāla-Period *Aṣṭasāhasrikā Prajñāpāramitā* Manuscript Distributed between Five Collections," *Vienna Journal of South Asian Studies* 51 (2007–8): 77–121.
2. Jinah Kim, *Receptacle of the Sacred: Illustrated Manuscripts and the Buddhist Book-Cult in South Asia* (Berkeley: University of California Press, 2013), 149–57.
3. I use the term "seriality" in a sense of having a sequential order. The term's usage in the modernist discourse is worth remembering given its decentralized, paradoxical significance. See Briony Fer, *The Infinite Line: Re-Making Art after Modernism* (New Haven, CT: Yale University Press, 2004); Firat Oruc, "Plebeianization, Un/Bound Seriality, and Global Modernism," *Criticism* (2013): 279–97. This parallels my juxtaposition of the term against the concept of maṇḍala, which is centralized and hierarchic.
4. The full title is given as "Icons Worthwhile to See, Taught in the Rinjung and Narthang Gyatsas and the Vajrāvalī (*Rin-'byuṅ sNar-thaṅ brgya-rtsa rDor-'phreṅ bcas-nas gsuṅs-pa'i bris-sku: Mthoṅ-ba don-ldan*)." The basis of this pictorial compendium came into being in eighteenth-century Mongolia, to illustrate the Rin-lhan by the Panchen Lama bLo-bzaṅ bsTan-pa'i ni-ma. Martin Willson, *Deities of Tibetan Buddhism: The Zürich Paintings of the Icons Worthwhile to See* (Somerville, MA: Wisdom, 2001), 3.
5. On the uniqueness of the "Tantric Devī series," see Terrence McInerney, "Mysterious Origins: The Tantric Devi Series from Basohli," in *Devi: The Great Goddess,* ed. Vidya Dehejia (Washington, DC: Smithsonian Institution, 1999), 119–35.
6. Vidya Dehejia, *Devi: The Great Goddess, Female Divinity in South Asian Art* (Washington, DC: Smithsonian Institution, 1999), 271.
7. Entries in the *Devi* catalog have it that the meaning will remain elusive until the meditational insight of the trained devotee comes to light. Dehejia, *Devi: The Great Goddess*, 272.
8. See the discussion in chapter 2 on Nepalese manuscripts of the DM. See also the discussion of the Punjab Hills and the trans-Himalayan manuscript culture zone connection in the introduction.
9. Sachindra Nath Siddhanta, *A Descriptive Catalogue of Sanskrit Manuscripts in the Varendra Research Museum Library,* vol. 1 (Rajshahi: Varendra Research Museum, 1979), 385.
10. The folios from this manuscript were included in the *Chefs-d'oeuvre du delta du Gange* exhibition scheduled to be held at the Musée Guimet, Paris. The exhibition was canceled, but the exhibition catalog was published. Vincent Lefèvre takes the date of the colophon as *terminus post quem* and gives the date of the manuscript as pre-1273. Vincent Lefèvre and Marie-Françoise Boussac, *Chefs-d'oeuvre du Delta du Gange: Collections des musées du Bangladesh* (Paris: Musée Guimet, 2007), 220.

11. Gudrun Melzer and Eva Allinger, "Die Nepalesische Palmblatthandschrift der Aṣṭasāhasrikā Prajñāpāramitā aus dem Jahr Ns 268 (1148 Ad), Teil Ii," *Indo Asiatische Zeitschrift* 20 (2012); Tanaka Kimiaki, "「インドの仏」展に出品された『八千頌般若経』装飾写本について (the Sanskrit Manuscript of the Aṣṭasāhasrikā- Prajñāpāramitā Exhibited at the Exhibition 'Indian Buddhist Art')," *東洋文化研究所紀要* 169.
12. The present whereabouts of folio 310, which would have a painted panel bearing a multiarmed tantric male deity, is unknown. Another remaining unaccounted-for folio is folio 531 bearing Vasudhārā and the original colophon.
13. See Kim, *Receptacle of the Sacred,* figure 5.8.
14. See, for example, a *Pañcarakṣā* manuscript dated Govindapāla's sixteenth year (1177 CE) in the National Archives collection in Kathmandu (Acc. No. 5.83).
15. Touching and holding each folio almost feels like handling a tightly woven, smooth fabric.
16. The original cord or metal rods holding the folios together do(es) not survive. The manuscript is kept together using a cord tied around the whole stack placed between two wooden protective boards. It is difficult to lift it up.
17. David L. Snellgrove, *The Hevajra Tantra: A Critical Study,* 2 vols. (London: Oxford University Press, 1959), 115; Pratapaditya Pal and Julia Meech-Pekarik, *Buddhist Book Illuminations* (New York: Ravi Kumar 1988), 31.
18. In fact, the ratio between the height of the stack (11.5 m, with additional folios and book covers, originally over 12 cm) and the width of each folio, 6.3 cm, is not far from the ratio recommended for an ablution altar for an installation ceremony in the VA.
19. This is achieved by allotting the whole area between the two columns that are usually divided up to accommodate a painted panel in the middle of the text.
20. See the discussion in chapter 3.
21. Allinger, "A Pāla-Period Aṣṭasāhasrikā Prajñāpāramitā."
22. The image is available at www.himalayanart.org/items/65003. According to the entry, this painting is part of a Vajrāvalī series commissioned for the fifth Dalai Lama mentioned in David Paul Jackson, *A History of Tibetan Painting* (Vienna: Verlag der Österreichischen Akademie der Wissenschaften, 1996). This image follows closely the description given by Jamgon Amezhab (c. 1597–1659).
23. Color terms are discussed in chapter 5.
24. The text is particular about the order of the attributes as it describes it. Also see the translation in Alex Wayman, *Yoga of the Guhyasamājatantra: The Arcane Lore of Forty Verses; A Buddhist Tantra Commentary* (Delhi: Motilal Banarsidass, 1977), 126–30.
25. The text of the NsP 2 is particularly specific about the color of the lotus for each tathāgata. Ratnasambhava's is a yellow lotus (*pita padma*), Amitābha's is a red lotus (*rakta padma*), and Amoghasiddhi's is a green lotus (*harita padma*). Akṣobhya's lotus is not identified by color but just given plainly as "*padma,*" which in nature may easily be reddish pink. Vairocana's lotus is described as "*puṇḍarīka,*" which seems to refer to a white lotus.
26. As seen in figure 4.6, folio 28v is in the Indian Museum, Kolkata. Figure 4.6 is a composite image, which intentionally unites the dispersed folios together.
27. This method of using a manuscript's interior space, that is, on pages of the manuscript strategically for containing Esoteric Buddhist deities, began to develop during the twelfth century. See Kim, *Receptacle of the Sacred,* 149–201.
28. See www.himalayanart.org/items/65115.

29. Iain Sinclair, "Envisioning Durjayacandra's Saptākṣarasādhana: On the Sources and Sponsors of a Twelfth-Century Painting of Seven-Syllabled SaṃVara," in *Himalayan Passages: Tibetan and Newar Studies in Honor of Hubert Decleer*, ed. Benjamin Bogin and Andrew Quintman (Boston: Wisdom 2014), 205–50.
30. The description reads, "the deity, the lord of this maṇḍala is four-legged, with two in *ardhaparyaṅka*, and two in *alīḍha*, with a matted hairdo with a five-buddha crown (*pañcabuddha mukuṭa*), dark blue or black (*kṛṣṇa*) in color, and sixteen armed and eight faced: the first face is red and three eyed, the root face is *kṛṣṇa*, the rest to the right is *sita* (white)-*kṛṣṇa* (blue black) and *kṛṣṇa*, and the left side is *rakta-kṛṣṇa* and *kṛṣṇa*. The top head is *dhūmra* (gray/smoky)," NsP, 20. Translation by author.
31. "*asya prajñā nairātmā nagnā kṛṣṇā kartrikapālāñcitasavyavāmabhujābhyāṁ bhagavantamāliṅgaya pratyalīḍhena nṛtyantī pañcamudriṇī raktavarttulatrinetradaṁṣṭrākarālaikamukhī jvaladūrdhvapiṅgalakeśī lalāṭataṭasthapañcamuṇḍagalāvalambiśuṣkanṛmuṇḍamālānupurādibhuṣitā*|" NsP, 20. Translation by author.
32. J. P. Losty, "An Early Indian Manuscript of the Kāraṇḍavyūhasūtra," in *Studies in Art and Archaeology of Bihar and Bengal*, ed. Debala Mitra and Gouriswar Bhattacharya (Delhi: Sri Satguru Publications, 1989).
33. Wedemeyer suggests that the semiotic possibility of transgressive acts of killing, sexual activities, cannibalism, and bodily engagement with the most polluting and revolting matters signifies a transcendent experience of nondual gnosis. Christian K. Wedemeyer, "Beef, Dog, and Other Mythologies: Connotative Semiotics in Mahāyoga Tantra Ritual and Scripture," *Journal of the American Academy of Religion* 75, no. 2 (2007): 383–417.
34. Ronald Davidson, *Indian Esoteric Buddhism: A Social History of the Tantric Movement* (New York: Columbia Uniersity Press, 2002), 242–43. Davidson uses this story to identify an important locus of the antinomian tantras and to explain the sociopolitical landscape in which these tantras developed.
35. Davidson, *Indian Esoteric Buddhism*, 242–43. The story is from Jñānamitra's *Prajñāpāramitānaya śatapañcāśatka-ṭīkā*.
36. Davidson, *Indian Esoteric Buddhism*, 242–43.
37. Christian K. Wedemeyer, *Making Sense of Tantric Buddhism: History, Semiology, and Transgression in the Indian Traditions* (New York: Columbia University Press, 2013), 189. Wedemeyer follows Sanderson's characterization of the nondual Śaiva tantra.
38. The image is credited as "Accession #851, Rajshahi Museum, Rajshahi, Bangladesh. Photographed by John C. and Susan L. Huntington, June 1994," and he expresses his gratitude to John, Susan, and Eric Huntington for the cover image in his acknowledgments. The image is not discussed anywhere in the book.
39. Snellgrove, *Hevajra Tantra*, 84–85; T 18 n. 892, vol. 3, http://tripitaka.cbeta.org/T18n0892_003.
40. This name along with the female deity's name appears in another similar AsP manuscript now in Mongolia. I thank Gudrun Melzer for this information. This must belong to a manuscript in the National Library of Mongolia. See a folio reproduced in Mark Elliott, Hildegard Diemberger, and Michela Clemente, eds., *Buddha's Word: The Life of Books in Tibet and Beyond* (Cambridge: Museum of Archaeology and Anthropology, 2014), 24.
41. The concept of "Ekapāda," or one-footed form of Śiva, is known from various textual sources, including the *Liṅga purāṇa*, and it is even mentioned as an aspect of Rudra in the Vedas. See Thomas Donaldson, "Ekapāda Śiva Images in Orissan Art," *Ars Orientalis* 13 (1982): 153.
42. This aspect deserves further exploration than is possible here. I am preparing a separate study on the tantric Śaiva-Buddhist relationship as articulated in artistic evidence.

43. Bulcsu Siklós, *The Vajrabhairava Tantras: Tibetan and Mongolian Versions, English Translation and Annotations* (Tring, UK: Institute of Buddhist Studies, 1996).
44. The two brothers and their wives appear on the bottom of this fantastic, large-scale woven maṇḍala. Based on this depiction, the commission of the maṇḍala is proposed to have been between 1328 and 1329, when both brothers were known to exist in harmony before the older brother was poisoned and died. See Patricia Berger, "Preserving the Nation: The Political Uses of Tantric Art in China," in *Latter Days of the Law: Images of Chinese Buddhism, 850–1850*, ed. Marsha Weidner (Lawrence, KS: Spencer Museum of Art, 1994), 104–5. The image is available at the Met's online collection (www.metmuseum.org/art/collection/search/37614).
45. This later Nepalese postcolophon records the patrons' more mundane wish along with the age old Mahāyāna stock phrase regarding the attainment of supreme knowledge by all sentient beings. It is fascinating that the wishes to be fulfilled through the meritorious act of the Prajñāpāramitā pūjā include being reborn in the Sukhavātī heaven. I thank Alexander von Rospatt for his help with the reading of this colophon.
46. For the relationship between individual visions and codified esoteric visual knowledge, see Jinah Kim, "Local Visions, Transcendental Practices: Iconographic Innovations of Indian Esoteric Buddhism," *History of Religions* 54, no. 1 (2014): 34–68; Jinah Kim, "Faceless Gazes, Silent Texts: Images of Devotees and Practices of Vision in Medieval South Asia," *Ars Orientalis* 46 (2016): 198–229.
47. Further exploration of sādhanas used in Nepal and those known in the Tibetan canon can be a fruitful venue of inquiry on this front.

CHAPTER 5. COLOR AS AN ENCODING TOOL

1. Fischinger's abstract animations were inspired by his study of the color theory and his familiarity with Kandinsky's works. Esther Leslie, "Where Abstraction and Comics Collide," *Tate Etc.*, issue 7, summer 2006 (accessed online on May 30, 2018, www.tate.org.uk/context-comment/articles/where-abstraction-and-comics-collide). The excerpt from his *Circles* (Kreise) is available on Vimeo from the Center for Visual Music (https://vimeo.com/55181698). Center for Visual Music, a nonprofit film archive based in Los Angeles, keeps an active research portal on Oskar Fischinger, see www.centerforvisualmusic.org/Fischinger/index.htm. I first learned about Fischinger's work from Jennifer Lynn Peterson at the Getty Research Institute during 2012–13 when the main theme of the scholars program was color.
2. See, for example, the research projects of the Gallant lab at the University of California, Berkeley. http://gallantlab.org/index.php/brain-viewer/.
3. Fischinger's abstract animation, too, is controlled and measured.
4. Such a transhistorical comparison can help explore how the interest in the workings of the mind was harnessed and expressed differently or similarly in medieval South Asia. The current Dalai Lama's serious interest in scientific studies of the brain is well known. Numerous recent and ongoing scientific studies on the brain activities and health benefits of meditation also suggest their commonality.
5. Alexander Huth et al., "Natural Speech Reveals the Semantic Maps That Tile Human Cerebral Cortex," *Nature* 532 (2016): 453–58.
6. http://gallantlab.org/huth2016/.
7. Andrew Skilton, ed., *How the Nagas Were Pleased by Harsha* (New York: New York University Press, 2009), 73. That a piece of red stone is fetched for drawing is also worth noting—the outlines and sketches for figures that we notice in palm-leaf manuscripts were often prepared in reddish brown pigment rather than black charcoal.

8. Although the definition of "*śilā*" includes red arsenic, whether it refers to this specific type of stone is uncertain. Given that this is being fetched from the "mountain" without much delay, this earth-based color could easily have been hematite, that is, red ocher, which would have been a more readily available material. For a study of geological deposits of ochers and white clay in India, see Geovanni Cavallo and Manoj Pandit, "Geology and Petrography of Ochres and White Clay Deposits in Rajasthan State, India," in *Geoarchaeology and Archaeomineralogy,* ed. R.I. Kostov, B. Gaydarska, and M. Gurova (Sofia: Publishing House St. Ivan Rilski, 2008).
9. Skilton, *How the Nagas Were Pleased,* 73.
10. Ronald Inden, "Imperial Purāṇas: Kashmir as Vaiṣṇava Center of the World," in *Querying the Medieval: Text and the History of Practices in South Asia,* ed. Daud Ali, Ronald Inden, and Jonathan Walters (Oxford: Oxford University Press, 2000).
11. Parul Dave Mukherji, ed., *The Citrasūtra of the Viṣṇudharmottara Purāṇa* (New Delhi: Indira Gandhi National Centre for the Arts and Motilal Banarsidass Publishers, 2001), 134.
12. G.K. Shrigondekar, ed., *Mânasollâsa of King Someśvara,* 3 vols. (Baroda: Baroda Oriental Institute, 1939), 2: 15.
13. Teun Goudriaan, *Māyā Divine and Human: A Study of Magic and Its Religious Foundations in Sanskrit Texts, with Particular Attention to a Fragment on Viṣṇu's Māyā Preserved in Bali* (Delhi: Motilal Banarsidass, 1978), 163–210.
14. The absence of color identification in the description of deities indicates an earlier layer in the development of Esoteric Buddhist iconography. Thus, *Aṣṭamahābhāyatārā sādhanam* does not provide any color value for the deity conjectured. Luis O. Gómez, "Two Tantric Meditations: Visualizing the Deity," in *Buddhism in Practice,* ed. Donald S. Lopez Jr. (Princeton, NJ: Princeton University Press, 1995), 320–21.
15. As attested in the early layers of the Pali canon, one of the thirty-two physical traits of the great man (mahāpuruṣa) that the Buddha Śākyamuni is born with is golden color. According to Paul Harrison's study, the *Pratyutpanna-samādhi sūtra,* an early Mahāyāna text that explains the practice of "buddhānusmṛti (lit. recalling the Buddha)," introduces an analogy of a golden image in explaining the visualization method and even makes "clear references to the use of images either two or three dimensional." Paul Harrison, "Commemoration and Identification in Buddhānusmṛti," in *In the Mirror of Memory: Reflections on Mindfulness and Remembrance in Indian and Tibetan Buddhism,* ed. Janet Gyatso (Albany: State University of New York Press, 1992), 222. Also see the passage in T418, 906a, and Harrison's translation in *The Pratyutpanna samādhi sūtra and the Śūraṅgama samādhi sūtra,* BDK English Tripitaka 25-II. 25-III (Numata Center for Buddhist Translation and Research, 1998), 23.
16. Imann Lai, "Scriptures and Images: Sarva-tathāgata-tattva-saṃgraha-nāma-mahā-yāna-sūtra and the Ninth-Century Vajradhātu Maṇḍala Excavated from the Famen Monastery, Xi'an, China," 회당학보 17 (2012): 202. Do-Kyun Kwon, "Sarva Tathāgata Tattva Saṃgraha: Compendium of All the Tathāgatas—a Study of Its Origin, Structure, and Teachings" (PhD diss., SOAS, University of London, 2002). The earliest known manuscript of the STTS has been paleographically proposed to be dated to the ninth century. See Lokesh Chandra and David L. Snellgrove, eds., *Sarva-Tathāgata-tattva Saṅgraha: Facsimile Reproduction of a Tenth-Century Sanskrit Manuscript from Nepal* (New Delhi: Rani, 1981). On Vajrabodhi's name, see the discussion in Iain Sinclair, "The Names of Nāgabuddhi and Vajrabuddhi," in *Esoteric Buddhism in Mediaeval Maritime Asia: Networks of Masters, Texts, Icons,* ed. Andrea Acri (Singapore: ISEAS, 2016).
17. Hudaya Kandahjaya, "Saṅ Hyaṅ Kamahāyānikan, Borobudur, and the Origins of Esoteric Buddhism in Indonesia," in Acri, *Esoteric Buddhism in Mediaeval Maritime Asia.*

18. Elizabeth Ten Grotenhuis, *Japanese Mandalas: Representations of Sacred Geography* (Honolulu: University of Hawai'i Press, 1998). Kuo Liying observes that in the Sino-Japanese tradition, the five colors of the five directions of the two world maṇḍalas are not always identical. Kuo Liying, "Maṇḍala et rituel de confession à Dunhuang," *Bulletin de l'École Française d'Extrême-Orient* 85 (1998): 238.
19. The identification of this ceiling's configuration as five tathāgatas depends heavily on the presence of double Vajra in the center of the ceiling. As seen in the details available on Artstor, http://library.artstor.org.ezp-prod1.hul.harvard.edu/asset/MIDA_104494, their hand gestures are not differentiated, suggesting a local understanding of the five-tathāgata scheme.
20. Even the *Vairocanābhisaṃbodhi sūtra* (T18, no. 848; also known as the Mahavairocana sūtra, MVS), which lays the ground for the Esoteric Buddhist tenets, characterizes color differentiation as arising from mind and treats color as ultimately superficial. In Rolf Giebel's translation, "Everything that is differentiated is all born of the mind; the distinguishing of white, yellow, red, and the like arises from the mind." *The Vairocanābhisaṃbodhi sūtra,* BDK English tripiṭaka series (Numata Center for Buddhist Translation and Research, 2005), 89. T18, no. 848, 22a. I thank the anonymous reader of my book for this reference.
21. As explained later in the chapter, a quantitative analysis of color terms is possible thanks to the digital tripiṭaka tools like the one available through cbeta.org.
22. Whether the entire text of the STTS as known in Sanskrit, Tibetan, and later Chinese translation was known at this time is debatable. Linrothe after Iyanaga suggests that the later portion of the STTS was probably known in the ninth century. Robert N. Linrothe, *Ruthless Compassion: Wrathful Deities in Early Indo-Tibetan Esoteric Buddhist Art* (Boston: Shambhala, 1999), 155–56. He posits that the STTS remained important until the eleventh century. I consider this renewed interest not as a continuation but rather as a reinvigoration with a more systematic attitude toward codification and canonization. A formation date for both the MVS and STTS is proposed as sometime around the early or mid-seventh century. Linrothe, *Ruthless Compassion,* 149.
23. Feng Shi, "自然之色与哲学之色—中国传统方色理论起源研究 (Natural Colors and Philosophical Colors—a Study on the Origin of the Cardinal Direction Color Theory in China)," *考古学报*, 04 (2016). Further research will determine whether a similar system existed in South Asia from as early as Neolithic era. We cannot overlook the possibility of the Chinese five-direction color system traveling westward.
24. In the Chinese system, the yellow color's central position seems to relate to the idea of golden light, and as the color for the emperor.
25. Lilla Bikfalvy Russell-Smith, "Wives and Patrons: Uygur Political and Artistic Influence in Tenth-Century Dunhuang," *Acta Orientalia Academiae Scientiarum Hungaricae* 56, 2/4 (2003): 401–28.
26. Another known example that follows this scheme is a Pelliot 2012 diagram, datable also to the mid-tenth century. Michelle M. Wang, "Changing Conceptions of 'Mandala' in Tang China: Ritual and the Role of Images," *Material Religion* 9, no. 2 (2013): 186–217; Liying, "Mandala et rituel." Liying reports this configuration in a text translated by Faxian during the Song dynasty in the late tenth century. Taisho 19 0939中心用黃色爲八輻輪。東方純白色。南方大青色。西方赤色。北方綠色.
27. A few monochromatic iconographic drawings like this one survive from Dunhuang and are also known in Japan, like the famous example of the *Gobushinkan* scroll. See the discussion in Cynthea Bogel, *With a Single Glance: Buddhist Icon and Early Mikkyō Vision* (Seattle: University of Washington Press, 2009), 74–78.
28. Even as a remote possibility, given the indications seen in the survey of colors in early Esoteric Buddhist material, it may be more reasonable to state that it follows a different model than being "not precisely correct," as Wang puts it. Wang, "Changing Conceptions of 'Maṇḍala,'" 203.

29. Wang, "Changing Conceptions of 'Maṇḍala,'" 203.
30. See the discussion of semiotic limitations of color terms in chapter 6.
31. See the twelfth-century examples in Susan L. Huntington, *The "Pāla-Sena" School of Sculpture* (Leiden: Brill, 1984). Donaldson dates some Odishan images that bear this feature as early as the ninth to tenth centuries, but his dating is not based on a rigorous stylistic analysis or comparative research with dated materials as conducted by Huntington. Thomas E. Donaldson, *Iconography of the Buddhist Sculpture of Orissa* (New Delhi: Indira Gandhi National Centre for the Arts; Abhinav Publications, 2001), figures 284, 305. This observation has already been made by Janice Leoshko among the corpus of sculptures from Bodhgaya. See Janice Leoshko, "Iconography of Buddhist Sculptures" (PhD diss., Ohio State University, 1987), 293.
32. For the painting's stylistic characteristics, see Eva Allinger, "The Green Tārā in the Ford Collection: Some Stylistic Remarks," in *The Inner Asian International Style 12th–14th Centuries* (Vienna: Verlag, 1998), 107–19.
33. The production date of this painting remains controversial. Jane Casey Singer proposes a date between 1057 (foundation date of the Reting monastery) and 1082, while Dan Martin argues for a twelfth-century date, a date between 1164 (foundation date of the Sphyil-phu monastery mentioned in the inscription) and 1175 (Chad-kha-ba). Steven M. Kossak and Jane Casey Singer, *Sacred Visions: Early Paintings from Central Tibet* (New York: Metropolitan Museum of Art, 1998), 54–59; Dan Martin, "Painters, Patrons, and Paintings of Patrons in Early Tibetan Art," in *Embodying Wisdom: Art, Text, and Interpretation in the History of Esoteric Buddhism*, ed. Robert N. Linrothe and Henrik Sørensen (Copenhagen: Seminar for Buddhist Studies, 2001), 139–84. Martin's argument is based on an improved reading of the Tibetan inscriptions on the back of the painting. His translation of *thugs dam* as the "high aspiration" instead of "meditational image" leads him to insist on the painting's production being tied to the person whose *thugs dam* this painting was, which in turn supports his argument for a twelfth-century date. Outright denial of the possibility of *thugs dam* being an actual image, however, seems to close a productive venue of inquiry regarding the relation between art and visionary experience: the distinct possibility of an object being the source of a vision not just the other way around that is frequently assumed in all textual studies of Buddhism.
34. For example, "bright/white" (*śukla*) of some forms of Avalokiteśvara, when Avalokiteśvara belongs to the Amitābha lineage, which is red.
35. The exceptional sheen of the polished black stone in the Tetrawan Tārā may have been an artistic response to the ritual need to have these images visible in "color" through reflexivity of the surface, as discussed in chapter 3.
36. Eva Allinger ("The Epsilon 1 Manuscript in the Wellcome Library, London") proposed a later date for this manuscript arguing that it was a Nepalese copy that retained its original colophon. While it is not completely impossible, it is most likely that this manuscript was in fact prepared in eastern India rather than in Nepal. See the discussion in Kim, "Illustrated Buddhist Manuscripts," in *History of Bangladesh: Early Bengal in Regional Perspectives (up to ca. 1200 CE)*, ed. Abdul Momin Chowdhury and Ranabir Chakravarti (Dhaka: The Asiatic Society of Bangladesh, 2018), 509–34.
37. Jinah Kim, *Receptacle of the Sacred: Illustrated Manuscripts and the Buddhist Book-Cult in South Asia* (Berkeley: University of California Press, 2013), 149–212.
38. As discussed in chapter 6, the palm-leaf surface was primed with a layer of white pigments. This white layer appears thicker and more opaque in most twelfth-century painted palm-leaf manuscripts.

39. The verse serves as a dharma relic, and it was customary to "attach" this relic at the end of the text, identified as a religious donation, to sanctify the act.

40. Examples include: the painted panel of folio 37r in a manuscript dated N.S. 191 (1071 CE), in the Asiatic Society, Kolkata, A15; and painted panels of a now-dispersed Gaṇḍavyūha manuscript, such as the panel depicting Sudhana's visit with a goddess (Harvard Art Museums, 1984.504). See the discussion in Kim, "Performing Texts, Engendering Merits: Manuscripts and Paubhas as Ritual Objects," in *Dharma and Puṇya: Buddhist Ritual Art of Nepal,* ed. Jinah Kim and Todd Lewis (Leiden: Hotei Publishing, 2019)," 90–91. Also notice a similarity in the treatment of physiognomic details on the five tathāgatas, including oval-shaped faces with slightly wide foreheads.

41. The manuscript is available on CUL's digital library (https://cudl.lib.cam.ac.uk/view/MS-ADD-01544/1). The sequence of scanning has this cover the first one, but the pūjā marks on the other cover indicate this one with the seven Mānuṣī Buddhas was the bottom cover.

42. Strangely, the two protector deities at either end are cut out of frame. The one on the left side end is missing about one-fifth of the full picture, while the one on the right end is missing nearly one-third of the picture. From the size and the shape, it is clear that the string hole on the right was modified at least once. It seems that the cover had to be modified after completion, with the painting made to fit the size of the manuscript, which resulted in trimming the ends unevenly.

43. The current state may suggest that the artists did not mix the ingredients but rather applied pigments in two layers—that is, blue over yellow or vice versa—and yellow discolored over time due to the light sensitivity of orpiment.

44. If the manuscript was indeed a product of N.S. 251, the reigning king's name would have been Ānandadeva; this would have required three letters, whereas it is clear that there were only two letters underneath what is now written as orthography for the letter "i" here. That the manuscript may date from earlier in the twelfth century, possibly the turn of 1100 CE, is also supported by the location of its production, which is identified as the Kīrtti maṇḍala; this likely refers to Kīrtipura, a principality southwest of today's Kathmandu, west of Patan. Kīrtipura seems to have been outside the direct rule of the kings claiming their hold over "Nepal maṇḍala." (A single political authority ruling over "Nepal maṇḍala" would have been a bold, fictive claim at the turn of the twelfth century!)

45. In SM 291, Ucchuṣma-Jambhala is described as blue black "*kṛṣṇavarṇa.*" Jambhala as a deity of prosperity and wealth seems to have developed from a much earlier practice of cultic deities, like the idea of yakṣa Kubera. A number of sādhanas report Jambhala's various forms, most commonly in yellow, but some sādhanas of a wrathful form called "Ucchuṣma (crackling) Jambhala" link him to Akṣobhya. S.K. Saraswati, *Tantrayāna Art: An Album* (Calcutta: Asiatic Society, 1977), LII.

46. Images of Nāgarāja are known to have been placed to protect a sacred site, like the eighth-century stone sculpture of Nāgarāja found in the southeast corner of Site No. 3 at Nālandā. The painting is, in fact, reminiscent of this two-armed image of Nāgarāja at Nālandā. Asher discusses and identifies the sculpture to be earlier than Devapāla's reign. The image was found with a two-armed goddess image of similar size. Asher rightly underscores the placement of Nāgārjuna and the goddess image as signaling their roles as "safekeeping of transcendent wisdom in the shadow of the site's Great stūpa." Frederick M. Asher, *The Art of Eastern India, 300–800* (Oxford: Oxford University Press, 1980), 82–83. The goddess image, which is identified as Sarasvatī, may in fact be an early attempt to depict the goddess Prajñāpāramitā. See the discussion in Jinah Kim, "Goddess Prajñāpāramitā and Esoteric Buddhism in Jayavarman VII's Angkor," in *Creative South,* ed. Andrea Acri and Peter Sharrock (Singapore: ISEAS, forthcoming).

47. D.C. Bhattacharya already speculated nearly half a century ago that the Pentad concept "may have been completed by the eleventh century," yet why this is so and what the implication of this late formulation may have been is not discussed. D.C. Bhattacharyya, "The Five Protective Goddesses of Buddhism," in *Aspects of Indian Art,* ed. Pratapaditya Pal (Leiden: Brill, 1972), 90.
48. G. Mevissen, "The Indian Connection: Images of Deified Spells in the Arts of Northern Buddhism," *Silk Road Art and Archaeology* 2 (1991/92). Both Mahāmāyūrī and Mahāpratisarā were circulating in manuscripts from early times as well: A Mahāmāyūrī manuscript is dated to the first half of the sixth century, and the Mahāpratisarā is known in a Gilgit manuscript that may date to the early seventh century. Gergely Hidas, "Mahā-Daṇḍadhāraṇī-Śītavatī: A Buddhist Apotropaic Scripture," in *Indic Manuscript Cultures through the Ages: Material, Textual, and Historical Investigations,* ed. Vincenzo Vergiani, Daniele Cuneo, and Camillo Alessio Formigatti (Berlin: De Gruyter, 2017), 449–85.
49. Paul Copp, *The Body Incantatory: Spells and the Ritual Imagination in Medieval Chinese Buddhism* (New York: Columbia University Press, 2014), 60–141.
50. G. Mevissen, "Images of Mahāpratisarā in Bengal," *Journal of Bengal Art* 4 (1999).
51. Florinda De Simini's recent study mentions a first half of the sixth-century manuscript that contains the Mahāmāyūrī as one of the Pañcarakṣā goddesses and assumes an early date for the Pañcarkṣā ("this collection of five early Sanskrit works"), but this is misleading. One does not stand in for the genesis of the Pentad set. Florinda De Simini, *Of Gods and Books: Ritual and Knowledge Transmission in the Manuscript Cultures of Premodern India* (Berlin: De Gruyter, 2016), 12.
52. Mevissen identifies the "Nepalese tradition," which corresponds closely with the SM 206, and the "Indian tradition," which more or less correlates to the descriptions of the deities in SM 194–200. See the discussion in G. Mevissen, "Transmission of Iconographic Traditions: Pañcarakṣā Heading North," in *South Asian Archaeology 1989,* ed. Catherine Jarrige (Madison, WI: Prehistory Press, 1992), 415–24.
53. See Kim, "A Book of Buddhist Goddesses: Illustrated Manuscripts of the Pañcarakṣā Sūtra and Their Ritual Use." *Artibus Asiae* 70, no. 2 (2010): 264–68.
54. Kim, "Book of Buddhist Goddesses," 270–79.
55. The five goddesses are in "borrowed," or makeshift, forms rather than articulating the distinct iconography described in the sādhana texts. It is certainly not the lack of expert knowledge on EB iconography that led to such a choice since other important EB goddesses like Vajratārā and Kurukullā are carefully articulated in this manuscript. This suggests that painters of the five goddesses may have remained open to new visual interpretations into the mid-twelfth century. For the discussion on this manuscript, see Kim, "Book of Buddhist Goddesses," 280–83.
56. See Kim, "Book of Buddhist Goddesses," figure 21.
57. David L. Snellgrove, *The Hevajra Tantra: A Critical Study,* 2 vols. (London: Oxford University Press, 1959), 1: 57–58.
58. For example, see the description in the seventeenfold Hevajra maṇḍala (NsP, 14) and the ninefold Heruka maṇḍala (NsP, 20).
59. Also see the discussion of color terms in chapter 6.
60. For a summary of this feature discussed in early Buddhist canonical texts, see Harrison, "Commemoration and Identification."
61. This observation is based on a search for color terms in the section under the esoteric teaching (Ch. *mijiao,* Kr. *milgyo* or Jp. *mikkyo*) in Taisho, especially those collected under T18 and T19. A quantitative analysis is possible thanks to the digital tripiṭaka. See, for example, http://tripitaka.cbeta.org.

62. T19 no 940 [0194a15] 從佛頂出無量百千光明。種種色類青黃赤白紫色. In a different part of the text, the colors of the light are described as blue, yellow, red, white, purple, *sphatika* (Sanskrit word meaning rock crystal or quartz), and silver, indicating the flexible use of color terms for describing the brilliancy of light.
63. Francesca Fremantle, "A Critical Study of the Guhyasamāja Tantra" (PhD diss., University of London, 1971), 37. The reading here is modified slightly based on the reading in Danapāla's translation of the GT (Taisho no. 0885), 0470c20. The date of the translation is believed to be either 985 or 1002 CE.
64. Alex Wayman, *Yoga of the Guhyasamājatantra: The Arcane Lore of Forty Verses; A Buddhist Tantra Commentary* (Delhi: Motilal Banarsidass, 1977), 153.
65. "alchemy consists of the fixing of the bodhicitta combining the ambrosial essences (*bdud rtsi*) of *prajñā* and *upāya*—and the cultivation of a "rainbow body" (*ra 'lus*) or a body of light." David Gordon White, *The Alchemical Body: Siddha Traditions in Medieval India* (Chicago: University of Chicago Press, 1996), 72.
66. The idea of the divine as light or divine light is common across numerous religious traditions, as Mathew Kapstein observes. Matthew T. Kapstein, "Rethinking Religious Experience: Seeing the Light in the History of Religions," in *The Presence of Light: Divine Radiance and Religious Experience,* ed. Matthew T. Kapstein (Chicago: University of Chicago Press, 2004).
67. Dominic Goodall, Alexis Sanderson, and Harunaga Isaacson, eds., *The Niśvāsatattvasaṃhitā: The Earliest Surviving Śaiva Tantra* (Paris: École Française d'Extrême-Orient, 2015), 71.
68. For example, in the *Nayasūtra* chapter 3: 39, "Vidyā is said to be four-coloured or uncolored: she should be visualized as white (*sita*), red (*rakta*), yellow (*pīta*) and black (*kṛṣṇa*), [or] as hollow/empty." Goodall, Sanderson, and Isaacson, *Niśvāsatattvasaṃhitā,* 456. Sanskrit text, 211.
69. Goodall, Sanderson, and Isaacson, *Niśvāsatattvasaṃhitā,* 463. *Nayasūtra,* 534.
70. Gudrun Bühnemann, "The *Śaradātilakatantra* on Yoga: A New Edition and Translation of Chapter 25," *Bulletin of the School of Oriental and African Studies* 74, no. 2 (2011).
71. Bühnemann, "*Śāradātilakatantra* on Yoga," 232.
72. Here "red lead" translates "*sindūr,*" but vermilion is also a possibility.
73. This suggestion is based on stylistic comparison with early Nepalese manuscript covers and some early dated manuscripts, like Add. 1643 in Cambridge. The Uma-Śiva iconography is very common in the late Licchavi period onward, and the celestial Gaṅgā diving from the sky is a distinct element seen in these sculptures, as seen for example in a stone image found in Nagal Tol, Kathmandu, which Pal stylistically dates to the eighth to ninth century.
74. For example, see a comparable stone image in the Asia Society collection (Rockefeller 1992.2), in Pratapaditya Pal, *Himalayas: An Aesthetic Adventure* (Chicago: Art Institute of Chicago, 2003), 29.
75. The four-armed form chosen for all goddesses and Śiva on the painted panels is consistent with the forms described in the NvS text.
76. We may take this three-headed form as depicting the four-faced vision of Īśvara described in the *Nayasūtra* since the face in the back may be assumed. On the other hand, the four faces are described as having different colors and forms (*Nayasūtra,* 3: 42–50), whereas the painting does not differentiate between them. The fact that the painting depicts him as white, holding a trident, a rosary, and a bowl, along with what seems to be a tiger skin wrapped across his chest, raises a possibility of connecting his form to the description of the fifth form that rises above the five-faced form of Śiva described in the *Nayasūtra* (3: 43–50). The editors of the NvS take "*vyāghrayajñopavītena*"—"a sacred thread made of a tiger or tiger skin"—as "impossible or unlikely." Goodall, Sanderson, and Isaacson, *Niśvāsatattvasaṃhitā,* 460. The painted image shows how the artist understood this feature as well as what this term may reference.

77. See the discussion in chapter 6.
78. Ellen Gough, "Shades of Enlightenment—A Jain Tantric Diagram and the Colours of the Tīrthaṅkaras," *International Journal of Jaina Studies* 8, no. 1 (2012): 1–47. The following analysis draws from Gough's pioneering study.
79. This is one of the artistic treatises surveyed by Nardi. Isabella Nardi, *The Theory of Citrasūtras in Indian Painting: A Critical Re-Evaluation of Their Uses and Interpretations* (London: Routledge, 2006). Whether this term *śyāma* means "black" is also uncertain. It can also mean green hued. See the discussion in chapter 6.
80. Gough, "Shades of Enlightenment," 8.
81. T.A. Gopinath Rao, *Elements of Hindu Iconography*, 2 vols. (Madras: Law Printing House, 1914), 1: 73–115.
82. The text remains unillustrated, but the scribe included a prominent wheel motif in the middle of folio 243v, almost 2 cm in height, and this image resonates well with the wheels depicted all over the painted cover, as an attribute of Viṣṇu as well as a dominant element of Viṣṇu's crown.
83. The choice of blue and its relationship to the term *kṛṣṇa,* which is often translated as "black" but in later centuries ubiquitously painted in brilliant blue, is discussed in chapter 6.
84. Michael T. Taussig, *What Color Is the Sacred?* (Chicago: University of Chicago Press, 2009).
85. Max Meehan, "Heavens and Hierarchies: Buddhist Textiles at Alchi," unpublished seminar paper for HAA184x Himalayan Art, Spring 2016. According to Meehan's analysis, red predominates in the textiles on royalty (71 percent), followed by the robes of tathāgatas, 62 percent of which are in red. The computational analysis was possible thanks to the de-bugging help from Artur Meller (Harvard College '16) and the digitization support from the Visual Resources Service, Fine Arts Library at Harvard. I thank Max Meehan (Harvard College '16) for allowing the publication of his analytical chart in this book.
86. The date of Alchi's Sumtseg is a matter of debate. Philip Denwood has repeatedly argued for the last third of the eleventh century as its foundation date, while Goepper is of the opinion that it must have been built at the turn of the thirteenth century. Luczanits supports Goepper's dating. Peter van Ham's new book argues for a late eleventh-century date. From the colorist perspective, the clear use of the IEB color system and the opacity of colors point to a date after 1100 CE, although given the sixteenth-century renovation inscription how much of the color we see today are of the original production remains a question to be explored further, which can be helped by further scientific analysis of the layers in painting.
87. Benoytosh Bhattacharyya, ed., Introduction to *Niṣpannayogāvalī of Mahāpaṇḍita Abhayākaragupta,* Gaekwad's Oriental Series, vol. 109 (Baroda: Oriental Institute, 1949), 16.
88. Masahide Mori, "The Installation Ceremony in Tantric Buddhism," in *From Materials to Deity: Indian Rituals of Consecration,* ed. Shingo Einoo and Jun Takashima, Japanese Studies on South Asia No. 4 (New Delhi: Manohar Publishers, 2005), 202. On Pañcarakṣā's ritual use, see Todd Lewis, *Popular Buddhist Texts from Nepal: Narratives and Rituals of Newar Buddhism* (Albany: State University of New York Press, 2000), 153–61.
89. I was the sponsor for the ritual that was held to wish for the well-being of my late mother-in-law. I thank the late Min Bahadur Shakya and his family for hosting this ritual. Ratna Raj Bajracharya of Kwā Bahā was the main priest conducting the ritual with his son, Hem Ratna Bajracharya.

CHAPTER 6. COLOR TO MATTER

1. Cited in Geeta Kapur, "Body as Gesture: Indian Women Artists at Work," in *Representing the Body: Gender Issues in Indian Art,* ed. Vidya Dehejia (New Delhi: Kali for Women, 1997), 170. Kapur cites this

passage to underscore the anachronism and the "modernist universalism of aesthetic affinities" in Amrita Sher-Gil's work.

2. Geeti Sen, *Feminine Fables: Imagining the Indian Woman in Painting, Photography, and Cinema* (Ahmedabad: Mapin, 2002), 79–80.
3. Sonal Khullar, *Worldly Affiliations: Artistic Practice, National Identity, and Modernism in India, 1930–1990* (Oakland: University of California Press, 2015), 61.
4. Ananda K. Coomaraswamy, *Rajput Painting* (New York: H. Milford; Oxford University Press, 1916), 4. Coomaraswamy cites Vincent Smith's rather fanciful theory that the "School of the Ancient West" mentioned in the early seventeenth-century account by a Tibetan Buddhist master, Tāranātha, originated in "Rājputāna during the 7th century, and became the model of the earliest Buddhist art in Nepal" to support his argument. More likely, this "school of the ancient west" in Tāranātha's account refers to the art of the Kashmir and Gilgit region.
5. Pramod Chandra characterizes this relationship between Ajanta paintings and the later Rajput paintings as that between "classical Sanskrit literature" and "the North Indian vernacular languages." Pramod Chandra, "Notes on the Study of Indian Miniatures," in *Indian Miniatures: The Ehrenfeld Collection*, ed. Daniel J. Ehnbom et al. (New York: Hudson Hills Press, 1985), 16.
6. See Sonya Rhie Quintanilla, Pramod Chandra, and John M. Rosenfield, *Rhythms of India: The Art of Nandalal Bose* (San Diego, CA: San Diego Museum of Art, 2008), 120.
7. For the discussion of early efforts for copying the murals, see Divia Patel, "Copying Ajanta: A Rediscovery of Some Nineteenth-Century Paintings," *South Asian Studies* 23, no. 1 (2007): 39–62.
8. It may be possible to reconstruct original colors virtually, as Harvard Art Museums did with Mark Rothko murals (see www.harvardartmuseums.org/visit/exhibitions/4768/mark-rothkos-harvard-murals), but I am not aware of any ongoing effort of this kind for Ajanta.
9. For example, see Manager Singh, "Microclimatic Condition in Relation to Conservation of Cave No. 2 Murals of Ajanta," *Current Science* 101, no. 1 (2011): 89–94; Manager Singh and Balasaheb Ramrao Arbad, "Ancient Indian Painting Recipes and Mural Art Technique at Ajanta," *International Journal of Conservation Science* 5, no. 1 (2014): 35–50; Om Prakash Agrawal, *Conservation of Wall Paintings in India: Achievements and Problems* (Lucknow: INTACH Indian Conservation Institute, 1995). Annamaria Giovagnoli et al., "The Mural Paintings of the Ajanta Caves, Part I: Documentation on Execution Techniques and Conservation Condition," paper presented at the 9th International Conference on NDT of Art, Jerusalem, Israel (2008); D. Artioli et al., "Mural Paintings of Ajanta Caves, Part II: Non Destructive Investigations and Microanalysis on Execution Technique and State of Conservation," paper presented at the Ninth International Conference on NDT of Art, Jerusalem, Israel (2008).
10. Singh and Arbad, "Ancient Indian Painting Recipes," 37. Its vibrancy until this date is quite remarkable. Green is most often begotten from a combination of yellow and blue pigments, and depending on the composition of the colorants, it can easily lose its original appearance.
11. That this pigment does not appear in the earliest layer of painting at the site does indicate the expanding trade network in which the patrons of Ajanta's heyday, in the fifth century, took part.
12. M. Singh, personal communication, November 23, 2017.
13. This is based on the analytical research conducted at Harvard. I thank Katherine Eremin and Penley Knipe (Straus Center for Conservation and Technical Studies) for their help.
14. A study on tantric alchemy by David Gordon White helps us forge an interesting three-way connection between tantric alchemy, artistic practices, and aesthetics in Indian painting. David Gordon White,

The Alchemical Body: Siddha Traditions in Medieval India (Chicago: University of Chicago Press, 1996), 184–217.

15. John Gage, "Black and White and Red All Over," *RES: Anthropology and Aesthetics* 16 (1988): 51–53.
16. John Gage, "Color in Western Art, an Issue?" *Art Bulletin* 72, no. 4 (1990): 521.
17. In European medieval manuscripts, the shortcomings have been addressed somewhat based on many scientific material analyses of pigments and other matters. For example, see Stella Panayotova, Deirdre Jackson, and Paola Ricciardi, eds., *Colour: The Art and Science of Illuminated Manuscripts* (London: Harvey Miller Publishers, 2016).
18. Alex Byrne and David R. Hilbert, "Color Realism and Color Science," *Behavioral and Brain Sciences* 26, no. 3 (2003).
19. The XRF analysis alone cannot confirm the identity of each pigment. It gives a reasonable possibility. For convenience, most likely pigments that are suggested in XRF analyses are referred to as those used in the paintings.
20. Coomaraswamy, "One Hundred References to Indian Painting," 51. Colors are supposed to have been prepared in individual containers according to traditional treaties.
21. This fluidity led scholars like U.P. Shah to argue that color terms for dark hues, like *śyāma, kṛṣṇa, nīla,* and *harita* are interchangeable, and used that way. U.P. Shah, "Iconography," in *Jaina Art and Architecture,* ed. A. Ghosh (New Delhi: Bharatiya Jnanpitha, 1975).
22. Edward Hopkins, "Words for Color in the Rig Veda," *American Journal of Philology* 4, no. 2 (1883): 166–91.
23. Sheldon Pollock, *A Rasa Reader: Classical Indian Aesthetics* (New York: Columbia University Press, 2016), 51–52.
24. Parul Dave Mukherji, ed., *The Citrasūtra of the Viṣṇudharmottara Purāṇa* (New Delhi: Indira Gandhi National Centre for the Arts and Motilal Banarsidass Publishers, 2001), 133–39.
25. Mukherji, *Citrasūtra,* 135n4; 150, 152; P. Shah, *Viṣṇudharmottara-Purāṇa, Third Khaṇḍa* (Baroda: Baroda Oriental Institute, 1958), 86.
26. Today's Patua painters in West Bengal use the seeds from the "achiote" (*Bixa orellana*) annatto tree to make red pigment. The annatto tree's Indic-language name includes *sindura.* However, this tree is believed to have been introduced to India from South America by the Spanish and Portuguese in the sixteenth century. Whether any materials derived from this *sindūra* tree mentioned in the VdhM can be used for making red pigment is difficult to determine as its usage seems to be limited to a protective ingredient rather than a colorant.
27. Shah, "Iconography," 469. U.P. Shah uses *harita, nīla, kāla, śyāma,* and *kṛṣṇa* interchangeably, but his argument seems to account for only textual sources. It is important to acknowledge the fluid semantic range of these terms, but at the same time, the confusion in the literature also may come from shortcomings in the process of translation into English. Considering artistic interventions in the shaping of the color terms and their meanings can also help locate these color terms in a more historically nuanced manner.
28. Charlotte Schmid's study suggests that "Kṛṣṇa" may have preexisted before the idea of Viṣṇu and his ten incarnations. See Charlotte Schmid, *Le Don de voir: Premières représentations Krishnaïtes de la région de Mathura* (Paris: École Française d'Extrême-Orient, 2010).
29. This attempt to adhere to the text is common in the process of cross-cultural translation. In contrast, those working in the tradition seem to have had no hesitation in depicting Rāma blue.
30. I was able to examine select folios from Books 5 and 6 of the Rāmāyaṇa (MS 15297[1] and IO San 3621) in person. The granular nature of blue pigments under 30X magnification indicates that the

pigment is mineral based. I thank Pasquale Manzo of the British Library for allowing me to examine the folios.

31. See the plates and the discussion in Ratan Parimoo, *Gujarati School and Jaina Manuscript Painting: N.C. Mehta Collection* (Ahmedabad: Gujarat Museum Society, 2010), 171–232.

32. Isacco and Darrah report that the blue pigment used for Kṛṣṇa's face is ultramarine, a pigment prepared from lapis lazuli. Enrico Isacco and Josephine Darrah, "The Ultraviolet-Infrared Method of Analysis, a Scientific Approach to the Study of Indian Miniatures," *Artibus Asiae* 53, 3/4 (1993): 490.

33. W. Norman Brown, *The Vasanta Vilāsa: A Poem of the Spring Festival in Old Gujarātī Accompanied by Sanskrit and Prakrit Stanzas and Illustrated with Miniature Paintings* (New Haven, CT: American Oriental Society, 1962), 148.

34. Isacco and Darrah, "Ultraviolet-Infrared Method."

35. Ten avatars of Viṣṇu as a set appear frequently in medieval stone sculptures, but whether a human figure in this set portrayal is Kṛṣṇa or Balarāma, another human incarnation of Viṣṇu, is far from clear. See the examples in Joan Cummins, ed., *Vishnu: Hinduism's Blue-Skinned Savior* (Ahmedabad; Nashville, TN: Mapin Publishing with Frist Center for the Visual Arts, 2011), 115–21.

36. In fact, some authors of the Esoteric Buddhist sādhanas seem to have been intimately aware of the theory of rasa. How the sādhana practice fits the switching of the emphasis from actors or objects in the product to the subject of experience, what Pollock terms as aesthetic revolution of Abhinavagupta, deserves further investigation.

37. An infrared spectroscopy performed at Harvard reveals that this local script was also used to write instructions for the painter, which is now covered under the red border.

38. This is true for most "dispersed series" of the period between the sixteenth and the seventeenth centuries, like the dispersed *Bhāgavata purāṇa* of the 1540s, which Daniel Ehnbom places somewhere around Mathura as a production site. Daniel J. Ehnbom, "Master of Dispersed Bhagavata Purana," in *Masters of Indian Painting*, ed. Milo C. Beach, Eberhard Fischer, and B.N. Goswamy (Zurich: Artibus Asiae Publishers, 2011), 77–88.

39. Initially, verse 39 of the *Rasamañjarī* was written on the top of the page. This was corrected by covering the verse text with a swath of orange paint.

40. *dayitasya nirīkṣyabhāladeśaṃ caraṇālaktapiñjaraṃ sapatnyāḥ|| sudṛśo nayanasya koṇasbhāsā śrutimuktāḥ śikhiropamāvabhūduḥ* 38.

41. Deborah Klimburg-Salter notes, "At Tabo and Tholing parts of the mandorlas, including the ring of vajras, are raised, giving an even greater sense of depth to the aureole diffused with rainbow-coloured waves of light." Deborah E. Klimburg-Salter, *Tabo: A Lamp for the Kingdom* (Milan: Skira, 1997), 210.

42. Eva Allinger and Christiane Kalantari, "Art, Mobility and Identity in the Western Himalayas," *Asian Art* (2012). Peter van Ham describes this feature as "a relief application of papier maché [*sic*] painted gold." Peter Van Ham, *Guge—Ages of Gold* (Munich: Hirmer, 2016), 76. He confirmed that whether a true "papier mâché" technique was used and how this feature was prepared remain to be explored. Personal communication with Peter van Ham, March 21, 2018. I thank him for sharing the image reproduced in figure 2.22.

43. The murals of Ellora remain understudied in comparison to those at Ajanta. Lisa Owen's recent study discusses painting as part of the larger iconographic program. Lisa N. Owen, *Carving Devotion in the Jain Caves at Ellora* (Leiden: Brill, 2012).

44. Modern science does not supply answers for all historical examples. It is important to remember that an identification of pigment is based on an interpretive maneuver. Much of the analytical data

generated from scientific analysis are subject to interpretation. The data do not provide a definite answer. See Christopher Krekel, Ursula Haller, and Andreas Burmester, "Artists' Pigments Reconsidered: Does Modern Science Match the Historical Context?" *Studies in Conservation* 51, no. 2 (2006).

45. Moti Chandra, *The Technique of Mughal Painting* (Lucknow: U.P. Historical Society, 1949), 27–28; Robert L. Feller, *Artists' Pigments : A Handbook of Their History and Characteristics,* 4 vols. (Washington, DC: National Gallery of Art, 1986), 1: 17–36.

46. See Brown, *Vasanta Vilāsa,* 147–49.

47. Rutherford J. Gettens, "Proposal for a Handbook on Analysis of Materials of Paintings," *Studies in Conservation* 6, no. 1 (1961).

48. B.B. Johnson, "A Preliminary Study of the Technique of Indian Miniature Painting," in *Aspects of Indian Art: Papers Presented in a Symposium at the Los Angeles County Museum of Art,* ed. Pratapaditya Pal (Leiden: Brill, 1972), 139–46.

49. Indrani Chatterjee, *Forgotten Friends: Monks, Marriages, and Memories of Northeast India* (Oxford: Oxford University Press, 2013).

50. One of the serendipitous incidents that contributed to further development in the scientific study of pigments in Tibetan thangkas is Richard R. Ernst's visit to Kathmandu in 1968. See Richard R. Ernst, "Arts and Sciences: A Perspective of Tibetan Painting," *Chimia* 55, no. 11 (2001); Sotheby's, "The Richard R. and Magdalena Ernst Collection of Himalayan Art," in *Sotheby's Auction Catalog,* ed. Sotheby's (New York: Sotheby's, 2018), 8.

51. Sabine Cotte, "Conservation of Thangkas: A Review of the Literature since the 1970s," *Studies in Conservation* 56, no. 2 (2011): 81–93. O.P. Agrawal's *Conservation of Manuscripts and Paintings of South-East Asia* (1982) remains a landmark publication, providing practical advice on how to protect and conserve manuscripts and paintings, including palm-leaf and birch-bark manuscripts unique to South and Southeast Asia. The last chapter of this book is devoted to "thangkas" from Tibet and the Indian Himalayas, following a chapter on Indian "miniature" painting on paper.

52. Tatjana Bayerová, "Buddhist Wall Paintings at Nako Monastery, North India: Changing of the Technology throughout Centuries," *Studies in Conservation* 63, no. 3 (2017): 171–88.

53. See, for example, studies by Manager Singh ("Microclimatic Condition in Relation to Conservation of Cave No. 2 Murals of Ajanta"; "Ancient Indian Painting Recipes and Mural Art Technique at Ajanta," with Balasaheb Ramrao Arbad).

54. For a succinct introduction to these methods, see the website on pigments developed by the Zurich-based scientist Juraj Lipscher: https://colourlex.com/methods/.

55. S. Panayotova, D. Jackson, and P. Ricciardi, eds., *Colour: The Art and Science of Illuminated Manuscripts* (London: Harvey Miller Publishers, 2016). Also see www.miniare.org.

56. What may fall under each of these categories, be it "Mughal," "Sanskrit," or "Tibetan," remains to be seen, and one wonders how comprehensive each category can be to do justice to such an ambitious scope. www.miniare.org/Project.php, accessed March 1, 2018.

57. Given that the current proposed scope includes "Mughal" and "Sanskrit" in addition to Tibetan illuminated manuscripts, it is hoped that a more comprehensive study of pigments and materials in the field of Indic manuscript painting will become available in the future.

58. Conducted in December 2012; the report was published in 2016. On the material culture of Tibetan books, see, for example, Agnieszka Helman-Wazny, *The Archaeology of Tibetan Books* (Leiden: Brill, 2014); Hildegard Diemberger, Karl Ehrhard, and Peter F. Kornicki, eds., *Tibetan Printing: Comparison Continuities and Change* (Leiden: Brill, 2016).

59. See, for example, Isacco and Darrah, "Ultraviolet-Infrared Method." This is a very helpful study, but it does not give detailed information on all the manuscripts that were analyzed. The points of analysis are only mentioned in a few exceptional cases.

60. The current URL for the project at the time of publication of this book is http://mappingcolor.fas.harvard.edu.

61. Anjan Chakraverty, *Indian Miniature Painting* (New Delhi: Roli Books, 2005), 12. This list is repeated verbatim in a recent publication on Sultanate manuscript painting. Éloïse Brac de la Perrière, *L'Art du Livre dans l'Inde des Sultanats* (Paris: PUPS, 2008), 101. That this inaccurate list is repeated in a recent publication also speaks to the fact that there remains a dearth of scholarship on pigment research on early Indic manuscript painting.

62. Research on Sanskrit manuscripts out of the Hamburg-based Centre for the Study of Manuscript Cultures already led to some new material analysis on early palm-leaf manuscripts. For example, see Martin Deheley et al., "Material Analysis of Sanskrit Palm-Leaf Manuscripts Preserved in Nepal," *Journal of the International Association of Buddhist Studies* 36/37 (2015). This study focuses on identifying the material properties of ink.

63. Laura Weinstein, Ananda K. Coomaraswamy curator of South Asian and Islamic Art, facilitated access to the manuscripts, and Joan Wright, Bertina Burr Conservator, made the investigation possible. Kaeley Fergusson and Michiko Adachi assisted Michele Derrick, Schorr Family Associate Research Scientist, in conducting analysis. I thank them all.

64. Indigo dye is prepared from leaves of plants, and types of plants used for blue dye production varies from region to region. Exactly which variety of this vast genus of indigo plant was used to create indigo dye used in a surviving painting from premodern India is difficult to prove, so is whether textual references to indigo, like "nīla" in the VdhM, refer to a particular variety of plant like *Indigofera tinctoria*, although it is most likely. This variety of indigo plant (*Indigofera tinctoria*) was an important cash crop for which the British colonial authorities aggressively pursued more cultivations and better yields. Prakash Kumar, "Scientific Experiments in British India: Scientists, Indigo Planters, and the State, 1890–1930," *Indian Economic and Social History Review* 38, no. 3 (2001). Another recent study examines labor and politics of indigo cultivation in colonial India. Natasha Eaton, "Nomadism of Colour: Painting, Technology, and Waste in the Chromo-Zones of Colonial India, C. 1765–C. 1860," *Journal of Material Culture* 17, no. 1 (2012).

65. This data will be made available on the MCH project website. "Ti" as minor trace is also noted on a fifteenth-century Jain manuscript in an earlier study. Isacco and Darrah, "Ultraviolet-Infrared Method," figure 4.

66. Isacco and Darrah, "Ultraviolet-Infrared Method." Only the Jain manuscript is identified in detail. Gettens's report is published in Brown, *Vasanta Vilāsa*.

67. Another possibility is a much later addition of cobalt blue, a synthetically manufactured pigment that started to be mass produced in the nineteenth century, although this is less likely since the elemental spectrum data of smalt on this manuscript differs from the elemental spectrum data of French manufactured smalt of the eighteenth century and later. I thank Katherine Eremin for sharing this observation.

68. Smalt's use in wall painting is reported in Khara Khoto fragments of the twelfth–thirteenth century, which was provided by Langdon Warner to Gettens while Gettens was at Harvard. Ashok Roy, ed., *Artists' Pigments: A Handbook of Their History and Characteristics* (Washington, DC: National Gallery of Art, 1993; reprint 2012), 2: 114; Rutherford J. Gettens and George L. Stout, *Painting Materials: A Short Encyclopaedia* (New York: Dover Publications, 1966), 157–59.

69. I thank Saryu Doshi for this reference regarding certain Gujarati Jain communities' ties to jewelers. Whether the enamel technique was already in use in fifteenth-century India needs further exploration. A more common method used in jewelry making in ancient India seems to have been inlaying pieces of precious stone on gold.
70. Feller, *Artists' Pigments,* 1: 188. Yellow chromate's usage as a pigment is attested in the nineteenth century or later.
71. Brac de la Perrière, *L'Art du Livre dans l'Inde des Sultanats,* 98–99.
72. Nancy Purinton and Mark Watters, "A Study of the Materials Used by Medieval Persian Painters," *Journal of the American Institute for Conservation* 30, no. 2 (1991): 135.
73. David J. Roxburgh, "Kamal al-Din Bihzad and Authorship in Persianate Painting," *Muqarnas* 17 (2000): 122.
74. Yves Porter, *Peinture et Arts du Livre: Essai sur la littérature technique Indo-Persane* (Tehran: Institut français de recherche en Iran, 1992), 103.
75. Adhyāya 40, verses 1–8, *Citrasutra,* 128–31; *Mānasollāsa,* 2: 13–14.
76. David Paul Jackson and Janice A. Jackson, *Tibetan Thangka Painting: Methods and Materials,* 2nd rev. ed. (London: Serindia, 1988), 20–22.
77. Burnishing is not the only technique that one can apply to achieve the smoothness of the finished surface. In the Tibetan thangka painting tradition, a different method—careful scraping of the surface with a knife—is used. Jackson and Jackson, *Tibetan Thangka Painting,* 101.
78. Desmond Lazaro, *Materials, Methods, and Symbolism in the Pichhvai Painting Tradition of Rajasthan* (Ahmedabad: Mapin, 2005), 105–8. A demonstration of this process by the Pakistani miniature artist Murad Khan Mumtaz can be seen online: https://youtu.be/hzkj_A3M-RY.
79. Vishwa Chander Ohri, *The Technique of Pahari Painting* (Shimla: Indian Institute of Advanced Study, 2001); on the history of this new traditional program being part of a growing contemporary artistic practice, see Nadeem Omar Tarar, "Framings of a National Tradition: Discourse on the Reinvention of Miniature Painting in Pakistan," *Third Text* 25, no. 5 (2011).
80. This is based on Joan Wright's observation, personal communication, April 20, 2018. On the order of scribing and painting, see Jinah Kim, "A Book of Buddhist Goddesses: Illustrated Manuscripts of the Pañcarakṣā Sūtra and Their Ritual Use," *Artibus Asiae* 70, no. 2 (2010): 259–329.
81. Porter, *Peinture et Arts du Livre,* 95. The list also includes methods for shading, mixing lapis plus cinnabar and lac for violet and realgar and indigo for blue night (*nilgun*).
82. Pigment loss on the painted panel and relatively fresh loss of the palm leaf's surface layer on the right side of folio 1 indicate that the folio may have been stuck to its board material, probably due to accumulation of moisture, and was rather forcefully removed from this "glued" condition prior to coming into the collection.
83. I conjecture that the missing penultimate folio 97 may have also had a painted panel planned. But this may not have been the case.
84. See the images on http://museum.asiasociety.org/collection/explore/1987-001-five-of-the-leaves-from-an-ashtasahasrika-prajnaparamita-manuscript/page/9.
85. Comparison may be made between three eastern Indian manuscripts that are written in the so-called Newari Bhujimol script, Wellcome Sansk. MS Epsilon 1, and Pañcarakṣā manuscript in National Museum, New Delhi. If the Nālandā connection that Allinger's study suggests for the Wellcome manuscript is tenable, there is a chance that this Pañcarakṣā manuscript in the MFA may in fact have been made in the area around Nālandā.

86. The Mahāmāyūrī text begins on folio 28v, where the preaching Buddha panel is placed, and here the text begins with an invocation to the goddess followed by a long list of the Buddhist litany instead of the traditional beginning of the text "*evam maya śrutam.*"
87. Brown, *Vasanta Vilāsa,* 148.
88. Ms_A's XRF result for a red spot indicates presence of arsenic element as well as Pb (lead), which according to Michel Derrek can suggest a possibility of realgar, an arsenic red pigment that sometimes occurs with orpiment. But realgar is known to have been used quite rarely.
89. The "Ca" pulse is consistently present in most areas analyzed in the *Pañcarakṣā* manuscript according to the XRF analysis data. Their relatively high pulse level vis-à-vis other elements detected in each area can be compared favorably to the low "ca" pulse level in the *Perfection of Wisdom* manuscript.
90. In the case of Tibetan thangkas, the priming layer was mostly calcium-based as indicated by material analysis on early Tibetan paintings (pre-1300 CE). See Robert Bruce-Gardner, "Realizations: Reflections on Technique in Early Central Tibetan Painting," in *Sacred Visions,* by Steven M. Kossack and Jane Casey Singer (New York: Metropolitan Museum of Art, 1998), 193–205.
91. The Tibet Museum manuscript was commissioned by a monk from Tibet and survives in Tibet. The Asia Society manuscript was commissioned by a donor possibly of a non-Sanskritic background; allegedly, it was once in the possession of Sakya Pandita and remained in Tibet until the twentieth century. The Asia Society manuscript is discussed in Susan L. Huntington and John C. Huntington, *Leaves from the Bodhi Tree* (Dayton, OH: Dayton Art Institute, 1990), 185–89.
92. Rutherford J. Gettens, Robert L. Feller, and W. T. Chase, "Vermilion and Cinnabar," in *Artists Pigments,* vol. 2 (Washington, DC: National Gallery of Art, 1993), 159–82.
93. Porter, *Peinture et Arts du Livre,* 83.
94. D.V. Thompson, in his "Artificial Vermilion in the Middle Ages," published in *Technical Studies in the Field of the Fine Arts* 2 (1933), notes that the manufacture of vermilion was a novelty in the eighth century, but it was commonplace in the fourteenth. Reported in *Artists Pigments,* vol. 2, 162.
95. White, *Alchemical Body.*
96. White, *Alchemical Body,* 194. From the material analysis perspective, White's discussion of red color and its use leaves much room for refinement both in terms of textual sources and practical references. In his discussion, vermilion (mercuric sulfide) and red lead are indiscriminately referenced. He also references mercuric oxide, a compound that is not used traditionally.
97. White suggests the possibility of identifying some areas of geothermal activity in India as a case where possibly cinnabar deposits are made in small amounts. White, *Alchemical Body,* 193–94.
98. White, *Alchemical Body,* 192.
99. "Mines and Mineral Occurrences of Afghanistan," US geological survey (2002). Accessed from mindat.org. February 12, 2018.
100. Karl Dasser, "Some Observations on the Technology of the Wall Paintings in the Sumtsek," in *Alchi: Ladakh's Hidden Buddhist Sanctuary,* ed. Roger Goepper (Boston: Shambhala, 1996).
101. Martin Deheley et al., "Material Analysis of Sanskrit Palm-Leaf Manuscripts Preserved in Nepal," *Journal of the International Association of Buddhist Studies* 36/37 (2015). The Vikramaśīla connection is established through a manuscript of the *Kalyāṇakāmadhenuvivaraṇa* (manuscript no. 1, NAK 5-20[K], KkV), which the authors report as bearing the name of a patron, Jinaśrīmitra, and the location of scribing, Vikramaśīla, in a colophon. It is interesting that only a single folio (folio 4) of this manuscript is kept in Kathmandu, and the rest is in Tibet (including the colophon folio), and the next manuscript in this Vikramaśīla group has one folio (also folio 4) missing, which is in Tibet. Unfortunately, the authors do

not provide any identifying information for the Tibetan repositories nor do they explain how they determined the single folio in the NAK as belonging to the Vikramaśīla KkV manuscript in Tibet.

102. The report suggests the possibility of iron gall ink used by a later hand correcting the text. Deheley et al., "Material Analysis," 130.

103. A laboratory experiment to simulate ink recipes with various mercury contents may prove useful in this regard. Experimenting through simulation of certain conditions and recipes is a common method used in the conservation lab. I thank Penley Knipe of paper lab at the Straus Center, Harvard Art Museums, and Joan Wright of MFA Asian paper lab, for teaching me the value of such experiments.

104. Dagmar Wujastyk, "Perfect Medicine—Mercury in Sanskrit Medical Literature," *Asian Medicine* 8 (2013).

105. One can only know the relative amount of mercury among the samples examined; it is difficult to compare their result with findings in other studies like the MFA project reported herein.

106. This is particularly the case in the United States and the United Kingdom.

107. Information from the public health statement for arsenic, www.atsdr.cdc.gov/phs/phs.asp?id=18&tid=3, accessed April 20, 2018.

108. Richard L. Burger and Jerrold B. Leikin, "Cinnabar Use in Prehispanic Peru and Its Possible Health Consequences," *Journal of Archaeological Science: Reports* 17 (2018).

109. Burger and Leikin also note that "the pre-Hispanic consumers of the pigment (cinnabar-based vermilion) would have been aware of the source of these health problems." Burger and Leikin, "Cinnabar Use in Prehispanic Peru," 733.

110. According to the study by N.S. Baer and his colleagues, the Act of 1908 that supposedly prohibited the further manufacture of Indian yellow is yet to be traced, but several Acts on the prevention of cruelty to animals passed under the colonial government of India (first in Bengal) from 1866 onward suggest its culmination by the early twentieth century. "Indian Yellow," *Artists' Pigments,* vol. 1, 19–21. Its manufacture may have continued past 1908, and Chandra reports that it could be obtained from Jaipur in his 1949 publication. Chandra, *The Technique of Mughal Painting,* 27–28.

111. Michael Taussig, "What Color Is the Sacred?" *Critical Inquiry* 33 (2006): 48.

112. Roy, *Artists' Pigments,* vol. 2, 113–30.

113. *Artists Pigments,* vol. 1, 170.

114. P.T. Craddock, L.K. Gurjar, and K.T.M. Hegde, "Zinc Production in Medieval India," *World Archaeology* 15, no. 2 (1983).

115. Zinc oxide, already known for its external use in the ancient Indic medical texts like the *Caraka saṃhitā.*

116. Sonya Rhie Mace, personal communication, March 23, 2018.

EPILOGUE

1. This is my translation of the second half of the verse based on the Benipuri edition. A recent translation of the first verse proposed by Paranjape reads as follows: "She who removes my existential distress is artful Radha / By the glimpse of whose body Shyama's darkness become lustrous green." Makarand R. Paranjape, "Enjoying God: The Divne Paramour," in *Radha: From Gopi to Goddess,* ed. Harsha V. Dehejia (New Delhi: Niyogi Press, 2014). I thank Harsha V. Dehejia for drawing my attention to this passage in the Satsai.

2. Ramvriksh Benipuri, ed., *Bihārī Satsai with Commentary by Śrī Rāmavṛkṣa Benīpurī* (in Hindi) (Patna: Pustak Bhandar, 1903).

3. Many pages have been cut to preserve only the painted panel; the back side has been pasted over with an additional sheet of blank paper, as if to mask or erase the text written in *nagari* (north Indian script).

One wonders if some early collectors and connoisseurs of Indian miniature painting found it problematic that the Indic text of these folios appears with paintings that bear so many stylistic features of the Mughal workshop.

4. Catherine Glynn, "Evidence of Royal Painting for the Amber Court," *Artibus Asiae* 56, no. 1/2 (1996); Steven Kossak, *Indian Court Painting, 16th–19th Century* (New York: Metropolitan Museum of Art, 1997), 43.
5. Sonia Wigh, "Politics, Patronage, and Polyvalence: Mirza Raja Jai Singh in Biharilal's Satsai," *Social Scientist* 43, no. 5/6 (2015).
6. In keeping with the Mughal imperial court's keen interest in verisimilar representations of nature, there seems to have been hesitation in using colors that lie outside the realm of optical possibilities for human skin color for the human incarnations of a god engaged in the activities of the human realm.
7. This darker color association with Kṛṣṇa also appears in classical Tamil literature where "Kṛṣṇa was described as having a body like blue sapphire or collyrium." D. Dennis Hudson, *Krishna's Mandala: Bhagavata Religion and Beyond* (New Delhi: Oxford University Press, 2010), 66.
8. This is based on a report from a contemporary Rajasthani artist's studio on the deep blue color of Shrinathji in Pichhvai paintings. Desmond Lazaro, *Materials, Methods, and Symbolism in the Pichhvai Painting Tradition of Rajasthan*. Ahmedabad: Mapin, 2005. According to an ongoing scientific analysis conducted at the Straus center, the deep blue color of Shrinathji in a painting in the Harvard Art Museums (acc. no. 2015.31) is mainly of smalt and possibly includes a mixture of tin.
9. The idea of timed light comes from the Rubin Museum's interactive display of some Tibetan thangkas in the *Second Buddha: Master of Time* exhibition, but this is a fictional scenario. One may imagine an experience stimulated in Yayoi Kusama's *Infinity Mirrored Room* (2013, Broad Museum, F-KUSA-2014.004), or in Choi Jeong Hwa's *Chaosmos Maṇḍala* installed at the MFA's *Megacities* exhibition (2016).
10. On the eight scenes of the Buddha's life becoming a codified iconographic set during the Pāla period, see Janice Leoshko, "Scenes of the Buddha's Life in Pala Period Art," *Silk Road Art and Archaeology* 3 (1993–94); and Hiram W. Woodward Jr., "The Life of the Buddha in the Pāla Monastic Environment," *Journal of the Walters Art Gallery* 48 (1990).
11. For the idea of the movement of the sun between these transcendental Buddhas, see Claudine Bautze-Picron, "Buddhist Painting during the Reign of Harivarmadeva (End of the 11th c.) in Southeast Bangladesh," *Journal of Bengal Art* 4 (1999).
12. Vidya Dehejia, *The Body Adorned: Dissolving Boundaries between Sacred and Profane in India's Art* (New York: Columbia University Press, 2009).
13. As cited in Gyula Wojtilla, "Contributions to the Cultural History of Emerald in Early India," *Acta Orientalia Academiae Scientiarum Hungaricae* 65, no. 4 (2012): 467.
14. Wojtilla, "Contributions to the Cultural History of Emerald, 465.
15. This list is based on my interview with Patua artists of Naya village in West Bengal in January 2017. Jamuna Chitrakar kindly demonstrated the process. I thank Frank Korom for his help with identifying Jamuna. For further discussion on the artists of Naya village, see Frank J. Korom, *Village of Painters: Narrative Scrolls from West Bengal* (Santa Fe: Museum of New Mexico Press, 2006).

SELECTED BIBLIOGRAPHY

Acri, Andrea, ed. *Esoteric Buddhism in Medieval Maritime Asia: Networks of Masters, Texts, Icons.* Singapore: ISEAS, 2016.

Adachi, Kiroku, ed. *大唐西域求法高僧傳* (*Daitō Saiiki Guhō Kōsō Den*). Tokyo: Iwanami Shoten, 1942. Reprint, 1980.

Adamjee, Qamar. "Strategies for Visual Narration in the Illustrated *Chandayan* Manuscripts." PhD diss. New York University, 2011.

Agnew, Neville, ed. *Conservation of Ancient Sites on the Silk Road: Proceedings of the Second International Conference on the Conservation of Grotto Sites, Mogao Grottoes, Dunhuang, People's Republic of China, June 28–July 3, 2004.* Los Angeles: Getty Conservation Institute, 2010.

Agrawal, Om Prakash. *Conservation of Manuscripts and Paintings of South-east Asia.* London: Butterworths, 1984.

———. *Conservation of Wall Paintings in India: Achievements and Problems.* Lucknow: INTACH Indian Conservation Institute, 1995.

———. *Wall Paintings of India: A Historical Perspective.* Lucknow: INTACH Conservation Centre, 1989.

Agrawal, R.C. "Khajuraho of Rajasthan: The Temple of Ambika Mātā at Jagat." *Arts Asiatiques* 10, no. 1 (1964): 43–65.

———. "Skanda with Cock and Peacock: A Rare Device in Gandharan Art." *Eastern Approaches* (1992): 130–32.

Agrawala, V.S. *The Deeds of Harsha: Being a Cultural Study of Bāṇa's Harshacharita.* Varanasi: Prithivi Prakashan, 1969.

Ahluwalia, Roda, and J.P. Losty. "Art Historical Overviews of the Mewar Rāmāyaṇa Books." www.bl.uk/ramayana.

Aitken, Molly Emma. *The Intelligence of Tradition in Rajput Court Painting.* New Haven, CT: Yale University Press, 2010.

———. *A Magic World: New Visions of Indian Painting.* Mumbai: Marg, 2016.

Aiyangar, Rangaswami, ed. *Kṛtyakalpataru of Bhaṭṭa Lakṣmīdhara.* Vol. 5, *Danakāṇḍa.* Baroda: Baroda Oriental Institute, 1941.

Ali, Daud. "Temporality, Narration, and the Problem of History: A View from Western India c. 1100–1400." *Indian Economic and Social History Review* 50, no. 2 (2013): 237–59.

Allinger, Eva. "The Epsilon 1 Manuscript in the Wellcome Library, London." *Wiener Zeitschrift für die Kunde Südasiens* 54 (2012): 151–84.

———. "The Green Tārā in the Ford Collection: Some Stylistic Remarks." In *The Inner Asian International Style 12th–14th Centuries,* 107–19. Vienna: Verlag, 1998.

———. "A Pala-Period Aṣṭasāhasrikā Prajñāpāramitā Manuscript Distributed between Five Collections." *Vienna Journal of South Asian Studies* 51 (2007–8): 77–121.

Allinger, Eva, and Christiane Kalantari. "Art, Mobility, and Identity in the Western Himalayas." *Asian Art* (2012).

Allinger, Eva, and Gudrun Melzer. "A Pañcarakṣā Manuscript from Year 39 of the Reign of Rāmapāla." *Artibus Asiae* 70, no. 2 (2010): 387–414.

Andhare, Shridhar. "Jain Monumental Painting." In *The Peaceful Liberators: Jain Art from India,* edited by Pratapaditya Pal, 77–87. Los Angeles: Los Angeles County Museum of Art, 1995.

Artioli, D., et al. "Mural Paintings of Ajanta Caves, Part II: Non Destructive Investigations and Microanalysis on Execution Technique and State of Conservation." Paper presented at the Ninth International Conference on NDT of Art, Jerusalem, Israel, 2008.

Asher, Frederick M. *The Art of Eastern India, 300–800.* Oxford: Oxford University Press, 1980.

Bahl, Kali C. "The Hindi 'Rīti' Tradition and the 'Rasikapriyā' of Keshavadasa: An Introductory Review." *Journal of South Asian Literature* 10, no. 1 (1974): 1–38.

Bailey, H.W. "Saka Studies: The Ancient Kingdom of Khotan." *Iran* 8 (1970): 65–72.

Bakker, Hans T. *The World of the Skandapurana—Northern India in the Sixth and Seventh Centuries.* Leiden: Brill, 2014.

Balbir, Nalini. "Le Monde Médian: Une peinture cosmologique Jaina sur tissu déposée au Musée Guimet." *Arts Asiatiques* 64 (2009): 27–41.

Balbir, Nalini, et al., eds. *Océan des Rivières de Contes.* Paris: Gallimard, 1997.

Banerjea, Jitendra Nath. *The Development of Hindu Iconography.* Delhi: Munshiram Manoharlal, 1974.

Barnard, Nick. "Jaina Paintings and Manuscripts in the Victoria and Albert Museum." In *Jaina Painting and Manuscript Culture,* edited by Julia A.B. Hegewald, 83–127. Berlin: EB-Verlag, 2015.

Barrett, Douglas E., and Basil Gray. *Painting of India.* Geneva: Skira, 1963.

Bautze-Picron, Claudine. "Between Men and Gods: Small Motifs in the Buddhist Art of Eastern India, an Interpretation." In *Function and Meaning in Buddhist Art: Proceedings of a Seminar Held at Leiden University, 21–24 October 1991,* edited by K.R. van Kooij and H. van der Veere. Gonda Indological Studies, 59–79. Groningen: Egbert Forsten, 1995.

———. "Buddhist Painting during the Reign of Harivarmadeva (End of the 11th c.) in Southeast Bangladesh." *Journal of Bengal Art* 4 (1999): 159–97.

———. "The Elaboration of a Style: Eastern Indian Motifs and Forms in Early Tibetan (?) and Burmese Painting." In *The Inner Asian International Style 12th–14th Centuries,* edited by Deborah Klimburg-Salter and Eva Allinger, 13–65. Vienna: Verlag, 1998.

Bayerová, Tatjana. "Buddhist Wall Paintings at Nako Monastery, North India: Changing of the Technology throughout Centuries." *Studies in Conservation* 63, no. 3 (2017): 171–88.

Beach, Milo Cleveland, Eberhard Fischer, Brijnder Nath Goswamy, and Jorrit Britschgi, eds. *Masters of Indian Painting.* 2 vols. Zurich: Artibus Asiae Publishers, 2011.

Beal, Samuel, ed. *Si-Yu-Ki: Buddhist Records of the Western World by Hsüan-Tsang.* London: Trübner, 1884.

Behl, Aditya. "Creating a New Genre: The Cāndāyan." In *Love's Subtle Magic: An Indian Islamic Literary Tradition, 1379–1545,* 59–108. New York: Oxford University Press, 2012.

Bendall, Cecil. *Catalogue of the Buddhist Sanskrit Manuscripts in the University Library, Cambridge.* Cambridge: Cambridge University Press, 1883. Reprint, Stuttgart: Steiner, 1992.

Benipuri, Ramvriksh, ed. *Bihārī Satsai with Commentary by Śrī Rāmavṛkṣa Benīpurī* (in Hindi). Patna, India: Pustak Bhandar, 1903.

Berger, Patricia. "Preserving the Nation: The Political Uses of Tantric Art in China." In *Latter Days of the Law: Images of Chinese Buddhism, 850–1850,* edited by Marsha Weidner. Lawrence, KS: Spencer Museum of Art, 1994.

Berkwitz, Stephen C., Juliane Schober, and Claudia Brown. *Buddhist Manuscript Cultures: Knowledge, Ritual, and Art.* London: Routledge, 2009.

Bhattacharya, Bhabatosh, ed. *Dānasāgara of Ballāla Sena.* Calcutta: Asiatic Society, 1956.

Bhattacharya, G. "The Newly Discovered Buddhist Temple at Nalanda." *South Asian Archaeology* 2 (1995): 719–40.

Bhattacharya, Vidhushekhar, ed. *Nagananda-Nataka of Sri Harsadeva.* Calcutta: Asiatic Society, 1957.

Bhattacharyya, Benoytosh, ed. *Niṣpannayogāvalī of Mahāpaṇḍita Abhayākaragupta.* Gaekwad's Oriental Series, vol. 109. Baroda: Oriental Institute, 1949.

———. *Sādhanamālā.* Vols. 1 and 2. Gaekwad's Oriental Series, vols. 26, 41. Baroda: Oriental Institute of Baroda, 1925–28; reprint, 1968.

Bhattacharyya, D.C. "The Five Protective Goddesses of Buddhism." In *Aspects of Indian Art,* edited by Pratapaditya Pal, 85–92. Leiden: Brill, 1972.

———. *Studies in Buddhist Iconography.* New Delhi: Manohar, 1978.

———. "The Vajrāvalī-nāma-maṇḍalopāyikā of Abhayākaragupta." In *Tantric and Taoist Studies in Honour of R.A. Stein,* edited by Michel Strickmann, 70–95. Brussels: Institut Belge des Hautes Etudes Chinoises, 1981.

Bhattasali, Nalini Kanta. *Iconography of Buddhist and Brahmanical Sculptures in the Dacca Museum.* Dacca: Rai S.N. Bhadra Bahadur, 1929.

Blaszczyk, Regina Lee. *The Color Revolution.* Cambridge, MA: MIT Press, 2012.

Bloom, Jonathan M. *Paper before Print: The History and Impact of Paper in the Islamic World.* New Haven, CT: Yale University Press, 2001.

Bogel, Cynthea. *With a Single Glance: Buddhist Icon and Early Mikkyō Vision.* Seattle: University of Washington Press, 2009.

Bollée, Willem B. *A Cultural Encyclopaedia of the Kathāsaritsāgara in Keywords: Complementary to Norman Penzer's General Index on Charles Tawney's Translation.* Halle an der Saale: Universitätsverlag Halle-Wittenberg, 2015.

Bose, Nandalal, and K.G. Subrahmanyam. *Vision and Creation.* Calcutta: Visva-Bharati Publication, 1999.

Boucher, Daniel. "The *Pratītyasamutpādagāthā* and Its Role in the Medieval Cult of the Relics." *Journal of the International Association of Buddhist Studies* 14, no. 1 (1991): 1–27.

Brac de la Perrière, Éloïse. "The Art of the Book in India under the Sultanate." In *After Timur Left: Culture and Circualtion in Fifteenth-Century North India,* edited by Francesca Orsini and Samira Sheikh, 301–38. New Delhi: Oxford University Press, 2014.

———. *L'art du livre dans l'Inde des Sultanats.* Paris: PUPS, 2008.

Brick, David. "The Dānakāṇḍa ('Book of Giving') of the *Kṛtyakalpataru:* A Critical Edition and Annotated Translation." PhD diss., Harvard University, 2009.

Bronner, Yigal. "Understanding Udbhaṭa: The Invention of Kashmiri Poetics in the Jayāpīḍa Moment." In *Around Abhinavagupta: Aspects of the Intellectual History of Kashmir from the Ninth to the Eleventh Century,* edited by Eli Franco and Isabelle Ratié, 81–148. Beaverton: LIT Verlag, 2017.

Brown, C. Mackenzie. "Purāṇa as Scripture: From Sound to Image of the Holy Word in the Hindu Tradition." *History of Religions* 26, no. 1 (1986): 68–86.

Brown, W. Norman, ed. *A Descriptive and Illustrated Catalogue of Miniature Paintings of the Jaina Kalpasūtra.* Washington, DC: Smithsonian Institution, 1934.

———. *The Story of Kālaka.* Washington, DC: Smithsonian Institution, 1933.

———. *The Vasanta Vilāsa: A Poem of the Spring Festival in Old Gujarātī Accompanied by Sanskrit and Prakrit Stanzas and Illustrated with Miniature Paintings.* New Haven, CT: American Oriental Society, 1962.

Buescher, Hartmut. *Catalogue of Sanskrit Manuscripts: Early Acquisitions and the Nepal Collection.* Copenhagen: NIAS, 2010.

Bühler, G. "New Jaina Inscriptions from Mathurā, No. XXI." *Epigraphia Indica* 1 (1892).

Bühnemann, Gudrun. "The 'Dhyana Collections' and Their Significance for Hindu Iconography." *Journal of Indian and Buddhist Studies* 40, no. 2 (1992): 1080–86.

———. "Erotic Forms of Gaṇeśa in Hindu and Buddhist Iconography." In *Script and Image: Papers on Art and Epigraphy,* edited by A. Gail, G. Mevissen, and R. Salomon, 15–28. Delhi: Motilal Banarsidass, 2006.

———. *Sādhanaśataka and Sādhanaśatapañcāśikā: Two Buddhist Sādhana Collections in Sanskrit Manuscript.* Vienna: Arbeitskreis für Tibetische und Buddhistische studien, Universität Wien, 1994.

———. "The Śāradātilakatantra on Yoga: A New Edition and Translation of Chapter 25." *Bulletin of the School of Oriental and African Studies* 74, no. 2 (2011): 205–35.

———. "Some Remarks on the Text of the Niṣpannayogāvalī as Found in Jagaddarpaṇa's Kriyāsamuccaya." *Zentralasiatische Studien des Seminars furs Sprach- und Kulturwissenschaft Zentralsiens der Universitat Bonn* 22–24 (1992): 18–21.

———. "Two Forms of Gaṇapati in the Indo-Tibetan Buddhist Tradition." *Wiener Zeitschrift für die Kunde Südasiens* 38 (1994): 201–11.

Burger, Richard L., and Jerrold B. Leikin. "Cinnabar Use in Prehispanic Peru and Its Possible Health Consequences." *Journal of Archaeological Science: Reports* 17 (2018): 730–34.

Byrne, Alex, and David R. Hilbert. "Color Realism and Color Science." *Behavioral and Brain Sciences* 26, no. 3 (2003): 3–64.

Canby, Sheila. "'Abd al-Samad." In *Masters of Indian Painting, 1100–1650,* edited by Milo Cleveland Beach, Eberhard Fischer, and B.N. Goswamy, 97–110. Zurich: Artibus Asiae Publishers, 2011.

Cavallo, Geovanni, and Manoj Pandit. "Geology and Petrography of Ochres and White Clay Deposits in Rajasthan State, India." In *Geoarchaeology and Archaeomineralogy,* edited by R.I. Kostov, B. Gaydarska, and M. Gurova, 147–52. Sofia: Publishing House St. Ivan Rilski, 2008.

Chakrabarti, Kunal. "A History of Intolerance: The Representation of Buddhists in the Bengal Purāṇas." *Social Scientist* 44, no. 5/6 (2016): 11–27.

Chakravarti, Ranabir. "Nakhudas and Nauvittakas: Ship-Owning Merchants in the West Coast of India (1000–1500)." *Journal of the Economic and Social History of the Orient* 43, no. 1 (2000): 34–64.

Chakraverty, Anjan. *Indian Miniature Painting.* New Delhi: Roli Books, 2005.

Chanchani, Nachiket. "From Asoda to Almora, the Roads Less Taken: Māru-Gurjara Architecture in the Central Himalayas." *Arts Asiatiques* 69 (2014): 3–16.

———. "Paper Prasada." *Artibus Asiae* 76, no. 2 (2016): 129–46.

———. "Telling Tales: The Freer Vasanta Vilāsa." *Artibus Asiae* 72, no. 1 (2012): 123–40.

Chandra, Lokesh. "The Rin-Ihan and Rin-Hbyun: To the Memory of Professor F. D. Lessing." *Oriens Extremus* 8, no. 2 (1961): 188–207.

———. *A Ninth Century Scroll of the Vajradhātu Maṇḍala.* Śata-piṭaka Series, vol. 343. New Delhi: International Academy of Indian Culture, 1986.

Chandra, Lokesh, and David L. Snellgrove, eds. *Sarva-tathāgata-tattva Saṅgraha: Facsimile Reproduction of a Tenth Century Sanskrit Manuscript from Nepal.* New Delhi: Rani, 1981.

Chandra, Moti. *Jain Miniature Paintings from Western India.* Ahmedabad: Sharabhai Manilal Nawab, 1949.

———. *New Documents of Jaina Painting.* Edited by Umakant Premanand Shah. Bombay: Shri Mahavira Jaina Vidyalaya, 1975.

———. "A Pair of Painted Wooden Covers of the Karaṇḍāvyūha Manuscript Dated A.D. 1455 from East India." In *Chhavi: Golden Jubilee Volume (1920–1970)*, 240–42. Varanasi: Bharat Kala Bhavan, 1971.

———. *Studies in Early Indian Painting.* London: Asia Publishing House, 1970.

———. *The Technique of Mughal Painting.* Lucknow: U.P. Historical Society, 1949.

Chandra, Moti, and Karl J. Khandalavala. *An Illustrated Āraṇyaka Parvan in the Asiatic Society of Bombay.* Bombay: Asiatic Society of Bombay, 1974.

Chandra, Pramod. "Notes on the Study of Indian Miniatures." In *Indian Miniatures: The Ehrenfeld Collection,* edited by Daniel J. Ehnbom, Robert Skelton, Pramod Chandra, and William K. Ehrenfeld, 15–18. New York: Hudson Hills Press, 1985.

Chandra, Pramod, and Sonya Rhie Quintanilla. "Nandalal Bose and the History of Indian Art." In *Rhythms of India: The Art of Nandalal Bose,* edited by Sonya Rhie Quintanilla, 26–41. San Diego: San Diego Museum of Art, 2008.

Chatterjee, Indrani. *Forgotten Friends: Monks, Marriages, and Memories of Northeast India.* Oxford: Oxford University Press, 2013.

Chowdhury, A.M. *Dynastic History of Bengal.* Dacca: Asiatic Society of Pakistan, 1967.

Cohen, Richard. "Setting the Three Jewels: The Complex Culture of Buddhism at the Ajaṇṭā Caves." PhD diss., University of Michigan, 1995.

———. *The Splendid Vision: Reading a Buddhist Sutra.* New York: Columbia University Press, 2012.

Contadini, Anna, ed. *Arab Painting: Text and Image in Illustrated Arabic Manuscripts.* Leiden: Brill, 2007.

Coomaraswamy, Ananda K. *Catalogue of the Indian Collections in the Museum of Fine Arts, Boston.* Part IV, *Jaina Paintings and Manuscripts.* Boston: Museum of Fine Arts, 1924.

———. "Illustrated Śvetambāra Jaina Manuscript of A.D. 1260." *Eastern Art* 2 (1930): 237–40.

———. "One Hundred References to Indian Painting." *Artibus Asiae* 4, no. 1 (1930): 41–57.

———. "Picture Showmen." *Indian Historical Quarterly* 5, no. 2 (1929): 182–87.

———. *Rajput Painting.* New York: H. Milford; Oxford University Press, 1916.

———. “The Technique and Theory of Indian Painting.” *Technical Studies in the Field of the Fine Arts* 3, no. 2 (1934): 59.

Copp, Paul F. *The Body Incantatory: Spells and the Ritual Imagination in Medieval Chinese Buddhism.* New York: Columbia University Press, 2014.

Cort, John E. “Contemporary Jain Maṇḍala Rituals.” In *Victorious Ones: Jain Images of Perfection,* edited by Phyllis Granoff, 141–57. New York: Rubin Museum of Art, 2010.

Cotte, Sabine. “Conservation of Thangkas: A Review of the Literature since the 1970s.” *Studies in Conservation* 56, no. 2 (2011): 81–93.

Cox, Whitney. “Literary Register and Historical Consciousness in Kalhaṇa: A Hypothesis.” *Indian Economic and Social History Review* 50, no. 2 (2013): 131–60.

Craddock, P.T., L.K. Gurjar, and K.T.M. Hegde. “Zinc Production in Medieval India.” *World Archaeology* 15, no. 2 (1983): 211–17.

Cummins, Joan. *Indian Painting: From Cave Temples to the Colonial Period.* Boston: MFA Publications, 2006.

———, ed. *Vishnu: Hinduism’s Blue-Skinned Savior.* Ahmedabad; Nashville, TN: Mapin Publishing with Frist Center for the Visual Arts, 2011.

Dachille, Rae Erin. “The Body Mandala Debate: Knowing the Body through a Network of Fifteenth-Century Tibetan Buddhist Texts.” PhD diss., University of California at Berkeley, 2015.

Dallapiccola, Anna L., ed. *Indian Painting: The Lesser-Known Traditions.* New Delhi: Niyogi Books, 2011.

Das Gupta, Rajatananda. *Eastern Indian Manuscript Painting.* Bombay: D.B. Taraporevala Sons, 1972.

Daston, Lorraine, ed. *Things That Talk: Object Lessons from Art and Science.* New York: Zone Books, 2004.

Davids, Caroline A.F. Rhys, ed. *The Visuddhi-Magga of Buddhaghosa.* London: Pali Text Society, 1920.

Davidson, Ronald M. *Indian Esoteric Buddhism: A Social History of the Tantric Movement.* New York: Columbia Uniersity Press, 2002.

———. “Revisiting the *Mañjuśriyamūlakalpa*’s Painting Chapters.” In *Reasons and Lives in Buddhist Traditions: Studies in Honor of Matthew Kapstein,* edited by Dan Arnold, Cécile Ducher, and Pierre-Julien Harter, 71–83. Somerville, MA: Wisdom Publications, 2019.

———. *Tibetan Renaissance: Tantric Buddhism in the Rebirth of Tibetan Culture.* New York: Columbia University Press, 2005.

De Simini, Florinda. *Of Gods and Books: Ritual and Knowledge Transmission in the Manuscript Cultures of Premodern India.* Berlin: De Gruyter, 2016.

DeCaroli, Robert. *Image Problems: The Origin and Development of the Buddha’s Image in Early South Asia.* Seattle: University of Washington Press, 2015.

Decleer, Hubert. “Review of Siklos, the Vajrabhairava Tantras, the Tibetan and Mongolian Versions, English Translations and Annotations.” *Indo-Iranian Journal* (1998): 290–301.

Dehejia, Vidya. *The Body Adorned: Dissolving Boundaries between Sacred and Profane in India’s Art.* New York: Columbia University Press, 2009.

———. *Devi: The Great Goddess; Female Divinity in South Asian Art.* Washington, DC: Smithsonian Institution, 1999.

———. *Discourse in Early Buddhist Art: Visual Narratives of India.* New Delhi: Munshiram,1997.

———. *Yoginī: Cult and Temples.* New Delhi: National Museum, 1986.

Deheley, Martin, Emanuel Kindzorra, Oliver Hahn, and Ira Rabin. “Material Analysis of Sanskrit Palm-Leaf Manuscripts Preserved in Nepal.” *Journal of the International Association of Buddhist Studies* 36/37 (2015): 119–52.

Desai, Vishakha N. “Painting and Politics in Seventeenth-Century North India: Mewār, Bikāner, and the Mughal Court.” *Art Journal* 49, no. 4 (1990): 370–78.

Devadhar, C.R., ed. *Dūtavākyam: A Sanskrit One Act Play by Bhāsa.* Poona: Oriental Book Agency, 1957.

Dezsö, Csaba. "Encounters with 'Vetālas' Studies on Fabulous Creatures I." *Acta Orientalia Academiae Scientiarum Hungaricae* 63, no. 4 (2010): 391–426.

Diemberger, Hildegard, Karl Ehrhard, and Peter F. Kornicki. *Tibetan Printing: Comparison, Continuities, and Change.* Leiden: Brill, 2016.

Dillon, Emma. "The Art of Interpolation in the Roman de Fauvel." *Journal of Musicology* 19, no. 2 (2002): 223–63.

Dine, Susan. "Sanskrit beyond Text: The Use of Bonji (Siddham) in Mandala and Other Imagery in Ancient and Medieval Japan." Master's thesis, University of Washington, 2012.

Donaldson, Thomas E. "Ekapāda Śiva Images in Orissan Art." *Ars Orientalis* 13 (1982): 153–67.

———. *Iconography of the Buddhist Sculpture of Orissa.* New Delhi: Indira Gandhi National Centre for the Arts, Abhinav Publications, 2001.

Doshi, Saryu. *Masterpieces of Jain Painting.* Bombay: Marg Publications, 1985.

Dundas, Paul. "Becoming Gautama: Mantra and History in Śvetāmbara Jainism." In *Open Boundaries: Jain Communities and Cultures in Indian History,* edited by John E. Cort, 31–52. Albany: State University of New York Press, 1998.

Durga, P.S. Kanaka. "Identity and Symbols of Sustenance: Explorations in Social Mobility of Medieval South India." *Journal of the Economic and Social History of the Orient* 44, no. 2 (2001): 141–74.

Dutt, N. "The Buddhist Manuscripts at Gilgit." *Indian Historical Quarterly* 9, no. 1 (1933): 227.

———, ed. *Gilgit Manuscripts,* vol. 1. New Delhi: Sri Satguru Publications, 1984.

Dwivedi, Vinod P. "A Rasamanjari Painting from Basohli." *Bulletin of the Cleveland Museum of Art* 56, no. 7 (1969): 262–68.

Eastman, Alvan C. "A Survey of Formulae in the Miniature Painting of Western India." *Art Bulletin* 20, no. 2 (1938): 133–44.

Eastwood, Bruce Stansfield. "The Elements of Vision: The Micro-Cosmology of Galenic Visual Theory According to Ḥunayn Ibn Isḥāq." *Transactions of the American Philosophical Society* 72, no. 5 (1982): 1–59.

Eaton, Natasha. *Colour, Art, and Empire: Visual Culture and the Nomadism of Representation.* London: I.B. Tauris, 2013.

———. "Nomadism of Colour: Painting, Technology, and Waste in the Chromo-Zones of Colonial India, c. 1765–c. 1860." *Journal of Material Culture* 17, no. 1 (2012): 61–81.

Eaton, Richard Maxwell. *The Rise of Islam and the Bengal Frontier, 1204–1760.* Berkeley: University of California Press, 1993.

Ehnbom, Daniel J. "An Analysis and Reconstruction of the Dispersed 'Bhagavata Purana' from the Caurapancasika Group." PhD diss., University of Chicago, 1984.

———. "Master of Dispersed Bhagavata Purana." In *Masters of Indian Painting,* edited by Milo C. Beach, Eberhard Fischer, and B.N. Goswamy, 77–88. Zurich: Artibus Asiae Publishers, 2011.

Ehnbom, Daniel J., Robert Skelton, Pramod Chandra, and William K. Ehrenfeld. *Indian Miniatures: The Ehrenfeld Collection.* New York: Hudson Hills Press, 1985.

Einoo, Shingo, ed. *Genesis and Development of Tantrism.* Tokyo: Institute of Oriental Culture, University of Tokyo, 2009.

Elias, Jamal J. *Aisha's Cushion: Religious Art, Perception, and Practice in Islam.* Cambridge, MA: Harvard University Press, 2012.

Elliott, Mark, Hildegard Diemberger, and Michela Clemente. *Buddha's Word: The Life of Books in Tibet and Beyond.* Cambridge: Museum of Archaeology and Anthropology, 2014.

Emmerick, R. "Some Khotanese Inscriptions on objets d'art." *Journal of the Royal Asiatic Society of Great Britain and Ireland* 3 (1968): 140–43.

English, Elizabeth. *Vajrayoginī: A Study of Her Visualizations, Rituals, and Forms.* Boston: Wisdom Publications, 2002.

Ernst, Richard R. "Arts and Sciences: A Perspective of Tibetan Painting." *Chimia* 55, no. 11 (2001): 900–914.

Feller, Robert L. *Artists' Pigments: A Handbook of Their History and Characteristics,* vol. 1. Washington, DC: National Gallery of Art, 1986.

Fenves, Peter D. *The Messianic Reduction: Walter Benjamin and the Shape of Time.* Stanford, CA: Stanford University Press, 2011.

Fer, Briony. *The Infinite Line: Re-Making Art after Modernism.* New Haven, CT: Yale University Press, 2004.

Fitshugh, Elisabeth West, ed. *Artists' Pigments: A Handbook of Their History and Characteristics,* vol. 3. Washington, DC: National Gallery of Art, 1997.

Fleming, Benjamin J. "Making Land Sacred: Inscriptional Evidence for Buddhist Kings and Brahman Priests in Medieval Bengal." *Numen* 60, no. 5–6 (2013): 559–85.

———. "Manuscripts and Shifting Geographies: The Dvādaśajyotirliṅgastotra from the Deccan College as a Case Study." In *Material Culture and Asian Religions: Text, Image, Object,* edited by Benjamin J. Fleming and Richard D. Mann, 59–72. New York: Taylor and Francis, 2014.

———. "The Materiality of South Asian Manuscripts from the University of Pennsylvania MS Coll. 390 and the Rāmamālā Library in Bangladesh." *Manuscript Studies* 1, no. 1 (2016): 28–51.

Flood, Finbarr Barry. *Objects of Translation: Material Culture and Medieval "Hindu-Muslim" Encounter.* Princeton, NJ: Princeton University Press, 2009.

Fogg, Sam, and Bob Miller. *Manuscripts from the Himalayas and the Indian Subcontinent.* London: Sam Fogg, 1996.

Formigatti, Camillo A. "A Forgotten Chapter in South Asian Book History: A Bird's View on Sanskrit Print Culture." In *Tibetan Printing: Comparisons, Continuities, and Change,* edited by Hildegard Diemberger, Franz-Karl Ehrhard, and Peter F. Kornicki, 72–134. Leiden: Brill, 2016.

———. "Sanskrit Annotated Manuscripts from Northern India and Nepal." PhD diss., University of Hamburg, 2015.

Foster, Hal. "An Archival Impulse." *October* 110 (2004): 3–22.

Foucher, Alfred. *Étude sur l'iconographie Bouddhique de l'Inde d'après des Documents Nouveaux.* Paris: A. Leroux, 1900.

———. *Étude sur l'iconographie Bouddhique de l'inde d'après des textes inédits.* Paris: Leroux, 1905.

Fraser, Sarah E. "Formulas of Creativity: Artist's Sketches and Techniques of Copying at Dunhuang." *Artibus Asiae* 59, no. 3/4 (2000): 189–224.

Fremantle, Francesca. "A Critical Study of the Guhyasamāja Tantra." PhD diss., University of London, 1971.

French, J. "Sansar Chand of Kangra." *Indian Art and Letters* 21 (1947): 89.

Furui, Ryosuke. "Rural Society and Social Networks in Early Bengal from the Fifth to the Thirteenth Century A.D." PhD diss., Jawaharlal Nehru University, 2007.

Gage, John. "Black and White and Red All Over." *RES: Anthropology and Aesthetics* 16 (1988): 51–53.

———. "Color in Western Art, an Issue?" *Art Bulletin* 72, no. 4 (1990): 518–41.

Galambos, Imre. "Manuscript and Print in the Tangut State: The Case of the Sunzi." In *Tibetan Printing: Comparisons, Continuities, and Change,* edited by Hildegard Diemberger, Franz-Karl Ehrhard, and Peter Kornicki. Brill's Tibetan Studies Library, 135–52. Leiden: Brill, 2016.

———. *Translating Chinese Tradition and Teaching Tangut Culture, Manuscripts, and Printed Books from Khara-Khoto.* Berlin: De Gruyter, 2015.

Gandhi, S.M. "Copper, Zinc, Lead Ores—Their Exploitation and Metal Extraction by the Ancients in the Northwestern India." *Journal of the Geological Society of India* 84 (2014): 253–66.

Gellner, David N. *The Anthropology of Buddhism and Hinduism: Weberian Themes.* New Delhi: Oxford University Press, 2001.

———. *Monk, Householder, and Tantric Priest: Newar Buddhism and Its Hierarchy of Ritual.* Cambridge: Cambridge University Press, 1992.

———. "Monkhood and Priesthood in Newar Buddhism." In *The Anthropology of Buddhism and Hinduism: Weberian Themes,* 106–33. New Delhi: Oxford University Press, 2001.

Gettens, Rutherford J. "Proposal for a Handbook on Analysis of Materials of Paintings." *Studies in Conservation* 6, no. 1 (1961): 26–28.

Gettens, Rutherford J., and George L. Stout. *Painting Materials: A Short Encyclopaedia.* New York: Dover, 1966.

Ghosh, Deva Prasad. *Mediaeval Indian Painting, Eastern School, 13th Century A.D. to Modern Times.* Delhi: Sundeep Prakashan, 1982.

Giovagnoli, Annamaria, et al. "The Mural Paintings of the Ajanta Caves, Part I: Documentation on Execution Techniques and Conservation Condition." Paper presented at the 9th International Conference on NDT of Art, Jerusalem, Israel, 2008.

Givens, Jean A., Karen Reeds, and Alain Touwaide. *Visualizing Medieval Medicine and Natural History, 1200–1550.* Aldershot, England; Burlington, VT: Ashgate, 2006.

Glynn, Catherine. "Evidence of Royal Painting for the Amber Court." *Artibus Asiae* 56, no. 1/2 (1996): 67–93.

———. "A Sixteenth Century 'Devīmāhātmya' Manuscript from Kangra." PhD diss., University of Southern California, 1979.

Goepper, Roger, ed. *Alchi: Ladakh's Hidden Buddhist Sanctuary.* Boston: Shambhala, 1996.

Goitein, S.D. "Portrait of a Medieval India Trader: Three Letters from the Cairo Geniza." *Bulletin of the School of Oriental and African Studies* 50, no. 3 (1987): 449–64.

Gómez, Luis O. "Two Tantric Meditations: Visualizing the Deity." In *Buddhism in Practice,* edited by Donald S. Lopez Jr., 318–27. Princeton, NJ: Princeton University Press, 1995.

Goodall, Dominic, Alexis Sanderson, and Harunaga Isaacson, eds. *The Niśvāsatattvasaṃhitā: The Earliest Surviving Śaiva Tantra.* Paris: École Française d'Extrême-Orient, 2015.

Goodman, Amanda. "The Ritual Instructions for Altar Methods (Tanfa Yize): Prolegomenon to the Study of a Chinese Esoteric Buddhist Ritual Compendium from Late-Medieval Dunhuang." PhD diss., University of California at Berkeley, 2013.

Goody, Jack. *The Interface between the Written and the Oral.* Cambridge: Cambridge University Press, 1987.

Gopalkrishnan, Sudha, ed., *Vijñānanidhi: Manuscript Treasures of India.* New Delhi: National Mission for Manuscripts, 2007.

Goswamy, B.N. "A Painter's Letter to His Royal Patron: An Old Takri Document." *Journal of the American Oriental Society* 86, no. 2 (1966): 209–16.

———. *The Word Is Sacred, Sacred Is the Word: The Indian Manuscript Tradition.* New Delhi: Niyogi Books, 2007

Goswamy, B.N., and Eberhard Fischer. *Pahari Masters: Court Painters of Northern India.* Zurich: Artibus Asiae Publishers, 1992.

Goudriaan, Teun. *Māyā Divine and Human: A Study of Magic and Its Religious Foundations in Sanskrit Texts, with Particular Attention to a Fragment on Viṣṇu's Māyā Preserved in Bali.* Delhi: Motilal Banarsidass, 1978.

———. "Some Beliefs and Rituals Concerning Time and Death in the Kubjikāmata." In *Selected Studies on Ritual in the Indian Religions: Essays to D.J. Hoens,* edited by Ria Kloppenborg, 92–117. Leiden: Brill, 1983.

Gough, Ellen. "Shades of Enlightenment—A Jain Tantric Diagram and the Colours of the Tīrthaṅkaras." *International Journal of Jaina Studies* 8, no. 1 (2012): 1–47.

Granoff, Phyllis. "The Gift of the Two Merchants: Defining the Buddhist Community through Story." *East and West* 55, no. 1/4 (2005): 129–38.

———. "Holy Warriors: A Preliminary Study of Some Biographies of Saints and Kings in the Classical Indian Tradition." *Journal of Indian Philosophy* 12, no. 3 (1984): 291–303.

———. "Jain Lives of Haribhadra: An Inquiry into the Sources and Logic of the Legends." *Journal of Indian Philosophy* 17, no. 2 (1989): 105–28.

———. "Luxury Goods and Intellectual History: The Case of Printed and Woven Multicolored Textiles in Medieval India." *Ars Orientalis* 34 (2004): 151–71.

———, ed. *Victorious Ones: Jain Images of Perfection.* New York: Rubin Museum of Art in Association with Mapin Publishing, 2009.

Greco, Gina L., and Peter Shoemaker. "Intertextuality and Large Corpora: A Medievalist Approach." *Computers and the Humanities* 27, no. 5/6 (1993): 349–55.

Griffiths, Arlo, et al. "An Inscribed Bronze Sculpture of a Buddha in Bhadrāsana at Museum Ranggawarsita Insemarang (Central Java, Indonesia)." *Arts Asiatiques* 68 (2013): 3–26.

Griffiths, Arlo. "Written Traces of the Buddhist Past: Mantras and Dhāraṇīs in the Indonesian Inscriptions." *Bulletin of the School of Oriental and African Studies* 77, no. 1 (2014): 137–94.

Gude, Tushara Bindu. "Between Music and History: Ragamala Paintings and European Collectors in Late Eighteenth-Century Northern India." PhD diss., University of California at Los Angeles, 2009.

Gupta, Parmeshwari Lal, ed. *Candāyana.* Mumbai: Hindi Grantha Ratnakara, 1964.

Guy, John. "Indian Painting from 1100 to 1500." In *Masters of Indian Painting,* edited by Milo Cleveland Beach, Eberhard Fischer, and B.N. Goswamy, 15–28. Zurich: Artibus Asiae Publishers, 2011.

Guy, John, and Jorrit Britschgi. *Wonder of the Age: Master Painters of India, 1100–1900.* New York: Metropolitan Museum of Art, 2011.

Gyaneswor Singh, Y. *A Report on Conservation and Preservation of Court Mural Paintings of Manipur, 1985.* Imphal: Mutua Museum, 1986.

Gyatso, Janet. "Letter Magic: A Peircean Perspective on the Semiotics of Rdo Grub-Chen's Dharani Memory." In *In the Mirror of Memory: Reflections on Mindfulness and Remembrance in Indian and Tibetan Buddhism.* Albany: State University of New York Press, 1992.

Hall, Kenneth R. "Ports-of-Trade, Maritime Diasporas, and Networks of Trade and Cultural Integration in the Bay of Bengal Region of the Indian Ocean, c. 1300–1500." *Journal of the Economic and Social History of the Orient* 53, no. 1–2 (2009): 109–45.

Hamburger, Jeffrey F. "Body vs. Book: The Trope of Visibility in Images of Christian-Jewish Polemic." In *Ästhetik des Unsichtbaren: Bildtheorie und Bildgebrauch in Der Vormoderne,* edited by David Ganz and Thomas Lentes, 112–45. Berlin: Reimer, 2004.

———. "The Iconicity of Script." *Word and Image: A Journal of Verbal/Visual Enquiry* 27, no. 3 (2011): 249–61.

———. *The Visual and the Visionary: Art and Female Spirituality in Late Medieval Germany.* New York: Zone Books, 1998.

———. "The Visual and the Visionary: The Changing Role of the Image in Late Medieval Monastic Devotions." *Viator* 20 (1989): 161–82.

Hamburger, Jeffrey F., and Brigitte Miriam Bedos-Rezak, eds. *Sign and Design: Script as Image in Cross-Cultural Perspective (300–1600 CE).* Washington, DC: Dumbarton Oaks, 2016.

Harimoto, Kengo. "In Search of the Oldest Nepalese Manuscript." *Rivista degli studi orientali, Nuova Serie* 84, no. 1/4 (2011): 85–106.

Harrison, Paul. "Commemoration and Identification in Buddhānusmṛti." In *In the Mirror of Memory: Reflections on Mindfulness and Remembrance in Indian and Tibetan Buddhism,* edited by Janet Gyatso, 215–38. Albany: State University of New York Press, 1992.

Harrison, Paul, and Christian Luczanits. "New Light on (and from) the Muhammad Nari Stele." In *Special International Symposium on Pure Land Buddhism,* 69–126. Kyoto: Research Center for Buddhist Cultures in Asia, Otani University, 2011.

Hayashi, Takatsugu. "On the Authorship of the Atthasalini." *Journal of Indian and Buddhist Studies (Indogaku bukkyogaku kenkyu)* 46, no. 1 (1997): 419–15.

Hayden, Brian. "Practical and Prestige Technologies: The Evolution of Material Systems." *Journal of Archaeological Method and Theory* 5, no. 1 (1998): 1–55.

Hazarika, Biman. "The World of the Sattriya School of Painting in Assam." In *Pelagic Passageways: The Northern Bay of Bengal before Colonialism,* edited by Rila Mukherjee, 425–42. Delhi: Primus Books, 2011.

Hegewald, Julia A. B., ed. *Jaina Painting and Manuscript Culture.* Berlin: EB-Verlag, 2015.

Heller, Amy. "The Paintings of Gra Thang: History and Iconography of an 11th Century Tibetan Temple." *Tibet Journal* 27, no. 1/2 (2002): 37–70.

———. "Three Ancient Manuscripts from Tholing in the Tucci Collection, Isiao, Roma, Part I: Manuscript 1329 E." In *Studies in Honour of Luciano Petech: A Commemoration Volume, 1914–2014.* Rome: Sapienza Università di Roma and Fabrizio Serra Editore, 2016.

———. "The Vajravali Mandala of Shalu and Sakya: The Legacy of Buston (1290–1364)." *Orientations* 35, no. 4 (2004): 69–73.

Hellwig, Oliver. "Materialgruppen in der Indischen Alchemie." *Zeitschrift der Deutschen Morgenländischen Gesellschaft* 164, no. 2 (2014): 451–68.

Helman-Wazny, Agnieszka. *The Archaeology of Tibetan Books.* Leiden: Brill, 2014.

Henss, Michael. *The Cultural Monuments of Tibet.* 2 vols. Munich: Prestel, 2014.

Hickman, Money L. "Notes on Buddhist Banners." *Boston Museum Bulletin* 71, no. 363 (1973): 4–20.

Hidas, Gergely. "Mahā-Daṇḍadhāraṇī-Śītavatī: A Buddhist Apotropaic Scripture." In *Indic Manuscript Cultures through the Ages: Material, Textual, and Historical Investigations,* edited by Vincenzo Vergiani, Daniele Cuneo, and Camillo Alessio Formigatti, 449–85. Berlin: De Gruyter, 2017.

Hines, Naseem Akhtar. *Maulana Daud's Cāndāyan: A Critical Study.* New Delhi: Manohar Publishers, 2009.

Hinzler, H. I. R. "The Book in Ancient Java: Books, Writing, Writing Material, and Reading in Written and Visual Evidence." In *Fruits of Inspiration: Studies in Honour of Prof. J. G. De Casparis,* edited by Marijke J. Klokke and Karel R. van Kooij, 157–90. Groningen: Egbert Forsten, 2001.

Hoffman, Eva R. "The Beginnings of the Illustrated Arabic Book: An Intersection between Art and Scholarship." *Muqarnas* 17 (2000): 37–52.

Holly, Michael Ann, et al. "Notes from the Field: Materiality." *Art Bulletin* 95, no. 1 (2013): 15–17.

Hopkins, Edward. "Words for Color in the Rig Veda." *American Journal of Philology* 4, no. 2 (1883): 166–91.

Hudson, D. Dennis. *Krishna's Mandala: Bhagavata Religion and Beyond.* New Delhi: Oxford University Press, 2010.

Huntington, John. "Early Tibetan Painting and the Bengal Connection." *Orientations* 34, no. 8 (2003): 32–40.

———. "A Gandharan Image of Amitāyus Sukhāvatī." *Annali Istituto Orientale di Napoli* 40 (1980): 651–72.

———. "The Technique of Tibetan Paintings." *Studies in Conservation* 15, no. 2 (1970): 122–33.

Huntington, John C., and Dina Bangdel, eds. *The Circle of Bliss: Buddhist Meditational Art.* Chicago: Serindia, 2003.

Huntington, Susan L. *The "Pāla-Sena" School of Sculpture.* Studies in South Asian Culture, edited by J. E. Van Lohuizen-de Leeuw. Leiden: Brill, 1984.

Huntington, Susan L., and John C. Huntington. *Leaves from the Bodhi Tree: The Art of Pāla India (8th–12th Centuries) and Its International Legacy.* Dayton, OH: Dayton Art Institute in Association with the University of Washington Press, Seattle, 1990.

Huot, Sylvia. "Visualization and Memory: The Illustration of Troubadour Lyric in a Thirteenth-Century Manuscript." *Gesta* 31, no. 1 (1992): 3–14.

Hussain, Syed Ejaz. "Silver Flow and Horse Supply to Sultanate Bengal with Special Reference to Trans-Himalayan Trade (13th–16th Centuries)." *Journal of the Economic and Social History of the Orient* 56, no. 2 (2013): 264–308.

Huth, Alexander G., et al. "Natural Speech Reveals the Semantic Maps That Tile Human Cerebral Cortex." *Nature* 532 (2016): 453–58.

Hutson, Matthew. "This 'Mind-Reading' Algorithm Can Decode the Pictures in Your Head." *Science* (January 2018).

Inden, Ronald. "Imperial Purāṇas: Kashmir as Vaiṣṇava Center of the World." In *Querying the Medieval: Text and the History of Practices in South Asia,* edited by Daud Ali, Ronald Inden, and Jonathan Walters, 29–98. Oxford: Oxford University Press, 2000.

Isacco, Enrico, and Josephine Darrah. "The Ultraviolet-Infrared Method of Analysis, a Scientific Approach to the Study of Indian Miniatures." *Artibus Asiae* 53, no. 3/4 (1993): 470–91.

Jackson, David Paul. *The Nepalese Legacy in Tibetan Painting.* New York: Rubin Museum of Art, 2010.

Jackson, David Paul, and Janice A. Jackson. *Tibetan Thangka Painting: Methods and Materials.* London: Serindia, 1988. Originally published 1984.

Jain, J. C. "Stories of Trading Merchants and Vasudevahiṇḍī." *Annals of the Bhandarkar Oriental Research Institute* 55, no. 1/4 (1974): 73–81.

———. *The Vasudevahiṇḍī.* Ahmedabad: L. D. Institute, 1977.

Jera-Bezard, Robert, and Monique Maillard. "Origine et montage des bannières peintes de Dunhuang." *Arts Asiatiques* 40 (1985): 83–91.

———. "Le rôle des bannières et des peintures mobiles dans les rituels du Bouddhisme d'asie centrale." *Arts Asiatiques* 44 (1989): 57–67.

Jhaveri, Amrita, and Rebecca Heald. *Thinking Tantra.* Tannery Arts and Plymouth University. London: Drawing Room, 2016.

Johnson, B. B. "A Preliminary Study of the Technique of Indian Miniature Painting." In *Aspects of Indian Art: Papers Presented in a Symposium at the Los Angeles County Museum of Art,* edited by Pratapaditya Pal, 139–46. Leiden: Brill, 1972.

Kalba, Laura Anne. *Color in the Age of Impressionism: Commerce, Technology, and Art.* University Park: Pennsylvania State University Press, 2017.

Kamalakar, G., V. Pandit Rao, and M. Veerender. *Conservation, Preservation, and Restoration: Traditions, Trends, and Techniques.* Hyderabad: Birla Archaeological and Cultural Research Institute, 1995.

Kandahjaya, Hudaya. "Saṅ Hyaṅ Kamahāyānikan, Borobudur, and the Origins of Esoteric Buddhism in Indonesia." In *Esoteric Buddhism in Mediaeval Maritime Asia: Networks of Masters, Texts, Icons,* edited by Andrea Acri, 67–112. Singapore: ISEAS, 2016.

Kapstein, Matthew. "Rethinking Religious Experience: Seeing the Light in the History of Religions." In *The Presence of Light: Divine Radiance and Religious Experience,* 265–300. Chicago: University of Chicago Press, 2004.

———. "Weaving the World: The Ritual Art of the Paṭa in Pāla Buddhism and Its Legacy in Tibet." *History of Religions* 34, no. 3 (1995): 241–62.

Kapur, Geeta. "Body as Gesture: Indian Women Artists at Work." In *Representing the Body: Gender Issues in Indian Art,* edited by Vidya Dehejia, 166–97. New Delhi: Kali for Women, 1997.

Kaviraj, Sudipta. "Two Literary Culture Histories in Bengal." In *Literary Cultures in History,* edited by Sheldon Pollock. Berkeley: University of California Press, 2003.

Keith, A. Berriedale. "The Date of the *Bṛhatkathā* and the *Mudrārākṣasa.*" *Journal of the Royal Asiatic Society of Great Britain and Ireland* (1909): 145–49.

Keith, A.W. "Notes on Somes Buddhist Remains in Magadha." *Bengal, Past and Present: Journal of the Calcutta Historical Society* 6 (1910): 57–68.

Keune, Katrien, et al. "Tracking the Transformation and Transport of Arsenic Sulfide Pigments in Paints: Synchrotronbased X-Ray Micro-Analyses." *Journal of Analytical Atomic Spectrometry* 30 (2015): 813–27.

Khandalavala, Karl J., and Moti Chandra. *New Documents of Indian Painting: A Reappraisal.* Bombay: Board of Trustees of the Prince of Wales Museum of Western India, 1969.

Khanna, Sunil. "Trans-Himalayan Caravans: Merchant Princes and Peasant Traders in Ladakh (Review)." *Journal of Interdisciplary History* 32, no. 2 (2001): 346–47.

Khokhlov, Yuri. "The Xi Xia Legacy in Sino-Tibetan Art of the Yuan Dynasty." *Asian Art* (2016). http://asianart.com/articles/xi-xia.

Khoroche, Peter, ed. *Once the Buddha Was a Monkey: Āryaśūra's Jātakamālā.* Chicago: University of Chicago Press, 1989.

Khullar, Sonal. *Worldly Affiliations: Artistic Practice, National Identity, and Modernism in India, 1930–1990.* Oakland: University of California Press, 2015.

Kim, Jinah. "A Book of Buddhist Goddesses: Illustrated Manuscripts of the Pañcarakṣā Sūtra and Their Ritual Use." *Artibus Asiae* 70, no. 2 (2010): 259–329.

———. "Emptiness on Palm Leaf: A Twelfth-Century Illustrated Manuscript of the 'Aṣṭasāhasrikā Prajñāpāramitā.'" *Bulletin of the Detroit Institute of Arts* 82, no. 1/2 (2008): 76–91.

———. "Faceless Gazes, Silent Texts: Images of Devotees and Practices of Vision in Medieval South Asia." *Ars Orientalis* 46 (2016): 198–229.

———. "Iconography and Text: The Visual Narrative of the Buddhist Book-Cult in the Manuscript of the *Aṣṭasāhasrikā Prajñāpāramitā* Sūtra." In *Kalādarpaṇa: The Mirror of Indian Art,* edited by Arundhati Banerji and Devangana Desai, 250–68. New Delhi: Aryan International, 2008.

———. "Illustrated Buddhist Manuscripts." In *History of Bangladesh: Early Bengal in Regional Perspectives (up to c. 1200 CE),* edited by Abdul Momin Chowdhury and Ranabir Chakravarti, vol. 2, 509–34. Dhaka: Asiatic Society of Bangladesh, 2018.

———. "Local Visions, Transcendental Practices: Iconographic Innovations of Indian Esoteric Buddhism." *History of Religions* 54, no. 1 (2014): 34–68.

———. "Painted Palm-Leaf Manuscripts and the Art of the Book in Medieval South Asia." *Archives of Asian Art* 65, no. 1/2 (2015): 57–86.

———. "Performing Texts, Engendering Merits: Manuscripts and Paubhas as Ritual Objects." In *Dharma and Puṇya: Buddhist Ritual Art of Nepal,* edited by Jinah Kim and Todd Lewis, 88–99. Leiden: Hotei Publishing, 2019.

———. *Receptacle of the Sacred: Illustrated Manuscripts and the Buddhist Book-Cult in South Asia.* Berkeley: University of California Press, 2013.

———. "Seeing in between the Space: Aura of Writing and the Shape of Artistic Productions in Early Medieval South Asia." In *History and Material Culture in Asian Religions,* edited by Benjamin Fleming and Richard Mann. London: Routledge, 2014.

———. "Unheard Voices: Women's Roles in Medieval Buddhist Artistic Production and Religious Practices in South Asia." *Journal of the American Academy of Religion* 80, no. 1 (2012): 200–232.

———. "Unorthodox Practice: Rethinking the Cult of Illustrated Buddhist Books in South Asia." PhD diss., University of California at Berkeley, 2006.

Kimura, Hideaki. "The Ritual of Initiation in the Mayajala Tantra." *Journal of Indian and Buddhist Studies* 39, no. 2 (1991).

Klimburg-Salter, Deborah E. "Along the Pilgrimage Routes between Uḍḍiyāṇa and Tibet: The Gilgit MSS Covers and the Tibetan Decorated Book Cover." In *Tibet in Dialogue with Its Neighbours: History, Culture, and Art of Central and Western Tibet, 8th to 15th Century,* 392–406. Arbeitskreis für Tibetische und Buddhistische Studien and China Tibetology Research Center, 2015.

———. "The Gilgit Manuscript Covers and the 'Cult of the Book.'" In *South Asian Archaeology 1987* (Part 2). Rome, 1990.

———. "Indo-Tibetan Miniature Painting from Himachal-Pradesh." In *Tibetan Studies: Proceedings of the 6th Seminar of the International Association for Tibetan Studies, Fagernes, 1992,* edited by Per Kvaerne, 441–53. Oslo: Institute for Comparative Research in Human Culture, 1994.

———. "A Note on the Origin of Tibetan Book Cover Decoration." *Tibet Journal* 16, no. 1 (1991): 115–27.

———. "The Painted Covers of the Saṃghāṭasūtra 627/28 and the Votive Objects from Gilgit." In *South Asian Archaeology 1989,* 395–402. Madison, WI: Prehistory Press, 1992.

———. *The Silk Route and the Diamond Path: Esoteric Buddhist Art on the Trans-Himalayan Trade Routes.* Los Angeles: UCLA Art Council, 1982.

———. *Tabo: A Lamp for the Kingdom.* Milan: Skira, 1997.

———. "Tucci Archive Report, 4: Dung Dkar/Phyi Dbang, West Tibet, and the Influence of Tangut Buddhist Art." *East and West* 51, no. 3/4 (2001): 323–48.

Klimburg-Salter, Deborah, and Eva Allinger. *The Inner Asian International Style 12th–14th Centuries.* Vienna: Verlag der Österreichischen Akademie der Wissenschaften, 1998.

Knuston, Jesse. *Into the Twilight of Sanskrit Court Poetry: The Sena Salon of Bengal and Beyond.* Berkeley: University of California Press, 2014.

Koch, E. "Visual Strategies of Imperial Self-Representation: The Windsor Padshahnama Revisited." *Art Bulletin* 99, no. 3 (2017): 93–124.

Koerner, Joseph Leo. "Factura." *RES: Anthropology and Aesthetics* 36 (1999): 5–19.

Komaroff, Linda. "Paintings in Silver and Gold: The Decoration of Persian Metalwork and Its Relationship to Manuscript Illustration." *Studies in the Decorative Arts* 2, no. 1 (1994): 2–34.

Konishu, Masatoshi. "Old Paper of Asutosh Museum Pancaraksa Manuscript—Its Significance in the History of Nepalese Paper-Making." *Journal of the Japanese Association for South Asian Studies* 2 (1990): 145-54.

Korom, Frank J. *Village of Painters: Narrative Scrolls from West Bengal.* Santa Fe: Museum of New Mexico Press, 2006.

Kossak, Steven. *Indian Court Painting, 16th-19th Century.* New York: Metropolitan Museum of Art, 1997.

Kossak, Steven M., and Jane Casey Singer. *Sacred Visions: Early Paintings from Central Tibet.* New York: Metropolitan Museum of Art, 1998.

Kramrisch, Stella. "Four Kangra Paintings." *Philadelphia Museum Bulletin* 50, no. 245 (1955): 41–47.

Krekel, Christopher, Ursula Haller, and Andreas Burmester. "Artists' Pigments Reconsidered: Does Modern Science Match the Historical Context?" *Studies in Conservation* 51, no. Supp. 2 (2006): 244–48.

Kuijp, Leonard W.J. van der. "A Text Historical Note on Hevajratantra II:V:1–2." *Journal of the International Association of Buddhist Studies* 8, no. 1 (1985): 83–89.

Kumar, Prakash. "Scientific Experiments in British India: Scientists, Indigo Planters, and the State, 1890–1930." *Indian Economic and Social History Review* 38, no. 3 (2001): 249–70.

Kumar, Saurabh. "Rural Society and Rural Economy in the Ganga Valley during the Gahadavalas." *Social Scientist* 43, no. 5/6 (2015): 29–45.

Kusukawa, Sachiko. "Copying and Coloring." In *Picturing the Book of Nature: Image, Text, and Argument in Sixteenth Century Human Anatomy and Medical Botany.* Chicago: University of Chicago Press, 2012.

Kwon, Do-Kyun. "Sarva Tathāgata Tattva Saṃgraha: Compendium of All the Tathāgatas—a Study of Its Origin, Structure, and Teachings." PhD diss., SOAS, University of London, 2002.

Kyan, Winston. "Family Space: Buddhist Materiality and Ancestral Fashioning in Mogao Cave 231." *Art Bulletin* 92, no. 1/2 (2010): 61–82.

Lacôte, Félix, ed. *Budhasvāmin-Bṛhat-Kathā Çlokasaṃgraha.* Paris: Imprimerie Nationale, 1908.

Lai, Imann. "Scriptures and Images: Sarva-Tathāgata-Tattva-Saṃgraha-Nāma-Mahā-Yana-Sūtra and the Ninth-Century Vajradhatu Mandala Excavated from the Famen Monastery, Xi'an, China." *회당학보* 17 (2012): 195–261.

Lajer-Burcharth, Ewa. *The Painter's Touch: Boucher, Chardin, Fragonard.* Princeton, NJ: Princeton University Press, 2018.

Lal, B.B. *Ajanta Paintings: Their Composition, Technique, Deterioration, and Preservation.* New Delhi: Islamic Wonders Bureau, 2007.

Laughlin, Jack. "Ārādhakamūrti/Adhiṣṭhāyakamūrti: Popular Piety, Politics, and the Medieval Jain Temple Portrait." PhD diss., Yale University, 2000.

Lazaro, Desmond. *Materials, Methods, and Symbolism in the Pichhvai Painting Tradition of Rajasthan.* Ahmedabad: Mapin, 2005.

Lee, Yong-Hyun. "『금강의 화환』(Vajrāvalī)에서 관정(灌頂)에 대한 아바야카라굽타의 해석 (Abhayākaragupta's Interpretations on the Consecration Ceremony of the Vajrāvalī)." 인도연구17, no. 1 (2012): 51–84.

Lefèvre, Vincent, and Marie-Françoise Boussac. *Chefs-d'oeuvre du delta du Gange: Collections des Musées du Bangladesh.* Paris: Musée Guimet, 2007.

Leoshko, Janice. "Scenes of the Buddha's Life in Pala Period Art." *Silk Road Art and Archaeology* 3 (1993–94): 251–76.

Lessing, F.D., and Wayman, A., eds. *Introduction to the Buddhist Tantric Systems.* Delhi: Motilal Banarsidass, 1978.

Lévi, Sylvain. "La Bṛihatkathāmañjarī." *Journal Asiatique* (1885): 397–554.

———. *Le Nepal: Étude Historique d'un Royaume Hindou.* 3 vols. Vol. 2. Paris: Ernest Leroux, 1905.

Lewis, Todd. "Mahāyāna Vratas in Newar Buddhism." *Journal of International Association of Buddhist Studies* 12, no. 1 (1989): 109–38.

———. *Popular Buddhist Texts from Nepal: Narratives and Rituals of Newar Buddhism.* Albany: State University of New York Press, 2000.

———. "The Tradition of Vajrācārya Storytellers." In *Dharma and Puṇya: Buddhist Ritual Art of Nepal,* edited by Jinah Kim and Todd Lewis, 156–60. Leiden: Hotei Publishing, 2019.

Lienhard, Siegfried, ed. *Svayambhūpurāṇa: Mythe du Népal; Suivi du Maṇicūḍāvadāna: Légende du Prince Maṇicūḍā.* Suilly-la-Tour: Éditions Findakly, 2009.

Lindberg, David C. *Theories of Vision from Al-Kindi to Kepler.* Chicago: University of Chicago Press, 1981.

Lindsey, Delwin T., and Angela M. Brown. "Universality of Color Names." *Proceedings of the National Academy of Sciences of the United States of America* 103, no. 44 (2006): 16608–13.

Linrothe, Robert N. *Collecting Paradise: Buddhist Art of Kashmir and Its Legacies.* New York: Rubin Museum of Art, 2014.

———. "Mirror Image: Deity and Donor as Vajrasattva." *History of Religions* 54, no. 1 (2014): 5–33.

———. *Ruthless Compassion: Wrathful Deities in Early Indo-Tibetan Esoteric Buddhist Art.* Boston: Shambhala, 1999.

Lippit, Yukio. "Goryeo Buddhist Painting in an Interregional Context." *Ars Orientalis* 35 (2008): 192–232.

Liying, Kuo. "Maṇḍala et Rituel de Confession à Dunhuang." *Bulletin de l'École Française d'Extrême-Orient* 85 (1998): 227–56.

Locke, John K. *Buddhist Monasteries of Nepal.* Kathmandu: Sahayogi Press, 1985.

Lohuizen-de Leeuw, Johanna E. van. *The "Scythia" Period: An Approach to the History, Art, Epigraphy, and Palaeography of North India from the 1st Century B.C. to the 3rd Century A.D.* Leiden: Brill, 1949.

Lopez, Donald S., Jr. *Elaborations on Emptiness: Uses of the Heart Sūtra.* Princeton, NJ: Princeton University Press, 1998.

———. *Prisoners of Shangri-La: Tibetan Buddhism and the West.* Chicago: University of Chicago Press, 1999.

Losty, J.P. *The Art of the Book in India.* London: British Library, 1982.

———. "The Art of Enlightenment: Buddhist Manuscripts from the Himalayas, India, China, Japan and Southeast Asia." Edited by Sam Fogg Ltd. London: Sam Fogg, 2008.

———. "Bengal, Bihar, Nepal? Problems of Provenance in 12th Century Illuminated Buddhist Manuscripts, Part 1." *Oriental Art* 35, no. 2 (1989): 86–96.

———. "Bengal, Bihar, Nepal? Problems of Provenance in 12th Century Illuminated Manuscripts, Part 2." *Oriental Art* 35, no. 3 (1989): 140–49.

———. "An Early Indian Manuscript of the Kāraṇḍavyūhasūtra." In *Studies in Art and Archaeology of Bihar and Bengal,* edited by Debala Mitra and Gouriswar Bhattacharya, 1–22. Delhi: Sri Satguru Publications, 1989.

———. *The Ramayana: Love and Valour in India's Great Epic.* London: British Library, 2008.

Luczanits, Christian. *Buddhist Sculpture in Clay: Early Western Himalayan Art, Late 10th to Early 13th Centuries.* Chicago: Serindia Publications, 2004.

———. "From Kashmir to Western Tibet: The Many Faces of a Regional Style." In *Collecting Paradise: Buddhist Art of Kashmir and Its Legacies*, edited by Robert Linroth, 109-49. New York: Rubin Museum of Art, 2014.

———. "The Life of the Buddha in the Sumtsek." *Orientations* 30, no. 1 (1999): 30–39.

———. "On the Earliest Mandalas in a Buddhist Context." In *Mahayana Buddhism: History and Culture,* edited by Darol Bryant and Susan Bryant, 111–38. Delhi: Tibet House, 2008.

Ludvik, Catherine. *Sarasvatī Riverine Goddess of Knowledge: From the Manuscript-Carrying Vīṇā-Player to the Weapon-Wielding Defender of Dharma.* Leiden: Brill, 2007.

Lyons, Tryna. "The Simla 'Devī Māhātmya' Illustrations: A Reappraisal of Content." *Archives of Asian Art* 45 (1992): 29–41.

Macdonald, Ariane. *Le Maṇḍala du Mañjuśrīmūlakalpa.* Paris: Adrien Maisonneuve, 1962.

Magaloni Kerpel, Diana. *The Colors of the New World: Artists, Materials, and the Creation of the Florentine Codex.* Los Angeles: Getty Research Institute, 2014.

Maggi, Mauro. "A Chinese-Khotanese Excerpt from the *Mahāsāhasrapramardanī*." In *Convegno internzionale sul tema la Persia e l'Asia Centrale da Alessandro al X Secolo,* 123–37. Rome: Academia nazionale del Lincei, 1996.

Maggi, Mauro, and Anna Filigenzi. "Pelliot Tibétain 2222: A Dunhuang Painting with a Khotanese Inscription." *Journal of Inner Asian Art and Archaeology* 3 (2008): 83–89.

Maguire, Henry. *The Icons of Their Bodies: Saints and Their Images in Byzantium.* Princeton, NJ: Princeton University Press, 1996.

Mahadihassan, S. "Indian Rasāyana and Chinese Alchemy." *Journal of the Asiatic Society of Bombay,* n.s., 52–53 (1977): 184–86.

Mainali, Sabitree. *Hindu Miniature Paintings of the Kathmandu Valley.* Kathmandu: Bishwa Kanta Mainali, 2009.

Mair, Victor H. "Xie He's 'Six Laws' of Painting and Their Indian Parallels." In *Chinese Aesthetics,* edited by Z. Cai, 81–122. Honolulu: University of Hawai'i Press, 2004.

Mallinson, James, ed. *The Emperor of the Sorcerers by Budhasvāmin.* New York: New York University Press, 2005.

Mallmann, Marie-Thérèse de. *Introduction à l'iconographie du tântrisme Bouddhique.* Paris: Librairie Adrien-Maisonneuve, 1975.

Mann, Richard D. *The Rise of Mahāsena: The Transformation of Skanda-Kārtikkeya in North India from the Kuṣāṇa to Gupta Empires.* Leiden: Brill, 2012.

Martin, Dan. "Painters, Patrons, and Paintings of Patrons in Early Tibetan Art." In *Embodying Wisdom: Art, Text, and Interpretation in the History of Esoteric Buddhism,* edited by Robert N. Linrothe and Henrik Sørensen, 139–84. Copenhagen: Seminar for Buddhist Studies, 2001.

Master, Alfred. "Gleanings from the Kuvalayamālā Kahā—II." *Bulletin of the School of Oriental and African Studies* 13, no. 4 (1951): 1004–16.

Matsunaga, Yukei. "The Character of Mayajala Tantra." *Journal of Indian and Buddhist Studies* 8, no. 2 (1960): 550–51.

McCombs, Jason. "Mahāyāna and the Gift: Theories and Practices." PhD diss., University of California at Los Angeles, 2014.

McCutchion, David, and Suhṛd kumāra Bhaumika. *Patuas and Patua Art in Bengal.* Calcutta: Firma KLM, 1999.

McGrath, Ann, and Mary Anne Jebb. *Long History, Deep Time: Deepening Histories of Place.* Canberra: Australian National University Press, 2015.

McHugh, James "The Disputed Civets and the Complexion of the God: Secretions and History in India." *Journal of American Oriental Society* 132, no. 2 (2012): 245–73.

———. "The Hindu Love of Writing, and the Manuscript as Event." Paper presented at Writing and the Inscription of Power in South Asia, Duke University, 2013.

McInerney, Terrence. "Mysterious Origins: The Tantric Devi Series from Basohli." In *Devi: The Great Goddess,* edited by Vidya Dehejia, 119–35. Washington, DC: Smithsonian Institution, 1999.

Mehra, V. R. "Note on the Technique and Conseervation of Some Thang-Ka Paintings." *Studies in Conservation* 15, no. 3 (1970): 206–14.

Meister, Michael. "Maṇḍala and Practice in Nāgara Architecture in North India." *Journal of the American Oriental Society* 99, no. 2 (1979): 204–19.

———. "Prāsāda as Palace: Kūṭina Origins of the Nāgara Temple." *Artibus Asiae* 49, no. 3/4 (1988): 254–80.

———. *Temples of the Indus: Studies in the Hindu Architecture of Ancient Pakistan.* Leiden: Brill, 2010.

Melzer, Gudrun, and Eva Allinger. "Die Nepalesische Palmblatthandschrift der Aṣṭasāhasrikā Prajñāpāramitā aus dem Jahr Ns 268 (1148 Ad), Teil II." *Indo Asiatische Zeitschrift* 20 (2012): 249–76.

Mevissen, G. "Images of Mahāpratisarā in Bengal." *Journal of Bengal Art* 4 (1999): 99–129.

———. "The Indian Connection: Images of Deified Spells in the Arts of Northern Buddhism." *Silk Road Art and Archaeology* 2 (1991/92): 351–82.

———. "Transmission of Iconographic Traditions: Pañcarakṣā Heading North." In *South Asian Archaeology 1989*, edited by Catherine Jarrige, 415–24. Madison, WI: Prehistory Press, 1992.

Meyer, Dirk. "Bamboo and the Production of Philosophy: A Hypothesis about a Shift in Writing and Thought in Early China." In *Material Culture and Asian Religions: Text, Image, Object*, edited by Benjamin J. Fleming and Richard D. Mann, 21–38. New York: Routledge, 2014.

Mishra, Biswajit, and Mihir Deb. "Mineral Deposits in India." *Proceedings of the Indian National Science Academy* 78, no. 3 (2012): 423–30.

Misra, R.N. "Silpis in Ancient India: Beyond Their Ascribed Locus in Ancient Society." *Social Scientist* 39, no. 7/8 (2011): 43–54.

Mitchell, W.J. Thomas. *Iconology: Image, Text, Ideology*. Chicago: University of Chicago Press, 1987.

Mitra, Debala. *Ratnagiri, 1958–61*. 2 vols. New Delhi: Archaeological Survey of India, 1981.

Mori, Masahide. "The Installation Ceremony in Tantric Buddhism." In *From Materials to Deity: Indian Rituals of Consecration*, edited by Shingo Einoo and Jun Takashima. New Delhi: Manohar Publishers, 2005.

———. "The Vajrāvalī of Abhayākaragupta: A Critical Study, Sanskrit Edition of Selected Chapters and Complete Tibetan Version." PhD diss., SOAS, University of London, 1999.

Mukherji, Parul Dave, ed. *The Citrasūtra of the Viṣṇudharmottara Purāṇa*. New Delhi: Indira Gandhi National Centre for the Arts and Motilal Banarsidass Publishers, 2001.

Murphy, Anne, and Heidi Pauwels. "From Outside the Persianate Centre: Vernacular Views on Alamgır." *Journal of the Royal Asiatic Society* 28, Series 3, no. 3 (2018): 409–14.

Murthy, S.R.N. "An Occurrence of Cinnabar in Rasarnavakalpa." *Journal of the Geological Survey of India* 14, no. 2 (1978): 83–86.

Nádasdi, Susan L. "Identical Stories in the Twenty-Five Tales of the Vetāla and in the Ocean of Story." *Acta Orientalia Academiae Scientiarum Hungaricae* 21, no. 3 (1968): 363–68.

Nahakpam, Indubala Joykumar. "A Cultural Study on the Jain (Western Indian) Illustrated Manuscripts That Are Preserved in the L.D. Institute of Indology, Ahmedabad." PhD diss., B.J. Institute of Learning and Research, 2011.

Nardi, Isabella. "Re-Evaluating the Role of Text in Indian Art." *South Asia Research* 29 no. 2 (2009): 99–126.

———. *The Theory of Citrasūtras in Indian Painting: A Critical Re-Evaluation of Their Uses and Interpretations*. London: Routledge, 2006.

Nath, Birendra. *Nalanda Murals*. New Delhi: Cosmo Publications, 1983.

Nawab, Sarabhai Manilal, Nachiket Chanchani, and Suthar Babu. "The Art of Gujarat Patronized by the Jains and Its History." *Art in Translation* 2, no. 3 (2010): 261–308.

Needham, Joseph. *Science and Civilisation in China: Chemistry and Chemical Technology*. Vol. 5, *Spagyrical Discovery and Invention: Physiological Alchemy*. Cambridge: Cambridge University Press, 1983.

Nelson, Donald. "Bṛhatkātha Studies: The Problem of an Ur-Text." *Journal of Asian Studies* 37, no. 4 (1978): 663–76.

Nichols, Stephen G. "Textes Mobiles, Images Motrices: L'instabilité textuelle dans le manuscrit médiéval." *Littérature* 99 (1995): 19–32.

Ohri, Vishwa Chander. *The Technique of Pahari Painting*. Shimla: Indian Institute of Advanced Study; New Dehli: Aryan Books International, 2001.

O'Neal, Halle. "Performing the Jeweled Pagoda Mandalas: Relics, Reliquaries, and a Realm of Text." *Art Bulletin* 97, no. 3 (2015): 279–300.

Orsini, Francesca, and Samira Sheikh, eds. *After Timur Left: Culture and Circulation in Fifteenth-Century North India*. Oxford: Oxford University Press, 2014.
Orzech, Charles D. "The 'Great Teaching of Yoga,' the Chinese Appropriation of the Tantras, and the Question of Esoteric Buddhism." *Journal of Chinese Religions* 34, no. 1 (2006): 29–78.
Östör, Ákos, Aditi Nath Sarkar, and Lina Fruzzetti. "Singing Pictures." Watertown, MA: Documentary Educational Resources, 2005.
Otter, Felix. *Residential Architecture in Bhoja's Samarāṅgaṇa-Sūtradhāra*. Delhi: Motilal Banarsidass, 2010.
Owen, Lisa N. *Carving Devotion in the Jain Caves at Ellora*. Leiden: Brill, 2012.
Pal, Pratapaditya. *The Arts of Nepal*. 2 vols. Vol. 2, *Paintings*. Leiden: Brill, 1978.
———. "Early Paintings of the Goddess in Nepal." *Ars Orientalis* 12 (1981).
———. *Himalayas: An Aesthetic Adventure*. Chicago: Art Institute of Chicago, 2003.
———, ed. *Indian Painting*. Los Angeles: Los Angeles County Museum of Art, 1993.
———, ed. *The Peaceful Liberators: Jain Art from India*. London: Thames and Hudson; Los Angeles: Los Angeles County Museum of Art, 1994.
Pal, Pratapaditya, and Julia Meech-Pekarik. *Buddhist Book Illuminations*. New York: Ravi Kumar 1988.
Panayotova, Stella, Deirdre Jackson, and Paola Ricciardi, eds. *Colour: The Art and Science of Illuminated Manuscripts*. London: Harvey Miller Publishers, 2016.
Paranjape, Makarand R. "Enjoying God: The Divine Paramour." In *Radha: From Gopi to Goddess*, edited by Harsha V Dehejia, 86–103. New Delhi: Niyogi Press, 2014.
Parimoo, Ratan. *Gujarati School and Jaina Manuscript Painting: N.C. Mehta Collection*. Ahmedabad: Gujarat Museum Society, 2010.
Passi, Alessandro, Cinzia Pieruccini, Elena Preda, and Fausto Freschi, eds. *Devī-Māhātmya: MS 4510 of the "Vincenzo Joppi" Municipal Library in Udine*. Udine: Società Indologica "Luigi Pio Tessitori," 2008.
Patel, Divia. "Copying Ajanta: A Rediscovery of Some Nineteenth-Century Paintings." *South Asian Studies* 23, no. 1 (2007): 39–62.
Pathak, S.K., ed. *The Album of the Tibetan Art Collections*. Patna: K.P. Jayaswal Research Institute, 1986.
Petech, Luciano. *Mediaeval History of Nepal (c. 750–1482)*. Rome: Instituto Italiano per il Medio ed Estremo Oriente, 1958.
Piotrovsky, M.B. *Lost Empire of the Silk Road: Buddhist Art from Khara Khoto (X–XIIIth Century)*. Milan: Thyssen Bornemisza Foundation and Electa, 1993.
Pollock, Sheldon. *The Language of the Gods in the World of Men: Sanskrit, Culture, and Power in Premodern India*. Berkeley: University of California Press, 2006.
———. *A Rasa Reader: Classical Indian Aesthetics*. New York: Columbia University Press, 2016.
———, ed. *Forms of Knowledge in Early Modern Asia: Explorations in the Intellectual History of India and Tibet, 1500–1800*. Durham, NC: Duke University Press, 2011.
———, ed. *Literary Cultures in History: Reconstructions from South Asia*. Berkeley: University of California Press, 2003.
———, ed. *Rāma's Last Act by Bhavabūti*. New York: New York University Press, 2007.
Porter, Yves. *Peinture et Arts du Livre: Essai sur la littérature technique Indo-Persane*. Tehran: Institut français de recherche en Iran, 1992.
Preisandanz, K. "On *ātmendriyamanorathasannikarṣa* and the Nyāya-Vaiśeṣika Theory of Vision." *Berliner indologische Studien* 4–6 (1989–91): 141–214.
Puri, Bharati. "Traveller on the Silk Road: Rites and Routes of Passage in Rahul Sankrityayan's Himalayan Wanderlust." *China Report* 47, no. 1 (2011): 37–58.

Purinton, Nancy, and Richard Newman, "Appendix 1: A Technical Analysis of Indian Painting Materials." In *Pride of the Princes: Indian Art of the Mughal Era in the Cincinnati Art Museum,* 107–113. Cincinnati: Cincinnati Art Museum, 1985.

Purinton, Nancy, and Mark Watters. "A Study of the Materials Used by Medieval Persian Painters." *Journal of the American Institute for Conservation* 30, no. 2 (1991): 125–44.

Quagliotti, Anna Maria. "Mañjuśrī in Gandharan Art: A New Interpretation of a Relief in the Victoria and Albert Museum." *East and West* 40, no. 1/4 (1990): 99–113.

Quintanilla, Sonya Rhie. *Mughal Paintings: Art and Stories: the Cleveland Museum of Art.* London: D Giles, 2016.

Quintanilla, Sonya Rhie, Pramod Chandra, and John M. Rosenfield. *Rhythms of India: The Art of Nandalal Bose.* San Diego, CA: San Diego Museum of Art, 2008.

Rao, T.A. Gopinath. *Elements of Hindu Iconography.* 2 vols. Vol. 1. Madras: Law Printing House, 1914.

Rathe, Saraju, ed. *Aspects of Manuscript Culture in South India.* Leiden: Brill, 2012.

Ray, Himanshu Prabha. "The Archaeology of Bengal: Trading Networks, Cultural Identities." *Journal of the Economic and Social History of the Orient* 49, no. 1 (2006): 68–95.

Repo, Joona. "Distinguishing 'Set' from 'Series' in Tibetan Painting." *Archives of Asian Art* 64 (2014): 59–73.

Rhi, Juhyung. "Early Mahāyāna and Gandhāran Buddhism: An Assessment of the Visual Evidence." *Eastern Buddhist* 35, no. 1/2 (2003): 152–202.

Rhie, Marylin M., and Robert A.F. Thurman. *Wisdom and Compassion: The Sacred Art of Tibet.* New York: Asian Art Museum and Tibet House, 1991.

Ricciardi, Paola, and Anuradha Pallipurath. "The Five Colours of Art: Non-invasive Analylsis of Pigments in Tibetan Prints and Manuscripts." In *Tibetan Printing: Comparisons, Continuities, and Change,* edited by Hildegard Diemberger, Franz-Karl Ehrhard, and Peter F. Kornicki, 485–500. Leiden: Brill, 2016.

Richardson, Sarah Aiofe. "Painted Books for Plaster Walls: Visual Words in the Fourteenth-Century Murals at the Tibetan Buddhist Temple of Shalu." PhD diss., University of Toronto, 2016.

Rosu, Arion. "Yoga et Alchimie." *Zeitschrift der Deutschen Morgenländischen Gesellschaft* 132, no. 2 (1982): 363–79.

Roxburgh, David J. "Kamal al-Din Bihzad and Authorship in Persianate Painting." *Muqarnas* 17 (2000): 119–46.

———. *The Persian Album, 1400–1600: From Dispersal to Collection.* New Haven, CT: Yale University Press, 2005.

———. "The Study of Painting and the Arts of the Book." *Muqarnas* 17 (2000): 1–16.

Roy, Ashok, ed. *Artists' Pigments: A Handbook of Their History and Characteristics,* vol. 2. Washington, DC: National Gallery of Art, 1993.

Russell-Smith, Lilla Bikfalvy. "Wives and Patrons: Uygur Political and Artistic Influence in Tenth-Century Dunhuang." *Acta Orientalia Academiae Scientiarum Hungaricae* 56, no. 2/4 (2003): 401–28.

Salomon, Richard. *Indian Epigraphy: A Guide to the Study of Inscriptions in Sanskrit, Prakrit, and the Other Indo-Aryan Languages.* Oxford: Oxford University Press, 1998.

———. "Review: On the Origin of the Early Indian Scripts." *Journal of the American Oriental Society* 115, no. 2 (1995): 271–79.

———. *Siddham across Asia: How the Buddha Learned His ABC.* Amsterdam: J. Gonda Fund Foundation of the KNAW, 2015.

Sander, Lore. "Remarks on the Formal Brāhmī Script from the Southern Silk Route." *Bulletin of the Asia Institute* 19 (2005): 133–44.

Sanderson, Alexis. "Remarks on the Text of the Kubjikāmatatantra." *Indo-Iranian Journal* 45 (2002): 1–24.

Sāṅkṛityāyana, Rāhula. "Second Search of Sanskrit Palm-Leaf MSS in Tibet." *Journal of the Bihar and Orissa Research Society* 23, no. 1 (1937): 1–57.

Saraswati, S.K. *Tantrayāna Art: An Album.* Calcutta: Asiatic Society, 1977.

Sastri, Hirananda. "A Pre-Mughal Citrapata from Gujarat." *Indian Historical Quarterly* 14, no. 3 (1938): 425.

Saunders, Barbara. "Revisiting Basic Color Terms." *Journal of the Royal Anthropological Institute* 6, no. 1 (2000): 81–99.

Saunders, Virginia. "Portrait Painting as a Dramatic Device in Sanskrit Plays." *Journal of the American Oriental Society* 39 (1919): 299–302.

Scherrer-Schaub, Cristina. "Printing versus Manuscript: History or Rhetoric? A Short Note Inspired by Pelliot Dic." In *Tibetan Printing: Comparisons, Continuities, and Change,* edited by Hildegard Diemberger, Franz-Karl Ehrhard, and Peter F. Kornicki, 153–70. Leiden: Brill, 2016.

Schlingloff, Dieter, and Monika Zin. *Guide to the Ajanta Paintings.* New Delhi: Munshiram Manoharlal, 1999.

Schmid, Charlotte. *Le Don de voir: Premières représentations Krishnaïtes de la région de Mathura.* Paris: École Française d'Extrême-Orient, 2010.

Schopen, Gregory. "The Book as a Sacred Object in Private Homes in Early or Medieval India." In *Medieval and Early Modern Devotional Objects in Global Perspective,* edited by Elizabeth Robertson and Jennifer Jahner. Hampshire, UK: Palgrave Macmillan, 2010.

———. "On the Absence of the Urtexts and Otiose Ācāryas: Buildings, Books, and Lay Buddhist Ritual at Gilgit." *Écrire et transmettre en Inde classique* 30 (2009): 189–219.

———. "Sukhāvatī as a Generalized Religious Goal in Sanskrit Mahāyāna Sūtra Literature." *Indo-Irananian Journal* 19, no. 3 (1977): 177–210.

———. "Taking the Bodhisattva into Town: More Texts on the Image of 'the Bodhisattva' and Image Processions in the 'Mūlasarvāstivāda-Vinaya.'" *East and West* 55, no. 1/4 (2005): 299–311.

Schoterman, J.A. "Kubjikāmata Tantra: The Laghvikāmnāya Version." In *The Sanskrit Tradition and Tantrism,* edited by Teun Goudriaan, 76–95. Leiden: Brill, 1990.

Sciacca, Christine. "Raising the Curtain on the Use of Textiles in Manuscripts." In *Weaving, Veiling and Dressing: Textiles and Their Metaphors in the Late Middle Ages,* 161–90. Turnhout: Brepols, 2007.

Sen, Geeti. *Feminie Fables: Imagining the Indian Woman in Painting, Photography, and Cinema.* Ahmedabad: Mapin, 2002.

Sen, Tansen. "Changes and Exchanges and Good Karma: Chinese Diplomatic Missions to Middle India in the Seventh Century." *India International Centre Quarterly* 36, no. 3/4 (2009): 34–47.

———. "In Search of Longevity and Good Karma: Chinese Diplomatic Missions to Middle India in the Seventh Century." *Journal of World History* 12, no. 1 (2001): 1–28.

Seth, Mira. *Indian Painting: The Great Mural Tradition.* New York: Abrams, 2006.

Seton, Gregory Max. "Integrating Non-Tantric and Tantric Doctrines through Prajñāpāramitā at Vikramaśīla during the Mid-Eleventh Century." Paper presented at the XVIIth Congress of International Association of Buddhist Studies, Toronto, University of Toronto, August 2017.

Sferra, Francesco, ed. *Sanskrit Texts from Giuseppe Tucci's Collection.* Rome: Istituto italiano per l'Africa e l'Orient, 2008.

Shah, P. *Viṣṇudharmottara-Purāṇa, Third Khaṇḍa.* Baroda: Baroda Oriental Institute, 1958.

Shah, Umakant Premanand. "Iconography." In *Jaina Art and Architecture,* edited by A. Ghosh, 465–93. New Delhi: Bharatiya Jnanpitha, 1975.

———. *More Documents of Jaina Paintings and Gujarati Paintings of Sixteenth and Later Centuries.* Ahmedabad: L.D. Institute of Indology, 1976.

———. *Treasures of Jaina Bhaṇḍāras.* Ahmedabad: L.D. Institute of Indology, 1978.

Sharf, Robert H. "Visualization and Mandala in Shingon Buddhism." In *Living Images: Japanese Buddhist Icons in Context,* 151–97. Stanford, CA: Standford University Press, 2001.

Shastri, M.S. "Report on the Gilgit Excavations in 1938." *Quarterly Journal of the Mythic Society* 30, no. 1 (1939): 1–12.

Shaw, Miranda. *Buddhist Goddesses of India.* Princeton, NJ: Princeton University Press, 2006.

Sheikh, Samira. *Forging a Region: Sultans, Traders, and Pilgrims in Gujarat, 1200–1500.* New Delhi: Oxford University Press, 2010.

Shi, Feng. "自然之色与哲学之色—中国传统方色理论起源研究 (Natural Colors and Philosophical Colors—A Study on the Origin of the Cardinal Direction Color Theory in China)." *考古学报*, no. 4 (2016): 445–64.

Shimizu, Tadashi. *The Bhāgavata-Purāṇa Miniature Paintings: From the Bhandarkar Oriental Research Institute Manuscript Dated 1648.* Tokyo: Toyo Bunko, 1993.

———. "The Meaning of Landscapes Depicted in the Viṣṇudharmottara-Purāṇa." *Journal of Indian and Buddhist Studies* 17, no. 1 (1968): 404–400.

Shivdatta, M.M., and Kashinath Pandurang Paraba, eds. *Bṛhatkathāmañjarī of Kṣemendra.* New Delhi: Panini, 1982. Originally published 1931.

Shrigondekar, G.K., ed. *Mânasollâsa of King Someśvara.* 3 vols. Vol. 2. Gaekwad Oriental Series, vol. 84. Baroda: Baroda Oriental Institute, 1939.

Siddhanta, Sachindra Nath. *A Descriptive Catalogue of Sanskrit Manuscripts in the Varendra Research Museum Library,* vol. 1. Rajshahi: Varendra Research Museum, 1979.

Siddiq, Mohammad Yusuf. "Calligraphy and Islamic Culture: Reflections on Some New Epigraphical Discoveries in Gaur and Pandua, Two Early Capitals of Muslim Bengal." *Bulletin of the School of Oriental and African Studies, University of London* 68, no. 1 (2005): 21–58.

Siegle, Lee, ed. *Gītagovinda: Love Songs of Rādhā and Kṛṣṇa by Jayadeva.* Clay Sanskrit Library. New York: New York University Press, 2009.

Siklós, Bulcsu. *The Vajrabhairava Tantras: Tibetan and Mongolian Versions, English Translation and Annotations.* Tring, UK: Institute of Buddhist Studies, 1996.

Sinclair, Iain. "Envisioning Durjayacandra's Saptākṣarasādhana: On the Sources and Sponsors of a Twelfth-Century Painting of Seven-Syllabled Saṃvara." In *Himalayan Passages: Tibetan and Newar Studies in Honor of Hubert Decleer,* edited by Benjamin Bogin and Andrew Quintman, 205–50. Boston: Wisdom 2014.

———. "The Names of Nāgabuddhi and Vajrabuddhi." In *Esoteric Buddhism in Mediaeval Maritime Asia: Networks of Masters, Texts, Icons,* edited by Andrea Acri, 389–92. Singapore: ISEAS, 2016.

Singh, Devika. "Indian Nationalist Art History and the Writing and Exhibiting of Mughal Art, 1910–48." *Art History* 36, no. 5 (2013): 1042–69.

Singh, Kavita. "Transfixed by the Arrow of Time: Phad Paintings of Rajasthan." In *Indian Painting: The Lesser-Known Traditions,* edited by A.L. Dallapiccola, 108–25. New Delhi: Niyogi Books, 2011.

Singh, Manager. "Microclimatic Condition in Relation to Conservation of Cave No. 2 Murals of Ajanta." *Current Science* 101, no. 1 (2011): 89–94.

Singh, Manager, and Balasaheb Ramrao Arbad. "Ancient Indian Painting Recipes and Mural Art Technique at Ajanta." *International Journal of Conservation Science* 5, no. 1 (2014): 35–50.

Siracusano, Gabriela. *Pigment and Power in the Andes: From the Material to the Symbolic in Andean Cultural Practices, 1500–1800.* London: Archetype Publications, 2011.

Skilling, Peter. "Paṭa (Phra Bot): Buddhist Cloth Painting of Thailand." In *Buddhist Legacies in Mainland Southeast Asia—Mentalities, Interpretations, and Practices,* edited by François Lagirarde and Paritta Chal-

ermpow Koanantakool, 223–57. Paris: École Française d'Extrême-Orient; Bangkok: Princess Maha Chakri Sirindhorn Anthropology Center, 2006.
———. "The Rakṣā Literature of the Śravakayāna." *Journal of the Pali Text Society* 16 (1992): 110–82.
Skilton, Andrew, ed. *How the Nagas Were Pleased by Harsha.* Clay Sanskrit Library. New York: New York University Press, 2009.
Skjærvø, Prods O. *Khotanese Manuscripts from Chinese Turkestan in the British Library: A Complete Catalogue with Texts and Translations.* London: British Library, 2002.
Ślączka, Anna A. *Temple Consecration Rituals in Ancient India: Text and Archaeology.* Leiden: Brill, 2007.
———. "The Two Iconographic Chapters from Devyāmata and the Art of Bengal." In *Tantric Studies: Fruits of a Franco-German Collaboration on Early Tantra,* edited by Dominic Goodall and Harunaga Isaacson, 181–246. Pondicherry: Institut Français de Pondichéry; Paris: École Française d'Extrême-Orient; Hamburg: Asien-Afrika-institut, Universität Hamburg, 2016.
Slusser, Mary Shepherd. *Nepal Mandala: A Cultural Study of the Kathmandu Valley.* 2 vols. Princeton, NJ: Princeton University Press, 1982.
Smith, John D. *The Epic of Pābūjī: A Study, Transcription, and Translation.* Cambridge: Cambridge University Press, 1991.
Snellgrove, David L. *The Hevajra Tantra: A Critical Study.* 2 vols. London: Oxford University Press, 1959.
Snodgrass, Adrian. *The Matrix and Diamond World Mandalas in Shingon Buddhism.* 2 vols. Śata-piṭaka Series, vols. 354, 355. New Delhi: International Academy of Indian Culture, 1988.
Sørensen, Henrik H. "Typology and Iconography in the Esoteric Art of Dunhuang." *Silk Road Art and Archaeology* 2 (1991/92): 285–349.
Spink, Walter M. *Ajanta: History and Development.* Leiden: Brill, 2005.
———. "Ajantā's Chronology: The Crucial Cave." *Ars Orientalis* 10 (1975): 143–69.
———. "The Caves at Ajanta." *Archaeology* 45, no. 6 (1992): 52–60.
Stein, Aurel. *Ancient Khotan: Detailed Report of Archaeological Explorations in Chinese Turkestan.* New York: Hacker Art Books, 1975. Originally published 1907.
Stein, Deborah L. *The Hegemony of Heritage: Ritual and the Record in Stone.* Oakland: University of California Press, 2018.
Steinkellner, Ernst. *A Short Guide to the Sudhana Frieze in the Temple of Ta Pho.* Vienna: Institute for Tibetan and Buddhist Studies, University of Vienna, 1996.
Stewart, Tony K. "Encountering the Smallpox Goddess: The Auspicious Song of Śītalā." In *Religions of India in Practice,* edited by Donald Lopez Jr., 389–97. Princeton, NJ: Princeton University Press, 1995.
Stoichita, Victor. *The Self-Aware Image: An Insight into Early Modern Meta-painting.* New York: Cambridge University Press, 1997.
Stout, George L. "Rutherfod John Gettens, 1900–1974." *Supplement to Studies in Conservation* 19, no. 3 (1974): 1–6.
Strauch, Ingo. "The Evolution of the Buddhist Rakṣā Genre in the Light of New Evidence from Gandhāra: The *Manasvi-Nāgarāja-Sūtra from the Bajaur Collection of Kharoṣṭhī Manuscripts." *Bulletin of the School of Oriental and African Studies* 77, no. 1 (2014): 63–84.
———. "Looking into Water-Pots and over a Buddhist Scribe's Shoulder—On the Deposition and the Use of Manuscripts in Early Buddhism." *De Gruyter* 68, no. 3 (2014): 797–830.
———. "Two Stamps with the Bodhigarbhālaṃkāralakṣa Dhāraṇī from Afghanistan and Some Further Remarks on the Classification of Objects with the ye dharmā Formula." In *Prajñādhāra: Essays on Asian Art, History, Epigraphy, and Culture in Honour of Gouriswar Bhattacharya,* edited by Gerd J.R. Mevissen and Arundhati Banerji, 37–55. New Delhi: Kaveri, 2009.

Subbarayappa, B.V., ed. *Chemistry and Chemical Techniques in India.* New Delhi: Munshiram Manoharlal Publishers, 1999.

Tanaka, Kimiaki. "「インドの仏」展に出品された『八千頌般若経』装飾写本について (the Sanskrit Manuscript of the *Aṣṭasāhasrikā-Prajñāpāramitā* Exhibited at the Exhibition 'Indian Buddhist Art')." *東洋文化研究所紀要* 169 (2017): 433–46.

Tarar, Nadeem Omar. "Framings of a National Tradition: Discourse on the Reinvention of Miniature Painting in Pakistan." *Third Text* 25, no. 5 (2011): 577–93.

Taussig, Michael T. *What Color Is the Sacred?* Chicago: University of Chicago Press, 2009.

Tawney, C.H., and N.M. Penzer, eds. *The Ocean of Story: Being C.H. Tawney's Translation of Somadeva's Kathā Sarit Sāgara; or, Ocean of Streams of Story.* 10 vols. Vol. 9. London: Chas J. Sawyer, 1928.

Teiser, Stephen F. *Reinventing the Wheel: Paintings of Rebirth in Medieval Buddhist Temples.* Seattle: University of Washington Press, 2006.

Ten Grotenhuis, Elizabeth. *Japanese Mandalas: Representations of Sacred Geography.* Honolulu: University of Hawai'i Press, 1998.

Thomas, Isaac Job. "Painting in Tamil Nadu A.D. 1350–1650 (Volumes I and II)." PhD diss., University of Michigan, 1979.

Topsfield, Andrew. *Court Painting at Udaipur: Art under the Patronage of the Maharanas of Mewar.* Zurich: Museum Rietberg, 2007.

Touati, Houari. *L'armoire à sagesse: Bibliothèques et Collections en Islam.* Paris: Aubier, 2003.

Trautmann, Thomas R. "Does India Have History? Does History Have India?" *Comparative Studies in Society and History* 54, no. 1 (2012): 174–205.

Trautmann, Thomas R., and Carla M. Sinopoli. "In the Beginning Was the Word: Excavating the Relations between History and Archaeology in South Asia." *Journal of the Economic and Social History of the Orient* 45, no. 4 (2002): 492–523.

Trier, Jesper. *Ancient Paper of Nepal: Results of Ethno-Technological Field Work on Its Manufacture, Uses, and History—With Technical Analyses of Bast, Paper, and Manuscripts.* Copenhagen: Jutland Archaeological Society, 1972.

Tuladhar-Douglas, Will. *Remaking Buddhism for Medieval Nepal: The Fifteenth Century Reformation of Newar Buddhism.* New York: Routledge, 2006.

Twist, Rebecca. "Patronage, Devotion, and Politics: A Buddhological Study of the Patola Sahi Dynasty's Visual Record." PhD diss., Ohio State University, 2008.

Urban, Hugh. *Tantra.* University of California Press, 2003.

Vajracarya, Gautam. *Nepalese Seasons: Rain and Ritual.* New York: Rubin Museum of Art, 2016.

Van Ham, Peter. *Alchi Treasure of the Himalayas: Ladakh's Buddhist Masterpiece.* Munich: Hirmer Verlag, 2018.

———. *Guge: Ages of Gold.* Munich: Hirmer, 2016.

Van Schaik, Sam. "A Definition of Mahāyoga: Sources from the Dunhuang Manuscripts." *Tantric Studies* 1 (2008): 45–88.

Vergiani, Vincenzo, Daniele Cuneo, and Camillo Alessi Formigatti, eds. *Indic Manuscript Culture through the Ages: Material, Textual, and Historical Investigations.* Berlin: De Gruyter, 2017.

Vira, Raghu, and Lokesh Chandra, eds. *Tibetan Maṇḍalas: Vajrāvalī and Tantra-Samuccaya.* New Delhi: International Academy of Indian Culture, 1995.

Von Hinüber, Oskar. "The Magnificent Bronze of Nandivikramadityanandi: A Delight for the Beholder, a Worry for the Epigraphist." *Orientations* 34, no. 4 (2003): 35–39.

———. *Die Palola Ṣāhis: Ihre Steininschriften, Inschriften auf Bronzen, Handschriftenkolophone und Schutzzauber; Materialien zur Geschichte von Gilgit und Chilas.* Mainz: P. von Zabern, 2004.

Von Rospatt, Alexander. "On the Monumental Scroll of the *Svayambhūpurāṇa* Now Kept in the VMFA Collection." In *Dharma and Puṇya: Buddhist Ritual Art of Nepal*, edited by Jinah Kim and Todd Lewis, 166–86. Leiden: Hotei Publishing, 2019.

Wallace, Vesna. "The Body as a Text and the Text as the Body: A View from the Kalacakratantra's Perspective." In *As Long as Space Endures: Essays on the Kalacakra Tantra in Honor of H.H. The Dalai Lama*, edited by Edward A. Arnold, 179–92. Ithaca, NY: Snow Lion Publications, 2009.

Wallis, Glenn. *Mediating the Power of Buddhas: Ritual in the Mañjuśrīmūlakālpa.* Albany: State University of New York Press, 2002.

Wang, Eugene. "Ritual Practice without a Practitioner? Early Eleventh Century Dhāraṇī Prints in the Ruiguangsi Pagoda." *Cahiers d'Extrême-Asie* 20 (2011): 127–60.

Wang, Michelle M. "Changing Conceptions of 'Mandala' in Tang China: Ritual and the Role of Images." *Material Religion* 9, no. 2 (2013): 186–217.

Wang-Toutain, Françoise. "Une peinture de Dunhuang conservée à la Bibliothèque Nationale de France." *Arts Asiatiques* 49 (1994): 53–69.

Wayman, Alex. *Yoga of the Guhyasamājatantra: The Arcane Lore of Forty Verses; A Buddhist Tantra Commentary.* Delhi: Motilal Banarsidass, 1977.

Wedemeyer, Christian K. "Beef, Dog, and Other Mythologies: Connotative Semiotics in Mahāyoga Tantra Ritual and Scripture." *Journal of the American Academy of Religion* 75, no. 2 (2007): 383–417.

———. *Making Sense of Tantric Buddhism: History, Semiology, and Transgression in the Indian Traditions.* New York: Columbia University Press, 2013.

Weissenborn, Karen. *Buchkunst aus Nālandā: Die Aṣṭasāhasrikā Prajñāpāramitā-Handschrift in der Royal Asiatic Society, London (Ms. Hodgson 1) und Ihre Stellung in der Pāla-Buchmalerei des 11./12. Jahrhunderts.* Vienna: Universität Wien, 2012.

White, David Gordon. *The Alchemical Body: Siddha Traditions in Medieval India.* Chicago: University of Chicago Press, 1996.

Whitehill, Walter Muir. "Edward Waldo Forbes, 1873–1969." *Boston Museum Bulletin* 67, no. 348 (1969): 93–96.

Whitfield, Roderick. "Four Unpublished Paintings from Dunhuang in the Oriental Collections of the British Library." *British Library Journal* 24, no. 1 (1998): 90–97.

Whitmore, Paul M., and Glenn R. Cass. "The Ozone Fading of Traditional Japanese Colorants." *Studies in Conservation* 33, no. 1 (1988): 29–40.

Widyalankara, Anuththaradevi. "Mapping Urban and Social Space of Mediaeval Cities as Depicted in 'Sandeśa Kāvyas.'" *Journal of the Royal Asiatic Society of Sri Lanka*, n.s., 57 (2011): 95–123.

Wigh, Sonia. "Politics, Patronage, and Polyvalence: Mirza Raja Jai Singh in 'Biharilal's Satsai.'" *Social Scientist* 43, no. 5/6 (2015): 47–64.

Williams, Joanna. "The Iconography of Khotanese Painting." *East and West* 23, no. 1 (1973): 109–54.

Willis, Michael. "Avalokiteśvara of the Six Syllables: Locating the Practice of the 'Great Vehicle' in the Landscape of Central India." *Bulletin of the Asia Institute*, n.s., 23 (2009): 221–29.

Willson, Martin. *Deities of Tibetan Buddhism: The Zürich Paintings of the Icons Worthwhile to See.* Somerville, MA: Wisdom, 2001.

Wisumperuma, Dhanesh. "Elephants in 'Sandēśa Kāvyas.'" *Journal of the Royal Asiatic Society of Sri Lanka*, n.s., 57 (2011): 71–94

Wojtilla, Gyula. “Contributions to the Cultural History of Emerald in Early India.” *Acta Orientalia Academiae Scientiarum Hungaricae* 65, no. 4 (2012): 463–78.

Woodward, Hiram W., Jr. “The Life of the Buddha in the Pāla Monastic Environment.” *Journal of the Walters Art Gallery* 48 (1990): 13–27.

Wujastyk, Dagmar. “Perfect Medicine—Mercury in Sanskrit Medical Literature.” *Asian Medicine* 8 (2013): 15–10.

Wujastyk, Dominik. “Indian Manuscripts.” In *Manuscript Cultures: Mapping the Field,* edited by Jörg B. Quenzer, Dmitry Bondarev, and Sobisch Jan-Ulrich. Berlin: De Gruyter, 2014.

Wulff, Donna. “Religion in a New Mode: The Convergence of the Aesthetic and the Religious in Medieval India.” *Journal of the American Academy of Religion* 54, no. 4 (1986): 673–88.

Yamasaki, Kazuo, and Yoshimichi Emoto. “Pigments Used on Japanese Paintings from the Protohistoric Period through the 17th Century.” *Ars Orientalis* 11 (1979): 1–14.

Xinjiang Institute of Cultural Relics and Archaeology, China, and the Academic Research Organization for the Niya Ruins of Bukkyo University, Japan, eds. *Dandanwulike yi zhi* (Dandan oilik site: Report of the Sino Japanese Joint expedition). Beijing: Wenwuchubanshe, 2009.

Zwalf, W. *Buddhism: Art and Faith.* London: British Museum, 1985.

ILLUSTRATIONS

FIGURES

MAP

TABLES

INDEX

Founded in 1893,
UNIVERSITY OF CALIFORNIA PRESS
publishes bold, progressive books and journals on topics in the arts, humanities, social sciences, and natural sciences—with a focus on social justice issues—that inspire thought and action among readers worldwide.

The UC PRESS FOUNDATION
raises funds to uphold the press's vital role as an independent, nonprofit publisher, and receives philanthropic support from a wide range of individuals and institutions—and from committed readers like you. To learn more, visit ucpress.edu/supportus.